ISLAMIC MODERNISM,
NATIONALISM, AND FUNDAMENTALISM

ISLAMIC MODERNISM, NATIONALISM, AND FUNDAMENTALISM

Episode and Discourse

MANSOOR MOADDEL

The University of Chicago Press

CHICAGO AND LONDON

Mansoor Moaddel is professor in the Department of Sociology, Anthropology, and Criminology at Eastern Michigan University. He is the author of three previous books including, most recently, *Jordanian Exceptionalism.*

The University of Chicago Press, Chicago 60637
The University of Chicago Press, Ltd., London
© 2005 by The University of Chicago
All rights reserved. Published 2005
Printed in the United States of America

14 13 12 11 10 09 08 07 06 05   1 2 3 4 5

ISBN: 0-226-53332-8 (cloth)
ISBN: 0-226-53333-6 (paper)

Library of Congress Cataloging-in-Publication Data

Moaddel, Mansoor.
    Islamic modernism, nationalism, and fundamentalism : episode and discourse / Mansoor Moaddel.
        p. cm.
    Includes bibliographical references and index.
    ISBN 0-226-53332-8 (cloth : alk. paper)—ISBN 0-226-53333-6 (pbk. : alk. paper)
1. Islam and politics—Islamic countries. 2. Religion and politics—Islamic countries. 3. Islamic countries—Politics and government. 4. Islamic modernism—Islamic countries. 5. Islamic fundamentalism—Islamic countries. 6. Nationalism—Religious aspects—Islam. I. Title.
    BP173.7.M63 2005
    320.5′57—dc22

                                         2004015731
♾ The paper used in this publication meets the minimum requirements of the American National Standard for Information Sciences—Permanence of Paper for Printed Library Materials, ANSI Z39.48-1992.

*To the fond memory of
my mother, Koukab Sultan Moaddel,
and my father, Hajj Muhammad Moaddel*

CONTENTS

ACKNOWLEDGMENTS

Writing this book took me a bit longer than I anticipated. In addition to the depth and breadth of the primary and secondary historical materials that it was necessary to collect, read, understand, analyze, and remember, it took me a long time to (1) figure out a pattern of stability and change in the production of discourse in Islamic countries, (2) explain this pattern in terms of the parameters of a social-scientific model drawn from the latest developments in the sociology of culture and cultural studies, and (3) incorporate meaningfully the sociological explanation into a broader process of historical development in the Islamic world in the modern period.

However, these tasks would have been very difficult to accomplish without the generous support of two grants from the National Science Foundation (SBR 96-01439, SBR 92-13209), one grant from the United States Institute of Peace (080-965), and fellowships from the National Endowment for the Humanities, the American Center of Oriental Research, and Eastern Michigan University. I am forever grateful for their support. Needless to say, none of these institutions bears responsibility for any of the shortcomings, errors, or opinions expressed in this book.

Several people provided insightful comments on different chapters of this book, among whom special thanks go to Professors Richard Lachmann, Donald M. Reid, James Jankowski, Israel Gershoni, Janet Afary, and Kamran Talattof. The invaluable comments of three anonymous reviewers for the University of Chicago Press are also gratefully acknowledged. I would also like to thank Abdul Hani Guend and Osama Kadi for their assistance with Arabic materials and Nicky Peters and Jon Merrison for their assistance with French materials. This book also benefited from the resources of the libraries at Eastern Michigan University, the University of Michigan, UCLA, the School of Oriental and African Studies at the University of London, the India Office Library and Records in London, the University of Chicago, the University of Tehran, the Presbyterian Historical Society in Philadelphia, the U.S. Congress, and La Maison Mediterranéenne des Sciences de l'Homme in Aix-en-Provence, France. Special thanks are also due to Douglas Mitchell, executive editor, Timothy McGovern, Erik Carlson, and other members of the staff of the University of Chicago Press.

I owe a great deal of gratitude to my wife, Marjan Sadeghi Moaddel, for her support and invaluable library assistance.

My deepest feeling of gratitude goes to my mother, Koukab Sultan Moaddel, and my father, Hajj Muhammad Moaddel (he liked very much to be called by the title "Hajj" before his name), whose unwavering love, encouragement, and support made it all possible. I am in particular grateful for my mother's occasional yet consistent exertion of tough love, which made me realize, among other things, that there may be care behind the anger one occasionally encounters in life. It is to their fond memory that I dedicate this book.

Sociological Theories of Ideology and Cultural Change

Over a Century of Cultural Change and Ideological Contentions

The social transformation of the Islamic world in the modern era did not produce a consensus among Muslims regarding the most fundamental principles of social organization. In an objective sense, this transformation was extensive: the traditional order declined, the modern state in the form of a massive bureaucratic and military organization was developed, new social classes and groups came into the limelight, and the indigenous economy became incorporated into the world capitalist structure. Yet Muslims reached no lasting agreement on the form government should take, the appropriate economic model, the relationship of Muslim nations with the outside world, the status of women, their national identities, and the relation of Islam to rational analysis and rule making. Instead, Islamic societies experienced a sequence of diverse cultural episodes characterized by serious ideological disputes and acrimonious debates followed by sociopolitical crises, ending in revolutions or military coups.

One of the key problems in building consensus was that the conflict between Islamic orthodoxy and the secular discourse that spread into the Islamic world either failed to produce a new synthesis or, where it did, produced a synthesis that was not widely institutionalized. In the nineteenth century, Muslim scholars made serious efforts to bridge the gap between Islam and the European Enlightenment, giving rise to Islamic modernism. Associated with this movement to some degree was liberal nationalism, whose aim was the construction of the modern national state. The decline of liberal nationalism and the overthrow of liberal governments brought new antiliberal regimes to power. These regimes subscribed to such ideologies as pan-Arab nationalism, Arab socialism, and monarchy-centered nationalism. With the decline of these ideologies, Islamic fundamentalism grew to become a dominant oppositional discourse. In this study, we attempt to uncover the basic parameters of the social conditions that promoted the rise of Islamic modernism, liberal nationalism, Arabism, pan-Arab nationalism, and Islamic fundamentalism. To this end, we develop a sociological model to explain the proximate conditions of ideology. We then subsume our sociological explanation in a historical narrative of the sequence of significant events that occurred in the Islamic world, the insertion of a Europocentric conception of secularism and universal progress in this sequence, the way secularism was understood by the indigenous intellectual leaders, the manner in which it shaped the policies of the modern state, and how this secularism generated its nemesis in the form of Islamic fundamentalism.

Islamic Modernism in India, Egypt, and Iran

Around the turn of the nineteenth century a new and extensive cultural encounter started between the West and the Islamic world. Virtually all native intellectuals strove to conceptualize the nature of this encounter, its contribution to the agonizing backwardness of their homeland, or, alternatively, its role in providing solutions to the problem of Muslim decline. The highbrow culture producers, however, went beyond formulating ideas simply to address the decadence of their society. They endeavored to devise a model for reorganizing the structure of authority, for providing a foundation to build a new society, and for drawing the basic principles of rule making. This encounter was multifaceted, and the native ideological resolutions were certainly diverse, but religion remained one of the encounter's most contested intellectual categories. Islamic modernism was the first Muslim ideological response to the Western cultural challenge. Started in India and Egypt in the second part of the nineteenth century, this movement was a remarkable intellectual development. It was reflected in the work of a group of like-minded Muslim scholars, featuring a critical reexamination of the classical conceptions and methods of jurisprudence and a formulation of a new approach to Islamic theology and Quranic exegesis. This new approach, which was nothing short of an outright rebellion against Islamic orthodoxy, displayed astonishing compatibility with the ideas of the Enlightenment. The central theological problems that engaged these thinkers revolved around the questions of the validity of the knowledge derived from the sources external to Islam and the methodological adequacy of the four traditional sources of jurisprudence: the Quran, the dicta attributed to the Prophet (*hadith*), the consensus of the theologians (*ijma*), and juristic reasoning by analogy (*qiyas*). They resolved to reinterpret the first two sources and to transform the last two in order to formulate a reformist project in light of the prevailing standards of scientific rationality and modern social theory. Such prominent intellectuals and theologians as Sayyid Jamal ud-Din al-Afghani, Sir Sayyid Ahmad Khan, Chiragh Ali, Muhammad Abduh, Amir Ali, Shibli Nu'mani, and their associates and disciples presented Islamic theology in a manner consistent with modern rationalist ideas. Some of these thinkers portrayed Islam as compatible with deistic and natural religion. They were impressed by the achievements of the West, ranging from scientific and technological progress, the Newtonian conception of the universe, Spencer's sociology, and Darwinian evolutionism to Western lifestyles. They all argued that Islam, as a world religion, was thoroughly capable of adapting itself to the changing conditions of every age, the hallmark of the perfect Muslim community being law and reason.

In India, the modernist interpretation of Islam became popular among a group of Muslim thinkers following the devastation caused by the Sepoy Rebellion of 1857–59. It was epitomized in Sir Sayyid Ahmad Khan's natural theology and in the different modernist trends of his associates: Chiragh Ali's radical modernism and legal reforms, Shibli Nu'mani's and Amir Ali's rationalist approach toward historical Islam and hagiographical studies, and Mumtaz Ali's feminism. Likewise, in Egypt, the Islamic modernists tackled such complex intellectual questions as the rise of the rational sciences and their implications for the Islamic belief system, the historical roots of Muslim decline, the apparent contradiction between Islamic tradition and the principles of social organization underpinning European civilization, the maltreatment of women, and Islamic conceptions of sovereignty and political theory. The movement started with Rifa'a al-Tahtawi but gained considerable momentum decades later when al-Afghani organized a circle of Muslim scholars to address the sociopolitical and theological issues facing Islam. It was further reflected in Abduh's theological works and Quranic exegesis, in Qasim Amin's reexamination of the status of women in Islam, in Muhammad Farid Wajdi's equation of Islam with civilization, and in Ali Abd al-Raziq's reconsideration of the Islamic conception of authority. Islamic modernism in Iran was not as strong as it was in India or Egypt. The major modernist attempt occurred during the Constitutional Revolution (1905–11), when the ulama were divided between the followers of monarchical absolutism and the followers of constitutionalism. A defense of constitutional law and representative government was formulated in Ayatollah Na'ini's response to the devastating traditionalist critique of constitutionalism.

Liberal Nationalism in Egypt and Iran, and Liberal Arabism and Arab Nationalism in Syria

Connected to Islamic modernism in the early stage of its development, liberal nationalism was a movement that filled the void left in the political-intellectual space by the retreat of Islamic orthodoxy and the decline of the absolutist state. Its ideologues addressed perplexing questions related to the constituting elements of the nation and the governing principles of its political institutions. Their nationalism was a new ideological response to the intervention of Western powers in the affairs of their countries. They favored national integration via cultural and educational reforms, the promotion of indigenous national languages, and the separation of religion and politics. Their democratic discourse, on the other hand, was aimed at checking the arbitrary rule of the monarch. As an emulative project, liberal nationalism adopted a Western conception of nation and Western principles of democratic institutions. Nevertheless, the political movements shaped by this ideology collided with the West's imperialistic advances.

Egypt was the first among Arab nations to experience the rise of liberal nationalism. The distinctive feature of its nationalist component was that it was territorial and revolved around Egyptian rather than Arab or Islamic identity. The intellectual leaders of this movement also viewed constitutionalism as the model of politics, secularism as superior to the traditional religious education, gender equality as preferable to gender hierarchy, and rationalism as the basis of science. It culminated in the formation of a constitutional government in 1924 based on a hereditary monarchy. This was followed by a period of liberal politics that spanned more than two decades. In practice, liberal politics was dominated by the landowning class, and the liberal intellectual leaders displayed an overly secularist and often antireligious outlook—both factors contributing to the decline of liberal nationalism and the rise of alternative discourses.

Like Egypt, Syria also experienced the rise of liberalism around the turn of the twentieth century. This political movement was crafted to Arabism as the key element of Syrian nationalist consciousness. Decades later, Arabism developed into a full-blown, illiberal, pan-Arab nationalism. Started in the works of Christian Arab intellectuals, the discourse of liberal Arabism was developed by Abdul Rahman al-Kawakibi and the Christian Najib Azoury, who suggested the Arab right to secede from the Ottoman Empire and establish an independent Arab caliphate. Al-Kawakibi's outlook was similar to that of the Islamic modernists. He attributed the decline of Islam to the the ulama's obstructionism, their stress on blind following, and despotic governments. Despotism, in his view, not only corrupts religion but the entire society as well. In the thirties, liberalism declined and the ideology of pan-Arab nationalism gained popularity among Syria's educated elite. Pan-Arab nationalists believed in the unity of Arab nations, that is, in an Arabism transcending religion and national boundaries, rejected parliamentary politics, considered the state the agent of revolutionary change and national emancipation, and had a secular orientation. Whereas in al-Kawakibi the deleterious effects of despotism were exposed and individual liberty was stressed, such harbingers of pan-Arab nationalism as Sati' al-Husri subordinated the idea of freedom to the notion of national emancipation and individual self-sacrifice for the liberation of the Arab land.

Finally, in late nineteenth-century Iran, anticlerical secularism and constitutionalism constituted the distinguishing features of the modern discourses adhered to by political thinkers. In this new intellectual movement, anti-Western nationalism was relatively weak. While the Constitutional Revolution of 1905 failed to establish the rule of law, the secular trend remained unabated under Reza Shah's authoritarianism (1925–41). Some of the leading intellectuals continued to attack various forms of religious practices, tribalism, and communal sectarianism. With the breakdown of Reza Shah's rule in 1941, a new liberal-nationalist episode was ushered in. In contrast to the earlier period, anti-British economic nationalism was the key feature of the political movement of the middle of the twentieth century. This episode ended in the U.S.-British-engineered coup in 1953 that overthrew Mohammad Mossadeq's nationalist government and restored the shah's power.

Islamic Fundamentalism in Egypt, Syria, Iran, Algeria, and Jordan

Following the decline of liberal nationalism and the overthrow of parliamentary politics through coups in all these Islamic countries, another cultural episode set in. The primary elements of this episode were the rise of an interventionist ideological state, on the one hand, and the increasing popularity of the Islamic opposition, on the other. In a marked contrast with the previous ideologies, Islamic fundamentalism categorically rejected the Western model and outlook. The precursors of fundamentalism, including Ayatollah Ruhollah Mussaui Khomeini and Ayatollah Morteza Motahhari from Iran, Hasan al-Banna and Sayyid Qutb from Egypt, Abul Ala Maududi from Pakistan, Mustafa as-Siba'i from Syria, and Abbasi Madani, Shaikh Nahnah, and Ali Belhaj from Algeria, insisted on unconditional fealty to Islam and questioned the validity of any sources of learning that were outside the Islamic cosmological doctrine. While Islamic modernism aimed at rationalizing religious dogma to show its consonance with modernity, fundamentalism aimed at Islamizing society through social and political action, the seizure of the state power being a necessary step in its overall Islamization project.

There are considerable variations in the discourse and orientations of Islamic fundamentalism among these countries, however. In Egypt, the liberal-nationalist ideology declined in the late 1930s before the onslaught of two cultural movements, united only by their hostility to constitutionalism, parliamentary politics, and the West. One was the movement of the Muslim Brothers (MB). It viewed Islam as a total system that transcended national boundaries, believed in the unity of religion and politics, considered Western culture decadent, denounced the "non-Islamic" currents in the universities, and condemned the mixing of the sexes in public places. The other was pan-Arab nationalism, which by the early fifties became an impelling force of cultural change in virtually all Arab countries. The overthrow of the monarchy by the Free Army Officers' coup in 1952 and the inauguration of

Gamal Abdel Nassir's pan-Arab regime brought the MB into a violent encounter with the government. The years following the coup gave rise to an extremist trend in the MB. The new trend was led by Sayyid Qutb, who rejected the existing order as an embodiment of the *jahiliyya*, the decadent cultural order that in the Muslim view prevailed in pre-Islamic Arabia.

Like Egypt's, Syria's liberal nationalism was commonly disliked by the pan-Arab nationalists and Islamic fundamentalists. With the decline of liberal politics and following a period of unification with Egypt in the United Arab Republic (1958–61), Syria drifted to the left when the Ba'athists seized power in 1963 through a military coup. The coup signified a major shift in political power. The urban notables who had long dominated Syrian politics gave way to radical politicians and an authoritarian, socialist-oriented state. In the postindependence period, the Syrian Muslim Brothers advanced the ideas of Islamic socialism, but from the 1960s on they avoided the term "Islamic socialism" and developed an antistatist free enterprise ideology. The program of the Islamic Front of the early 1980s developed the idea that the state was doomed to fail when acting as a merchant, defended freedom of commerce and ownership, ensured freedom of the press and political parities, and guaranteed equality among citizens. It did not eschew political violence against the regime, however.

In Iran, parliamentary politics also ended with a coup, in 1953. It marked the rise of a new bureaucratic state that intervened heavily in the economy and culture. From the sixties on, there was a cultural shift away from secularism and toward radical Islamism. The religious opposition attacked the shah as an anti-Islamic, pro-foreigner, Western puppet and a promoter of decadent Western culture under the guise of women's freedom. A distinctive feature of the opposition was the rise of clergy-centered Islamic discourse.

The experience of Algeria in many respects was not different from that of Egypt, Syria, and Iran. As in these countries, Islamic fundamentalism in Algeria was a postfifties phenomenon. As in these countries, liberal nationalism and Islamic modernism were among the dominant oppositional discourses in Algeria in the first quarter of the twentieth century. The radicalization of the Algerian independence movement, culminating in the revolutionary war against the French in 1954–62, resulted in the rise of socialist and Arab nationalist ideologies. The achievement of independence in 1962 set the stage for culture production. The rise and consolidation of the socialist-oriented authoritarian state paralleled the transformation of the Algerian religious movement from reformism to militant Islamic radicalism. It was first reflected in al-Qiyam, a movement formed in 1964 in opposition to the state's cultural policies and official Islam under Ahmed Ben Bella. Linked to al-Qiyam, Ahl al-Da'wa (People for the Call) was formed in the late seventies to express Algerians' dissatisfaction with many of the state's policies. By the 1980s, militant

Islamic fundamentalism was the dominant religious and cultural movement in the country. In 1989, the Islamic Salvation Front (FIS) was formed with the explicit purpose of establishing an Islamic state.

The cultural turn in Jordan was not as dramatic as it was in Algeria, Egypt, Iran, and Syria, although the kingdom faced serious challenges from pan-Arab nationalists in the fifties. As a marked departure from the history of the Islamic movement in those countries, the relationships between the Hashemites and the Islamic movement in Jordan were characterized by moderation and peaceful coexistence. During the fifties, the Jordanian branch of the Muslim Brothers went so far as to defend the regime against the menace of radical pan-Arab nationalism. After the democratization process launched by the late King Hussein, a secular trend emerged in the Islamic movement. This trend was characterized by organizational differentiation and the rationalization of religious discourse. The history of the Muslim Brothers and these developments after 1989 displays a pattern of religious activism that was quite different from, if not opposite to, the pattern of relations between the state and religion in the other Islamic countries. This difference justifies the application of the term "Jordanian exceptionalism."

Historically Significant Issues

These discourses were diverse: they posed different questions, rested on dissimilar conceptual scaffolding, and shaped various strategies, orientations, and attitudes. They varied in terms of social support, having different relationships with the ruling regimes and significant groups and social classes. There were also variations within and between the cultural contexts that gave rise to these discourses. Nevertheless, the issues in relation to which the precursors of Islamic modernism, liberal nationalism, Arabism and Arab nationalism, and Islamic fundamentalism formulated their ideas remained remarkably invariant. Among them were such issues as those related to (1) the status of rational, empirical sciences and their relationship with Islam, (2) the relationship between religion and politics, (3) the ideal form of government, (4) national identity, (5) the relationship of Muslim nations with the outside world, and (6) the status of women.

Some of these ideological movements addressed a more exhaustive set of issues than others. In some countries, these issues were discussed more comprehensively than in other countries. In all cases, however, these issues mediated the relationship between variations in social conditions and variations in the utterances of culture producers. Why in different periods were different ideas formulated to address these issues? What is the relationship between these ideas and the prevailing social conditions? What were the basic features of the historical conditions that promoted heightened ideological activity among the educated elite of these countries? What were the key factors underpinning the changes and variations in Islamic

modernism, liberal nationalism, and fundamentalism cross-nationally and historically? Who created the necessary social space and resources for the production and
growth of these discourses? What factors determined their basic themes, content,
and sociopolitical orientations? We address these questions in order to explain the
determinants of these ideologies. We first discuss the rise of Islamic modernism in
India, Egypt, and Iran. We then examine the rise of territorial nationalism in
Egypt, liberal Arabism and pan-Arab nationalism in Syria, and anticlerical secularism, constitutionalism, and economic nationalism in Iran. Finally, we analyze
Islamic fundamentalism in Egypt, Iran, Syria, Algeria, and Jordan. By carefully an-
alyzing the rise and demise of diverse ideological movements in these countries, our
goal is to advance the social-scientific understanding of the relationship between
the production of ideas and broader social conditions.

Issues, Islamic Cultural Traditions, the Inequality of Power, and Ideas

In explaining the pattern of stability and change in the production of discourse,
this study stresses the contextual specificity of the cases. This specificity is historical: it is derived from the particular combination of concrete social and cultural
forces that give national-historical character to a given ideological movement. It is
markedly different from the formalistic, text-based, and reductive specificities that
have characterized the analyses of Islamic culture by various Islamicists (so-called
Orientalists). Such notions as that Islam does not recognize the separation of religion and politics, that in Islamic cultural tradition there is no legal recognition of
corporate persons, that the conceptual repertoire in the Islamic culture promotes
authoritarianism, and that Islamic political theory is tilted toward conservatism and
patrimonial domination are not only debatable but also methodologically hopelessly inadequate to explain, say, the failure of secular discourse and democracy and
the rise of religious extremism in the Islamic world.[1] It is insufficient, if not flatly
wrong, to try to explain Islamic society—its concrete political and social institutions and Muslim social behavior—in terms of textual analysis. The analysis of the
text is important, but it must be complemented by a systematic comparative analysis of historical cases.

This study also departs from the perspective of the historians of colonial culture,
drawn from Michel Foucault's notion of the relation of knowledge to power and the
use of his perspective by Edward Said to criticize Western scholarship on the Orient,
in which inequality in the distribution of power between Islamic countries and
Western powers featured prominently in explaining culture.[2] This study certainly
considers the relationship between power and ideological production. Nevertheless,
we argue that the manner in which power shapes the production of discourse is
more specific to its national setting than to the generality of Western domination.
Contrary to the Saidian perspective, the nearness to or distance from power does not

necessarily decide the validity of a discourse. In fact, by using a text-based and reductive method to invalidate the views of the Islamicists, Said has brought himself methodologically very close to the same scholarly tradition that he has so vehemently rejected. The Islamicists' assertions about Islamic culture and politics need to be assessed in terms of a systematic comparative analysis of the cases; a simple statement that they are tied to colonial power does not invalidate their assertions.[3] Moreover, Western domination, as we will attempt to demonstrate in this work, may be a poor predictor of the kind of ideas being produced. Militant anti-Western oppositional discourses such as Islamic fundamentalism and pan-Arab nationalism in fact emerged in independent national states that the West was no longer directly dominating. Finally, there are considerable historical and cross-national variations in ideological production among Islamic countries, and these variations may not be explained by the dynamics of Western hegemony or the lack thereof.

Far from reflecting Islamic cultural traditions or unequally distributed power, Islamic modernism, liberal nationalism, Arabism and Arab nationalism, and Islamic fundamentalism were ideas produced by groups of like-minded individuals. These individuals had different level of resources, cultural capital, and institutional ties. They had varying relations with the ruling elite and different degrees of access to the position of power within the state's bureaucracy. They also faced varying ideological obstacles in their attempt to formulate the conceptual schema for the construction of a new sociopolitical community. To identify and analyze the key of aspects of the historical contexts in which their perceptions were formed and discourses formulated, this work employs a disinterested perspective by constructing a formal analytical model based on abstract theories developed in the sociology of culture, cultural studies, and theories of language. This model advances three central propositions: (1) Ideological production is a discontinuous process and proceeds in an episodic fashion. (2) While the availability of resources and space are important, the actual production of ideas—the content of what is being produced—takes place within the existing discursive context and the location of this context in the sociopolitical space of the social formation. Finally, (3) ideas are produced within the international context of cultural diffusions and transfer of meaning.

Cultural Studies and the Legacy of the Classical Tradition

Models drawn from the correspondence perspective have thus far guided research on ideology. Robert Wuthnow departs from this perspective by formulating an alternative articulation model, while Randall Collins offers an amended Durkheimian two-step model of intellectual creativity. While all these models have advanced the social-scientific understanding of ideological change, none adequately explains how ideas are actually produced and how the specific contents of ideologies are constructed. This study formulates an alternative episodic discourse model in order to explain the proximate conditions of ideological production.

The correspondence perspective presumes a duality between social structure and ideology and presumes that ideology corresponds to social structure in a determinate manner. Émile Durkheim has a *mimetic* conception of religious ideas—they are the symbolic representations of social arrangements. Because religion reflects a vital aspect of collective solidarity, the form of religious unity changes step by step with each stage of structural and functional transformation.[4] For Karl Marx, too, ideology corresponds to social structure. It is "interwoven with the material activity and the material intercourse of men."[5] Max Weber's approach is much more analytical and rich with detailed subtlety than either Durkheim's or Marx's position. He questions the purely materialistic analysis of ideas by arguing that, for example, religious ideas do not neatly intermesh with interest. Instead, he introduces the notion of "the metaphysical needs of human mind." Nevertheless, on a lower level of abstraction, Weber concedes that there is an elective affinity between diverse social grouping (for example, warrior classes, peasants, business classes, and intellectuals) and different religious tendencies. He establishes this correspondence through a secondary intellectual process of "reinterpretation of ideas."[6]

Using this perspective, social scientists have attempted to explain concrete ideologies. For example, Guy Swanson, following Durkheim, connects varying conceptions of God's immanence in Protestantism and Catholicism to the nature of political institutions existing in Europe prior to the Reformation.[7] Using a Marxist approach, Immanuel Wallerstein claims that the rise of liberal ideology was functionally related to its underlying hegemonic power in the world economy.[8] Applying a corollary of this view to India, Partha Chatterjee argues that third-world nationalism was a derivative discourse, manifesting a general "problem of the bourgeois-rationalist conception of knowledge, established in the post-Enlightenment period of European intellectual history."[9] A more general argument corresponding to the hierarchically organized economic zones envisaged by world systems theory is that of the "new discursive histories" on how colonial discourse constrained the people of the periphery to ensure the hegemony of the core nations.[10] Finally, David Harvey connects cultural changes in contemporary capitalist society to changes in the regime of accumulation, maintianing that "postmodern fiction . . . mimics the conditions of flexible accumulation,"[11] and that "the transition from Fordism to flexible accumulation . . . ought to imply a transition in our mental maps, political attitudes, and political institutions."[12]

Even in Foucault there is a trace of the correspondence perspective that relates the development of the modern concept of the individual to "the experience which became increasingly prominent in the eighteenth and nineteenth centuries of ordering individuals according to strict arrangements in military regiments, of treating individuals' bodies medically, of incarcerating them in separate classes, and later of organizing work into specialized tasks."[13] Further, in *Discipline and Punish*, Foucault is explicit in considering "punitive methods not simply as consequences of legislation or as indicators of social structures."[14] Yet he holds that the development of penal law and the human sciences is a reflection of a single process of which the technology of power is the organizing principle. The correspondence premise is also evident in the works of his followers. For Timothy Mitchell, for example, the new system of representation in Egypt is a reflection of the colonial design imposed by the British, and the order of modern life in Egypt reflects the colonial order.[15] Likewise, Said believes that Orientalism has less to do with the Orient than with the Western world, shaped to a degree by the exchange with various kinds of power.[16]

Each version of the correspondence theory has its own particular difficulties. Durkheim is criticized for taking a "reductionistic attitude toward belief in God,"[17] and for his dated ethnographic evidence.[18] Alexander Goldenweiser and Edward Evans-Pritchard have questioned the Durkheimian mimetic conception of religion and argued that "it is no longer accepted that the primitiveness of a social system assures the primitiveness of the form of religion associated with it."[19] Marxian cultural theory is also criticized for being one-sidedly materialist or class reductionist. Finally, Weber's approach is considered inadequate because "the manner in which ideology is conceptualized has resulted in what sometimes appears as an overly subjectivist view of its nature and function."[20] The major problem of the perspective, however, is the absence of a specific mechanism that connects ideas to social structure. None of the legacies of the classical tradition provides an objective clue that links the production of ideas to social structure. In virtually all the versions of the correspondence perspective, the key explanatory variable has remained psychological and subjectivist. For Marx, the reality of class exploitation is masked by the unreality of the social relations projected by the ideological superstructure. Ideologies generate false consciousness in the oppressed masses and at the same time, like a tranquilizer, provide psychological comfort. The neo-Marxist reformulation of the source and functions of ideas does not fully resolve the Marxist problem of causal inadequacy and subjectivism. Louis Althusser, for example, uses the concept of interpellation (addressing) to explain the reproduction of the social relations of production, where the process of subjective orientation fits individuals into a given social location (i.e., the constitution of the subject).[21] Similarly, Durkheim stresses the psychological functions of rituals as the key variable connecting cultural symbols to collective solidarity. The Durkheimian approach flourished in the works of Victor Turner. For him, symbolic behaviors and ritual performances are phases in broad social processes that transform the obligatory and constraining into something desirable. "The irksomeness of moral constraint is transformed into the 'love of virtue.'"[22] Weber also considers the subjective orientation formed by certain religious beliefs such as the doctrine of predestination to be the crucial link connecting ideas to the emergent social conditions—capitalism.[23]

The emphasis on the subjective component of ideology was also the predominant feature of various cultural adaptation models that were in vogue around the middle of the twentieth century. In the seminal works of Talcott Parsons and others, value assumed the highest position in the cybernetic hierarchy of the elements of social structure, and value analysis constituted the standard approach in explaining culture. Cultural change and the production of meaning in Parsons's view is portrayed as a diffusing process in which autonomous development in any or all of the subsystems of society produces social differentiation. The latter in turn leads to the emergence of a new set of problems that the old cultural pattern cannot address or resolve. A more general, rational, and systematic value pattern is thus necessary to provide the basis of social stability by cementing the emergent cleavages in society.[24]

Ideology is viewed as the constitutive feature of the social structure. Yet there is still a duality between structure cum culture and other "objective" social conditions that are guided and regulated by values and norms. Above and beyond reference to the process of rationalization, cultural diffusion, innovations in science, changes in belief systems, and the emergence of charismatic leaders, it is unclear how social differentiation and value generalization are connected, who it is that is responsible for the production of meanings, and how the production of meaning occurs. The functional significance of value generalization for the stability of a differentiated social system does not necessarily lead to its emergence. As in other theories in the correspondence perspective, however, the key explanatory mechanism connecting social conditions to ideology in the Parsonian tradition is clearly psychological. For example, theorists working within this framework have considered individual psychological orientation the link connecting rapid social change to the rise of alternative ideologies.[25] Likewise, subjectivism and stress on psychological predisposition featured prominently in early theories of development and economic change. For both Everett Hagen and David McClelland, innovative and creative ideas are the necessary ingredients for economic progress. The psychological impediments to the production of such ideas are removed when the hierarchical-authoritarian social system is disturbed[26] or the early socialization pattern is altered.[27]

New Departures: Wuthnow and Collins

The absence of a mechanism that connects ideas to the regularities of social life is symptomatic of a more serious problem in the correspondence perspective—the central assumption that ideas and social structure correspond to each other. Wuthnow departs from the correspondence perspective by problematizing this assumption, arguing that ideas and social structure "always relate in an enigmatic fashion."[28] Rather than being the inevitable reflections of social reality, ideologies are produced, and for them to be produced, there must be sufficient resources for their production and a social space that permits them to grow. Since social structure and ideology are autonomous processes without one necessarily determining the other, there must be "specific historical conjunctures that [make] cultural innovation possible."[29] Hence the relation of ideology to social environment is posed in terms of the problem of articulation.

Articulation occurs under favorable *environmental conditions* that provide resources, within an *institutional context* where resources are molded, and in accordance with the *action sequences* of culture producers and consumers. The process of articulation involves *production,* that is, nonanonymous *selection,* meaning that certain genres adapt to a new environment better than others, and *institutionalization,* that is, the establishment of routinized mechanisms for the production and dissemination of ideas. What is articulated and in what ways ideology becomes free of contextual determination are described by the terms *social horizon,* specific events and experiences that become the texts of ideology, *discursive field,* the symbolic space within the ideology itself, and *figural action,* ideologically defined behavior. For Wuthnow, exceptional economic growth in Europe provided the necessary resources for the Reformation, the Enlightenment, and socialism. The state, on the other hand, by providing the necessary social space, played the most important mediating role in the emergence of these cultural episodes.[30]

Wuthnow's emphasis on the significance of social resources and social space for culture production, his understanding of cultural change as a discontinuous process, and his conceptual scaffolding that specifies the way the social environment structures ideological production and, in turn, the manner in which ideologies through their discursive fields determine the central categories that shape figural actions are important for understanding ideological production. Nevertheless, being exclusively concerned with how meanings are articulated within the social environment, but not with how meanings are produced, his model still, despite the employment of a conjuncture of complex historical factors, ends up with indeterminacy.[31] Further, while he abandons the reductionism of the correspondence perspective, it is unclear what it is that generates the internal dynamics of ideological processes.

Collins addresses some of the theoretical issues left out of Wuthnow's model. He first notes that the process of reflection and abstraction systematically reduces the vast range of philosophical erudition to a small number of rival positions, hardly more than half a dozen. This principle, which he calls the law of small number,[32] sets the upper and lower bounds of philosophical expositions and debates.[33] Within this structure, intellectual creativity takes place through personal contacts, fueled by emotional energy and cultural capital. The mechanism of intellectual creativity is contrasting positions, which are generated by the dynamic of creation through opposition.[34] Collins relates the microlevel intellectual network and broader social conditions in a two-step model of causality. External social conditions affect intellectual diversity by "rearranging its material base."[35] Thus, when external conditions disrupt the intellectual attention space, internal realignment takes place, and this in turn unleashes creativity for formulating new positions and new tensions among the privileged arguers at the core of the network.[36]

Collins's goal is to formulate a global theory of intellectual change applicable to all diverse intellectual traditions of human societies. Being concerned with a general dynamic common to all these traditions, Collins, like Wuthnow, is silent about the specific issues and crucial nuances involved in philosophical disputations leading to the creation of diverse worldviews. In fact, both theoreticians fail to explain how the actual content of ideas is constructed and what factors determine its theme and sociopolitical orientation. Collins's contention that creativity moves by oppositional interactions is too general to account for the variations in the content of philosophical production that give rise to diverse historical patterns.[37]

An Episodic Discourse Model

The production of sociopolitical ideas involves (1) the expression of opinions and beliefs, and (2) the dissemination and consumption of these opinions and beliefs. The first refers to the actual production of meanings, and the other to the reproduction of the conditions that gave rise to those meanings. Resources and social space, while crucial in the dissemination of ideas, are factors *external* to ideological production. The actual production of ideas involves the content of what is being produced—that is, the message being communicated and the conceptual vehicle used. These include conceptual innovation, the formulation of the themes, the resolution of issues, and the shaping of the sociopolitical orientations of ideology. This *internal* aspect of ideological production cannot be explained in terms of the parameters of the articulation model.

Ideologies constitute organized sets of signs: concepts, symbols, and rituals. They have social referents. They are about historically significant problems. The producers of sociopolitical ideas make reference to these problems, for example, economic backwardness, poverty and inequality, race and gender differences, political domination and arbitrary rule, and national security. What they actually say, however, cannot be directly derived from these problems. Expression takes place through the medium of signs. And although signs make reference to elements of social life, "they define and interrelate them in an 'arbitrary' manner, that is, in a manner that cannot be deduced from exigencies [of social life]. . . . The arbitrary status of a sign means that its meaning is derived not from its social referent—the signified—but from its relation to other symbols, or signifiers within a discursive code."[38]

Meanings are thus produced within the context of relationships among symbols.[39] "Understanding," in Michael Holquist's explication of Mikhail Bakhtin, "comes about as a response to a sign with signs."[40] Expressions are made, meanings come about, and ideas are produced in relation to other expressions, meanings, and ideas that are present, occupying simultaneous but different spaces.[41] This relationship is mutual—words are responded to with words, rituals with rituals, symbols with symbols, and body movement with body movement. Idea causes idea.[42]

Target and the Production of Discourse

Because innovative ideas are developed in differential relations to existing discourses, all new ideologies are in essence oppositional. Ideological production is a function of the kinds of discourses that are dominant in the social environment. Ideological producers develop their ideas vis-à-vis the conceptual framework, symbolic order, and ritualistic practices, that is, the discursive fields of competing ideologies. In addressing social problems, they reevaluate, revisit, or reject the claims, the arguments, and often the conceptual foundations of competing ideologies. At the same time, ideological producers beget responses, rebuttals, and counterarguments from their adversaries. Debates, back-and-forth discussions, and ideological disputations set the *internal* dynamic of ideological production, as each side of the debate structures the kind of argument its opponent is likely to advance against it. Each side constitutes the *target* of ideological production for the other.

A target is any set of discourses in relation to which ideas are formulated. The nature of the target may vary from being a single discourse to a plurality of discourses. The constituting elements of the target itself can vary from being a simple set of ideas to a set of complex theoretical or philosophical systems. The simplicity or the complexity of the target decides the level of sophistication, elegance, and rigor of the ideas being produced. The target may also vary in terms of its site. The carriers of a discourse are individuals with organizations and power. They may enjoy the support of the state, powerful groups, or social classes. This support enhances their power in controlling the means of culture production. Whoever supports the target ideology, whether it is a self-sustaining, stand-alone establishment or not, its connections to significant social classes or the state have considerable implications for shaping the orientation of ideological production. It is the nature of the power of the target ideology and its location within the sociopolitical space of the social formation that determine the social or political orientation of the new ideology. This is because the production of a new ideology involves not only a critique of the target ideology, but a critique of its institutional basis as well.

The cross-tabulation of the two variables—the nature of the target and the location of the target vis-à-vis the state—will yield four possible conditions for ideological production.

Pluralistic versus Monolithic Targets

(1) If the target is characterized by diverse ideologies and, hence, a plurality of discursive fields, then the new ideological production tends to develop a multiplicity of themes and display eclectic, pluralistic, and moderate characteristics. (2) If, on the other hand, the target includes only a single ideology, that is, a monolithic discursive field, then the new ideology tends to develop a set of centralized themes and display monistic and fundamentalist characteristics. Where there is cultural pluralism, the market of ideas is strengthened, expanded, and diversified. Cultural pluralism enhances competition among ideological groups. In this intellectual environment, ideological producers must "compete for the patronage of potential consumers of *Weltanschauungen*."[43] To be successful in marketing their ideas, ideological producers must consider the diverse views of the adherents of competing ideologies. Given the market character of ideology,[44] eclecticism and moderation may have a better chance of success in attracting interested audiences in a pluralistic context. Moreover, the presence of competing ideologies subjects ideological producers to crisscrossing ideas, reinforcing the belief in the complexity of social life, directing ideological producers toward the development of synthetic models in which elements of competing ideologies are also taken into consideration. In a monolithic intellectual environment, on the other hand, ideological producers encounter a single, often unambiguous, dominant ideology. Their alternative idea is defined most often in terms of its opposition to the target. In a simplistic sense, the production of ideas in this context is driven by the assumption that whatever the ideology of the target is, it is not right. Ideological producers facing a monolithic target tend to overlook alternative possibilities in dealing with the same social problems. In attacking a monolithic target, they often tend to reproduce in a different form an idea system structurally similar to what they are criticizing.

We may thus propose that the higher the level of intellectual pluralism in society, the higher the level of competitions among ideological groups, and the higher the likelihood of the production of an eclectic, general, and universalistic discourse; and the stronger the monolithic cultural environment, the stronger the likelihood of the rise of a fundamentalist and monistic discourse.

The State and Ideological Outcomes

Intellectual markets are always regulated by the state or the dominant cultural authorities. This regulation may vary from the formulation of a set of objective rules that are uniformly applied to all groups in society to an extreme case where cultural authorities themselves are maintaining a monopoly of the means of expression. Culture production tends to take a political or a social orientation depending on whether the source of this regulation comes from the state or influential cultural (or religious) institutions outside the state. Thus, considering the location of the target in the sociopolitical space of society, (3) if the target is loosely connected to the state or the ruling elite remains indifferent to ideological debates, then ideological production is confined to civil society and tends to remain predominantly social and nonpolitical in orientation. Nonpolitical targets beget apolitical oppositional discourse. Finally, (4) if the target is strongly connected to the state, or the ruling elite extensively intervenes in cultural affairs to promote a certain ideology, then ideological production becomes politicized and tends to develop a political orientation. This is the context where political ideologies emerge.

We may propose that, in fact, the closer the target to state power, the higher the likelihood of the rise of oppositional political ideologies. That is, the greater the state's intervention in culture, the higher the likelihood of the rise of political ideologies; and the lower the state's intervention in culture, the higher the likelihood of the rise of social ideologies.

The State, Discursive Context, and Ideological Production in the Islamic World

We propose that Islamic modernism in India, Egypt, and Iran emerged under conditions of a pluralistic intellectual market and minimal state intervention in culture. Liberal nationalism emerged under conditions of a weak monarchical absolutism (hence liberalism) and foreign domination (hence nationalism). A third alternative is possible when ideological production is directed against the dominant cultural institution in civil society. In nineteenth-century Iran, for example, a weak absolutist state coexisted with a powerful religious institution. The Babi movement in the middle of the century was against the Shi'i orthodoxy. Finally, when the target of attack is the totalitarian ideology of the bureaucratic-authoritarian state, then ideological production tends to display monistic and fundamentalist characteristics and take a political orientation (table 1).

Inductive and Deductive Constraints

The model in table 1 assumes that the factors relevant to the production of ideas are the nature of the intellectual market and its relationship to power. It also assumes that ideological producers enjoy absolute freedom of expression constrained only by the existing sets of signs and their own intellectual capacity (cultural capital and emotional energy). There are, however, other constraints on their utterances. These constraints are principally of two kinds. One set consists of *deductive* constraints. It is hardly the case that ideological producers utter anything out of the blue. Whatever they say is structured by the axioms, parameters, and rules of reasoning of the ideological universe to which they adhere. In this sense, the freedom of expression of ideological producers is limited by the conceptual, methodological, canonical constraints of their own worldviews. Luther could go

Table 1. Ideological movements in the Islamic world

Discursive Field of Target	Location of Target	
	Civil Society	*The State*
Pluralistic	Islamic modernism: India, Egypt, and Iran from the second part of the nineteenth century until the early twentieth	Liberal nationalism: Egypt, Iran, and Syria from the second part of the nineteenth century to the middle of the twentieth
Monolithic	Sectarian ideological movement: Babism in Iran in the middle of the nineteenth century	Islamic fundamentalism: Algeria, Egypt, Iran, "Jordan," and Syria from the 1930s to the 1990s

only so far in attacking the prerogatives of the pope and Catholicism without questioning the basic tenets of Christianity. Likewise, in their formulation of the modernist exegesis of the Quran, the Muslim thinkers of the late nineteenth century were obliged to establish the consistency of their views with the basic Islamic creed in order to avoid the charge of infidelity to their faith and the loss of the right to speak. Similarly, the ideologues of the international communist movement had to carefully monitor their expressions to escape the accusation of opportunism, revisionism, and the betrayal of revolutionary Marxism-Leninism. Deductive constraints are always present, but their boundaries vary depending on the ideology in question. Certain ideologies allow greater freedom of thought than do others. Leninism, for example, appears to display a much more clear-cut definition of socialist democracy than Marxism of the Second International or Western Marxism in the period after the sixties. Likewise, the methodology of Quranic exegesis in Islamic orthodoxy leaves much less room for theological speculations than does the rationalist and naturalistic approach espoused by the Islamic modernists.

All ideologies display a hierarchy of constraints: some are the *core* while others are *peripheral*. For example, all Islamic thinkers must accept as their core constraints that Muhammad is the prophet from God and the Quran is the word of God. In addition to these core constraints, orthodox Muslim theologians adhere to the peripheral constraint that the traditional method of jurisprudence must be followed, whereas Islamic modernists reject this methodology and favor a more rationalistic approach. Likewise, to remain Marxist, one must adhere to the core constraint of the economic determination of the political and cultural institutions and processes (at least in the final analysis). A Marxist-Leninist is further constrained by the peripheral idea of the revolutionary communist vanguard party, the necessity of smashing the "bourgeois state," and imperialism as the highest stage of capitalism.

The deductive constraints may also include the parameters of the world ideological context. The nature of the discourse that is dominant globally, or regionally, may influence the minds of ideological producers. International ideological context involves the definition and codification of the world in terms of such binaries as Christendom versus Heathendom in a Christian worldview; the abode of Islam versus the abode of war in Islamic orthodoxy; civilization versus savagery in the Enlightenment; East versus West, North versus South, and first world versus third world in various "third-world" ideologies; class society versus classless social order in communism; and imperialism versus socialism in Marxism, Leninism, and Maoism. These categories impose certain modes of thinking on ideological producers. It would certainly make a world of difference in the political expressions of, say, native thinkers in the Islamic world whether they subscribed to the image of the West as a civilized order or as an aggressive imperialistic system.

International transfer of meaning and civilizational osmoses also function as deductive constraints. Ideas that are developed in a given community of ideological producers are often transferred to other places. The strategies and tactics for ideological mobilization that are proved effective in one context are replicated by others, and the success of an ideological movement in one country stimulates interests among people in another country with a similar cultural profile. The rise of the idea of revolution and the success of the French Revolution might have contributed to the glorification of the "concept of revolution" and inspired activists in other places to emulate the French model. Because it formed a part of the notion of social evolution and progress, the concept itself became historicized. The Russian Revolution in 1917 convinced many Marxist activists that not only was socialism possible but also Leninism was the correct method of achieving it, and other interpretations of Marxism were instances of revisionism and opportunism. When, on the other hand, an ideological movement fails to solve social problems or improve the life situations of its followers, its validity is called into question. When a given ideological system loses its validity it is tantamount to the removal of the deductive constraints it had on the minds of ideological producers. They need not concern themselves with its conceptual and methodological prerequisites.

Other constraints are related to the effect of social forces outside the realm of ideas. These are *inductive* constraints. Deductive constraints shape the original formulation and development of ideas. Not all ideas, however, find interested audiences and gain institutional support. Certain sets of beliefs may be more attractive than others, and a given constellation of ideas may be popular only among certain groups and classes. A particular ideology may become a dominant discourse under a specific historical condition. In short, ideas correlate with social processes, or, as

Karl Mannheim stated, are "always bound up with the existing life-situation of the thinker."[45] When ideas are adhered to by a significant number of people, gain institutional support, and become a permanent feature of society, people tend to believe that they have been proved correct, verified by the empirical facts of human practice. Marx was probably right when he stated that "idea has always disgraced itself when differed from interests." Ideological producers are often conscious of these real-life impediments to their expressions. They often modify their ideas to fit existing political arrangements.

Inductive constraints determine the likelihood of the dissemination and institutionalization of ideologies. These constraints may operate on three levels. First, the production of ideas is a collective endeavor, and the community of ideological producers often develops its own identity, forming a collective action frame.[46] Collectivity generates power, and this power shapes ideas in a manner that resonates with the organizational interests of the collectivity. Second, beyond collectivity, the institutionalization of an ideological movement depends on the supports of powerful groups, social classes, or the state. Finally, inductive constraints operate on the broader context of the existing international structure, consisting of the world economy, interstate relations, and international nongovernmental organizations.

Episode

Meaning is produced within the context of the present. The present in the life of the ideological producer is a niche generated by his or her emotional energy, cultural capital, lifestyle, life chances, memory, and social network. These factors always undergo changes, but the changes are often minor and incremental. There are occurrences in the ideological producer's life, but they are of small magnitude, and life appears continuous. The continuity of life, however, is interrupted by dramatic events that may cause a change in the social order or in people's perception of existing social arrangements. The interim between such events constitutes an episode: a bounded historical process that has a beginning and an end, and displaying a certain distinctiveness by virtue of its difference from the preceding and following episodes. Episodes begin and end with such events as a military coup, a significant social and political upheaval, the outbreak of a war or a revolution, or dramatic changes in a government's policies, a sudden economic swing, or an important innovation, whether indigenously created or imported. These events have significance because they provide empirical data in relation to which ideological producers confirm or negate a given system of ideas. Such historical events, says William Sewell, Jr., "tend to transform social relations . . . they reshape history, imparting an unforeseen direction to social development and altering the nature of the causal nexus in which social interactions take place."[47]

We use the concept of episode to stress discontinuity in ideological production. A currently dominant cultural movement may have no conceptual, symbolic, or methodological affinity with the preceding cultural movement. The preceding cultural movement may even constitute the target of ideological production. Depending on the social context, the present discourse may be an antithesis of, a reaction to, or simply an ideological innovation within the preceding discourse. This discontinuity is more pronounced in the unsettled social context of the contemporary Middle East. While past discourses may provide clues to the understanding of the present, it is important to consider the specific political, social, and cultural arrangements that were formed following a major event in society—a coup, a revolution, an act of terrorism, or a sociopolitical crisis or social upheaval. These events and the subsequent rearrangement of the social forces may cause changes in the worldviews of ideological producers and determine the domination of a particular discourse in society. Hence, ideology is conceptualized as episodic discourse.

An episode delineates the immediate context of ideological production—where social resources and cultural schema come into play in the production of meaning.[48] In a settled environment, one may expect a functional compatibility between inductive and deductive constraints. There is an overlap between the limits imposed on one's discourse by the belief system and the limits imposed by the societal hierarchy. In an unsettled social environment, changes in class relations or state structures relax the constraints imposed on ideological producers. Or, alternatively, the dynamics of debates, ideological disputations, and the international transfer of meaning may also provide a context for ideological change. These factors may stimulate awareness among intellectuals of alternative modes and methods of viewing social reality.

The Methodology and Strategy of Comparison

We use these propositions to analyze the determinants of diverse ideological production in the Islamic world. Our observation of Islamic modernism in India, Egypt, and Iran covers a period from the nineteenth century to the early twentieth, our observation of territorial nationalism in Egypt, Arabism and pan-Arab nationalism in Syria, and anticlerical secularism and constitutionalism in Iran covers a period from the second part of the nineteenth century to the the middle of the twentieth, and our observation of Islamic fundamentalism in Algeria, Egypt, Iran, Jordan, and Syria covers a period between the nineteenth thirties and nineteenth nineties. We employ two sets of variables. One set pertains to such broader social factors as changes in the economy, demographic expansion, changes in state structures and policies, and changes in class relations and class formation. The other sets measures the proximate conditions of ideological projection—the structure of the intellectual market and its connection to power.

Our comparative methodological strategy is based on John Stuart Mill's criteria of causality: methods of agreement, difference, and concomitant variations.[49] In the first part of this book, our analysis of the origins of Islamic modernism in India, Egypt, and Iran proceeds in two stages. First, we assess the role of the social forces—in particular, the state and social classes—in providing the requisite social resources and space for Islamic modernism. Next, we evaluate the effect of discursive pluralism on the development of new religious positions on key issues. Discursive pluralism is reflected in the number of ideological groups in society.[50] It is also measured in terms of the degree of conceptual diversity of existing discourses and the diversity of the positions taken by ideological groups on historically significant issues. Taking both indicators together, we may argue that the higher the number and the higher the conceptual heterogeneity of the discourses that are present in an intellectual market, the higher the level of discursive pluralism. We try to show the effect of variations in discursive pluralism on the worldviews of Muslim intellectual leaders. Likewise, we attempt to assess the relationship between variations in the role of the state in the intellectual market and rise of social or political discourses. In this part, our comparative analysis conforms to Mill's method of agreement.

In the second part of this study, we analyze the origins of territorial nationalism in Egypt, anticlerical secularism and constitutionalism in Iran, and liberal Arabism and Arab nationalism in Syria. We assess the degree to which these discourses were related to changes in the institutional structures and policies of the state, class politics, the ideologies of the absolutist state, and Western intervention. We also consider such other factors as the rise of the indigenous educated elite, the rise of or a renewed emphasis on the need for a national language, an awareness of the ancient and pre-Islamic history of the homeland, the demarcation of national boundaries, and the rise of Christian and Jewish intellectuals. Our objective is to show the variations in liberal nationalism in terms of the differences in the nature of the ideological targets in opposition to which this discourse was produced. To what extent, for example, can territorial nationalism in Egypt, the change in Syrian political discourse from emphasis on individual liberty to the subordination of this liberty for the emancipation of the Arab land, and the change of Iranian anticlerical secularism and constitutionalism to economic nationalism be related to the kind of ideological targets faced by the intellectual leaders? The strategy of comparison in this part converges on Mill's method of concomitant variation[51] and Charles Tilly's variation-finding comparison.[52]

In the final part of this book, Algeria, Egypt, Iran, Jordan, and Syria are compared and contrasted in terms of changes in state structure and policies, class formation, demographic changes, and the nature of the intellectual market. Our objectives are (1) to uncover the common features of the social conditions of Islamic fundamentalism and the way in which the variations in these conditions can explain the variations in the discourse and orientations of the Islamic fundamentalist groups, and (2) to demonstrate how these common features display a sharp contrast with the conditions of Islamic modernism. Although the comparative analysis of Islamic fundamentalism in Egypt, Iran, and Syria may provide adequate data to uncover the common factors underpinning this movement, Algeria and Jordan were included to rule out the validity of rival explanations of Islamic fundamentalism. These include the extent to which Shi'i institutional development explains the strength of fundamentalism and the relative weakness of Islamic modernism in Iran. Thus, Iran's sharp contrast with other cases may lend credibility to the argument that Iran is a special case whose religious experience was shaped principally by the specific development of Shi'ism. The analysis of the Algerian case provides a strong empirical basis for the assessment of this argument. This is because in terms of strength, the Islamic movement in Algeria was similar to the movement in Iran. That is, Algeria *agrees* with Iran. Yet, in contrast with Iran, the Algerian ulama were not as politically strong as their Iranian counterparts. Further, some of the prominent Algerian ulama had in the past displayed a fairly strong tendency toward modernity, rather than the traditionalism that had been the predominant feature of the Iranian ulama. In terms of past historical experience of religious movement, Iran and Algeria are in *contrast*. In accordance with Mill's methods, what is common to both Algeria and Iran must then be considered the cause of fundamentalism, not the singularity of Iran's religious experience.

Another rival explanation is related to Western intervention. Conventional explanations of Islamic fundamentalism revolve around the issue of Western cultural invasion, economic infiltration, and political domination of the region and the ensuing socioeconomic inequality and arbitrary rule. Considering the view of the fundamentalists on diverse subjects ranging from Western democracy to the role of women, this explanation seems persuasive. There are considerable differences between Western culture and the cultural outlook of Islamic fundamentalists. This explanation is particularly applicable to the countries that had close ties to the West. It may thus be argued that the ruling elite's alliance with the West was consequential for the rise of fundamentalism. This alliance resulted in the influx of foreign ideas, material culture, and consumerism—all of which were perceived as violating Islamic tenets, provoking the hostility of the Islamic groups and their mobilization against the state. An anlysis of Jordanian fundamentalism provides the empirical data for assessing the adequacy of the conventional argument. The Kingdom of Jordan was a Western ally, yet it managed to maintain a peaceful relationship with the Muslim Brothers. Thus, if the causal model advanced in this work is correct, the factors that were present in the cases of Algeria, Egypt, Iran, and Syria must necessarily be absent or weak in the case of Jordan.

Storytelling: The Interaction between Sociology and History

In this study, we cover the period beginning with the decline of the Islamic empires in the seventeenth century to the rise of Islamic fundamentalism in the second half of the twentieth century. From this broad historical period, we select certain episodes and then advance a cross-national and historical comparative analysis of the social conditions in each episode in order to illuminate key sociological variables governing the patterns of stability and change in the production of discourse. We propose that the variations in the immediate social and discursive context— whether it is pluralistic or monolithic and its proximity to power—had a determinate impact on the expressions of the intellectual leaders as they tried to address the significant issues facing their society. Our approach is disinterested. We do not make any teleological assumption about the dynamic of historical change. Nor do we subscribe to the notion of evolutionary history and its offshoot in the twentieth-century modernization perspective. Nevertheless, the fact that these countries contemporaneously experienced Islamic modernism, then liberal nationalism, and finally Islamic fundamentalism may signify that what was at work was certainly more than the interactions among several historical variables sociologically constructed. At the same time, these intellectual leaders, be it Islamic modernists, liberal nationalists, national royalists, liberal Arabists, Arab nationalists, or Islamic fundamentalists—were all part of a larger saga of the systematic cultural encounters between the West and Islam that started sometime around the turn of the nineteenth century and are still going on.

We cannot reduce the history of this encounter to the interplay of a set of sociological variables. Certainly, our sociological model casts serious doubt on certain teleological readings of the Islamic history in the modern period, which range from various conspiratorial theories to more sophisticated variants of Orientalism perspective to the criticisms of Orientalism that have treated Western scholarship on the Orient as a function of various forms of power. There are always inequalities in the distribution of power both within and between societies. This study, however, disengages the Foucauldian notion, and its Saidian offshoot in the area of Middle Eastern studies, of the connection between ideas and power. If power plays a crucial role in the generation of discourse, it is not the structure of power per se. It is rather the nature of the interconnections between the power structure and the structure of the ideological market that, I propose, shapes the orientation of ideological producers. This disengagement is particularly crucial because the existing power structure cannot harness ideological production as effectively as it maintains obedience to its rule in economic activity and the fulfillment of roles in a social hierarchy. Even under unequally distributed power, the subject population often devises ways to change or revise the dominant discourse.[53] Likewise, our model raises serious questions about the adequacy of the text-based and reductive account of the Islamicists. Certainly, Islam's teachings on politics, gender, and international relations and other issues may have a bearing on the expressions of Muslim intellectual leaders. Nevertheless, one cannot explain the variations in various Islamic discourses in terms of their analysis of the text.

The broader Islamic cultural tradition, the similar sequence of ideological movements experienced in the selected Islamic countries, and the invariance of the issues addressed by the intellectual leaders—all are indicative of a wider historical story in the modern period that started with Islamic modernism and ended with fundamentalism. Our sociological model is intended to explain the different scenes of this story, not its overall dynamic. We try to demonstrate how the diversity of these scenes would account for the diversity of the ideas formulated by various thinkers. We argue that it is in these scenes that various thinkers faced one another, debated pertinent issues, mutually structured their utterances, and formulated their ideological resolutions. Nevertheless, the scenes do not tell the story, the plot, and they do not reveal the hero or the villain.

We contend that the experience of ideological movements in the Islamic world in the modern period constitutes a story. The major setting is cultural encounters between Islam and the West and the establishment of Western hegemony in the Islamic world. In this encounter, the major debate is over the meaning and the status of secular reasoning. The protagonists of the story are the intellectual leaders. The story is about attempts by these thinkers to control arbitrary rulings—in politics and culture. If the expansion or contraction of the intellectual space was the key factor contributing to the ability of these intellectual leaders to produce a more generalized, abstract, and universalistic discourse, the villain of the story, as we shall try to demonstrate in the third part of this book, is the character who was responsible for narrowing this space—the exclusionary secular ideological state.

THE RISE OF
ISLAMIC MODERNISM

Introduction to Part One

Many of the ad hoc explanations of the origins of Islamic fundamentalism in the twentieth century refer to historical factors that were also present in the Islamic countries in the nineteenth century—Western domination, the invasion of the cultural landscape by various alien ideologies, incorporation into the world economy and vulnerability to the economic fluctuations in the world market, the existence of socioeconomic inequality, and arbitrary rule and authoritarianism. Yet the responses of Muslim intellectual leaders to the encounter with Western culture were predominantly modernist, not fundamentalist. In fact, the countries that experienced the most notable expansion of Islamic modernism—Egypt and India—were also under the direct colonial rule of a Western power. Generally, across India, Egypt, and Iran (and Algeria), the ulama were favorably disposed toward the construction of a modern political order.

While variations in the social structures and social processes may explain the variations in the religious outcomes in the two different periods, on the level of thought processes, it seems, the key factor was the presence of a discursive space in the Islamic intellectual movement that made it possible for Muslim intellectual leaders to see somewhat clearly, despite their country's low level of industrial and commercial development in the late nineteenth century, the benefit of the European model of social engineering in constructing a new sociopolitical order. This intellectual space was made possible by two developments. The first was changes in the conception of sovereignty in historical Islam from from one that emphasized the unity of religion and politics in the early Islamic theory of the caliphate to a conception that progressively amounted to the admission of the reality of secular politics. This secular politics was thought to be Islamic to the extent that the ruler defended the faith and maintained an alliance with the ulama and sought and implemented their advice. The decline of the absolutist state from the eighteen century on constituted a favorable condition for such thinkers as Shah Waliallah in India and Muhammad Ibn Abd al-Wahhab on the Arabian Peninsula to reflect on and criticize the Islamicity of the current political order. Their thought provided an Islamic precedent for the modernists to question the adequacy of Islamic orthodoxy.

Second, the social transformation of the nineteenth century and the emergence of a pluralistic intellectual environment further expanded this discursive space. In addition, the philosophical debates and religious disputations among diverse ideological groups contributed to the rise and crystallization of several issues that Muslim intellectual leaders found difficult to resolve within the traditional framework of Islamic orthodoxy. The Islamic modernist discourse was thus produced as these intellectual leaders attempted to formulate their responses to serious questions posed to their faith by the followers of the Enlightenment, Westernizers, and missionaries. Their answers were certainly constrained by the existing sociopolitical arrangements as well as by the depth and breath of the social transformation that their countries were experiencing. The variations in the content of their discourses were determined by the variations in the nature of the existing intellectual markets. At any rate, the contraction of the discursive space by the secular ideological state in the twentieth century provided the intellectual condition for the rise of Islamic fundamentalism.

In chapter 1, we shall try to describe the Islamic conceptual scaffolding, the status of secular politics (i.e., the ruler's discretionary power), and rational reasoning in historical Islam, the relationship between religion and politics in premodern India, Egypt, and Iran, the crises of the traditional order in these countries, and the variations in the social transformation that these countries experienced in the nineteenth century. Chapter 2 has dual objectives. First, it summarizes the views of Shah Waliallah and Muhammad Ibn Abd al-Wahhab and then discusses the diffusion of Western culture in Islamic countries, Muslims' perception of the West, and the West's of Islamic countries. In chapters 3–5, we shall try to explain the rise of Islamic modernist discourse in India, Egypt, and Iran and the variations in this discourse in terms of variations in the targets (regimes of signification) Muslim thinkers encountered in these countries.

ONE

Social Transformation
and the Origins of Islamic Modernism

India, Egypt, and Iran had already experienced different yet profound social transformations when a group of Muslim scholars found themselves in a favorable social environment to reexamine the Islamic belief system in light of modern sociopolitical thought. This transformation involved the expansion of commerce, incorporation into the world capitalist economy, the development of capitalism, the decline of old and the rise of new social classes, the rise of the modern state, and the emergence of new and diverse cultural movements. As a result, the requisite social resources and space for culture production were provided, a pluralistic discursive field emerged, and the formulation of Islamic modernism became possible.

Three sets of historical factors contributed to the genesis of Islamic modernism: those that removed the institutional barriers to ideological innovation, those that provided the social space, resources, and need for this innovation, and those that formed the intellectual context in relation to which this new discourse was actually produced. The destruction of the absolutist state and the decline of Islamic orthodoxy were among the first set, the rise of the modern state and the formation of new social classes and class alignments were among the second set, and the emergence of a pluralistic intellectual market and the illumination of a series of ideological targets were among the last set.

The last of the three sets constituted the proximate conditions of Islamic modernism. The Islamic modernists developed a new set of ideas in relation to several distinctive ideological targets. One was the discourse of Islamic orthodoxy, which claimed a monopoly of legitimate religious expressions. The others were the secular discourses and religious ideologies that, as a result of the European interventions, started to invade the cultural landscape of Islamic countries with powerful force from the late eighteenth century on. These included the secular discourse of the Enlightenment, the narrower Europe-centered rationalist discourse of the think tanks connected to British colonial administrations and Westernizers, and the cultural and religious discourse of Christian Evangelicals. Islamic modernism was an ideological resolution of a group of Muslim intellectuals who attempted to address the intellectual problems that beset Islam as a result of the sweeping criticisms leveled against it by adherents of theses discourses. These criticisms by arousing the need among Muslim thinkers to defend their faith, compelled them to take new positions on various issues facing Islam, which resulted in the emergence of an Islamic modernist discourse. Understanding the determinants of Islamic modernism thus requires an understanding of traditional Islamic discourse and diverse critiques of it.

The process of change in India, Egypt, and Iran was by no means homogeneous. It carried different types of constraints and opportunities for the actors involved. In India, the decline of the Mughals and the outbreak of internecine conflicts among the Muslim and Hindu power contenders drove the *zamindars* (landowners) and merchants toward an alliance with the East India Company. The breakdown of the Mughal Empire and the establishment of British colonial rule over the Indian territories removed the institutional barriers to cultural change and facilitated the spread of Western culture on the subcontinent. In Egypt, cultural change was preceded by the rise and massive expansion of the bureaucratic and military apparatuses of the state in the first half of the nineteenth century. The state's need for skilled personnel knowledgeable in European military technology promoted the establishment of modern educational institutions, which in turn facilitated the diffusion of new ideas from Europe in Egypt. The state thus provided the necessary social space for the rise of modern discourses. In Iran, in contrast, the state remained conservative throughout the nineteenth century, and the Shi'i establishment maintained a strong grip on culture, effectively exhausting any attempt at cultural innovation and modernization. Iranian merchants, on the other hand, resentful of the increasing encroachment on their domestic market by Russian and British concerns and angered by the state's indifference to their interests, became the principle force behind nationalist demands for constitutional change. Ironically, a section of the ulama aligned with these merchants and, along with secular intellectuals, led the revolutionary movement of the early twentieth century that overthrew absolutism and established a constitutional system.

Religion and Politics in the Premodern Period

Premodern India, Egypt, and Iran were part of the three great empires, the Mughal, the Ottoman, and the Safavid, which sheltered almost the entire territory of dar ul-Islam (abode of Islam) from the early sixteenth century to the end of the eighteenth. Although this gives the history of Islam during these centuries a recognizable political and cultural pattern,[1] there were considerable variations in social structure, state administration, and religious institutions not only among these empires but also within them. Each empire had its own political and security concerns. The Mughals were a Muslim minority ruling a majority of Hindu and other non-Muslim subjects. The Ottomans faced Europe and the political challenges of various rulers in different regions and principalities within their dominion. The Safavids were at work consolidating Shi'ism as the state religion and subduing challenges from diverse tribal groups in the country. These empires also had different religious profiles. Mughal India was religiously nonunified, the Ottomans belonged to the majority Sunni sect of Islam, and Iranians adhered to Shi'ism, a minority sect. The relationships between these three political entities, while mostly peaceful, on occasion broke into military confrontations. The wars between the Ottomans and the Safavids in the sixteenth century, with concomitant violent repression of their Shi'i and Sunni minorities living in their respective dominions, and between the Mughals and Nadir Shah of Iran in the eighteenth century are prime examples. It is thus difficult to find a pattern of historical behaviors and social relationships that are common to these empires or are constituting elements.

On Islam and the role of Islamic institutions under these empires historians are divided. One pole in the spectrum of views considers Islam an integral part of the traditional order. As a belief system, this view considers Islam impervious to change, incompatible with democracy and modern social institutions.[2] Another pole considers Islamic theology rational and rejects the notion that Islam was a monolithic faith by emphasizing the presence of Islamic pluralism in the premodern period.[3] There may be elements of truth in both positions. Our objective here is not to pass judgment on the role of Islam in history or, alternatively, assess the adequacy of the judgments passed on Islam by its nineteenth-century critics. It is rather to present an adequate description of traditional Islamic discourse, the structure of Islamic institutions, and ties to the existing power in order to gain an understanding of the nature of the issues being contested as a result of the cultural encounter between the West and the Islamic world and to explain why this encounter shaped the rationale for Muslim thinkers to reexamine their faith.

Islamic Jurisprudence and the Limiting of Rational Analysis: Closing of the Gate of Ijtihad

Generally, Islamic worldviews rested on a series of binaries, which defined Islam as a religion and its followers as members of a religious community (*umma*). These included *wahy* (revelation) versus *'aql* (reason), *towhid* (divine unity) versus *shirk* (idol worshipping), *shari'a* (Islamic law) versus *jahiliyya* (the state of ignorance), *dar ul-Islam* (the abode of Islam) versus *dar ul-harb* (the abode of war), *wilaya* (delegation by God) versus *mulk* (hereditary rule), *khilapha* (spiritual authority) versus *sultanate* (temporal authority), and *umma* (universalistic Islamic community) versus *asabiyya* (particularistic tribal solidarity). The Islamic regulative and normative codes of conduct, which covered virtually all aspects of human endeavor, were formulated during centuries of doctrinal development marked by intense discussions and often acrimonious debates. By the medieval period, these codes had grown into a full-blown system of laws specifying the Islamic way of life (*shari'a*). The *fiqh,* or the knowledge of the practical rules of religion, was to regulate the actions of all Muslims, which fall into five categories: (1) required (*wajib*), (2) forbidden (*mahzur*), (3) recommended (*mandub*), (4) disapproved (*makruh*), and (5) merely permitted (*mubah*).[4]

Four schools of Islamic jurisprudence laid the methodological foundation of Islamic laws in the Sunni sect. These schools were a medieval legacy, which came to fruition in order to address the problems Muslim administrators and generals faced as a result of the passage of time and the expansion of Islam into new territories. For these problems, there were no specific guidelines in the scripture or in the tradition of the prophet. They stimulated the need for rational reasoning to establish new principles that were Islamic and at the same time controlled the rule of the judges and regulated the conduct of the Arab administrators. Abu Hanifa was the first to introduce a new rule of reasoning known as *qiyas* (analogy), which went beyond the literal meaning of the Quranic text to uncover its causal (*'illa*) underpinnings.[5] Because unfettered employment of *qiyas* resulted in abuse and encouraged casuistry, Malik Ibn Anas, the founder of the second school, gave primacy to the tradition of the prophet or local custom after the Quran, with *qiyas* to be used only as a last resort.[6] Yet these two positions dissatisfied the founder of the third school, Muhammad al-Shafi'i, who extended the principle of *ijma* (consensus) beyond the jurists of Medina to include all the ideas and decisions that were agreed upon by all the competent authorities in Islam. The four roots of Islamic jurisprudence in the Shafi'i school of law were thus the Quran, the hadith, ijma, and qiyas. Ahmad Ibn Hanbal, the fourth and final authoritative figure in Sunni jurisprudence, attacked qiyas. For him, rationalist interpretation of the Quran and tradition was permissible, and thus the ijma was unlawful innovation (*bid'a*). After the death of Ibn Hanbal, the gate of *ijtihad* was considered closed among the Sunnis, and all the jurists were instructed to follow one of these four orthodox schools.[7]

The early Shi'i believed that all laws were implicit in the Quran and the hadith and were to be discovered by the jurists, and that there was no need for ra'y (opinion), its offshoot qiyas, or ijma. With the passage of time, however, these theologians started to face practical problems similar to those encountered by their Sunni counterparts, which could not be resolved by reference to the Quran or the hadith.

The Shi'i fiqh thus developed in a fashion similar to the Sunni and came to rest on the Quran, the hadith, ijma, and *'aql*.[8]

Islam and the Problem of Secular Politics

Islamic conceptions of politics also underwent profound changes after their early formulation in the doctrine of the *khilafa* (caliphate). As the successor to Muhammad, the *khalifa* (caliph) was to assume the activities and privileges exercised by Muhammad save the prophetic functions.[9] The question of who had the necessary qualifications to be the leader of the Islamic community and how the Islamic conception of authority was to be reconciled with changing political reality after the death of the Prophet remained the arduous task of Muslim theologians cum political theorists. The Sunni theorists are unanimous about the legitimacy of the first four caliphs, given the honorific title of the *Rashidun*—exemplars of rightful Muslim rulers. Nevertheless, the changing political realities of the post-Rashidun caliphate under the Umayyads (661–750), the Abbasids (750–1258), and thereafter provided serious problems for Muslim jurists: How is one to reconcile the Islamic notion of sovereignty with the claims of a self-made caliph among the continuously emerging military leaders and tribal chiefs in different parts of the Islamic world?

In their sustained efforts to reconcile the theory of the caliphate and the existing political reality, Muslim scholars more and more departed from the conception of politics as the unity of the political and religious leadership in the person of the caliph to take positions that progressively amounted to the admission of the reality of secular politics—the differentiation between religious and political leadership. First Abu al-Hasan Ali al-Mawardi (972–1058), in his *Ordinances of Government,* attempted to legitimize the authority of the caliph vis-à-vis the challenges of the Muslim rulers who had effective power within their own territories. It bound the ruler of each successor state to the centralized spiritual authority of the Abbasid caliphate and gave him delegated legal authority in his own territory and a claim to the loyalty of his subjects.[10] Later development, however, undermined al-Mawardi's formula. Effective power was in the hands of the Kurdish, Turkish, or Caucasian military elite, whose actions were dictated by the exigencies of political power rather than the shari'a. Thus, "to maintain that the sultan derived his power from the caliph was increasingly difficult as it became clear that in fact the caliph was set up and deposed by the sultan."[11] A further concession to expediency was offered by Imam Muhammad al-Ghazali (1058–1111)—the celebrated Shafi'i theologian, religious scholar, and mystic. Al-Ghazali argued that as long as the authority of the caliph was recognized, the sultan should be treated as lawful. Trying to unseat the sultan by declaring his power illegal would result in lawlessness and chaos (*fitnih*), a condition more detrimental to the welfare of Muslims than having a tyrant in power.[12]

Clearly, in al-Ghazali's thinking there was a definite shift "from the origin of political power to its use."[13] This shift was necessitated by the changing condition of the Muslim community. At the same time, it reflected the influence of Greek philosophy—in particular, the views of Plato and Aristotle—on Islam. Muslim philosophers like Abu Nasr Farabi (870–950) and al-Husayn Ibn Abdullah Ibn Sina (Avicenna, 980–1037) were impressed by classical Greek views and attempted to resolve the problem of leadership in a manner acceptable to the philosophic mind and at the same time remain loyal to their faith. Their basic conclusion was unorthodox when they argued that, in Albert Hourani's summary, "the content of the divine law was attainable in principle by the unaided human intellect, and failing a prophet a good system of law could grow up in society in other ways."[14] While such orthodox thinkers as al-Ghazali and Taqi al-Din Ahmad Ibn Taymiyya (1263–1328) were suspicious of philosophy, traces of Greek philosophy and the views of Farabi and Ibn Sina could be detected in their works.

Noting a poor fit between the ideal Islamic state and the political reality of their time, later scholars as diverse as Ibn Taymiyya and Abd al-Rahman Ibn Khaldun (1333–1406) conceded that the caliphate had ceased after the fourth caliph and that the sovereignty exercised by the Umayyads and the Abbasids had never been more than a "royalty."[15] For Ibn Khaldun, royal authority was a form of social organization that "requires superiority and force, which expresses the wrathfulness and animality (of human nature)."[16] Like their predecessors, these thinkers did not suggest the overthrow of the existing ruler. They worked out a formula for observing the shari'a while recognizing discretionary power. Ibn Taymiyya expanded the concept of the shari'a to bring within its scope the ruler's "discretionary power without which he could neither maintain himself nor provide for the welfare of the community."[17] He did so by applying the principle of *maslaha*. Since God's purpose in giving laws was human welfare, the ruler's discretionary power was necessary not just for his own protection but also for providing for the welfare (i.e., maslaha) of the community. While his doctrine assured the legitimacy of the Mamluk government in Egypt, it also contained the precept that a "good government depended on an alliance between amirs, political and military leaders, and 'ulama,' interpreters of the law."[18] In a similar fashion, Ibn Khaldun offered a way to incorporate Islam into the "natural life span" of dynasties so that a more stable and universalistic regime would be created.

In Shi'ism, the doctrine of *imamat* states that the political authority of the Prophet devolves on Ali (the Prophet's son-in-law and the fourth caliph in Sunni Islam) and his male descendants. Ali is considered the first rightful imam, followed by eleven imams in twelver Shi'ism. Following the occultation of the twelfth imam, the world was left without a legitimate authority. Since the Shi'i lived as a minority in a hostile Sunni environment, the Shi'i ulama took the practical course of renouncing the legitimacy of the existing order while abstaining from any rebellious action.[19] The elevation of Shi'ism to the status of state religion under the Safavids (1501–1722) paralleled a significant shift in Shi'i political theory in a direction remarkably similar to that of Sunni. In this new development, the doctrine of imamat, which initially embodied the twin functions of religion and politics in the twelfth imam, was differentiated: the ulama assumed religious authority and the shah political leadership. Mutual assistance and cooperation between the ruler and the ulama was considered necessary for the betterment of the country and religion.[20]

The Sociopolitical Status of the Ulama

The recognition of the ruler's discretionary power legitimized the institutional separation of religion and politics. This legitimacy, however, was predicated upon an alliance between the ulama and the sultan, a precept laid down by Ibn Taymiyya. In Mughal India, Mamluk Egypt, and Safavid and Qajar Iran, there were fairly cordial relations between the religious and political hierarchies.[21] At the apex of the Islamic establishment were the ulama who attained the approval of a great body of jurists or a level of intellectual competence to be able to settle differences and decide questions of general discipline. These ulama enjoy the honorific title of Sheikh ul-Islam or Sadr us-Sudur in different parts of the Islamic world.[22] These religious notables were appointed by the rulers.[23] Under the Ottomans, the title of Sheikh ul-Islam was bestowed by the sultan upon the *mufti* of Constantinople, whose office carried a religious and political significance unparalleled in other Muslim countries,[24] and in Mughal India, Sadr us-Sudur was appointed by the emperor.[25] These ulama endorsed the power of the ruler and read the Friday sermon (*khutbah*) in his name. The emperor and these religious leaders often had friendly relationships. For example, a certain Sheikh Abdul Nabi, appointed Sadr us-Sudur by Mughal Emperor Akbar in 1565, was given authority that no other holder of the office had ever enjoyed. The emperor had such a great faith in the sheikh that he would bring and place his shoes before his feet.[26]

In addition to the mosques, the schools of higher learning known as *madrasas* were the ulama's major institutional support. These schools gained increasing significance in the Islamic world from the eleventh century on.[27] Political stability under the Saljuqs in the eleventh century promoted the expansion of Muslim education as the ruling elite established madrasas to educate the leaders and governors of their country. In 1078, Nizamul Mulk—the all-powerful vizier of the early Saljuq period (1063–92) founded the military school in Baghdad.[28] Effectively controlling the content of the school curricula, the ulama maintained their control over the religion. The ulama often revealed an astonishing degree of ruthlessness in persecuting the unorthodox and devastating the unfaithful. In India in

1577, Sadr us-Sudur Sheikh Abdul Nabi ordered the execution of a rich Brahman who had cursed the Prophet.[29] In Egypt and Iran the ulama also went out of their way to suppress the unorthodox and severely punish those they considered unfaithful to the faith.

Naturally, their religious and political influences brought them substantial wealth. Some of the ulama were wealthy landowners, and some were even engaged in commerce. In premodern Egypt, the ulama managed the wealth of minors and orphans, schools, mosques, and hospitals and above all managed the funds of charitable endowments, the *awqaf* (plural of *waqf*), which in the early nineteenth century covered almost one-fifth of the total cultivable land and which included perhaps even a higher proportion of real estate and other forms of urban property. They were also involved in every form of commercial transaction, since all sales, purchases, and transfers of property had to be authorized by a judge and in the presence of a witness.[30] Baer places the ulama on a level with the Mamluk elite; they were among the chief multazims, built luxurious palaces, and surrounded themselves with servants and hangers-on.[31] The Iranian ulama also owned considerable landed property in the nineteenth century, partly a Safavid legacy and partly the result of proulama practices of Qajar rulers.[32] In certain parts of the country, notably Azarbaijan and Isfahan, the ulama were an important element in the landowning class.[33] In Mughal India, the ulama formed an open-ended petty bourgeois class, although people with aristocratic backgrounds could be found in their midst.[34] At the court of Akbar, for example, there was a powerful Makhdum-ul-Mulk, who accumulated so much wealth that when he died, thirty million rupees in cash were found in his house, and several boxes containing gold blocks were buried in a false tomb.[35] Religious leaders, jurists, muftis, qadis (judges), theologians, judicial officers, and important poets and writers were known as *ahl-i saadat* (virtuous) and were conscious of their superior social position.[36]

Revenue grants, known as *madad'i ma'ash* (aid for subsistence), were a principal source of income for the ulama in India. Abul Fazl, a noted historian in the Aurangzeb court, specified four classes of persons who were the recipients of these grants: men of learning; religious devotees; the destitute; and people of noble lineage, who could not take any employment. The bulk of these grants were given to the first two groups.[37] A department was charged with looking after these grants and presided over by the Sadr us-Sudur at the court, provincial sadrs (*sadr-i juzv*), and, at the lowest level, *mutawallis*.[38] In 1769, Aurangzeb issued a decree making this assistance hereditary, but with the proviso that it was to be governed by imperial orders, not by the shari'a.[39] In short, a structural harmony characterized the relationship between the Islamic institutions and the bureaucratic and military organization of the state in premodern India, Egypt, and Iran.

Although Muslim rulers enjoyed absolute power in pursuing their political interests and military goals, the ulama often put up stiff resistance against what they consider undue intervention in religious affairs and protested any serious violation of Islamic laws by the incumbent ruler.[40] Even in religiously nonunified India, Emperor Akbar could go only so far in modifying his religious policy. When in addition to the Muslims, the scholars of other faiths, such as Hindu pandits, Parsi mobeds, and Jain sadhus were invited to his *ibadat khana* (house of worship), serious disaffection developed among the ulama, some of whom even declared Akbar an infidel, leading to an open rebellion in 1581.[41]

The Crisis of the Traditional Order and Social Transformation

The traditional order in India, Egypt, and Iran was undermined by the gradual intensification of economic, political, and cultural crises in the course of the seventeenth century and thereafter, which led to a social transformation involving incorporation into the world economy, the development of capitalism, and the emergence of modern social institutions. On the nature of the crises that brought down the formidable bureaucratic and military organizations of the Islamic empires and on the patterns of social transformation, historians are not able to settle their debates on each case, let alone reach consensus on the causes of change that were common to all. Nevertheless, after the tumult of economic dislocation was replaced by some degree of serenity and the chaos of conflicts gave way to a more clear configuration of political and social hierarchies, the picture that emerged in nineteenth-century India, Egypt, and Iran showed similar types of actors whose varying levels of resources and various political alliances broadly accounted for the variations in culture production among these countries. These actors were the ulama, merchants and landowners, the state, modern intellectuals, the missionaries, and the colonial powers.

India

Historians are by and large unanimous that a structural crisis set the Mughal Empire on a course of rapid disintegration.[42] Yet they differ on the cause and nature of this crisis. For some, it was rooted in the problem of the *jagirdari* system. *Jagirdar* was the right to collect revenues on the state lands that was given to provincial Mughal governors in lieu of their salaries. "The jagirdari crisis" ensued as a result of a widening gap between the salary demands of the jagirdars (who was appointed for no more than four years) and the revenues that could be squeezed from the peasants working on these lands.[43] As a result, cultivation fell off as oppression increased and peasants left the land because they could not survive. Squeezed between the jagirdars and the peasantry, the zamindars rose in armed revolt at the head of their peasant dependents.[44] Another view considers that recovery from the shortage of *jagir* was possible but attributes the cause of the crisis to the political conflict and internecine wars between rival factions of the ruling elite in the early eighteenth century.[45] Finally, for C. A. Bayly, the crisis of India in the eighteenth century was complex, having three distinct aspects: the cumulative indigenous changes reflecting commercialization, group formations, and political change; the wider crisis of western and southern Asia signaled by the decline of the Mughal, Ottoman, and Safavid empires; and massive European expansion and intervention.[46]

The restiveness of the Hindu warriors and peasant farmers coupled with the invasion of the country by the Persian Nadir Shah in 1739 and later the Afghans (1759–61) sped up the decline of imperial power. As a result, provincial governors in Awadh, Bengal, and the Deccan surreptitiously consolidated their own regional bases of power. In 1757, the East India Company seized control of the rich province of Bengal, and in 1759 it removed the last vestige of Mughal influence at Surat on the west coast. After a brief rearguard action in defense of the core area of Delhi, the Mughal emperor submitted in 1784 to the "protection" of the greatest of the Maratha war chiefs, Mahadji Scindia. With the latter's defeat by the British armies in 1803, Delhi was occupied by the company. The emperor was reduced in European eyes to the status of a pathetic "tinsel sovereign," surrounded by the emaciated ladies of his harem and chamberlains who maintained the shadow of his authority through the reiteration of court rituals.[47]

The decline of the Mughal Empire signified a major social transition in which the Indians "remained active agents and not simply passive bystanders and victims in the creation of colonial India."[48] Social groups and classes such as the Hindu and Muslim revenue farmers, Indian merchants who were largely Hindus of the traditional commercial castes or Jains, and local gentry and the zamindars emerged into the limelight. By the middle of the eighteenth century, the indigenous merchants were a powerful interest in all the major states that had emerged from the decline of the Delhi power. The zamindars began to tax markets and trade and to seize prebendal lands that the Mughal elite had once tried to keep out of their hands.[49] Many of these elements later provided capital, knowledge, and support for the East India Company, thus becoming its uneasy collaborators in the creation of colonial India.[50] According to Farhat Hassan, Calcutta, which formed the nucleus of British expansion in India for a considerable period, was a haven for influential merchants' communities, literati-officials, brokers, and bankers. A complex set of factors that involved the cooperation of indigenous merchants, the generous support of Mughal officials and service families, and the mobilization of regional political actors underlay the the preeminence of Calcutta in British rule in India.[51]

Egypt

Egypt was incorporated into the Ottoman Empire in 1517, when Sultan Selim I defeated its Mamluk rulers, and, for almost three centuries, political power was divided among three rival elites: the viceroy, or governor, who represented the imperial authority; a body of Janissaries, ostensibly established to serve the imperial military force but actually there to checkmate any dangerous ambitions of the viceroys; and the Mamluk beys, who had declared their allegiance to the sultan and were therefore appointed governors of various provinces in Egypt. The country gained considerable autonomy as the Ottoman Empire fell into a steady decline, and by the 1700s the Turkish viceroy was a mere pawn in the hands of the local Mamluk.[52] The despotic rule of the Mamluks was abruptly ended by the French occupation of the country in 1798–1801. This brief interlude, by weakening the Mamluks and exposing the natives to a new superior Western power, proved to be consequential for the transformation of the country in the subsequent decades. This event marked the beginning of the modern era in Egypt.

Napoleon's departure from the country brought back the old conflict between rival Mamluks and Ottoman forces. The native notables and the ulama in particular remembered too vividly the notorious reigns of Murad Bey and Ibrahim Bey (1775–98) to allow the restoration of power to the Mamluks in their homeland. They instead rallied behind Muhammad Ali, an ambitious young officer who had come to Egypt in 1801 with the Albanian detachment in the Turkish expeditionary force against the French.[53] The ulama played a key role in the revolt against the *wali* (governor) of Egypt and in assisting Muhammad Ali's ascent to the throne of Egypt. The ulama deposed "the *vali* [*wali*] on religious grounds, based on their traditional power to declare a ruler 'rebellious.'"[54] "Those set in authority," declared Umar Makram, "are the ulama, and those who uphold the *sharia* and the righteous sultan. This man [the governor] is a tyrannical man, and it is the tradition from time immemorial that citizens depose a *wali* if he be unjust."[55] With the support of the ulama, the merchants, and the guilds, Muhammad Ali became the governor of Cairo in 1805.[56] By 1810, he had defeated all his rivals and secured order in the country.

Muhammad Ali departed from the Mamluk type of government. He initiated a new administrative apparatus, bringing under the firm control of the government such institutions of traditional society as semiautonomous guilds, village administration, the Sufi orders, and orthodox religious establishments. Between 1810 and 1815, a comprehensive system of state trading monopolies was created to augment the state's revenues and at the same time establish some sort of discipline among the artisans and small traders of the cities and the environs.[57] A modern industry replete with iron foundries, tanneries, bleaching establishments, a printing press, and twenty-nine cotton factories were also established in 1837.[58] Muhammad Ali also drastically changed the system of land ownership. The old Mamluk ruling class was dispossessed, the system of tax farming (*iltizam*) was changed, tax exemption from waqf lands was eliminated, state lands were managed more efficiently, and a more effective system of tax collection was introduced. The government thus acquired considerable financial autonomy.[59] The multazims cum ulama were gradually squeezed out of the alliance, unless they accepted the redistribution of land. Some ulama accepted this secondary role, while others, like Makram, sought to block it (and in so doing lost more than their land).[60] Moreover, Muhammad Ali's elimination of tax farming expanded his popularity in the countryside and thus made it even more difficult for the dispossessed landowners and the ulama to challenge the pasha, an honorary title for military and civilian officers.[61] By setting up a special *divan,* collecting information, and hearing fellah grievance, Muhammad Ali undermined the standing of the multazims in the countryside.[62] Since taxes had to be collected and land supervised, the rural local elites, such as sheikhs and village leaders, were co-opted and given the tasks previously assigned to the multazims. In that fashion the new government earned the support of the village sheikh and was assured of getting his village's taxes.[63]

As was also the case in India, social transformation in Egypt brought about new political developments, destroyed the old landowning class, undermined the ulama, and later in the second half of the nineteenth century led to the rise of the new landowning class and merchants.

Iran

Given the scale of social transformation in Egypt and India, nineteenth-century Iran in comparison was remarkably stable and conservative. The Qajar rulers displayed no serious desire to modernize the country. The state's administrative and military structures remained fragile and primitive. The Qajars' standing army was not larger than a contingent of Qajar tribesmen and a bodyguard of four thousand Georgian slaves. The rest of the army was composed of a poorly trained mass militia, estimated at around one hundred fifty thousand men, broken down into regional forces and a tribal cavalry of some eighty thousand. Its prebendal bureaucracy was nothing more than a haphazard collection of hereditary accountants (*mostowfis*) and secretaries (*mirzas*) in the central and provincial capitals.[64] Attempts at social and political reforms by some of the more enlightened Qajar viziers, such as Amir Kabir and the Sipahsalar, remained abortive mainly because they faced stiff resistance from the ulama and the court's intrigues.

Nineteenth-century Iran was eventful and conflict ridden, however. John Foran has suggested that many of Iran's conflicts were caused by the country's insertion into the international system of interstate competition and incorporation into the world economy. The reorganization of the structure of domestic production according to the external dictates of the world economy arrested Iran's autonomous development, which in turn provoked resistance to foreign interests among the indigenous forces.[65] True, both Egypt and India were even more deeply incorporated into the world economy than Iran, but the key differences were that (1) inter-state competition considerably weakened the Qajar state, particularly following two humiliating defeats by Russia in 1813 and 1828, the Qajars' failed siege of the city of Herat in 1837 and then occupation of the city in 1856, which prompted the British to invade southern Iran from the Persian Gulf and occupy Bushehr (leading to the 1857 peace treaty in which Iran gave up all claims to Afghan territories, including Herat), and the rise of the Babi movement around the middle of the century; (2) the Qajar rulers showed no serious interest in modernizing the state and society; and (3) the infiltration of the domestic market by European and Russian commercial interests produced class alliances quite different from those of India and Egypt. While in India the merchants and the landowners were allied with the East India Company, and in Egypt they benefited from the breakdown of Muhammad Ali's monopoly system and the general process of economic development, in Iran, in contrast, the merchants and the guilds were undermined by the increasing infiltration of the domestic market by foreign concerns and by the state's indifference to their needs. As early as the 1830s, the merchants were alarmed by foreign competition, but they lacked the administrative capabilities as well as the capital necessary to meet these challenges. The Qajars' granting of concession to foreign concerns worsened their situation. As a result, these merchants were antagonized and began supporting protest movements against the state.[66]

One of the most celebrated events of nineteenth-century Iran was the granting of the tobacco concessions that sparked the protest movement of 1890–92, in which the merchants and the guilds widely participated. The movement was a rebellion against a concession granted by the shah to Major G. F. Talbot, a British citizen, in 1890 for the monopoly of buying, selling, and manufacturing tootoon and tobacco in the interior or exterior of the Kingdom of Iran for fifty years in return for an annual rent of fifteen thousand pounds, a quarter of the annual profits after paying all expenses, and a 5 percent dividend on the capital.[67] The concession was particularly damaging to the merchants and retail traders whose income depended on this profitable tobacco trade. Tobacco was one of the country's major exports, and had the concession come into force, it would have affected the livelihood of a significant section of the population in Iran. Between March 20, 1890, when the concession was signed, and late January 1892, when it was canceled by the shah, there were intense conflicts between the British and the shah, on the one hand, and the merchant-led resistance movement and a segment of the ulama on the other.[68]

The historical event that produced the greatest social transformation was the Constitutional Revolution (1905–11). A host of historical factors prompted the merchants, retail traders, craftsmen, educated elite, and a significant section of the ulama to demand, with an astonishing unity, constitutional change from an ailing monarch.

TWO

Historical Discontinuity and International Transfer of Meaning

Why the decline of the absolutist state and the weakening of the orthodox ulama should stimulate reflective thought among Muslim scholars is hard to answer. Nevertheless, we cite three factors that might have prompted these scholars to re-examine Islamic sociopolitical views. First, accepting the ruler's discretionary power in Islamic political theory, without suggesting a procedure to check his arbitrariness, and closing the gate of ijtihad, without offering the means of officially ascertaining the consensus on a given point of law, remained deficient solutions to the innovative minds of Muslim scholars.[1] Second, the emphasis on obedience in the medieval theory of government and the appreciation of order, which in Ann Lambton's view tended to strengthen traditionalism in all aspects of intellectual life, were hard to sustain given the declining power of the absolutist monarch and his impotence in defending the land of Islam from the eighteenth century on.[2]

Finally, the shift in the conception of the ruler from being patriarchal (as it is generally understood in a shepherd analogy) in classical theory to that of an autocrat in medieval theory entailed a shift in the basis of government from right religion to justice. "Kingship," said Nizam ul-Mulk, "remains with the unbeliever but not with injustice."[3] Although the doctrine of just rule and the people's right to rebel against the unjust ruler became central in Islamic political theory, it was applied only under exceptional circumstances—when all necessary conditions for successful rebellion were present. Generally, however, rebellion against an unjust ruler in historical Islam was a pragmatic solution to an issue that required a theoretical resolution.

Whether the procedural inadequacy, the unsustainability of the principle of obedience to an incompetent autocrat, or simply the right to rebel against an unjust ruler were the real intellectual factors that gave rise to the reformist fundamentalism of the eighteenth century is certainly debatable. We may, however, reasonably postulate that these factors had given rise to a feeling of nonaccomplishment of historical Islam, something lacking in existing political and religious institutions, or, conceptually, on a higher level of abstraction, a discursive space that permitted the rise of the religious outlook of Shah Waliallah (1703–62) in India and Muhammad Ibn Abd al-Wahhab (1703–87) in Arabia. In formulating their alternative views, however, these thinkers fell back on the conception of religious and political authority in pristine Islam, which early Muslim scholars thought inadequate to address the emergent problems Islam faced during the heyday of its imperialistic expansions. In the absence of a pluralistic intellectual environment of debates and discussions, these thinkers were unable to transcend the limits of orthodoxy, although, undeniably, they furnished a discursive framework that facilitated the rise of Islamic modernism in the next century.

Islamic Reformist Fundamentalism of the Eighteenth Century

Shah Waliallah and Muhammad Ibn Abd al-Wahhab were inspired by the intellectual tradition that went back to the orthodox discipline of Ibn Taymiyya and Ibn Khaldun's thesis on the circulation of political dynasties.[4] The political formulas offered by these intellectual figures to resolve the problem of leadership remained intact until about when the process of the disintegration of the Islamic empires began to accelerate. Nevertheless, their fundamental precept that the *khilafa* had ceased to exist after the Rashidun caliphs became the point of departure for these new thinkers. Further, the views of Shah Waliallah and Muhammad Ibn Abd al-Wahhab were also directed against the static formalism of orthodox Muslim jurisprudence. These movements were thus aimed at political as well as religious and social reforms.

Islam, according to Muhammad Ibn Abd al-Wahhab, is based on the rejection of all gods except God. Assigning partners to God (shirk), said Ibn Abd al-Wahhab, "is evil, no matter what the object, whether it be 'king or prophet, or saint or tree or tomb'; to worship pious men is as bad as to worship idols."[5] He argued that the true Islam was that of the first generation and protested against all those later innovations that had in fact brought other gods into Islam. The Islam the Ottoman sultan protected was not the true Islam, and thus he was not the true leader of the umma.[6] In a similar fashion, Shah Waliallah concluded that the development of monarchy, as opposed to the early republican tradition of Islam, and the closing of the gate of ijtihad, were the causes of the prevailing deterioration of Muslim societies. Shah Waliallah declared that Muslim jurisprudence should be totally subordinated to the Quran and the traditions of the Prophet. He insisted that the meanings of the Quran were accessible to the ordinary audience, and its message was as applicable today as it had been in the days of the Prophet. In his endeavor to make the Quran understood, he considered it proper to accept or reject the approved *tafsir* (Quranic exegesis) wisdom from the past.[7] "His object was primarily to convey the word of God in translation to the average educated Muslim and secondarily to break the monopoly of the theologian, who had become petty minded and far too preoccupied with externalities of ritual, converting himself into the Muslim counterpart of the Hindu Brahmin."[8]

To Shah Waliallah, Islamic culture was described as the sunna and shari'a minus the bid'a. In the Indian environment bid'a became a synonym for the Hindu folkways and mores which were retained by the converts and thus diffused into Muslim society. Consequently, social reform meant a greater Islamization of the society to keep Islam free from shirk—from associationism of all kinds with Divine Unity, Divine Will, and Divine Power.[9] In his reformist efforts to bring the religious law of Islam into the open fully dressed in reason and argument,[10] Shah Waliallah initiated a renewed emphasis on independent reasoning (i.e., *ijtihad*) as "an exhaustive endeavour to understand the derivative principles of canon law."[11] This emphasis on ijtihad remained Shah Waliallah's main contribution to modernist thinking in Muslim India. His works inspired the neo-Mu'tazilite modernism of Sayyid Ahmad Khan, Shibli's scholasticism, and religious reconstruction in the thought of Muhammad Iqbal.[12] In short, his principles of exegesis favored a modernist Muslim approach to the Quran because they cleared the way for the reading of the Quran by the "average educated Muslim."[13] In this sense the effect of Shah Waliallah's principles resembled the effect of the opening up of the Bible to a wider audience through the Protestant Reformation in sixteenth-century Europe. If the Shah Waliallah was indeed discerning a "sign of the times," perhaps he perceived that in the midst of a failing Mughal Empire political fortunes might not guarantee the survival of Islam.[14]

More directly, however, the teachings of Ibn Abd al-Wahhab and Shah Waliallah produced something quite different from modernism—militant movements for the rehabilitation of Islam. The Wahhabi militants first gained control of central Arabia and the Persian Gulf and then sacked Karbala, on the fringes of Iraq, and occupied the Hijaz until at the request of the Ottoman sultan their power in Arabia was destroyed by Muhammad Ali in the nineteenth century.[15] Labeled "Wahhabi" by the British and "mujahidin" by its followers, the Indian movement was led by Sayyid Ahmad Barelvi (1786–1831), a disciple of the divine's son and successor Abdul Aziz, whose circle he joined in 1807. Two learned scions of the family of Shah Waliallah, Shah Isma'il and Abdul Hayy, joined him as his disciples, marking the progress of Shah Waliallah's program "from theory to practice, from life contemplative to life active, from instruction of the elite to the emancipation of the masses, and from individual salvation to social organization."[16] Barelvi declared dar ul-harb the territories of India occupied by the

British and other non-Muslim forces and called upon the regional Muslims to join him in a holy war against the infidels.[17] The movement was crushed by the British in 1858, suffered another defeat in 1863, and was persectued all over India.[18]

Given their anti-British and militant nature, there is little historical continuity between these movements and the moderate and pro-Western orientations of Islamic modernism. If they had any influence on Islamic modernism, it might have been diffused, general, and indirect—setting an ideological precedent and some doctrinal groundwork for rebelling against Islamic orthodoxy. The movement of the mujahidin, in Aziz Ahmad's perceptive remark, although it represented an archaic effort to recover India from the British and their Hindu and Sikh allies, "inspired the technique of religious reform in later pro-Western Indian Wahhabism as represented by Sayyid Ahmad Khan."[19] In fact, by attacking the spiritual claim of the sultan, the dogmatism of the ulama, unlawful innovations (bid'a) in Islam, reverence for the saints and the worship of their shrines, and various forms of superstition that had crept into Islamic theology and rituals since the first generation of Islamic history, Shah Waliallah and Ibn Abd al-Wahhab opened the Pandora's box of rational criticism that expanded the range of permissible expressions in Islamic theology.[20] They weakened the ideological rigidity of Islamic orthodoxy and gave a religious authenticity to the worldviews of the Islamic modernists, enabling the latter to more effectively respond to the biting criticisms of their conservative colleagues. On various occasions, for example, the Indian Sayyid Ahmad Khan claimed that he was a Wahhabi and the Egyptian Muhammad Abduh expressed sympathy for Wahhabism.[21]

The Diffusion of Western Culture in the Islamic World

It is unclear to what extent Shah Waliallah and Muhammad Ibn Abd al-Wahhab were influenced by modern ideologies. Their critiques of the existing order were fundamentalist and untainted by non-Islamic outlooks, although they might have been aware of Western technological progress. This is particularly true of Shah Waliallah, whose period of intellectual activity coincided with the rapid expansion of the East India Company. At any rate, the increasing contact between the Islamic world and Europe in the eighteenth and nineteenth centuries stimulated mutual curiosities among the people of both cultures. The European involvement in Islamic countries was dictated by economic interests as well as a sense of curiosity and desire to discover the exotic land of the Orient. Talking about sixteenth-century India, François Bernier wrote: "the rich exuberance of the country, together with the beauty and amiable disposition of the native women, has given rise to a proverb in common use among the *Portuguese,*

English, and *Dutch,* that the kingdom of *Bengale* has a hundred gates open for entrance, but not one for departure."[22]

Modern technological innovations in the means of transportation and communication brought Europe much closer to the Islamic world. Travel became easier and faster, durable commodities and material culture were produced and transported on a larger scale, and written texts were reproduced more rapidly and, through translations, made available to a larger audiences and consumers in the world. Of special significance in enhancing this process was the invention of the printing press, which was one of the three things, along with gunpowder and the compass, that, in the words of Francis Bacon, changed "the appearance and state of the whole world."[23] The introduction of print in the Islamic world in the nineteenth century—that is, four hundred years after it was established in Christendom—contributed enormously to Muslim cultural transformation. Oral transmission of knowledge gave way to written, and ideas were exchanged in a more systematic, less personal, less immediate, more abstract, and more intellectual manner, on a much larger scale, and in much greater volume.[24]

The process of cultural exchange between the West and Islamic countries was active and nonanonymous. It was conducted by and through a group of individuals with certain resources. This exchange was focused, not haphazard, and revolved around crucial points of differences between the West and the East. It was also asymmetrical. Muslim commentators viewed the West with fascination. The Westerners, convinced of their cultural superiority, tended to criticize mercilessly all the major institutions of Islamic society. This asymmetry was reinforced not only by inequality in power but also by different levels of technological development and scientific progress between the two cultures. Although Western powers were seriously competing with one another for the control of the underdeveloped world, ideologically they were remarkably in unison, as all subscribed to the seminal ideas of the nineteenth century: progress, civilization, and human evolution. The Enlightenment was the dominant ideological universe, and it contributed significantly to the shaping of the development of culture in the Islamic world.

Early Impressions:
The East's Perception of the West and the West's Perception of the East

Europe was almost always applauded by its Muslim visitors for what they saw there and what was absent in their homeland in the nineteenth century. Expressing his astonishment and bewilderment during his sojourn in Europe in the latter part of the century, Nasir ud-Din Shah of Iran was particularly impressed with the status of the European women. "The women," said the shah, "are very much occupied in business and at work especially at agriculture and in gardening do they labour much more than their husbands."[25]

The Memoirs of Mirza Abu Talib Khan

One of the most systematic assessments and panegyrical descriptions of Europe was presented by Mirza Abu Talib Khan in the memoirs of his travel to Europe, Africa, and the Middle East during 1799–1803. Abu Talib Khan spent most of his time in England. He was possibly the first Indian Muslim to have visited abroad with the ostensible purpose of traveling only and to have left an account of his visits for the purpose of communicating to his readers "the curiosities and wonders which he saw, and to give some account of the manners and customs of the various nations he visited, all of which are little known to Asiatics," and for affording "a gratifying banquet to his countrymen."[26] He believed that, if emulated, the customs, inventions, and sciences of Europe would bring great advantages to Muslim nations.

About the social status and liberty of the European women that amazed Nasir ud-Din Shah, Abu Talib Khan was much more eloquent and appreciative several decades earlier. He was perhaps among the first to praise monogamy in Britain. Nothing, said he, conduces more to the British success in raising children "than the *single marriages* of the Christians, where the progeny being all of the same stock, no room is left for the contentions and litigations which too often disturb the felicity of a Mohammedan family perhaps the off spring of a dozen mothers."[27] His appraisal of Europe's progress was positive and often mixed with awe. He was cognizant of the role of machines and the Industrial Revolution in facilitating labor and cheapening the price of commodities. At the same time, he commended the organization of labor and the regularity of work in England.[28] Impressed by the prevalence of liberty in Britain,[29] he described the British constitution as a "union of the monarchical, aristocratical, and democratical governments, represented by the King, Lords, and Commons; in which powers of each are so happily blended, that it is impossible for human wisdom to produce any other system containing so many excellences, and so free from imperfection."[30] His visit to the House of Commons was for him as amazing as it was amusing: "The first time I saw this assembly, they reminded me of two flocks of Indian paroquests, sitting upon opposite mango-trees, scolding at each other; the most noisy of whom were Mr. Pitt and Mr. Fox. . . . . It is not however to be inferred, from this circumstance, that Parliaments are of no utility; on the contrary, they are of the greatest service."[31] The British were not free of defects, however. Abu Talib Khan pointed to their want of faith, their pride, their passion for money, their desire for ease and dislike of exertion, their irritability of temper, their habit of wasting time in sleeping, eating, and dressing, their luxurious manner of living, their vanity and arrogance, their selfishness, their want of chastity, their extravagance, and their contempt for the customs of other nations.[32] Among their virtues were their sense of honor, their reverence for possessors of superior excellence, their dread of offending the rules of propriety, their desire to improve the situation of the common people, their adherence to the rules of fashion, their passion for mechanisms, their plainness of manners, their good natural sense, and their soundness of judgment.[33] Other prominent Muslim visitors also praised Europe, but in a more measured manner than Abu Talib Khan. Not without reservations, the Egyptian Rifa'a al-Tahtawi admired Parisians for "the sharpness of their intellects, the precision of their understanding, and the immersion of their minds in deep matters . . . they are not prisoners of tradition, but always love to know the origin of things and the proofs of them. . . . but among their ugly beliefs is this, that the intellect and virtue of their wise men are greater than the intelligence of the prophets."[34]

James Morier and the Adventures of Hajji Baba

In a sharp contrast, the European assessments of other cultures, Islamic cultures included, were almost always devastatingly critical. James Morier's fictional satire *The Adventures of Hajji Baba of Ispahan* is a good example. The fiction was a result of the author's unique diplomatic experiences in Iran and sensitive observations. It was first published in 1824 and received high praise from literary men including Sir Walter Scott, who declared that Morier "described the manners and vices of the Eastern nations not only with fidelity but with the humor of Le Sage and the ludicrous power of Fielding himself."[35] *The Adventures of Hajji Baba* portrayed a decadent society characterized by religious intolerance, superstition, deception, patriarchy, and polygamy and a political institution whose king's arbitrary power had no limit. It showed the unpredictability of social life, "where an individual, especially if possessing talents, may rise and sink as often as a tennis-ball, and be subjected to the extraordinary variety of hazards in one life, which the other undergoes in the course of one game."[36]

Hajji Baba was a teenage son of Kerbelai Hassan, a celebrated barber in Isfahan. He convinced his father to let him accompany the merchant Osman Aga on a journey to Mashhad. On the way, they were robbed and taken prisoner by a band of Turkmen. Osman Aga was placed in charge of taking care of a string of fifty camels, with threats from the chief that his nose and ears would be cut off if any one of the camels was lost or stolen. Because of his skills as a barber, Hajji Baba received better treatment. After more than a year in captivity and, spotting government troops, he escaped from the Turkmen. But the troops took him prisoner, disarmed him, and took all his belongings. Upset at his mistreatment by the government's agent, he was consoled by an old muleteer, Ali Katir, who told him that one could not contend with fate. "Smoke your pipe now and be happy."[37] He arrived in Mashhad, where he became a water carrier, selling water drawn from a filthy reservoir as "equal to the sacred well of *Zem Zem*," making a considerable amount of money. He participated in water-carrier competitions in commemoration of the slaying of

Imam Hussein, sprained his back, and was no longer able to carry water. He then became a tobacco seller and a swindler, got caught, and received corporal punishment. Bitter at the way he was treated, he left Mashhad for Tehran. From his dervish friends, he learned "the art of deception"[38] and became a dervish en route to Tehran, writing talismans for women. He arrived in Tehran and through a series of events emerged as an assistant to the king's physician, Mirza Ahmak. The physician was concerned about a European doctor whose knowledge of modern medicine was threatening his business. "What is worse than all," said Mirza Ahmak, this infidel "pretends to do away with the small-pox altogether, by infusing into our nature a certain extract of cow, a discovery which one of their philosophers has lately made. Now this will never do, Hajji. The small-pox has always been a comfortable source of revenue to me; I cannot afford to lose it, because an infidel chooses to come here and treat us like cattle."[39]

The physician then instructed Hajji Baba to spy on the foreign doctor, but warned Hajji Baba of the customs of the Europeans that were "totally different to ours . . . instead of shaving their heads, and letting their beards grow, as we do, they do the very contrary, for not a vestige of hair is to be seen on their chins, and their hair is as thick on their heads as if they had made a vow never to cut it off: then, they sit on little platforms, whilst we squat on the ground; they take up their food with claws made of Iron, whilst we use our fingers; they are always walking about, we keep seated; they wear tight clothes, we loose ones; they write from left to right, we from right to left; they never pray, we five times a day; in short, there is no end to what might be related of them; but most certain it is, that they are the most filthy people on earth, for they hold nothing to be unclean; they eat all sorts of animals, from a pig to a tortoise, without the least scruple."[40]

At the house of the physicians, Hajji Baba met Zeenab, among slave girls at the physician's harem. On one day, when everybody was gone to the funeral of a lady from the king's harem, Hajji Baba and Zeenab found themselves alone in the doctor's house, where they dined, drank wine, sang, and made love. Hajji Baba's affair with Zeenab was short lived, however. In the meantime, the doctor received the shah as his guest, the shah met Zeenab and became interested in her, and Zeenab joined the shah's harem, for it is his "privilege to enter every man's harem at pleasure, and to inspect his women unveiled."[41]

Hajji Baba left the doctor to "become the sub-lieutenant to the chief executioner of Persia—a character, whatever my readers may think of it, of no small consequence" in a state where various gradations of violence constituted the chief forms of punishment. In this position, Hajji Baba witnessed the tragedy of the execution of Zeenab, whom he had made pregnant. Suspected of impregnating Zeenab, Hajji was deprived of his post. Running for his life, he took sanctuary in Qum. There, he managed to get the attention of the city's chief *mujtahid* (a high-ranking member of the clergy), Mirza Abul Qasim. Being apprehensive about his visit with the mujtahid, he began to recite whatever he knew about his religion: Those who did not believe in Muhammad and Ali his lieutenant were infidels and heretics, worthy of death, and all men would go to hell, "excepting the true believers; and I further believe that it is right to curse Omar—I am certain that all the Turks will go to Jehanum—that all Christians and Jews are *nejis* (unclean)."[42] In the meantime, the shah receiving a Georgian slave girl as a gift, his wrath at the loss of Zeenab considerably subsided, and through the mujtahid's intervention, Hajji Baba was pardoned. He returned to Isfahan only to be informed that his father was dead that he was plundered of his inheritance.

After a series of adventures he escaped to Baghdad and then to Istanbul, where he set up as a vendor of pipe sticks. Here, he assumed the character of a rich merchant of high extraction and married a wealthy widow, but, being revealed as an imposter, he was forced to divorce his bride. Hajji Baba then met the Iranian ambassador, Mirza Firouz, and his final adventure began when he displayed a great assiduity in acquiring and compiling some knowledge of the European character. Hajji Baba "wrote" the history of Europe. Upon his return to Iran, he gained the protection of the grand vizier, and of the shah himself.

Despite its favorable reception in Great Britain, the book's real impact on Iran came only in the early twentieth century, when it was ably translated by Mirza Habib Isfahani, an Iranian intellectual and political activist of the Constitutional Revolution of 1905–11. Nevertheless, the country's educated elite, religious leaders, and high-ranking governmental officials were aware of its content before the translation appeared. Its publication caused angry reaction of the Iranian government and some religious leaders.[43]

The Adventures of Hajji Baba was fiction. Yet it was real in its portrayal of the predominant manner in which Westerners viewed Iranian society and for that matter the Islamic world as a whole. It was also real in its demarcation of the basic line of difference between the West and the East. The issues raised by Morier's criticism and ridicule of Iran's traditional social order became, in the latter period, more clearly the fundamental points of contention among diverse ideological producers in India, Egypt, and Iran. The fiction is a modernist critique of Iran written in terms of British ethnocentrism. Morier believed in the superiority of British culture. Like Kipling, he also held that one should "let West be West and East be East:"

> A distinct line must ever be drawn between "the nations who wear the hat and those who wear the beard;" and they must ever hold each other's stories as improbable, until a more general intercourse of common life takes place between them. What is moral and virtuous with the one, is wickedness with the other,—that which the Christian reviles as abominable, is by the Mohamedan held sacred. Although the contrast between their respective man-

ners may be very amusing, still it is most certain that the former will ever feel devoutly grateful that he is neither subject to Mohamedan rule, nor educated in Mohamedan principles; whilst the latter, looking upon the rest of mankind as unclean infidels, will continue to hold fast to his bigoted persuasion, until some powerful interposition of Providence shall dispel the moral and intellectual darkness which, at present, overhangs so large a portion of the Asiatic world.[44]

Islam as a Target of Polemics and Locus of Contested Issues

The diffusion of modern ideas in India, Egypt, and Iran diversified the intellectual climate in these countries. As a result, the conceptual schema of Islamic orthodoxy came into head-to-head collisions with alternative sets of codes in the discourse of the followers of the Enlightenment, British Westernizers, and Christian Evangelicals. These codes included binaries like *human reason* versus *superstition, scientific rationality* versus *traditionalism, civilization* versus *savagery, women's freedom* versus *male supremacy, freedom* versus *despotism,* and *Christendom* versus *heathendom.* In practical terms, too, any serious thought about the reorganization of sociopolitical life had direct implications for the social role and function of Islamic orthodoxy. Was it possible to discuss Europe's technological progress and the principles of modern science without considering its contrast with the Islamic sciences? Could serious intellectuals admit the superiority of Western civilization without recognizing the decadence of the abode of Islam? How could one raise the issue of woman's education and her role outside the home without visiting the problem of male supremacy? And could any intellectual bring forward the idea of the people's sovereignty without contemplating its congruity, or lack thereof, with the Islamic conception of political authority?

In their attempts to answer these questions, the Islamic modernists considered the orthodox ulama to be ill equipped to effectively respond to the challenges facing their faith. They drew from the norms and standards of the Enlightenment and advanced new positions on these issues, bringing into relief a new modernist discourse in Islam.

THREE

Europocentric Rationalism
and Islamic Modernism in India

The proximate condition of Islamic modernism in nineteenth-century India was the emergence of a pluralistic cultural environment. This pluralism was characterized by intense ideological debates and religious disputations among the followers of such diverse groups as rationalists, Westernizers and the ideologues connected to British colonial administration, Evangelical Christianity, and the ulama. We are not arguing that premodern India was a homogeneous culture. On the contrary, it was a diversified society in terms of language, religion, and ethnicity.[1] Islam too was far from being a monolithic religion. In the early nineteenth century, for example, there were three principal centers of theological education. One was the school of Shah Waliallah in Delhi, which was shifting in emphasis from reformism to eclectic traditionalism. Another was the apolitical school of Farangi Mahal at Lucknow. The third was the Khayrabad seminary, in which medieval philosophy and logic predominated. In the second half of the century, the Deoband conservative school synthesized the three traditions and rose to prominence.[2]

These schools, while indicative of the depth and breath of the intellectual dynamism of Islam, generally operated within conceptual and methodological frameworks that were traditionalist, which imparted a subtle discursive unity to these diverse intellectual movements. Without a serious change in the cultural and political order, such modernists as Sayyid Ahmad Khan, Chiragh Ali, and others would have had a difficult time expressing their ideas.[3] Besides, the political difficulties entailed in reexamining Islamic orthodoxy notwithstanding, the crucial factors in the origins of Islamic modernism were the specific issues raised by diverse ideological contenders. Muslim thinkers certainly had their own views on the role of Islam in history and on Islamic conceptions of politics, orientations toward women, assessments of the rights of followers of other religions, and opinions of the status of rational inquiry. To change these views, some one should be able to turn them into issues, criticize them from different angles, and be powerful enough so that those who are being criticized could not use force to silence their critics. Whether the British occupation of India was condoned or condemned for allegedly destroying a valued way of life, there was no escaping for reflective Muslim thinkers that the issues raised by nineteenth-century critics of Islam in India constituted serious anomalies for their faith—the decadence of Muslim societies, impressive European scientific discoveries and technological innovations, religious tolerance, the relationship between religion and politics, and the role and status of women.

British Reforms and Cultural Outcomes in India

The British entered India in 1615. It took about two hundred years and considerable changes in the country's sociopolitical profile for the East India Company to accumulate the power and ideological justification to embark on implementing a series of social reforms. All that Ambassador Sir Thomas Roe procured from the Mughal emperor Jahangir was a concession that allowed the English to live according to their own religion and laws without interference. Any disputes that arose between them and the Mughal subjects were to be settled by the Mughal authorities. In 1661, Charles II extended the legislative power of the company to include Indian elements of the company's settlements. The British judicial system was marginal and hardly came in contact or conflict with the Mughal judicial system, and its foothold on the Indian soil was scarcely noticed in the Mughal imperial records.[4]

A multitude of factors—including the growing disparity between the authority and the power of the Mughal emperor, the slow accumulation of wealth resulting from the expanding commercial economy of the seventeenth century, the rise of literate Muslim gentry and of Hindu landholders and merchants, the emergence of semiautonomous kingdoms within the ambit of the imperial domain, the rapid disintegration of the Mughal empire after 1707, and the ensuing half century of predatory civil strife—all provided ample opportunities for the East India Company to begin a phase of rapid imperial expansion in 1757 with large-scale acquisitions of Indian territory.[5] In 1764, it obtained a legal executive status in the provinces of Bengal, Bihar, and Orissa from the nominal and powerless Mughal emperor Shah Alam II.[6] By the turn of the nineteenth century, India was a company state. In the first quarter of the century, the company launched a major offensive against India's major cultural institutions.

Early Romantic Discourse

The rationalist discourse that shaped British reformist policies was well-articulated in James Mill's *History of British India*. This was preceded by the Romantics, "whose object was not to use the East for any propagandist purpose of their own, nor to judge it by a standard of their own, but simply to study it for itself and enjoy its achievements for their own sake."[7] This theme gained strength in the work of Sir William Jones, the pioneer of Sanskrit studies and "the first of the great Orientalists, of those ardent enthusiasts who have done so much to spread abroad in Europe appreciation of Asiatic culture and learning."[8] For Jones, the most important project was the completion of a digest of Hindu and Islamic laws, to be compiled by the most learned of the native lawyers, to form a basis for legal decision. In his view, "nothing indeed could be more obviously just, than to determine private contests according to those laws, which the parties themselves had ever considered as the rules of their conduct and engagements in civil life."[9] Informed by such ideas, the original policy of the East India Company was one that "patronized both Hindu and Muslim religions. Offices were open on Sunday but closed on Indian holidays. Troops were paraded in honour of Hindu deities. A coco-nut was solemnly broken at the beginning of each monsoon, and British officials assisted in the management of Hindu religious trusts."[10]

This school fell before the onslaught of two parties united only in their hostility to Indian civilization: the Evangelicals and the rationalists.[11] The Evangelicals were in particular irritated by the company's strict religious neutrality. They were dismayed to observe that "civil and military officials were compelled to honour heathen and Muhammadan festivals with their presence, and even in many cases to present the sacrificial gifts of the Government to the Brahmans. On the occasion of festive processions the idols were greeted with a 'royal salvo' of cannon."[12]

Europocentric Rationalist Discourse

The Romantic phase ended early in the nineteenth century. "The Company," in Garratt's words, "gave up being 'wet nurse to Vishnu,' and 'churchwarden to Juggernaut.' It became strictly secular, and hence more and more aloof in a country where religion permeates every human activity."[13] Whereas Warren Hastings had acquired a proficiency in Persian and supported the foundation by Sir William Jones of the Bengal Asiatic Society, Lord William Bentinck (governor general in 1828) proposed the demolition of the Taj Mahal and the sale of its marble. He was only diverted from this intention because the test auction of materials from the Agra Palace proved unsatisfactory.[14] This changed outlook was carried by a new generation of administrators who came to India for a few years. Endowed with a full consciousness of their racial superiority, they viewed Indian civilization as "a subject only fit for the antiquary."[15] They believed that through educational reforms and the natural operation of knowledge and reflection, changes in the religious outlooks of Indians would be effected, without any effort to proselytize or interfere in their religious liberty. As William Wilson Hunter predicted, "no young man, whether Hindu or Muhammadan, passes through our Anglo-Indian schools without learning to disbelieve the faith of his fathers. The luxuriant religions of Asia shrivel into dry sticks when brought into contact with the icy realities of Western Science."[16]

One of the pioneers of Anglicist and Westernizing policy, Thomas Macaulay, "urged on the Government the need for teaching Indians the English language and the Western arts and sciences with a view to creating an Indian intelligentsia which would form the connecting link between the imperial power and the masses ruled by it."[17] "The question now before us," said Lord Macaulay,

> is simply whether, when it is in our power to teach this language, we shall teach languages in which by universal confession there are no books on any subject which deserve to be compared to our own; whether, when we can teach European science, we shall teach systems which by universal confession whenever they differ from those of Europe differ for the worse; and whether, when we can patronize sound philosophy and true history, we shall countenance at the public expense medical doctrines which would disgrace an English farrier, astronomy which would move laughter in girls at an English boarding-school, history abounding with kings thirty feet high and reigns 30,000 years long, and geography made up of seas of treacle and seas of butter.[18]

The "scientific" justification for the Westernizers' views like that of Macaulay was provided by James Mill (1773–1836). The criteria of civilization used by Mill were drawn chiefly from "conjectural" history, the Benthamite principles of utility, and the general intellectual heritage of the Enlightenment. He quoted John Millar's *Origin of the Distinction of Ranks* as the authority for the test of civilization provided by the status of women. "The condition of the women," says Mill, "is one of the most remarkable circumstances in the manners of nations. Among the rude people, the women are generally degraded; among civilized people they are exalted."[19]

For Mill, the organizing principle of history was the "scale of nations." Conjecturing that the place of Indians on the scale was low, he condemned every single aspect of their way of life as barbarous—not only their science, but their philosophy, art, and manners as well. Utilitarian standards of "completeness" and "exactness" were used to judge Hindu laws. And, ultimately, because the Hindus did not view God's works as "just, rational and sublime"—in other words, because they did not believe in a Newtonian universe—it was impossible for them to have "elevated and pure and rational" ideas of God.[20] In Duncan Forbes's assessment, "given the 'scale of nations' as the organizing principle of history, and the uniformitarianism of Rationalist historiography, the logical result is an extreme form of Europocentricism, 'scientifically' established."[21]

Mill's *History* and his official connection to the East India Company effected a complete change in the system of British administration and set its intellectual foundation.[22] This new outlook gave the British a legitimacy that went far beyond that which would flow from their function as the protector of social order and security. It lent credibility to their self-proclaimed mission of civilizing and uplifting the conditions of "backward" nations—epitomized in Kipling's famous phrase, the "white man's burden."[23]

The judiciary was among the first institutions to undergo reform. In time the British grew increasingly critical of the Islamic penal code. They condemned as barbarous such forms of punishment as death by stoning, amputation of hands, retaliation (revenge), and other forms of corporal punishment. The Islamic penal code was also found wanting for carrying no distinction between private and public law and for making it difficult to get convictions for certain offenses.[24] Charles Cornwallis (whose tenure was 1786–93) was convinced that the prevailing criminal justice system was entirely useless, futile, and rotten to the core, contrary to natural justice and the good of society.[25] The British thus began making changes in the Muslim Law of Crime to adapt to new social exigencies—intent was made the criterion of murder, in 1791–92 mutilation was abrogated and the law of homicide was revised, the doctrine of *ta'zir* (discretionary punishment) was changed in 1803, and a regulation of 1817 rationalized the law dealing with adultery.[26] Finally, in 1832, Islamic law ceased to be the general law of the land. This process continued until the Indian penal code was formulated in 1860.[27]

The administration of Lord William Bentinck (1828–35) marked a period of major economic and cultural reform as the British began to address such deplorable customs as widow burning (suttee), child marriage, the ostracizing of untouchable castes, and the practice of female infanticide, which was discovered to be prevalent among certain tribes of India. British authority claimed that in the districts of Bengal no fewer than 5,997 widows were burned alive in ten years, and only too often the unfortunate women were induced to submit to this rite or were thrown by force into the flames of the burning pyre. Lord Bentinck forbade suttee and other customs, such as the drowning of children in the sacred rivers, the exposure of the aged and the sick on the banks of the Ganges, self-sacrifice by throwing oneself beneath the wheels of the idols' cars in great processions or by submitting to the tortures of hook-swinging.[28] The practice of female infanticide also aroused British indignation.[29] The British claimed that all imaginable expedients, whether of a coercive, persuasive, or sumptuary character, had been tried. By all the ruling authorities, supreme and subordinate, the crime itself had been unsparingly reproved. Inhuman, unnatural, revolting, atrocious, horrid, disgusting, disgraceful, shocking, grievous, sinful, wicked, wretched, detestable, execrable, dreadful, abominable, barbarous, aggregately murderous, diabolical—these were the denunciatory terms that ran freely through the gravest and calmest official documents.[30]

Female infanticide and suttee were never sanctioned in Hindu scriptures and were forbidden by Sikh and Muslim authorities. Emperor Jahangir, having heard of a village in which the inhabitants were wont to put their daughters to death, ordered, "the barbarous practice to be discontinued, and [a law] enacted that whoever should commit it in future should be put to the torture."[31] He also forbade suttee.[32]

The Evangelicals

The mass influx of Christian missionaries to India paralleled the expansion of British colonial power, a process that was reinforced by Evangelical revival in Europe. By the second quarter of the nineteenth century, the missionaries had established an overwhelming propaganda machine in India. Speaking of the breadth of missionary polemics against Islam, a mid-nineteenth-century commentator noted that within the preceding ten or twenty years, "the amount of facts carefully collected, and of data philosophically weighed . . . [had been], perhaps, of greater value than all the labours of Christian writers during the twelve preceding centuries."[33]

The missionaries began slowly, but the charter of 1813 paved the way for large-scale missionary activities and allowed their merciless criticisms of Islam and "heathen" religions to go on unhindered by the exigencies of British rule in India.[34] By the late 1830s, Protestant missionaries had spread to the centers of Muslim culture in the North-Western Provinces, their activities ranging from written and oral debate to preaching in the bazaars and distributing copies of the Bible in vernacular languages.[35] This process was enhanced by the rising influence of Evangelical outlooks within the ranks of the East India Company, which, although it publicly supported the principle of religious neutrality, was privately sympathetic to the goals of the missionaries.[36]

Although united in their common hostility toward Indian culture, the Evangelicals and the rationalists had separate agendas. The missionaries had passion but no interest in the philosophy of history. They were quick, however, to attribute Western progress to the influence of Christianity, while deeming Islam "an active and powerful enemy" of their faith.[37] Their criticisms of Islam ranged from assaults on the Prophet Muhammad to the censure of historical Islam—its political institutions, conception of the family, and treatment of women. They questioned Muhammad's knowledge of Christianity, claiming that his "confused notions of the Trinity and of the Holy Ghost" had been received through a Jewish informant, himself imperfectly acquainted with the subject.[38] The Prophet of Islam was described as "melancholic," "low-spirited," "a man of semi-barbarous habits,"[39] a ruthless conqueror, who was involved in "frightful butchery of the Bani Coreitza" and "numerous assassinations,"[40] and polygamous.[41]

The authenticity of the miracles attributed to Muhammad was publicly debated between the missionaries, led by a certain Henry Martyn, and Muslim doctors. Martyn's controversial tracts had already evoked responses from the Iranian clerics Mirza Ibrahim in Shiraz and Muhammad Reza in Hamadan. They became influential through Samuel Lee's *Controversial Tracts on Christianity and Mohammedanism* (1824).[42] For Mirza Ibrahim, a miracle was an effect exceeding common experience, accompanied by a prophetic claim and a challenge to produce the like. He held that a miracle might be proved by particular experience or confined to any single art but must be attested by the evidence and confession of those best skilled in that art. The miracle of the Quran belonged to the science of eloquence, in which the Arabs were perfect adepts. The Quran was accompanied by a challenge, and when the Arab challengers professed their inability to produce an equal, their evidence became universally binding.[43] In rebuttal, Henry Martyn asserted that, "to be conclusive, a miracle must exceed *universal* experiences,—that the testimony and opinion of the Arabs is therefore insufficient, besides being that of a party concerned,—that, were the Koran allowed to be inimitable, that would not prove it a miracle,—and that its being an *intellectual* miracle is not a virtue, but by making it generally inappropriate a defect."[44]

In the early 1840s, William Muir (who later became secretary to the government of the North-Western Provinces) took a deep interest in missionary activities by publishing what he regarded as the bizarre and superstitious aspects of Islamic beliefs. His intention was not to ridicule Islam but to lure his Muslim audience to convert to Christianity, since he believed that educated Muslims would be astonished to read about the multitude of "ridiculous stories" deemed Muhammad's miracles: "A dirty handkerchief cast into an oven, came out of the flames, white and unsinged, because it had been used by Mohammed. His spittle turned a bitter well into a sweet one; removed a scald; cured the ophthalmia; restored sight to a blind man; mended a broken leg, and healed instantaneously a deep wound. A man's hand was severed in battle from his arm; he carried it to Mohammed, who, by applying his spittle, rejoined it as before. . . . A dumb boy was cured by drinking the water he had washed his mouth and hands in. He laid his hands upon a lunatic child, who was cured, a black reptile being immediately discharged from his body."[45]

Muir deplored what he called with derision "a few specimens of wonders" mentioned in *Maulud Sharif* that Muslims believed to have happened following the birth of Muhammad: "All the Kings of the earth were struck with dumbness, and remained inarticulate for a day and a night: the vault of Kesra was rent; fourteen of its battlements fell to the grounds."[46] This book, Muir then concluded, "is a type of the Mohammedan mind of India;—credulous beyond belief. It is an important illustration of the position that although Mohammedans are captious, and pseudocritical to the utmost, when attacking other religions, they are incredibly simple and superstitious . . . in reference to their own faith."[47]

The Treatment of Women

The critiques of gender hierarchy and the maltreatment of women featured prominently in the missionaries' and Westernizers' cultural warfare against Islam and other religions. They viewed such practices as suttee, female infanticide, gender segregation, early marriage, and a lack of education for girls as indications of the cultural backwardness of India.[48] In their literature, they proudly stated, "the fight against the abomination of the suttee was one of the first of the great humanitarian movements set in motion by the missionaries. Child-marriages and the enforced celibacy of widows are a twofold scourge, against which not only missionaries but also many of the most intelligent natives have striven for a century past with little success."[49] Another report indicated that "a most bitter prejudice exists in the minds of the people in many parts of India against female education, and this prejudice is deep-rooted. . . . . These people think that the highest duty of a woman is to marry, and devote herself with all her thoughts and energies to the comfort of her family. If she should learn to read, they say she will be so occupied with her books that she will neglect these duties."[50]

As part of their work among women, the missionaries erected orphanages and asylums.[51] They also founded the Calcutta Female Juvenile Society for the Education of Native Females and the Calcutta School Society in 1819, and the Ladies' Society for Female Native Education in Calcutta and the Vicinity in 1824. Witnessing men's prejudice against women, some missionaries held that "this sad state of things would only be remedied when the young men of India had become so far familiar with Western culture as to be able no longer to tolerate wives who were wholly illiterate."[52] Around the middle of the nineteenth century, an increasing number of educated men became interested in educating their daughters and other female relatives. Over a decade later, Christian missionary women used this opportunity to extend their message to secluded women at home.[53] In April 1870, the Woman's Foreign Missionary Society of the Presbyterian Church was founded. A year later, the society started the publication of *Woman's Work for Women*, which continued until the 1920s.[54]

The Ulama's Response and Counterattack

Muslim responses gained momentum around 1840s. The ulama of both Sunni and Shi'i sects produced and disseminated a large number of pamphlets, letters, and books and participated in enlivening public disputations, refuting the missionaries' arguments. "In former times," said a Muslim theologian, "when the Christians were not in power, and the noisy violence of their abrogated religion was therefore concealed, our

Professors seldom turned their thoughts towards its refutation; but upon the learned of *this* age, it is incumbent and their sacred duty to use every endeavour to overturn their faith, otherwise these people by their insidious efforts will gradually mislead whole multitudes."[55] The criticisms the ulama leveled against Christianity in the nineteenth century contained nothing that was distinctively different from those raised by their predecessors during the prime period of Islamic expansion: Trinitarianism was a travesty of the real Christianity, Jesus's mission was not universal and was intended only for the Jews, as Christ had said, "I am not sent, but unto the lost sheep of the house of Israel,"[56] the divinity of Christ and the Trinity were absolute impossibilities,[57] and the Bible was no longer a genuine scripture.[58]

The years 1855–57 marked the consolidation of the Muslim counteroffensive. One of the most outstanding disputations occurred between a German missionary, the Reverend Karl Gottlieb Pfander (1803–65), and Muslim theologian Rahmat Allah Kiranawi, assisted by a Westernized scholar, Dr. Wazir Khan. The latter, while in England for medical studies in the 1830s, carried out extensive research on Christianity and collected books of biblical criticism by German authors. His knowledge of Christianity from Western sources provided much of the materials for Rahmat Allah in his attack on the missionaries.[59] Pfander, whose *Mizan-ul-Haqq: Treatise on the Controversy between Christians and Muhammedans* (published in German in 1829) was published in Persian in 1835 and created considerable uproar among Muslim theologians in both Iran and India.

The subjects of discussion were the abrogation and corruption of the Bible, the doctrine of the Trinity, the prophecy of Muhammad, and the inspiration of the Quran.[60] The disputation was held in the presence of a number of British officers, including the scholar-polemicist Sir William Muir, Hindu, Christian, and Muslim scholars, and the general public, and it raged for three days. After presenting the Quranic doctrine of abrogation (*naskh*)—that the revelations in the Quran had abrogated certain passages of earlier revelations—Rahmat Allah and Wazir Khan took Pfander to task on the crucial Muslim argument that the text of the New Testament contained contradictions which can only be explained as "interpolations." The discussion on this point, according to Muslim accounts, came to an end when Pfander admitted that abrogation of the scriptures was a theoretical possibility. Rahmat Allah and Muslim opinion hailed the 1854 debate as a great victory for Islam, and Pfander was clearly disturbed about the outcome.[61]

The Sepoy Rebellion of 1857–59

By 1820, the East India Company had subdued virtually all the major Indian states and practically replaced the Mughal emperor, although his authority was still nominally revered and respected. At the same time, it faced all the problems that naturally came with conquests and centralization of power. The conquests demanded resources for establishing and maintaining security, which were to be obtained through further conquests. On a magnified scale, the company inherited the conflict between the desire of the Indian kingdoms to squeeze revenue from the land and the entrepreneurship of merchants and peasants. There were also periodic revolts of zamindars, who were fighting off demands for higher revenue, as well as revolts in cities and town. Finally, there was the threat to the sepoys' interests and status from British cost-cutting reforms, the trimming of their perquisites, and the widening of the area of recruitment.[62]

All these factors contributed to the rebellions of 1857–59. Yet the form of the rebellion developed not so much from these economic and political exigencies as from the uniform cultural treatment of the indigenous people by the Anglicist-missionary alliance. The missionaries' attack on Indian culture roused a hostile reaction from both Hindus and Muslims. Their anger turned against the East India Company, when in the decades preceding the rebellion such British administrators of the predominantly Muslim provinces of the Punjab and Sind as Sir Henry Lawrence and Sir Robert Montgomery provided moral and financial assistance to the missionaries.[63] In 1853, Sir Herbert Edwardes, commissioner and agent of the governor general of the Muslim frontier areas of the North-Western Provinces, stated, "our Mission . . . is to do for other nations what we have done for our own. To the Hindoos we have to preach one God; and to the Mahomedans to preach one Mediator."[64]

Such assertions and the increasing emphasis on the use of English in schools and colleges, education for girls, the partial implementation of legislation to ensure a convert's right to inherit his family property, the interest in missionary schools taken by some of the Evangelically-inclined government officials, and grants given to these schools—all aroused suspicions about the religious intentions of the company. Added to the explosive situation was a circular by a certain Father E. Edmund sent in 1855 to all government employees suggesting that as the whole of India had come under British rule, linked together through railways, steam vessels, and the electric telegraph, it was desirable that all embrace the same system of religion.[65]

Sensing the gathering storm, the lieutenant governor of Bengal promptly issued a notice indicating that the government had no intention of interfering in the religion, rites, and ceremonies of the Hindus and Muslims.[66] The notice, however, failed to calm the excited public, as a rumor spread quickly that the new cartridges being introduced in the Indian Sepoys numbering over 230,000 men were greased with the fat of oxen and swine. To take them between one's teeth or even to touch these cartridges was to make a Brahman Hindu soldier break caste and a Muslim become unclean. A mutiny thus broke out at Meerut in the North-Western Provinces on May 10, 1857, and "spread like wildfire from garrison to garrison and from province to province. In a few weeks almost the whole of North India was in flames."[67] The British, however, managed to control the rebellion through brutal force, and peace was restored throughout India on July 8, 1859.

The Aftermath of the Mutiny: A New Episode for Culture Production

The mutiny was a traditionalist response to British colonialism, and its catastrophic defeat decisively ended any hope of revitalizing the old order. It marked a new episode for culture production. The Mughal rule was formally ended. The control of India passed from the board of directors of the East India Company to the British parliament and electorate, and major economic developments, including the construction of railroad and other infrastructures, took place after 1860.

The mutiny was atrocious. British men, women, and children were cut to pieces in cold blood. The rebels received equally harsh penalties and were subjected to meaningless cruelty. The brutality displayed in the first Cawnpore massacre by the rebels against the British and then in the second Cawnpore massacre by the British against the rebels epitomized the extent of the horror and human tragedy experienced by both sides.[68] The conservative reaction was mercilessly crushed, and as far as the Muslims were concerned, the defeat in no uncertain terms signified not only the reality of the British presence in India but also the dynamics of the culture and social organization that underpinned their military invincibility.

British power notwithstanding, there was no real political alternative. Given the existing pluralistic context of ideological contention, the problem for Muslim scholars became more cultural and theological than political. Diverse ideological contenders were raising serious issues about Islam and Islamic history. In their attempts to resolve these issues, the Islamic modernists found it necessary to revise the methodological foundation of Islamic orthodoxy, to give primacy to reason in their interpretation of religion, to equate revelation with natural law, to reject polygamy and a strict gender hierarchy that gave men too much power over women, and to devise a rationalist approach to Islamic history.

Empirical versus Islamic Sciences:
Natural Theology and Rationalization of Religion

Sayyid Ahmad Khan (1817–98) was influenced by the problems of Muslim India—in particular, the significant events of his time, the most important of which were the startling effects of the mutiny. He was not a passive bystander in the unfolding gruesome drama. He was drawn into the action not as a participant in the fight for or against the British, but as a man desperately striving to save human lives from belligerent parties. This terrible event of Indian history, said Altaf Husain Hali, his biographer, brought about "a momentous revolution in Sir Sayyid's way of thinking."[69] In Hafeez Malik's assessment, the trauma of 1857 provided the essential background to his greatness. Had not the wars of 1857 broken out, Sayyid Ahmad Khan would probably have ended his life as a minor judicial official with a dozen mediocre books to his name.[70] Like Hali and Malik, Christian W. Troll argued that "after the Indian Mutiny of 1857 and the traumatic events accompanying and following it, Sayyid Ahmad Khan entered the field of theology proper, that is, a rational interpretation of religious faith, practice and experience."[71]

When Queen Victoria proclaimed a general amnesty, Sayyid Ahmad Khan urged the members of his defeated and demoralized community to gather at the famous shrine of Shah Bulaqi Sahib to thank Her Majesty for her clemency. The whole population of his community complied, and on July 28, 1859, some fifteen thousand Muslims gathered, distributed food to the poor, prayed, and listened to his speech.[72] Throughout his life, Sayyid Ahmad Khan maintained a cordial relationship with the British and considered their rule in India "the most wonderful phenomenon the world has ever seen."[73] This is not to say that he displayed a servile submission to foreign rule. His loyalist approach was an element in his ambitious project for uplifting the conditions of Indian Muslims. He acknowledged the decadence of Muslim society and the striking backwardness of his people vis-à-vis the Europeans. It was his firm conviction that India could never rise unless "the Europeans and natives mixed with each other not as the rulers and the ruled but as friends and brethren."[74]

Sayyid Ahmad Khan's ideas, however, were developed in relation to the intellectual problems of Islam that had been raised by missionaries, British civil servants, and Westernizers, and in relation to the scientific discoveries that were challenging his faith. True, his theological speculation was rooted in the antitraditionalism of Shah Waliallah and the rationalist views of the Mu'tazila school and of the Ikhwan al-Safa (Brethren of Purity).[75] For him, the ulama were ill equipped to deal with the intellectual problems that had besieged Islam in the modern period. In the past, the ulama advanced *Ilm-i Kalam* (lit. "rhetoric") to combat the incursion of Greek philosophy into Islam. "Greek philosophy," said Sayyid Ahmad Khan, "was based largely on conjecture and hypothesis; our ancestors, therefore, had the relatively simple task of answering conjecture with conjecture and hypothesis with hypothesis. The propositions of modern science, however, are proved empirically and obviously that which is shown to be true cannot be disproved merely by conjectural reasoning."[76] To establish the truth of Islam and reconcile Islamic tenets with the principles of natural law, he refused to accept the decisions of the ulama and the orthodox as final. The Quran, he said, is the final authority in all matters of judgment. He enunciated the principle that he would accept only "tafsir al-Qur'an bil Qur'an"—the explanation of the text of the Quran by reference to the Quran itself, and not to any tradition or the opinion of any scholar.[77]

This exegetic premise was to serve his natural theology: God as the creator of the universe sent prophets, including Muhammad, to guide mankind. The Quran is the word of God revealed to Muhammad through revelation. There is nothing in the Quran that is incorrect or antihistorical. God has also created the laws of nature. The Quran, as the word of God, and the laws of nature, as his work, having one creator, cannot contradict each other. Revelation and natural laws are therefore compatible.[78] For Sayyid Ahmad Khan, the eschatology and cosmology of any true religion cannot run counter to the laws of nature discovered by modern science. A religion's conformity with human nature or nature in general is a clear proof of its coming from God. On the other hand, "if that religion is against human nature and constitution, and against his [mankind's] powers and the rights which follow from these powers, and stands in the way of putting them to useful purposes, then undoubtedly that religion cannot be claimed to issue forth from the hands of the Author of Nature, for religion, after all, is made for men."[79] In keeping with these propositions, Sayyid Ahmad Khan went as far as claiming, "Islam is nature and nature is Islam."[80]

He used this methodology to rationalize various supernatural events, attributes, and entities mentioned in the Quran. For example, he held that the Darwinian theory of evolution and the Islamic tenets of Creation are compatible. The Quran affirms that the law of evolution is observable in relating one species of created being to another. "Semen" or "seed" are symbolic imagery of the nucleus of life, referring to the primeval movement of life emerging from inert matter. The concept of the angel is the divine moral support for man's struggle in life, while Satan signifies the dark passion of man. The word *jinn* is used in the Quran to refer to anything hidden, like a child in its mother's womb, the pagans of Mecca who hid themselves to eavesdrop on the Prophet, and the savages who used to remain hidden in the wilderness.[81] Likewise, the crossing of the sea by Moses and the drowning of Pharaoh meant that God had made the sea fordable, but by the time Pharaoh and his army arrived, the water had risen, and as a result they were all drowned. Noah's flood was a local occurrence. Miracles were not the evidence of prophecy: a prophet's function was to enlighten, to guide, and to appeal to reason, not to dazzle, to mystify, and to appeal to superstition. Dismissing the attribution of miracles to Muhammad as an imitation of the Jews and the Christians, Sayyid Ahmad Khan maintained that the Prophet of Islam had had no miracles to exhibit. All miracles rested with God. These and many other statements made by Sayyid Ahmad Khan reflected the depth of the impression rationalist scientific discourse had made on his thought and the extent to which he strove to make Islam accessible to reason.[82]

The theological modernism of Sayyid Ahmad Khan paralleled his subscription to the dominant nineteenth-century paradigm on society and history. Through him and virtually all the modernist thinkers, the notion of evolution, progress, and human civilization crept into Islamic social theory. Societies were no longer judged in terms of the ethical criteria of right and wrong that were based on such binaries

as dar ul-Islam versus dar ul-harb and shari'a versus jahiliyya. The level of technological advancement and the development of modern social institutions became the
yardstick for evaluating societies. Civilization, in his view, "connotes the advanced,
cultured, and humanized form of Europeans, who stand in glaring contrast to the
wild and barbarized peoples of North America, aborigines of Australia, Tartars and
inhabitants of East Africa."[83] He held that some nations are intrinsically superior
to others in their capability of benefiting from natural and social factors of progress.
He believed in laissez-faire and assigned a limited role for government in the
advance of civilization.[84]

Impressed by Joseph Addison and Sir Richard Steele's *Spectator* and *Tatler*,
Sayyid Ahmad Khan published *Tahzib al-Akhlaq* (*Social Reform*) to bring progressive ideas before Indian Muslims. Although the name was taken from the ethical
treatise of Ibn Miskawayh, the journal was modeled on these authors' journals. He
intended the word *akhlaq* to convey the same meanings that the English word "civilization" did—manners, customs, scholarship, the arts and crafts, human occupations and profession, and the use of leisure time, within the broad areas of society
and culture.[85] The journal raised storms of bitter controversy, and in fact the shock
of its content was the most important factor in the journal's quick rise to prominence. Praise was poured on things which the Muslims had always been taught to
mistrust, scorn, or hate, such as Western eating customs, Hindu progressiveness,
and English education. Censure was heaped on much that characterized Muslim
attitudes: blind following (taqlid) of customs sanctioned by religion, "professional"
asceticism, theological rigidity.[86] He argued that "freedom in following one's own
likes and dislikes is every man's privilege, as long as others are not harmed."[87] It is
the right of every individual.[88] "In its brilliant pages," in Aziz Ahmad's assessment,
"modernism emerged as a potent force and considerably changed the course and
the direction of Islam in India."[89]

Sayyid Ahmad Khan spoke in favor of intellectual pluralism in which diverse
views were discussed and debated. "When people are forced to hear arguments on
both sides of a matter," he said, "there is always hope of justice, but when they hear
only one side, falsehoods become obdurate and turn into prejudice. Even truth
does not retain the effect of truth because it tends to get more and more exaggerated until it turns into a lie."[90] In his commentary on the Bible, Sayyid Ahmad
Khan did not accept the Muslims' position that the Bible was altered and tampered
with. In his view, belligerent disputations among Muslims and Christians over the
issue of abrogation (naskh) were nothing more than arguments about words, and
much of the evidence the Christians had taken from the Bible to attack the tenets
of Islam was based on misunderstanding.[91]

A corrective to Sayyid Ahmad Khan's natural theology and a more conservative
restatement of some of his view was presented in the religious thought of Mahdi Ali

Khan, known as Muhsin al-Mulk (1837–1907). He, like Sayyid Ahmad Khan, departed from taqlid (emulation) and moved to ijtihad (independent reasoning), and considered that the hadith, as a source of law, should be accepted with great caution. One cannot be absolutely certain that the actual wording of a hadith was Muhammad's exact statement. Impurities might have mixed with Muhammad's statement and changed its meaning. While Muhsin al-Mulk did not reject the other source of law, the consensus (ijma) of the ulama, he claimed it could not be accepted entirely. It should be reevaluated and judged according to the findings of physical sciences and the standards of contemporary ethics. Muhsin al-Mulk, however, departed from the natural theology espoused by Sayyid Ahmad Khan, arguing that nature was a vague concept and the laws of nature were being continuously rediscovered and reinterpreted by modern science. The Quran, by interpreting extranatural agencies as allegorical, laid down the principle of possible exceptions to these laws. Thus, instead of explaining them away in terms of a naturalistic rationality, Muhsin al-Mulk claimed that supernatural phenomena such as miracles, angels, and Satan could be considered among these exceptions.[92] His exegetical approach therefore provided room for the independence of Islamic theology from naturalistic interpretation and thus for a conservative reassertion that what was immutable was the law of God revealed to Muhammad, and that it was the laws of nature and society discovered by humans that were fallible and subject to change.

Rational Law versus the Shari'a

Sayyid Ahmad Khan's objective in rationalizing religious dogma and establishing the congruity between Islam and science was to construct a religious basis for the existence of a modern Muslim, rejecting the Anglicist notion that the educated could be Muslim no more. At the same time, he appropriated European sciences by claiming that scientific discoveries were in fact forecast in the Quran. Islam was thus removed as the source of the backwardness of Muslim societies. Given the identity of Islam with science, a virtuous Islamic society and modern society were one and the same. As Sir Sayyid's principal associate, Chiragh Ali (1844–95) followed a similar approach in rationalizing religious dogma and reformulating Islamic laws in a manner congruent with the standards of European civilization. He too was oriented toward natural theology. For him, Islamic culture contained certain intellectual traditions, such as the investigative methods used in biographical dictionaries and the principles of rational criticism, and had advanced the dialectical methodology currently in vogue in Europe. This methodology, however, had been ridiculed by the orthodox ulama throughout the centuries.[93]

The rationalizing of dogma, however, had a limit. The rigidity and outmoded nature of certain aspects of Islamic laws were used by its critics as evidence of Islam's incompatibility with modernity. These laws could not be explained away by a rationalist interpretation. The Reverend Malcolm MacColl, for example, claimed that the Islamic states were branches of a cosmopolitan theocracy bound together by a common code of essentially and eternally unchangeable civil and religious rules. Formulated twelve centuries ago to guide the rude and ignorant Arabs, these rules must be followed forever by all Muslims. The inviolable sanctity of Muhammad's decrees was guarded by a most powerful and wealthy corporation whose duty and interest it was to prevent the introduction of any of the reforms the European cabinets had periodically recommended to the favorable consideration of the sultan.[94]

Rather than provide a rational justification for religious laws, Chiragh Ali conceded that in fact certain aspects of Islamic laws are irreconcilable with the modern needs of Islam, whether in India or Turkey, and required modifications. "The several chapters of the Common Law, as those on political Institutes, Slavery, Concubinage, Marriage, Divorce, and the Disabilities of non-Moslem fellow-subjects are to be remodeled and re-written in accordance with the strict interpretations of the Koran."[95] He thus removed these laws from the level of religion (i.e., sacred laws to be discovered via exegesis) and placed them within the category of the secular (laws that were manmade). He did so by making a distinction between the Muhammadan revealed law of the Quran and the Muhammadan common law that had been developed in the course of Muslim history. He argued that Islamic states had not usually been theocratic in their system of government. The early caliphs had been appointed by election. There had been no common code for the guidance of the government during the republican period, or during the Umayyid dynasty. In these periods, there had been a total absence of any ecclesiastical law books except the Muhammadan revealed law of the Quran. The Muhammadan common law was the unwritten law which had been compiled from a very few verses of the Quran, as well as from the customs and usages of the country, supported by traditions contradictory in themselves and based on the consensus of the Muslims. The common code of Islam or Islamic jurisprudence had been compiled in a very late period, and as such it could not be considered essentially and eternally unchangeable. Nor could it be binding on any other nation than the Arabs, whose customs, usages, and traditions it contained and upon which it was based.[96]

The pure Islam taught by Muhammad in the Quran, said Chiragh Ali, is capable of progress. What MacColl called "the inviolable and absolutely unchangeable law of Islam," which impelled the ulama to resist the introduction of European reforms, was only the Muhammadan common law and in no way could be considered infallible.[97] This distinction not only enabled Chiragh Ali to refute MacColl's claim about the rigidity of Islam, but also set a theological basis for reinterpreting the Quran and the conduct of Muhammad in terms of the standards of modernity. For Chiragh Ali, "the fact that Mohammad did not compile a law, civil or canonical, for the conduct of the believers, nor did he enjoin them to do so, shows that he left to the believers in general to frame any code, civil or canon law, and to found systems which would harmonize with the times, and suit the political and social changes going on around them."[98]

Gender Hierarchy, Polygamy, and Islamic Feminism

The situation of women was among the most visible targets of the missionaries' and Westernizers' polemics. Sayyid Ahmad Khan contended that while Islam treated women more favorably than other religions, the condition of women in the advanced nations was much better than that of women in Muslim countries. In advanced countries, good fellowship, courtesy, consideration, love, and encouragement characterized relations between men and women. Men paid attention to their women's comfort, ease, happiness, and pleasure. Muslims, in contrast, made no progress in these areas, and in India there were such unworthy and humiliating carryings-on that one could only cry out, "May God have mercy on us!"[99] On the sensitive issue of polygamy, he and Chiragh Ali reexamined the Quranic injunction on polygamy and concluded that the practice was illegal in Islam. The pertinent verse in the Quran stated, "marry such women as seem good to you, two, three, four; but if you fear you will not be equitable, then only one." They contended that justice in marriage could be synonymous only with love, and since a man was emotionally incapable of loving more than one woman equally at once, polygamy was therefore prohibited.[100] Chiragh Ali argued that reducing the unlimited polygamy practiced in Arabia was Muhammad's preliminary measure toward its abolition, but "his declaring in the Koran that no body could fulfill the condition of dealing *equitably* with more than one woman" was the final step.[101]

Sayyid Mumtaz Ali (1860–1935) went beyond the prohibition of polygamy. In his works, women's rights and the campaign for gender equality gained central significance. His *Huquq un-Niswan* (*Women's Rights*) and the journal *Tahzib al-Niswan* (*Reforming Women*), which he founded with his wife, were among his major publications on women. Although Mumtaz Ali was trained in the conservative school of Deoband, his association with Sayyid Ahmad Khan and involvement in religious disputations between the ulama and the missionaries affected his views of Islam. For a time he came under the influence of the missionaries.[102] In his treatise on the rights of women, Mumtaz Ali first systematically presented the traditional arguments for male supremacy: God gave men greater physical strength and capacity to rule; men were more rational, less emotional, and endowed with greater intellectual powers; men were the exclusive recipients of divine favors, for God had sent only male prophets, not prophetesses; the Quran was repeatedly quoted in support of male domination; God first created man and then created woman for his comfort; according to the Quran, the testimony of two women was equal to that of one man, and in the inheritance of property, a daughter's share was only half that of a son;

because men might have as many as four wives at once, God had given them more powers; and even after life women were to assume an inferior position because God had granted men the company of beautiful women (*houris*) but had decreed that women should be chaste in paradise. Mumtaz Ali refuted every one of these arguments by recourse to reason, and through his modernist exegetical approach he explained away the Quranic injunctions that were brought to bear in support of the traditionalist views on women. For example, he held that physical strength could not be considered a criterion for establishing the superiority of men over women. Nor did physical strength establish the right to rule, even though in the dark ages "might made right." It was not strength, but wisdom that would determine the right to rule. "When women have been called upon to rule, as in the case of the current Queen-Empress, Victoria, they have ruled with great skill, wisdom, and justice."[103]

Mumtaz Ali rejected the traditionalist interpretation of the Quranic verse that justified men's authority over women: "Men are the managers of the affairs of women for that God has preferred in bounty one of them over another, and for that they have expended of their property. Righteous women are therefore obedient."[104] For him, this verse dealt only with activities such as business transactions, in which men had greater knowledge than women, but it did not declare that women should be subordinate to men in all spheres of activities. In the case of court witnesses, in which the testimony of two women was equal to that of one man, Mumtaz Ali argued that the Quran referred specifically to business matters in which women might be less experienced than men. This lack of experience was the result of social conditions, not an inherent defect in woman's character. In such other areas as marriage, divorce, and adultery, in which both sexes were equally experienced, however, the Quran did not make a distinction between the testimony of men and women.[105]

On the issue of veiling, he maintained that modest behavior was natural to humans and a characteristic of civilized societies. Veiling did not mean that women should hide their faces or refrain from being seen in public. Extreme isolation had deleterious effects on women. Confined to the home environment, women did not get fresh air and sunshine, and as a result their health was affected. And when women did go out, a bevy of servants held up curtains to shield them from all eyes. "This is stupid and wasteful," said Mumtaz Ali. In this form of extreme isolation, even the word "wife" was used only in purdah. A husband, instead of referring to his spouse as "my wife," would say something like "the person in my house" or use another form of verbal effusion. This practice was not only injurious to women, but also harmed the entire society, for it promoted narrow-mindedness and mistrust even within the same family. As a remedy, Mumtaz Ali suggested changes in the form of women's dress, relaxation of the restrictions on women's movement, and establishment of the freedom for women to attend public gatherings with their husbands. He also recommended that the current practice of marriage be changed; it should be based on the consent of the individuals involved, dower (*mahr*) should be reasonable, and women should be given the right to initiate divorce under certain conditions.[106]

Civilization and Islamic History

The glaring contrast between Europe and Islamic nations gave rise to a pervasive consciousness of decadence among the modernists, which necessitated an account of Muslim decline. True, this question was not the exclusive concern of the modernists. The traditionalists (*ahl-i hadith*), for example, viewed Islamic history as that of a consistent retrogression from its golden age of the Prophet. There was also the need to defend and rehabilitate early Islamic history against the assaults of its critics. Much of the criticisms of historical Islam revolved around the issues of jihad and Muslims' alleged intolerance of other faiths. Jihad was a particularly sore point in Muslim-Christian history. People like William Muir, Robertson Smith, George Sale, and Aloys Sprenger as well as Christian missionaries like T. P. Hughes and Samuel Green argued that in his zeal to spread Islam, Muhammad, holding the Quran in one hand and a scimitar in the other, pursued aggressive wars of conquest against the Qureish, other Arab tribes, the Jews, and Christians, compelling them to convert to Islam. They also portrayed Islam as an intolerant religion, and Muhammad himself as a person who plotted the assassination of his enemies and was cruel to his prisoners.

Chiragh Ali rejected these claims by first presenting the historical context within which Muhammad's alleged actions had taken place. Then, with recourse to international law, religious liberty, and the legitimacy of defending one's freedom, he claimed that Muhammad's conduct was justified. In his view, none of his wars were offensive, nor did he in any way use force in the matter of belief. All his wars were defensive. Chiragh Ali also explained that defensive war was only one of the senses of the concept of jihad used in Islam. Jihad also pointed to one's utmost efforts, exertion, labor, or toil. Further, the alleged assassinations attributed to Muhammad were in fact executions of several individuals for the crime of high treason against the Muslim Commonwealth. All were in conformity with the laws of war.[107] On slavery, he held that the Quran mentioned the practice as de facto but not de jure—that is, as a matter of practice of the pagan Arab—but it took measures in every moral, legal, religious, and political realm to abolish it. The Quran never allowed the enslavement of captives of war, nor did it sanction the turning of female captives into concubines.[108]

Shibli Nu'mani (1851–1914) and Amir Ali (1849–1928) went beyond Chiragh Ali's defensive statement and offered a more comprehensive depiction of Islamic history. Shibli Nu'mani was among the conservative members of the Aligarh College. Yet his writings, far from being traditionalist, reflected the historical methods and normative criteria in vogue in Europe. He used this method to refute the charges Western authors leveled against Islam on the treatment of Christians and Jews living under its domain and on slavery. He suggested that Islamic historiography must go beyond the style of the early Muslim writers on the Prophet. These writers had been preoccupied with reporting the facts without caring how these facts affected their religion.[109] Shibli's *Sirat al-Nabi* intended to elaborate the proper methods of writing on the life of Muhammad and respond to the charges made against his character and conduct. His responses had a more conservative orientation than that of other modernists. For example, to explain how three hundred footsoldiers of Muhammad followers managed to defeat an army of one thousand armed soldiers that included one hundred horsemen of the Qureish tribe, Shibli advanced a rational argument only to satisfy Western historians "to whom everything in this world of cause and effect appears to be the result of some evident cause." That is, Muhammad and followers were victorious because there was a lack of unity among the Qureish; because, as a result of the rains, the ground where the Qureish had encamped had become muddy; and because the Qureish had miscalculated the strength of the army of Islam. Nevertheless, Shibli was quick to indicate that "these are the causes, and in fact Divine intercession only meant the combination (and coming together of all these causes). If you compare the Muslim army with that of the Quraysh [Qureish] will it appear according to military calculations that the victory of the former was inevitable?"[110]

Where modernity had the greatest influence on Shibli was in his method of historical analysis, emphasizing the standard of evaluating evidence and systematic presentation of argument. He argued that "the standard of evidence and narration changes with a change in the nature of the event."[111] For example, if a child of five related that the Prophet used to take him in his arms, then there is no room to doubt that narration. But if he related that such and such a person had explained an intricate ruling of law, then it would be doubted whether the child had correctly understood the ruling. While admittedly the traditionalists were not unaware of the standard of evidence, his main critique of their method of writing history was of their preoccupation with military successes.[112] For him, "this method was not right even for the history of kings and their government; and for writing the *Sirat* of the Prophet it was positively unsuited. War sometimes becomes unavoidable in the life of a Prophet. In these circumstances he appears to be a mere conqueror or commander, but this is not his real character. The minutest details of the life of a Prophet are marked by holiness, purity, tolerance, generosity, universal sympathy and a spirit of sacrifice."[113]

Shibli's analysis of the rule of Omar, the third caliph, is indicative of his investigative approach. In explaining Omar's success in conquests, he considered the emphasis of Western historians on the weakness of Eastern Roman Empire and the Persian Empire to be inadequate. The real cause of the Muslim conquest was "the enthusiasm, resolution, steadfastness, courage and daring which the Holy Founder of Islam had instilled in them [followers of Islam] and which Omar had further sharpened and fortified."[114] These conquests were also successful because these empires did not enjoy much popular support. The system of government under Omar, and other Rashidun caliphs, was democratic, not autocratic. There was a consultative assembly, citizens had a role in his administration, and no special privilege was accorded the caliph. Omar also promoted democracy in the conquered areas.[115] On the treatment of non-Muslims (*dhimmis*) living within the domain of Islamic rule, Shibli maintained that their lives and properties were placed on the same level with the Muslims'. They were also consulted in matters of administration concerning their welfare. They enjoyed complete freedom of religion and were at liberty to perform their religious rites, ring their bells, take out the cross in procession, and hold religious fairs.[116] On slavery, Shibli argued that while Omar did not abolish slavery, which he probably could not have succeeded in doing even if he had tried, he used various means to curtail the practice.[117] Turning to a more recent Islamic history, Shibli defended Alamgir, a Mughal ruler who was judged harshly by the Orientalists. Shibli claimed that Alamgir was a reasonable ruler. He exceeded his predecessors by promoting education in India, and although he did not claim to be a caliph, he was a Muslim ruler and promoted Islamic traditions in his administration.[118]

Similarly, Amir Ali advanced a rationalist approach in presenting historical Islam, but there are differences between the two scholars. First, Amir Ali belonged to the Calcutta school of modernity, Westernization, and loyalism, which was independent of the Aligarh school though unmistakably influenced by it. A distinctive feature of this school was that its chief adherents, such as Abd ul-Latif Khan, Karamat Ali, and his disciple Amir Ali, were orthodox Shi'i.[119] Second, in contrast with Shibli, Amir Ali was liberal, and much of his work was aimed at a Western audience. Because of his pioneering and systematic work in reexamining Islamic history and his championing of the cause of Islam in terms of the ethical standards of modernity, he is certainly a leader of the pan-Islamic intellectual movement for the defense of Islam in the West. His *Spirit of Islam* ran to nine editions and *A Short History of the Saracens* to thirteen in Great Britain.

Yet despite these differences the two scholars shared a broad methodological orientation in defending historical Islam on such issues as slavery, polygamy, and the treatment of non-Muslims living under Islamic rule. As a Shi'i, it was an article of faith for Amir Ali to consider Ali the Prophet's legitimate successor. Nevertheless, if the intellectual pluralism of nineteenth-century India directed such a thinker as Sayyid Ahmad Khan to bridge the gap between Christianity and Islam, it was all too natural to expect Amir Ali to search for a formula that transcended the Shi'i-Sunni division and discord. To this end, Amir Ali made a distinction between the Shi'i notion of apostolic imamat and the pontifical caliphate of Abu Bakr, Omar, and Osman, who preceded Ali. For Amir Ali, the two forms of leadership, apostolic and pontifical, could coexist and even play positive functions for the Muslim community, as evidenced by Ali's being the principal adviser to Abu Bakr and Omar. He disagreed with the traditional Shi'i position that the caliphate of the first three caliphs was illegitimate. For him, these caliphs were elected by the unanimous suffrage of Muslims. For the sake of Muslim unity, Ali was perceptive in forfeiting his claim and pledging allegiance to Abu Bakr.[120] Amir Ali even spoke favorably of the Ottoman caliphate of the Sunni sect.[121]

Amir Ali presented his views on women, slavery, religious tolerance, and other issues from an evolutionary perspective. This perspective gave him the rationale to go on the offensive against the missionaries: historical Judaism, Christianity, and other religions had displayed many instances of immorality, oppression, and cruelty against humans. Female infanticide, for example, which was common among the pagan Arabs, must have also been common in the seventh century of the Christian era. Whether it was under Zoroastrians or Christians, the condition of women during the centuries preceding the advent of Islam was deplorable.[122] Further, "concubinage, the union of people standing to each other in matrimony, existed among the Arabs, the Jews, the Christians, and all the neighboring nations. The Prophet did not in the beginning denounce the custom, but towards the end of his career he expressly forbade it."[123] On polygamy, Amir Ali's position was similar to that of Chiragh Ali and other modernist writers in equating justice in marriage with love.[124]

Amir Ali criticized Christianity because it had raised "no protest against slavery, enforced no rule, inculcated no principle for the mitigation of the evil."[125] In contrast, slavery in historical Islam was based on racial tolerance. Social mobility and progress of slaves were possible under the Islamic civilization. Such was not the case in Christendom or present Europe: "In Islam the slave of to-day is the grand vizier of to-morrow. He may marry, without discredit, his master's daughter, and become the head of the family. Slaves have ruled kingdoms and founded dynasties. The father of Mahmud of Ghazni was a slave. Can Christianity point to such records as these? Can Christianity show, in the pages of history, as clear, as humane an account of her treatment of slaves as this?"[126] It should be noted that in his defense of Islamic history, Amir Ali might have gone a bit too far, and, in Aziz Ahmad's apt remark, "such embarrassing episodes as the Zanj (Negro) revolt (870–83) against the 'Abbasids and their underlying economic and social motivation have been conveniently overlooked."[127] On the status of non-Muslims living under Muslim rule, Amir Ali's position was similar to that of Shibli.[128]

While Amir Ali's reasoning was similar to that of Shibli and Chiragh Ali in showing the peaceful and tolerant nature of Islam, he employed a more offensive approach in discussing historical Christianity, raising the same charges against Christianity as the missionaries did against Islam. "Every action of violation was sanctified by the Church, and, in case of extreme iniquity, absolution paved the criminal's way to heaven. From the first slaughters of Charlemagne, with the full sanction of the Church, to the massacre and enslavement of the unoffending races of America, there is an unbroken series of the infringement of international duties and the claims of humanity. . . . The rise of Protestantism made no difference."[129] However various groups within Christianity disagreed among themselves on doctrinal and theological matters, they were in perfect agreement with each other in denying rights and interests to nations outside the pale of Christendom. Islam, on the other hand, was opposed to isolation and exclusiveness. To be sure, religion, Islam and Christianity alike, had in the past often provided "a pretext for the gratification of ambition" by "designing chieftains." The Muslim casuists like their Christian counterparts divided the world into the dar ul-harb and the dar ul-Islam, the counterparts of heathendom and Christendom. These concepts in Islam, said Amir Ali, differentiated only the condition of belligerency and that of peace, and by no means implied waging wars and invading the territories of nations whose inhabitants were non-Muslims.[130]

FOUR

The French Enlightenment and Islamic Modernism in Egypt

In many respects, Egypt in the nineteenth century was different from India in the same period. India was religiously nonunified, culturally heterogeneous, was highly populated, had a complex system of social stratification, and was dominated by a differentiated system of colonial administration. Egypt, in comparison, was religiously unified, culturally homogeneous, and less populated and had a simpler system of stratification and a uniformed system of political administration. Yet the two countries displayed striking similarities in the discursive context in which Islamic modernism was produced. This context was pluralistic, displaying several major discourses including the European Enlightenment, British Westernizing discourse, the proselytizing discourse of the Evangelicals, and the discourse of the orthodox Islamic establishment.

Egypt provides the additional utility of ruling out an alternative explanation that cannot be ignored if we focus on only India: that is, that Islamic modernism was produced within a network of like-minded Muslim scholars to enhance their social position and occupational interests. Except for Amir Ali, all the modernists were part of the Aligarh movement. These individuals knew one another, resided in the same locality, and along with Amir Ali enjoyed friendly relations with the British. Thus, their common position on some key issues facing their faith was a reflection of their organizational interests rather than an outcome of their scholarly exertion to defend their religion against the onslaught of both the rationalists and the missionaries. Without such an organized network, Islamic modernism might not have emerged.

Organization and network are certainly important in shaping the development of ideas. But our objective here is to show the significance of targets in determining the content of ideological production. In defending their interests, even calculating opportunists are constrained by the existing debates and war of positions. Egypt, however, provides a useful case to shed further light on the import of culture, rather than organization and network, in shaping discourse. The works of the Egyptian modernists—from Tahtawi's account of life in Paris in the 1830s to al-Raziq's controversial book *Islam and the Principles of Authority* in the mid-1920s—span almost a century. Although a modernist theme tied their works, Tahtawi, al-Afghani, Abduh, Wajdi, Amin, and al-Raziq did not form a network. Since they are so separated in time, it is difficult to pinpoint the existence of a lasting organizational context that shaped the discourses of these thinkers. Different organizations and networks might have influenced these people. Tahtawi was part of the bureaucracy of a modernizing despot, Abduh was the mufti of Egypt, and al-Raziq was connected to the liberal-nationalist movement. Certainly, varying organizational contexts constrained their discourses, but the fact that they took similar positions on key issues facing Islam was associated with their common encounters with similar cultural dynamics and ideological targets as they experienced, like their Indian counterparts, a similar kind of systematic assault on Islam by the followers of the Enlightenment, the missionaries, and Westernizers and a similar kind of resistance on the part of their conservative colleagues. The variations of emphasis in their discourses appeared to have been a function of the variations in the kinds of ideological targets they faced.

The State and Culture Production

Under Muhammad Ali, the change in the land tenured system, the expansion of government control over traditional institutions, the restriction of the power of the ulama, and the massive construction of the administrative and military organizations of the modern state—all promoted the rise of modern ideas. Of considerable significance were the continued decline of the madrasas throughout the century and the establishment of modern state schools. Students were also sent to Europe to gain knowledge in military technology. By 1840, a total of 349 students were sent to Europe to study various branches of science. Most of these students were initially drawn from Turks or Levantine Christians, but later the proportion of native Egyptians grew. This latter group formed the first intelligentsia of modern Egypt.[1] As far as the development of culture is concerned, in Panayiotis Vatikiotis's assessment, "the founding of a printing press and the School of Languages and Translation were perhaps the two greatest achievements of the Muhammad Ali period within Egypt."[2]

Muhammad Ali was assisted by the followers of Henri de Saint-Simon who arrived in Egypt in the 1830s. With the cultural and industrial development of Egypt as their avowed objective, Saint-Simonites worked as doctors, engineers, and teachers and helped to design and execute the first great modern work of irrigation in the country, the barrages on the Nile.[3] Muhammad Ali's principal interest lay in building a strong military. Having an imperial design of his own,[4] he sent students to Europe, set them to translating technical works when they returned, and established a press to print the translation and an official newspaper to publish the texts of his decrees and decisions. Saint-Simon's vision of a model society directed by a priesthood of scientists had little or no appeal for Muhammad Ali.[5] He was interested in modern techniques of warfare, not modern ideas. There had been disappointing occasions for the khedive when he encountered students who had shown interests in matters of civil administration. "One, on being asked what he had studied, replied, 'Civil Administration,' 'And what is that?' asked Muhammad 'Ali, to which the unfortunate student replied 'the study of the government of affairs'; 'What!' exclaimed Muhammad 'Ali, 'you are not going to get mixed up in the administration! What a waste of time! It is I who govern. Go to Cairo and translate military works.' "[6]

He reorganized social life to centralize power and build his military, but the laws and manuals issued to regulate military life "offered a model of how society in general could be organized, as indeed it was."[7] Muhammad Ali showed little interest in culture. Although he was called upon by the Ottoman sultan to suppress the Wahhabi movement, his policy toward religion was one of moderation. When the Europeans interceded with him for a woman who had been condemned for apostasy, he ordered her to be brought before him. "He exhorted her to recant; but finding her resolute, reproved her for her *folly*, and sent her home, commanding that no injury should be done to her."[8] Sultan Abd al-Majid's decree on religious liberty further favored religious pluralism. Under Khedive Ismail, a more-than-tenfold increase in the educational budget expanded the requisite resources for culture production. Directed by capable administrators like Ibrahim Pasha and Ali Mubarak Pasha, cultural development forged ahead. The School of Languages and Administration was reopened and in 1886 became the first secular law school under the direction of Vidal Pasha, a French jurist. Founded in 1872, the Dar al-Ulum teachers' college played a leading role in the revival of Arabic literature. The khedive also supported such journals as *Rawdat al-Madaris* to spread science and scholarship among Egyptians. Private foreign and local educational institutions, foundations, and missions strengthened the state's educational program.[9] The British also assisted the rise of modern culture by implementing measures of reform. Under their tutelage, the Egyptian press became a medium for public debates. Favorable political conditions encouraged an influx of Syrian and Lebanese émigrés to Egypt, and they played a prominent role in the country's culture. Men of letters like Adib Ishaq and Salim al-Naqqash were followed by others like Faris Nimr and Ya'qub Sarruf. They published the dailies *al-Muqqattam* and *al-Ahram* and the monthlies *al-Hillal* and *al-Muqtataf.*[10]

After occupying Egypt, the British did not completely break away from the exist-ing system of government. The statesman Frederick Temple Hamilton-Temple-Blackwood, Lord Dufferin, who went to Egypt in 1882, after the British occupied the country, concluded that most of the institutions of government were suitable instruments and recommended that Britain not tamper with them. Nor did the British attempt to interfere in the religious affairs. The professed cultural policy of Evelyn Baring, Lord Cromer, the British consul general in Egypt, was one of reli-gious neutrality. The Englishman, said Cromer, "will scrupulously abstain from interference in religious matters. He will be eager to explain that proselytism forms no part of his political programme. . . . He will scrupulously respect all Moslem observances. He will generally, amidst some twinges of his Sabbatarian conscience, observe Friday as a holiday, and perform the work of the Egyptian Government on Sunday."[11] This policy, however, angered the missionaries.[12] "The power occupying the country," they protested, "would take no special care of the Christian popula-tion, nor manifest any special interest in converts from Islam."[13] They demanded that "the government of Egypt should be for Egyptians—whether Moslems, Copts, or Protestants, matters not,—and the Christians, forsooth, as much Egyptians as the Moslems—more so, if history be examined.[14] They also criticized the persist-ence of favoritism that was accorded the Muslims against the Copts.[15]

The Pluralistic Intellectual Environment

While the decline of the traditional institutions removed the barriers on culture production, the flooding of Egypt's cultural landscape by Western ideologies diver-sified the structure of ideological contentions in the country, creating a pluralistic cultural environment. As the diffusion of modern culture in Egypt accelerated, the conceptual schema of Islamic orthodoxy collided with alternative sets of codes in the discourse of the followers of the Enlightenment, British Westernizers, and Christian Evangelicals.

The European Enlightenment

Saint-Simon and Auguste Comte believed in social evolution, according to which humans would abandon theological and metaphysical doctrines for scientific knowledge. They were the architects of a positivist project in which society would be organized according to rationalist principles and the scientists were assigned the task of supreme priesthood to guide society. "Saint-Simon correctly foresaw the industrialization of the world, and believed that science and technology would solve most of humanity's problems."[16] As early as the 1830s, this new doctrine entered Egypt with his followers, who were engaged in various technical projects. Moreover, many of the students who were sent abroad became familiar with mod-ern thinking on society and government. Already in the 1830s, they were beginning to play a part in affairs: they were translating and publishing books that were not purely technical, they were working closely with the Saint-Simonites to reorganize the schools, and from their ranks came the first substantial political thinker of modern Egypt, Rifa'a al-Tahtawi (1801–73).[17] His stay in Paris (1826–31) was important in his intellectual life. Tahtawi read books on ancient history as well as on the French thought of the eighteenth century, such as the works of Voltaire, Racine, Condillac, Montesquieu, and Rousseau. Impressed by the last author, he invented an Arabic equivalent for the term "social contract"—*iqd al-ta'annus wa'l-ijtima al-insani.*[18] "The thought of the French Enlightenment left a permanent mark on him, and through him on the Egyptian mind."[19]

The discoveries of the European sciences were disseminated in Egypt through such journals as *Rawdat al-Madaris* and, later, *al-Muqtataf.* Edited by Tahtawi, *Rawdat al-Madaris* enriched the Arabic language through translations and by strengthening a new critical literary movement, spread science, and educated Egyptians for modern social change.[20] *Al-Muqtataf* played even a more prominent role in spreading scientific discourse and introducing its readers to modern ideas and discoveries.[21] Articles were published on a variety of subjects ranging from breakthroughs in medicine, technological inventions, literature, and the causes of Western progress and Eastern backwardness to the role of women in society. Among the articles that appeared in the journal were the biographies of prominent scientists, eulogizing such personalities as Isaac Newton,[22] Galileo,[23] Louis Pasteur,[24] Charles Darwin,[25] Ernest Renan,[26] Humphry Davy,[27] Maria Mitchell,[28] and Herbert Spencer.[29] *Al-Muqtataf* also informed its readers of inventions like electricity, the telephone, the phonograph, and photography that had astonished people in the Islamic world.[30] These momentous contributions to human progress enhanced the prestige of the Western sciences among the educated elite, stimulating the desire to uncover the secret of Western advancement.

Al-Muqtataf promoted the idea that the regularities of the temporal world were governed by causal laws, which could be discovered via human intellectual exertion. Some of the views expressed in the journal raised storms of controversy within both Muslim and Coptic conservative establishments. The journal's reports of Darwin's theory of evolution and such discoveries as the roundness and movement of the earth angered these communities.[31] In response to criticisms, the editors portrayed themselves as noncommittal, arguing that at least Darwin should be credited for his contribution to science.[32] To defuse the conservative protests, some writers tried to uncover in Islamic history an intellectual pedigree for Darwin and Galileo. A commentator stated that the idea of the roundness of the earth could be found in al-Ghazali.[33] A certain Amin Shameal established an affinity between Darwin and Ibn Khaldun's views of dynastic changes.[34] In reaction to Shibli Shumayyil's works on Darwinism, Abduh translated al-Afghani's "Refutation of the Materialists" into

Arabic. While religious conservatives, both Muslim and Christian, rejected Darwinism, their Westernizing counterparts were positively disposed toward it.[35] Sarruf and the Lebanese-Egyptian journalist Farah Antun replied to al-Afghani's commentary on Darwinism. Antun went so far as comparing al-Afghani's simplistic interpretations of Darwinism to those of a primary school boy.[36]

Women's social status also gradually became an issue in the ideological debates. *Al-Muqtataf* contributed to this development by defending a woman's right to an education and to work outside her home.[37] It published articles in favor of women, arguing that women, like men, are intelligent, and emphasized the significance of motherhood, education for women, and the task of teaching women their rights in society.[38] Writers and contributors also debated a woman's role outside her home and her rights. A certain Abu Khatir and Salim Shakra exchanged ideas on women's right to education.[39] Another commentator, Wadeh al-Khouri, praised the situation of women in England, France, and the United States, indicating that they had the mental capability to perform important social functions if they were given opportunities similar to those that men had. A Najeeb Antonios criticized al-Khouri for going too far in imputing rights to women.[40] Shibli Shumayyil, in his essay "Are Men and Women Equal?" enumerated the physiological differences between men and women.[41]

British Westernizers

The British also contributed to the nineteenth-century debate over the culture of Islamic Egypt. While they openly pursued a policy of religious neutrality, their critical attitudes toward Islam were known to the country's intellectual leaders. Lord Cromer's *Modern Egypt* summarized such critical attitudes. In this book, he portrayed the history of Britain as a prime example of historical progress in contrast to Islamic history, which was dismal. He condemned Egypt for its intolerant religion, barbaric criminal law, and degradation of women. For him, Islam as a social system was a complete failure. This failure emanated from its keeping women in a position of marked inferiority, the rigidity of its law, its tolerance of slavery, and its intolerance of other religions.[42] The founder of Islam, said Cromer, "launched fiery anathemas against all who would not accept the divinity of his inspiration, and his words fell on fertile ground, for a large number of those who have embraced Islam are semi-savages, and often warlike savages, whose minds are too untrained to receive the idea that an honest difference of opinion is no cause for bitter hatred."[43]

On no point did the new critics of Egyptian society find themselves in greater accord than in condemning the mistreatment of women, their seclusion, and polygamy. Cromer criticized Egypt for its institution of male domination and pointed to the superiority of European civilization for its favorable treatment of women. "In the first place, the face of the Moslem woman is veiled when she appears in public. She lives a life of seclusion. The face of the European woman is exposed to view in public. The only restraints placed on her movements are those dictated by her own sense of propriety. In the second place, the East is polygamous, the West is monogamous."[44] He further stated that "the whole fabric of European society rests upon the preservation of family life. Monogamy fosters family life, polygamy destroys it."[45] Cromer also believed that "Islam cannot be reformed . . . reformed Islam is Islam no longer; it is something else."[46] Echoing the view of his colleagues in India, he was convinced that the educated Egyptians were "demoslemised Moslems and invertebrate Europeans."[47] This is because "in passing through the European educational mill, the young Egyptian Moslem loses his Islamism, or, at all events, he loses the best part of it."[48]

When we clear our minds of the twentieth-century perspective on imperialism, we may appreciate the British ability, despite their high-handedness, to legitimize their presence in Egypt. The British, said Wilfred Blunt, "were popular everywhere in Mohammedan lands, being looked upon as free from the political designs of the other Frank nations. . . . England . . . appeared in the light of a bountiful and friendly providence very rich and quite disinterested, a redresser of wrongs and friend of the oppressed."[49] Even if we question this assessment, we may be justified in arguing that the British presence contributed to cultural pluralism in Egypt because, as Charles Wendell stated, "European Powers paradoxically did the native press an unquestionable service by removing the threat of arbitrary suppression by the will or whim of the khedive."[50] At the same time, while undermining the traditional barriers to modern discourses, they managed not to interfere in religious disputations. This fact most probably hindered the politicization of cultural exchange between Egypt and Europe despite the inequality in the distribution of power. This relative freedom in all likelihood prompted the modernists to avoid oppositional politics. For Abduh and his followers, British rule, while in principle unacceptable, left the only viable opportunity for the gradual education of their fellow Egyptians. The British would also be easier to get rid of than the khedivial autocracy. This outlook was based on a theory of Abduh's which he had learned from the Indian reformer Sayyid Ahmad Khan. It was also in line with the views advanced by al-Ghazali, Ibn Taymiyya, and Ibn Khaldun. In Rashid Rida's summary of Abduh's view,

Political authority in all Muslim lands—no matter who is the master, a conquering foreigner or a national of the land—is in oppressive or despotic hands. To support conqueror or despotic fellow countryman on grounds of religion or learning in fact corrupts both religion and learning. To resist them, on other hand, is to invite persecution for men of religion and learning. The best possible course under the circumstances is to avoid conflict with such authorities and persuade those who wield power that progress is useful for the people and cannot be harmful to them. The reformer in these countries must be satisfied at present if, by this conciliatory method, he can obtain the help he needs from government.[51]

Christian Evangelicals

The spread of mission Christianity in the Ottoman Empire was made possible by the protective measures the European powers obtained for the Christians and Jews living in its domain. Without these measures any success at conversion was deemed impossible, for apostasy in Islam was punishable with death.[52] Further, this protection brought them not only political advantages but commercial, financial, and cultural advantages as well. In Egypt, this change in fortune was also a result of Muhammad Ali's policy of welcoming Christians and Jews to the country.[53] These developments naturally provided the necessary resources for the churches to embark upon their proselytizing efforts. In scope and organization, the missionary project of the Church Missionary Society of Great Britain paralleled the political and economic magnitude of the country's lay adventurers. With a history going back to 1799, it claimed to be one of the oldest and the most extensive missionary agencies in the world, with an annual budget of more than two million dollars and with missions in West Africa, Uganda, Egypt, India, China, Japan, the northwest of America, and elsewhere.[54] Its missionaries arrived in Egypt in 1819,[55] and those of the United Presbyterian Church of North America in 1854.[56] The activities of these missionaries, however, were almost exclusively confined to work among the Copts, principally because "the door of the Copts was opened wide, while the door to the Muhammadans was generally closed and double barred."[57]

Like their counterparts in India, the missionaries started their activities in Egypt by criticizing Islamic history, questioning the integrity of Muslim rulers, assaulting Muhammad's character, and self-righteously condemning Islam for the degradation of women. A conspicuous fact throughout the history of Muslim rule in Egypt, said the Presbyterian Charles Watson, "is the superiority of the Christian, whether Copt or Protestant, to the Moslem in mental ability."[58] The twelve centuries of Muslim history are "for the most part a story of war, revolution, and tyranny."[59] As regards the integrity of the Muslims, he said, "honesty does appear, here and there . . . but for the most part the history of Moslem Egyptian actions presents a record of treachery parried only by greater treachery."[60] And "morality, as the word is commonly used in Christian parlance in the sense of loyalty to one's legal wife, can scarcely be applied to Moslem life."[61]

The missionaries hammered away at Egypt for the situation of women, claiming that in nothing did Islam appear worse when compared with Christianity than in its treatment of women. Polygamy practiced by Muslim men was the twin sister of barbarism.[62] "In the West," he stated, "woman is honored; in Egypt, she is despised. If a man should find it necessary to refer to his wife, he will seldom say My wife, or call her by her name . . . but will say, the family, or the company, and if he should say, My wife, he will likely add, May God preserve thee from dishonor."[63] As a result of being kept in an inferior status, Watson concluded, Muslim women have become inferior to women in the West. "The intelligence, the patience, the culture, the self-denial of the western women, have their exact contrast in the ignorance, the superstition, the irritability, the boorishness and the selfishness of the Egyptian women."[64]

The establishment of schools, begun in the late 1820s, was among the missionaries' principal methods of establishing contact with young Egyptians. It took them four years to manage to have Copts and a few Muslims boys attend these schools. This was followed by the opening of a school for girls. In 1838–39, fifteen Muslims attended the mission schools, and they did not object to religious instruction. A missionary woman, Mrs. Lieder, even gained access to the Ibrahim Pasha's harem to teach his wife and two daughters. The following year, the mission school was visited by the minister of public instruction and others who expressed their pleasure at its methods of instruction.[65] Muslim opposition to the missionaries, however, began to mount in the years 1840–41. The schools lost favor and were saved from being shut down only through the intervention of the United States consul. To avoid future trouble, Muslim boys had to be barred from the mission's schools.[66] During the Urabi rebellion, missionaries were harassed and threatened in Alexandria.[67] In sum, although their activities were not as extensive as they were in India, missionaries had an active presence in Egypt in the nineteenth century. By 1905–6, there were eight missions working among native Egyptians. Altogether, these missions had a total of 141 foreign workers and 664 native workers. They had established 170 elementary schools with 11,312 pupils, 25 boarding and high schools with 4,576 pupils, 3 colleges or seminaries with 687 pupils, 4 hospitals with 3,586 in-patients, 10 clinics, and a native church with 62 organized congregations.[68] According to Samir Raafat, an Egyptian historian, "back then . . . a lot of people found . . . [the] American evangelical system as a way out of the dogma of their own churches. American education was more liberal. It was co-educational. It was new and modern."[69]

Pioneers of Islamic Modernism

Like their Indian counterparts, Egyptian Muslim intellectuals were concerned with the problems facing their community. They were aware of Europe and realized the agonizing backwardness of their society: the archaic technology, the primitive level of scientific knowledge, the despotic political institutions, and the poverty and illiteracy of the masses. Naturally, these historical exigencies had instilled a sense of urgency in their minds. Their ideological resolution, however, neither directly emanated from nor was dictated by these exigencies. It was formed in a different manner. The followers of the Enlightenment, the Westernizers, and the Evangelicals created enormous controversies on various sociopolitical and cultural aspects of Islamic tradition. These intellectuals formulated their discourse within the context of these controversies. In doing so, they realized the inadequacy of the methodological framework of Islamic orthodoxy that had dominated the Azhar and other institutions of higher learning in Egypt.

To formulate an alternative method of Quranic exegesis, these thinkers reinterpreted the scripture in terms of the normative and cognitive standards of the Enlightenment. Islamic jurisprudence was reexamined, some of its key concepts and principles were reinterpreted in the new light, and at the same time new terminology was added to the Islamic conceptual repertoire. Of the four sources of Islamic jurisprudence, the Quran and hadith were reinterpreted, and ijma and qiyas were fundamentally transformed. The door of ijtihad was pushed open, as human reason competed with prophetic revelation, maslaha turned into utility, *shura* (consultation) into parliamentary democracy, ijma into public opinion, the ideas of natural selection and the survival of the fittest crept into Islamic views of change, polygamy became a questionable (even unlawful) institution, and Islam itself became identical with civilization—all congruent with the norms of nineteenth-century social thought.[70]

The Differentiation of Knowledge: Rational versus Islamic Sciences

Rifa'a Badawi Rafi' al-Tahtawi was among Egypt's first modern thinkers. The modernism that Tahtawi espoused was not an intellectual outgrowth of his background as a graduate and then teacher of the Azhar, although it had undeniably affected the way he approached modern ideas. Tahtawi's thorough knowledge of Islam had admitted him to the top echelon of orthodoxy. Being involved in the state's educational program, he came into a close contact with the ideas of the Enlightenment and the European lifestyle during his sojourn in Paris (1826–31).

Some of the views of the Enlightenment were not far fetched for Tahtawi, who was brought up in the tradition of Islamic political thought. The view that individuals realize their potential within the context of social life, that the good society is based on justice, that the purpose of government is the welfare of the ruled, or that, as Rousseau held, a good legislator was one with the intellectual ability to conceive laws framed in religious symbols that the public could understand and recognize as valid were consistent with the views of Muslim philosophers on the role of the Prophet. Other views that influenced him, such as the notion that the people should participate in governmental affairs, that they should be educated for this purpose, and that laws must change according to circumstances, and those that are good at one time and place may not be so at others, were quite new for the ulama of Egypt. Tahtawi's views about nation, country, and nationalism were derived from Montesquieu. In Paris, he met Orientalists like Silvestre de Sacy and through them became aware of the discoveries of the Egyptologists. His awareness of ancient Egypt and its glories filled his mind and became an important element in his thought.[71]

How did Tahtawi develop his ideas? One thing is clear: Tahtawi could not have remained strictly loyal to his orthodox upbringing while performing the task of modernizing Egypt's educational system. His position as a man in charge of expanding modern educational institutions in the country was indeed congruent with a differentiated conception of knowledge that constituted a core element in his modernist thought. In Islamic orthodoxy, knowledge had a uniform structure, and the ulama embodied both rational and religious scholarship. Thus, when he introduced the rational sciences to learned Egyptians, he clarified a distinction not quite known in Muslim academia between scientists, who knew the rational sciences, and the ulama, who were scholars of the religious sciences (i.e., theology). Tahtawi informed his readers that one should not assume that French scientists were also priests. Priests were only knowledgeable on religious matters, even though some might also be scientists. In France, many scientists were not familiar with Christian theology. This fact, in his view, explained why Christians had surpassed Muslims in sciences: Europeans had emphasized rational sciences, while the Azhar and other Muslim universities were all preoccupied with traditional sciences.[72]

Nevertheless, it may not be enough to argue that his job had automatically led him to be receptive to the ideas of the Enlightenment. There were other forces at work that prompted Tahtawi and other educated Egyptians to develop a modernist interpretation of Islam. His ideological position was shaped at the points of difference between two cultures: the advance of Europe and the decadence of Egypt. If Europe made progress while Egypt remained stagnant, it must be due to differences in their principles of social organization. It is thus not accidental that many themes that appeared in Tahtawi for the first time, which were later to become familiar in Arabic and Islamic thought, were derived from these differences: that, within the universal umma, there were national communities demanding the loyalty of their subjects; that the object of government was human welfare in this world as well as the next; that human welfare consisted in the creation of civilization, which was the final worldly end of government; that modern Europe, and specifically France, provided the norms of civilization; that the secret of European strength and greatness lay in the cultivation of the rational sciences; that the Muslims, who had themselves studied the rational sciences in the past, had neglected them and fallen behind because of the domination of Turks and Mamluks; and that they could and should enter the mainstream of modern civilization, by adopting the European sciences and their fruits.[73]

The recognition of the differentiated conception of knowledge in Tahtawi had an important implication. It provided a discursive space for the rise of modernism while effectively undermining the conceptual framework of the traditional educational institutions. For the acceptance of the utility of the separation of the rational from religious sciences had legitimized the foundation of the modern school for fulfilling the technical needs of the country. At the same time, it was tantamount to an admission of the possibility that the advance of the rational sciences would render religious claims about social life and the physical universe superfluous. Tahtawi did not see this contradiction, and here one may detect the influence of religious training on his thought. For him, as for many other modernist thinkers, it was an article of faith that there was not much difference between the principles of the Islamic law and those of natural law on which the codes of modern Europe were based. To support this claim, he often made reference to the Quran and the hadith. He realized, however, the new challenges facing Islam. He demanded a more intellectual activism from the ulama, arguing that they were not simply the guardians of a fixed tradition. He believed that it was necessary and legitimate to adapt the shari'a to new circumstances. This assertion implied that the closing of the gate of independent reasoning by traditionalists was no longer acceptable. It was for later generations of Islamic scholars, however, to push it open.[74]

Many of the issues that Tahtawi dealt with were elaborated and expanded by later modernists.[75] There was, however, an element of discontinuity between his experiences and those of Sayyid Jamal ud-Din al-Afghani (1839–97). Given the vast progress Egypt was making under Muhammad Ali, Tahtawi had every reason to be optimistic. For al-Afghani the situation was different. His extensive travels and close observations of the deteriorating condition of Muslim nations and the European domination of the Islamic world prompted him to reflect upon the causes of Muslim decline and the way to bring back Muslim glory of the past. Al-Afghani's pan-Islamic ideas broadly corresponded to the emerging nationalist cum Islamic movement against foreign domination. He visited India about 1857, when he was still young, and might have witnessed the Indian mutiny of 1857–59. He was involved in anti-British movements in various countries. In Egypt, he became the guide and teacher of a group of young men, mainly from the Azhar. In addition to Abduh, the group included Saad Zaghlul, who became the leader of the Egyptian nation fifty years later.[76]

Nevertheless, it would be hard to argue that al-Afghani's general ideas about religion, science, and society corresponded to the exigencies of the anti-imperialist struggle. In his ideological reflections, he fixed his gaze on three distinct targets: European powers, the despotic rulers of Muslim nations, and the orthodox ulama. His worldview displayed three elements: (1) the idea of Islamic unity against Western political domination, (2) a consciousness of decadence, and (3) a positive philosophical exposition of the rational sciences and critique of the orthodox ulama. Al-Afghani's quarrel with the West, Britain in particular, was political. His views, on the other hand, were influenced by the seminal ideas of the nineteenth century, in particular François-Pierre-Guillaume Guizot's *History of Civilization.*

For Guizot, the word *civilization* meant progress—the improvement of social life and the development of the human mind.[77] The world is regulated and marches on according to the ideas, sentiments, and moral and intellectual dispositions of man himself. "It is upon the intellectual state of man that the visible form of society depends."[78] Al-Afghani used this perspective to explain the decline of Islamic civilization. In the past, he said in *al-Urwa al-Wuthqa,*[79] Muslims were superior in all fields of human endeavor. Their doctrine prevailed, their power was complete, their literature rose above other literature, and their norms and values dominated those of their predecessors and contemporaries. Islam thus enjoyed all the elements of a flourishing civilization. But, "today, Muslims are stagnant in education and knowledge." The reform suggested by some Western-educated individuals was not successful in treating the malady of the umma. This is because for these individuals reform meant taking pride in emulating the West, belittling the indigenous culture and people, and running to the service of the foreigners. The solution was a return to the fundamentals of Islam. Muslims must realize that their strength in the past was due to their adherence to Islam.[80] Islam had declined because of the weakening of the solidarity among Muslims and the division of Islamic territories into different kingdoms, each ruled by a despot who was interested in fulfilling only his own desires and working according to his whims. Muslims should unite and learn from the experience of other nations.[81] Dignity and honor could not be compromised. Humans worked to preserve their dignity, striving toward perfection, and there was no end to human progress. How could Muslim people, after a glorious and dignified past, accept humiliation and forgo the essential qualities of their humanities, living like animals, succumbing before tyrants, and allowing their prudence to be taken away from them? It was time for them to wake up to the bare essentials of their humanity.[82]

In al-Afghani's more abstract philosophical exposition, there were scarcely any traces of the influence of the pressing need for a pan-Islamic movement. He countered the critics of Islam in terms of the criteria of the Enlightenment. He (with Abduh) took issue with European writers who had considered Islam the cause of the backwardness of Muslim societies. They rejected the claim that the belief in *al-qada wa al-qadar* (predestination) was responsible for Muslim decadence. These critics, they said, were mistaken because they had confused this term with *al-jabr* (compulsion). All sects in Islam agreed that belief in *al-qada wa al-qadar* did not mean a submission to the status quo. Nor did it justify lagging behind other nations and accepting a retrogressive state as a fateful decree from God. *Al-qada wa al-qadar* indicated the "omniscience" and "omnipotence" of God, not compulsion. The knowledge of God was not in contradiction with free will. In fact, free will within the broader knowledge of God would make humans accountable for their deeds. God had decreed that Muslims must observe their religious beliefs and perform their duties, which also included striving for progress and defending their rights and freedom of choice.[83]

Al-Afghani's modernist view is not consistent with his political idea of Muslim unity against Europeans. In response to Renan, who had attacked Islamic Arabs for allegedly being hostile to rational inquiries, he used an evolutionary perspective to explain the relationship between Islam and science. He argued that prophecy was necessary because all peoples in their early stage of development were incapable of accepting reason to distinguish good from evil. They had to follow their preachers in the name of the Supreme Being. "This is no doubt for men one of the heaviest and most humiliating yokes . . . but one cannot deny that it is by this religious education, whether it be Muslim, Christian, or pagan, that all nations have emerged from barbarism and marched toward a more advanced civilization."[84] Al-Afghani further argued that "all religions are intolerant, each one in its way."[85] On science and religion, he provocatively attacked Muslim religion, the orthodox ulama, and the despotic rulers of Muslim nations. "Whenever it became established," said he, "this religion tried to stifle the sciences, and it was marvelously served in its designs by despotism. . . . Religions, by whatever names they are called, all resemble each other. No agreement and no reconciliation are possible between these religions and philosophy. Religion imposes on man its faith and its belief, whereas philosophy frees him of it totally or in part."[86]

Yet al-Afghani's anti-imperialist and pan-Islamic politics often tended to override his modernist discourse. On many occasions, he glorified the early Islamic civilization, arguing that the people of early Islam had no science, "but, thanks to the Islamic religion, a philosophic spirit arose among them, and owing to that philosophic spirit they began to discuss the general affairs of the world and human necessities."[87] He often portrayed himself a staunch believer. In "The Refutation of the Materialists," delivered in 1880–81, al-Afghani advanced a pragmatic defense of religion, that is, the utility of the orthodox for the majority and the danger of sects including the materialists.[88] He argued that religion was the mainstay of nations and the source of their welfare and happiness, while naturalism was the root of corruption and source of foulness. He criticized Darwin and such worldviews as socialism, communism, and nihilism. His fierce criticism also extended to Sayyid Ahmad Khan and the Aligarh movement in India.

Nikki Keddie has explained away these contradictory elements by arguing that "Afghani was profoundly influenced by a tradition, particularly strong among the Islamic philosophers, that it was correct and proper to use different levels of discourse according to the level of one's audience. Like the philosophers, he believed that the masses, 'amma [umma], were not open to rational philosophical argument."[89] This may be the case. Alternatively, however, these inconsistencies can be explained in terms of two major sides of al-Afghani. As a modernist thinker and in exchange with philosophers on his level, he was critical of religion. But as an anti-British activist, his discourse was oriented toward pan-Islamic oppositional politics. Given his anti-imperialist project, he naturally viewed pan-Islamism as the most effective way of combating foreign domination of the Muslim world. His modernism was as much radical and provocative as that of the Aligarh movement, and there was not much in his philosophical view that could not be reconciled with that of Sayyid Ahmad Khan and associates. If, for him, their naturalism was undesirable and their commitment to Islam suspect, it was because of their "complicity" with the British.

Revelation and Reason, Traditional and Secular, and a Comtean Problematic

Political conditions structure discourse. Al-Afghani's radicalism came at the cost of his residential stability. In every country he visited, he stirred up controversy, which led to his expulsion. And his position in the religious hierarchy was too tenuous to constrain his daring philosophical utterances. This form of politics was not to the liking of his closest associate, Muhammad Abduh (1849–1905).[90] Abduh's discourse was constrained by the reality of the British presence in the country, and by the power of the orthodox Islamic institutions that he ended up heading in 1899 as the mufti of Egypt. For him, moderation was the only alternative. True, he was swept up in the rising nationalism in the 1870s, which led to his arrest, imprisonment, and exile. On intercession from various quarters, including the British, he was allowed to return to Egypt in 1888. From that time on, he held that priority must be given to education so that the people could perform the duties of a representative government with intelligence and firmness. Both the government and the people must gradually become accustomed to the giving and receiving of advice, and if the country were ready for participation in the Government, there would be no point in seeking such participation by force of arms.[91] Abduh was prepared to cooperate with the rulers of Egypt insofar as they were helpful in his educational project. He was on a good terms with Prime Minister Mustafa Pasha Fahmi and Lord Cromer.

The starting point of his thought was the decline of Islam, but he held that the general line of development in Egypt was both inevitable and beneficial. Yet this development carried the danger of dividing the society into two spheres without a real link. One sphere, always retreating, was based on the laws of Islam, and the other, always expanding, gave sway to principles derived by human reason from consideration of the utility of worldly affairs. It also resulted in the emergence of two diverse educational systems, each creating its own category of educated elite with a corresponding cultural orientation. One was dominated by the conservatives, who had resisted all change, and the other by the younger generation, which had embraced all ideas of modern Europe. Just as Sir William Jones had had misgivings about the rationalists in India, Abduh doubted the possibility of successfully transplanting European laws and institutions to Egypt. Given the inevitability of change, it was irrelevant to ask whether devout Muslims could accept the ideas of the modern world. For him, the question was whether someone who lived in the modern world could still remain Muslim.[92] Inspired by the Enlightenment,[93] he viewed Egypt's cultural predicament from a Comtean perspective. Like Comte, who searched for a universally acceptable system of ideas that were to transcend both the rationalist zeal of the French Revolution and those who wanted to return to the old order, Abduh was preoccupied with showing that Islam contained the universalistic creed that could link the two cultures and form a moral basis of modern Egypt.[94] Further, reforming Islam had another utility: that of being the only available and plausible method. Reforms by secular means required the erection of a new structure for which neither materials nor the necessary personnel were present.[95]

The key element in Abduh's modernist project was to demonstrate to the younger generation that Islam supported change while at the same time convincing his conservative colleagues that this change did not entail violating the fundamentals of religion. He made a distinction between the essential and inessential aspects of Islam, a distinction that paralleled Chiragh Ali's dichotomy of Muhammadan revealed law and Muhammadan common law. Following Ibn Taymiyya and other thinkers who had made a distinction between acts directed toward the worship of God (*ibadat*) and those directed toward other men and life in the world (*mu'amalat*), Abduh maintained that there was a systematic difference between the teaching of revelation in regard to the one and the other. While Islam laid down specific rules about worship, it contained only general principles about relations with other men, leaving it to men to apply them to all the circumstances of life. This was the legitimate sphere of ijtihad, which was not only permitted but essential as well. Although it was possible to reach a collective judgment of the community in time, such a consensus was never infallible and could not close the gate of ijtihad. For Abduh, the real rejection of Islam, the real *kafir*, was the refusal to accept the proof of rational argument, the hallmark of the perfect Muslim community being both law and reason. Thus if, for Comte, the development of the new discipline of sociology was to produce a rational system of social morality and a science of human happiness, for Abduh, Islam was the true sociology, the science of happiness in this world as well as the next. It could serve as the basis of modern life. In a fashion parallel to Comte's, he aimed to create a new type of ulama that could articulate and teach the real Islam, that could bridge the gap between the traditional and revolutionary forces of his society. When Islamic law is fully understood and obeyed, society, he believed, will flourish; when it is misunderstood or rejected, society will decay.[96]

Abduh's employment of reason was to demonstrate the affinity of Islam with modern scientific thinking. In his exegesis of the Quranic story of the prophet David and his war with the Philistines, for example, Abduh deduced from the verses of the Quran fourteen propositions concerning sociopolitical change, progress, and war, calling them "sociological laws of the Quran." This reflected the imprint of Herbert Spencer and social Darwinism on his views. He argued that Allah's will was executed according to a general law. War among nations was one of these general laws. War was natural among humans because it was an instance of the struggle for existence. Part of this general law was the Quranic verse which stated that "Were it not for the restraint of one by means of the other, imposed on men by God, verily the earth had been utterly corrupted."[97] Abduh claimed that the idea of natural selection did not contradict Islam. He considered false sociologists those who believed that this idea was the discovery of contemporary materialists. For him, the Quran admitted that life could not be right without natural selection. People fight each other for truth and benefit. This struggle saves the earth in the way that it will save truth and righteousness.[98] Abduh's rationalism did not mean that he had subscribed to the Mu'tazilite philosophy of the universe as "a rationally integrated system governed by laws of cause and effect, which God had created and set in motion once and for all."[99] Adopting this view might have impaired his relationship with the Ash'arite theologians of the Azhar, who denied that the universe was governed by causal laws and stressed the working of the universe as the expression of the omnipotence of the divine being. Rather, he used reason in a parallel competence with revelation, both belonging to the same sphere, accepting neither separation nor conflict between them.[100]

Yet Abduh had to modify his theological eclecticism in order to meet secular challenges to his faith. In particular, the French historian Gabriel Hanotaux and Farah Antun criticized Islam from a rationalist and secular perspective. In these debates, Abduh appeared to have taken a position quite close to rationalism and the notion of natural law. Hanotaux's article "Face to Face with Islam and the Muslim Question" appeared in the *Journal de Paris* (1900). Hanotaux claimed that Christian belief in the Trinity or God's immanence in human life formed the theological foundation for appreciating man's worth and his nearness to God. Muslim belief in God's unity and transcendence, in contrast, underlay the thought of man's insignificance and helplessness. Further, active use of means and self-dependence among Christians had emanated from the idea of free will, while the stagnation of Muslim nations was rooted in the doctrine of predestination and blind submission to law. In his rebuttal, Abduh indicated that discussions of predestination were not peculiar to any one religion. Christians were not in agreement on the question of man's free will. On the doctrine of the unity of God, Abduh resorted to reason by arguing that compared to the ideas of God existing among other groups, the Islamic doctrine was based on the highest form of reasonable belief that was attained by the intellect, whereas reason played no role in the belief in the Trinity, as Christians themselves would confess.[101] In the second controversy, Antun criticized Islam for being less tolerant toward learning and philosophy than Christianity. On the other hand, the emergence of modern civilization in Europe was made possible because learning had triumphed over persecution in Christian Europe. Abduh responded by arguing that Christianity had also persecuted its own scholars as well as the adherents of other faiths, while Islam had historically contributed to civilization and learning. He acknowledged, however, that there were historical reasons for the current rigidity of Islam.[102] In these two debates, we may detect a clear shift in Abduh's statement away from the Ash'ari and toward a more explicit Mu'tazilite stance, a theological position Abduh had consciously attempted to eschew.[103]

Islam and Civilization

A major change in the Islamic conception of the world in the nineteenth century involved the increasing irrelevance of the binary of dar ul-Islam versus dar ul-harb. This change was associated with the prevalence of the consciousness of decadence among modern Islamic thinkers and, at the same time, the rising popularity of a new conception of the world based on the dichotomy of civilization versus savagery. It created an intellectual problem, however, for the modernists. The civilized order in Europe, having its own laws to be discovered by sociology in contradistinction to the revealed laws of Islam, was an anomaly that al-Afghani, Abduh, and other modernist thinkers had to reckon with. For if a non-Islamic order surpassed Muslims in science and technology, understanding its sociological laws would not only uncover the secrets of its progress but also reveal the existence of new principles of social organization that had yielded a better society than that of Muslims. How could one reconcile the tension between this new mode of social organization, which had produced civilization, and the Islamic religion, which, in the Muslim view, was far superior to that of Europe? How could a superior religion (i.e., Islam) and a decadent social order (Muslim countries) coexist? Further complicating the issue was the nineteenth-century debate on the relevance of religion to social progress.[104]

Al-Afghani and Abduh tried to resolve this dilemma by attributing the decline of Muslims to certain historical causes while at the same time remaining loyal to the scholarly tradition of their religion. Another way of tackling this anomaly was an apologetic trend that sought an easy way out by trying to establish a Muslim pedigree for modern ideas of Europe. Traces of this trend were visible in *al-Muqtataf*, as some of its contributors claimed that such views as Darwin's theory or the movement of the earth had already been alluded to in the works of Muslim scholars like al-Ghazali or Ibn Khaldun. Muhammad Farid Wajdi (1875–1954) took this argument to its logical extreme by presuming that Islam was a perfect model of civilization. His central premise was that everything the modern world had discovered and approved was foreseen in the Quran and hidden in its verses. "There is no principle," said Wajdi, "that has been discovered by experience and no theory that has been established by the testimony of the sense, which have had an influence in the progress of man and in uplifting civilization, but are an echo of a verse from the Kur'an or of a tradition of the Prophet; so that the observer imagines that all effort and energy on the part of the scholars of the world towards the uplift of mankind have no other purpose than to bring practical proof of the truth of the principles of Islam."[105] While for Abduh a true society was based on the teaching of Islam, in Wajdi there was a subtle change in the relationship between the two, and true Islam conformed to civilization.

In Hourani's view, Wajdi was polemical and lacked the vivid sense of responsibility Abduh and other thinkers had displayed toward Islam.[106] But how do we explain Wajdi's apologetics? Abduh's scholarly responsibility was certainly an aspect of his intellectual erudition. He was also constrained by the discursive context within which he was advancing his reformist ideas. His academic position as the head of the Azhar and his background in Islamic scholarship placed an effective limit on his expressions. Wajdi, on the other hand, had fixed his gaze on the debates in Europe, France in particular. He was taking issue with such writers as Benjamin Constant, Ernest Renan, and Joseph Geyser. His book, published in French, was intended for a French audience, without being too concerned with such other Muslim views as Islamic orthodoxy. Too anxious to defend Islam vis-à-vis the Europeans, Wajdi had dissolved Islam in modernism. Again, the character of one's target—the French Enlightenment—shapes one's discourse.

Gender Hierarchy and the Rise of Islamic Feminism

As it was in India, the status of women in Egypt was among the most hotly debated issues in the cultural encounters between the followers of traditional Islam and its opponents. In the late nineteenth century, there was also a growing gender awareness in the country, reinforced by the extension of education to women. The missionaries played an important role in extending European-style education to women. By 1875 an estimated 5,570 girls were attending missionary schools, among them 3,000 Egyptians; and by 1887 about 4,000 of 6,160 were Egyptians. Although the majority of these girls were Copts, a small number of Muslims also attended. In the 1870s, the state also took steps to institute education for girls, and, by 1875, 890 girls were attending the government-run primary schools.[107] Feminist consciousness was promoted by such examples of the women's press as *al-Fatah* (*The Young Woman*, 1892), *al-Firdaus* (*Paradise*, 1896), and *Mir'at al-Hasna'* (*Mirror of the Beautiful*, 1896).[108] *Al-Muqtataf* also played a role in elevating women to a subject of national debate. Favorable attitudes toward women were reinforced by Muslim intellectual leaders. Abduh, for example, argued that "such matters as divorce, polygamy, and slavery do not belong to the essential of Islam."[109]

The Missionaries' and Westernizers' attack on Islam, the rise of Islamic modernism, and the extension of education to women and the increasing visibility of women in the public sphere constituted the sociocultural context in which the Islamic feminism of Qasim Amin (1865–1908) was formulated. Amin was provoked when the French writer the duc d'Harcourt criticized Egypt for its backwardness, the low status of women, and the use of the veil. Amin responded by defending the veil and criticizing the promiscuity of the European social life. Thenceforth, he studied European views on women and concluded that the advancement of Egypt lay in the uplifting of its women.[110]

Amin's feminism began by considering tradition, despotic political institutions, and the orthodox ulama as the root of the continued subordination of women to the powerful tyranny of men. Egypt's backward tradition itself had been perpetuated by a succession of despotic governments. "These despotic systems have also influenced the relationships between men and women—man in his superiority began to despise woman in her weakness."[111] Amin also attacked the ulama for their views on female education, seclusion, the veil, polygamy, and divorce. With few exceptions, these theologians manipulated Islam, making it an object of ridicule. The Islamic jurisprudence and the subjects that were taught at the Azhar were useless unless they were based on scientific truth and preceded by a familiarity with scientific methods, for Islamic theology must be the seal of all the sciences and the summary of all knowledge. Amin denied that Christianity had played a role in the advancement of Western women. It did not protect women's rights through either specific or general rules.[112] On the other hand, "Islam declared women's freedom and emancipation, and granted women all human rights during a time when women occupied the lowest status in all societies."[113] The low status of women in contemporary Egypt is therefore no fault of Islam.

On the veil, Amin argued that the shari'a allowed a woman to uncover her face and her palms. Covering the face had been part of pre-Islamic ancient traditions that had survived to the present. He further maintained that it "is no more appropriate for a woman to cover her face than for a man to cover his." On marriage, Amin again assailed the ulama for considering it a contract by which a man has the right to sleep with a woman. A true marriage must be based on both physical attraction and a harmony of spirit, which was possible only when one realized that it was just as important for a woman to have a say in the choice of her husband as it was for a man to have a say in the choice of his wife. On polygamy, his position was identical to that of Indian modernist Muslims: that justice in a polygamous relationship was impossible. The practice was therefore prohibited in Islam.[114] Finally, divorce was permissible in Islam, but it should not be a man's prerogative only. "If women are given the right to initiate divorce, then indeed we will have brought about more just and humane conditions for them."[115]

Amin was cautious. He made systematic reference to the Quran and other authoritative sources in advancing his themes. Yet a barrage of criticisms was directed against his views, which caused him to adopt a more critical attitude toward Islamic history. In *al-Mar'a al-Jadida* (*The New Woman*), the appeal was no longer to the Quran and the shari'a, but to science and Western political freedom: "Look at the eastern countries; you will find woman enslaved to man and man to the ruler. Man is an oppressor in his home, oppressed as soon as he leaves it. Then look at the European countries; the governments are based on freedom and respect for personal rights, and the status of women has been raised to a high degree of respect and freedom of thought and action."[116] In a counteroffensive against his critics, Amin further stated, "the civilization of Islam began and ended before the lid was taken off science as we know it today."[117] He objected to the preoccupation with the past and the glorification of the early Islamic history. His alternative portrayal of the Islamic past came as a shock to the conservatives, as Amin got even closer to the Westerners' critique of historical Islam. The Muslims were mistaken when they believed that the past was already past, and their duty lay in keeping it intact and unaltered. They were misguided by chroniclers and historians who presented Islamic civilization as a perfect one. For Amin, past Islamic civilization contained many flaws and was inadequate as a pattern for the modern world. For contemporary Muslims, their past should have only a historical significance as a source from which they could draw valuable lessons on the causes of the rise and fall of nations. Islam could furnish the spiritual basis of their daily lives, but it provided little guidance for solving the problems of modern life. "The main historical function of Islam," in Jamal Mohammad Ahmed's summary of Amin, "was to provide a simple and warlike people with cohesion and faith. It made a nation of warring tribes and enabled them to conquer nations far superior to themselves in the arts of civilization, and to give them a unified government and law. But as time went on the Muslim mind became stationary, under the rigorous supervision of theology. . . . Those who looked upon the West as an implacable enemy were not

helping Egypt. Europe was in a position to teach the East not only about its industries and arts but also about that art which was the key to all others—civic virtues,
an art almost unknown in the contemporary East."[118]

The Amin controversy extended well into the late twentieth century, when Leila
Ahmed, following Edward Said's general critique of Orientalism, presented a dis-
approving portrayal of Qasim Amin, accusing him of expressing "not just a generalized contempt for Muslims but also contempt for specific groups, often in
lavishly abusive details." In particular, "those for whom Amin reserved his most
virulent contempt—were Egyptian women."[119] In her view, Amin's description of
the condition of Egyptian women was suspect and inadequate because of "his
exceedingly limited access to women other than members of his immediate family and their retinue, and perhaps prostitutes."[120] These assertions are anachronistic and full of biases and contain little factual evidence. One of the ways in which
Ahmed attempts to discredit Amin is to show the similarities between the views
expressed in selected passages from his book and those of the British and the missionaries. Ahmed claimed that "the ideas to which Cromer and the missionaries
gave expression formed the basis of Amin's book."[121] Since a generalized dislike if
not hatred of the British and the missionaries are presumed (or expected from her
readers)—they are all bigots in Ahmed's assessment—Amin's views are therefore
worthy of condemnation and his character suspect. We do not deny that the missionaries, Westernizers, and the French Enlightenment had affected in different
ways the worldviews of Muslim intellectual leaders in this period. However, a critical attitude toward Islam by a missionary or a Cromer could not be assumed to
be false. It should be assessed by historical facts, and Ahmed is not always convincing in this regard.

Her subtle expressions on such other issues as veiling are not any more telling.
She says, "when one considers why the veil has this meaning in the late twentieth
century, it becomes obvious that, ironically, it was the discourses of the West, and
specifically the discourse of colonial domination, that in the first place determined
the meaning of the veil in geopolitical discourses and thereby set the terms for its
emergence as a symbol of resistance."[122] One should bear in mind the self-evident
fact that people who experienced British domination in the late nineteenth century
were not the same people who used the veil in the late twentieth century to attack
the Western lifestyle. Nor was there a colonial power in the Arab world in the late
twentieth century. We may thus ask against whom the veil had become "a symbol
of resistance." Often the line demarcating the people who defended the veil as a
symbol of resistance and her own view of the subject is blurred and indistinguishable. Her proposition on the veil is debatable, however. The colonial power—the
British in Egypt or the French in Algeria—was much less secular and less interventionist on matters of religion than the national states that were formed in the

twentieth century. The veil became significant within the context of feminism imposed from above by the secular ideological states, not by the colonial power. Finally, Amin's works on women were published contemporaneously with the works of Indian Islamic feminist Mumtaz Ali.[123] Although it is not clear how these two authors might have influenced each other, there are remarkable similarities and consistency in their criticisms of Muslim tradition, in their feminist exegesis of the Quran, and in their ideological resolution of how women's role and status in society should be viewed and uplifted. Is Leila Ahmed willing to argue that Mumtaz Ali also had contempt for Muslim India and women?

Constitutionalism and Political Authority in Islam

The question of political authority in Islam did not feature prominently in the works of Egyptian modernists before the twentieth century. The heterogeneity of the ruling elite, discursive pluralism, and the British policy of religious neutrality, and even Muhammad Ali's repeated defeats of the Ottoman army in the first half of the nineteenth century—all resulted in the progressive irrelevance of such concepts as that of the caliphate in their discourse. Moreover, the traditional ruler-ulama alliance had little appeal among these thinkers. The Ottomans were still the nominal rulers, with the conservatives tending to support their rule while modern intellectual leaders demanded independence and constitutionalism. In the national liberation movement, even pan-Islamist nationalists like Abd Allah Nadim (1845–96) and Mustafa Kamil (1874–1908) did not wish to establish an Islamic government in their country. True, the idea of an Arab caliph was part of the Arab nationalist discourse that originated in Syria in response to Abdülhamid's authoritarianism and the Turkish nationalism of the late nineteenth and early twentieth centuries.[124] The liberal version of this discourse first appeared in the works of Abdul Rahman al-Kawakibi who, along with the Christian Najib Azoury, proposed the Arab right to secede from the Ottomans and establish an independent Arab caliphate.[125] However, the issue of caliphate gained significance in the Islamic world after the Turkish National Assembly abolished the sultanate and set up a shadow caliphate with spiritual power in 1922 and then did away with the caliphate altogether in 1924. Mustafa Kemal provided the rationale:

> The notion of a single Caliph, exercising supreme religious authority over all the Muslim people, is one which had come out of books, not reality. The Caliph has never exercised over the Muslims a power similar to that held by the Pope over the Catholics. Our religion has neither the same requirements, nor the same discipline as Christianity. The criticisms provoked by our recent reform [separating the caliphate from the sultanate] are inspired by an abstract, unreal idea: the idea of Pan-Islamism. Such an idea has never been

translated into reality. We have held the Caliphate in high esteem according
to an ancient and venerable tradition. We honour the Caliph; we attend to his
needs, and those of his family. I add that in the whole of the Muslim world,
the Turks are the only nation which effectively ensure the Caliph's livelihood.
Those who advocate a universal Caliph have so far refused to make any contribution. What, then, do they expect? That the Turks alone should carry the
burden of this institution, and that they alone should respect the sovereign
authority of the Caliph? This would be expecting too much [of us].[126]

In Egypt, the caliphate became the rallying cry of the conservatives, and Abbas
Hilmi was more interested in becoming the caliph than establishing a constitutional system.[127] After the revolution, his son, King Fuad, did not give much support to the constitution either. After 1924, The king schemed to become a caliph.[128]
Although the caliphate movement in Egypt faded within a few years, the issue for
the first time in modern Egypt became a socially significant topic of political
debate. The treatise of Ali Abd al-Raziq (1888–1966) in *al-Islam wa Usul al-Hukm*
(*Islam and the Fundamentals of Authority*, 1925) contributed to this debate. In this
work, al-Raziq went far beyond the assessment of the necessity of the caliphate; he
questioned whether there had ever been an Islamic system of government. The fact
that the historic caliphate had ceased to exist after the Rashidun was a matter of
agreement among Muslim thinkers. The crux of al-Raziq's argument was that the
very concept of the caliphate was itself un-Islamic. He thus questioned what had
been regarded as the core of Muslim doctrine. In his view, the caliphate had no
basis in the Quran, tradition, or consensus among the ulama. Theoretically, the
caliphate was a vice-regency on behalf of the Prophet and embodied both religious
and secular authorities, and it was held by those who had succeeded him. Nevertheless, the examination of the proofs presented in support of this institution provided an insufficient basis to sustain the claim of this form of government. "If we
were to collect all his direct teachings on the question of government, we would get
little more than a fraction of the principle of law and organization needed for maintaining a state."[129] Al-Raziq then argued that the chief purpose of Muhammad had
been purely religious and spiritual, not political. His intention had not been to
establish an empire. Nor had his mission required him to exercise power over his
followers or opponents. The political changes Muhammad brought about in the
life of the Arabs had been the incidental consequences of his moral revolution.
From this al-Raziq went on to attack the historical experience of the caliphate by
declaring that the institution had hindered the progress of the Muslims. It had been
the source of all corruption in Muslim history and an instrument of obstruction
against intelligent thinking. Religion had therefore nothing to do with one form of
government rather than another, and there was nothing in Islam that prevented

Muslims from destroying the old and establishing a new political system on the basis of the newest concepts and experiences.[130]

Abd al-Raziq thus dismantled what was hitherto considered the building block of the Islamic conception of political authority. He had a twofold objective. One was to formulate an Islamic basis for the construction of a new political order based on the separation of religion and politics. This was accomplished through his thorough theoretical assessment of the concept of the caliphate in the early Islamic sources. The other was to further undermine the already weak ideological hegemony of the Turk over Egypt—and hence to further galvanize the nationalist movement. This was done through his stormy attack on the historical caliphate, which had symbolized and provided the ideological justification for Turkish rule in Egypt.

The Reaction of the Orthodox Ulama

Once the traditional Islamic methods of interpretation were abandoned, the gate to independent judgment was reopened, and the Islamic belief system was placed before the judgment seat of reason, then anything perceived as good, desirable, and rational might be considered Islamic. As a result, Islam could be engulfed by innovations of all sorts, which would undermine, in the final analysis, its very integrity as a belief system and identity as a religion distinct from other belief systems—an outcome against which the orthodox had fought ceaselessly for centuries. Naturally, the modernists were under the watchful eyes of the orthodox ulama. The former could go only so far in rationalizing Islam without arousing the suspicion of the ulama that what they were preaching was not in tune with the Islamic tenets and effectively forfeiting their right to speak. Abduh and al-Afghani were accused of infidelity to Islam. "What kind of a sheikh is this," one of the conservatives said of Abduh, "who speaks French and travels in European countries, who translates their writings and quotes from their philosophers and disputes with their learned men, who gives 'fatwas' of a kind that no one of his predecessors ever did, and takes part in benevolent societies and collects money for the poor and unfortunate?"[131] The orthodox rebuttals and reactions were serious matters for the Islamic modernists. The charge of disloyalty to Islam, and even apostasy, had placed effective limits on their utterances.[132] Throughout the nineteenth century, the conservative ulama showed their open hostilities to what they considered unlawful innovation in Islam. Their opposition to change was not simply over theological matters. They even expressed their dislike of switching to European clothes, the wearing of a hat, the study of arithmetic, the dissection of the human body, and the efficacy of quarantine.[133]

The views of the conservative ulama had naturally limited the rationalist exegesis of Abduh, who had cautiously stated that one cannot "explain away" the principles of the Quran or hadith and that if there was anything in them which seemed incompatible with reason, one must either search for the real sense of the words or else submit himself to God and accept without understanding.[134] Those who in their reexamination of Islam had gone far beyond the limits deemed acceptable to the conservatives were punished severely. The controversy that Abd al-Raziq had generated did not end in mere bitter discussions and invectives. Soon a court consisting of twenty-four of high-ranking ulama of the Azhar was convened and rendered a unanimous decision confirming the charges of unorthodoxy and declaring him guilty of conduct "unbecoming the character of an alim" (*alim,* a learned religious scholar, is the singular of *ulama*). He was dismissed from the body of the ulama, his name was expunged from the records of the Azhar and other mosque schools, and he was barred from filling any religious office.[135]

FIVE

Iran: The Bastion of Traditionalism and Conservative Reaction

The similarities between India and Egypt in the determinants of Islamic modernism were striking, despite their differences in social structure and historical experience. The Iranian case further supports our explanatory model. In this case, the weakness of Islamic modernism is associated with the absence of a major social transformation and discursive pluralism. The contrast between Iran and Egypt is particularly illustrative given their similarities in social structure and religion in the early nineteenth century. Both countries were religiously unified, displayed similar economic structures and class profiles, exhibited analogous traditional social institutions, were demographically alike, and were governed by a sort of unified system of political administration. Yet throughout the century, Iran remained imposingly conservative. Attempts at social reforms fell victim to the court's intrigues and the ulama's uncompromisingly forceful reactions. Shi'i modernism emerged during the Constitutional Revolution of 1905–11, when a group of ulama acknowledged the significance of constitutional ideas for Iran's development and attempted to reconcile these ideas with the Shi'i conception of political sovereignty.

Iran also has the utility of providing a natural control case to assess the degree to which ideological change was possible within the very institution of the ulama in the absence of a direct foreign influence. This factor is especially significant given that the British promoted Western culture in India and Egypt. True, the formative years of the modernist discourse in people like Tahtawi, Abduh, and al-Afghani predated the British occupation of Egypt. Nevertheless, because there was an affinity between the British colonial staff and the modernists in both countries, Islamic modernism could be viewed as a cultural change that was primarily fostered by the British, while a relatively weak cultural influence of a European power ensured Iran's conservatism. A corollary of this argument would be that the conservative ulama were the uncompromising opponents of modernism in all three countries. Our analysis of the Indian and Egyptian cases indicated that the ulama were in fact highly critical of the Islamic modernists. But were they also uniformly the proponents of traditionalism? Although considerably weaker than either Egypt's or India's, Shi'i modernism during the Constitutional Revolution is an example of an autonomous development of discursive pluralism in the absence of the direct influence of a Westernizing alien power. Moreover, the case of Shi'i modernism removes a possible Europe-centered bias that our analysis may carry—the assumption that Western-style social transformation is a precondition for modern cultural change. Lacking a social transformation and the rise of a modern state, the Iranian case demonstrates that modernist ideas may still gain a foothold in society, if a pluralistic context emerges. We do not deny the role of the British in affecting the rise of Islamic modernism in India and Egypt. This role was significant insofar as it generated a discursive pluralism.

Iran's cultural conservatism was reinforced by the confluence of several historical factors. In contrast to Egypt, the Iranian state remained weak throughout the nineteenth century. This weakness was a result of two major defeats by Russia and the conclusion of humiliating treaties in 1813 and 1828. These defeats made the state vulnerable to challenges from below in the rise of the Babi movement around the middle of the century. This weakness also paralleled the rise in the power of the ulama in the same period. The ulama, coupled with their conservative allies within and outside the court, exhausted attempts at reforms, rebuffing challenges to their authority. They were also effective in blocking the missionaries' efforts in the country. At the same time, the activities of the merchants and craft guilds against European and Russian economic encroachments granted the ulama the opportunity to lead protest movements in defense of "national interests" against foreigners. All these factors contributed to the solidification of a "monolithic" religious environment in the society. The institutions of Shi'ism, however, remained structurally pluralistic, as prominent ayatollahs maintained their individual rights to independent ruling. There was no formal organizational hierarchy that would consolidate the ulama into a single bureaucratic structure. This pluralism made their unity vulnerable to the crisscrossing pressures emanating from diverse social forces—the state and property-owning social classes. As a result, they almost always displayed disunity vis-à-vis virtually all historically significant issues facing the public. This disunity was displayed in the emergence of opposing factions in the Tobacco Movement (1890–92) and the Constitutional Revolution (1905–11), when a group of the ulama supported the constitution while others opposed it and remained royalist. The religious division over the constitution was extensive, and the conflict between the warring factions of the ulama was fierce. It was concluded when the revolutionaries executed one of the most prominent outspoken critiques of constitutionalism, Sheikh Fazlullah Nuri.

The Usuli-Akhbari Controversy
and the Solidification of the Shi'i Orthodoxy

The center of Shi'i learning in the *Atabat*—the Shi'i holy places in Iraq—was a scene of acrimonious debate among the ulama in the late eighteenth century. This debate was concluded in the resolution of a long-standing controversy in Shi'i jurisprudence. Up until that time, there had not been much consensus among the ulama on the extent to which rational argument could be applied in the interpretation of religious laws and the settlement of important doctrinal problems facing the discipline of jurisprudence. There were competing schools. The Akhbaris denied any independent ruling on the part of the ulama above and beyond the tradition of the Prophet and the imams. The Usulis, on the other hand, asserted the legitimacy of the function of the mujtahids in the interpretation of law and doctrine and in making independent judgments. For the Akhbaris, the ulama's basic function was the transmission of doctrine (*naql*), which was given precedence over the application of reason ('aql), and ijtihad or independent reasoning was considered unlawful innovation similar to Hanafi rationalism in Sunni Islam. While for the Akhbaris all believers should be followers (*muqallid*) of the imam (who is believed to be in occultation), for the Usulis all believers should choose a living mujtahid to follow and abide by his judgment—hence the divisions of the faithful into followers (*muqallid*) and spiritual leader (*marja'*).[1] This is not to argue that because the Shi'i ulama emphasized independent rulings they had accepted the principle of rational interpretation of religion. Still, the ulama had to follow the principles of Shi'i jurisprudence, which was not fundamentally different from that of the Sunnis. Finally, Sufism was attached to the esoteric rather than to the law. It rejected the validity of any interference of the ulama in worldly affairs while claiming that the Sufi doctrine was identical to the esoteric knowledge of the imams.

The leading proponent of the Usuli position was a certain Aqa Muhammad Baqir Bihbahani (1705–1803), who ended the supremacy of the Akhbaris in the Atabat. Firmly establishing as his motto the Quranic injunction that a Muslim should "enjoin good and prohibit evil," Bihbahani vigorously championed the Usuli position and attacked both the Akhbaris and the Sufis by formally denouncing them as infidels (i.e., *takfir*). The means Bihbahani employed were often brutal. Known as *sufikosh* (Sufi killer), Bihbahani was accompanied by a number of *mirghadabs* (executioners of corporal and capital punishment).[2] The ulama thus established their religious supremacy in the early nineteenth century through an effective use of repressive measures to undermine the influence of the Akhbaris and the Sufis.

The consolidation of the Usuli position went hand in hand with the rise of the Qajars. These two processes, although they had different sources and dynamics, tended to mutually reinforce each other. The Qajar were of nomadic decent, and for them the administration of the country was far more complex than that of a tribe. The tribal background of Qajar leaders provided neither the legitimacy nor the administrative structure necessary to rule a country. The growth of the Usuli ulama was thus reinforced by their ability to perform educational, judicial, and legitimation functions for the Qajar state. The ulama held a monopoly of the institutions of traditional education. The juridical system of the Qajar state was divided into two parts—the 'urf (nonreligious) and the shar' (religious, or shari'a) courts. While the 'urf courts covered the areas related to state administration and crimes against the state, the shar' courts covered the areas of civil laws and disputes. The ulama had full control over the shar' courts, which gained considerable importance as the general economic conditions in the country began to improve in the early nineteenth century.[3] The development of Shi'i' political theory under the Qajars also reflected this process.[4]

Yet the ulama's religious and cultural supremacy made them a clear target of ideological attack from the Babi religious movement, which around the middle of the nineteenth century managed to win many followers, shaking the foundation of state authority and the ulama's prerogatives. The Qajars' repeated defeats in wars with imperial Russia led to the collapse of governmental authority in various parts of the country.[5] These defeats also placed the peasants under considerable pressure, because they were the ones who had to carry the main burden of the wars.[6] Although the economic hardships of the postwar periods underpinned the rise of Babism, however, the ideology of the Babi movement was developed in defiance of the ulama's religious orthodoxy.

The Babi faith originated in the thought of Sheikh Ahmad Ahsa'i, a forerunner of Gnostic Shi'ism (irfan) and the founder of the Sheikhi school. Of the five Shi'i principles—towhid (the unity of God), nabovvat (the prophecy of Muhammad), resurrection, imamat, and justice—the sheikh accepted only towhid, nabovvat, and imamat, while rejecting justice and resurrection. He also rejected the material nature of the mi'raj, the Prophet's journey to heaven. He then added a fourth pillar (rokn) to Shi'ism. This added pillar refers to the mediators between the twelfth imam, who is in occultation, and the people. These mediators are bab (the gate) through which one can communicate with the hidden Imam. The mediators are the pious spiritual leaders who are closer to God than the ordinary people.[7]

In 1844, Sayyid Ali Muhammad Shirazi (1819–50), a disciple of the Sheikhi school and the founder of Babism, claimed that he was the Bab in communication with the hidden Imam and the bearer of a new revelation from God. He soon attracted followers, which led to serious uprisings against the religious order in 1848–53. Historians have attributed these uprisings also to the revolutionary thought and leadership capability of the martyred Babi heroine Tahira, known as the Qurrat al-Ayn (Consolation of the Eyes), Mulla Hosein Bushruyeh, and

Mulla Muhammad Ali Barforushi.[8] In their mobilizing efforts, these leaders did not simply attack the ulama. They also took the side of the downtrodden by criticizing social inequality and the maldistribution of wealth, preaching that "ownership is a social corruption," the accumulation of wealth "by a small group when the majority is deprived of it is the worst corruption. . . . You, the peasants, should take a share from these properties in order for poverty to fade away." In the teaching of Babism, it was said, the rich accumulated their wealth at the peasants' expense. "You, the oppressed people of Iran . . . arise."[9] These ideas gained considerable support among the impoverished masses in both rural and urban areas.[10] In Gilan, Mazandaran, and Khorasan, villagers joined the Babi movement in large numbers. In cities people refused to pay taxes. In Zanjan, people attacked prisons, attempting to free those incarcerated for failing to pay their taxes.[11] Even considerable numbers of the ulama joined the Babi movement. The total strength of the movement was estimated at nearly one and a half million, or about 20 percent of the country's total population.[12]

The Babi movement posed a threat to the state, but even more to the ulama's guardianship of religious orthodoxy. The ulama and the state acted in unison in brutally repressing the Babis.[13] The movement, far from weakening the ulama, indeed resulted in the enhancement of their political strength. In the aftermath of the Babi defeat, the ulama further consolidated their power: the shari'a courts were strengthened, the awqaf came under the ulama's control, the administrators of the endowments (*mutawalli-bashis*) became more important than the governors in some provinces, and some state lands were also given to the ulama. The ulama annually received considerable cash payments from the government to spend on various purposes. The marriage of one of the ulama and a royal court member sealed the alliance, when Mirza Abulqasim, the Imam Jom'eh of Tehran, who gave the fatwa for the massacre of the Babis, became the shah's son-in-law.[14] As Firouz Kazemzadeh remarked, "the close cooperation between the mullas and the government in opposing the Babi-Baha'i movement was almost entirely to the advantage of the clergy, which increased its hold on the Shah and the bureaucracy, and stigmatized as a Babi any Persian who dared to open his mind to Western influence."[15]

However, contradictory pressures from the state and property-owning classes undermined the ulama's political unity during the major events of the late nineteenth and early twentieth centuries. The Tobacco Movement of 1890–92 was a prominent example of the effect of such social forces in giving rise to diverse political factions in their ranks. For example, in places such as Isfahan, where the landowners opposed the tobacco concession granted to Major Talbot, the ulama became actively involved in the movement. In Tehran, on the other hand, Ayatollah Bihbahani was bribed and became allied with Amin us-Sultan (the prime minister) and so refused to support the movement. In Azarbaijan, while the merchants and retail traders organized the movement, the ulama were initially reluctant to participate.[16] This reluctance prompted the anticoncession activists to distribute an anonymous placard in the Tabriz, the province capital:

> Ulemas [Ulama] of the town! Law is the law of religion and not the law of the European!
>
> Woe to those Ulemas who will not co-operate with the nation! Woe to those who will not spend their lives and property! Any one of the Ulemas who will not agree with the people will lose his life. Woe to anyone who may sell one muskal of Tobacco to the Europeans! Woe to the Europeans who may wish to enforce these customs of the Infidels. We will kill the European first, and then plunder their property. Woe to the Armenians, who will be killed, and will lose their property and their families. Woe to those who will keep quiet.[17]

In Mashhad, when the tobacco merchants and traders organized opposition to the concession, they managed to attract the support of only a few of the ulama. The ulama predominantly supported the shah and the concession. In their telegram to the shah, a group of the ulama stated: "The tobacco sellers and some ruffians who know nothing about the affairs of the state and the nation and do not understand all aspects of the issue behaved ignorantly, causing the disappointment of His Majesty, the refuge of Islam. . . . While praying for the shah's well being, we began calming down the people; thanks to God . . . and to the intelligence and competence of Sahibdivan, the people were calmed down and dispersed. In every respect, obeying the command of the king of kings, the refuge of Islam, is our duty."[18]

The shah was forced to cancel the concession when Iranians observed a fatwa allegedly issued by the eminent Shirazi,[19] which declared, "In the name of God, the Merciful and the Forgiving. As of now, the consumption of tobacco and tootoon in any form is tantamount to war against the Imam of the Age."[20]

Obstacles to the Missionaries

Given the ulama's enormous resources and the general conservative nature of the society, missionaries faced serious barriers to their activities. The first horrific warning to the missionaries was the murder of the Russian ambassador, Aleksandr Griboyedov, and the massacre of about eighty of his staff in Tehran. When the latter attempted to protect two Christian women who had converted to Islam but later decided to return to their former faith, a certain Haj Mirza Masih issued a fatwa that it was lawful to rescue these Muslim women from the hands of the unbelievers. A mob gathered around the residence of Griboyedov, the Cossacks opened fire, and the mob attacked the residence, killing the entire Russian mission.[21] Although there were no further such incidents, it lingered in the memory as a chilling reminder to any foreigner of the consequences of careless meddling in the religious affairs of the natives.

The missionaries, however, attempted to make some headway into Iran's traditional order. A pioneer of missionary activities in the country was Henry Martyn (mentioned in chapter 3). During his stay in Shiraz (1811–12), he made a Persian translation of the New Testament and the Psalms of David and set out for Tehran to present a copy to the shah. When Martyn became ill, Sir Gore Ousely, the British ambassador, presented the translation to the shah on his behalf. "The king was much pleased with the gift," reported Ousely, "and expressed his approbation of it by a public acknowledgment."[22] About his experience in Iran, Martyn wrote that "public curiosity about the gospel, now for the first time, in the memory of modern Persians, introduced into the country, is a good deal excited here and at Shiraz, and at other places; so that, upon the whole, I am thankful for having been led hither, and detained."[23]

The missionaries started their activities among non-Muslims, the Nestorians and Assyrians in Urumiah, a northwestern city. In 1836, the American missions opened a seminary for boys, and in 1838, a seminary for girls. In 1870, there were 700 people attending the Protestant celebration of Communion and about 960 children in the school,[24] certainly not a small number in a relatively backward country. In 1872, the Presbyterian missionaries were supporting a number of "Bible-women" in Urumiah and one in Abadan.[25] In 1880, the Women's Foreign Missionary Society of the Presbyterian Church reported that it had seven missionaries in Iran.[26] And in 1907, there were in the "reformed Church" 2,658 communicants, belonging to 961 families, 38 percent being men and 62 percent women.[27] The missionaries also attempted to expand their activities to other major cities, including Tehran, Hamadan, and Tabriz.

Proselytizing among Muslims proved to be extremely difficult. In 1881, after a decade of missionary work, there was hardly a change in the situation. The missionaries failed to gain permission from authorities for religious activities. After the conservatives complained to the shah that Muslims had attended religious meetings on mission premises in Tehran, the shah issued an order that not only forbade the missionaries to proselytize among Muslims, but also instructed them to ban Muslims from attending their religious services.[28] The missionaries had no choice but to comply.[29] Heightened antiforeign sentiments among Iranians also made the missionaries an easy target of attack, and it became too dangerous for Christians, especially the missionaries, to attend religious ceremonies. It was reported that, for example, "the population of Tabriz is exceedingly fanatical. Last year, foreigners were in some danger of being massacred during the holy frenzy of the religious festivals. In 1885, the missionaries had to close down temporarily in the town because of the fear of massacres."[30] Julius Richter also mentioned that a missionary was killed by a religious fanatic in the north of Urumiah.[31]

There were, however, some positive reports about missionary activities in Iran. For example, against his grandmother's advice that "you must not go as missionary to Persia, for if you do the Persians will convert you," a missionary asked rhetorically, "Was my grandmother right in thinking that my pleasure in Persia was likely to be a detriment to my usefulness? Was I less likely to do good to the Persians because I thought well of them to begin with? And would it have been a waste of time if, after a term of years, I had partly converted the Persians and the Persians had partly converted me? May there not be a profitable reciprocity in spiritual influence?"[32] Missionaries also managed to circulate their criticisms of social orders in certain parts of the country. In biting criticisms, one report enumerated Iran's unforgiving conditions of social life:

> The real cause of all the wretchedness lies in the fact, that there is so little to
> do to earn a living, and, perhaps, the *prime* cause is the ignorant priesthood
> and the government, dead to everything except extortion. I don't think it pos-
> sible for people at home to understand that there are no manufactories of any
> description, no forests, no mines of gold, sliver, copper, iron, coal; no railroads
> to furnish employment, no turnpikes, no printing presses, no canals, no ship-
> ping, no wagons, no public vehicles of any kind, no public charities, or private
> either, no poorhouses, no orphan asylums, or asylums of any kind, no hospi-
> tals; but all the widows and orphans, and the old, the blind, and lame, and
> dumb, and insane, are turned into the streets. Then think of the religion and
> government of this country. Think of the degradation of poor women.
> A woman! What is she but a slave from childhood? Think of her when mar-
> ried, a slave to her husband and her bigoted, ignorant, superstitious mother-
> in-law. Even the girls who go out from our seminary, what can they do who
> cannot stir out alone or speak a loud word for years?[33]

Referring to the condition of girls, another reported, "the interest I feel in our girls as they are leaving our school is much deeper than when they enter. My heart aches for them as they go forth to their monotonous, sometimes slave-like lives. There is so much in their surroundings to drag them down."[34]

Considering anecdotal evidence, including Fereydoun Adamiyat's brief comment that the missionaries had stirred controversy in Urumiah,[35] one may postulate that their proselytizing activities had some impact on their immediate surroundings.[36] Overall, however, the environment of Iranian culture remained closed to the mission-aries throughout the nineteenth century. The extent of the missionaries' frustration in their efforts to disturb Iran's monolithic religious order can be inferred from an article published in 1923, "Are the Persians Worth While?" Referring to women's deplorable condition, the author took issue with those who argued that it was "a waste of money, time and effort to do anything for the Persians . . . in a missionary way."

Some one will say, "What do these people need of us? Are not their conditions all right as they are?" It seems to me that if Christianity did no other thing for Persia than to abolish loveless child marriages and polygamy, it would have done a well-worth-while work. Possibly some one even here in America may think that polygamy is not so bad. To such a one I would extend an invitation to come with me and talk with some of our Persian sisters and get their view-point. Many a woman has said to me, when I was still single, "You do well not to marry; our lives are very bitter." Not long before we left Meshed, a lady came to Dr. Hoffman for medical treatment, and I called with him at her home. A relative explained to me that she was sick from "eating grief" because her husband's *other* wife had just arrived home from Kazvin.[37]

Had the missionaries obtained freedom of expression in Iran, it could be postulated that their disputations with the ulama would have created a "breathing space" large enough for reform-minded Muslims to develop their modernist interpretations of Shi'ism.

State Officials and Culture Production

The Qajars had little interest in modernization, and the reformist measures initiated by such capable viziers as Mirza Abul Qasim Qa'im Maqam (under Muhammad Shah), Amir Kabir, and the Sipahsalar (both under Nasir ud-Din Shah) remained abortive. They soon found themselves out of a job. Even worse, Muhammad Shah ordered the execution of Qa'im Maqam, and Nasir ud-Din Shah ordered the execution of Amir Kabir. Both were succeeded by ineffectual premiers.[38] The fifty-year rule of Nasir ud-Din Shah was a period of intense conflict between the reformists and conservatives over cultural change. Although he occasionally supported change, the shah displayed no serious interest in reforms. As Edward Browne wrote, "he does everything in his power to prevent the diffusion of those ideas which conduce to true progress, and his supposed admiration for civilisation amounts to little more than the languid amusement which he derives from the contemplation and possession of mechanical playthings and ingenious toys."[39]

Ironically, though, it was the state itself that provided the channel for the transfer of modern ideas to Iranians. Modern Europe and its scientific and technological achievements were first discovered by state officials. They had the chance to visit Europe and experience the lifestyle and sociopolitical norms of its people. The government, by sending students abroad to study and by building modern public schools, contributed even further to the spread of Western culture in the country. The members of the educated elite that was thus formed not only became aware of their country's marked backwardness vis-à-vis Europe but also acquired the knowledge of the intellectual foundation of European civilization. Being attached to the government, they had the means of effecting cultural change in their native land. As early as 1811, Crown Prince Abbas Mirza sent two students from Tabriz to London to study medicine, and in 1815, five more to England for study.[40] Mirza Salih Shirazi and Mirza Ja'far Khan Tabrizi were two graduates of British schools who played a role in the political reform movement and the dissemination of modern ideas. Mirza Salih introduced the ideas of democracy, freedom, the Magna Carta, and constitutionalism to educated Iranians. He called England the land of freedom (*vilayat-i azadi*) and praised the House of Commons, to which every person was eligible to be elected.[41]

Amir Kabir, the grand vizier, initiated the first serious attempts at reform. Believing that the country's reform and modernization would not succeed as long as the ulama retained their extensive power, he moved to curb their interference and meddling in politics by initiating judicial reforms.[42] But soon he faced their fierce opposition, the court's intrigues, and the conniving of the his rivals, which resulted in his failure and demise. He succeeded only in founding a modern state school in Tehran, Dar al-Fonun, for the spread of modern education and the training of state personnel. Established in 1851, Dar al-Fonun overcame the opposition of the ulama and became an important institution for the recruitment, education, and support of the nationalist reformers. In its first year, it admitted 105 students, and by the early 1890s, enrollments reached 387. Its faculty at first was mostly of foreign nationals, but afterward Iranian graduates of European schools began to fill the teaching positions. Modern ideas were disseminated through translations by the Dar al-Fonun instructors and with the assistance of foreign teachers.[43] Despite the introductory level of its courses, Dar al-Fonun became an effective channel for the transformation of thought, having considerable social impact and throwing doubt on the adequacy of the curriculum in the traditional schools.[44]

Foreign diplomats also contributed to cultural change in Iran. Morier's devastating critique and ridicule of Iran's traditional order in *The Adventures of Hajji Baba* was known to the educated elite. The translation of the novel into effective Persian prose by Mirza Habib Isfahani in 1905 further expanded its intellectual impact, contributing to the enhancement of secular movements. On a philosophical level, Arthur de Gobineau, a French diplomat and scholar, collaborated with Iranians in translating Descartes' *Discours sur la Methode*. The works of Newton and segments of Charles Darwin's *Origins of Species* were also translated.[45] With the dismissal of Amir Kabir, the reforms came to a halt. Between his fall in 1851 and the appointment of the reform-minded Sipahsalar as the vizier in 1870, there was a hiatus of twenty years in the reform movement. The first seven years were a period of stagnation under ineffectual Aqa Khan Nuri, the Itimad ud-Dowleh (1851–58); this was followed by a short period of some progress (1858–61) and then a decade of political and economic crises (1861–71). Aqa Khan Nuri was a conservative politician, if not an outright leader of the reactionaries. He disliked innovation and modern thought. He even tried to shut down the Dar ul-Fonun and send its professors back to Europe.[46] These setbacks did not hamper the rise among the educated public of such ideas as the separation of religion and politics, social evolution, the ruler's accountability to the public, and the people as the government's raison d'être. In a marked departure from religion as the source of knowledge, these new intellectuals emphasized human reason and adopted Descartes' famous dictum "I think therefore I am."[47] In 1858, several treatises on political criticism were published, forty-two students were sent to France to study, the first draft of the constitutional law was presented to the shah, the state council (*shoura-ye doulat*) was formed, the first political grouping, Majma'eh faramoush-khaneh (The House of Oblivion), modeled on freemasonry societies of Europe but not connected to them, came into existence, and other measures were taken to improve the economy, finance, and the system of communication.[48]

The conservative ulama again seriously resisted these ideas and used every opportunity to prevent the shah from implementing reforms. The 1860s were a period of economic hardships exacerbated by drought, which caused the outbreak of extensive urban riots. The shah reacted violently by harshly suppressing the riots. He also ordered the execution of Tehran's chief of police for his failure to control the disturbances. The shah's display of ruthlessness, signified by the his wearing of red attire to show "majestic rage," was the direct negation of his promise to improve law and order in the country.[49] In 1861, he also halted the progressive movement. The faramoush-khaneh was dissolved because, as its opponents argued, it was a place for *fitnih* and corruption, filled with "the rogues and the ruffians." The students who were sent to France were ordered back home, the rationale being that "those who studied and trained in France would become republicans and anti-religion."[50]

The intellectual movement, however, continued, as the French Enlightenment and reformist ideas coming from the Ottoman Empires offered a new concept of the state, elaborated different types of government, presented the idea that the "national will" was the source of state power, emphasized the significance of laicized politics and the idea of freedom as a right, and introduced the principle of natural right.[51] These ideas and concepts reverberated in the works of enlightened Iranians. One author suggested the significance of scientific knowledge for the affairs of the state and the nation while attacking the traditional sciences as archaic and futile. Another enumerated the country's shortcomings: the people's sufferings, the governors' arbitrary rule, the unpredictability of the government's decisions, a lack of security for people and property, the people's lack of awareness of their rights, the prevalence of bribery, the absence of tax law and regulations in the government's spending, the prevalence of foreign influence, and the country's weaknesses vis-à-vis foreigners. This author sought the remedy in the adoption of Western civilization with the provision that it not contradict Islam. He also emphasized the significance of personal freedom, political freedom, and freedom of the press. Still another author demanded orderliness in the government, a constitution, and the rule of the people.[52] A fourth author addressed Iranians in 1863: "If you could realize the advantage of liberty and human rights, you would have never tolerated slavery."[53] Finally, in 1870 a leading reform-minded, high-ranking state official, Majd ul-Mulk, wrote an influential essay on Iran's economic, political, and social decline, and the need for reform at all levels. The essay rose to prominence not simply as an effective political commentary but also as "a masterpiece of the new literary genre of social criticism that developed in this period."[54]

In 1871, the shah appointed a new liberal vizier—Mirza Hosain Khan Mushir al-Daula, the Sipahsalar. His tenure coincided with the rise of the Ottoman Tanzimat and the first decade of the Meiji restoration (1868–1912) in Japan.[55] Inspired by these movements, the new premier brought together prominent intellectuals, among them Mirza Malkum Khan, Mirza Yusef Khan Mostashar al-Daula, and Majd ul-Mulk. Malkum Khan, a Muslim convert of Armenian background, is considered an intellectual leader of the Constitutional Revolution. During his sojourn in Paris, Malkum Khan became interested in contemporary political philosophy, particularly in Saint-Simon's school of social engineering and Auguste Comte's religion of humanity. He drafted a *Daftar-i Tanzimat* (*Book of Reform*) as a proposal for reform. Its preamble started with the warning that Iran would be engulfed by foreign powers unless the shah decreed laws for reform. He used the term *qanun* (law) for these laws and to differentiate them from the shari'a and the existing state regulation ('urf). Malkum insisted that these new laws must be based on the principles of improving public welfare and the equality of all citizens.[56]

With the support of these intellectuals, the premier tried to establish the rule of law in the country. He set up a new Ministry of Justice to carry out his judicial reforms. New laws were formulated, the judiciary gained some autonomy, and a constitutional law was written. Influenced by the Napoleonic Code, a new legal code applying to secular issues based on science and reason and aiming at justice and equality was thus formed. The Sipahsalar believed that the ulama should be treated with reverence and that the government should refrain from interfering in such matters as prayer, religious services, marriage and divorce, and the resolution of religious issues. At the same time, he held that the ulama should not be allowed to interfere in governmental affairs. He also implemented measures to curb the arbitrary power of the governors.[57] These reforms were again resisted by the ulama and the conservatives. The Sipahsalar's chief adversary was the chief of the ulama, Hajji Mulla 'Ali Kani, who had close ties with some of the Qajar princes. He possessed a vast fortune.[58] "While Hajji Mulla 'Ali Kani had a granary full of corn and the people were dying of hunger," complained the Sipahsalar to the shah,

"I brought out the supplies of my family and household and distributed them among the poor. They offered him 50 tomans for each kharvar (=1 cwt. appro.), but he refused to sell, hoping that the price would increase. Meanwhile, the people were perishing. . . . Now they [Hajji Mulla 'Ali and his associates] are guardians of the Holy Law, while I am a subverter of the faith!"[59]

The Reuter concession in 1872, which stipulated, among other things, the construction of a railroad by a British concern, was used by the ulama as a sign of foreign domination of the country. The ulama and the conservatives in the court spread the rumor that the railway was to pass through the shrine of Shah Abd al-Azim in a suburb of Tehran. Hajj Mulla Kani issued a fatwa declaring the necessity of the premier's dismissal. Another leading religious figure of Tehran, Sayyid Salih Arab, even declared that it was a religious duty to kill (*vajib al-qatl*) the Sipahsalar.[60] Should the shah fail to dismiss him, the ulama threatened to leave the city and even Iran.[61] The ulama also declared Malkum Khan and Mostashar al-Daula heretical. In their defense, the two reformers coined the terms *mashrutiyyat* (constitutionalism) and *mashru'iyyat* (from the shari'a), arguing that the two concepts, far from being incompatible, were in fact identical in spirit.[62]

The conservative pressures resulted in the dismissal of the Sipahsalar in 1872. Malkum Khan was sent to London as Iran's ambassador. Losing his ambassadorship in 1889, he took a harder position against the shah. He founded the famous newspaper *Qanun* to convey his views to Iran. The paper aroused considerable interest in Tehran and contributed to the outbreak of the Constitutional Revolution. The first issue, published in 1890, carried the slogan "Unity, Justice, and Progress." Starting with an Islamic prayer in Arabic, the paper stressed the need for the establishment of rational law and the introduction of a national consultative assembly. The government banned the paper, and its mere possession was considered a capital offense.[63] Other papers dedicated to reforms and constitutionalism included *Habl ul-Matin*, originally published in Calcutta years before the revolution, considered the most important Persian paper of the opposition in exile; *Ruznama-ye Majles*, edited by Sadeq Tabataba'ie (the son of the constitutionalist mujtahid Sayyid Muhammad Tabataba'ie), who was to abandon his clerical garb after the first *majles* (parliament); *Nedaye Vatan*, edited by Majd al-Islam; *Roh al-Qods*, edited by Sultan al-Ulama; *Kuakab al-Darri*, edited by Nazem al-Islam; and *Tadayyon*, edited by Fakhr al-Islam.[64]

The Constitutional Revolution and Shi'i Modernism

A variety of historical factors contributed to the Constitutional Revolution: the radicalization of the merchants and the guilds, the movement of the intellectuals for constitutional change, and the wider difficulties that were partly a result of poor harvests and partly the effect of the fluctuations in the world market on the domestic

economic conditions around the turn of the century, coupled with the assassination
of Nasir ud-Din Shah in 1896, which removed a master politician skilled in the art
of "divide and rule," the new shah's ill health, interelite political rivalries, and the
support for a constitutional system within an influential section of the ulama.[65]
Among these factors, however, the participation of the ulama appeared to be
anachronistic and counterintuitive. Why did the ulama participate in the constitutional movement against a monarchy that had often been credited as the defender
of the faith (*Islam panah*)? Qajar absolutism had benefited the ulama not only financially and politically but also in terms of maintaining a monolithic religious order
under their exclusive sway. To give one prominent example, the ulama indeed owed
a lot to the Qajars for repressing Babism, a movement that would have made the
institution of Shi'i orthodoxy superfluous, had it succeeded. True, the ulama had
their own reasons for participating in the movement to end the shah's arbitrary
power and establish the house of justice. After all, the idea of resisting injustice and
tyranny was not new in Islam. Historical Shi'ism carried a rich repertoire of anec-
dotes on the rise of religious leaders against unjust rulers.

Nevertheless, joining the movement for the formation of the National Consultative Assembly to debate issues and to legislate was a different order. The
Fundamental Law ratified in 1905 by the ailing monarch, carried practical implications that went far beyond ending absolutism. A secular document modeled on the
Belgian constitution, it considered the assembly the representative of "the whole
people of Persia." Elected by the people in accordance with the electoral law, which
was to be separately promulgated, the assembly was granted extensive power,
including "the right in all questions to propose any measure which it regards as con-
ducive to the well-being of the Government and the People. . . . All laws necessary
to strengthen the foundations of the State and Throne and to set in order the affairs
of the Realm and the establishment of the Ministries, must be submitted for
approval to the National Consultative Assembly."[66] The assembly removed not
only the monarch but also the ulama's prerogative in interpreting and implementing the law within the framework of the shari'a. The Fundamental Law was aimed
at changing the state and curbing the shah's arbitrary power. At the same time, it
usurped from the ulama the very normative and regulatory functions that had been
in their exclusive domain. This fact did not remain concealed from the keen eyes
of the prominent Sheikh Fazlullah Nuri, "the celebrated reactionary mujtahid," to
use Browne's phrase.[67]

At the outset, Nuri and his associates faced a serious dilemma. On the one
hand, the revolution was supported by a wide cross section of the population,
monarchical absolutism was a discredited ideology, and the rule of law was far
superior to the rule of an erratic despot. On the other hand, lawmaking by the
people's representatives was contrary to the laws of the shari'a. How could they

oppose the constitution without opposing the revolution, which could expose them to the risk of being isolated? From November 1905, when two leading members of the ulama, Sayyid Abdullah Bihbahani and Sayyid Muhammad Tabataba'ie, started the revolution by opposing the government, to January 1907, when the shah died and his son Muhammad Ali succeeded him, the enthusiasm for the revolution was strong, and Nuri had no choice but to join, reluctantly, the movement for change.

When Muhammad Ali Shah started to rebel against the constitutional government, Nuri found an opportunity to express his conservative views. Claiming that the Fundamental Law was un-Islamic, he drafted a constitutional amendment that gave a council of the ulama the right to supervise all legislation put before the parliament to ensure that it was in accordance with the shari'a. Following considerable debate, an amendment was made to the constitution as article 2. The amendment, however, was not in the form that Nuri had originally intended. Article 2 left the final selection of the members of the council to the parliament. The Supplementary Fundamental Laws ratified on October 7, 1907, was, rather, a compromise between the religious groups and the liberal secular activists. It considered Twelver Shi'ism the country's official religion, instructing the lawmakers that "at no time must any legal enactment of the Sacred National Consultative Assembly . . . be at variance with the sacred principles of Islam." As a major concession to the religious establishment, the document declared that "it is for the learned doctors of theology (the *ulama*)—may God prolong the blessing of their existence!—to determine whether such laws as may be proposed are or are not conformable to the principles of Islam; and it is therefore officially enacted that there shall at all time exist a Committee composed of not less than five *mujtahids* or other devout theologians, cognizant also of the requirement of the age, which committee shall be elected in this manner" (articles 1 and 2). Other articles of the constitution, on the other hand, although ambiguously worded, reduced the power of the ulama. For example, article 71 states, "the Supreme Ministry of Justice and the judicial tribunals are the places officially destined for the redress of public grievances, while judgment in all matters falling within the scope of the Ecclesiastical is vested in just *mujtahids* possessing the necessary qualifications." Similarly, article 86 had undermined clerical influence: "In every provincial capital there shall be established a Court of Appeal for dealing with judicial matters in such wise as is explicitly set forth in the laws concerning the administration of justice." On the other hand, the Supplementary Fundamental Laws declared that "The powers of the realm are all derived from the people; and the Fundamental Law regulates the employment of those powers" (article 26). The king's sovereignty was not derived from God but from the people: "The sovereignty is a trust confided (as a Divine gift) by the people to the person of the King."[68]

Intellectual Pluralism and Ideological Contention

The Fundamental Law of 1905 and the Supplementary Fundamental Laws of 1907, far from resolving the problem of political sovereignty, gave added momentum to the dynamic of ideological debates and gave rise to the crystallization of diverse viewpoints upheld by different groups. Indicative of this intellectual vitality was the rapid development of journalism, which peaked in 1907, when the number of newspapers approached ninety.[69] Groups that were united in their demand for the establishment of the National Consultative Assembly now began to debate the form of government, the scope and content of parliamentary democracy, the necessity of social reforms, and, most important, the relationship between the new political order and religion. Three major groups contended for hegemony. The Westernizers formed the radicals of the Constitutional Revolution. They fought for the establishment of secular laws and the implementation of social reforms that also included elements of socialism. The moderates were led by the proconstitutionalist ulama, who searched for a compromise that took into account the role of the religious establishment, prerevolutionary practices, and social customs. Finally, there were the conservative ulama, who by now strove to upend the revolution and restore the old order.

The Absolutist Ulama and the Constitution

The Supplementary Fundamental Laws satisfied neither the radicals nor the conservatives. An article in *Sur-i Israfil* attacked the ulama as "money grabbers" who concealed their slimy interests with sublime sermons. *Habl ul-Matin* criticized the Supplementary Fundamental Laws for granting considerable power to the ulama: "This makes as little sense as having a supreme committee of five merchants to scrutinize the commercial validity of all laws deliberated by the people's representatives." It went further by blaming the problem of the Middle East on the ignorance, superstitions, petty-mindedness, obscurantism, dogmatism, and interference in politics of the clerics.[70] The absolutist ulama were equally dissatisfied for different reasons. Boosted by the strong backing of the shah, the conservative notables, and the fief holders who were affected by the financial reforms proposed by the parliament, they rose against the revolution. For Nuri, the supplement was too weak to curb constitutionalism. He used the pretext of the article of the Fundamental Law granting equality before the law to Muslims and non-Muslims alike to declare open opposition to constitutionalism.[71]

He took the position of an enthusiastic adherent of the traditional division of authority between the shah and the ulama. He began his argument with the premise that "the divine law is the best of all laws,"[72] which had been completed, perfected, and finalized by Muhammad, the last of the prophets. "If anyone," said

Nuri, "believes that the exigencies of time may change some of the articles of the faith or complement it, such a person is outside the bounds of the shari'a."[73] Nuri's point of departure was the nineteenth-century conception of political authority based on a division of labor between the ulama, in charge of religious affairs, and the shah, in charge of governmental affairs, according to which it was "the responsibility of each, with the assistance of the other, to guard and preserve the religion and the world of worshippers . . . so that the roots of Islam may be protected in the absence of the Imam."[74] Nuri further stated: "The ulama's responsibilities are to deduce the general commands [ahkam] which are the articles of divine law from four religious sources and disseminate them to the people. These four sources are the Quran, the akhbar [tradition], consensus [ijma], and reason ['aql]. The established deductive method must be followed and the ulama are not allowed to use qiyas [analogy] or istihsan [judgment or ruling that may sound right and proper], for these latter approaches are forbidden in the imamat jurisprudence."[75]

Based on these premises, Nuri set out to expose the un-Islamic nature of the constitution: If the function of the assembly was to formulate new laws, this was forbidden. If it was to formulate Islamic laws, this was the function of the ulama and should be done in accordance with the methodology of the jurisprudence. If it is to govern the behavior of state officials, then there is no need to call it Islamic. If the purpose of the constitutionalists, in Nuri's interrogation, "is to determine, strengthen, and implement the divine law, then what is the business of the common people and different groups to interfere in religion? Why do the constitutionalists seek their votes in the affairs of society but make reference to its religious bases?"[76] Following the royalist coup and ensuing bloody conflict, during which a number of prominent constitutionalists were killed, and confident of the power of the royalists, Nuri forged ahead in his censure of the constitutionalists, referring to the constitution as the great sedition (fitnih-yeh kubra), which from its emergence, rise, and decline had gone through three stages: (1) discourse and presentation (taqrir va unvan); (2) writing and declaration (tahrir va i'lam); (3) practice and test ('amal va imtihan). The first stage had been presented in such a pleasant way that it had attracted both the learned and the common people. In the second stage, the constitutionalists had first confined themselves to obscure statements and had then begun formulating laws and regulations so that they could write freely against religion and the ulama. In the third stage, the constitutionalists had begun to practice whatever oppression they could.[77]

Nuri further attacked on the constitutionalists by arguing that the concepts of equality and freedom were a heresy, traced the contemporary problems of instability, immorality, and ideological insecurity to the subversive influence of that "atheist Armenian Malkum," and declared that the majles liberals, like the French Jacobeans, were paving the way for socialism, anarchism, and nihilism.[78] Aroused by these words, the royalists attacked any passerby who happened to be wearing the short, European-styled hat as an "atheistic constitutionalist" and prepared to march on the National Consultative Assembly.[79] The royalist forces, however, were eventually defeated. Nuri was captured and subsequently executed.[80]

The Rise of Shi'i Political Modernism: Na'ini's Conception of Sovereignty

One of the most important efforts at a modernist interpretation of the Shi'i conception of political authority was a defense of constitutionalism by Mirza Muhammad Hussein Gharavi Na'ini (1860–1936). Na'ini's commentary on the legitimacy of the constitution was a new development in Shi'ism. It was formulated, as it were, within the context of ideological warfare among diverse groups for the control of the direction of cultural change in Iran. The social forces favoring change were mobilized, the royalist forces were crushed, diverse groups were actively promoting their ideas, and the ulama were deeply divided. Thus emerged favorable conditions for ideological innovation by a most prominent Shi'i theologian. Na'ini's ideas developed in direct response to Nuri's claim regarding the illegitimacy of the constitution from the Islamic perspective.

It should be noted that the influence of modernity on the Iranian Islamic movement predated Na'ini and can be traced to the works of such thinkers as al-Afghani, Sheikh Hadi, and Tabataba'ie. As was also the case in Egypt, modernism in Iran was associated with the works and activities of Sayyid Jamal ud-Din al-Afghani. Al-Afghani was involved in Iran's protest movements and had cooperated with the antigovernment activists. He was disliked by the conservatives, who questioned his fidelity to Islam.[81] A contemporary of al-Afghani, Haji Sheikh Hadi Najmabadi (1834–1902) held modernist ideas as well, arguing that reason was the most important prophet for leading humans to the right path, while superstition, fear of criticism, and bad habits and customs were like human diseases. Najmabadi was critical of the ulama, considering the wicked ones evil humans.[82] He was denounced as a heretic. Even Sayyid Muhammad Tabataba'ie, who was originally his disciple, later "denounced his opinions as heretical to his father, Sayyid Sadiq, who publicly banned him as an infidel. This denunciation, however, so far from injuring him, actually added to his prestige and increased the number of his disciples and admirers."[83]

A prominent leader of the Constitutional Revolution, Sayyid Muhammad Tabataba'ie opposed despotism and fought for a constitutional regime primarily on practical grounds: "I have not seen constitutionalism," said Tabataba'ie, "but according to what I have heard, and been told by those who had visited the constitutional countries, constitutionalism will bring security and prosperity to the country. Therefore, I also became an enthusiast of constitutionalism and interested in setting up a constitutional system for Iran."[84] He was a nationalist. According to Hadi Hairi, Tabataba'ie "was the only distinguished *mujtahid* to pronounce statements bearing a nationalistic sense. He frequently mentioned that he was devoted to his country, Iran, and that his service to Islam lay within the country."[85] In his defense of the constitution, Tabataba'ie went so far as to threaten Nuri for his counterrevolutionary activities:

> In the Name of God the Merciful and Forgiving. I guarantee that if His Reverence Hajji Saykh Fazlullah should act contrary to the undertaking which he has given, I will in person expel him from Tihran. Mulla Muhammad of Amul and Hajji Mirza Lutfullah must also go. [June 20, 1907][86]

In his monograph *Tanbih al-Ummah wa Tanzilh al-Millah* (*The Admonition of the Umma and the Enlightenment of the Nation*), Na'ini went beyond a simple affirmation of the goodness of a constitutional regime for Iran. Writing during the years when bloody struggles over the constitution were unfolding, Na'ini attempted to show the superiority of a constitutional regime to the sultanate or any other form of government that was based on the arbitrary decisions of the ruler. Like all other modernist thinkers of this period, he took as his point of departure the decline of Islam and the progress of Christian nations. For him, this change in Muslim fortunes was particularly striking given the glaring backwardness of Christianity vis-à-vis the Islamic civilization in the Middle Ages. The root cause of this decline, for Na'ini, was deviation from the basic principles of Islam.[87]

Na'ini's started by stressing the necessity of the state. For him, the stability of social order depended on the existence of the state, whether it was based on a single person or a group of individuals, legitimate or illegitimate, and whether the ruler or rulers assumed power through violence, heredity, or election. A government was stable when it relied on the wishes, thoughts, and beliefs of its people. The state functioned for the stability of social order in two ways. One refers to domestic concerns such as establishing security, educating its citizens, administering justice, and maintaining law and order. The other was the protection of national interests from foreign intervention, awareness of foreign intrigues, and the provision and organization of defensive forces. The performance of these functions meant "protecting the citadel of Islam" in the language of the experts of the shari'a, and "protecting the country" in the language of others. So far, nothing was new in his exposition. Both Shi'i and Sunni political theorists had long realized the utility of having a government for safeguarding the Islamic community.

The innovative aspect of Na'ini's political commentary was in his comparative evaluation of despotism and constitutionalism. Here, his argument is a point-by-point refutation of Nuri's defense of absolutism. A despotic regime, for Na'ini, displayed three negative aspects from a religious viewpoint. It had usurped the authority of God and hence had committed an injustice against him. It had oppressed the imam by usurping his authority. Finally, it was based on the oppression of the people. A constitutional government, on the other hand, was free of the first and third kinds of oppression. It had usurped only the authority of the imam. Thus, there was no doubt that a constitutional government was far superior to a despotic one.[88]

THE RISE OF
LIBERAL NATIONALISM, ARABISM,
AND ARAB NATIONALISM

Introduction to Part Two

Islamic modernism was an outcome of the efforts of a group of Muslim scholars to resolve the intellectual problems facing their faith in the changing social context of India, Egypt, and Iran from the second half of the nineteenth century to the first quarter of the twentieth. Two parallel and interrelated processes of the rise of the modern state and the emergence of a pluralistic intellectual market constituted the proximate conditions of Islamic modernism. In India and Egypt, these conditions emerged as a result of the decline of the traditional order, the rise of new social classes (most notably merchants and landowners), state formation, and the expansion of the educated elite connected to the administrative bureaucratic structure of the modern state. In Iran, in contrast, no major social transformation took place, and as a result the conditions favoring Islamic modernism were not as extensive as they were in India and Egypt. In all three cases, however, modernist ideas in Islam were produced as Muslim intellectuals addressed the sociopolitical issues they encountered. These ideas (1) were the outcomes of the existing sociopolitical and cultural environment insofar as they constituted a set of ideological resolutions of the issues that were generated by the debates and disputations in this environment, (2) had a social and nonpolitical orientation as long as the ruling elite remained by and large aloof from cultural debates, and (3) displayed a moderate tendency insofar as they were shaped within a pluralistic context.

In the following three chapters, we shall trace the historical development of modern political thought in Egypt, Syria, and Iran from the late nineteenth until about the middle of the twentieth century. In broad conceptual terms, liberal nationalism was a derivative of European political theories. It flowed in the works of indigenous culture producers from the belief that since the European constitutional model of politics was associated with Europe's technological achievements and economic development, if implanted in their homelands it would bear similar fruit for their people.

We should not, however, exaggerate the role of cultural diffusion in explaining the rise of new political discourses in these countries. This is true for two principal reasons. First, the growth of modern political ideologies in Islamic countries was facilitated by the existence of an intellectual space in Islamic political thought. This space was provided by the recognition of the reality of secular politics in historical Islam. However, for reflective Muslim political thinkers, the secular politics that was represented by the absolutist states in various Islamic countries was far from an ideal form of government—the ruling elite not only lacked the necessary Islamic credentials but also were corrupt and tyrannical. The decline of these states from the eighteenth century on further expanded this intellectual space and gave an impetus to the search for an alternative politics that would transcend the limits of absolutism. While some of the ulama resisted change, Muslim scholars predominantly opted to support the formation of an independent, transparent, and responsive state. Such a pronationalist and liberal tendency on their part is understandable. There was little religious justification for the defense of the old absolutist regime. Moreover, the minimalist argument that a constitutional state was far superior to a despotic one had a high currency among them. On a more concrete level of political action, there was also an affinity between liberal-nationalist intellectual leaders and the modernist ulama during the early stage of the nationalist and constitutional movement in Islamic countries.

Second, there were significant historical and cross-national variations in political thought in this period, which cannot be explained in terms of cultural diffusion. In Egypt, liberal nationalism was Egyptian and territorial. Arab identity was not among its defining features. In Syria, in contrast, the notion of Arabism was at the center of political thought among the country's intellectual leaders. In the decades surrounding the beginning of the twentieth century, this movement had a liberal-Arabist orientation. It addressed the problem of despotic rule and emphasized the significance of freedom for the construction of modern society. After World War I, however, liberal Arabism gradually gave way to pan-Arab nationalism, in which the idea of individual freedom was subordinated to or superseded by the idea of individual self-sacrifice for the cause of the liberation of the Arab land from foreign domination and the unification of the Arab people into a single nation. In Iran, on the other hand, the ideology of the Constitutional Revolution (1905–11) had a distinctly anticlerical and secularist orientation while conveying a notable pro-Western attitude. In the 1941–53 period, however, Iran experienced the rise of economic nationalism, and anticlerical secularism gradually became less significant in Iranian political thought, even though this secularism remained a distinctive feature of the ideology of the Pahlavi state.

As was true in the case of Islamic modernism, the factors that constituted the broad conditions of liberal nationalism were numerous and not confined to the process of economic development and the rise of the national bourgeoisie. Among them were the rise of the educated elite, the rise of or a renewed emphasis on the need for a national language, an awareness of the ancient and pre-Islamic history of the homeland, the demarcation of national boundaries, the rise of indigenous dominant classes, the consolidation of the modern secular state, and further diffusion of liberal and nationalist ideas from Europe in these countries. These factors constituted only the broad conditions of liberal nationalism, however, and by themselves they do not explain how this discourse was actually produced.

We shall try to explain these diverse ideological outcomes in terms of the nature of the regimes of signification indigenous political thinkers faced in their attempt to formulate a political project for the construction of a modern national state. We shall argue that liberal, constitutional, and nationalist thought was developed in oppositional relation to three major discourses. One was the ideology of monarchical absolutism. Another was the discourse of the orthodox ulama. The third was the ideology of colonial domination. We shall argue that the variation in the extent of the domination of these discourses in politics, the content of these discourses, and the manner in which these discourses were combined or connected with one another shaped the nature and orientations of the political ideologies that emerged in these countries.

SIX

Egypt: The Rise of Liberalism
and Territorial Nationalism

Islamic modernism and liberal nationalism were interrelated ideological movements in Egypt. There were conceptual consistencies between the two discourses, and until the nationalist revolution of 1919, the two movements tended to reinforce each other. The Islamic modernists reexamined Islamic jurisprudence in light of rationalist principles, questioned the Ottomans' Islamic conception of political authority, abandoned the dichotomy of the abode of Islam and the abode of war in favor of the ideas of civilization and progress, and displayed favorable attitudes toward the social role of women and religious minorities—all congruent with the liberal-nationalist aim of establishing an independent Egypt within the framework of constitutionalism and parliamentary politics. The two movements were also interconnected. The leaders and activists in both movements were part of the same network of liberal thinkers. They knew one another and circulated among the same political and cultural salons. Indeed, Islamic modernism contributed to the widening of the intellectual space that permitted the growth of liberal nationalism. In the 1920s and 1930s, nationalist intellectual leaders, however, took a radical secularist turn by displaying an overly critical attitude toward religion. This strong secularist orientation weakened their ties with modern Islamic activists and contributed to the vulnerability of liberal nationalism to the onslaught of both Arab nationalism and Islamic fundamentalism.

Islamic modernism and liberal nationalism were also the outcomes of the same general social transformation Egypt experienced in the nineteenth century. A similar set of circumstances influenced their discourses and orientations. Nevertheless, the intellectual problems faced by the two movements were different. The Islamic modernists tried to resolve the anomalies facing their faith in the modern period so that the shari'a could once again become the guiding principle of social life. The liberal nationalists, on the other hand, struggled to formulate an intellectual foundation for building an independent Egypt with a responsive nationalist government. In this endeavor, they encountered a set of ideological targets that were analytically different from those faced by the modernists—although historically these targets were not separable.

A series of binaries defined the liberal-nationalist discourse. These included such opposing ideas as *watan* (nation) versus *umma,* Egyptian primordial identity versus the Ottomans' suzerainty, self-rule versus the British protectorate, secular law versus the shari'a, utilitarian principles versus traditional values, constitutionalism versus hereditary rule, freedom versus despotism, and Egyptology versus Islamic history. The concept of watan was at the center of Egyptian political thought and formed the basis of Egyptian nationalist philosophy. It pointed to the existence of an Egyptian community, transhistorical and eternal, having a distinctive Egyptian identity and thus entitled to a separate political presence. The admission of the idea of watan by the culture producers naturally begged a number of important questions around which revolved the political debates of the period: How was this nation to be organized politically and socially? How was its history to be understood and written? Who were the members of this nation? What were the criteria of citizenship? What would be the role of religion in this new political community? How were the religious and ethnic minorities to be treated? What were the conditions for self-rule and how to achieve it? The debate over the nature and significance of the Egyptian nation within the liberal-nationalist framework continued from the second part of the nineteenth century through the 1930s, until its significance was challenged by Arab nationalism and Islamic fundamentalism.

Historians are unanimous about the reign of Muhammad Ali in contributing to the rise of Egyptian nationalist consciousness. But they are divided on how his rule effectuated the development of this political identity. Nationalist historians and commentators have considered Egypt a preexisting nation, which had always been endowed with its own distinctive sense of identity. The rise of Muhammad Ali and the construction of the modern state liberated the country from centuries of Mamluk and Ottoman tyrannical rule and thus gave the national spirit the opportunity for free expression. The fellahin (peasants) who were conscripted into the new army and participated in the numerous campaigns Muhammad Ali launched to carve out an empire for Egypt out of Ottoman territories discovered their true sentiments: that they were fighting for Egypt, and that they were Egyptians first and foremost, and not Muslims or Ottoman subjects. Muhammad Ali himself was portrayed as the prototype of a national hero, who had delivered Egypt from her misery and restored her past glory and grandeur—thus awakening and bringing to life the unadulterated Egyptian identity that had always been present but had been repressed through centuries of foreign occupation. The failure of Muhammad Ali to build a truly independent Egypt was then attributed to foreign intrigues, as the Ottoman sultan caved in to British pressure by signing in 1838 the Balta Lima commercial treaty that abolished commercial monopolies throughout the empire, and by the *firman* (decree) of 1841, which reduced Muhammad Ali's army to eighteen thousand men.[1]

Another group has questioned this interpretation. They have argued that Egypt cannot be treated as having an existence separate from centuries of Mamluk and Ottoman rule. Even mid-nineteenth-century Egypt had an Ottoman character, as the occupiers of the top echelon in various institutions of the state were Ottoman-Egyptians, who spoke Turkish and shared the values and heritage of Ottoman culture.[2] Khaled Fahmy, in particular, argues that far from displaying nationalist sentiments, the fellahin offered considerable resistance to their conscription into the national army, that Muhammad Ali engaged in dynastic wars of imperialistic expansion rather than wars of independence, that he was interested in building a dynasty for his family and cared little about Egyptians, that he was ambivalent about the Ottoman sultan, and that British hostility was due to his military expansion, not his efforts at modernization.[3] For Fahmy, if the Pasha's army managed to turn the inhabitants of Egypt into loyal citizens of Egypt, he did so "not by 'opening their eyes' to their true identities, or helping them to discover their hidden sentiments, but by subjecting them to a rigorous and tight disciplining regime whereby their bodies and minds were minutely controlled so that the Pasha and his elite could accomplish their own ambitions."[4] Moreover, the ruling elite contributed to the rise of nationalist consciousness not by the conscription of Egyptians into the national army, but rather by their antinationalist policy of making sure that none of these Egyptians was promoted to senior ranks, thus turning thousands of Egyptian army officers and soldiers into a homogenized community. According to Fahmy, "the deeply felt sentiments of injustice, frustration and animosity that the Arabic-speaking soldiers and their junior officers had towards the Turkish-speaking military elite was a powerful ingredient in forging the rising national consciousness and was made even more potent by being echoed in the civilian society at large. For the ethno-linguistic 'division of labor' that characterized the Pasha's army was mirrored by a similar one in the civilian administration where the ruling elite remained 'Turkish' and where 'Arabs' were prevented from being promoted to higher posts."[5]

The reality may be somewhere in between, however. The nationalist historians have not necessarily erred when they have pointed to the existence of an Egyptian entity that existed above and beyond the Mamluk and Ottoman period. Nor can we question the insight that, since the fellah was a pawn in the pasha's dynastic design, a nationalist feeling was not rekindled in his heart as a result of being transformed from a peasant to a soldier. In the formation of nationalist consciousness, the multiple institutions of the state certainly played a crucial role. So also did such other factors as the rise of an educated elite, the rise and consolidation of the Egyptian landowning class, the expansion of the economic, cultural, and political influence of religious minorities, the increase in the number of influential Syrian émigrés, economic development and stability under British rule, the heterogeneity of the elite, and a weak khedive. All these factors, however, do not explain how the nationalist discourse was produced. Why did Egyptian intellectual leaders glorify Muhammad Ali as the hero of Egypt, despite his brutality? Why did they blame the British and the Ottoman sultan for his failure? Where was the source of such other ideas as constitutionalism, equality, secular law, and utilitarianism?

We argue that far from being a reflection of the sociopolitical changes, the discourse of liberal nationalism was formulated in relations to two distinct target discourses. The first and foremost was the Westernizing discourse of British colonialism, which presumed the Egyptians' inability to rule themselves and hence the need for British tutelage. The other was the traditional conception of authority under the Ottomans that gave legitimacy to khedivial power in Egypt. These discourses were diverse, originating from different, if not opposing, ideological universes. As a result, two major trends emerged within the overall framework of liberal nationalism, each displaying the imprint of one or the other target discourse on its worldview and orientation. As a movement, the nationalists were united by a general opposition to British rule and by a consensus on the idea of Egyptian nationhood. They diverged on the specific conception of an independent and constitutional Egypt and on the method of achieving it. The discourse of such liberal thinkers as Ahmad Lutfi al-Sayyid was a secular outgrowth of Islamic modernism as well as a derivative of the political thought of the Enlightenment. Another major trend was the ardent nationalism of Mustafa Kamil, which flowed from al-Afghani's and Nadim's anti-British pan-Islamism.

Indigenous Grievances and Ideological Outcomes

Egypt's socioeconomic and cultural development in the nineteenth century not only expanded the requisite social resources of the dominant classes but also shaped and gave legitimacy to their grievances. The Ottoman law of the 1840s regarding private landownership, the breakdown of Muhammad Ali's monopoly system, the establishment in 1866 of the Consultative Assembly of Delegates by Khedive Ismail—all gave rise to a new landowning class as an important political force. It was only, however, after they gained "notable" status as members of the Consultative Assembly that they were able to claim the right to criticize the state for excessive taxation and inadequate representation, to object the existence of the abusive system of capitulation that had accorded extra territorial privileges to European immigrants and commercial interests, and to participate in the nationalist movement against arbitrary rule and for the liberation of Egypt. Likewise, the recruitment of indigenous Egyptians into the military preceded their demand for the further expansion of their power and the removal of the rigid ethnic ceiling that blocked access to the top positions within the military hierarchy. Finally, the involvement of educated Egyptians in the state bureaucracy provided a foundation for protesting the increase in the number of Syrian Christians in the government.[6]

The development of the liberal-nationalist movement was tied to the sociopolitical problems Egypt faced under Khedive Ismail. These included the khedive's arbitrary rule, the financial crisis of the state, which undermined Egypt's ability to pay its massive foreign debt, excessive taxation, and the restiveness of the indigenous army officers. The formation of al-Hizb al-Watani al-Ahli (The National Popular Party), the ascent of Ahmad Urabi Pasha to the pinnacle of the nationalist movement, and the slogan "Egypt for the Egyptians"—backed by a trilateral coalition of the army, the educated elite, and the landowners—were a nationalist solution to these problems. The Urabi rebellion (1879–82) reflected the grievances of the indigenous forces against both the khedive and the British.[7]

The people's grievances were naturally the crucial points of reference for the liberal-nationalist ideologues. Nevertheless, these by themselves do not provide adequate clues to how the ideology of liberal nationalism was produced. This is because some of these grievances had existed in Egypt for centuries, but Egyptians' response was something other than liberal or nationalist. In the past, unpaid or underpaid army officers simply revolted. The disgruntled dominant classes often opted to support another faction of the ruling elite or sought the ulama's patronage in the defense of their interests. From the dynamics of interest-based class actions or the army's contention for power in nineteenth-century Egypt it would be difficult to arrive at the rise of liberal nationalism, although it was undeniably connected to these interests.

Further, to appreciate the complexity of the relationship between "national" or class interests and liberal nationalism, we may even consider that the rise of this ideology in the last quarter of the nineteenth century was an unintended consequence of the actions of diverse groups who were not necessarily in favor of or opposed to nationalism. In fact, the forces that became the targets of the nationalist attack contributed to its genesis and growth. One was Khedive Ismail, who strengthened the landowners' political power by creating in 1866 the seventy-five-member Consultative Assembly of Delegates. He did not, of course, desire a representative government. But to impress his European creditors with his constitutional posture, Ismail had to consult the assembly on many issues. At the time, however, there was no sign of a possible conflict between the khedive and his assembly. The 1860s was a decade in which Egypt enjoyed a prosperity that was made possible by a lucrative world cotton market—reinforced by the American Civil War (1860–65), which benefited

Egypt—an influx into Egypt of Europeans with interests in economic development, and the building of the Suez Canal. The single-commodity export-enclave economy, however, was vulnerable to fluctuations in the world market as a decline in the international demand for cotton transformed the 1860s' boom to the economic bust of the 1870s and led to a financial crisis of the state. This brought to the fore multiple conflicts involving Khedive Ismail, the assembly, the army, and the European financiers who had underwritten the khedive's modernization program. The polarization of these conflicts set the stage for the later Urabi uprising. Khedive Ismail, hoping to free himself from European control, gave a free hand to journalists to attack foreign intervention, further aiding the rise of nationalist spirits.[8]

Another factor was the Europeans. Concerned about their financial commitments in the country, they forced Ismail to accept the principle of ministerial responsibility. The involvement of Anglo-French controllers in 1876 in supervising the financial administration, while creating difficulties for the khedive, afforded the assembly cause for bolder intervention in the state's affairs when certain of its members proposed their right to control such financial matters as the reduction of taxes and the accountability of European ministers to the assembly.[9] Third, there were the landowners, who advanced a constitutional argument to resist taxation. For them, naturally, if the Europeans had the right to check the khedive's decision, so did the landowners. Fourth, the indigenous officers in the army were drawn into action because the existing restrictions limited their upward mobility and, more seriously, the economic measures introduced by the government resulted in trimming their perquisites, a cut in the expenditures of military schools, and the retirement of Egyptian officers to the inactive list. Officers' pay and benefits fell into arrears.[10] Finally, educated Egyptians, native and foreign journalists, and al-Afghani, who arrived in Egypt in the early 1870s, helped the rise of anti-British agitation. Ironically, the only group that jeopardized the movement was the rebels themselves, whose miscalculation and spirit of brinkmanship led to the British occupation.[11]

Determinants of Liberal Nationalism

These historical exigencies had certainly influenced the minds of political thinkers. Their solutions to Egypt's problems were naturally directed against those who were in a position to make major political and economic decision. Who was responsible for Egypt's insolvency? The khedive? The European financiers? The greedy landowners or state bureaucrats? For Urabi and his associates, the answer was simple—Egypt should rid itself of the Europeans and their puppet, Khedive Tawfiq, and establish a constitutional regime. For the highbrow ideological producers, the question was much more complex. Being against arbitrary rule and foreign domination was one thing; being for the formation of a constitutional system in Egypt was quite another. People like Muhammad Abduh had serious misgivings about the readiness of the public for constitutional change and, even more, about the military as the method of realizing it, but observing "how seriously the notables, Sultan Pasha and Urabi, were working at creating a constitution, he threw in his lot with them, saying that 'then and then only, along with Sultan Pasha and all Egypt, I became a follower of Ahmad Arabi' [Urabi]."[12] Even if Urabi had realized the complexity of the constitution making and nation building, the revolutionary crisis that engulfed Egypt in the late 1870s and the polarization of society into the pro-Egypt revolutionary camp, on the one hand, and domineering non-Muslim foreigners, on the other, would not have left much political space for formulating an intellectual justification for a gradualist and reformist method of political change. Even a farsighted intellectual like Abduh saw no choice but to support the rebellion.

Economic Development, Elite Heterogeneity, and Political Salons

That the British occupied Egypt to protect their interests is hardly debatable.[13] They crushed the nationalist movement and reinstalled Tawfiq as the khedive. Tawfiq in the nationalist perception was a figurehead and a British puppet. The real power was wielded by Lord Cromer, who ruled Egypt as consul general (1883–1907). Naturally, the British occupation gave rise to nationalist sentiments through the clashes of interests and symbols between the occupying and the indigenous forces. Nevertheless, these facts alone cannot explain the rise of liberal nationalism as the dominant ideology of the Egyptians' resistance to foreign rule. What factors prompted the intellectual leaders to adopt the European models of politics and nation building? Why was there no conspicuous Islamic fundamentalist or Arab nationalist response to British colonial rule? Why, for the first decade of the occupation, did no significant nationalist movement arise in the country?

Far from producing a militant political and religious extremism, the occupation by Great Britain (1882–1922), despite its being a non-Muslim, alien power, generated a situation that prompted the intellectual leaders to appreciate the complexity of the problem of political order, to engage in ideological reflection on a higher level of abstraction than their extremist counterparts did in the twentieth century, to shy away from immediate political controversy, and to reach toward a comprehensive understanding of the prerequisites for establishing a modern democratic state. In fact, under the occupation, the economic, social, and cultural development of Egypt forged ahead. The newly gained security, the development of communications, the application of a measure of sanitation, and the introduction of cotton cultivation contributed to demographic expansion. The population increased from about 6.8 million in 1882 to 11.3 million in 1917. Railroad construction continued and expanded from 1,300 kilometers in 1880 to 4,800 kilometers in 1909. Security and development fostered a great boom in foreign investment. By 1914, the total capital of joint stock companies was estimated at £E100 million, 92 percent of which had been invested by foreigners. The British presence also contributed to the country's political culture. Modern Egyptian literature developed extensively during this period. The movement to revive Arabic literary masterpieces accelerated during the occupation and inspired such influential poets as Mahmud Sami al-Barudi (1840–1904), Ismail Sabri (1854–1923), Ahmad Shawqi (1868–1932), Muhammad Hafiz Ibrahim (1872–1932), and Khalil Mutran (1871–1949). In 1898, one hundred sixty-nine papers and journals were in existence, and two hundred and eighty-two in 1913.[14]

Equally important in the rise of the liberal-nationalist ideology was a change in the structure of power from being absolutist and authoritarian under Muhammad Ali to a pluralistic system characterized by elite heterogeneity and interelite rivalries. Under British occupation, decision making was far from being the sole prerogative of an absolutist ruler. What is more, in Nadav Safran's assessment, "by the example of their administration, their efficiency and devotion, their vigilance, and such actions as the abolition of the *kurbaj* (whipping) and forced labor, the British communicated to Egyptians . . . the notion that power is a social function and not simply domination; that office is a public service and not a fief to be exploited in return for personal service to a prince; that the people are really equal before the law; and that their rights, even if unstated in constitutions, can exercise a restraint on the power of the government."[15]

The plurality of power, though unequally distributed, and elite heterogeneity promoted different political alignments and diverse political salons. One such salons was that of Nazli Fazil, who, because of contempt for her cousin Tawfiq and belief in liberal principles, supported Urabi. Following his downfall, she turned intensely pro-British. Her salon was a meeting-ground for such prominent individuals as Saad Zaghlul (who became the leader of the independence movement after the First World War), Abduh, Amin, and prominent British civil servants, including Cromer. Another salon was that of Ali Mubarak Pasha, one of the foremost educators of Egypt. Many of the country's notables visited his house, including Mustafa Kamil. A third was that of Riaz Pasha, which had close connections to the Islamic religious hierarchy and the antioccupation groups. Riaz helped Ali Yusuf, a sheikh from the Azhar, to found *al-Muayyad* in 1889, which became a mouthpiece of nationalism.[16] Finally, there was the political salon of Fuad Salim al-Hijazi, a son of Latif Salim, who was the head of the military college and had been one of Urabi's supporters in 1879. Frequented by people like Mustafa Kamil, this salon provided a link between Urabi nationalism and that of Mustafa Kamil.[17] These political salons, with shifting coalitions and crisscrossing political alignments, in all likelihood tended to encourage political moderation and eclecticism.

They also broadly reflected the range of the country's political alignments and formed the organizational settings for training and supporting future political leaders. Naturally, within these salons different ideologues and activists tested the waters and gained a sense of the existing arrangements of political opportunity. Because the intellectual leaders, political activists, and ruling elite were tied in informal networks of social and political gatherings, they all had the opportunity for sustained interactions and exchanges of ideas. Power unequally shared is the recipe for conflicts, but continued interaction among people of different rank and status would reduce the likelihood that conflicts would turn toward extremism. As we shall discuss in part 3, the state's exclusionary policies and the low level of interaction between the ruling elite and the intellectual leaders in the second half of the twentieth century were crucial factors underpinning the rise of Islamic fundamentalism.

The Discourse of Power: British Colonialism

On how the occupation was first perceived, experienced, and tolerated, historians have offered different interpretations. For Safran, the occupation was met by Egyptians with despair, but gradually they realized that the British encroached on Muslim institutions much less than the Muslim rulers who had preceded them, and as their various projects unfolded, most sections of the population found good, practical reasons for tolerating their presence.[18] Jacques Berque, on the other hand, argued that imperialism brought into play such concrete forces and set up such turmoil in the country that they stifled or discouraged resistance.[19] Berque did not demonstrate how these forces would discourage resistance above and beyond pointing to the fact that the economy was in disarray and that the military was the decisive weapon of the British.[20]

Whether we consider the rise of nationalism a reflection of what Safran considered the conflict between Cromer's pious intention—a combination of "civilized" values and "Christian" ethics—and colonial mentality,[21] or simply a form of resistance to imperialism after the disarray it had created in social life had subsided, as Berque tended to believe, we cannot deny that British rule carried certain crucial ingredients that significantly shaped the ideology of the Egyptian response to imperialism. These ingredients, in addition to establishing a healthier economy, a standardized bureaucracy, and a relatively tolerant and free cultural environment, included a series of ideas that the intellectual leaders used in formulating their oppositional discourse to British rule in the first quarter of the twentieth century.

The British political discourse was drawn from a wider ideological universe—a rational and secular Europocentric perspective—that was not necessarily imperialistic. The neutrality of this perspective, in fact, transcended the narrow imperialistic mission of Great Britain, giving it an aura of legitimacy. This perspective was also congenial with the outlooks of the expanding indigenous educated elite and

the Syrian émigrés, who saw in the "temporary" British presence a favorable opportunity for cultural change. If, later in the twentieth century, Egyptian liberal
nationalists collided head-to-head with the British, it was not because they were
defying the Enlightenment's teachings on liberalism and nation building. It was
because the British did not remain loyal to the very principles upon which they had
justified their veiled protectorate of the country—teaching Egyptians the art of
governing constitutionally. The British in the twentieth century appeared as a foreign force whose objective was to expand and protect their particularistic interests
in the country. With the deposition of Abbas II in 1914, the British became a clear
target of nationalist agitation.

The British justified their occupation as a means to maintain order and security,
resolve the country's financial crisis, and prepare Egyptians for self-rule. It was to
be a temporary presence.[22] On the necessity of the occupation, Alfred Milner, the
British undersecretary for finance, claimed that "Great Britain did save Egypt from
anarchy, and all European nations interested in Egypt from incalculable losses in
blood and treasure, to say nothing of the deep dishonour which those losses, foreseen and yet unhindered, would have brought on civilized mankind."[23] In his view,
the Urabi movement "possessed great destructive force, but it had not within itself
the elements necessary for the construction of anything enduring."[24]

Lord Dufferin had little confidence that a constitutional system would succeed
in Egypt. In his view, "despotism not only destroys the seeds of liberty, but ren-
ders the soil, on which it has trampled, incapable of growing the plant. A long-
enslaved nation instinctively craves for the strong hand of a master, rather than
for a lax constitutional regime. A mild ruler is more likely to provoke contempt
and insubordination than to inspire gratitude."[25] Similarly, Cromer had little
confidence in the ability of Egyptians to rule themselves, claiming that he had yet
to come across a single man among the Pasha class who could really "understand
the main elements of the local political problem with which the Egyptian government" had to deal.[26] What Egypt needed most of all was order and good government. "Perhaps, *longo intervallo,* liberty would follow afterwards. No one but
a dreamy theorist could imagine that the natural order of things could be
reversed, and that liberty could first be accorded to the poor ignorant representatives of the Egyptian people, and that the latter would then be able to evolve
order out of chaos."[27]

In Cromer's view, the Egyptian's inability to rule was rooted in his incapacity to
reason. The European was "a natural logician, albeit he may not have studied logic."
The mind of the Oriental, on the other hand, was "slipshod."[28] The Egyptians "are
often incapable of drawing the most obvious conclusions from any simple premises
of which they may admit the truth."[29] The high powers of organization displayed by
the European would find their contrast in "the feeble organizing power of the

Oriental, with his fatalism which accepts the inevitable, and with his submissiveness to all constituted authority."[30] A general "muddle-headedness" characterized the ordinary uneducated Egyptian.[31] Cromer complained:

> Tell an Egyptian cook that he puts too much salt into the soup. He will abstain altogether from the use of salt. Or, on the other hand, tell him that he does not use salt enough; he will throw in a bucketful. He cannot hit the happy mean; moderation in the use of salt, or in anything else, is foreign to his nature; he cannot grasp the idea of quantity.[32]

A firm believer in the cultural superiority of the Westerner, Cromer evoked "the white man's burden" as the British central mission among the world's downtrodden. He lectured on ancient and modern imperialism, proclaiming that the duty of the Englishman lay in the direction of developing self-governing principles in the colonies.[33] He conceded, "it may be that at some future and far distant time we shall be justified . . . in handing over the torch of progress and civilization in India to those whom we have ourselves civilized."[34] Nevertheless, this development would involve a process of racial and religious change, as he warned that "until human nature entirely changes, and until racial and religious passions disappear from the face of the earth, the relinquishment of that torch would almost certainly lead to its extinction."[35]

Donald Malcolm Reid has demonstrated how the French and the British invoked the cultural symbols of the classics in their encounter with Egypt. Bonaparte masqueraded as Alexander and Lord Cromer measured himself against the proconsuls of imperial Rome.[36] The classics did not simply provide nineteenth-century imperialists the grandeur of imperial Rome to imitate, thereby establishing a historical continuity in the transfer of civilization from Europe to Egypt. They also furnished a perspective from which the Europeans conjured up Egypt. In the frontispiece of the *Description de l'Egypte*, "Roman/French eagle standards top the honour roll of battles running down the frame. Inside the frame, a telescoped view of the Nile valley from Alexandria to Aswan brims with ancient remains, but—tellingly—Cairo, Islamic monuments, and modern inhabitants are nowhere to be seen."[37] Cromer blended classics with Orientalism in viewing Egyptians as unchanging: "The Romans . . . assure us that the Egyptians were proud of the scourge-marks for perpetrating frauds in taxation. As it was in the days of Augustus, so it was in the days of Ismail."[38] Likewise, Milner referred to the classical era to describe his impression of the country. "Egypt is still, like the Egypt of Herodotus, the chosen home of what is strange and unexampled and paradoxical. . . . Amit [*sic*] countless changes, the country retains one unchanging attribute. . . . eternally abnormal. This genius for eccentricity is something that no change can exorcise."[39]

Westernization, Religious Minorities, and Syrian Immigrants

For the growing religious minorities and recent immigrants to Egypt, the British Westernizing mission was not empty rhetoric. The British occupation favored these groups, expanding their interests and cultural influence enormously. For Christians and Jews residing in Egypt, British reforms were crucial steps in the secularization of politics and depoliticization of religion. Likewise, Syrian émigrés, some having escaped from Ottoman repression in Syria and some having been pushed out by an economic crisis in their homeland, naturally supported the British. Toward the end of Ismail's reign and during the occupation, Syrian immigration to Egypt rose sharply. The British in turn reinforced this process by giving preference to Syrians in hiring for administrative positions. A large-scale flow of Syrian population into Egypt gave the government ready-made material for stabilizing its administrative system.[40]

The decades between 1870 and about 1920 represented the heyday of Syrian intellectual activities in Egypt. Dedicated to the Westernization process, most of the newcomers had a strong influence on the climate of opinion in the country. These émigrés did the most to spread in Egypt the liberal and scientific currents of thought that were in vogue in France and Britain. Jurji Zaydan (1861–1914) promoted Western standards of literary and historical criticism. He published his five-volume history of Arab civilization and his four-volume history of Arabic literature in terms of a secular framework. Shawqi wrote romances which sought to express the splendor and glory of ancient Egypt. Syrians also contributed extensively to the development of the press. As the editor of *al-Muqtataf*, Ya'qub Sarruf (1852–1927) defended rationalism and, along with Shibli Shumayyil, introduced Egyptians to the ideas of Darwin. Farah Antun (1861–1922), the editor of *al-Jami'ah*, published French literature, including the works of Jean-Jacques Rousseau and Ernest Renan.[41] Three Lebanese Christians, Sarruf, Faris Nimr, and Shahin Makarius, founded the pro-British *al-Muqattam* to oppose the influence of *al-Ahram*, which since its inception in 1876 had upheld the cause of nationalism before and during the Urabi revolt. Now impressed by the freedom afforded to the press by Cromer—which was denied by the Turks in Syria—and by the financial and economic reforms of the British in Egypt, the proprietors of *al-Muqattam* threw their weight wholeheartedly in favor of the occupation.[42]

The Khedives and Nationalism:
From Collaborative Tawfiq to Rebellious Abbas II

For the nationalists, the self-proclaimed civilizational mission of the British was too closely associated with their interests to carry much credibility. If they were serious, why did they fail to invest in education, to promote indigenous Egyptians to high-ranking positions in the civil service, and to industrialize the country? Questions like these convinced the nationalists of British callousness and lack of sincerity.

Nevertheless, considering such other options as defending Egyptian independence within the context of khedivial absolutism or supporting Ottoman rule, which meant at first supporting Sultan Abdülhamid's despotism and then bowing to the national chauvinism of the Committee of Union and Progress, the British "temporary" occupation appeared a more effective alternative for Egypt's economic and social development. For such enlightened intellectuals as Abduh and Amin, British presence, although in principle unacceptable, was better than khedivial arbitrary rule and could provide favorable conditions for the development of a constitutional government.

What is more, Egypt's cultural shift under Muhammad Ali and then more forcefully under Ismail removed the traditional framework from politics. This shift involved, on the one hand, a departure from the historical ruler-ulama alliance and, on the other, a weakening of the economic and cultural ties with the Ottomans. Instead, Egypt become oriented toward cultural pluralism, changing the status of religious minorities from dhimmis (protected second-class citizens of an Islamic state) to citizens, including these minorities in the state bureaucracy, and encouraging an influx into Egypt of Europeans (whose number increased from a few thousands to around one hundred thousand in the 1860–76 period). The rise of Arabic as the official language of the country, the expansion of modern education, and judicial reform contributed to the development of a modern Egyptian nation. This process brought Egypt closer to Europe, pushed it away from the Ottomans, and broadened the political space for the rise of modern nationalism.

Yet despite the divorce of the power and authority of the Ottoman sultan, the rulers of Egypt were still technically walis—representatives of the Sublime Porte, the Amir of the Faithful, who had the ultimate authority in Egypt, as he could depose the wali and designate a successor. This authority became increasingly intolerable for educated Egyptians and constituted a target of nationalist agitation in the country. Had not the British occupied Egypt, if we take our cues from Iran and Syria, we may postulate that the collision between khedive absolutism and, at one remove, Abdülhamid's suzerainty, and the political aspirations of the Egyptian educated elite would have directed liberal nationalism toward the appreciation of Arabism, secularism, and alliance with Europe. The occupation, however, changed the course of the nationalist movement in the country. While in greater Syria the nationalist movements were directed against the Ottomans' despotism and rested on the Arab identity (see chapter 7), British rule in Egypt gave its nationalism a distinctly Egyptian character. Even though Tawfiq was a dictator who could not be trusted by the nationalists,[43] his lack of legitimacy was primarily a consequence of his complicity with the British.[44]

In terms of their proclivity toward absolutism, there was not that much a difference between Tawfiq and his successor, Abbas II (reigned 1892–1914). Having the ambition of becoming an absolutist ruler, the latter could not tolerate British

tutelage. He first openly resisted the British over the appointment of top governmental officials and over the army. Then, learning that he had little control over
either and realizing his precarious position, he began to pursue a pinprick policy
against England from 1895 on.[45] Abbas II's power struggle with Cromer did not
produce the desired result, and the British signing of the Entente Cordiale with
France in 1904 ended any hope that he would rule Egypt without the British. His
popularity among Egyptians nonetheless increased as he placed himself at the forefront of the nationalist struggle.[46]

The khedive's anti-British stance, however, split the nationalist movement, giving credibility to pan-Islamic and pro-Ottoman nationalism. For liberal nationalists, however, being anti-British was not enough to be part of the movement.
They had serious misgivings about the khedive's sincerity. For them, the divine
nature of the Ottoman sultan and for that matter his representative in Egypt was
too unconvincing to require philosophical consideration. Stripped of his traditional ideological garb, what was left of the khedive's power was his arbitrary rule,
which became a subject of criticism in Egypt's constitutional thought. For liberal
nationalists, a ruler was considered legitimate insofar as he followed the rule of
law, something that Khedive Abbas II was unwilling to accept. He envied
Abdülhamid as he tried to imitate his police system. He went so far as to cooperate with the sultan in the persecution of the Young Turks.[47] And when he told
Mustafa Kamil in 1900 that public opinion meant nothing to him and if he "were
to put on a hat and walk around the streets of Cairo, no one would say anything," Mustafa became so angry that he announced his break with the khedive
in a letter to al-Ahram.[48]

The Rise of Liberal Nationalism

Abbas II was deposed in 1914. The number of British people occupying high-
ranking administrative positions in the state bureaucracy at the expense of both
other Europeans and indigenous Egyptians increased considerably.[49] These facts in
conjunction with the demeaning attitudes of the British toward Egyptians gave
rise to the common perception that the real intention of the British was to dominate
and plunder rather than to educate and prepare Egyptians for self-rule. This perception gained full support in the unfolding drama surrounding the Dinshawai
incident of June 1906. The summary and severe punishment inflicted on the villagers in Dinshawai, after a British officer died as a result of an attack by villagers,
provided the impetus for the rise of nationalist agitation.[50] Ali Yusuf wrote twenty-
three articles in al-Muayyad, Mustafa Kamil used the incident fully in Paris, and
hardly a poet kept silent. Qasim Amin recorded that "Every one I met had a broken heart and a lump in his throat. There was nervousness in every gesture—in
their hands and their voices. Sadness was on every face, but it was a peculiar sort of

sadness. It was confused, distracted and visibly subdued by superior force. . . . The spirits of the hanged men seemed to hover over every place in the city."[51]

The cruelty with which the sentence was carried out—the condemned men were flogged and hanged in their own village, while their families were looking on— caused indignation among Egyptians. But the extensive emotions that the incident aroused signified something broader that was happening in the country's political landscape: the rise of a generalized nationalist consciousness that enabled educated Egyptians to make common cause with the peasants against the British.[52]

Watan and Nationalism

British people had been attacked in Egypt before the Dinshawai incident, and they had displayed their unshaken resolve in punishing the perpetrators swiftly. Nevertheless, for the incident to become a symbol of national indignation Egypt had to undergo considerable political and cultural change. This change entailed the rise in historical significance of the notion of watan and the associated political, cultural, and emotional attachment to it in the form of nationalism.

The use of the concept of watan in the Egyptian political literature was associated with the general historical process of modernization, the rise of modern social classes, and state formation. The awareness of the glory of pre-Islamic ancient Egypt, the rise of Arabic as the official language of the country, the demarcation of its borders after Muhammad Ali's failed campaign in Syria, the formation of a national army based on countrywide conscription, and the decline of Turkish cultural influence made the idea of Egyptian nationhood highly attractive. Also important was the movement of Egyptians against foreign occupation—first in revolts against Bonaparte in 1798, then in support of Muhammad Ali in 1805, and finally against the British from the late 1870s on. Given that this particularistic idea of the Egyptian nation was formed in the context of the struggle against foreign and non-Islamic subjugators, its apparent contradiction with the notion of the universal Islamic community was not noted by the people leading the movement in the first half of the nineteenth century. Nor did it matter to the highbrow culture producers whether the nature of the struggle being waged against foreigners was nationalistic or Islamic. After all, the enemy was both foreign and non-Muslim, and the exigencies of the struggle against that enemy overshadowed the conflict between Islam and nationalism. Fighting for Egypt and fighting for Islam were the same.

The ulama did not find it worrisome to observe the Egyptian conception of nationhood rousing a sense of loyalty mixed with deep emotions as potent as the conception of religious affiliation. Evidently, this struggle opened a new cultural space that enabled writers, poets, political activists, and even men of religion to use allegiance to watan as a yardstick to judge the legitimacy of the rulers. The poet Salih Magdi (died 1881) provocatively attacked the ruler: "Normal men take a woman for a wife. He wants a million wives. Normal men take a house for a living. He takes ninety. O Egyptians, there is disgrace all around; Awake, Awake."[53] In another poem, he left the khedive out and attacked foreigners: "Egyptians all, awake. Defend your faith and your land. Your wealth is looted and Your sons are nothing but slaves."[54] The new conception of an Egyptian nation also influenced the manner in which old terminology was interpreted. The Azhar professor Hussein al-Marsafi discussed words, such as "watan," "umma," "justice," "oppression," "freedom," "education," "politics," and "government," that were in vogue in the political literature about 1880 in light of the new conceptual development. For him, religion was no longer the only unifying feature of the umma. "The *umma*," he said, "is a collectivity of people who are brought together by a unifying factor, this being, on the basis of investigation, language, locality, or religion."[55] Similarly, for a Syrian émigré, Adib Ishaq, who wrote under the general title "Political Life, Rights and Duties" to clarify the meaning of such terms as rights, duties, patriotism, and freedom: "*Al-Watan,* la patrie—the home country—linguistically means man's place, his abode. Politically, it is the place where his rights are secure and towards which he has duties. There can be no *Watan* without freedom."[56] The political struggle against foreigners pacified the conflict between religion and nationalism and made it possible for "the concept of 'la Patrie,'" in Hourani's apt remark, to conquer "without a struggle."[57]

Pan-Islamism versus Western Civilization

One way to measure the significance of nation and to appreciate the cultural distance Egypt had traversed in the course of the long nineteenth century from Islamic to nationalistic sentiments and from the primacy of religious sensibility to an emotional attachment to national symbols was to listen as one of the most eloquent spokespeople of Egyptian nationalism, Mustafa Kamil (1874–1908), addressed Egyptians about Egypt as if he were talking about a *person* dear to one's heart and to imagine the excitement his words aroused among his subjugated compatriots. For him, it was not language or religion, but the feeling of belonging to the land of Egypt that was the most potent unifying force in bonding Muslims and Copts alike to struggle against foreign rule. Such emphasis on the psychic unity of Egyptians was naturally a meaningful vehicle of mobilization against the occupying power.[58] Kamil fostered and glorified the sentiment of nationalism:

> Nationalism is a sentiment before which all nations and all communities
> bow because it is the feeling of the worth and dignity of man, of the bounty
> of God and His care, of the meaning of existence itself. . . .
> Nationalism is the food which the body and soul of Egypt need before any
> other food. . . . It is the mainspring of all miracles and the principle of all

progress . . . it is the blood in the veins of nations and the life of all living things. . . .

Nationalism is the noblest tie for men and the solid foundation upon which great and mighty kingdoms are built. . . . Life is merely transitory and it has no honor without nationalism and without work for the welfare of the fatherland and its children. . . .

Fatherland, O fatherland: To you my love and my heart. To you my life and my existence. To you my blood and my soul. To you my mind and my speech. . . . You, you, O Egypt are life itself, and there is no life but in you.[59]

Mustafa Kamil was addressing Egyptians, who were also Muslims. It was natural for him to speak of "the Egyptian nation," and "of the Islamic nation." He saw no conflict in giving allegiance to both: "for every living nation there are two great obligations: the obligation towards its religion and its creed, and its obligation towards its *watan* and the land of its fathers."[60] His pro-Ottoman orientation, however, cannot be explained simply by his emphasis on the religious allegiance of the nation. "We are," he said, "concerned more than others with the integrity of the Ottoman Empire, because the integrity of its domains is the foundation upon which our legal rights against the action of the English is based. We must not forget that whatever we demonstrate which has to do with the support of Turkey is viewed and considered by us as part of the Egyptian cause against the English."[61] In the Urabi movement, there was also a call for Egyptian solidarity with the Ottoman sultan Abdülhamid, putting the anti-British struggle in the context of a holy war, and popular sentiment dubbed the Urabi forces the party of God (*hezbollah*).[62] This is curious because the call for "Egypt for the Egyptians" by Urabists was not only directed against European intervention, but aimed in equal measure at the arrogant exclusivity of the predominantly Turco-Circassian power-elite as well.[63] Why did Urabi and, a couple of decades later, Kamil continue to profess solidarity with the Ottomans? Were the Ottomans not responsible for Muhammad Ali's economic and military decline? Had they not caved in to the British pressure in order to undermine Egyptian nationalist aspirations? What kept these nationalists from recognizing the Ottomans as the historic nemesis of Egyptian independence? In comparative terms, we may argue that the reality of the British presence and the decline of the political, socioeconomic, and cultural influence of the Ottomans in Egypt had naturally removed the latter as a target of nationalist ideological attack. Further, Abdülhamid's pan-Islamism, as well as the anti-British attitudes of Abbas II and the latter's sympathy for the sultan, might have inspired Mustafa Kamil to a take a pro-Ottoman position.

For more reflective political thinkers, the issue was not just defeating the occupying forces. It was the formulation of a political agenda for the construction of an independent Egypt. The consciousness of decadence that drove the intellectual project of Islamic modernism was also the point of departure for the liberal-nationalist ideologues. For them, however, the question was more narrowly conceived. It was not why Muslim nations had failed to achieve a modern civilization. It was rather why Egyptians were unable to form a prosperous and dynamic nation similar to those of the Europeans. Abd Allah Nadim (1845–96), who was among the country's first nationalist ideologues, addressed this issue in a somewhat systematic manner. He was in the vanguard of indigenous protests against the growing power of the Europeans, who he thought were living off the fellahin in the countryside, and against the khedive, who was a source of the miseries inflicted upon Egyptians.[64] His comic stories illustrated the high-handed way in which the Europeans treated Egyptians.[65] Nadim was not simply attempting to liberate Egypt from the Europeans or check the arbitrary power of the khedive. He was also in search of a model for Egypt that would make it strong and affluent. In this search, he had fixed his gaze on principles of social organization other than tradition and Islam. For him, language was one of the most important organizing principles of a nation, the unity of language being as important as the unity of race. He sought the reason for the fall of the Arab, Turkish, and Persian states in the existence of many languages within their borders, which had become rallying points for dissent and provided excuses for foreign intervention.[66] In addition, the Oriental kings, their ignorant and superstitious subjects, the self-indulgent rich, and the ineffectual ulama had also contributed to the demise of Muslim nations: "The people of the East wasted their money on amusements (malahi), and on religious mendicants, candles for mawlids (saints' birthdays), and vows at shrines, 'and so knowledge suffered a setback in Eastern countries, and ignorance became general among the common people. The ulama restricted themselves to religious instruction in some countries, and the exact sciences were abandoned.'"[67]

The Western commercial classes, on the other hand, did not allocate their profits to bodily pleasures. They instead subsidized scientific and religious societies, founded schools and institutions, and sent their scientists and clerics all over the world to learn about and win over the people who were different from themselves. He cited America as an example of a successful, science-oriented culture.[68]

Although the ancient glories of the Pharaonic era featured prominently in the works of some of the liberal nationalists of the later period, Nadim, being a sheikh and an alim, naturally conceived of the past golden age as the time of the Prophet and the early Islamic movement. He was a puritan and criticized the missionaries, whose system of education was dangerous to the language and culture of Egypt. He also criticized Ismail, for having brought in Europeans, who opened theaters, dance halls, and other places of corruption.[69] From this standpoint, in contrast with the fundamentalists of the period after the 1930s, he did not conclude that the Western model should be rejected. Nor did he believe that Egypt could prosper using only its own resources. Instead, he suggested emulating Europe as the method of uplifting the condition of Egypt. "The acquisition of civilization," said Nadim, "is conditional on [our] imitating them and accepting their ways. Savagery consists of being at variance with them, and acting against their opinions. We, the people of the East, must compete with the civilized nations in order to emerge from the slough of barbarism attributed to us, so long as we persist in [following] the teachings of our ancestors. We shall never arrive at this goal except by the means Europe has employed, and all of these are subsumed under educational methods. These consist of their having combined religious with academic instruction, and having made them one system [of education]."[70]

His attitude toward Europe, however, was not always consistent. On the one hand, following the Urabi defeat, he basically reiterated Cromer's proclaimed mission in Egypt: "But we do not forget that we are under the watchful eye of a great power that is striving to advance our civilization, and to bring us to an awareness of our national rights. She is doing all she can to spread European education throughout the various sections of our country, and her ministers and deputies are proud of having led us to civilization, and taught us many ways of improving [our lot] that we had not known of."[71]

He also displayed an anti-Western attitude while defending a pan-Islamic alternative. He suggested that if the Easterners closed the breaches in their common defenses and "give one another support, and present a united Oriental front— Egyptian, Syrian, Arabian, and Turkish—we shall be able to say to Europe: 'We go our way and you go yours.'"[72]

Liberal Nationalism

The discourse of liberal nationalism was clearly directed against two targets. One was Turkish despotism, and the other British colonialism. One of the most sophisticated spokespeople of this trend was Ahmad Lutfi al-Sayyid (1872–1963). In his many articles and editorials, he forcefully promoted the reorganization of Egyptian society and government around two pivotal ideas: Egyptian nationhood and freedom. Al-Sayyid's reasoning about the significance of these ideas for Egypt, however, was formed, as it were, within the context of diverse discourses: the ideology of the Enlightenment, British colonial discourse, the Islamic modernism of Abduh, pan-Islamism, and the nationalism of the khedive.

Al-Sayyid's view reflected the influence of the idea of the evolution of human society expressed by such thinkers as Rousseau, Comte, Renan, Mill, Spencer, and Durkheim. Following these scholars, he accepted the view that the natural law of progress was the governing principle of social evolution and led to a constant expansion of individual liberty, the domination of reason, increasing social differentiation and complexity, the decline of religion and custom, and the employment of individual self-interest as a basis of the social contract and government. He studied Aristotle's *Ethics,* was influenced by the didactic writing of Tolstoy, and followed Gustave Le Bon's thought on nationalism. The latter attributed a fixed mental constitution to each people that was created throughout history, consisting of two basic elements: reason and character. Le Bon also suggested that religion was the most important factor in shaping national character and that the birth of a new religion is the birth of a new civilization.[73]

Al-Sayyid insisted on the utilitarian principle as a basis of political action and on the necessity of the Egyptians' learning the meaning of freedom and individual responsibilities. "Our political actions," he said, "must be based on the utilitarian principle because we are living in a time when this is the way things are done, and because the modern civilization from which we draw all our strength is so constituted. The West fights with this weapon, and the greatest danger could befall us if we do not imitate it in this respect."[74] From this principle he concluded that the basis of government was free agreement, although he believed no less that there were certain human associations so old and stable that they could be thought of as natural and possessing the same rights as individuals.[75] The consistency of his views with Western liberalism is clear. But al-Sayyid went a step further by accepting, broadly speaking, Cromer's agenda for Egypt on the necessity of training Egyptians for self-rule. He believed that Europe should provide guidance. The British occupation, in fact, was hailed as the "guiding authority." Al-Sayyid, however, warned that the British would never win the friendship of Egyptians unless they reassured them through their efforts that they were working for the advancement of Egypt. "We are a nation," said al-Sayyid, "who more than any other stand in need of training in constitutionalism, training in freedom, for the minds of both individuals and groups, and education in [the principle that] there is accord between private and public interests. And if the two interests should conflict—though this seldom happens—the public interest must be placed before the private. Our need for such training is recognized by all Egyptians irrespective of their differences of class or creed."[76]

Al-Sayyid's conception of nationalism was also formed in relation to the opposing views of two groups who had the common denominator of denying the Egyptian national identity. One was that of the British, who presumed the Egyptians' inability to rule themselves—the justification for British domination of Egypt—and the other was that of the pan-Islamists, who stressed religious loyalty. Al-Sayyid criticized British rule not because it was foreign, but because it was absolute. While acknowledging the benefit it had brought to Egypt, he did not view improvements in economic conditions and finances as solutions to the problem of the lack of a moral relationship between rulers and ruled. Likewise, he chastised the proponents of pan-Islamism for claiming that Egypt was the nation of every Muslim who settled on its soil. According to this reasoning, Egyptian nationhood was eliminated, which made the idea of independence difficult to understand. He ridiculed pan-Islamism and pan-Arabism as delusions and fancies. Islamic nationalism seemed to him not to be true nationalism. The idea of dar ul-Islam was an imperialistic principle, useful only to imperialistic nations that were eager to enlarge their territories.[77]

There was a certain affinity between al-Sayyid's views and Abduh's Islamic modernism. Al-Sayyid followed the latter in subscribing to the gradualist method of educating and training. He disagreed with Cromer's portrayal of Islam. According to al-Sayyid, the defects Cromer attributed to Islam were in fact inherent in the Eastern absolutism that dominated the Islamic world. He also pointed out that Cromer's notion of "typically Islamic" fatalism and apathy had also been present in Christian Europe during the Middle Ages. While praising Islamic democracy, al-Sayyid was critical of Islamic orthodoxy. The Prophet Muhammad, in his view, had decreed the sovereignty of the nation and followed the opinion of the community. He had strongly urged and recommended fidelity to this rule. The Rashidun caliphs had followed in his footsteps in this matter. The ulama, on the other hand, had distorted the sacred law for the benefit of the worldly rulers who later came to power. They had used learned opinion to please the sultans and excuse their criminal acts.[78]

In al-Sayyid's thought, the Islamic theory of government was irrelevant, and he abandoned some of its key concepts. He also questioned the concept of jihad, which al-Afghani had tried very hard to resurrect. In a response to Egyptian newspapers that took up the cause of the Ottoman Empire in the Tripolitanian War with Italy (1911–12), he argued that "the Egyptians must not, in the interests of the country, make religion—under these circumstances—the basis for their political acts. They must repudiate today as they have in the past, any accusation of religious bigotry . . . 'pan-Islamism and fanaticism.' For they have found out that this accusation was one of the major pretexts employed by the British for remaining in Egypt, and that they are still making use of it up to the present moment."[79] For him, the Islamic conquerors—from the Arabs to the Turks—were all imperialists, as long as they used religion as a mask for political ends. In the history of his own country, Lutfi placed the Turks on the same level as the British, namely, as foreign invaders and despots. "If the Egyptians are agitated by the English administration of their country, they were agitated before that by the Turkish administration."[80]

For al-Sayyid, the pan-Islamic principle that beliefs were the basis for political action was a dangerous credo. Instead he suggested the vital principle of utilitarianism for adoption as a guiding principle of politics: "We believe categorically that making utility the basis for action is a credo which does not conflict with the monotheistic [Islamic] faith. Let people act as they wish in actual life for their own benefit, with the proviso that they do not legalize the forbidden, nor forbid the legal, and that they comport themselves in conformity with the teachings of their religion, which commands the good and forbids the evil."[81]

In his view of the history of the Egyptian nation, al-Sayyid took the historical perspective of Tahtawi and the Pharaonists. In response to his European adversaries, who argued that Egypt had never been independent, al-Sayyid argued that those who were against Egypt's independence were only a rabble, which did not possess the ancient national identity of the Egyptian nation, or its well-defined homeland, or its social institutions when the world scarcely knew the first step to take for creating such social institutions. The ancient Egyptians were the most tolerant of nations in their imperialist policy, since they adopted the course of decentralization in their pursuance of that policy, preserving the religion, customs, and government of the conquered nation and allowing it to be free within its own territories in return for recognizing Egyptian sovereignty.[82]

SEVEN

Syria: From Liberal Arabism to Pan-Arab Nationalism

Nationalism in Egypt was Egyptian and territorial. Arab identity did not feature prominently in the political discourse of its intellectual leaders, notwithstanding the rise of Arabic as the official language of the state and considerable development in Arabic literature in the last quarter of the nineteenth century. In Syria, in contrast, Arab consciousness came to play an increasingly central role in the formation of the nationalist discourse from the late nineteenth century on. The full-fledged doctrine of twentieth-century Arab nationalism recognized the inhabitants of the region from the Atlantic Coast in North Africa to the Persian Gulf (with the exclusion of Persians to the east and Turks to the north) as an indivisible Arab people. It considered the Arab homeland a natural geographical unit, a living body, and the Arabic language the most advanced and the most ancient of the Semitic languages.[1]

The development of nationalist thought in Syria was also different from that of Egypt in displaying two distinct periods with diverse orientations toward the questions of nation and individual liberty. One was a period of liberal Arabism between the second half of the nineteenth century and the early twentieth, and the other was the era of the rise of pan-Arab nationalism, between the two world wars. Liberal Arabism was an eclectic discourse, based on a series of loosely connected ideas that distinguished Syria from the Turkish Ottomans in terms of such binaries as centralized Ottomanism versus decentralized Arab autonomy, Arabism versus Turanianism, Arabization versus Turkification, religious equality versus religious hierarchy, individual citizenship versus ethnic and religious sectarianism, rational rule making versus the shari'ah, representative government versus dynastic rule, and the rule of law versus arbitrary rule (*istibdad*). Although the significance of these categories changed with the changes in the regimes of signification from the pan-Islamic despotism of Sultan Abdülhamid and the Turkish nationalism of the

Committee of Union and Progress (CUP) to the imposition of the French mandate, the key ideas that, by and large, remained invariant until the rise of pan-
Arab nationalism were the notions of liberty, the wickedness of despotism, and
Arab independence. Pan-Arab nationalism, in contrast, was based on a different set
of dualities: Arab nationalism versus country nationalism, Arab organic unity versus the colonial partitioning of the Arab land, the liberation of the Arab people versus imperialist domination, Arabism versus Islamism, Arab unity versus tribalism
and sectarianism, and individual self-sacrifice versus individual liberty.

The development of and changes in political discourses in Syria were connected
to the considerable social transformation the country experienced in the nineteenth
and twentieth centuries. This connection, however, is complicated by the presence
of, and interaction among, varied forms of nationalist consciousness arising among
diverse groups in different parts of the Arab world that, unlike Egypt, enjoyed little independence of Ottoman rule in the nineteen and early twentieth centuries.
Historians are engaged in a lively debate on (1) the beginning of Arab nationalism—whether it was in the second half of the nineteenth century, the decade or so
before the First World War, or after the overthrow of Faisal's government in Syria
in 1920 and the establishment of his kingship about a year later in Iraq; (2) the role
of Muslims and Christians in the genesis of Arab nationalism; (3) the variations in
historical dynamics that gave rise to different Arab nationalist movements in
Lebanon, Syria, Iraq, and Arabia; (4) the role of economic and class dynamics, such
as the influence of the Syrian landowning class, class fraction, and interelite competition for economic and political supremacy in Syria and Arabia; (5) the ideological roots of Arab nationalism—Islamic modernism or Muslim secularism—and
the effect of various nationalist ideologies entering the Arab world in the nineteenth and twentieth centuries; (6) the role of the Iraqi Kingdom in promoting
Arab nationalism; and (7) the connection between CUP policies of nationalization
and Turkification and the rise of Arab nationalist discourse. In this debate, there are
also other issues: Arabism versus Arab nationalism, Syrian nationalism versus Arab
nationalism, local Arab politics and revolt versus regional movements, and the
Arab nationalist movement versus the Arab nationalist ideology.[2]

From the depth and breadth of this historical debate one thing becomes clear:
Arab nationalism was not a monolithic discourse that had a unified characteristic,
was not governed by a single dynamic, and was not supported by similar social
groups and classes. There were certainly considerable differences among the secular discourse of Arabist Christians, the liberal-Arabist discourse of Muslim political
thinkers, the ideology of Arab revolt, and the pan-Arab nationalist ideology that
was promoted by the Iraqi Hashemite Kingdom. In this chapter, we select two of
the most important poles in the spectrum of Arab political discourses. One pole
consisted of the set of ideas that was presented by Butrus al-Bustani (1819–83), other

Syrian Christians, and prominent Muslim thinkers like Abdul Rahman al-Kawakibi (1849–1903). The other was the political discourse of pan-Arab nationalism that was developed by people like Sati' al-Husri (1880–1968). While it is debatable whether the intellectual roots of Arab nationalism can be attributed to al-Bustani and al-Kawakibi, we follow the distinction historians have made between "Arabism" as a protonationalism describing a pre–World War I Arab movement and "Arab nationalism" as a mature form of nationalism with the concomitant desire for separation of the Arabs from the Ottoman Empire and the formation of a single Arab state.[3] Our object is then to assess the degree to which our model explains the production of these two different political discourses on how to view and organize the Syrian nation, the nature of its government, the status of individual liberty, and the conception of the enemy of the nation.

We argue that Syrian liberal Arabism first emerged as a part of the loosely defined ideology of Ottomanism. Then it was further developed as a truly liberal and antidictatorial discourse, having oppositional relations to Abdülhamid's authoritarian pan-Islamism and finally to Turkish nationalism of the early twentieth century. Pan-Arab nationalism emerged in a historically different context, which was characterized by the colonial partitioning of the Arab land and the imposition of the French mandate on Syria between the two world wars. Turkish nationalism and French colonialism were two subsequent signifiers in reference to which this new political awareness among Syrians was generated, debated, and at last accepted as the most essential component in the making of the Syrian state after the 1950s.

In the first period, Syrian Arab intellectual movements had a liberal orientation. The rapid disintegration of the Ottoman Empire following its defeat in the First World War, the overthrow of the nascent Faisal kingship in Syria, and the imposition of the French mandate on the country paralleled a gradual shift in Syrian nationalist discourse from liberalism and antiauthoritarianism to militant pan-Arab nationalism. Under the French mandate, the liberal-nationalist framework adopted by the National Bloc gradually lost credibility as a result of the decline of French cultural influence and France's failure to protect Syria's territorial integrity. In its place, the idea of pan-Arab unity gained increasing popularity in the works of the country's political thinkers. The transformation of Syrian nationalism from liberalism to radical pan-Arabism was associated with the imposition of the French and British spheres of influence on Greater Syria, Jordan, and Iraq. The longer the European powers remained in the region, the more prominent became the concept of pan-Arabism in Syrian nationalist discourse. The more Syrian territories the French ceded to the neighboring states, the more central became the notion of the emancipation of the homeland in Syrian nationalist discourse. The end result was the subordination of the idea of freedom to the notion of national emancipation and individual self-sacrifice for the homeland. These changes in the concept of nationalism are mirrored in the work of Sati' al-Husri, who became one of most effective spokespeople of pan-Arab nationalist thought.

It must be noted that although we argue that Arab consciousness was first developed in dialogical relation to the target ideology of Turkish nationalism, its later development into a well-articulated nationalist doctrine was made possible not so much by the ideology of foreign domination as in response to a growing perception of the collective mistreatment of the Arab people and the political fragmentation of their land by the colonial powers. More crucially, Arab nationalism was also forcefully promoted by the Iraqi Kingdom in its attempt to transform the existing tribal and sectarian loyalty into a nationalist sensibility and thus create the social cement to anchor the emerging state to various institutions in civil society.

Social Transformation and Cultural Change: The Crisis of 1860

Syria was incorporated into the Ottoman Empire in 1516. Before the annexation, Syria enjoyed a central position in the Old World as a great junction for overland and sea routes from central and eastern Asia and India to the Mediterranean, Africa, and Europe as well as for exchanges among its neighbors, Mesopotamia, Egypt, and Anatolia. (Some of the routes developed in prehistoric times. By 3000 BC caravan trade was so well established that its methods were standardized, and commercial exchanges regularized.)[4] Aleppo developed as the Levant's chief market city, where European merchants established their trading stations and consulates. Damascus flourished as the principal staging post for the annual haj (pilgrimage) to Mecca, for which it supplied the provisions and transport.[5] Far from undermining its regional economic preeminence, incorporation into the empire served Syria by bringing an empirewide market to the country and making it the main communication link between the Ottoman Empire and Europe while at the same time protecting Syria from foreign encroachment.[6]

The Ottomans' rule was not unproblematic, however. The Turkish governors were appointed by and responsible to the Sublime Porte. They were perceived by Syrians as outsiders. Syria's political stability was thus contingent upon the cooperation of the urban notables, a powerful group of scholar-landowner families that had effective control over the economy and culture.[7] The relationship between the Ottoman central authority and these notables was that of cooperation and competition. When the central authority was weak, as it had been in the first half of seventeenth century and the second half of the eighteenth, they enjoyed considerable power, which won them significant tax concessions. Overall, however, and despite their linguistic and ethnic differences, the Turks and Syrians were bound together by their shared acceptance of the religio-dynastic basis of the state and by their mutual interest in protecting the unity and integrity of the abode of Islam from the threat of the neighboring Christian powers.

In the modern period, several factors changed the relationship between Syria and the Ottoman's central authority, including the gradual incorporation of the Ottoman Empire into the world capitalist economy, the diffusion of modern ideologies in the Islamic world, and successive defeats of the Turkish army by European powers after the Ottoman retreat from Vienna in 1683. These defeats underscored the reality of Ottoman decline and European military superiority.[8] The increasing inequality of power between a decaying empire and thriving imperialisms changed the framework for economic transaction in favor of Europe. The treaty of capitulation limited the Ottomans' customs duties on imports from European states and accorded various extraterritorial privileges to them. The European goods paid very low customs duties on entry into the empire, while Syrian and other Ottoman goods seeking to enter Europe were subject to prohibitive duties or barred outright.[9] The commercial treaties signed by the Ottomans in 1838 were applied to Syria and further reinforced the already great advantages enjoyed by foreign merchants.

Another crucial factor that further changed the basis of economic competition to European advantage was the expansion in maritime transport, which brought Syria's preindustrial economic system into a close encounter with European innovation. The use of steam navigation in the eastern Mediterranean by the Austrians and the French in the 1850s (it was first used by the British in 1835), who replaced the British as Syria's principal European trade partners, flooded the country with less expensive cotton goods from European factories. The construction from 1859 to 1863 of a carriage route from Beirut to Damascus by the French stimulated the rapid growth of foreign trade and rendered the country even more closely dependent upon the European economy. A small group of merchants, who acted as European trade agents, benefited immensely, while the craftsmen whose source of livelihood was ruined became dependent on European production.[10] This dependence made Syria's economy so vulnerable to fluctuations in the European economy that a French financial crisis in 1857–58 beset Syrian businesses, causing numerous bankruptcies, and it was further aggravated by two years of poor of harvests.[11]

There was also a change in the balance of social and cultural power within the heterogeneous population of Syria. In the middle of the nineteenth century, the population of the provinces of Aleppo, Damascus, and Sidon—commonly known as Syria and Palestine—was about 1.5 million. More than 1 million were Muslims. Most were Arab Sunnis, but among them there were also substantial numbers of non-Sunni Arabs (Alawis, Druzes, and Mutawalis) and non-Arab Sunnis (Kurds and Turkomans). The second largest group was about half a million Christians (including some two hundred thousand Maronites in Lebanon). The number of

Jews in Syria and Palestine was only about twenty-five thousand.[12] Not only did social change bring considerable wealth to these religious minorities, but also the Tanzimat (the series of Ottoman reforms instituted between 1837 and 1876) expanded their religious and cultural freedoms. In particular, such reforms as the Hatt-i Sherif (Noble Rescript) of Gülhane in 1839, which recognized the right to life, property, and honor and the equality of all religious groups before the law, the *Hatt-i Humayun* (Imperial Rescript) in 1856, which guaranteed the right of non-Muslims to serve in the army, and a new civil code, the Mejelle, issued in 1870, changed the very concept of Ottoman society and challenged the notion of Muslim supremacy.[13]

The outbreak of violence against religious minorities in Damascus in 1860 resulted from aggravated social tensions brought about by such changes as the increasing European influence in the city, the enrichment of the Jews and Christians who acted as agents of European commercial interests, the threat to the interests of the ulama, and a general economic decline that started with the Egyptian occupation of Syria (1831–41).[14] It was also fueled by the ulama, who had resented the Tanzimat and other reforms that curtailed their social privileges. "The mobs certainly consisted of many unemployed Muslim artisans, especially textile workers, out of work owing to the displacement of their crafts by European man-ufactured goods, who vented their anger on the more prosperous local Christian community, popularly identified with European interests."[15] The crisis, however, was the only major upheaval in post-1860s Syria in which the religious element played a violent part. From this period until the consolidation of the Ba'ath regime in the early 1960s, political movements in Syria were expressed predominantly in secular rather than religious terms.

In the aftermath of the 1860 crisis, the process of change accelerated. The Syrian economy continued to develop as a result of European investments in sericulture, the construction of the Beirut seaport and of railways, and commercial and bank-ing businesses, while the Ottoman administration, despite its inherent imperfec-tions, became more regular and efficient. The revival of trade within the area of Islamic civilization, demographic change that favored modernization, and security maintained and even increased the need for urban craft and agricultural produc-tion.[16] These developments also brought about changes in class relations. The decline of the role of Syrian merchants in international trade and the development of a profitable cash crop economy prompted the merchants to invest in land. Further, the Ottomans' land code of 1858, which was devised to ensure the occu-piers stability of holding and thus to provide a basis for increased tax revenues, con-tributed to the making of a landowning class in Syria. As a result, the tripartite power structure in Syria that consisted of scholar-landowner families of the ulama and *ashraf* (claimants of descent from the Prophet), the *aghawat* (singular *agha,* an

Ottoman title meaning "chief" [of the military]) of the local garrisons, and tax farmers and merchants merged and was transformed by the turn of the century into a comparatively cohesive landed bureaucratic class as a provincial aristocracy of service.[17] The second part of the nineteenth century also witnessed the rise of the Christian commercial bourgeoisie.[18] Parallel with these sociopolitical changes was a change in culture and cultural hierarchy. The ulama's control of culture loosened as the missionaries' schools were opened, changes were made to the Islamic judicial systems that resulted in the emergence of civil and mixed courts, and the process of the diffusion of modern European ideologies into Syrian territories accelerated. For the development of modern ideas in Syria, the crisis of 1860, according to Antonius, "deserves to be regarded . . . as the decisive event of the nineteenth century. It awakened men's minds to the horrors of their moral stagnation and rekindled the zeal of those who saw that at the root of the country's tribulations was the sectarian hatred that thrives on ignorance. It led to a renewal of activity in the establishment of schools and to an intensification of effort in favour of breaking down barriers of obscurantism."[19]

Determinants of Arab Nationalism

How did these changes contribute to the rise of Arabism as a significant cultural and political movement? Why did Syrian intellectual leaders identify themselves as Arab, an identity that became increasingly defined in contradistinction to Turkish? What were the political and cultural processes that gave legitimacy to the notion of Arabism as the core organizing principle of the Arab community in Syria? Who was the agent of this distinctly Arab self-reassertion in the twentieth century? One thing seems clear: the Ottomans' reforms (1839–76), by changing the traditional Islamic principle of the empire, set the stage for the rise of Arabism. By the time Sultan Abdülhamid (1876–1909) decided, after he had initially promoted the first Ottoman constitution, to halt the process of change under the banner of pan-Islamism, the force of social transformation was too strong to be contained by a ruling despot. Different groups and social classes, most notably a new class of Arab entrepreneurs and religious minorities, had already stepped into the limelight, which resulted in the emergence of a dynamic, pluralistic cultural environment. As historians have noted, foreign cultural and economic influences had penetrated most of the region. There was a striking expansion of state, missionary, and private education along the coast of Syria.[20] In Beirut province (*wilayat*), the number of state schools alone rose from 153 in 1886 to 359 in 1914, a growth rate faster than that of the population. Different cities and newspapers also played a role in promoting Arabism: *al-Muqtabas* was published in Damascus and *al-Mufid* (the organ of the Arab nationalist secret society al-Jam'iyya al-arabiyya al-fatat) in Beirut, and Palestine was a source of Arab awakening against Zionists' expansionism. Among other cities that played a role in the Arabist movement were Istanbul, where local struggles were quite often resolved in terms of national politics in Majles al-mab'uthan (Chamber of Deputies), the lower chamber of the Ottoman parliament, and Cairo, home to a large Syrian community and the headquarters of the influential Hizb al-lamarkaziyya al-idariyya al-uthmani (Ottoman Administrative Decentralization Party). Visiting scholars from Egypt had a great impact on Syria. Abduh, for example, taught Shakib Arslan and Sheikh Ahmad ʿAbbass al-Azhari, founder of Beirut's influential Ottoman Islamic College, which became the train-ing ground for a whole generation of prewar Beirut Arabists.[21] All these factors, however, although they may explain the emergence of a cultural renaissance in Syria, cannot explain why this renaissance took the Arabist form.

Nor can we attribute the rise of Arabism to the interests of the emergent mer-chant and landowning classes and religious minorities, even though they consti-tuted major social forces demanding cultural change and political inclusion. The indigenous merchants commonly mistreated by the system of unequal taxation installed by the Ottoman's capitulation treaties with the Europeans might have used Arabism as a conceptual vehicle to express their localized and particularistic grievances in general and nationalist terms. Here we may see a parallel with Iranian merchants in the second half of the nineteenth century, whose economic interests constituted the prime motivating force underpinning their oppositional nationalis-tic activities. In addition, being involved in trade with Europe, Syrian merchants adopted a liberal and nationalist view of politics.[22] Their support for Arabism, how-ever, remained inconclusive. Ernest Dawn's analysis of the occupational and family backgrounds of a sample of Arab nationalists and Ottomanists indicated that both groups were predominantly from the Syrian upper class—landowners and mer-chants. He found that the principle distinction between the Arabists and the Ottomanists was the holding of state office.[23] He concluded that "in Syria, those members of the Arab elite who had a vested interest in the Ottoman state were Ottomanists. Those who were without such a stake were Arabists. Thus was a tra-ditional intra-elite conflict defined in terms of a new ideology."[24] This conclusion is also supported by Philip Khoury's analysis of the politics of urban notables in Damascus.[25] All that can be said about the significance of class politics in shaping ideology is that liberal Arabism in Syria and liberal nationalism in Egypt and Iran (see chapter 8) were appropriated by economically dominant classes to further their interests. Even then, far from providing a dynamic and vitality to this ideology, the close identification of liberal politics with these classes tended to undermine its credibility, contributing to its demise and the rise of various supranational ideolo-gies (such as militant Arab nationalism and Islamic fundamentalism). Generally, it would be hard to argue that class politics directly shaped the ideas of such harbin-gers of Syrian liberal Arabism as al-Bustani or al-Kawakibi.

Nevertheless, as in other cases, factional conflicts and interelite competitions can be said to have contributed to the rise of Arabism not only by producing the requisite political space for the growth of this discourse, but also by providing an alternative option for the section of the Syrian dominant classes who were excluded from gaining access to the high-ranking positions in the state's bureaucracy. This still does not mean that Arabism was a reflection of intraclass rivalries for political power. There had always been competitions among Syrian notables for closer access to the ruling elite or bureaucratic positions, and those who had temporarily or permanently fallen out of favor had not resorted to Arabism as an oppositional ideology. Thus, the historical processes that gave credibility to Arabism as a viable option to be used by the members of the Syrian economic elite must be located somewhere outside the dynamic of class action or interelite competition. Besides, economic expansions, the rise of indigenous classes, a cultural renaissance, and interelite rivalries were also present in Egypt in the same general period. Yet Egypt gave rise to territorial nationalism, and Syria to Arabism and, later, Arab nationalism. Some other historical factors must have been present in Syrian and absent in Egypt (and vice versa) that explain the considerable difference between these two nationalist discourses.

From Ottomanism to Abdülhamid's Pan-Islamism and Then to Turkish Nationalism

The crucial factor that explains the contrast between Syrian and Egyptian nationalism rests in the changing discourses of the Ottomans and their effects on Syria. Egypt was culturally too distant from Istanbul and too closely involved with Europe to be affected by what the Ottomans had said and done. Serious Muslim scholars gave little credence to the claim that Ottoman sovereignty was bestowed by God to ensure the virtue of the Muslim community. This sovereignty was, rather, utilitarian, a political power necessary to ensure the protection of social order. Insofar as the sultan was able to defend the abode of Islam and upheld the shari'a, he was a legitimate sovereign, although he did not possess all the necessary credentials. His Islamic rule bound together disparate Muslim elements of the empire, and his political domination was justified in terms of the exigencies of maintaining and defending the umma. And the empire as a whole was organized into different religious communities (*millets*) such as Greek, Armenian, and Jewish millets, but there was no millet based on language or ethnicity like Turkish, Arab, or Kurdish.[26]

Turkish was the official language of administration and government, and the majority of the Turks never learned Arabic. They were not, however, in a position of cultural domination in Syria. The Arabs had considerable cultural influence on the Turks. Not only had numerous Arabic words found their way into the Turkish language, but also prayers and readings from the Quran in the mosques of Constantinople and other Turkish towns were always in Arabic.[27] There was thus little interest on the part of the Arabs in establishing an independent state of their own. "Leading Muslims," said Zeine N. Zeine, "as well as the vast majority of the inhabitants of the Arab Near East, remained loyal to the Ottoman Government. Thus, the over-worked phrase 'Arab Awakening' was originally an awakening to the abuses, the corruption and the despotism of the Turkish regime and a desire to reform it, i.e., to put an end to misgovernment, to demand for the Arab equal rights with the Turks and a greater measure of political freedom and civil liberty. The alternative of establishing an independent sovereign Arab State as a result of separation from or extinction of the Ottoman Empire did not occur to the vast majority of the Muslims either as desirable or as possible."[28]

This is not to argue that the Arabs were unaware of themselves or of the Turks, who appeared negatively in the Arab's perception as a more or less constant and homogeneous ethnic group.[29] "But in the nineteenth century," said Zeine, "there was as yet no 'Arab Question' in international politics. Indeed, the word 'Arab' itself as a designation for the inhabitants of the Arab provinces of the Ottoman Empire rarely occurred in the books and documents of the period. It was reserved mainly for the Bedouins of the desert and for all the non-town dwellers in the Near East. The general terms 'Muslim' and 'Christian' were used to describe the two principal classes of inhabitants in this area."[30] And the religious bond connecting Syria to the Turks overrode any ethnic awareness.

The Tanzimat changed the relations between the Ottomans and their diverse subject population. One of the most important cultural manifestations of this change was the gradual transformation of the ideology of the empire from Islamic universalism to a loosely defined and contentious notion of Ottomanism. This new discursive framework was intended to reconstitute the empire in terms of the equality between Muslim and non-Muslim subjects, individual liberty and the security of personal property, and the elimination of the sultan's arbitrary rule while at the same time attempted to preserving the empire's Islamic identity. Ottomanism had considerable appeal to diverse intellectual leaders within the empire. Even Christian Arabs like Adib Ishaq (1856–1885), Ibrahim al-Yaziji (1847–1906), Ahmad Faris al-Shidyaq (1801–87), and Butrus al-Bustani defended Eastern civilization in terms of Islamic greatness and concentrated their efforts on Ottoman reform rather than on Arab separatism.[31] Ottomanism was effectively undermined by Sultan Abdülhamid's pan-Islamism. His overthrow by the CUP (formed in 1907), however, did not produce a decentralized constitutional system as was understood and demanded by the non-Turkish Ottomanists. To preserve the unity of the fragile empire, the CUP increasingly moved toward authoritarianism and governmental centralization, and by 1913 the CUP had firmly established its leadership in the form of a virtual military dictatorship under Enver Pasha, Cemal Pasha, and Talaat Pasha.

The decline of Islamism paralleled the rise of Turkish nationalism in the late nineteenth century, and by the turn of the twentieth century, the press was glorifying Anatolia as the homeland of the Turks, and peasants as the backbone of a Turkish nation. Such literary clubs as the Turkish Homeland Society and Turkish Hearth propagated Turkish ideas and nationality. These clubs waged a campaign to simplify the Turkish language, making it more accessible to the public.[32] As a leading spokesperson of Turkish nationalism, Ziya Gökalp abandoned both Islam and Ottomanism as the basis of the empire. Although he was ostensibly concerned with education, Gökalp's main objective was to promote Turkish nationalism. He argued that educators were mistaken in taking psychology as their guide and considering the individual as the object of education. Instead, he took his lead from sociology, claiming that the nation should be the educational object. Education should be national in the sense that it stressed not an individualistic approach to various personality and academic problems, but, rather, a collectivist inculcation of the particular Turkish national culture in which "the individual becomes a genuine personality only as he becomes a genuine representative of his culture."[33]

This process was accelerated by the Young Turk revolution of 1908. While promising equality of all Ottoman subjects before the law, the new Ottoman leaders were not able to carry out this promise.[34] Although the CUP members were not at the outset nationalist and their chief objective was to maintain the integrity of the empire, they realized that the Turks were the only element that was not opposed to centralization. They fell back on their Turkish nationality and came to think of Turkification as the means of achieving their objectives.[35] As a result, according to Zeine, "the newly born Turkish nationalism of a most chauvinistic type asserted itself and clashed with the Arabs' pride in their race, religion and language. One can rightly say that the seeds of an Arab separatist movement began to sprout from the soil of Turkish nationalism from 1909 onward. This expression of Turkish nationalism has been called 'Pan-Turanianism'—a supernational propaganda for a rapprochement between all the Turkish-speaking peoples, on the same lines as Pan-Slavism."[36] A distinctly Arab identity gained meaning to the Syrian politicians and intellectuals as the religious bond between Syrians and the Turks seriously eroded and as the Turkish elite began to stress their Turkish identity and reorganize the empire on national chauvinistic principles that were too localized and narrow to transcend its ethnic diversity in a universalistic direction.

Syrian Nationalist Discourse

The changes in the ideology of the Ottomans from Islamic universalism to Ottomanism in the Tanzimat period, to Abdülhamid's pan-Islamic despotism, and finally to Turkish nationalism from 1909 on appeared to have created parallel changes in the nationalist discourse of Syrian intellectual leaders. The imposition of the French mandate following the short-lived Faisal kingship was the next important factor that shaped the orientation of the nationalist discourse. Our contention is that since the Ottomans and the French constituted two successive, rather than simultaneous, regimes of power and symbols, the political expression of Syrian political thinkers, in contrast to that of their Egyptian counterparts, did not display synchronically liberalism and nationalism. The shift in their political thought from preoccupation with individual freedom and other liberal issues to militant pan-Arab nationalism was associated with changes in the nature and the discourse of power.

The rise of Ottomanism for Syrian Christian intellectuals, who had obtained knowledge of Europe (through travel, missionaries, or the American University of Beirut), was a welcome opportunity to promote liberalism, at the center of which was their long-yearned-for idea of equality with Muslims. The early and the most sophisticated spokesperson of this trend was Butrus al-Bustani. He was for the reinvigoration and modernization of the Arabic language, the equality of all before the law, the separation of the religious and secular realms, and respect and love of one's country; he used the Prophet's statement "hubb al-watan min al-iman" (love of country is an article of faith) as the motto of his most famous periodical. He wrote as an Ottoman subject, and in his writing there was no hint that he wished to break away from loyalty to the sultan. His nationalism was a territorial one. He appealed to those who lived in Syria, his watan, who shared its land, customs, and language. For him, religious fanaticism was a major obstacle to Syria's development. He emphasized that all Syrians should recognize the significance of national unity and cooperate with one another on the basis of equality. For him, all religions were the same in essence, and Eastern and Western people shared the same human nature, descended from the same parent, and worshipped the same God.[37]

Other authors like Ibrahim al-Yaziji, the son of Nasif al-Yaziji, a prominent figure in the revival of classical Arabic literature, spoke in his poems of Arab pride and the glory of Arabic literature, and he incited the Arabs to insurgence. He argued that the Arabs declined after the Turks dominated them and reduced learning to religious sciences and religion to bigotry.[38] The historical novels of Jurji Zaydan also created a romantic image of past Arab history. In addition to language, the report of the glory of ancient Syria published in 1861 by one of the earliest of Arabic journalists, Khalil al-Khuri, in a little book entitled *Kharabat Suriyya* (*The Ruins of Syria*) led to the wide use of the name "Syria" with undertones of pride and self-identification, something not too different from what the discovery of Pharaonic Egypt contributed to Egyptian nationalism.[39]

The idea of Syrian independence was first developed by a few young Arab Christians, educated in the Syrian Protestant College. In 1875 (two years before the accession of Abdülhamid), these individuals formed a secret society. They became even more radicalized in reaction to Abdülhamid's rise to power. His Islamism and revival of the caliphate ran contrary to what former Christian intellectuals were preaching about religious tolerance and the equality of all Ottoman subjects before the law. Naturally, young Christians had little choice but to take a more radical approach toward Turkish rule in Syria. As early as 1880, an anonymous placard in Arabic appeared in the streets of Beirut, Damascus, Tripoli, and Saida, denouncing the evils of Turkish misgovernment and exhorting the population to overthrow it. The placard appealed to the Arabs, to their patriotism (*wataniyyah*) and "glorious past," urging them to rise and expel the Turks from their lands and emancipate themselves from Turkish despotism.[40]

While Christian intellectuals equated Arabism with secularism and religious equality, Muslim intellectuals could not totally divorce it from religion. Islam was the Arab contribution to history—the Prophet of Islam was an Arab, the Quran was in Arabic, and the glorious accomplishments of the Islamic movement in the early period were under Arab leadership.[41] Further, the nationalism of Christian intellectuals was not to the liking of Muslim Arabs. They were in fact outraged "at the spectacle of Christians assuming the air of masters of Arab learning. Attacks on the pretensions of Yaziji and other Christian literary men were popular."[42] Dawn even claims that the Arabism of Muslim intellectuals was rooted in Islamic modernism.[43] The modernists' emphasis on the glory of Islam under the Rashidun caliphs and on the Quran and the Arabic language as the only means to understand it and their belief that the degeneration of the basis of the Islamic polity was a result of the rise of dynastic rules implied that an Islamic political system that was rooted more firmly in the Arabic tradition, language, and leadership would overcome the weakness of the Ottomans' Islamism. It could also be argued that the Ottomans' decline had revealed their incapacity to defend the land of Islam, undermined the legitimacy of the Turkish claim to the caliphate, and in certain Arabic quarter highlighted the difference between the Ottomans' Islamic credentials and the basis of sovereignty in Islam.[44]

Nevertheless, Arabism cannot be traced to Islamic modernism or to the Ottoman decline. Fearing that the breakdown of the empire would be equal to the total domination of Islamic countries by European powers, a modernist like Abduh in the final analysis favored Ottomanism.[45] And the decline of Ottoman power gave an impetus to the pan-Islamic movement, not Arabism. We therefore contend that the nationalism of Muslim Arabs, like that of their Christian counterparts, was produced in oppositional relationship to the Ottomans' ideology of domination. Reflecting this process were the antidespotic and liberal ideas espoused by Abdul Rahman al-Kawakibi in *Taba'yi al-Istibdad wa Masari' al-Isti'bad* (*The Attributes of Tyranny and the Defects of Oppression*) and *Umm al-Qura* (*The Mother of Cities*). Like other thinkers, al-Kawakibi was heavily influenced by nineteenth-century European writings, such as the works of Charles Fourier, Rousseau's *Social Contract,* Blunt's *Future of Islam,* and, most of all, Vittorio Alfieri's *Della Tirannide.*[46] There were also political influences on the writings of both al-Kawakibi and Azoury. Khedive Abbas Hilmi of Egypt, having his own ambition of becoming the caliph, paid al-Kawakibi a monthly stipend of fifty pounds. Even *Umm al-Qura* might have been a piece of khedivial propaganda.[47]

Certainly, in formulating ideas, thinkers like al-Kawakibi drew from diverse cultural sources and sought support from politically weighty individuals or groups. Both are necessary—one provides the conceptual scaffolding to frame ideas and the other the requisite social resources that make the reproduction and dissemination of ideas possible. Nevertheless, al-Kawakibi's selection of the very subject of tyranny, emphasis on how tyranny would retard social development and individual character, and exhortation to secede from the Ottomans and establish an Arab state—all became significant and meaningful, as it were, within the context of and in opposition to Abdülhamid's despotic rule, even though he ostensibly indicated that he was not attacking a particular tyranny but pointing to the distemper of the East and its origin.[48] He believed that Islam had declined because of the obscurantism of the ulama, passive taqlid, and the denial of the rights of reason—all promoted by despotic rulers. In this regard, there is not much difference between him and other modernists like al-Afghani and Abduh. Al-Kawakibi's distinctive contribution was his greater emphasis on the attributes of tyranny and the corruptive influence of oppression on not only religion but the entire society as well.[49]

He considered tyranny the willful and arbitrary conduct of public affairs without the fear of retribution. In his view, the tyrant would keep people ignorant, fear science and its products (but would not fear the theological sciences), promote false honors, facilitate the accumulation of wealth, turn individuals into hypocrites who falsely profess virtue and religion, shield villains from criticism and exposure, and destroy individual will power. Tyrannical rule would thus corrupt every class, type of society, and individual. The nation, in his view, was also to be blamed for tyranny. If the majority of its people did not feel the pains of tyranny, they did not deserve to be free. On the method of fighting tyranny, al-Kawakibi suggested peaceful means. Tyranny was not to be fought with violence, but slowly and with gentleness. Before people began fighting tyranny, they must know what was to replace it.[50] Al-Kawakibi suggested reforming the law, creating a modern and unified system of law by the use of ijtihad, and proper religious education. He also suggested that something else was necessary as well—"a shift in the balance of power inside the *umma,* from the Turks back to the Arabs."[51] With this, in Sylvia Haim's interpretation, al-Kawakibi became the first true intellectual precursor of modern pan-Arabism. His political views, however, were not traditionalist, for by launch-

ing the idea of a merely spiritual caliphate he took the first step toward a purely secular politics. "For all his preoccupation with the state of Islam al-Kawakibi, once
he introduced the idea of a spiritual caliph, was led to consider politics as an
autonomous activity divorced from divine prescription, and fully subject to the will
of men. Such an idea is an essential prerequisite of nationalism."[52] The Christian
Arab Najib Azoury (circa 1873–1916) also suggested that Muslim power be transferred from the Turks to the Arabs.[53] He believed in a single Arab nation in which
Christians and Muslims would be treated equally. An independent Arab state, in
his view, should be a constitutional and liberal sultanate with an Arab Muslim sultan. In the Hijaz, he argued for a temporal kingdom for an Arab caliph.[54]

As long as Abdülhamid remained in power, the constitutional movement in the
Ottoman dominion remained united. With his overthrow, the movement split up
between the Turkish nationalists, who supported a centralized system, and the liberals, who favored administrative decentralization. (There were also conservative
elements among the Arabs who disapproved of the Ottomans' reforms.) The Young
Turk revolution of 1908 and the national chauvinistic policies pursued by the CUP
resulted in the solidification of Arab nationalism. The most conservative trend
within this movement was that of the Arab revolt. The revolt itself was not initially
ideological. It was set in motion by the dynamics of the contention for power
among the house of Sharif Hussein (1853–1931, the last of the Hashemite Sharifians
that ruled over Mecca, Medina, and the Hijaz in unbroken succession from 1201 to
1925; he also launched the great Arab revolt in June 1916 against the Ottoman
army), the CUP leadership, and local contenders.[55]

One of the spokespeople of the Arab revolt, Amir Abdullah, Sharif Hussein's son,
had a religious conception of Arab nationalism. Despite their exceptional qualities,
wrote Abdullah in his memoirs, "the Arabs, by virtue of the geography, extreme heat,
and aridity of their land, had no inclination to form powerful governments to put their
affairs in order; rather, for these reasons, their inclination was to live scattered and dis-
united, engaging in battles and raids, with irreligiousness, idolatry, and the errors of
the *Jahiliya*."[56] Arabs had gained when the religion of Islam arrived. "Accordingly and
as a result of their existence as a single element having a single tongue, they were unified, converted to a single faith, and turned in a single direction."[57] In Dawn's assessment of Abdullah's view, "the requirements of Arabism are fulfilled by membership in
an Islamic state which enforces the Koran and the sunnah, rather than by possessing a
separate independent Arab state.[58] For Abdullah, the Ottomans' departure from Islam,
the reforms of the Tanzimat, and the orientation toward Western form were the factors, underpinning the Arab revolt. According to Abdullah,

In the last century and earlier, there occurred some of the changes which
shook this unifying bond between the Arabs and the non-Arabs. The decree of

the *tanzimat* issued in the time of Sultan Mahmud II was the first step in the revolt against the Arab teachings handed down from their Koran and the sunnah of their Prophet in favour of the alien Western form which its devotees themselves did not understand. Then there were reversals, contradictions, falterings in progress, and dilatoriness in action. Among these were the sudden change in the form of the army and administration, the extermination of the Janissary corps and the creation of the troops called the "New Army."[59]

Syrians did not play a prominent role in the Arab revolt, and their contribution (as well as the Iraqis') to the Hashemite Arab Army consisted of Arab Ottoman officers and men who were taken prisoner by the British or Arab forces.[60] King Faisal, during his brief rule of Syria, expressed only a rudimentary theory of Arab nationalism. In a speech of May 1919, he rebutted the idea, which he attributed to Europeans, that the Arabs of the desert and those of the towns were two distinct groups. "We are one people," he said, "living in the region which is bounded by the sea to the east, the south, and the west, and by the Taurus Mountains to the north." He also declared that he was an Arab first and a Muslim second. "We are Arabs," he used to say, "before being Muslims, and Muhammad is an Arab before being a prophet." He also said, in a speech in Aleppo in June, 1919: "there is neither minority nor majority among us, nothing to divide us. We are one body; we were Arabs even before the time of Moses, Muhammad, Jesus, and Abraham."[61]

The French Mandate and the Rise of Pan-Arab Nationalism

The outlooks of Syrian political thinkers before World War I were heterogeneous and eclectic. The Christian nationalist trend displayed secularism, stressed the idea of religious equality, and regarded the Arabic language and territory as the most essential components of the Syrian nation. The Muslim trend, on the other hand, was multifaceted. The people leading the Arab revolt were promoting Islamic Arab nationalism, while the modernists called for religious and political reforms in the direction of qualified secularism and liberalism. During the two decades of French rule (1920–45), however, a major shift occurred in the discourse of Syrian political ideologues away from liberalism and criticisms of tyranny and toward the glorification of the Arab nation and Arab land. Its Islamic component weakened as the views of Muslim and Christian thinkers merged into a somewhat unifying nationalist discourse in which the notion of pan-Arabism and the emancipation of the Arab land overrode other considerations, such as the idea of individual liberty, the evils of tyranny, parliamentary democracy, and constitutionalism.

The liberal-nationalist movement was led by the urban notables—individuals drawn from about fifty families in Aleppo, Damascus, Hama, and Homs. These families consisted of those who had possessed wealth for a number of generations and those who had gained it, largely in industry, since World War I. They had extensive holdings in the agricultural and industrial sectors.[62] As in the Ottoman period, political power was city based and rested on a personal support system. Liberal constitutionalism was the framework in terms of which the deputies, the politicians, the urban notables, and men of standing expressed their political opposition to French rule and demanded independence. Nevertheless, as these politicians succeeded in leading the independence movement, the liberal-nationalist discourse gradually lost credibility in the works of the leading Syrian political thinkers during the same period. Instead, pan-Arab nationalism rose to become the dominant, all-encompassing political discourse that informed the country's political activists. Why? While class polarization and the deterioration of economic conditions might have contributed to the decline of liberal politics, changes in the dominant regimes of signification were the factors that prompted the intellectual leaders to consider pan-Arab nationalism as the appropriate model of politics for the Arab people.

The French contributed to the concentration of landed properties by encouraging the private appropriation of land especially by those who collaborated with the mandate. The State and waqf lands were sold to large landowners, concession companies, and tribal chiefs. Moreover, the landlords who were the principal recipients of loans from state agricultural banks simply relent the money to the fellahin at much higher interest rates. Small and landless peasants had to turn to moneylenders, merchants, and landlords, who charged exorbitant rates, which in periods of bad harvests could reach 150 percent.[63] The result was a high concentration of landed property. Until 1958, large estates, which covered 45 percent of the irrigated area and 30 percent of the rain-fed land, were held by only 2.5 percent of the total number of landowners. About two-thirds of the large estates were owned by absentee landlords. For the most part, they were merchants who had invested their earnings from trade in agricultural land. About 70 percent of the rural population did not own any land at all but subsisted either as sharecroppers or laborers.[64] Landowners and tribal chiefs consistently formed the largest group of Syrian deputies in the 1919–59 period. Their numerical superiority precluded legislation designed to modify the existing economic inequality, and it thus explains the steadily growing gap between the government and the needs and desires of the masses.[65]

Further, rapid population growth, social dislocation due to the collapse of the traditional industries, and change in the intellectual climate undermined the ability of the personal patronage system of the urban notables to accommodate the needs of the population. By the late 1930s, this inability became evident, as an increasing number of politically active individuals sought services and support outside the old patronage system and moved toward such new social and cultural institutions as secondary schools, universities, and youth organization as well as modern districts where these institutions were located.[66] This process, on the one hand, led to a decline in the popularity of the urban notables. On the other hand, it gave rise among aspiring middle-class activists to the notion that democratic parliamentary politics was nothing but a tool of a small group of wealthy individuals.

In the absence of comparative figures, it is hard to assess the difference in class polarization between the late nineteenth century and the post–World War I period. As far as the production of ideas is concerned, the shift in Syrian political discourse away from liberal Arabism to pan-Arab nationalism may be due to the changes in the nature of the ideological targets faced by Syrian political thinkers. The collapse of the Ottoman Empire had removed many issues such as Turkification, the centralization of power, the sultan's arbitrary rule, and the evils of despotism from the intellectual agenda of these thinkers. There was no arbitrariness of the sultan to inspire demands for constitutional rule, no Turkification to inspire glorification of the Arabic language, and no attempt at centralization to inspire agitation for a federated system.

Instead, there was the French mandate, which was illegitimate from the start.[67] France's situation in Syria was not even like that of Britain in Egypt. Although the British had established their protectorate over Egypt by force, they were able to save Egypt from financial insolvency, promote freedom of the press, and patronize modern culture. In the Syrian nationalist perception, on the other hand, French rule had ruined Syria. The nationalists had every reason to doubt the genuineness of France's civilizational mission in their homeland. Reinforcing their misgivings about its intention were France's continued territorial concessions—first, it renounced all Syria's claims on Palestine and Transjordan in the Sykes-Picot Agreement in 1916, then gave up the Wilayat of Mosul to British Iraq, next ceded to Turkey the richest region of northern Syria, Cilicia, in 1921, and, finally, gave to Turkey the Sanjaq of Alexandretta in 1937.[68] The French were also suspect because of their historical role as the protector of the Christians living under the Ottomans, a suspicion that was even more intensified when they disregarded Syrian religious sensibility and pursued policies favoring religious minorities that inflamed traditional sectarian conflict.[69]

In the aftermath of the 1925–27 revolt the French realized the necessity of making concessions to the nationalists, and the nationalists realized the prudence of dropping the tactic of armed confrontation. The French political role in the country, however, was far from aiding Syrians to achieve political maturity. The French first allowed the promulgation of a constitution. In 1928, the nationalists drafted a constitution based on a parliamentary republic and universal suffrage, equality between citizens of all sects, and freedom of religion. It promised to provide specific representation of the religious minorities in the chamber. The constitution also—written from the nationalist perspective, disregarding the actual course of Syrian history since 1918 and the reality of the mandate—declared Syria to include Transjordan, Palestine, and Lebanon as one and indivisible. It gave to the Syrian government the power to organize the armed forces, and to the president the power to conclude treaties, grant pardons, appoint ambassadors, and proclaim martial law.[70] France rejected the constitution, however. It also failed to ratify the 1936 treaty that was signed by the National Bloc and the French Popular Front government.[71]

Jamil Mardam Bey, one of the spokespeople of the liberal politicians, stated in 1939 that France's failure to maintain Syria's territorial integrity was the major cause of the decline of its influence: "The maintenance of French influence in Syria and its intellectual and economic supremacy are not irreconcilable with the aspirations of the Syrian nation. If France had succeeded in retaining Syria's natural borders, a Syrian federation might have been conceivable. Filled with unlimited confidence in French policies, our country would willingly have lent all its resources and means to the services of a generous and allied power. Unfortunately the Syria entrusted to France, which France should have guided towards the day when it could govern itself alone, has been relentlessly torn apart."[72]

In the Syrian perception, the French, imbued with a colonizing spirit, had shown no interest in improving the country's economic conditions or in maintaining its territorial integrity. Thus, the mandatory idea that Syrians ought to emulate the French model of parliamentary republic to govern themselves was losing appeal. Already the left-leaning Syrian nationalists were expressing their opposition to the ill-fated 1936 treaty that had been signed by the National Bloc and the French Popular Front. And the leadership of the Bloc, anxious to secure independence from the French, intentionally avoided pan-Arabism.[73] With the decline of liberalism, the pan-Arabist element in the nationalist discourse in Syria gained centrality.

Dawn's analysis of the history textbooks that were designed for use in the schools of Palestine, Syria, and Iraq provides the parameters of pan-Arab nationalism. The earliest was *Tarikh Filastin,* by Umar Salih al-Barghuthi and Khalil Tuta (Totah). Next appeared an elementary school text by Muhammad 'Izzat Darwaza, *Mukhtasar Tarikh al-Arab wa-al-Islam.* Darwaza followed this with two other elementary school textbooks: *Durus al-Tarikh al-Mutawassit wa-al-Hadith* and *Durus al-Tarikh al-Qadim.* By the end of the 1920s, a more or less standard formulation of the Arab self-view had appeared and received comprehensive statement in a textbook for intermediate schools, *Tarikh al-Umma al-'Arabiyya,* by Darwish al-Miqdadi.[74]

These texts portrayed the Arab homeland as a natural geographical unit, consisting of the "Arab Island"—a living body of which "the head" was the Fertile Crescent, "the heart" central Arabia, and "the extremities" the Arabian coastlands from the Gulf of Aqaba to "the Gulf of Basra." This "Island" was "the cradle of the Arabs and their fortress." The ancient pre-Islamic Arabs were only a small part of the glorious history of the Arab, and Arabic was the most advanced among the ancient Semitic languages. Semito-Arab history was divided into two periods of greatness. One was the ancient Semitic and the other Islamic, each followed by periods of decline in which aliens dominated the Arabs. Miqdadi introduced the concept of the jahiliyya to characterize present conditions. In both ages, imperialism had reduced the Arab nation to subjugation, humiliation, and abasement. The identity of the contemporary Arab predicament with the jahiliyya gained a literary significance in a play by Miqdadi, which he gave the title *Between Two Jahiliyya*. The ancient Arabs had become rich and famous from their share in international commerce. The advance of Persian and Romano-Byzantine imperialists, who had seized the Fertile Crescent and southern Arabia in order to control the trade routes, had radically changed this happy situation. The Arabs' dangerous enemy had been one: the Aryans—that is, the Persians in the east and the Greeks, Romans, and Franks in the west.[75] In the case of two cultural lenders, the Persians and the West, these texts unanimously believed that borrowing from them had been nearly fatal. The Persians were commonly portrayed as having been filled with hatred of the Arabs and a fanatical desire for revenge for the loss of their sovereignty and glory.[76]

All Arabs, including the Bedouins, had noble qualities. Women enjoyed equality with men. Arabs loved freedom and equality. They possessed "great excitability, intensity of sensation, and sharpness of intellect." The great success of the Arabs after the coming of Islam had been aided by their natural qualities.[77] Islam had been brought the Arab nation to greatness, but it had not eradicated the Arabs' principal defect, which was their great virtue carried to excess—that is, individualism, egoism, and tribal asabiyya. The Persians, however, were blamed because under their influence the position of women, the family, and Arab culture and society had been corrupted.[78]

When Miqdadi wrote his textbook, the condition of the masses and class relationships had been receiving attention from Arab intellectuals for some time. Miqdadi explicitly stressed proletarian opposition to the capitalist collaborators with foreign imperialism in the Hijaz. He depicted the Prophet Muhammad as a proletarian revolutionary. Under present conditions, the second jahiliyya, false religion was providing the means for the upper classes to exploit and utilize the populace. The rulers, the usurers, and the ulama were collaborating to extirpate religion and fetter the masses with superstition.[79]

In the thirties and forties, Syrian intellectual leaders also defended similar ideas. In their works, pan-Arab nationalism was based on the unity of language, the natural frontier of the Arab territories, and common history. While the Arabists of the earlier period, like Amir Abdullah, Rashid Rida, and Shakib Arsalan, in different ways suggested the unity of Islam and nationalism—an approach that was not congruent with the nationalism of Christian Arabs—from the thirties on, Islam was treated as only one of the Arabs' major contributions to history. Islam as the Arab national religion, the Arabic language, and the geographical area with its natural frontiers constituted the bases of Arab nationalism.[80] Similarly, the Lebanese Muslim Abdullah al-Alayili included in his *Dustur al-Arab al-Qaumi (The National Constitution of the Arabs)* the language as the essential pillar, the climate as the generator of a common temperament, the natural frontiers, and history. For him, religion was also a manifestation of the nation. In his view, religion was the sum of the spiritual and intellectual characteristics of a nation, which were based on "an organic response" to a particular environment.[81] All these expressions signify the turning of Arab nationalism in the direction of secularism, the notion of the organic unity of the Arabs, and portrayals of foreign forces as the key factor in Arab disunity and decline.

One of the most sophisticated spokespeople of pan-Arab nationalism was Sati' al-Husri (1880–1968). His life and work exemplify how changes in the social conditions of pre- and post–World War I Syria affected the process of ideological change from liberal Ottomanism to pan-Arab nationalism. This change signified the decline of the idea of individual liberty and democratic rule and the rise of the notion of the Arab nation and Arab land and the subordination, or even the sacrifice, of individual liberty to the nationalist aim.[82] Before World War I, al-Husri was a staunch defender of Ottomanism. He took issue with Gökalp, arguing that the Ottoman Empire could adopt Western values and technology without resorting to Turkish nationalism. He believed that administrative decentralization and regional autonomy were the most effective method of preserving and modernizing the empire. While rejecting language as a basis of nationalism, he stressed emotional identification with Ottoman territory as a motivating symbol for invigorating Ottomanist nationalism.[83] In short, Sati's political desires and demands were not all that different from those of Arab compatriots who fought against Abdülhamid's tyranny and for a constitutional government. Even after the outbreak of the war and the declaration of the Arab revolt, al-Husri remained at his post in Istanbul. When the war ended in Ottoman defeat, he adopted the cause of Arab nationalism and became one of its foremost advocates.[84]

The shift in al-Husri's political discourse was in a direction that resembled that of Gökalp. To be sure, he was influenced by the nationalist ideas coming from Europe. His approach to nationalism, like the approach of the Germans, was cultural and romantic. He strove to inspire the sentiments required to produce national unity. For him, as explained by William Cleveland, "patriotism (*al-wataniyyah*) is love of the fatherland (*al-watan*) and a feeling of inward commitment (*irtibat batin*) toward it; nationalism (*al-qaumiyyah*) is love of the nation (*al-ummah*) and a similar feeling of inward commitment."[85] For al-Husri, unity of language and history are the foundations for creating a nation and building nationalism. This is because unity in these two spheres leads to unity of feelings and inclinations, unity of sufferings and hopes, and unity of culture, thus making the people feel that they are the sons of one nation, distinguished from other nations."[86]

Al-Husri gives a secondary role to the idea of national will as a basis of government and nation. National will, in his view, is the result of a shared language and history, the result of national ties rather than an independent formative force in itself. To argue that the will of the masses as expressed in voting is determinative is to support a practice which fluctuates by habit and can be manipulated by propaganda; it is to support a practice which splits the nation from its natural groupings and causes it to resemble artificial parties. This is a further indication of al-Husri's concern for national unity at the expense of individual political freedom.[87]

Since all Arabs share the bond of unity through language and history and since this unity is a necessity for the progress and independence of the Arab people, only the followers of imperialism and regionalism are the enemy of this unity. Accordingly,

> There is left no room to doubt that the division of the Arab provinces into several states took place because of the bargaining and ambitions of the foreign states, and not according to the views and interests of the people of the countries. So, too, were the borders of these states determined by the wishes and agreements of the foreign powers, and not according to the natural demands of the situation or the requirements of indigenous interests. . . . Is it possible for us to consider, for example, the peoples of Syria as forming a true nation, different from the people of Iraq and Lebanon? Never, gentlemen. All that I have explained indicates clearly that the differences we now see between the people of these states are temporary and superficial. . . . We must always assert that the Syrians, Iraqis, Lebanese, Jordanians, Hejazis, and Yemenis all belong to one nation, the Arab nation.[88]

Solidarity and self-sacrifice are the means to realize the goal of Arab nations. Al-Husri even goes so far as to glorify military life as a valuable instrument in the service of the nation; it is a life of order and discipline, of sacrifice and altruism.[89] In his comment in support of conscription in 1928, al-Husri argued that

> He [the soldier] lives with a group of the sons of his fatherland who are from different towns and classes and who hold various beliefs and positions. He lives with them subject to a system in which they are all included without exception. He lives there, not with the intention of returning to his original personality or of being confined to his family and a life centered in his village. On the contrary, he works for a purpose which is loftier than all these, for a purpose which ensures the life of the fatherland and the welfare of the

nation. . . . Military life makes him feel clearly the existence of nation and fatherland. He learns true sacrifice of blood and self in the cause of the nation and the fatherland.[90]

For al-Husri, the idea of Arab nation gained significance above and beyond individual freedom, the undesirability of arbitrary behavior by the ruling elite, the significance of parliamentary democracy and constitutionalism—the issues which were central in the thinking of al-Kawakibi. His pan-Arab nationalist discourse consisted of three main elements: First, the idea of Arab unity and its consistency with Islamic unity. He argued that pan-Arabism neither contradicted nor was inimical to Islam. Second, and as a logical extension of his ambitious pan-Arabist project, he strongly argued that Egypt was part of the Arab nation. Finally, the most provocative aspect of his theory of pan-Arab nationalism is the notion that he gave primacy to the nation, beyond which individual freedom and happiness did not exist. According to al-Husri,

> I wish it realized that freedom is not an end unto itself, but is a means to a higher life. The patriotic interests which may sometimes demand a person to sacrifice his life and soul, may also demand the sacrifice of his freedom. He who does not sacrifice his personal freedom in the cause of his nation's freedom when the situation demands it, may then lose his personal freedom along with the freedom of his nation and his fatherland. He who does not consent to "lose" (*yufni*) himself in the nation to which he belongs, may then be "absorbed" (*al-fana*) by a foreign nation which could someday conquer his fatherland. Therefore, I say continuously and without hesitation: "Patriotism and nationalism above and before all else, even above and before freedom."[91]

In speaking of a man's having to "lose" (*yufni*) himself in his nation, al-Husri, according to Haim's commentary, is speaking of the genuine metaphysics of nationalism, which invested the relation between the individual and his political group with religious significance; indeed, the term *yufni* (infinitive: *fana*) had been used hitherto in the literature of the Islamic mystics to denote the union of the worshipper with the God. The practical consequence of this doctrine is that the citizen must practice complete solidarity with, and implicit obedience to, the state.[92]

The nationalist political discourses produced by these ideologues in the 1930s and thereafter were to galvanize and mobilize the Arab intellectuals and the public at large in a movement against European domination. We have argued that these discourses were directly related to the nature of the French domination of Syria and its inability, unwillingness, or failure to establish a viable democratic system in cooperation with the country's notables. Had the French assisted urban notables in establishing an independent parliamentary republic, where diverse political groups shared power, the faith of the country's liberal-nationalist movement would have been different.

It should be noted that the pan-Arab nationalist discourse espoused in the textbook and fully articulated by al-Husri cannot be entirely explained in terms of French-Syrian conflicts. This nationalist doctrine was also forcefully promoted by King Faisal, who governed Iraq. The overly anti-Iranian attitudes promoted in these textbooks did not have much to do to with the political reality of Iraq-Iran relationships (both countries were being manipulated by British imperialism), but given that Iraq had a long history of territorial disputes with Iran, and that Iranians, like Europeans, considered themselves Aryans, these ideologues naturally took the side of their government.[93]

Iran: From Constitutionalism and Anticlerical Secularism to Economic Nationalism

The discourse of Iranian liberal nationalism exhibited interesting similarities to and differences from the Egyptian and Syrian discourses. In all these countries, nationalism conveyed a romantic feeling about the land and territories of the nation, a common awareness of the country's significance throughout history, and the utility of national self-determination based on the national will (except for the Arab nationalism of Sati' al-Husri, which subordinated the national will to the liberation and organic unity of the Arab nation), which could be realized through the formation of a constitutional democracy and parliamentary politics. These countries also shared broad social conditions that gave rise to this political ideology—a weak absolutist monarch, a heterogeneous ruling elite and power structure, Western cultural diffusion, and certain historical events such as military defeats in wars, on the one hand, and archeological discoveries that provided new knowledge of the country's past glory and power, on the other. Unlike Egypt or Syria, however, Iran constituted a nation. Before the emergence of modern nationalism in Europe, all the constituting elements of nationalism were present and recognized in Iran. According to Adamiyat, "the image of the land of Iran, the existence of the Aryan nation and racial pride, the common language and religion, and, most important of all, a common historical awareness and viewpoint were not something that was imported from abroad."[1]

Other variations of liberal nationalism among the three countries are also noteworthy. In Egypt, the nationalist element in the liberal-nationalist movement predominated. This nationalism was territorial and displayed a distinctly Egyptian identity. In Syria, in contrast, the rise of nationalist consciousness was less tied to the Syrian territory as such. It was first reflected in the liberal-Arabist movement and later in pan-Arab nationalism. Likewise, there were two distinct episodes in Iran's liberal nationalism. The first was the liberal nationalism of the early twentieth century, and the second occurred in the middle of the twentieth. In a hiatus of thirty years separating the two episodes—from 1911, when the constitutional period ended, until 1941, when Reza Shah abdicated the crown—Iran experienced pressure from foreign powers, most notably Great Britain and imperial Russia, and the intensification of sociopolitical conflicts among various social groups and tribes, which led to the Reza Khan coup in 1921, the abolition of the Qajar dynasty in 1925, and the establishment of the Pahlavi dynasty in 1926. The primary feature of the first episode of the liberal-nationalist movement was its antimonarchical and anticlerical nature. Another noteworthy feature was the absence of any anti-Western element. The second episode of liberal nationalism began after the Reza Shah's abdication, which led to the formation of a coalition between different nationalist groups, the rise of the National Front, Mosaddeq's premiership, the nationalization of the oil industry, and the overthrow of Mosaddeq's liberal-nationalist government through a coup jointly engineered by the United States and Britain in 1953. The key feature of this second movement was anti-British economic nationalism. We argue that the change in the discourse and orientations of liberal nationalism during these two episodes from anticlerical secularism, constitutionalism, and pro-Westernism to anti-Western economic nationalism was associated with the change in the dominant ideological targets in relation to which liberal-nationalist ideologues formulated their political discourse.

The Dual Target of Constitutional Thought in the Late Nineteenth Century

All the constituting elements of nationalism were present in Iran before the nineteenth century—a common language and religion, a common historical awareness of the distinctiveness of Iran (its land, people, and ethnicity), and the prevalence of a general national identity of "Iranianness." In the second half of the century, intellectual leaders reconstituted these elements into a new political ideology. How did this reconstitution result in the formation of anticlerical constitutionalism? We argue that while defeats in wars, weak absolutism, and Western cultural diffusion provided the setting, two elements formed the proximate conditions that shaped this new political ideology. One was a combination of the political practices of the Qajar rulers and the political thought underpinning their absolutism. The other was the institutional practices of the ulama in the field of education and the administration of justice as well as the religious discourses that justified these practices. The predominance of these two targets in Iran's political culture oriented the ideological producers toward constitutionalism, anticlerical secularism and, at one remove, anti-Arab nationalism.

The Political Discourse and Practices of the Qajars

In chapter 1, we discussed some of the factors that contributed to the weakness of the Qajars—the defeats in the wars with imperial Russia, the debacle in Herat, the rise of Babism, British occupation of Bushehr, and the radicalization of the protest activities of the merchants and the guilds in the second half of the nineteenth century. In this section, we focus only on the manner in which the Qajars responded to these problems and how their responses shaped the oppositional ideology, leading to the Constitutional Revolution of 1905–11.

The Nasir ud-Din Shah period is important for understanding the genesis of constitutionalism. In the course of his long rule (1848–96), the political universe that he helped creating increasingly became identified with him and his arbitrary and capricious decisions. Abbas Amanat's detailed analysis of Nasir ud-Din Shah's system of government revealed a process that he described as "the beginning of monarchical absolutism in the modern sense."[2] Traditionally, he argued, the monarch's principle function was to maintain a balance in the "cycle of equity," involving a tripartite interplay between the ruler, the government, and the subjects. To this end, the shah was given the rights of dismissing and promoting, punishing and rewarding. The performance of this function naturally required the shah to remain distanced and detached to a degree from the everyday decisions of the government's agents. These rights "were bestowed upon him [the king] because he was considered the locus of divine glory and possessor of royal charisma (*farr-i shahi*). He was the 'shadow of God [*zillullah*] on earth,' but if he was not capable of maintaining the delicate balance between the government and the subjects he was destined to lose his divine mandate and with it his glory and his throne."[3] The laudatory titles that followed the shah's name in public sermons and ceremonies, as well as in the official records and chronicles, were to signify his position as the supreme regulator with divine rights. According to Amanat,

Drawing on the glories of the Persian mythical and dynastic past, the Qajar shah was acclaimed by court chroniclers and in official records as a "world conqueror" (*gity sitan*) of "Alexandrian magnitude" (*sikandar sha'n*), a possessor of Jamshid's glory (*Jam jah*), of Faridun's charisma (*Faridun farr*), and of Khusraw's splendor (*Kisra shawkat*). During the times of war and punishment he was a Turk with the ferocity of Genghis (*Changiz sawlat*) and the vehemence of Tamerlane (*Timur satwat*). In peacetime he was acknowledged as a "joyous king" (*shahryar-i kamkar*) and a fortuitous sultan (*sultan-i sahab-qaran*) whose religious and civil duties were also couched in his titles. Above all he was the "shadow of God" (*zillullah*) upon earth, a "refuge of Islam" (*Islam panah*) and a "shield of the Islamic shari'a" (*shari'at panah*), but he was also a "guardian of the Persian kingdom" (*hafiz-i mulk-i ajam*) and more frequently the king (*padshah*) of the "Guarded Domains" (*mamalik-i mahrusa*) of Iran.[4]

Nineteenth-century Iran, however, was facing a new set of problems. There was an upsurge of popular dissent, the most organized of which was the movement of the mercantile community for protection against foreign economic encroachments. On the cultural level, the emerging modern intellectuals demanded reforms, particularly in the areas of education and the judiciary. The all-powerful conservative Shi'i establishment, on the other hand, considered any such reform contrary to Islam (that is to say, contrary to their occupational interests and cultural prerogatives). On the international level, Iran was facing powerful imperialism, as Great Britain and imperial Russia were vying for political influence and economic concessions in the country.

Naturally, these crisscrossing pressures emanating from diverse sources could not be resolved by maintaining an equilibrium within the traditional framework of the cycle of equity. As an alternative, Nasir ud-Din Shah had several options. First, he could have dispensed with the ulama and launched a program of modernization in order to transform the traditional order and construct a modern military and administrative apparatus of the state. This was the option that was pursued by Muhammad Ali in Egypt and, in the twentieth century, by the Pahlavis. Second, he could have given in to British pressure by allowing the expansion of their political and economic influence—a course that was followed in Mughal India as early as the seventeenth century. Finally, he could have supported ministerial autonomy and his modernizing ministers in their attempts at educational and judicial reforms and the modernization of other state apparatuses (something that was haphazardly pursued by the Ottoman sultans in Istanbul in the nineteenth century). While the shah failed to commit himself fully to any of these options, he picked and chose from the alternatives only to increase his personal power and guarantee his survival. "The Shah," said Amanat, "combined shrewd diplomacy, often playing off rival European powers against each other, with selective reforms and equally shrewd weakening of traditional checks and balances to increase his own political power at the expense of ministerial autonomy."[5]

After the murder of Iran's first reformist vizier, Amir Kabir, on the shah's direct order, the first phase of reform ended in 1860s. Attempts at reforms that were initiated later in 1870s by another modernizing minister, Mushir al-Daula, to rationalize the government apparatus, to restrict the abuses of officeholders, to implement a code of administrative law, to regulate the judicial process and government courts, and to allow a degree of consultative representation on the model of the neighboring Ottoman Empire were again compromised by the shah to suit his own wishes. Underlying his intolerance of reform was his suspicion of Western education. The promotion of modern education, in his view, was an invitation to social innovation and, ultimately, political trouble. He even placed a ban on traveling abroad save for government-sponsored missions. He also kept to a bare minimum the number of graduates of Western institutions in the government. He skillfully managed to maintain his absolutist rule through "an endless game of chesslike maneuvers and counter maneuvers, dismissals, reinstatements, grants of royal favor (*iltifat*), infliction of royal wrath (*ghazab*), exiles, secret murders (most notoriously by means of a poisonous brew known as "Qajar coffee" [*qahva-yi Qajar*]), palace intrigue, bribery, annual auctioning of offices (provincial governorships as well as ministerial appointments), extortion in the guise of gifts (*pishkish*) and estate taxes imposed on deceased members of the government and court, and compromise and coercion."[6] His desire to circumvent any long-term administrative procedure in effect placed a heavy burden on the shah's own shoulders, making him directly responsible for all decisions, great and small.[7]

The shah was certainly performing a balancing act, but this act was not in terms of the traditional formula of maintaining equity, which required a degree of detachment from ordinary, everyday affairs. He micromanaged the affairs of his entourage and the nation in order to foster the universe at the center of which was the desire to protect and maintain his absolutism. An absolutist ruler who was present at all levels of decision making naturally offered a clear target of ideological attack at all these levels. This presence certainly provided useful materials for reflective ideological producers as they attempted to understand the causes of Iran's backwardness and to devise a strategy of what to do to overcome obstacles to progress and prosperity for their nation.

The Ulama

Any attempt at codifying, regulating, and rationalizing state policies and procedures and checking the monarch's arbitrariness entailed a reexamination and reorganization of the ulama's institutional power and prerogatives. Reforms entailed, as it did in nineteenth-century Egypt, the modernization of the educational institutions and the system of the administration of justice. Both these institutions were under the ulama's domain and represented the major pillars on which the powerful religious establishment rested. This institutional power in conjunction with the ulama's ownership of considerable landed properties and control of the vast resources of the religious endowments gave them formidable power. Following their success in defeating alternative schools in Shi'ism and the Babi movement, the ulama from the middle of the nineteenth century on managed to maintain almost a total cultural control of the country. This significant, clear, and identifiable cultural power had a drawback, however. It turned the ulama and their institutions into a target of cultural opposition.

Modernization initiated and sponsored by the state in nineteenth-century Egypt undermined the economic and cultural resources of the ulama while at the same time generating some sort of pluralistic cultural environment. And the process of cultural transformation went hand in hand with the rise of Islamic modernism. As early as the 1830s Tahtawi began to publish his reflections on the congruity of Islam and modernity. In the emerging nationalist movement from the last quarter of the nineteenth century on, Islam, far from being a target of the nationalists' ideological attack was one of its constituting parts. In fact, some of the harbingers of Egyptian liberal nationalism were the disciples and associates of Muhammad Abduh. The liberal-nationalist criticisms of Islam and the dissociation of liberal nationalism and Islamic activism did not occur until the 1920s and the 1930s. Until that time, liberal nationalism in Egypt had a predominantly territorial and anti-British orientation. In Syria, too, the institution of the ulama had to accommodate the rising economic, political, and cultural influence of religious minorities.

In Iran, on the other hand, the ulama's power in the nineteenth century was unrivaled in comparison to that of their counterparts in Egypt or Syria. Throughout the century they not only managed to defeat attempts at reform by state officials but also to stifle any religious reflection that sought to bridge the gulf between Islam and modernism. As was discussed in some details in chapter 5, the ulama were instrumental in resisting and undermining the modernization efforts of reformist viziers like Amir Kabir in the middle of the nineteenth century and Mushir al-Daula, the Sipahsalar, in the 1870s. They were also effective in narrowing the political space for those who hoped to advance a modernist interpretation of religion. These efforts naturally generated resentment among political thinkers and activists. An important consequence of the ulama's intransigence was that liberal-nationalist thought turned as much against clerical obstructionism as it did against monarchical absolutism.

Social Transformation and Cultural Change

In previous chapters we argued that the rise of the modern state and class formation preceded the rise of new cultural movements in India, Egypt, and Syria. In nineteenth-century Iran, such changes did not occur to any significant extent. How, then, did modern ideas enter the country? Who provided the social space and resources for the emerging modern oppositional intellectuals? How do we explain the rise of constitutionalism as a powerful movement in a traditional society? Historical analyses of this period have pointed to several factors. One is the role of the state itself. As was indicated in chapter 5, the reforms of the Qajar shah, though aborted, nonetheless generated a limited set of occupational positions in the state bureaucracy, providing the basis for a small group of modern intellectuals. These positions, however, were too few and the state officials were watched too closely by the conservative court and the ulama to be able effectively to propagate their ideas. Another factor in the spread of modern ideas was the European embassies.

A third factor was what Mongol Bayat called "the Transcaucasian connection." This connection was made possible as a result of treaties of Golistan (1813) and Turkomanchai (1828), signed after two disastrous, humiliating defeats in wars with Russia. By the terms of these treaties, Iran gave up all claims to political rule in Caucasus. The Turkic-speaking province of Azarbaijan was permanently divided in two, the south remaining part of Iran and the north, with an estimated population of half a million Muslims, falling under Russian dominance. Russian rule undermined the supremacy of the Muslim gentry as well as the ulama's authority. In addition, several factors contributed to the rise of modern nationalist and liberal ideas among Muslims. These included the discriminatory policies of imperial Russia toward its Muslim subjects, the rise of an Islamic modernist movement among Central Asian Muslims, which was influenced by a Tartar cleric, Shehabeddin Margani (1818–89), and the implementation of certain measures to modernize the traditional Islamic madrasa system by a Tartar from the Crimea, Ismail Beg Gaspraly (Gasprinski, 1851–1914). During the period in which Iranian intellectuals were cautiously promoting their ideas, their northern counterparts, being under the rule of a non-Muslim power, enjoyed considerable freedom of expression.[8] Tiflis and Baku became two major centers of new Muslim intellectual movements. Baku, in particular, was one of most industrialized cities in the Russian Empire, forming an important focal point for the maintenance of economic and cultural ties between the Russian and Iranian portions of Azarbaijan. A more fertile and liberal intellectual climate, along with employment opportunities in the Baku oil fields, attracted both the educated and the mercantile classes, as well as unskilled laborers from Iranian Azarbaijan. At the turn of the century, Iranian migrant workers made up 15 and 12 percent of the labor force in Baku and Elisavetpol (Gandzha), respectively. Between 1891 and 1904, the Russian consulate in Tabriz issued 312,000 entry visas.[9] This context provided the social support for the rise of Iran's important liberal-nationalist thinkers, such as Mirza Fath Ali Akhundzadah and Abdul Rahim Talibov.

The fourth important factor giving impetus to nationalist constitutional thought was the movement of the Iranian merchants. These merchants were primarily economic actors, involved in the national and regional trade according to the golden rule of trade, buying cheap and selling dear. From the middle of the nineteenth century on, these merchants received stiff competition from British and Russian companies. The failure of the Qajars to protect these merchants and the granting of concessions to British concerns antagonized the mercantile community. The common mistreatment naturally tended to transform the merchants' localized concerns into a national issue, and the idea of forming a nationalist government that would protect domestic commerce gained considerable support among them.

During the Constitutional Revolution, they used their network and vast resources in defense of constitutionalism.

The Rise of Nationalist and Constitutional Thought

Like their Egyptian and Syrian counterparts, Iranian intellectual leaders used modern European political thought as a perspective from which to view the political problems of their society. This new perspective did not provide solutions to these problems, however. The solutions that these intellectuals offered were, rather, shaped by other systems of signification that at the same time appeared to them to be obstacles to their desire to found an independent, prosperous Iran. These were the ideology of the absolutist monarchy and the ulama's exclusionary religious discourse. The monarch's absolutism and the ulama's traditionalism structured the way such intellectual leaders as Mirza Fath Ali Akhundzadah (1812–78), Mirza Aqa Khan Kirmani (1854–96), Abdul Rahim Talibov (1834–1911), Mirza Malkum Khan (1833–1908) and others understood the meaning of constitutionalism, secularism, and nationalism within the Iranian context. The duality of the shah-ulama target defined the parameters of their discourse—constitutionalism, anticlerical secularism, the latter reinforcing a sense of hostility to Arab culture and all manners of Arabism. Anti-imperialist nationalism was relatively weak in the first episode of the liberal-nationalist movement.

For the sake of clarification, if Nasir ud-Din Shah had been farsighted to some degree and if the ulama had been more tolerant of dissenting views, we might reasonably speculate that modern educational institution would have developed fairly extensively in Iran and the ideas of Europe would have been used in a more transcendental manner. These intellectuals might have been able to realize that in historical Islam and Iranian political history there was enough intellectual space to build a modern politics that would also take into account the religious concerns of the ulama. After all, the reality of secular politics was recognized by leading Islamic theologians cum political theorists as early as the time of Imam al-Ghazali. Given nineteenth-century political and cultural limitations, the secularism that these intellectuals finally espoused was developed as a political opposition to the ulama. Far from being a transcendental discourse, this secularism ended up forming a discourse on religion that was as restrictive as the very religious discourse that these intellectuals were opposing. We shall attempt to elaborate this point further in our analysis of Islamic fundamentalism.

Nationalism and Discourse on Land and Language

A key component of Iran's nationalism has been a romantic portrayal, glorification, and consecration of its territories as a sacred place where the nation resides. Tracing the discourse on land in historical writings from the early nineteenth century to the middle of the twentieth, Firoozeh Kashani-Sabet has argued that "land and fron-tiers served as the intellectual fulcrum of nationalist politics and polemics."[10] "Just as every nation," she further states, "ferreted out a territory to animate its frontier fictions, so too did it select a language to disseminate its lore and to cohere its human fellowship. It is unsurprising then that the discourse on land and language in Iranian nationalism went hand in hand, though linguistic interests intensified in response to territorial rivalries and threats."[11] Kashani-Sabet reports that the Zoroastrian cosmology Eran-Vej in ancient Iran placed the origin of the Ayrans in the middle of the central circle of the earth. A tenth-century geographer, Abu Ishaq Ibrahim bin Muhammad al-Farisi al-Istakhri, mapped the world of Islam with a particular fondness for "the kingdom of Iranshahr," which exceeded all other lands in development, completeness, and prosperity. Istakhri's view persisted in the work of Hamd Allah Mustawfi, who wrote under Mongol rule.[12]

Iran's defeats in the wars with Russia, its loss of territories, and the debacles in Herat in 1837 and 1856 were grim reminders that the nation had lost its former imperial grandeur and territorial expanse. These failures added an element to the nationalists' oppositional discourse of the nineteenth century. Their grief over the destruction of the empire was at the same time a statement against the ineptitude of the current rulers. Mirza Fath Ali Akhundzadah, sketching the frontiers of the old Iran, "bounded in the north by the River Jayhun and the Aral Sea and the port of Darband, in the south by the Persian Gulf and the Sea of Oman, in the east by the River Sutlej between Sind and Hindustan, and in the west by the Bosphorus," went on to deplore the present regime: "Alas, oh Iran, what has become of the government, that grandeur, that might, that prosperity."[13] A similar lamentation echoed in the writings of another leading intellectual, Mirza Aqa Khan Kirmani: "what a pity and regret for you, oh Iran. Where is that grand government (dawlat-i 'azim)? Where is that enormous glory (shukat-i jasim)? What happened to that famous might (qudrat-i kaza'i)? Where did that divine kingdom go (saltanat-i khuda'i)? Where is that honor (sharaf), and where is that prosperity (sa'adat)?"[14]

This discourse of decline, however, did not mean "the land of Iran" (Iranzamin) had lost its purity and natural beauty. On the contrary, in Mirza Aqa Khan's pan-egyric description of the country—or what he occasionally called the "mother-land" or the "fatherland"—Iran is portrayed as a beautiful and lovely bride: "from its borders come ambergris breezes, its soil is more valuable than gold, its land fresh and lush, its mountainsides wonderful, its prairies pleasant and heartily, its air clean, its water pure, and its fruits delicious. There is no doubt about the healthy nature of Iran's climate—there is no native epidemic. Syphilis has come from the West [farang], typhus is a 'gift' from Egypt or has come from India via Arabia, influenza from Russia and Italy, and diphtheria from Arabia, and sore throat [dard-galu] from Europe."[15]

The nationalist writers were as laudatory about Iran's glorious ancient history as they were about its natural beauty and purity of climate. For Akhundzadah, ancient Iran and the Islamic era following the Arab invasion of the country were historical contrasts: one representing the era of power and splendor and the other weakness and decline. The Arab domination was the beginning of the political and spiritual decline of Iran. The hungry and shabby Arabs had destroyed Iran's civilization. These thieves had ended the happiness of Iranians and brought in a bunch of nonsense and baseless beliefs. In confirming Firdawsi, the legendary Persian poet, who believed that the Arabs used religion as an excuse to plunder the wealth of other nations, Akhundzadah made reference to Ibn Khaldun's statement that predatory strife was the art of the Arabs.[16] "The wild and savage Arabs destroyed the relics of the angelic Persian kings, annihilated their traditions of justice, and instead imposed their despotic tradition and religion on Iran."[17]

Like Akhundzadah, Mirza Aqa Khan praised ancient Iran—its political institutions, language, and religion. For him, Zoroastrianism was one of the most complete and progressive faiths in ancient times. He attributed the largesse and greatness of the Aryan nation and race to its "Iranian essence." Due to this essence, Iran, unlike many other ancient nations which disappeared from the face of the earth, managed to continue its existence through periods of decline in order to rise again.[18] For him, as they were by other nationalist writers of this period, all the elements of nationalism—land, language, religion, and history—were considered parts of a single totality, which constituted the basis of the philosophy of Iranian nationalism. For Kirmani, debilitating historical circumstances had destroyed the national awareness and solidarity among Iranians and paralyzed the society. The nerves of unity, national solidarity, and ethnic harmony—the principle sources of the life of a nation—were broken, and the sense and understanding of nationhood were gone. And the nation was in the state of civil paralysis. This condition of national paralysis enabled the despots to impose their rule on the nation, and the people experiencing the oppression, instead of protesting, were praising their oppressors. Kirmani thus strove to empower and mobilize Iran's social spirit for the emergence of the nationalist movement. To this end, he coined a new vocabulary, including "the strength of nationality" (qovvat-i milliyyat), "the disposition toward honor and community" (rag-i gheirat va jami'yyati), "the survival of kind, nationality, and race" (baqa'i nou'eiyyat va qoumiyyat vs jinsiyyat), "unity and national solidarity" (yaganigi va itihad-i milli), and "racial unity" (vahdat-i jinsiyyat).[19]

With the glorification of pre-Islamic Iranian civilization and panegyrical portrayal of Iran's natural exquisiteness and climatic purity came an attempt to purify and simplify the Persian language. To be sure, as Adamiyat explains, the idea of reforming or changing the alphabet was developed within the context of East-West encounters. At the time, it was held that the complexity of Oriental languages in contrast with the spoken languages of Europe was a factor in the backwardness of the Orient. A complex language would make learning difficult. The reformers pointed to such problems in the Persian and Arabic alphabets as the similarities of the letters, excess of periods, lack of vowels, and changes in the shapes of letters according to their location in words. Akhundzadah followed this perspective. He first suggested that the Persian alphabet be reformed but then pushed forward the idea of changing the entire alphabet to Latin.[20] One may speculate that Akhundzadah's dislike of the Arabs and anything Arabic underscored his desire to change the alphabet. In fact, he believed that one of the negative consequences of the "savage Arab's" domination of Iran was the imposition on the country of a language that made education very difficult. His real reason, however, was his firm conviction that changing the alphabet was one way of promoting modern thought and science among Iranians.[21]

In addition to the people's attachment to the land, the Persian element was a key aspect of the nationalist discourse, as Akhundzadah professed unequivocally, "even though I am a Turk, I belong to the Persian ancestry."[22] Likewise, for Mirza Aqa Khan Kirmani, language was an important element of nationalism. He believed that the national strength was predicated upon the strength of its language. A nation was a people who speak the same language. The nation that lost its language would also lose its nationality.[23]

Despotism, Political Corruption, and Constitutionalism

The prevalence of corruption in the state's administrative system and the shah's arbitrary behavior were among the most important reasons cited by the intellectual leaders to demand constitutionalism. To be sure, reactions to corrupt and despotic rulers were recurrent phenomena in Iranian history, giving rise to the famous dictum that a kingdom may survive with the unbeliever but not with injustice. And such reactions do not necessarily give rise to liberal ideas. As will be discussed in the third part of this book, the intellectual leaders of Islamic fundamentalism also referred to such problems in condemning the existing (secular) regime. If nineteenth-century ideological producers reached for an anticlerical constitutionalist resolution, it was because, first, the institutions of the monarchy and the religious establishment were perceived as obstacles to the foundation of a modern prosperous state and, second, their worldviews were shaped by such seminal ideas as civilization, progress, and secularism. Using these ideas, political ideologues for more than fifty years—from 1850, when Akhundzadah started writing his plays through the reformist activities of Malkum Khan—were so successful in their united onslaught on the ideology of monarchical absolutism and Shi'i orthodoxy that, despite their small numbers, were able to shape a revolution that overthrew monarchical absolutism, sent one of the most staunch defender of the Shi'i orthodoxy, Sheikh Fazlullah Nuri, to the gallows, and established a constitutional monarchy.

Criticism of the sociopolitical order constituted a major theme of Akhundzadah's plays. In one, he exposed the charlatanism of a certain alchemist who was deceiving the public about his knowledge to turn silver into gold. In another, he described the encounter between science and religious superstition, while at the same time satirizing the ineffectual vizier, Mirza Aghasi. In yet another play, his political satire targeted the nature of Oriental government.[24] Akhundzadah was also the first among his group to address the condition of women. In his plays, he portrayed women as intelligent and independent individuals, capable of making important decisions on matters ranging from the choice of a spouse to personal finances.[25] Mirza Aqa Khan Kirmani was also critical of religious and political institutions while defending constitutionalism, individual liberty, rights, and responsibilities. In criticizing the ulama, he wrote: "the rights of nations, the right of monarchy, the rights of the state, the right to work, the right to life, the rights of honor and scientific superiority, the rights of commerce, the rights of ethic and largesse—all are unknown to their excellencies. They are ignorant of the science of chemistry, astronomy, earth, politics, wealth and progress of nations, the expansion of commerce, occupations, and industry."[26] His political thought on the emergence of the state, the philosophy of law, and the principles of natural rights were influenced by Rousseau and Montesquieu. In his view, the bases of the modern state—civil society, liberty, equality, and justice—are rooted in natural law. The happiness of man is in equality and justice. A despotic government is contrary to the law of nature and is the cause of the destruction and ruin of society. The standard of ethics—right and wrong—is rational law, which is also based on natural principles.[27] Although he believed in socialism, he made reference not to the proletarians (for Iran was not an industrial society) but to the movement of peasants and the middle class.[28]

For the survival of civilization and the establishment of security and safety, the state, Kirmani thought, is a necessity. Nevertheless, real justice and moderation can exist only in the presence of opposing forces. The force of the state and the force of the nation should be equal to each other for justice to prevail. The rights of liberty include freedom of thought, writing, expression, religion, commerce, style of dress, habitation, marriage, wealth, custom and mores, and nationality. Without them, no justice is possible. These constituted the charter of human rights.[29] Like Akhundzadah, Kirmani defended women's rights. In his view, men and women should be treated as equal in all rights. Just as there is no difference between the two hands and both are used equally, men and women are also equal members of society. "Humanity will never reach its height of excellence unless women become equal to men in all rights and affairs."[30] For him, state absolutism is a result of the public's ignorance of its rights and of the benefits of liberty and equality. The rule of a despotic government and the lack of freedom and participation of people in the affairs of the country are among the principle causes of corruption in high

places, the decline of the country, the degeneration of national morality, and historical weakness and lawlessness.[31]

Liberal, nationalist, and constitutional ideas gained practical significance in the
intellectual and political activities of Malkum Khan (1833–1908), an Armenian
born to a pro-Western family in Isfahan who later converted to Islam. While
Akhundzadah and Kirmani were attempting to promote liberal and antidespotic
ideas in the country, Malkum Khan was among the first who initiated a reformist
movement for constitutional change. His career also displayed the transformation
of liberal ideas to a movement for revolutionary change. He first created the House
of Oblivion (Faramushkhanah), modeled on but not attached to the European
Freemasonry society, to train the new educated elite as state officials to implement
reforms.[32] As a high-ranking state official and inspired by the Tanzimat movement
in the Ottoman Empire, he drafted for the court a *Daftar-i Tanzimat* (*Book of
Reform*). Its preamble summarized the conditions of the country while emphasizing its readiness for reform; it described the dreadful conditions of the peasants, the
poor system of transportation, governmental corruption (which Khan called "governmental typhus"), military weakness, disorganization in the state's administration, and the extravagance of state officials and courtiers. After conceding that the
regime was based on an absolutist hereditary monarchy and that legislative and
executive functions were the shah's prerogative, it suggested a series of laws on the
nature of the government, the conditions for legislation, the rights of the nation,
the organization of the parliament, the codification of existing laws, the differentiation of governmental responsibilities in the country, the formation of an army, the
creation of a department of taxation, the introduction of a modern educational system, the construction of roads, and the creation of a state bank for improving the
financial condition of the country. Malkum Khan used the term *qanun* for these
laws, to differentiate them from both the shari'a and the existing state regulations
('urf). These new laws, Malkum Khan stressed, must be based on two fundamental principles: the improvement of public welfare and the equality of all citizens.

Following the debacle at Herat and Iran's military defeat by the British in Bushehr,
which had gravely concerned Nasir ud-Din Shah, Malkum found it an opportune
time to present the *Daftar* to the shah. Initially, the shah appeared sympathetic to the
proposal, but once the ulama in Tehran denounced the concept of qanun (law) as a
"heretical innovation" and accused the House of Oblivion of having connections
to the "atheistic republican" Freemasons in Europe, he banned the society, shelved
Daftar-i Tanzimat, and exiled Malkum Khan to Istanbul.[33] The resistance to the
reforms he suggested and his exile naturally disillusioned Malkum Khan about the
possibility of implementing reform from within the government and made him
increasing critical of the government and the religious institutions. In his *Traveler's
Tale,* Malkum Khan parodied court intellectuals, scribes, and poets for their obscure

language, meaningless phraseology, obsession with trivia, and flattery of the power-ful, and the religious authorities for their pomposity, ignorance, intolerance, distrust of modern science, use of incomprehensible Arabic, resort to esoteric mumbo jumbo, enflaming of sectarian passions, and financial exploitation of the community of the faithful.[34] By 1890s, Malkum Khan changed his political orientation from that of a reformist trying to change the government from within to that of a revolutionary advocating the overthrow of the absolutist monarchy. He founded the famous *Qanun* newspaper to spread his views in the country from abroad.

Secularism and the Pro-Western Orientation

There was something paradoxical about the Constitutional Revolution. It was led by two of the ulama—Bihbahani and Tabataba'ie—yet secularism was its organiz-ing principle. On one level, and to those of the ulama who participated in the rev-olution, it was not paradoxical at all. The constitution was a solution formulated in general terms in order to resolve the particular problem of arbitrary power. It took away the monarch's power to rule as he wished. A new power—the power to legis-late—was generated and given to the people's representatives. Realizing that this new power aimed at curtailing dramatically the ulama's legislative hermeneutics,[35] Nuri unsuccessfully challenged the constitution. The ulama, however, managed to amend the constitution by adding a proviso that the Islamicity of any legislation passed by the majles should be assessed and approved by a council of the ulama. The paradox, however, was a result of the tremendous social pressures brought to bear on the Shi'i establishment, which prompted a group of the ulama to forgo their own occupational interests in order to stay with the people and the revolu-tion. In the absence of a formal religious hierarchy, the ulama were in fact vulner-able to social pressure. The modernist Ayatollah Na'ini had exhibited great social foresight when he realized that between absolutism and constitutionalism, the lat-ter was the lesser of two evils.

The influence of modern Western political ideologies that sought the replace-ment of religious discourse with scientific ideas as the organizing principle of pol-itics and the increasing historical awareness of the power and magnanimity of ancient Iran shaped the secular-nationalist revolutionary movement of the early twentieth century. Besides, nineteenth-century intellectual leaders had more than fifty years of accumulated grievances against the ulama's uncompromising resis-tance to reforms and modernization. Now that the ulama's daunting power was no more and they were divided into pro- and antiroyalist camps, these intellec-tuals were determined to bring down this institution as effectively as possible. The three main ideological trends detected by historians of the constitutional revolution—Shi'i radicalism, Western liberalism, and Russian social democ-racy—were all united in their common aim at curtailing the authority of the

conservative ulama in Iran's public life. Modernist concepts and ideas were introduced by religious dissidents who mobilized the masses, preaching the merit of
the movement in the mosques and religious schools, wrapping their thought in
the traditional language of the Quran and the holy texts. The Hemmat Party of
Baku, which founded, on the eve of the revolution, branches in Tabriz, Ferqeh-
yi ijtima'iyun amiyun (a social democratic group) and other major Iranian cities,
was successful in recruiting members from among the low-ranking ulama and
religious dissidents.[36] Nevertheless, this reactive and angry secularism, which
was later espoused by twentieth-century intellectuals, did not take a critical
assessment of the Islamic theory of government as its point of departure. It was
partly political movement, insofar as it was a reaction to the ulama's power, and
partly a haphazardly emulative discourse.

Another noticeable feature of the Constitutional Revolution was its pro-Western
orientation. While Western interventions generated nationalist consciousness
among various politically active segment of the population and even leading intellectuals like Akhundzadah went so far as to proclaim that a homegrown despot
was preferable to colonialism,[37] the cultural movement in this period counted
on Western support. In addition to the affinity between the ideology of the
Constitutional Revolution and the Western ideas of liberalism and nationalism, the
diplomats connected to Western embassies contributed both intellectually and
organizationally to the resources of the constitutional movement. A noteworthy
indicator of this orientation was the selection of the British legation in Tehran by
revolutionary activists as the site of the sanctuary that played a significant role in
mobilizing the public for constitutional change—a political tactic that became
unthinkable in the excessively anti-Western opposition movements in the second
half of the twentieth century. What is more, the sanctuary, which lasted twenty-
three days (from July 19 to August 10, 1906) enjoyed the active support of the leading ulama. Fearing repression by the government, and since the authorities had
earlier violated sanctuary at the Shah Abd ul-Azim Shrine in southern Tehran and
had fired at the demonstrators around the Friday Mosque, protesters decided to
turn to the British legation for support. In a bold political move on July 9,
Bihbahani and several members of the secret societies sent a letter to the secretary
of legation, Evelyn Grant Duff, requesting his assistance, but were turned down.
To the second letter sent on July 18, inquiring whether the nationalists could peace-
fully take sanctuary in the legation compounds in Tehran, Grant Duff responded
that while he wished they would not occupy his legation, "it was not in his power,
in view of the acknowledged custom in Persia and the immemorial right of 'bast,'
to use, or cause to be used, force to expel them if they came."[38] The sanctuary
started when five merchants and theology students moved into the British legation
on July 19, and by August 2, their numbers had soared to fourteen thousand,

representing nearly one-third of the labor force of Tehran.[39] The sanctuary resulted in the shah's consent to the formation of parliament.

The Rise of the Pahlavis: A New Context for Culture Production

Ideological debates among the leading figures of the revolution contributed to the formulation of the Fundamental Law and the Supplementary Fundamental Laws. The secular politicians suggested new conceptual scaffolding as a foundation for the formation of the modern state. Their secular-nationalist view was reflected in 1906 in such slogans as "Long live the nation of Iran." When the royal proclamation consented to the formation of parliament, the nationalists rejected the proclamation because it did not include the phrase "the *nation* of Iran." While a second draft incorporated the phrase "the nation of Iran," it was still rejected because it called for the formation of an "Islamic consultative parliament." The nationalist leaders were still not satisfied. The government continued to argue that the majles should be an "Islamic majles," but the opposition insisted that the majlis must be called a "national majles."[40] Telegrams from Baku and Tiflis threatened to send armed volunteers, and even the Cossacks were preparing to defect if the court did not capitulate to the demands of the revolutionaries. The secular nationalists continued to call for a third draft of the proclamation in which the terms "Islamic consultative majlis" were changed to "national consultative majlis."[41] These changes naturally contradicted the views of the ulama and prompted the royalist Sheikh Fazlullah Nuri to reject the constitution and the parliament altogether.

Although the revolution gave birth to modern types of political organizations, such as a parliament, city councils, modern political parties, and a women's movement, it failed to produce consensus among Iranians about the political and cultural direction of the country. Following Nuri's defeat and subsequent execution, conflicts between moderate clerics and secularists cum socialists continued. The assassination of Bihbahani by radical social democrats,[42] the conflict between the socialists and the landowners, ethnic and tribal strife, and British-Russian political rivalries[43]—all worked against the reorganization of the political order on the basis of constitutional principles. In the 1909–21 period, Iran experienced a process of disintegration: by mid-1910, the National Assembly was sharply divided into rival parties, and tribal warfare broke out a year later, British and Russian troops moved into the main northern and southern cities, Ottoman contingents invaded the western regions in 1915, autonomous governments were formed in Azarbaijan and Gilan by 1920, various tribes controlled much of Kurdistan, Arabistan, and Baluchistan, and the central government lost control beyond the capital in about 1920.[44] This historical juncture determined the political fortunes of Reza Khan, a Cossack brigade commander. Backed by the British general William Edmund Ironside, Reza Khan and a group of Anglophiles headed by Sayyid Zia ud-Din

Tabataba'ie carried out a coup in February 1921. Through successful military oper-ations that put an end to autonomous movements and tribal rebellion and effective political maneuvering, Reza Khan managed to become first the prime minister, then overthrow the Qajar dynasty, and finally install himself as the new shah of Iran and establish the Pahlavi dynasty in 1926.

Politics and Culture under Reza Shah

The rise of Reza Shah to power, the formation of the modern centralized admin-istrative organization of the state, and the state's extensive involvement in the eco-nomic and cultural reorganization of society created a new environment for culture production and set the stage for the rise of a new liberal-nationalist move-ment in the 1941–53 period. A key feature of this movement was economic nation-alism. It consisted of a set of interrelated presuppositions about the foundation of Iranian society and who controlled that foundation: (1) the oil industry was the foundation of the economy, (2) the oil industry was controlled by the British, (3) the Pahlavis had come to power with the aid of the British in order to ensure the continued British suzerainty over Iran; and (4) the Pahlavis' overall policies in the economic, social, and cultural realms were primarily designed to maintain Iran's dependent and dominated position vis-à-vis the Western capitalist countries. A wide variety of Marxist, nationalist, and Islamic historians and activists treated this view as an article of faith, but each group worked out a different solution to what they commonly perceived to be the Pahlavi problem. Although there are ele-ments of truth in some of these claims, none explains such anomalous cases as Reza Shah's decision to shy away from the British and ally with the Germans in the thirties, a serious miscalculation that led to the Allied invasion and occupation of Iran during World War II and his forced abdication in 1941. Moreover, the struggle to protect the national economy—most notably national trade—by mer-chants and the guilds started as early as the second part of the nineteenth century, and although the foundation of a prosperous and independent economy was one of the goals of the Constitutional Revolution, it was not its defining feature. Why, then, did economic factors become so significant in the discourse of the political activists in the twentieth century?

The diffusion of various brands of leftist ideology, and more significantly the political impact of the socialist revolution in Russia in 1917, certainly contributed to the rise of economic nationalism. As social historians Ervand Abrahamian and Janet Afary have demonstrated, socialist ideas had a considerable following in the Constitutional Revolution and during the period of disintegration. The socialism of this period, however, was interfused with liberalism and placed great emphasis on the ideas of the Enlightenment. If nineteenth-century intellectual leaders had emphasized the necessity of liberal, constitutional, and secular ideas for the construction of a modern political order, for many political thinkers in the twentieth century, the economic category became the most important organizing principle of politics. And as a result, their political views were shaped from the standpoint of determining who controls the economy. Further, the meddling of the British in Iran's internal affairs, particularly their unsavory deal with imperial Russia in 1907 (which divided the country into British and Russian spheres of influence), exposed their imperialism and disillusioned Iranian intellectuals about the true nature of the British mission in the country. While on the eve of the Constitutional Revolution Iranians were counting on British support when they took sanctuary in the British legation, later they viewed the British as the enemy of Iran's national interests. For the later Iranians, it was not too difficult to revise the history of British actions as demonstrations of intrigue and conspiracy to ensure Britain's influence in the country. This new perspective could be supported by ample evidence from several historical instances: the British attack on and seizure of the port city of Bushehr in 1856, the Reuter concession, the tobacco concession, the British-Russian conspiracy of 1907 to divide Iran, and the British monopoly of the Iranian oil industry.

Cultural change under Reza Shah further reinforced anti-British economic nationalism. His ties to the British, however, did not appear to have been the key factor in the rise of this new oppositional discourse. The form of domination certainly shapes the nature of oppositional discourse, and Iranians opposing the British over the control of the oil industry may seem a self-evident response. But for the issue of oil to gain centrality in the nationalist agenda favorable cultural factors had to be present. This was so because, first of all, the British took credit for the discovery of oil in the country, for building one of the world's largest oil refineries, and, therefore, for contributing to the Iranian economy. Further, during the first quarter of the twentieth century, there was considerable dissension among Iranians over many issues related to the nature and form of government, the role of religion in politics, the nature of the economy, the role of the ulama in modern educational institutions, and the social role and status of women. The issue of oil was one among many. We thus argue that changes in Iran's cultural profile under Reza Shah contributed to the transformation of the British presence into a clear symbol of domination worthy of becoming a target of nationalist attack and popular agitation. By realizing many of the goals of the Constitutional Revolution—promoting secularism and undermining the power of the ulama, fostering national unity, achieving territorial integrity, and forming a centralized state—Reza Shah in effect removed these goals from the nationalist agenda. He effectively ended all the autonomous governments, brought tribal power under control, established security in the country, formed a powerful and modern centralized state, founded and expanded the institutions of secular education, brought the institution of religious endowments (awqaf) under governmental control, initiated and enforced considerable changes in the people's style of dress, including the forced unveiling of women, and downplayed the importance of religion and religious holidays, while his ideologues glorified pre-Islamic Iranian kingship and culture.[45] The revival of the Persian language—in particular, an attempt to purify the language of Arabic words—was also a key component of Reza Shah's cultural policies. According to Kashani-Sabet, "Persian revivalism found its most lavish display in the Firdawsi International Conference of 1934, which commemorated the thousand-year birthday of Iran's most celebrated poet."[46]

These policies were congruent with the dominant cultural trend in society. In fact, the secular trend unleashed by the Constitutional Revolution continued unabated under the Pahlavis until the sixties. The country's leading intellectuals and social critics continued to attack Iran's traditional culture, at the center of which were various religious practices, tribalism and ethnic divisions, and communal sectarianism. The solution was sought in the formation of a centralized state with an emphasis on pre-Islamic kingship and culture, the expansion of secular education, the spread of the Persian language among non-Persians, the adoption of Western philosophy and technology, and the destruction of the clerical influence. Modern secular ideas were often expressed in major periodicals of the twenties, such as *Iranshahr, Farangistan,* and *Ayandeh.* Abrahamian's content analysis of these periodicals reveals their socioeconomic and political orientation. Of the 236 articles published in *Iranshahr,* 73 stressed the importance of public and secular education, 45 emphasized the need to improve the status of women, 30 eulogized pre-Islamic Iran, and 40 discussed aspects of modern technology and Western philosophy. Similarly, of some 70 articles published in *Farangistan,* 15 dealt with modern education, 8 with the status of women, 10 with industrial technology, 9 with Western political philosophy, 3 with pre-Islamic Iran, 3 with Azarbaijan, 2 with the secular movement in Turkey, 4 with international relations, and 16 with Persian literature. The contents of the monthly *Ayandeh* were similar, but they focused mainly on the need to form a centralized state and a unified national identity.[47]

One of the most effective spokespeople of modern secular discourse was Ahmad Kasravi (1891–1946), Iran's famous social critic and iconoclastic historian. Kasravi began his career as a student of religion. His dislike of the clergy soon prompted him to leave traditional education and enter the American Memorial School in Tabriz to study the English language and modern sciences. Kasravi was a prolific writer. He founded the monthly *Payman* in 1933 and the newspaper *Parcham* in 1941. In addition, he published more than fifty books and theses concerning various aspects of Iranian society viewed from critical and historical perspectives.[48] Like other thinkers, Kasravi began by acknowledging the decline of Iran. In his view, this decline was caused by tribal, linguistic, and sectarian divisions. He was particularly critical of various religious rituals commemorating the martyrdom of

Imam Hussein on the grounds that these practices reflected superstitions and were incompatible with a modern lifestyle.

Kasravi was also critical of the Islamic establishment. For him, there were two kinds of Islam. One was the Islam that had been founded by Muhammad more than thirteen hundred years ago, and the other was today's Islam, which was divided into such diverse sects as Sunni, Shi'i, Ismaili, Ali-allahi, Sheikhi, and Karim-khani.[49] The Islam of today was controlled by the clergy. The clerical institutions not only had failed to benefit the people, but was also the source of many problems and misfortunes. It was a major source of Iran's misery, ignorance, underdevelopment, and inferiority vis-à-vis the Europeans. Kasravi believed that the ignorance propagated by the clergy was so extensive that it had made Muslims arrogant. Being so convinced of the rightness of their religion, they even wished Europeans to convert to Islam. Moreover, the clergy blocked innovation and progress. Foreign powers also used the clerical establishment to pursue their policies and realize their political objectives. Finally, this kind of Islam even belittled the name of God.[50] Of course, the Muslims also had their own excuses, said Kasravi. Whenever one raised the problems facing Muslim nations—the people's ignorance and sectarianism—they would quickly respond, "if people are bad, it is not the fault of Islam." When this argument lost validity, they would then say; "people do not act according to the principles of religion. If they do so, every thing is going to be all right." They also claimed that the existing divisions and sectarianisms were not caused by religion. Islam was in essence clean and pure. They would say, "we should return to the fundamentals of religion," or "we should reform religion." For them, said Kasravi, "the book of Islam is the Quran, and as long as it exists, Islam also exists."[51]

Thus, the cultural outlooks of the intellectual leaders in the 1920s and 1930s were consistent with the cultural policies of Reza Shah. His repression of the tribal and ethnic movements in different parts of the country during the turbulent years following the Constitutional Revolution was not a conspiracy dictated by the British to curb the social revolutionary movement. The shah succeeded in building a new, centralized monarchy because his regime rested on the dominant interests in the country, and many of his objectives were in keeping with the aims of the revolution. When he so daringly outlawed the veil and traditional ethnic clothes, obliged the people to wear Western-style dress, expelled the ulama from the state bureaucracy, and initiated many other secular reforms, he did so not simply because of his leadership capability and military might. Reza Shah was riding a favorable cultural trend, a discourse whose adherents were both inside and outside his regime and included both the flatterers of the monarchy as well as its critics. These measures were supported by his critics, although on the whole they were ambivalent about his authoritarianism.

The Rise of the National Front and Economic Nationalism

The allied invasion of Iran and the abrupt end of Reza Shah's rule contributed to the conditions that allowed liberal nationalism to grow in the period 1941–53: the weak political position of Reza's son and successor, Muhammad Reza Shah, heterogeneity and conflict among the elite, the rise of mass political parties, and rivalries among world powers. These conditions were also favorable to the rise of revolutionary and ethnic autonomy movements. In this period, the Democratic Party of Azarbaijan, with a total membership of seventy-five thousand, was established, and this led to the formation of an autonomous government in Azarbaijan in 1945. A similar autonomous government was also formed in Kurdistan in the following year. In the rural areas, the conflict between peasants and landowners intensified. Peasant movements culminated in the formation of peasant associations in various parts of the country. With the central government's power highly diminished, peasants were able to win concessions from landowners. Similarly, the workers' movement gained considerable strength. In 1944, the Central Council of Unified Trade Unions of Iranian Workers was formed. By 1945, it claimed a membership of two hundred thousand workers and, by 1946, a membership of four hundred thousand, with 186 affiliated unions.[52] The increasing radicalization of the ethnic minorities and the peasants' and workers' movements frightened the dominant classes as well as foreigners, the British in particular. The common fear of a possible social revolution spreading from these groups underlay their de facto unity in suppressing these movements, and by 1949 the power of the monarchy was considerably restored.

The relative ease with which these movements were repressed may be instructive on the relationship between culture and the success or failure of movements of dominated groups and classes. How did the state manage to repress all these movements, particularly since there were internal feuds and dissension among the political elites in the 1940s? One indication of such interelite rivalries is that Iran experienced the inauguration of thirteen premiers and seventeen cabinets in the 1941–53 period. Yet despite the inability of the elites to cooperate, the social movements were crushed because of the absence of a revolutionary discourse. No overarching ideology existed to connect Iran's independence and development to the idea of regional and ethnic autonomy, the workers' right to unionize, and land reform. These movements simply aimed to take advantage of the political vacuum generated by the decline of the authority of the central government. More crucially, the idea of maintaining national unity and territorial integrity had a considerable currency among different leaders of the nationalist movement. Thus, we may postulate that it was this very idea that transcended differences among politicians, the courts, and the military, causing them to form a united front against the movements of ethnic minorities for autonomy and of workers and peasants. The argument advanced against the autonomy movement in Azarbaijan is a case in point. For example, even the Iran Party, which was the most significant democratically oriented nationalist party, attacked the autonomy movement in Azarbaijan on the grounds that "the Democratic Party of Azarbaijan had used a favorable international situation. Its birth was under the supervision of foreigners and through their military support. Many Iranians considered this an unforgivable sin. Especially when it demanded the protection of the Turkish language and other things that wounded the hearts of Iranian patriots."[53]

With the removal of what was perceived to be a domestic threat to national unity, the British exploitation of Iranian oil became a clear target of ideological attack and a focus of economic nationalism, transcending ethnic and class division and ensuring national unity. Moreover, landowners and merchants were too disgruntled by the arbitrary rule of Reza Shah to allow the rise of another dictator. Whoever among the politicians was able to articulate most effectively the themes of nationalism and restrictions on the arbitrary power of the monarch had a better chance to lead the masses and rally them to action. It was within the discursive field of national interests versus the British, and democracy versus arbitrary rule, that the National Front grew to become the strongest political force in the country in the early fifties.[54] The front's democratic objective was to check the arbitrary power of the monarch by demanding that he reign and not rule. Its nationalist objective was to eliminate British control of the Iranian oil industry. The National Front appeared close to realizing both objectives when Mosaddeq was elected prime minister in the early 1950s.

This is not to argue that the nationalist ideology covered up the reality of ethnic and class differences by virtue of constituting the dominant discourse. Its transcendental power to a large extent rested on the interest in controlling the country's most important natural resource. The nationalist leaders and agitators made effective use of Iran's right to control its natural resources in their mobilizing efforts against the British. In addition, the economic thinking of this period constituted a favorable context for the rise of Tudeh Party (the communist party formed in 1941). The collapse of Reza Shah's regime, the release of large groups of political prisoners, and the attraction of the communist ideology for young educated Iranians contributed to rapid rise of the Tudeh Party as a significant political party with an extensive following among workers and ethnic minorities. The popularity of the economic category in sociopolitical thought might in fact have been a crucial factor in the considerable involvement of the educated elite among the Tudeh activists. The influence of economic thinking in this period was so pervasive that even Muslim activists expressed their outlook in socialist terms. For example, an organization calling itself the Movement of God-Worshipping Socialists was formed in this period. At any rate, the materialism of the Tudeh Party in turn contributed to the rise of economic nationalism, and to the perception that much of Iran's economic difficulties could be resolved if the oil industry were brought under the government's control.

The weak monarch and the strong British presence in the country, along with effective control of the oil industry by the British, shaped the nationalist discourse and the rise of economic nationalism. Iran's grievances against the British-controlled Anglo-Persian Oil Company (APOC) were indeed extensive. First, the oil concession of 1901, which had been granted by the shah of Qajar to a British engineer, William Knox D'Arcy, had not been ratified by the parliament of the post-constitutionalist period. Second, the APOC did not consistently follow the terms of the 1901 agreement. For example, the British government granted a rebate to the Royal Navy in 1920 without the agreement of the Iranians. Furthermore, the Iranians began to demand back payments and royalties that had been discontinued during the war period of 1916–20 and their share in the profits of subsidiaries. Finally, while the company had made a profit of £200 million by 1933, Iran had received only some £10 million of the £32 million due it contractually. Third, from the Iranian perspective the 1933 agreement signed by Reza Shah and the British was not much better than the 1901 concession. For example, according to article 19 of the 1933 agreement, prices for refined petroleum products in Iran were based upon the average Romanian or Gulf of Mexico FOB price, whichever was lower, plus actual transportation and distribution costs, less a 10 percent discount. The unfairness of the agreement is evident when one considers that the production cost of oil in the Middle East averaged $1.20 per ton compared to $12.45 per ton in the United States. After World War II, Iran's grievances against APOC continued to mount. It was indicated that the profit of the company in 1950 alone, after deducting the share pid to Iran, was more than the entire sum of £114 million paid to Iran in the past half century.[55]

The rise of the National Front was aided by two additional factors. One was the strong support it received from the guilds and the merchants. Under Mosaddeq there was an upsurge in guild activity in politics and street demonstrations. The merchants were also quite influential in the politics of this period. The bazaar as a whole served as a social basis for the front. As early as 1944, in the fourteenth parliamentary elections, the bazaar supported Mosaddeq, giving him the largest number of votes of all representatives. Mosaddeq's nationalist economic policies in turn helped promote local industries and expanded the export of local products.[56] At the same time, the liberal-nationalist discourse provided the ideological context for the formation of the Society of Merchants and Guilds (Jaami'ih-ye Bazarganan va Pishevaran-i Bazaar), which was in turn used as a vehicle for the mobilization of the members of the bazaar against the shah and for the nationalist cause. Another factor was the active involvement of the United States in international politics under the banner of anticolonialism and liberal internationalism, an ideology that was well articulated under the Wilson administration. The support of the United States for the nationalist cause in Iran was further reinforced by the conflict between American and British oil companies. In turn, the front's leaders were counting heavily on U.S. support for the realization of their democratic and nationalist objectives. The United States was praised even by one of the most radical members of the front:

> From the other side of the Atlantic Ocean, from the State of Liberty and from the Land of George Washington, these days we hear the message of affection. The United States of America that, with its invaluable material and moral assistance, has saved many nations of the world from death and starvation, and the hungry and destroyed Europe from embracing Communism, today is going to assume a much heavier responsibility.
>
> The United States must help us at the mouth of the volcano [implying the Soviet Union]. . . . We do not interpret the United States' assistance but as a reflection of humanitarian feelings and love for the humanities.[57]

The United States, however, not only failed to support the democratic movement but even collaborated with the British in the coup that overthrew Mosaddeq and reinstalled the shah in 1953. The coup set the stage for the radicalization of Iran's nationalist movement and later for the emergence of Islamic revolutionary discourse.

THE RISE OF
ISLAMIC FUNDAMENTALISM

Introduction to Part Three

We attempted to explain the variations in nationalist discourse in Egypt, Syria, and Iran in terms of the variations in the regimes of signification that were connected to the dominant sociopolitical institutions in these countries. In Egypt, British colonial rule, on the one hand, and arbitrary khedivial power, on the other, framed the discourses of nationalist intellectual leaders in terms of Egyptian identity and territories. In Syria, nationalist discourse revolved around Arab identity. Its liberal-Arabist phase was shaped, as it were, in oppositional relation first to Abdülhamid's pan-Islamic despotism and then to Turkish nationalism. In the post–World War I period, the domination of the Arab region by Western powers and the colonial partitioning of the Arab region into disparate states gave rise to the ideology of pan-Arab nationalism. In Iran, the dual targets of the ulama's obstructionism and Qajar absolutism oriented the development of political thought in the direction of anticlerical secularism and constitutionalism. British control of the Iranian oil industry signified the economic category in nationalist thought, promoting economic nationalism in the middle of the twentieth century.

Insofar as the liberal nationalists were struggling to secure independence for their country and establish a responsive government, there was no serious quarrel between them and the modernist ulama. But in the postindependence and postrevolutionary period, nationalist ideologues and policy makers did not confine their activities to the realm of politics. Subscribing to a Europe-centered secularist project, these ideologues began to narrow down the cultural and social spheres of religious institutions: they rewrote history to fit their nationalist conception of the past and to overlook the Islamic period, glorified pre-Islamic kingship and ancient history, reformed the educational institutions in contradistinction to the religious institutions, attacked religion and religious rituals in terms of Western standards, and limited the sphere of activities of religious groups. These actions naturally politicized religion, generating a favorable context for the rise of Islamic fundamentalism.

The broad environmental factors that promoted the rise of the Islamic fundamentalist movement included rapid economic development, demographic expansion, the development of modern social classes—in particular, the rise of the new middle class—and the expansion of institutions of higher learning. These developments were followed by an economic downturn and social dislocation. The discourse of Islamic fundamentalism, however, was produced in oppositional relation to the overly secularist outlooks of the nationalist intellectual leaders. Islamic fundamentalism assumed a radical and militant orientation after the military overthrow of the existing regimes and the formation of an intrusive bureaucratic ideological state in Algeria, Egypt, Iran, and Syria.

Islamic fundamentalism represented a marked departure from both the Islamic modernist and the nationalist discourses that preceded it. Like these discourses, Islamic fundamentalism constituted a set of positions taken by Muslim intellectual leaders on a series of issues facing their society. In many respects, these positions were diametrically opposed to those adopted by the harbingers of Islamic modernism. In many respect, too, the worldviews of the fundamentalists in different Islamic countries on the sociopolitical role of religion, the relationship between religion and science, the status of women, Western culture, and the function and form of government were quite similar. Our contention is that these similarities are related to similarities in monolithic ideological discourses imposed from above by the secular ideological states in Algeria, Egypt, Iran, and Syria.

We analyze the exceptional Jordanian case to underscore the significance of the state structure and state culture in shaping religious movements in society. The Hashemite state, despite its authoritarianism, displayed certain pluralistic features and little interest in directly interfering in culture. As a result, the Islamic movement tended toward moderation and had a peaceful relationship with the ruling elite. The controlled democratization process launched by the late King Hussein in 1989 and the emergence of a semipluralistic political environment were associated with the secularization of the Islamic movement, reflecting the organizational differentiation and rationalization of religious discourse.

NINE

The Rise of the Muslim Brothers in Egypt: From Moderate to Revolutionary Activism

The late thirties represent a turning point in Egypt's cultural history. They mark the decline of liberal nationalism and the rise of alternative discourses. Many of the ideas proposed by the liberal intellectual leaders and the secular policies implemented by the nationalist government collided forcefully with diverse ideologies of "supra Egyptianism," to use Israel Gershoni and James P. Jankowski's phrase.[1] Two major institutions of Egyptian constitutionalism, the parliament and the political parties, became the targets of strident criticism from different groups within the opposition movement. A significant part of educated Egyptians and opinion leaders in the forties and fifties departed from liberal nationalism and began following alternative discourses in their attempt to find solutions to the problems facing their society. Among them, the discourse of the Muslim Brothers was the most significant.

Founded in 1928 by a schoolteacher, Hasan al-Banna (1906–49), the Society of the Muslim Brothers (MB) has been one of the most powerful and resilient organizations representing Islamic fundamentalism in modern Egypt. Its rise to a position of considerable sociopolitical influence—it commanded a membership of over five hundred thousand activists in the forties—signified a major shift in the country's cultural movement. In a marked departure from liberal nationalism, the discourse of the MB rejected the Western model, Egyptian territorial nationalism, the idea of the separation of religion and the state, parliamentary politics, and the Islamic modernist conception of gender relations. As an alternative, al-Banna proposed a vision of Islam as an all-encompassing religion: "We believe the provision of Islam and its teachings are all inclusive, encompassing the affairs of the people in this world and the hereafter. And those who think that these teachings are concerned only with the spiritual or ritualistic aspects are mistaken in this belief because Islam is a faith and a ritual, a nation (*watan*) and a nationality, a religion and a state, spirit and deed, holy text and sword. . . . The Glorious Qur'an . . . considers [these things] to be the core of Islam and its essence."[2]

The MB constructed its religious niche as an activist religious movement in contrast with what it perceived as the Azhar's political detachment and Sufi's otherworldliness. The overall outline of this activism was sharply defined in its opposition to liberal nationalism, Western capitalism, and international communism. A series of binaries defined its identity and distinguished the MB from other movements: Islamic activism versus religious retreatism and apathy, Islamic unity versus the political parties' disunity and factionalism, puritanism and modesty versus sexual laxity, gender segregation versus mixing of the sexes, Egypt's Islamic essence versus Pharaonism, spiritualism versus Western materialism.[3]

The rise of the MB after almost a century of the expansion of modern discourses and the spread of secular education in Egypt appeared anachronistic and counterintuitive. If the MB was a traditionalist response to the British imperialistic objectives, why did this movement fail to appear much earlier, when the British were directly ruling the country? How did the MB's leadership justify the rejection of the constitution and the idea of multiparty parliamentary politics? Why did they turn against the liberal-nationalist Wafd party but not the monarchy? What factors shaped the political and religious outlook of the MB?

In attempting to explain the determinants of the MB's sociopolitical discourse, we focus on the interplay of the same set of variables that were also employed in explaining the rise of Islamic modernism and liberal nationalism. The rise of the MB was certainly connected to the sociopolitical and cultural transformation Egypt experienced between the 1919 revolution and the 1930s. In more specific terms, changes in class relations and the dynamics of interelite political rivalries undeniably shaped the resources and the opportunity structure from which the MB drew in its contention for political power and cultural supremacy. In addition, the economic difficulties of the 1930s, the rising unemployment, and the exclusionary policies commonly pursued by diverse segments of the ruling elite contributed to the rise of the MB and shaped its political orientation. Nevertheless, we contend that the MB's discourse, far from being a reflection of the emergent social classes or the traditional Arabic and Islamic culture, was rather produced in an oppositional relation to the dominant ideology of liberal nationalism. To be sure, the MB was an Islamic movement that drew its legitimacy from the shari'a. But its leaders' interpretations of the shari'a, as the guiding principles of their movement, were influenced by the kinds of obstacles they perceived to be hindering the realization of their Islamic objectives.[4] The changes in their discourse were thus a function of the changing nature of these obstacles. We argue that in the thirties and forties, liberal nationalism, while serving as a target for the MB's ideological attack, in a dialogic manner shaped its discourse. The existing political pluralism, despite the Brothers' strong criticism of parliamentary and party politics, had nevertheless directed the MB in a moderate direction as it attempted to participate in electoral competitions. As pluralism declined and the MB's participation in the parliamentary politics was blocked, an extremist trend prevailed in the movement. This process was reinforced after the 1952 coup, when Nassir's authoritarian regime imposed a monolithic ideological structure on Egyptian society—and hence brought about the emergence of a new set of targets in relation to which the Brothers further advanced their sociopolitical views.

Social Differentiation and Changes in Class Relations: The Landowners versus the New Effendiyya

The cultural turn in the late thirties followed the social differentiation and structural transformation that were produced as a result of a whole array of developments in demographic growth, occupational expansion, and education after the 1919 revolution. The population increased rapidly, rural to urban migration accelerated, the traditional social classes continued to decline, a new, educated middle class connected to the expanding bureaucratic structure of the state and to an emerging industrial sector grew swiftly, a working class emerged, and the landowning class continued to expand its power and interests in the society. That social differentiation and demographic expansion would bring a new set of actors to the country's increasingly contested political arena was understandable. After all, the revolution, being a mass-based movement, was fought on the premise that Egypt was for the Egyptians and that the people were the source of legislation and national sovereignty. Naturally, politics was no longer the exclusive realm of a tripartite of power elite—a group of notables who formed the Wafd party (founded in 1918) and led the revolution, the king who had his own prerogatives, and the British who still maintained considerable influence in the country. The emergent middle class, the new *effendiyya*, became among the most vociferous challengers of the postrevolutionary regime.

The economic historian Charles Issawi meticulously documented Egypt's demographic shift, social dislocation, economic inequality, and deteriorating economic conditions in the thirties. The population increased from 11,287,000 in 1907 to 18,947,000 in 1947 and 26,080,000 in 1960 (an increase of over 130 percent), while the crop area expanded from 7,700,000 *feddans*[5] in 1912 to 9,300,000 feddans in 1952 and 10,050,000 feddans in 1957 (an increase of about 31 percent).[6] In 1920–50, the volume of agricultural production managed to keep pace with the population.[7] Parallel with the demographic change was an increase in rural-to-urban migration. Between 1917 and 1937, the population of Cairo rose from 791,000 to 1,312,000 and that of Alexandria from 445,000 to

686,000, representing an increase of 66 and 55 percent, respectively, compared with 25 percent for the country as a whole. During the same period, the population of the twenty largest towns rose from 1,883,000 to 2,944,000, an increase of 54 percent. In other words, every year some 30,000 people were drifting from the countryside to the towns.[8] It was not just the demographic change that produced social dislocation, however. There were also changes in the occupational profile, as the number of traditional craftsmen in the cities and villages fell from 150,000 in 1914 to 95,000 in 1937 and then to 60,000 in 1958. The number of new artisans increased very slowly, from 380,000 in 1907 to 715,000 in 1958—an annual growth rate of 1.3 percent.

In class terms, the landowners enjoyed much more influence in the revolution of 1919 and its aftermath than any other group. The establishment of a constitutional monarchy considerably expanded their power and influence. Of the eighteen-member commission responsible for drafting the constitution, eleven members, or 61 percent, were large landowners. Similarly, of the total of thirty-two members of the Constituent Assembly, twenty, or 62 percent, were large landowners.[9] The landowners had been active in politics since the days of Khedive Ismail, and their participation in the revolution was in resonance with their interests in the hydraulic economy, since the government-controlled irrigation could make or break a large landowner.[10] Naturally, they pushed for a constitutional government in order to be able to check the government's arbitrary behavior.[11] The Egyptianization of economic enterprises further expanded the power of the dominant classes, as the percentage of Egyptian businessmen investing in companies increased from 47 percent in 1934–39 to 84 percent in 1946–48[12] (or as the share of Egyptians in joint-stock companies increased from 9 percent before 1933 to 79 percent of the newly formed companies in 1933–48 and 39 percent of the total).[13] The capital of industrial joint-stock companies rose from £E16.3 million in 1938 to £E28.5 million in 1945 and £E56.8 million in 1950.[14]

Historians have pointed to the existence of a structural unity between the landowners and the emergent industrial bourgeoisie as the latter did not challenge the landowners' economic and political supremacy. Rather, a close link between the two was forged, as individuals who were landowner-industrialists or landowner-merchants became the rule. Afaf Lutfi Marsot observes that "the links among political activity, economic enterprise, and landowners were positive and strong, and explain why there was no challenge to the power of the landowners from the new industrial elite, for they were to a large extent one and the same, or wanting to be."[15] Further, the white-collar professionals who had led the nationalist struggle, through intermarriage or the acquisition of landed property, were gradually dissolved into the ranks of the landowning class. While the first Wafdist delegation to Parliament appeared to its opponents shockingly plebeian, in every subsequent delegation an increasing number of members listed their main occupation as landowner.[16]

In the postindependence period, there was also an increase in the number of salaried professionals, including teachers, intellectuals, technicians, and engineers. According to Gershoni and Jankowski, the number of doctors and engineers in Egypt each more than doubled between 1927 and 1947, while the number of lawyers nearly doubled. Posts in the government bureaucracy grew by 61 percent over the period from 1941 to 1954, and the number that required educated employees grew particularly (from 47,000 to 170,000). Overall, in the decade from 1937 to 1947 occupational groups of a primarily effendi character (government clerks, teachers, medical and legal specialists, engineers, and "writers and journalists") are estimated to have increased by almost 40 percent (from 155,500 to 216,500).[17] The newly established modern industry also absorbed a portion of the urban population. The population censuses put the number engaged in manufacturing, mining, and building at 610,000 in 1937 and 835,000 in 1947, and there was a further increase of 81,000 between 1947 and 1951.[18]

Class Politics, Economic Difficulties, and Ideological Change

With these changes came a new set of demands from the emerging groups and social classes for economic benefits, cultural enrichment, and political participation. The 1920s were a happy decade for Egypt. In addition to the feeling of empowerment that would naturally come following a successful revolution, in economic terms "high cotton prices seemed to promise continued prosperity for all."[19] The 1930s, however, were a different order. They were a decade of economic bust, following the boom of the 1920s. As in the decade preceding the Urabi rebellion and British occupation, Egypt's economic problem was externally induced, resulting from the vulnerability of its single-commodity export economy to fluctuations in the world market—in this case, the world economic depression of the early thirties. According to table 9.1, the value index of agricultural crops declined sharply, from 145 in 1924–28 to 75 in 1931, and, with some fluctuations, increased to 94 in 1940. It then increased steadily during the war years, to 267 in 1945. The value index declined again, to 209 in 1946, but it began to considerably increase annually, reaching 442 in 1950. The volume index fluctuated between 83 and 103 in the prewar years, and between 94 and 75 during the war years, but it steadily increased from 98 in 1946 to 118 in 1951. The sharp decline in the value of agricultural crops in the 1930s naturally undermined the government's ability to expand or even maintain social services to meet the needs of the growing population. It also impoverished a significant portion of the population whose livelihood was tied to export trade.

We should not, however, exaggerate the intensity of economic difficulties and class polarization as causal factors leading to social protests and cultural change. For

Table 9.1. Volume and gross value of agricultural crops in Egypt

Year	Volume	Value
Prewar years:[a]		
1924–28	83	145
1929	93	118
1931	80	75
1933	92	78
1935	94	94
1937	103	97
1938	93	89
War years:[b]		
1940	94	94
1941	89	115
1942	79	184
1943	75	187
1944	79	229
1945	81	267
Postwar years:[c]		
1946	98	209
1947	100	258
1948	112	285
1949	110	325
1950	119	442
1951	118	

Source: Charles Issawi, *Egypt at Mid-century: An Economy Survey* (London: Oxford University Press, 1954), p. 79, table 8.
Note: Volume and value in 1939 are set at 100, and other values are in relation to that.
[a] For the pretwar years, volume is a measure of fourteen main crops; value is a measure of twelve main crops.
[b] For the war years, volume is a measure of all crops and livestock products.
[c] For the postwar years, volume is a measure of all crops, based on 1934–38 = 100; value measures twelve main crops.

one thing, an impoverished society does not have enough resources to engage in effective ideological contention. And Egypt's impoverishment was not as severe as has sometimes been maintained. The massive growth in the number of writers and journalists—from 1,200 in 1937 to 8,200 in 1947—which indicated heightened cultural activities,[20] required a sustained inflow of resources. As table 9.1 indicates, there was a consistent increase in the value index of agricultural production throughout the forties. Its increase in the postwar period was quite impressive. The increase in the volume index for agricultural production in the postwar period was also significant. For another thing, many of the socioeconomic factors singled out to explain the cultural shift also existed before the 1919 revolution. Beginning in

1907, Egypt experienced a major economic downturn that contributed to the rise of anti-British protest movements but not to antiliberal Islamic activism.

Further, the connection between the inequality in land distribution in the thirties and forties and the decline of liberal nationalism may take on a different meaning if we consider changes in this inequality over a longer period of time.[21] Although many Egyptian activists self-righteously attacked large landowners, it is not convincing to argue that inequality in landownership contributed to Egypt's cultural turn and the rise of the MB. This is particularly so when we consider that while large landownership persisted through the first half of the twentieth century, the share of large holdings in the total declined between 1896 and 1948. As table 9.2 shows, the percentage of small landowners (with holdings of less than 5 feddans) in the total holdings steadily increased from 19.87 percent in 1896 to 34.62 percent in 1948. Their number and area increased from 611,000 landholders and 994,000 feddans in 1896 to 2,565,000 landholders and 2,056,000 feddans in 1948. The numbers of middle-sized (with holdings of 5–40 feddans) and large (with holdings of more than 50 feddans) landowners changed little, and their areas declined somewhat, from 1,816,000 to 1,754,000 feddans for the middle-sized and from 2,192,000 to 2,128,000 feddans for large holdings in the same period, but their percentage in all holdings declined from 36.31 percent and 43.82 percent in 1896 to 29.54 percent and 35.84 percent in 1948, respectively. To be sure, one may argue that much of the decline in inequality in landed properties was due to a considerable increase in the number of very small landowners (holders of less than 1 feddan) between 1913 and 1948, from 60.5 percent to 72.77 percent, and in their area, from 7.67 percent to 13.79 percent of the total. Nevertheless, it may be argued that in the 1930s there were more landowners to resist any significant increase in the land-tax assessment than simply the middle-sized and large landowners. From these data, it would be hard to derive the antilandowner attitudes of the opposition from the fact of the land distribution.[22]

Likewise, the notion that liberal nationalism declined because it did not have mass support in the 1919 revolution, and that, as Safran claimed, the masses' participation in the revolution was motivated by their deep hatred of a religiously alien power disregards the extensive cultural changes Egypt experienced in the nineteenth and twentieth centuries. Before the 1919 revolution, there was no significant fundamentalist movement in Egypt. Even the pan-Islamic anti-British movement that was inspired by the teachings of al-Afghani was influenced by the European Enlightenment. Gershoni and Jankowski's claim that a revolution in Egyptian literacy brought into active involvement in public life social strata who were more deeply rooted in Arabic and Islamic modes of expression than the Westernized elite who led the revolution is equally suspect and amounts to reading history backward: Because these groups ended up supporting the MB, they therefore must have been more

Table 9.2. Distribution of land holdings in Egypt, 1896–1948

Year	All Holdings		Holdings of <1 Feddan		Holdings of <5 Feddans		Holdings of 5–40 Feddans		Holdings of >50 Feddans	
	Number	Area (thousands of feddans)	Number	Area (thousands of feddans)	Number	Area (thousands of feddans)	Number	Area (thousands of feddans)	Number	Area (thousands of feddans)
1896	767	5,002			611	994	144	1,816	12	2,192
	(100)	(100)			(79.66)	(19.87)	(18.77)	(36.31)	(1.56)	(43.82)
1913	1,557	5,293	943	406	1,411	1,419	133	1,633	13	2,241
	(100)	(100)	(60.56)	(7.67)	(90.62)	(26.81)	(8.54)	(30.85)	(0.83)	(42.34)
1929	2,176	5,794	1,476	569	2,019	1,708	144	1,759	13	2,327
	(100)	(100)	(67.83)	(9.82)	(92.78)	(29.48)	(6.62)	(30.36)	(0.60)	(40.16)
1939	2,481	5,837	1,752	702	2,323	1,915	146	1,674	13	2,180
	(100)	(100)	(70.62)	(12.03)	(93.63)	(32.81)	(5.88)	(28.68)	(0.52)	(37.35)
1948	2,721	5,938	1,980	819	2,565	2,056	144	1,754	12	2,128
	(100)	(100)	(72.77)	(13.79)	(94.27)	(34.62)	(5.29)	(29.54)	(0.44)	(35.84)

Source: Charles Issawi, *Egypt at Mid-century: An Economy Survey* (London: Oxford University Press, 1954), p. 126, table 18.
Note: Values in parentheses are percentages (computed by the author).

engrossed in the Arabic and Islamic tradition than their predecessors.[23] First, these authors have not provided evidence indicating that there were significant differences between the social position of the members of the middle class who actively participated in the revolution and the new effendiyya. Second, even if there were in fact such differences, we still need to explain why they followed the MB. In many crucial respects, the discourse of the MB was a new innovation in the Islamic movement, which cannot be deduced from the Arabic-Islamic traditions of the marginal social strata that were brought into the limelight as a result of the revolution in literacy. Given that the MB's discourse was produced, rather than being the inevitable reflection of the prevailing socioeconomic conditions, the connection between the Arabic-Islamic essence of the new effendiyya and the formulation of the MB's discourse cannot be adequately explained in terms of class dynamics. An important factor in Gershoni and Jankowski's historiography, however, is posing the process of cultural change within the broader regional context of the diffusion of pan-Arabist ideas in Egypt, which had become possible as a result of the increasing contact between Egyptians and their neighbors in the postrevolutionary period.[24] While one may counter by pointing out that in the 1920–36 period, of the 1,450 students sent abroad, 1,229 went to Britain and France for study,[25] and thus Egypt in this respect had greater contact with Europe than with its Arabic and Islamic neighbors, we cannot overlook the impact of neighborly contacts on domestic cultural conditions. If the migration of Syrians to Egypt in the nineteenth century contributed to the rise of liberal and secular discourse, Egyptians becoming aware of the Syrians' struggle against the French or Iraqis against the British had naturally fomented pan-Arabist solidarity in their midst.

Granted, the economic difficulties of the thirties created mass discontent and contributed to the decline of the legitimacy of constitutional rule and parliamentary politics. These factors in fact provided the issues in reference to which culture producers formulated their ideas about the appropriate model of politics, the desirable mode of social organization, and Egyptian identity. But whether the landowners were responsible for these difficulties cannot be deduced from the fact of these difficulties. This is so particularly in light of the fact that the dynamics of capitalist agricultural development in the first half of the twentieth century did not enhance the concentration and centralization of productive wealth. Thus, if the landowners came under attack, it was not because they were a selfish group of people. It was rather because their active presence in the parliament had made them a visible target of ideological attack. And their unwillingness to share power with other groups, including the Muslim Brothers, transformed the universalism of the parliamentary system into a particularistic tool tied to the landed interests.

In fact, the political visibility of the landowners and the state's exclusionary policies underpinned the frustration of the intellectuals and opinion leaders with the parliament, shaping the perception that the parliament was a corrupt, unrepresentative, and self-serving body concerned only with promoting the interests of its members and the class they represented, as Gershoni and Jankowski have meticulously documented. Tawfiq al-Hakim, perhaps an outstanding example of a former enthusiast of the post-1919 national order, in the 1930s was criticizing the parliament, which had turned into an instrument of the large landowners, who had deprived it of any real democratic quality. Political commentators charged that Egypt had a system of "parliamentary rule without real democracy," that the purpose of this system was to "guard the material interests of the upper classes only" and "to blind the masses and exploit them most shamefully and vilely," that it was driven solely by "lust for office" and "desire for personal gain," and that it turned the country into "a stage for oratory and theatrics." Equally vehement criticism was directed at the established political parties. Party politics was portrayed as partyism, viewed as an incurable sickness spreading through the body of the nation, as "factions" without "any clearly defined program" or, in the case of those which had split off from the Wafd, with "no program and no defined aim except fighting with the Wafd and collaborating with the British as a means of gaining power." Revulsion with "politics" had the effect of "reverberating negatively upon the Western-inspired form of territorial nationalism which had taken hold in Egypt in conjunction with the parliamentary order." The mood of discontent and frustration extended beyond politics. Intellectuals characterized Egypt in the 1930s as a country in "crisis" and experiencing social "confusion," intellectual "perplexity," emotional "anxiety," and moral "chaos." Sayyid Qutb saw contemporary Egyptian culture as being in a state of "confusion" in which the values of the "materialist European civilization" spreading in Egypt did not fit with the country's beliefs and customs; the result was bound to be a prolonged period of "perplexity" and "anxiety."[26]

The State and Culture Production:
Secularism and the Politicization of Religion

The rise of the liberal-nationalist state in the postrevolutionary period did not create consensus among the principle actors about Egypt's cultural and national priorities. The revolution, the declaration of independence, and the constitution (while ending the British protectorate, recognizing Egypt as an independent sovereign country, and considerably curtailing the power of the king)[27] failed to resolve successfully the two central issues facing the liberal-nationalist movement. Egypt did not attain full independence from Britain. Nor was it able to eliminate totally the monarch's arbitrary power. Instead, the revolution resulted in the formation of a new power block in which the revolutionary leaders shared power with the king and the British, without the three being in agreement about the constitution as the guiding principles of political action.[28] Indeed, there was among the contending factions of the ruling elite a mutual nonrecognition of one another's constitutional rights and responsibilities.[29] The British and the king seriously limited the Wafd's ability to implement its policies,[30] and the Wafd leaders were unwilling to share power with or recognize the political interests of new groups. These rivalries, however, provided a favorable space for the MB to mobilize support against the Wafd's "un-Islamic" tendencies. The khedive, who saw in entertaining the idea of becoming a caliph a useful tool to combat his liberal-nationalist rivals, was the Brothers' natural ally.

Crucial in the development of the Islamic opposition were the rise of the secularist state and the rationalist outlooks of the intellectual leaders connected to it. On the one hand, the state's expanding bureaucracy, particularly in the field of education, more than any other institution in Egyptian society contributed to the genesis of the new middle class—the new effendiyya.[31] The Egyptianization of the state's personnel further expanded the occupational positions to be filled by educated individuals; the number of British staff in the military and civil administration continually declined after the 1919 revolution.[32] On the other hand, the state's decidedly secular educational function and reformist policies contributed to the politicization of religion. One relevant example of the state's secularism that raised the suspicion of religious groups is related to the reorganization of the Egyptian University as a full-fledged state institution in 1925.[33] The layout of its campus, reflecting Parisian beaux arts conventions, and its stately neoclassicism broke with the Islamic past. Although the original plan of the university included a main mosque, it remained unbuilt, symbolizing the school's secular priorities.[34] A predominantly non-Egyptian faculty strengthened and promoted the university's secular liberal orientation (the Egyptianization of its faculty took place only gradually).[35]

Likewise, nationalist politicians and deputies implemented policies that came into conflict with the religious views of the conservative Islamic establishment. They questioned the wisdom of retaining the shari'a courts, the necessity of having a mufti, and the rationale for maintaining the institution of the waqf. They also proposed to reform the marriage and divorce laws and to prohibit colorful local, popular practices connected with burials and visits to cemeteries. In the field of women's rights, the family, gender relations, and matters of personal status, reforms were introduced in the shari'a and the religious courts. A series of legislative acts from 1923 to 1931 ameliorated the abuses involved in child marriages and the facile repudiation of wives by husbands using the traditional formula of divorce. In 1927, draft legislation that further restricted polygamy was introduced. A number of feminist magazines and journals wholly devoted to the problems of Egyptian women appeared in this period.[36] In the tumultuous March of 1919, a crowd of about three hundred veiled "revolutionary gentlewomen" marched through the streets of Cairo demanding independence. After the 1922 declaration of independence, Huda

Sharawi and her friends raised issues specific to women. In 1923 Sharawi dramatically discarded her face veil and founded the Egyptian Feminist Union. Many upper-class women followed Sharawi's example in dress. Beginning in the late 1920s, they slowly forced their way into the Egyptian University.[37]

The action of the liberal intellectual leaders also contributed to the politicization of religion. Firmly committed to a rationalist Europeanizing model of social organization, these leaders found it necessary to subject historical Islam and Islamic orthodoxy to ardent criticisms. They glorified the pre-Islamic sociopolitical order and emphasized the distinctive Egyptian entity that in their views transcended religion and language. Leading intellectuals associated with the liberal-nationalist movement used their newly acquired cultural capital and institutional position to further advance their views on politics, the nation, literature, gender relations, and the proper methods of historical analysis. These views questioned many of the core Islamic principles. Influenced by the earlier writings of Shibli Shumayyil (1850–1917), several Egyptian writers now carried on the propagation of the idea of evolution. Thus, *Fasl al-maqal fi falsafat al-mushu' wa'l-irtiqa'*, by Hasan Hussein, appeared in 1924; Ismail Mazhar's (1891–1962) translation of *The Origin of Species* (*Asl al-anwa*) four years later. A general treatise on the theory of evolution (*Nazariyyat al-tatawwur wa asl al-insan*) by Salama Musa (1887–1958) also appeared around that time. Two works on Islam created the most controversy in the 1920s. One was Ali Abd al-Raziq's reexamination of Islamic political theory in 1925, in the wake of Mustafa Kemal's abolition of the caliphate in 1924. The other was Taha Hussein's *Pre-Islamic Poetry*, which appeared in 1926.[38]

In chapter 4, we discussed the uproar caused in conservative circles by al-Raziq's reinterpretation of the traditional Islamic conception of sovereignty in favor of constitutionalism. Likewise, Taha Hussein's analysis of the historical context of jahiliyya poetry produced angry reactions and acrimonious debates. For Taha Hussein questioned a popularly held Muslim belief that the early Islamic movement was a reaction against the decadence of the pre-Islamic era, as was reflected in its poetry. He argued that the so-called pre-Islamic poetry was not genuine in the sense of belonging to the period before the rise of Islam. "The greater part of what we call pre-Islamic literature does not belong to the pre-Islamic period at all, but was forged only after the appearance of Islam. It is, therefore, Islamic, representing the life, the tendencies and the predilections of the Muslims, more than it does the life of pre-Islamic period."[39] The remains of genuine pre-Islamic literature were very scanty and not an adequate portrayal of the pre-Islamic culture. As to why this poetry was attributed to the pre-Islamic period, Taha Hussein enumerated a number of factors, such as the desire to promote political designs, gratify national and tribal rivalries, and serve the interests of the narrators, storytellers, grammarians, tradition collectors, theologians, and commentators on the Quran.[40] Taking a more conservative approach, Ahmad Amin (1886–1954) began work in the 1920s on a subtle attack upon tradition. He argued for a system of ethics based on reason and intuition, and against one based solely on tradition derived from religious teachings and custom.[41] To defend the idea of Egyptian identity, he argued that the secession of Ibn Tulun in the ninth century from Baghdad and the establishment of the Fatimids and later the Mamluks were instances of the Egyptian will to independence against the Umayyad and Abbasid conquerors. The breakdown of the unity of umma that, in the common Muslim historical view, was the greatest disaster that had befallen Islam, was thus treated as a cause for celebration because it signified Egypt's early self-assertion.[42]

The liberal intellectual leaders also made intricate efforts to establish a distinct Egyptian cultural personality: through the centuries Egypt, for al-Sayyid, had molded a "pharaonic core"; it had carried "the religious lights," in the view of Muhammad Hussein Haykal (1888–1956); it had displayed a Mediterranean sensibility that blended, as Taha Hussein maintained, a material and spiritual subjectivity; it was, for al-Hakim, obsessed with the notion of time and space.[43] Following the discovery of the tomb of Tutankhamen in all its dazzling splendor in 1922, the Pharaonic era appeared as the real legacy of the new independent Egypt: it was both pre-Islamic and pre-Christian, so that the spirit of the new Egypt was to be an amalgam of both the Islamic and Christian cultures. For half a century after 1919, Taha Hussein led the campaign to establish classical studies in Egypt. A nationalist and a liberal reformer, he saw classics as indispensable to building a modern, secularized nation-state.[44] Taha Hussein capped his preference for Hellenic and Roman classical culture with the thesis that Egypt had always belonged to a wider, general Mediterranean civilization. The future of Egypt's development therefore lay in retaining this old link. In effect, Taha was rejecting both the Islamic and African civilizational orbits for Egypt in favor of an older—and closer to Europe—southwest Asian and eastern Mediterranean cultural heritage.[45]

In short, Vatikiotis's summary of the views of the liberal intellectual leaders in the postrevolutionary period reveals that they had an outlook not too different from the Europe-centered perspective of James Mill and Lord Macaulay. If the latter was part of the sequence of events that led to the Indian mutiny of 1857–58, the former shaped the discourse of the Muslim Brothers:

> This brand of liberal, secular rationalism constituted a far more dangerous attack upon Islam and its tradition. Salama Musa, Ismail Mazhar and Husayn [Hussein] Fawzi did not equivocate over the proclamation of Man as the hero of modern civilization; over the assertion that law must be man-made if it is to be dynamic and creative. Nor did they hesitate in introducing a socioeconomic interpretation of history, culture and politics. Above all, they

proclaimed Western civilization as the highest stage of man's spiritual and
material development; declared Islamic civilization and culture dead and useless; and advocated the adoption of Western civilization and culture without
reservations as the only way for the advancement of their country. . . . Moreover, unlike the *literati,* their secular humanism and commitment to the application of science to the study of society were so strong as to lead them to
an attack on Islamic reformers. Thus to them al-Afghani was an "ignorant
reactionary." Evolution, science and a positivist philosophy constituted the
formula which they advocated for the advancement of Egypt.[46]

The Muslim Brothers versus the Liberal-Nationalist Intellectuals

The rise of the Society of the Muslim Brothers was a response to these developments. To be sure, one may cite the diffusion of such antidemocratic and antiliberal ideologies as Fascism and communism from Europe in Egypt in the thirties to
have shaped a discursive context that was congruent with the all-encompassing discourse of the Muslim Brothers. In the same way that such seminal ideas of the nineteenth century as evolution, progress, and civilization gained a superior status in
the thought processes of the Islamic modernists, the totalitarianism of Fascism and
Nazism, stress on militarism and individual heroism, and antimaterialist socialism
seemed to have affected the way al-Banna formulated an Islamic response to the
problems of the Muslim community. According to Wendell, "whatever he may
have said or written in adverse criticism of European Fascism and imperialism,
there can be little question that Hasan [al-Banna] was deeply impressed by the
organization of the Nazi, Fascist, and Communist parties, and by no means rejected the tactics they employed to gain and sustain their power."[47] In addition, the
economic difficulties coupled with the failure of the Wafd party to resolve the
national issue of total independence naturally made the Egyptian public suscepti-
ble to pro-Fascist and pro-Nazi propaganda. In the 1930s, Misr al-Fatat (Young
Egypt), which adhered to the idea of imperial Egyptian nationalism and religious
extremism, emerged. Its paramilitary organization—the Green Shirts—was formed
to pursue its political objectives. The rise of religious activism was also a reaction
to the missionaries. The Young Men's Muslim Association (YMMA) was founded
in 1927 to counter the program and propaganda of Christian missionaries. The
same aim was pursued by the Hassafi Welfare Society, which was organized by
al-Banna and friends to build the individual moral character and check the missionary activities of the Christian Biblical Mission which was "preaching Christianity in the guise of nursing."[48] In trying to copy the missionaries, al-Banna went
so far as to send his cadres to the School of Social Service, a Western school. Although he believed that the school was established to "serve the missionaries and

imperialists" in Egypt, he maintained that "whatever the case, there is no doubt that its scientific and practical programme will greatly facilitate the training [of the Brothers] in social welfare works. There is no doubt that this will open doors to our efforts to penetrate Egyptian society."[49]

The crucial factors that shaped the discourse and political orientation of the Muslim Brothers were the ideology of liberal nationalism and the policies implemented by the nationalist government. To a disinterested observer, the Egyptian version of liberal nationalism would not have appeared to be simply a discourse to resolve the problem of politics in a constitutional direction. It would rather have appeared to be an all-encompassing and comprehensive ideology, dictating a worldview that ranged from a philosophy of history to a style of dress. To a Muslim observer, in particular, the feature of this ideology was defined less in terms of the necessity of liberating Egypt from the vestiges of foreign domination than in terms of opposition to an Islam that was, in the nationalist perception, deleterious to the construction of modern Egypt. In about one decade, the liberal nationalists and policy makers attacked virtually all aspects of the Islamic tradition from a predominantly secularizing model of social evolution and universal progress. This ideology naturally produced its own antagonists. The rise of the Islamic movement from the 1930s on was a reaction to the ideas of the liberal intellectual leaders and, in some crucial respects, a "mirror image" of secular liberalism. Whatever extremism could be attributed to the MB would find its counterparts in the Wafd and in the liberal-nationalist discourse, however rationally constructed. As the liberal nationalists were hard at work attempting to replace Islam with their own version of secularism, the ideologues of the MB in a parallel fashion portrayed their version of Islam as a total system, applicable to all times and to all places. For al-Banna, Islam was "a religion, a nationality, and a creed uniting all Muslims."[50]

This is all the more true because the new effendiyya had serious misgiving about the politically visible dominant classes. Excluded from political participation, they perceived constitutionalism and parliamentary politics as the tool of the landowning class and a symbol of their domination. Indicative of their attitudes toward the ruling elite was al-Banna's admonition to his followers that "chiefs, leaders, and men of rank and authority will hate you, all governments will rise as one against you, and every government will try to set limits to your activities and to put impediments in your way."[51] How the existing regime of signification—that is, secularist liberal politics—shaped the MB's worldview can be inferred from the fact that initially the MB did not have a clear idea about the nature of its role in society. The Brothers developed their sociopolitical discourse during the first ten years of their activities. At the fifth conference (which was also the tenth anniversary of the movement) the Brothers offered a general sketch of their program. It was, said Hasan al-Banna,

(1) a salafi message, i.e., The Book of God and the *Sunnah* of His Messenger;
(2) a Sunni path: for the *Ikhwan* [Brothers] oblige themselves to following the
purified *sunnah* in all their deeds, especially in the domain of beliefs and acts of
worship . . . ; (3) a Sufi reality: for the *Ikhwan* know that the basis of righteousness is the purification of the soul, transparency of the heart, perseverance in
work . . . and love for the sake of God . . . ; (4) a political organization: for the
Ikhwan demand the reform of political order from within and the revision of the
relationship of the Muslim *ummah* with other nations . . . ; (5) a sporting group:
for the *Ikhwan* look after their bodies and know that a strong Muslim is better
than a weak Muslim . . . ; (6) a scientific and cultural league: for . . . Islam makes
the seeking of knowledge a religious duty . . . ; (7) an economic enterprise: for
Islam is interested in the acquiring of money . . . ; (8) a social endeavour: for the
Ikhwan are interested in the ills of society and try to find ways for their cure.[52]

If we brush aside the extensive quotations from the Quran that al-Banna brought
to bear in support of his views, there would remain few Islamic arguments that
were deductively formulated. For the most part, al-Banna appeared to have constructed a sociopolitical position in terms of his differences with what he perceived
as anti-Islamic tendencies in Egypt: liberal nationalism, positive law, and the glorification of pre-Islamic Egypt. He made reference to such concepts as patriotism and
nationalism without systematically assessing their status in Islam but only to state
the superiority of his Islamic movement over all other movements. For him, "love
of this land, attachment to it, sentiment toward it. . . . [making] every effort to free
the land from its ravagers, to increase its independence, and to instill the principles
of freedom and greatness in the souls of its sons. . . . reinforcing the bonds which
unite individuals within a given country"—all are prescribed by Islam.[53] If "patriotism" meant "the conquest of countries and lordship over the earth, Islam has
already ordained that, and has sent out conquerors to carry out the most gracious
of colonization and the most blessed conquests."[54] Al-Banna rejected the notion
of nationalism that entailed division "into parties which engage in mutual throat-
cutting, hatred and vituperation, hurling accusations at one another, deceiving one
another, and banding together to further a positivist course of action dictated by
their desires, informed by their personal motives and goals, and interpreted by their
minds to accord with their own selfish interests."[55] He said "we define patriotism
according to the standard of credal belief, while they define it according to territorial borders and geographical boundaries."[56] Further elaborating his difference with
secular nationalism, al-Banna proclaimed that,

If . . . what is meant by "nationalism" is the revival of the customs of a pagan
age which have been swept away, and the reconstitution of extinct manners

that have gone by, while a benevolent civilization which has long been established is effaced, and the bonds and attachments of Islam are dissolved by the
propaganda of national and racial self-aggrandizement, as some states have
done by taking extremes measures to annihilate the characteristic traits of
Islam and Arabism—extending even to personal names, the letters of the
alphabet and the vocabulary, and to the reviving of long-dead pagan customs—then this ingredient of nationalism is reprehensible, deleterious in
its consequence and evil in its results.[57]

Al-Banna's disapproval of the secularist policies of the nationalist government,
the public involvement of women in society and the mixing of the sexes, and the
views of liberal intellectual leaders was so intense that he equated them with a disease that afflicted Eastern nations. This disease was characterized, on the intellectual side, by "anarchy, defection, and heresy which destroy their religious beliefs
and overthrow the ideals within their sons' breasts. . . . . [and] on the sociological
side by licentiousness of the manners and mores, and through the sloughing off of
the restraints of the humanitarian virtues they inherited from their glorious, fortu-
nate ancestors; while through imitation of the West, the viper's venom creeps insid-
iously into their affairs, poisoning their blood and sullying the purity of their
well-being. They have been assailed through the workings of a positive law which
does not restrain the criminal, chastise the assailant, or repel the unjust; nor does it
even for one day take the place of the divinely revealed laws."[58]
   Since the liberal intellectual leaders drew from Western thought in their criticisms of Islam, the MB's rejection of liberalism entailed the rejection of the West
as well. Writing in 1936, during the Great Depression, al-Banna argued that " 'the
civilization of the West,' proudly strong in its science, and for a period able to sub-
jugate the world, is now 'in bankruptcy and in decline,' its political fundamentals
destroyed by dictatorship, its economic systems racked by crisis, its social order
decaying."[59] Egyptian writers who shared or adopted the "false ideas" of the
Orientalist about Islam were regarded as having abetted, "intentionally or not," the
cultural imperialism of the West. Well-known writers accused of this tendency were
Taha Hussein, Ali Abd al-Raziq, Khalid Mhummad Khalid, and Amin 'Uthman.[60]
   In the same way in which Saad Zaghlul and Mustafa al-Nahhas (who became the
head of the Wafd party following the death of Zaghlul) portrayed the Wafd as the
representative of the whole nation and regarded non-Wafdist political groups as
outside the pale of the nationalist movement,[61] the MB leadership considered their
movement the embodiment of the true spirit of Islam, criticizing the Islamic orthodoxy of the Azhar for its political ineffectiveness and Sufism for its focus on withdrawal. Just as the Wafd claimed exclusive national leadership, al-Banna went so far
as to suggest the abolition of all political parties and the creation of a single party

with an Islamic reform program.[62] The government's secular policies provoked anger among the MB leaders and other prominent Muslim activists. Reacting to the Egyptian University's secularism, al-Banna denounced the university for its "non-Islamic" currents and for acting as though it "could not be a lay university unless it revolted against religion and fought the social tradition which derived from it."[63] Rashid Rida, a prominent Muslim scholar, assailed the university as "a haven for heretics and a breeding ground for atheism," and the Muslim Brother Muhammad al-Ghazali said the liberals were "puppets and slaves of the European and serving the cause of Christian imperialism."[64] And around 1938, a group of students burst into the office of Taha Hussein and denounced him for backing coeducation.[65] The Wafd and the MB being mutually exclusive, the decline of one benefited the rise of the other. In the post–World War II era, the Wafd lost its unique role as the principal voice of articulate nationalist discontent; the MB had seriously eaten into the traditional Wafdist strongholds: the university, the civil service, and the countryside.[66]

Nassir's Military Coup and the Radicalization of the Muslim Brothers

Except for occasional Muslim reactions to missionary activities, the dominant cultural trend in Egypt since the Napoleonic invasion at the turn of the nineteenth century had remained moderate and peaceful for well over a century. Even the Society of the Muslim Brothers, despite its totalistic discourse and demand for unquestionable loyalty from its members, opted for moderation and eschewed militant activities for more than a decade after it was founded in 1928. The society could be best conceived of as an Islamically organized contender in an intricate power struggle among the palace, the conservative pan-Islamic groups, the pan-Arabists, the Wafd, and the British. They often allied with the right-wing faction of the Wafd party, the king, and other conservative forces against the communists and the left-leaning faction of the Wafd party. The Brothers did not even attack the British presence in Egypt until the mid-1940s. Their list of fifty demands, which included an attack on colonialism couched in general terms, contained neither any mention of independence for Egypt nor anything about the withdrawal of British troops from Egyptian territory.[67] The MB's first general conference, held in May 1933, concerned itself primarily with the problem of Christian missionaries—an issue not too different from the concerns of the nineteenth-century modernists in India and Egypt. In a letter to King Fuad, the Brothers urgently requested that such activities be brought under control.[68] Furthermore, on the occasion of the coronation of the much-loved young King Faruq in 1937, the Brothers called their fourth conference to celebrate his accession. Following a long and joyous celebration, they gathered at the gates of 'Abidin Palace chanting a traditional oath of loyalty: "We grant you our allegiance on the Book of God and the Tradition of His Prophet."[69] For the palace and its conservative allies at the Azhar, led by the king's mentor, Shaykh Mustafa al-Maraghi, the Muslim Brothers (as well as Young Egypt) were useful as counterweights to the Wafd—a relationship which caused membership defections from the Wafd in 1939.[70] In short, as long as pluralistic political and cultural conditions existed, the MB tended to operate within the existing political framework and refrain from extremist actions, their difference with other political parties being that they derived the legitimacy of their mission from the shari'a.

There was also an affinity between the MB and Islamic modernism. The Brothers did not believe in orthodox jurisprudence. For them, the shari'a was not inclusive of the four schools of law. Like the Islamic modernists, al-Banna considered the Quran and the tradition of the Prophet the primary sources of the Islamic law.[71] For Qutb, the legal scholars were important guides to the present, but Muslims were free to adjust Islam to their times and situations. The MB members often displayed critical attitudes toward the orthodox exegeses, indicating that no useful exegesis existed except those of Muhammad Abduh, Rashid Rida, and Ibn Kathir.[72] Further, the MB did not have much faith in the orthodox theory of the caliphate, arguing that the political structure of the Islamic state included consultation, the nation as the source of power, and the relation between ruler and ruled as a social contract.[73] On occasion, it even commended the West for its respect for individual freedom and the right of workers, widespread social spirit, and the responsibility of its rulers to their people.[74] As Brynjar Lia concludes, far from being an aggressive reassertion of religious traditionalism, the rise of the Muslim Brothers in the 1930s was an instance of the rise of modern mass politics in Egypt.[75]

Although the economic difficulties of the forties might have promoted extremism in the ranks of the Brothers, the ruling elite's exclusionary policies were a far more important factor in shaping the MB's political orientation. For example, at its sixth general conference, in January 1941, the MB decided to participate in the parliamentary elections. Al-Banna declared himself a candidate for the district of Isma'iliyya, the birthplace of the movement, but soon he was summoned by Prime Minister Mustafa al-Nahhas Pasha and asked him to withdraw. Without much debate, he consented. Although in return the prime minister removed many of the restrictions imposed on the MB's activities, at the end of 1942 he again closed down all the MB's branches, excepting only the headquarters.[76] In 1944, the Wafd was dismissed, and the palace selected Ahmad Mahir Pasha to form the government. The latter immediately made preparations for new general elections. The Brothers prepared to enter the contest for a second time. Al-Banna again opted for Isma'iliyya, and five of his chief colleagues chose other areas in Egypt, intending to campaign on the basis of their Islamic program. In January 1945, the elections—believed to have been among the more obviously dishonest held in Egypt—took place, and al-Banna and all the other Brothers were defeated in constituencies where they had been certain of victory.[77] This political mistreatment naturally gave credibility to al-Ghazali's claim that "corruption in the parties and party leaders had a crucial political consequence: parliamentary life and democratic government failed. The 'upper class,' the seat of politico-economic power, 'monopolized' government. The people were 'compelled' to choose the parliament from among their 'oppressors': the landlord commanded the votes of his tenants; the 'lord of finance' those of his debtors—'the hungry ones.' . . . 'all the elections since 1923 . . . are spurious.'"[78] The dissolution of the MB in 1948 and the assassination of al-Banna in 1949 further frustrated the MB's attempts to use legitimate channels to propagate its ideas in society.

It may be hard to speculate on what would have been the practical application of the Brothers' notion of the unity of politics and religion had the institutions of the constitutional monarchy and parliamentary politics been able to function smoothly (the Jordanian case might provide some interesting clues; see chapter 13). The military coup of 1952 swept all away. Representing a turning point in Egypt's political history, the coup not only overthrew the monarchy and multiparty politics, but also transformed the state into an active agent of social change, bringing about a revolution in the economic and social relationships. While the military regime expanded its popular basis by mobilizing the middle and lower classes against the landowners, the members of other economically dominant classes, and the British, it dissolved all the political parties and created a one-party state. The MB cooperated with the Free Army Officers in overthrowing the constitutional monarchy in the early years of the coup.[79] The regime, however, would not tolerate the existence of the MB as an autonomous movement. Regime-MB confrontations escalated into sporadic armed conflicts between the military forces and the MB's secret apparatus, which was by and large out of the control of the MB's leadership. A failed assassination attempt on Nassir by an MB member gave the government the excuse to launch a severe crackdown on the MB in 1954. The regime staged a speedy trial of several its leaders, six defendants were hanged, and hundreds were imprisoned in camps. With the period of collective responsibility lasting barely two years under the Free Army Officers regime, the system of rule became personalized, and by 1954 Nassir emerged as "a native *sultan*."[80]

Adopting a socialist economic strategy and portraying itself as the champion of progress and social justice, the military regime launched a land reform program.[81] It also Egyptianized and then nationalized industries and the banking system.[82] In the course of a decade, the state became the sole political, economic, and cultural agent in the nation. The bureaucracy swelled from 350,000 employees in 1952 to approximately 1.2 million by 1970. The number of ministries increased from fifteen to twenty-eight during the same period. Public corporations, an artifact of the nationalization of foreign firms and socialist law, jumped from one in 1957, the first year of the expropriations, to thirty-eight in 1963. By 1970 their number had reached forty-six.[83] The 1964 constitution declared Egypt, now called the Arab Socialist Republic, a part of the Arab nation; its system of government was democratic socialist, based on the alliance of the working people, the religion of the state was Islam, and the economic foundation of the state was the socialist system.[84] The elections of Nassir as the president of the republic were all based on plebiscite, rather than electoral competition. Nassir was glorified as the hero and spokesperson of Arab nationalism, a true defender of the Arab people against all forms of imperialistic aggression.

These changes in the structure, policies, and ideology of the state had a determining impact on the discourse of the Muslim Brothers. The state's totalitarianism and extensive political repression produced its counterpart in the rise of an equally totalitarian Islamic movement in Egypt. The most effective and celebrated ideologue of this new Islamic trend was Sayyid Qutb (1906–66). Qutb's intellectual career reflected changes in the sociopolitical and cultural environment. A literature major at Cairo University, he became a modernist literary critic. Until the late thirties he was associated with Abbas Mahmud al-Aqqad. At that time, according to Adnan Ayyub Musallam, Qutb "distinguished himself as an outspoken partisan of the new school of poetry, especially the views advanced by al-Aqqad, a leader of the Diwan group whose writings and theories appear to have been greatly influenced by English writers, such as Hazlitt, Coleridge, Macaulay, Mill and Darwin."[85] During the formative years of his intellectual career, Qutb was under the influence of liberal nationalism and believed in such secular ideas as the separation of religion and literature, which he expressed forcefully in his writings in the 1930s.[86] He was also a member of the Wafd party until the midforties. Disenchanted, he resigned from the party and started writing against the British and the monarchy. He joined the MB in 1950 and rose quickly in its organizational hierarchy in 1952.[87]

Qutb's shift to Islamic subjects paralleled the general decline of liberal nationalism. In 1939, he took issue with Taha Hussein's ideas, presented in *The Future of Culture in Egypt,* that Egypt and Europe had had a common intellectual heritage since the time of the Pharaohs and that Egypt was a Western, not an Eastern, nation. Qutb rejected the unity of culture between Egypt and the West. As an alternative, he divided the West into its culture and civilization. Egypt, in his view, could maintain its cultural and Islamic identity, while emulating Western civilization, which included its scientific achievements.[88] He accepted Western industry and natural sciences, while rejecting its culture and even its social sciences. Qutb countered the perception that Islam pales next to what the West had to offer. "There is nothing in Islam for us to be ashamed of or defensive about. . . . During my years in America, some of my fellow Muslims would have recourse to apologetics as though they were defendants on trials. Contrariwise, I took an offensive position, excoriating the Western jahiliyya, be it in its much-acclaimed religious beliefs or in its depraved and dissolute socioeconomic and moral conditions: this Christian idolatry of the Trinity and its notion of sin and redemption which make no sense at all; this Capitalism, . . . that animal freedom which is called permissiveness, that slave market dubbed 'women's liberation.'"[89]

The state's exclusionary policies and the imposition of a monolithic Arab national-socialist discourse on Egyptian society further amplified Qutb's extremism. The assassination of al-Banna during the critical precoup period, the victims of the 1954 hangings, the appalling conditions of Tura Prison in Cairo's southern suburbs, where most of the leaders of the MB were held, the extensive use of physical and psychological torture—all made a deep impression on the thinking of the Brothers. Such inhumane treatment prompted Qutb to question the Islamic nature of the regime, defying the existing order as a state of jahiliyya, ignorance. Jahiliyya, said Qutb,

> signifies the domination (*hakimiyya*) of man over man, or rather the subservience to man rather than to Allah. It denotes rejection of the divinity of God and the adulation of mortals. In this sense, jahiliyya is not just a specific historical period (referring to the era preceding the advent of Islam), but a state of affairs. Such a state of human affairs existed in the past, exists today, and may exist in the future, taking the form of jahiliyya, that mirror-image and sworn enemy of Islam. In any time and place human beings face that clear-cut choice: either to observe the Law of Allah in its entirety, or to apply laws laid down by man of one sort or another. In the latter case, they are in a state of jahiliyya. Man is at the crossroads and that is the choice: Islam or jahiliyya. Modern-style jahiliyya in the industrialized societies of Europe and America is essentially similar to the old-time jahiliyya in pagan and nomadic Arabia. For in both systems, man is under the domination of man rather than of Allah.[90]

For Qutb the condition of jahiliyya prevailed in Egypt, where the people were no longer worshipping God but revering Nassir and his regime.[91] The rejection of Nassir also entailed the rejection of his pan-Arab nationalism. In 1953, Qutb did not object the use of Arabism as a basis for unity as long as it was understood that Arabism was a mere stage in the realization of pan-Islamic unity. Less than a decade later, however, he disapproved of pan-Arab nationalism because "there was no sense in liberating the land from a Byzantine or a Persian tyrant in order to put it in the hands of an Arab tyrant. Any tyrant is a tyrant."[92] In a later text, he flatly rejected pan-Arabism as incompatible with Islam:

> The homeland (*watan*) a Muslim should cherish and defend is not a mere piece of land; the collective identity he is known by is not that of a regime. . . . Neither is the banner he should glory in and die for that of a nation (*qawn*).

. . . His jihad is solely geared to protect the religion of Allah and His Shari'a and to save the Abode of Islam and no other territory. . . . Any land that combats the Faith, hampers Muslims from practicing their religion, or does not apply the Shari'a, becomes ipso facto part of the Abode of War (*Dar al-Harb*). It should be combated even if one's own kith and kin, national group, capital and commerce are to be found there. . . . A Muslim's homeland is any land governed by the laws of Islam. Islam is the only identity worthy of man. . . . Any other group identity . . . is a jahili identity of the type humanity has known during its periods of spiritual decadence.[93]

Repression and incarceration is believed to have contributed to the rise of a prison mentality among Muslim activists. In Hasan Hanafi's assessment, "their deep motivation was a hatred of reality, a need to revenge what nationalism, Arabism, socialism, secularism, and all that Nasser and the Ba'th party stood for. It was a desire to destroy everything and to build a new, a rejection of the other, a refusal of dialogue, a denial of all compromises, etc. The actual world was a world of disbelief, a Jahiliyah world which had to be destroyed completely and totally in order to build a new world of belief where everyone could live and practice his own faith. . . . Even the socialist trend in Qutb's thought has disappeared."[94] Gilles Kepel makes a similar assessment: "Sayyid Qutb was horrified by the barbarism of the camp guards, by the inhumanity with which they had let the wounded die. Various witnesses report that it was then that he lost his last remaining illusions as to the Muslim character of the Nassir regime."[95] Other Muslim activists who had similar political experiences denounced the ruler of Egypt, calling him "the pharaoh," an unsavory character who was condemned in the Quran for his acts against the prophet Moses.[96]

Researchers have noted that Qutb was influenced by the writings of Muhammad Asad and Abul Ala Maududi, which were translated into Arabic and became available in Egypt in 1951. His early writings in this period were filled with references to their work. His later works were in fact the radical conclusion of the ideas expressed by them.[97] Likewise, Emmanuel Sivan has attributed Qutb's rejection of the West to the influence of Maududi as well as the ideas of the fourteenth-century theologian Ibn Taymiyya—hence, a medieval theology is used to address modern politics.[98] These contentions may be true, but Qutb's decision to use the concept of jahiliyya to categorically reject the existing order, his invocation of the Islamic injunction regarding the duty of Muslims under the condition of jahiliyya, and the wide reception of this idea among Egyptian Muslim activists all constituted an ideological orientation that became meaningful only within the monolithic cultural context imposed from above by the military regime. As Chapter 13 will argue, this idea was also introduced to the Jordanian Islamic movement, but the Jordanian

MB, having a diametrically different experience under the Hashemites, decided to exclude the writings of Sayyid Qutb from its educational curricula. It should also be noted that, as was discussed in chapter 7, the idea of jahiliyya was employed by pan-Arab nationalists, like Darwish al-Miqdadi, in history textbooks that were used in Iraq, Palestine, and Syria.[99] It did not, however, gain the wide popularity and ideological significance that it gained in postcoup Egypt.

TEN

Ba'athist Socialism and Militant Reformist Fundamentalism in Syria

As was the case in Egypt, Islamic fundamentalism in Syria was a twentieth-century phenomenon. Formed in Aleppo in 1935 and then moved to Damascus in 1944, the Syrian branch of the Muslim Brothers (MB), started as a moderate Islamic movement. While the Brothers in Egypt and Syria operated autonomously, they had similar organizational structures and, along with the Jordanian branch (see chapter 13), regarded themselves as parts of a single Islamic movement. The Brothers had a modest beginning, but after the persecution of the Egyptian branch, many of its members escaped to Jordan and Syria, strengthening the movement in those countries. Following the Ba'ath coup in 1963, the MB and all other political parties were banned. From this period on, the MB adopted a militant orientation, trying to overthrow the Ba'athist regime through armed conflict and establish an Islamic state. In 1979, the MB militants launched an attack on the Aleppo military school, massacring more than sixty cadets, and in 1980 an assassination attempt was made on President Hafiz al-Assad. The regime responded by killing thousands of the members of the Muslim Brothers in 1982.

There are interesting similarities in political history between Egypt and Syria. In both countries, political developments in the twentieth century were shaped by nationalist struggles for independence against foreign rule. Independence was followed by a period of liberal politics and political pluralism. In both countries, the liberal-nationalist episode effectively ended with a military coup that was followed by the rise of the Arab nationalist and then socialist-oriented authoritarian state. As was the movement in Egypt, the Islamic movement in Syria was affected by the changes in the nature of the dominant discourse in society and in the structure and policies of the state. These changes involved the decline and eventual overthrow of the patrimonial and pluralistic politics of the postindependence period, the rise of the Ba'athist regime, and the imposition of a monolithic secular socialist discourse on society from the sixties on. In parallel with these changes, the Muslim Brothers were transformed from a moderate Islamic movement with a professed commitment to pluralism and Islamic socialism to a militant antisocialist and antistatist Islamism.

To underscore the distinctiveness of the political and cultural context that gave rise to militant fundamentalism, we may recall that after the crisis of 1860, in which religious minorities were attacked by Muslim mobs, Syria did not experience similar extremism for more than a hundred years. From that date on, the dominant trend in the Islamic movement was characterized by modernism in discourse and moderation in politics. In addition to such harbingers of liberal Arab nationalism as al-Kawakibi, scholars like Jamal al-Din Qasimi (1866–1914), Sheikh Tahir al-Jaza'iri (1851–1920), and Muhammad Kurd Ali (1876–1953) admired Western civilization, attempting to bridge the gap between Islam and modern Western thought. The broad social conditions that gave rise to Islamic modernism in Syria were similar to the conditions in Egypt and India. The Tanzimat movement (1839–76) undermined the ulama's control of the educational institutions, the judiciary, and the awqaf. These changes were further promoted by the reformist policies of Midhat Pasha, who came to Syria in 1878. As governor of Syria, he undertook a variety of reforms in the educational, social, political, and economic institutions. He obliged notables in Damascus to found a society for promoting the establishment of schools (al-Jam'iyya al-khayriyya li-insha' al-madaris). His efforts resulted in the establishment of thirty schools in various parts of Syria, including schools for girls and vocational schools. As a leading Islamic modernist, al-Jaza'iri was an active member of this society, and for some time he was the inspector of education in charge of examining the qualifications of teachers.[1]

The ideas of the Syrian Muslim Brothers were different from the pro-Western attitudes of the Islamic modernists of the earlier generation. In general, they shared the religious and sociopolitical outlooks of their Egyptian counterparts—having a strong anti-Western orientation, stressing independent reasoning in their interpretations of the Quran and the sunna of the Prophet, and showing a critical attitude toward the traditionalist ulama. The specific political discourse and program of the Syrian MB were, however, shaped by the political and social conditions of their country. In the forties and fifties, they attempted to establish an affinity between Islam and socialism; with the advent of the Ba'ath Party and the establishment of an authoritarian Arab socialist regime, they moved away from socialism and began to criticize the regime's socialist measures, particularly the nationalization of private enterprises, as well as its secularist orientation. While the Egyptian Muslim Brothers in the 1940s emphatically considered political parties a source of national disunity and called for their dissolution, the program of the newly constituted

Islamic Front (which included the Muslim Brothers) in Syria in the 1980s promised freedom for all political parties. Unlike the teachings of al-Banna, the program of the front displayed distinctive features of reformism and liberalism.

The Fragility of the Postindependence State:
The Decline of the Urban Notables

The urban notables who successfully led the nationalist movement against France were able to maintain only a shaky control over the politics of Syria after independence. The unifying power of the National Bloc fell into a spiral course of decline and disintegration once independence was won in 1943. While its members remained popular representatives of the nation vis-à-vis the French, in reality they were a loose amalgam of local power contenders who could command loyalty only in their own towns and among their own clans and dynasties. Just one year after the French troops left Syria, a serious split emerged in the National Bloc, as the dominant faction formed the National Party, under the control of Shukri Quwatli, who had led the Bloc since 1940 and held the presidency since 1943. His opponents formed the People's Party in 1948. The social origin of the split was the conflict between Quwatli's Damascene backers and the business community in Aleppo, whose traditional role as a trading center for the Fertile Crescent had practically been terminated by the creation of the Syrian state. The People's Party also gained the support of the powerful Atasi family, which controlled the Homs region.[2] These parties and the independents who successfully contested the 1949 elections generally consisted of personal followers of individuals who were drawn from the landed interests, tribal chiefs, and the professions (doctors, lawyers, teachers, and merchants). While their political power precluded legislation designed to modify the inequality in landownership, a patrimonial system connected the members of this class to the people they ruled.

The rapid decline of the urban notables was set in motion by a host of socioeconomic and cultural factors, the most important of which was the general process of social change that had begun to work against their interests since the thirties. Demographic growth, the social dislocations caused by the collapse of the traditional industries, and the rise of the new middle class undermined the effectiveness of the personal patronage network in meeting the demands of the expanding population. At the same time, outside this hierarchical network, such new social and cultural institutions as secondary schools, universities, and youth organizations emerged, and these provided an alternative setting and support for an increasing number of politically active individuals. Dissatisfied with the interest-conscious members of the dominant classes, these individuals naturally developed critical attitudes toward the parliamentary system that these classes controlled. The process of change accelerated after independence. The landowners and merchants began adopting capitalist methods and invested their land rents in industry; large merchants became agricultural and industrial entrepreneurs. Tribal chieftains, feudalists, and merchants often bought shares in industrial corporations, which led to the gradual development of a modern capitalist class within the ranks of the traditional ruling class of wealthy landowners and traders.

Parallel with the change in class relations were changes in the lifestyle of the wealthy. With the departure of the French, the rich urbanites moved away from the cities' old quarters, where their homes, decorated with abundant Oriental luxuries inside, were outwardly indistinguishable from ordinary homes. They now lived in the expensive villas vacated by the French in the new quarters of the city. The new bourgeoisie bought cars, hired chauffeurs, and acquired a taste for conspicuous consumption.[3] If in the past they had tended to cover up the extent of their wealth and conceal, in their public behavior, their differences from the people below their rank, their newly acquired lifestyles now accentuated their differences from the rest of the society. A certain General Za'im (who led the first military coup in Syria, on March 30, 1949) shocked Damascene society out of its puritanism when he let it be known that he disapproved of the traditional Arab clothing and headgear, and the streets blossomed with a curious collection of European hats; women appeared more freely in public and danced to American tunes in night clubs.[4] This new lifestyle increased the expanding gap between the rich and the poor.

In the postindependence period, the new middle class also expanded considerably. A great increase in the number of educational institutions after 1944, coupled with urbanization, the development of modern institutions, and the extension of state services, generated new employment opportunities for educated Syrians. The number of civil servants more than tripled during 1939–47 period.[5] Consisting of teachers, doctors, lawyers, army officers, and students, this group of individuals demanded inclusion in the political process, cultural empowerment, and economic benefits. The landowning and capitalist class, which controlled the political institutions and was now clearly recognized by a distinctive lifestyle, became a clear target of attack by the educated elite, who had now made common cause with workers and peasants.[6] From the late forties on, they seriously challenged and ultimately supplanted the urban notables,[7] a process not too different from what Egypt was experiencing in the same general period.

Twentieth-century Syria also witnessed the rise of the peasants' movement. In his in-depth study of Syrian peasantry, Hanna Batatu pointed to the nature of their specialized crops and geographic locations as crucial factors determining the peasants' level of political consciousness and militancy. Of significance in the movement of the peasantry were the peasant-gardeners, who enjoyed a degree of organization and a high level of literacy in their ranks. Their long organizational experience accounted for their marked ability to protect their interests and resist the arbitrariness and importunities of tax farmers or tax collectors—a characteristic that set them apart from most other peasants. They were also among the most enterprising of Syria's peasants.[8] As for the geographic location, the peasant mountaineers were more prone to rebellion than the peasants of the open plains. From the beginning of the nineteenth century to the great Syrian revolt of 1925–27, Druze peasants were involved in no fewer than eighteen major raids against villages in the Hawran or armed risings against—or military encounters with—the Egyptians, the Ottomans, or the French. In the same period, the montane Alawi peasants defied or took up arms against the established government on at least thirteen different occasions.[9] Nevertheless, as Batatu observed, during the centuries of Ottoman rule and down to the immediate postindependence period the peasants did not constitute a homogeneous or cohesive social group. Thanks to the efforts of Akram Hourani and the fusion of dissident intellectuals with the peasantry, Syria saw a fairly strong peasant movement in the organization of the Arab Socialist Party in 1950. This new and modern political platform gave the peasants the opportunity to obtain considerable power and shape the political and social history of their nation. Of great import was Hourani's encouragement of many of his young partisans from rural or urban families of humble status to enroll in the cost-free Hims Military Academy in order to gain a foothold in the officer corps, which in retrospect constituted a significant factor in the rise of power and influence of people with rural origins in the armed forces and eventually over the state.[10]

The shift in the intellectual climate also undercut the power and social influence of the urban notables. Forcefully promoted by the Hashemite Kingdom in both Iraq and Jordan, Arab nationalism had become the dominant political discourse among the intellectual leaders in Syria, Iraq, and Jordan by the late thirties. Liberal ideas and the stress on individual liberty had been on the decline for some time, and instead the ideas of liberating the Arab lands from the yoke of colonialism, forming a united Arab nation, and sacrificing oneself for the cause liberation were gaining ground among Syrians. Thus, the nonideological and increasingly ineffective political parties of the urban notables had little appeal for the aspiring members of the middle class and the educated elite. This is true despite the fact that in 1945 Syrian President Quwatli pledged his loyalty to pan-Arabism and coordinated his efforts with other leaders to cofound the Arab League.[11]

During the two short periods of parliamentary politics, in 1946–49 (followed by military dictatorships in three coups in the 1949–54 period) and in 1954–58, Syria's political scene was a cafeteria of diverse political parties, which included the National Party (the Damascus-based ruling wing of the National Bloc which had led the independence movement), the People's Party (the Aleppo-based dissident wing of the National Bloc), and the independents (mostly landowners, tribal chiefs, and heads of the largest and most powerful families). There were also several ideological parties which challenged the political power of the ruling class. These were far-right Syrian National Party, the Ba'ath Party, the Communist Party, the Cooperative Socialist Party (a right-wing pan-Islamic movement), and the Arab Liberation Movement. The outcomes of parliamentary elections in 1949 and 1954 indicated the cultural trend in the country in favor of pan-Arab nationalist groups (table 10.1). The impressive success of the Ba'ath Party and the decline of the People's Party was a good measure of the change in the country's ideological climate. While in both elections groups and parties that were tied to the ruling class managed to maintain the majority in the parliament, the 1954 elections are believed to have been among the most vital in Syrian history. They signified the end of the era dominated by traditional political forces and the rise of the left wing of the Arab nationalist movement.[12] By the end of 1957, the conservatives were virtually eliminated as a factor on the political scene.[13]

The electoral success of the Ba'ath Party was also due to its merger with Hourani's peasant-based Arab Socialist Party. Historically, Ba'athism did not

Table 10.1. Strength of political parties in parliamentary elections in Syria

1949		1954	
Political Party	*No. of Seats*	*Political Party*	*No. of Seats*
Independents (including 9 tribal representatives)	31	Independents	64
Independents tied to the People's Party	20		
People's Party	43	People's Party	30
Ba'ath Party	1	Ba'ath Party	22
National Party	13	National Party	19
Syrian National Social Party	1	Syrian National Social Party	2
Cooperative Socialist Party	1		
Islamic Socialist Bloc	4		
		Arab Liberation Movement	2
		Communist Party	1
TOTAL	114	TOTAL	142

Source: Patrick Seale, *The Struggle for Syria: A Study of Post-war Arab Politics* (London: Oxford University Press, 1965), p. 183.

Note: The 1949 figures are only a rough guide; no exact comparison is possible. In 1949, party boundaries were fluid and candidates' affiliations unclear; the chamber then consisted of 114 members, as against 142 in 1954; the National Party officially boycotted the 1954 election, although many of its members stood; in 1954 no Islamic party contested the election.

represent a single force but a plurality of elements, each having different social goals and mental horizons. The Ba'ath Party of 1943–52 was not peasant oriented but wedded to the idea of pan-Arab nationalism. Its pan-Arab orientation was characteristic of many of the members of the urban intelligentsia as well as of the mercantile class, to whom the breakup of the Arab provinces of the Ottoman Empire after 1917 created a grave impediment to the free flow of native commerce and the economic viability of the fragmented territories. In the mid-1940s the adherence to the Ba'ath Party of many young Alawi refugees who had lost their homes in the wake of the 1939 annexation of the predominantly Arab district of Alexandretta by Turkey imbued the party's pan-Arab nationalist feeling with greater fervor.[14] However, the merger of the Ba'ath Party with Hourani's party in 1952 contributed to its electoral success and to the rise of a socialist vision in the party. The merger also contributed to the rise of a politically conscious rural intelligentsia. Many of the students in the party's ranks and teachers in its cadres were of peasant or rural origin and had been won over by its strong animus against social injustice and discrimination between the sects.[15]

Finally, the antimilitary attitudes of the urban notables were the last nail in the coffin of the notables' formely extensive sociopolitical influence. Despite their formal control of the state bureaucracy and political parties, these notables failed to consider the armed forces as a source of political power. According to Patrick Seale,

> After 1946 the great majority of cadets at the Homs military college came from the lower middle class, molded no doubt in their schooldays by one or other of the doctrinaire youth movements which had sprung up in the 1930s and 1940s. The Muslim landed families, being predominantly of nationalist sentiments, despised the army as a profession: to join it between the wars was to serve the French. Homs to them was a place for the lazy, the rebellious, the academically backward, or the socially undistinguished. Few young men of good family would consider entering the college unless they had failed at school or been expelled. The conservative "right" in Syria neglected the army as a source of political power, with disastrous consequences, as it was the army, an eager and indoctrinated instrument, which later destroyed the power of the landed families and urban merchants, with the result that a veteran Syrian politician of the 1940s would find little to recognize or approve of in the political scene fifteen years later.[16]

This process was reinforced by the French. Their military recruitment focused heavily on the dissident rural communities, which the French administration considered to be less nationalist than the urban Sunni.[17]

As far as the politics of religion is concerned, during the period of political pluralism there was no significant militant fundamentalist tendency among the

Islamic groups. Like other emerging political contenders, Muslim activists formulated their discourse in opposition to the policies of the urban notables and within the general framework of the prevailing intellectual climate—leftist politics, socialism, and anti-Westernization. Reflecting this climate, the Muslim Brothers summarized the country's problems in economic terms: the villagers were oppressed by the gendarmes; the poor suffered from hunger, disease, and negligence; the merchants were being driven to bankruptcy by high taxes; laborers were held down by the nonenforcement of the labor laws; and general disorder and cruelty prevailed while the responsible authorities were asleep.[18] The Brothers even tried to show the consistency of Islam with socialist ideas. The MB leader Muhammad Mubarak once declared that the brotherhood was a "Marxist beverage in an Islamic cup."[19] While the League of the Ulama was not a party, it proclaimed itself a "directive front" for the propagation of "good deeds." Certain candidates who were affiliated with the league formed a new organization called the New Islamic Socialist Front. Mustafa as-Siba'i, its leader, declared that it would work for the realization of Islamic "socialism," as had been advocated by the Prophet, the achievement of social justice, and maintenance of human rights. The front entered its own candidates in the 1954 elections, which included as-Siba'i and Muhammad Mubarak.[20]

The Rise of the Ba'ath Party: A New Context for Culture Production

The rise of the Ba'ath Party and its control of state power in the sixties created a new context for the production of culture. The ideology of the new state originated in the thought of two Damascene schoolteachers, Michel Aflaq and Salah al-Din al-Bitar, one Christian and the other Muslim, who in 1943 founded the Ba'ath Party. The change in their outlook from the nationalist ideology espoused by the urban notables to radical Arab nationalism was an instance of the cultural turn occurring in Arab countries. This cultural shift also paralleled a change in the country's political climate in the postindependence period. According to Aflaq, "Before going to France I was simply a nationalist, I had been greatly influenced by my father who had taken an active part in the struggle against the French and had been imprisoned several times. Nationalism was our local reality, but Bitar and I discovered socialism in France. On our return we were eager to pass on these ideas to a new generation."[21] Describing their impressions of the Syria's rulers when they returned home following their sojourn in France (1929–34), Aflaq and Bitar indicated that "We returned to Syria to find that the national leaders were men who could not see beyond their economic and family interests . . . To be effective, the struggle against the colonizer had to involve a change of mind and of thought, a deepening of national consciousness and of moral standards; it was related to the nation's intellectual and moral life."[22]

As an alternative to the nationalism of the urban notables, which was bound to the Syrian territory, these ideologues blended Arab nationalism with socialism, using the trinity "Unity, Freedom, and Socialism" as the hallmark of their movement.[23] In its first communiqué, issued in July 1943, the Ba'ath Party stated: "We represent the spirit of Arabism against materialistic Communism. We represent living Arab history against dead reaction and contrived progressivism. We represent complete Arab nationalism expressing the product of the personality against the empty nationalism which does not go beyond lip-service and which all ethics refute. We represent the gospel of Arabism against professional politics. We represent the new Arab generation."[24] In its first national convention, held in 1947, the Ba'ath Party called for the Arab League to take measures toward achieving Arab unity. In the sphere of domestic politics, the party advocated the protection of local industry, levying progressive income taxes on the rich, the supervision of domestic and foreign trade, and the restriction of private property.[25] The central feature of Ba'ath ideology in the 1940s and 1950s, however, was Arab nationalism. "The basic idea in Ba'th [Ba'ath] doctrine," said Tabitha Petran,

> is that the Arab nation is a permanent entity in history. The Arab nation is considered, philosophically speaking, not as a social and economic historic formation, but as a transcendent fact inspiring different forms, one of its highest contributions taking the form of Islam. It was not Islam that modeled the peoples of Arabia, the Fertile Crescent, and North Africa, equipping them with Islamic values, especially the Arabic language and Arabic culture, but the Arab nation that created Islam. This conception of the Arab nation implicitly advantages the Arab contribution to history. On the other hand, Arab decadence can be overcome through a purifying and spiritual action, not religious but moral.[26]

Before the seizure of power, the Ba'ath Party advocated parliamentary democracy, social justice, and Arab socialism. The last was presented as a moderate and spiritual socialism in contrast with materialistic Western socialism. In addition, socialism in Ba'ath ideology had a secondary significance, particularly when the party was engaged in anticommunist polemics. Islam was acknowledged as the basis of the most glorious phase of Arab history, but it was considered a past that had now become part of the heritage of Christian (and other non-Sunni) Arabs as well.[27] The socialism of the Ba'ath Party, however, gained importance and centrality following its merger with Akram Hourani's Arab Socialist Party in 1952. The merger produced the more powerful Arab Socialist Renaissance Party (al-Hizb al-ba'ath al-arabi al-ishtiraki).[28] Following its success in the 1954 parliamentary election, the new Ba'ath Party combined forces with other leftist parties and the left-leaning military in order to challenge the power of the dominant classes in and outside the government.

The post-1954 parliament was the scene of forceful encounters between political actors that were determined to change drastically the existing social hierarchy and those who were equally determined to resist change. The military was also actively involved in political affairs. The ensuing controversy and intense rivalry among opposing groups and factions culminated in the political crisis of 1957. The crisis prompted the Ba'ath leaders and their allies to seek union with Egypt as the only way out of the factional clashes and the country's disintegration. The result was the United Arab Republic, formed in 1958. This union was also "an implementation of the call for unity which the Ba'ath had been preaching for almost 20 years."[29] However, political development in the early 1960s, including the collapse of the United Arab Republic in 1961 and the failure of the two Ba'athist governments that had come to power in Baghdad and Damascus in the spring of 1963 to form a federal union, undermined the traditional assumptions of Ba'athist ideology.[30] These failures, while serious blows to the idea of Arab nationalism, provided breathing space for the communists to expand their influence in the Ba'ath Party; thus, from the early 1960s on the party moved toward socialism. The idea of Arab unity was relegated to a secondary position in the party's doctrine as Marxist-Leninist terminology was integrated into Ba'ath thinking and with it a more radical conception of socialism.[31] Although direct reference to Marxism was decidedly avoided, Marxist concepts abounded in the party's rhetoric. One of the party's documents, for example, stated: "The second characteristic of our Party is revolutionism, since the point of departure for the scientific, nationalist socialist thinking in social and economic analysis is a dialectical one. It starts from the affirmation of a contradiction in the national society and the existence of a struggle between the classes, which in turn is characterized by its tendency to achieve two simultaneous goals: national unity and the liquidation of exploitation."[32]

The Ba'ath Party bestowed upon itself the role of the "revolutionary vanguard" to direct revolutionary changes and to lead the downtrodden in the exercise of popular democracy. The concept of "popular democracy" was "presented as an antithesis to the discarded Western parliamentary democracy that offers freedom only to the wealthy few and proved to be unsuited for the needs of the developing nations. 'Popular Democracy' will, on the other hand, guarantee freedom to those classes who constitute the true people and ensure the country's rapid development. The new regime will centre in the party, leading the popular organizations and councils and operating according to the principle of 'democratic centralism.'"[33] The regime's commitment to this vanguard ideology and the centrality of the army in implementing it was clearly stated in a 1964 cabinet statement by none other than the party's chief ideologue, Salah al-Bitar, who professed that "an ideological army is one that exercises its right of debating the country's policies in congress and popular assemblies and of delegating the execution of that policy to a political leadership, which the people and its organized military and civilian vanguards have chosen."[34]

Equipped with this radical outlook and backed by the military in the coup of 1963,[35] the Ba'ath ruling elite initiated a new era in Syria's history: the state power was effectively reorganized in the fusion of the party and the military, a radical program of economic restructuring launched, a fundamental change in the system of class hierarchy effected, and the state-society relationship transformed. The economic restructuring had three major objectives: (1) to initiate a land reform program that would eliminate the concentration of landownership, (2) to destroy the monopolistic merchant families and their businesses by nationalizing most of the organized business sectors, and (3) to give the government a more decisive role in the management of the economy through central planning. By 1967 these three objectives had been realized.[36] As a result, an elite predominantly recruited from the Sunni landlord and merchant bourgeoisie was displaced by a new one of rural, lower-middle-class, and disproportionately Islamic minority origins.[37] The state extensive intervention in the economy naturally entailed a considerable expansion of its bureaucracy. The first government, which was announced within a week of the takeover, was made up of twenty-six ministers, of whom thirteen were Ba'athists and the remainders were Nassirites, Arab Socialists, Communists, and independents. This was already the largest government Syria had known since independence in 1943. Subsequent reshuffles increased the number of ministers to thirty (but the balance between Ba'athists and non-Ba'athists remained unaltered).[38]

The Ba'athists' shift toward socialism was associated with a decidedly secularist outlook, which often gave rise to a wide perception among conservative groups that the party was undermining the role and function of religion in society. In the Arab nationalist discourse of the 1950s, nationalism and Islam were given an equal standing in every respect. Nationalism was the determination of the Arabs to continue the mission of Muhammad. "Thus the Prophet became the founder of the Arab nation, and Islam was the product of the Arab national genius."[39] With Arab nationalism assuming a secondary status in Ba'ath thinking, religion was judged according to the principles of socialism and the evolutionary transformation of society, in which it was to wither away and give space to the scientific understanding of society and nature. A version of such a view was boldly expressed by one of the Ba'athist ideologues when, in an article published in the army magazine, he went so far as to assault religion and urged its readers to sweep away all the traditions of the past—feudalism, capitalism, colonialism, God, and religion. In their place the author proposed "absolute belief in man's ability." The publication of the article, however, produced a furor among the ulama and, for the first time, among Christian clergymen. The government quickly backed down and attributed the article to an "imperialist conspiracy."[40]

The secularism of the regime was also reflected in the Permanent Constitution of the Syrian Arab Republic (1973), which was adopted by the Syrian Council of the People. The new constitution, unlike the provisional constitution of 1964, did not affirm that Islam was the state religion.[41] The only concession made to religion was in article 3 of the constitution, which stipulated that "the Islamic Fikh [*fiqh*] 'jurisprudence' is a principle source of legislation."[42] This deliberate oversight provoked a clash between the Ba'athist regime and the predominantly Sunni population; religious leaders throughout the country protested and urged believers to boycott the plebiscite on the constitution to take place in March 1973.[43] President Hafiz al-Assad and the Council of the People made a small retreat by adding a compromise amendment to the constitution that stipulated that "the religion of the President of the Republic is Islam."[44] At the same time, in his letter to the council, the president adamantly stated that "we reject every retrogressive interpretation of Islam that implies detestable Puritanism and abominable fanaticism."[45] This amendment failed to dampen rising religious fervor, and more religious riots broke out on the occasion of the Prophet's birthday in April 1973. The Muslim fundamentalists demanded the insertion in the constitution of a statement that the president must be a Sunni Muslim, and that Islam must be the religion of the state. None of these revisions were accepted, and the constitution stood as it was proposed by the government.[46]

The Radicalization of the Islamic Movement

Like their Egyptian counterparts, Syrian Muslim activists were certainly striving to establish a religious order in their country. The formulation of their program and strategy for the realization of this religious state was shaped, as it were, within the political and discursive context of an intrusive ideological state. Changes in the practices, concrete programs, and slogans of the Islamic opposition were associated with changes in the political conditions in the country from the patrimonial political pluralism of the forties and fifties to the monolithic discourse imposed on civil society by the Ba'ath regime. In the late 1940s, the Muslim Brothers were the principle rivals of the Ba'ath and Communist parties for influence among the members of the middle and lower classes.[47] The political competition for followers shaped the programs and slogans of the Brothers and their decision to advance the idea of "Islamic socialism." Mustafa as-Siba'i (1915–64) even insisted that "the Brotherhood not the Communist or Ba'ath parties had the means and competence to bring an end to social and economic injustice." The Islamic solution to Syria's social and economic problems was a leftist-inspired agenda, as it stressed an end to the country's dependence on foreign powers, to feudalism, and to the domination of the upper-class elite. The Brothers in coalition with other Islamic groups went so far as to form the Islamic Socialist Front, an organization not too different from the

Movement of God-Worshipping Socialists in Iran during the heyday of liberal politics and economic nationalism. However, after 1954, when the military regime fell, the Muslim Brothers did not take part in the elections. "It seemed to shrink from politics, and many of its branches turned toward politically neutral areas concerned with the 'religious and moral education' of the people."[48]

The pluralistic environment of the 1940s and 1950s and the existence of a multiparty system that reflected the interests of diverse groups and classes naturally subjected the competing groups to crisscrossing ideological pressures, hindering the development of discursive or political extremism among the Islamic groups. The big merchants and landowners of Damascus threw their principal weight behind People's Party and National Party, but they and their supporters also voted for the Muslim Brothers, not out of sympathy for them but out of their fear of the Communists and the Ba'athists.[49] However, with the ascendance of the left the picture began to change. The Ba'ath regime's policy of systematically disrupting and disorganizing the political parities and collectivities that were mainly connected to the urban mercantile establishments and rural landowners channeled oppositional politics through the religious medium. The state's economic and cultural orientations in fact structured the Brothers' concrete political agenda. The implementation of socialist measures and the destruction of the economic and political supremacy of the urban notables effectively removed economic categories from the discourse of the opposition groups in the sixties through the eighties. At the same time, the state's secularism gave rise to a religious definition of the new social conflicts that originated in the state's policies and the socioeconomic changes Syria experienced in this period.

The transformation of economic relationships under the Ba'ath Party also changed the nature and dynamics of class politics. It moved the center of the oppositional activities from the rural areas to the major cities. Before the Ba'athist coup, workers, peasants, and other less privileged groups were among the key supporters of the radical movements against the existing economic hierarchy and the political institutions that supported it. After the coup it was the property-owning classes who were antagonized by the state's policies. In the 1964 uprising against the regime, the Muslim Brothers and notable merchants were clearly in the forefront. The opposition movement took the form of disturbances in Syria's major cities. In Hama, the Brothers, the ulama, and great notable families led the uprising; government buildings came under attack, street barricades were erected, merchants protested, and the "godless" Ba'ath Party was denounced from the mosques. The merchants' strikes and disturbances spread to Aleppo, Homs, and Damascus. In the capital, the Chamber of Commerce called for the repeal of restrictions on foreign commerce and a guarantee against further nationalization. In addition, the bitterness of conservative Muslims' opposition to the Ba'ath Party was intensified by what they regarded as Ba'athist atheism and the prominence of Christians and heterodox Muslims among the new ruling groups.[50] The major role in organizing active resistance to the Ba'ath Party was played by the Muslim Brothers. The Friday sermon in the mosques furnished them with an effective religious instrument for mobilizing a large segment of the population to act against the regime. Unlike secular right-wing politicians, who were easily labeled reactionary supporters of the exploiting classes, the Brothers did not appear to represent merely personal and material interests. They had launched a religious war on the regime. At a time when socialism and revolution were elevated to the level of sacred Arab nationalism and opposition to them carried the stigma of otherness, the MB naturally had the important advantage of speaking in the name of another, still as respectable and potent, ideology.[51] At any rate, the government responded with tanks against the barricades and artillery against the mosques in Hama, while in Damascus Ba'athist militants forcibly opened shops and clashed with the Muslim Brothers. In 1965, Ba'ath radicals launched a major assault on the urban establishment, nationalizing most of the modern industrial sector, all foreign trade, and segments of wholesale internal commerce, and speeding up the land reform.[52]

While the protests of the sixties were motivated by the resistance of the landed interests and conservative Muslims to the regime's socialism and secularism, the violent protests of the late seventies and early eighties were largely a result of the politicization of the members of the new middle class that had emerged as a result of the state's bureaucratic expansion and economic development. The militants involved in the campaign against the regime in the early 1980s were mostly young men between their late teens and early thirties. They were mainly secondary school or university students, teachers, and members of the professions. This was suggested by the occupational distribution of the activists—mostly Muslim Brothers but also vocal members of the secular opposition parties and of professional associations—who were arrested by the government between 1976 and May 1981. Out of a total of 1,384, about 28 percent were students, 8 percent schoolteachers, and 13 percent professionals, including 79 engineers, 57 physicians, 25 lawyers, and 10 pharmacists. The profiles of the chiefs of the militant groups and of the key members of the leadership bore out that the movement's guiding layer emanated from the professional middle class. While maintaining that artisans and shopkeepers formed a significant component of the society's membership, its deputy superintendent general confirmed in 1982 that its militants were drawn by and large from their offspring or their educated elements—primarily college students and, to a lesser extent, teachers and other members of the intelligentsia.[53]

By 1980, different Islamic opposition groups, including the Muslim Brothers, had formed a united Islamic Front. The objective of the front was "to integrate the dispersed Muslims' efforts and orient them . . . toward the establishment of God's

rule on earth, by putting forward a plan for joint action to which all would agree
. . . to give added force to the Islamic tide and revive the duty of *jihad*."[54] The proclamation that the front issued, while reflecting the interests and the outlook of the
urban and Sunni trading and manufacturing classes,[55] contained point-by-point
refutations of the ruling Ba'ath ideologies and policies. At the same time, it displayed a considerable number of liberal attitudes toward politics and government
as well as the economy. The proclamation consisted of two parts: the manifesto and
the program of the Islamic revolution of Syria. The manifesto started with a historical analysis of the decline of Islam from its perfect state, after which "the deviation began, and 'jahiliyya' raised its ugly head again through people who, in their
pursuit of personal desires and striving for power gains, denied the nation its rights
and transgressed against its interest."[56] It also contained a more specific account of
political change and the seizure of power by the Ba'ath Party in Syria. It considered
the postcolonial regime of the forties "a false democratic regime which controlled
the country through leaderships that gained power through their wealth and landownership."[57] It also explicitly mentioned Hafiz al-Assad and his brother Rif'at as
people directly responsible for the decline of Syria and its failure to gain true independence. The ruling elite were also challenged on the grounds of being sectarian.
This sectarianism, the front argued, had led to the overrepresentation of the Alawis
(a religious minority constituting less than 10 percent of Syria's population) in the
Ba'ath Party and the military (President Hafiz al-Assad himself being an Alawi). In
reaction to the underrepresentation of the Sunnis, who constituted about 69 percent of the total population, the front addressed "wise men" of the Alawi community, warning them that, as 10–15 percent of the population, they could not
reasonably expect to continue their domination of the majority for long. Enough
time remained for them to avoid bloody conflict, it said, if they ceased to support
Hafiz al-Assad and his brother Rif'at and helped bring them to justice.[58] For the
front, the "horrible decline" of the Ba'athist regime into the "mire of sectarianism"
constituted one of its greatest crimes and a fatal mistake. The Ba'ath Party was,
according to the front, "sectarian fascist." It was also referred to as "the sectarian
party" and its dictatorship as a "sectarian dictatorship."[59] The first objective of the
front was to bring an end to the regime of Hafiz al-Assad and the dictatorship of
the sectarian Syrian Ba'ath Party.

Except for references to Islam and quotations from the Quran, the program of
the Islamic Front appeared as a secular document that based itself on constitutional
principles of "equality between the citizens," the "protection of the citizens" against
government autocracy, unjust laws, and emergency legislation, the "preservation of
the dignity of the citizens" against personal and psychological torture, the "abolition of political prisons and detention centers," and "the system of mutual consultation (democracy)," "separation between the authorities," "freedom to form

political parties," and "freedom of thought and expression" (unless it was connected to a foreign power or violated the constitution or faith of the nation), "freedom of the trade unions" from the domination of the state and the single party, and the protection of "the rights of ethnic and religious minorities."[60] In rejecting the state's socialist policies, the program stated, "it is now clear to all people that Islam has its own economic system which is based on the recognition of the natural human incentives that cannot be ignored."[61] The Brothers' decision to excise the term "socialism" from their political vocabulary in the early 1960s was in all likelihood a reaction to the domination of the Left in the Ba'ath Party in this period. According to the front, capitalism was at fault because it exploited the workers, but socialism, depriving them of the right to strike, was an even harsher tyranny. It further argued that "the Ba'th system mixes the worst of the West—rampant materialism—and of the East—an unproductive state sector that destroys incentives and is corrupted to enrich a small political clique. An Islamic economy would encourage private enterprise, investment, and the 'natural incentives' of a fair profit, while avoiding excessive concentration of wealth and class conflict."[62] The program emphasized that "individual ownership should be protected and private capital encouraged to actively participate in strengthening the national economy. . . . The state is bound to fail in achieving its purpose when it becomes a merchant."[63] The front also proposed to transfer "the ownership of the factories and industrial establishments from the state to the workers. In return, the workers pay installments that can be deducted from their benefits and wages over a long period of time without affecting the livelihood of their families."[64] The rejection of usury is among the few subjects on which the front made direct reference to Islamic law. Even then the front based its argument on non-Islamic sources, saying, for example, that "the rest of the world realized the harms of usury, and prominent economists like Keynes considered it the source of economic crisis."[65] However, the front added that all laws contrary to Islam had to be abrogated.[66] Foreign schools would be closed, and the national educational system would be fully developed to meet the educational, cultural, and spiritual needs of the Syrian people. Ethnic and religious minorities, however, would have the right to develop and maintain their private schools.[67]

Encouraged by the success of the Islamic opposition in Iran, Syrian Islamic militants accelerated their attack on the regime. Assassination and sabotage were stepped up. In June 1979, a massacre of more than fifty military cadets took place in Aleppo. In the spring of 1980, the Islamic opposition staged a major offensive in northern Syria that took on the character of overt urban guerrilla warfare against the government.[68] It also made an unsuccessful attempt on Assad's life in June 1980. The regime responded with a massive military attack on the organization and networks of the Islamic opposition, which resulted in the killing of several thousands of its members and supporters. Although at present there is no way of verifying the accuracy of the number of people killed in the militant uprising, Amnesty International reported that "estimates of the number of dead on all sides range from 10,000 to 25000." The veteran socialist leader Akram Hourani and the secular parties insisted that through the whole of February 1982 no fewer than 25,000 civilians lost their lives.[69]

Although the issue of legislation remained vague in its program, the authors of the proclamation of the Islamic Front assumed considerable latitude in their proposed post-Ba'athist Islamic state. Its stands against socialist planning, the state's control of the economy and other major social institutions, and the single-party system were in direct opposition to the Ba'ath Party's ideology and policies. The front's antisectarian Islamism was also shaped by the secularism and the sectarian character of the regime. The militant and violent approach to the problem of politics is also related to the violent nature of the Ba'ath Party and the manner in which it maintained power. The front's support for a multiparty system, political pluralism, and various forms of freedom within a loosely defined Islamic framework, however, cannot be defined solely in oppositional relations to the features of the Ba'ath Party's secular ideological state. It can be speculated that the exigencies of building a wide coalition against the regime prompted the Islamic leadership to modify some of the restrictive elements of the teachings of the Muslim Brothers that were proposed by al-Banna. This is all the more true given the realization among the opposition groups of the adverse effects of the military for democracy and the country, as Akram Hourani, the politician who played a central role in encouraging people of humble origins to get involved in the military, stated clearly in 1970.[70] The moderation of the teachings could also be a reflection of the front's members' backgrounds in modern education and the weak presence of the organized Islamic establishment in their midst.

The weak presence of the ulama in the opposition (in contrast with Iran) may also explain the regime's success in splitting the Islamic movement in the country and successfully crushing the challenge of the Islamic Front. The regime's largesse toward the ulama and religious institutions attenuated the anxiety created by its secularist policies. From the beginning of his regime President Assad sought to contain the more intractable elements within the Muslim Brothers by stretching out his hand to the ulama. He missed no opportunity to honor them or attend to their concerns. In 1971 he arranged for the seating in the People's Assembly, which was then appointive, of several Muslim dignitaries, including Sheikh Ahmad Kaftaru, the mufti of the republic, and Sheikh Muhammad al-Hakim, the mufti of Aleppo. In 1973 he made large personal contributions to Islamic law schools in the province of Hamah and to a religious organization devoted to charity in Hims. In 1974 he raised the pay of the country's 1,138 imams (prayer leaders), 252 *mudarris* (teachers), 610 *khatibs* (preachers) 1,038 *mu'azzins* (announcers of the hour of prayer), and 280 *qaris* (reciters of Quranic verses). He augmented their remuneration further in 1976, and again in 1980. Under his auspices 5.4 million Syrian pounds were earmarked in 1976 for the constructions of new mosques. Every year on a specified day in Ramadan, the month of abstinence, he broke fast with the principal ulama. "You and I," he told them on one such occasion, "need one another: I need to hear from you yearly, for through your words I sense not only your feelings but the feelings and desires of the people, anxious as I am, being a fellow countrymen at the topmost point of responsibility to seek only what the people want."[71]

There were also other factors that may explain the failure of the Islamic opposition in Syria to overthrow the regime despite its success in Iran (see chapter 11). The Ba'ath Party was socialist and, along with its ally and sometimes rival, the Communist Party, had systematic connections with the peasants and workers. Syria's strong peasant movements grew out of the condition of the poor peasants, who by the early 1950s were still mainly landless and lived under a form of tenancy that amounted to serfdom. (The movement in the Hama region, however, included some of the better-off peasants as well as the poorest.) From the early 1940s on the Hama movement forced changes in Syrian society through militant activity in the countryside and the vigorous political representation of Akram Hourani, its leader.[72] Hourani's peasant-based populist movement joined the Ba'ath Party in the late forties and strengthened the party's ties to the peasants.[73] A working-class movement, although relatively small, had also been present in Syria for some time. Beginning in 1926, workers' struggle for a wage increase, a minimum wage, and the eight-hour day led to the formation of the Federation of Trade Unions of Syria in 1938. By the mid-1950s the labor movement had called for assistance to the unemployed, protection for agricultural workers, and an economic development program for Syria. It also became active in opposing alliance with the West, especially the Baghdad Pact. Militancy increased within the movement, forcing the government to adopt some of the workers' demands. By this time the Ba'ath Party had gained some influence in the unions, and Communist influence was growing.[74]

When the Ba'athists seized power, the peasants benefited considerably from their land reform program. The nationalization of industry and tax policies were favorable to workers and urban poor.[75] Thus, in its conflict with the Islamic opposition, the Syrian regime, in addition to its well-organized party bureaucracy and military, enjoyed the supports of the peasants and workers. In the rural areas, the Alawis, in particular, strongly supported the regime, while in the cities Ba'athist militants forcibly opened shops and clashed with the members of the MB.[76] The Brothers, in contrast, had scarcely any foothold in the countryside, despite their vitality in Damascus and other Syrian cities.[77] Moreover, the Syrian Islamic movement probably lacked the populist appeal needed to mobilize the whole society against the

Ba'ath Party. Indeed, the secular Left, organized workers, the peasantry, and the salaried middle class were bound to be wary of any change likely to return power to merchants and landlords.[78]

Syrian religious and ethnic diversity was also a factor affecting politics, simultaneously enabling and constraining the collective capacity of both the opposition and the regime. Some figures may help to provide an idea of this diversity. More than 82 percent of the country's population was Arabic-speaking, and about 69 percent was Sunni Muslims. In language and religion, the Arab-speaking Sunni Muslims constituted 57 percent of the population. The major religious minorities in Syria were the Alawis (11.5 percent), Druzes (4.0 percent), Isma'ilis (1.5 percent), and Christians (14.1 percent), of whom the Greek Orthodox Christians (4.7 percent) constituted the most important community.[79] It is interesting to note that the Sunni and Christian confessions cut across the urban-rural gap, whereas the Islamic heterodox sects were chiefly rural and—the Alawis in particular—traditionally deprived.[80] Thus, when the Ba'athists took power, given the overrepresentation of religious minorities among their leaders, they could rely heavily on their coreligious rural peasants. Considering the Alawis' strong distrust of the Sunnis, who had so often been their oppressors,[81] they tended to defend the government in the face of Sunni revolutionary challenge. On the other hand, the very predominance of religious minorities in the top government's position had made the Ba'ath Party's rule in the cities problematic.[82] The government's reforms, however, had considerable support among the lower classes, especially in the rural areas.[83]

Finally, the regime in the 1970s took a favorable orientation toward the merchants, and at the same time attempted to play down its ideological differences with Islam. In this respect, the Syrian experience approached that of Egypt under Anwar el-Sadat when he initiated a new economic strategy away from socialism and toward a free market economy. While in many respects the Ba'ath Party's socialist ideology helped define the Islamic identity of the opposition movement, in the seventies the Syrian rulers began taking a conciliatory approach toward Islam (a policy that was quite different from that of the shah of Iran when he disregarded the Islamic sensibility of the public by unilaterally changing the Islamic calendar into a monarchical one; see chapter 11). In particular, when Hafiz al-Assad came to power in 1971, he pursued policies to mute the secularism of his predecessors. He tried to portray himself as a pious Muslim, reintroduced the abolished religious formulas into public ceremonies, and cultivated the ulama with honors and higher salaries.[84] Assad also launched an economic liberalization program in the 1970s, which was designed both to appease the merchants and to stimulate economic growth, a policy that most probably reduced the tension between the state and the merchant class.[85]

ELEVEN

Iran: Monarchy-Centered Nationalist Discourse and the Origins of Clergy-Centered Revolutionary Shi'ism

Iran, the country that the shah boasted was an island of peace and tranquility in the stormy waters of world politics, first displayed signs of political unrest in 1977. By 1979, this unrest had developed into a mass revolutionary movement that toppled one of the oldest institutions of monarchy in the world and brought about the establishment of the Islamic Republic. Iran thus became the first Islamic country in the modern period that successfully overthrew a secular government and formed a religious regime. The rise of Shi'i revolutionary discourse as the all-encompassing ideology of the Iranian Revolution was to many observers an astonishing phenomenon, particularly given the county's considerable experience of secularization in the twentieth century. To appreciate the extent of the change in the worldviews of Iranians that gave rise to the popularity of the religious ideology, we may consider the contrasting fates of two prominent leaders of the ulama—Sheikh Fazlullah Nuri in the Constitutional Revolution (1905–11) and Ayatollah Khomeini in the Iranian Revolution of 1979. Nuri was sent to the gallows for moving against the constitution, insisting on the ulama's prerogatives as the sole interpreters of the law, and defending monarchical absolutism. About seventy-three years later, when, in the debates over the nature of the post-revolutionary regime, Ayatollah Khomeini attacked democracy as a Western concept and thus alien to Islam, he was hailed by millions.

In fact, the unpopularity of Western-style democracy in the revolutionary movement formed a favorable context for the Ayatollah to create a system that not only gave the jurisprudent (the *faqih,* or supreme religious leader) the ultimate political and legal authority but also paradoxically displayed a power structure that was not much different from the monarchical absolutism he so vehemently opposed. To further underscore the novelty of Khomeini's ideas, we should mention that even as recently as the middle of the twentieth century, there was no sign that the ulama would be interested in founding an Islamic government. In the late forties, Grand Ayatollah Burujirdi instructed the clergy to stay away from getting involved in politics. In the sixties and seventies, however, not only did the ulama gradually become united in opposition to the shah, but also many middle-class intellectuals turned to Islam as a medium for political expression, significantly contributing to the formulation of Islamic revolutionary discourse. What were the social conditions of Islamic fundamentalism? Why did the ideology of liberal nationalism decline? Why was secular politics rejected by a large section of the educated elite? Who created the social space and resources for the harbingers of Islamic fundamentalism? What factors shaped the discourse and sociopolitical orientations of revolutionary Shi'ism?

To answer these questions, we focus on the social transformation Iran experienced in the period after the 1953 coup: economic development, demographic expansion, changes in class relations, and the expansion of the bureaucratic and administrative structure of the state. This transformation shaped the conditions for new culture production and generated the social actors interested in Islamic subjects. To be sure, there were certain historical factors specific to Iran, including the bazaar as an important source of support for religious activism and the unprecedented political power of the Shi'i ulama, which was unrivaled by the power of their Sunni counterparts in Arab countries. These factors may explain the success of the revolutionary Islamic movement in Iran and its failure in Algeria, Egypt, and Syria. Nevertheless, in terms of the proximate social conditions for the production of Islamic fundamentalist discourse, there were no significant differences among Algeria, Egypt, Iran, and Syria—expansion of the bureaucratic and administrative structure of the state, a monolithic discursive context generated by the state's extensive intervention in culture to shape society according to a certain secular-nationalist ideology, politicization of religion, and rapid expansion of the middle class.

The Coup, Social Transformation, and Cultural Outcomes

From the viewpoint of Iranian nationalists, the 1953 coup was an illegitimate seizure of power. This illegitimacy became particularly striking because (1) the royalists conspired with foreign forces to overthrow a democratically elected premier and (2) they collaborated with international oil companies to compromise Iran's national interests. For the nationalists, opposition to the shah's regime in the sixties and seventies was rooted in this lack of legitimacy. Their charges may be true, but the very fact of the coup cannot be said to have been the cause of the rise of the revolutionary Islamic movement. There are several reasons for this. First, a significant section of the ulama either directly participated in the coup or tacitly approved the military overthrew of Premier Mosaddeq. In fact, between 1941, when Reza Shah was overthrown by the Allies, and 1959, the ulama were more often aligned with the monarch than in opposition to him.[1] Second, after the coup, major nationalist and religious figures were willing to accept the shah's rule, provided that he abided by the constitution. Finally, stating that the regime was illegitimate is one thing, but explaining the decline of secular politics and the rise of revolutionary Islam in the 1960s through the 1970s is quite another.

The coup contributed to the rise of militant Islamic fundamentalism because it set the stage for subsequent changes in the structures and policies of the state, the economy, and class and group relations. It marked the beginning of a new episode for culture production because (1) the state's major initiatives for economic development started after that date; (2) it displayed a new international alignment between the regime, the Western states, and international capital; (3) it showed a major expansion in the bureaucratic administrative structure of the state; and (4) it indicated a change not only in the economic and cultural policies of the state but also in the alignment of the regime with the domestic social forces. Although complex social processes were at work in producing the revolution of 1977–79, we argue that the key factors explaining the formulation of Islamic fundamentalist discourse were the state's exclusionary policies and the imposition of a secularist monolithic discourse on society from above.

Economic Development and the Patterning of Class Conflict

The revolutionary movement of 1977–79 was preceded by two decades of impressive economic development, prosperity, and social differentiation. The GNP grew by 11.6 percent during the period covered by the Fourth Development Plan (1968–72). Agriculture had the lowest growth rate, at 3.9 percent per annum; oil and services achieved the highest rates, at 15.2 and 14.2 percent per annum, respectively. Industry grew at an average annual rate of 14 percent in real terms. With this growth came new occupational positions, resulting in the expansion in the number of jobs, which increased by 1.2 million during this four-year period. The Fifth Development Plan began in 1973 and was completed at the end of 1977. During this period, the economy grew at a rate faster than that of the Fourth Development Plan. Economic development was reinforced by the shah's success at striking a favorable deal with the oil companies. As a result, oil revenues quadrupled between 1969 and 1974, which enhanced the level of economic prosperity in the country. From the midseventies on, however, a series of economic difficulties, including a high inflation rate and a scarcity of basic commodities, lowered the level of people's prosperity, causing public dissatisfaction and contributing to the outbreak of the protest movement.

The State and Class Formation

Modernization initiated and promoted by the state contributed to the distribution of wealth, the formation of social classes, and the pattern of class conflict. The main beneficiaries of the sixties' and seventies' economic development were international enterprises and a small group of wealthy capitalists who, through their close ties to the state, were able to dominate the economy and reap substantial profits. Consisting of about one thousand families, this class included the royal family, the owners of private banks and modern commercial centers, industrialists, and those involved in agribusiness. These people owned not only many of the large commercial farms but also some 85 percent of the major private firms in banking, manufacturing, foreign trade, insurance, and urban construction.

Estimated at nearly 1 million families, the petty bourgeoisie (craftsmen and retailers) and the merchants, particularly those connected to the bazaar, and landowners were antagonized by state economic policies. Industrial development, state policies of various sorts (such as the licensing system), credit allocation, and the establishment of farm corporations and agribusiness undermined the interests of these classes. The traditional ("feudal") landowning class was destroyed through the land reform of the sixties. In its place, a capitalist landowning class emerged in the postreform period. On the eve of the revolution, agricultural landholders were divided into three categories. The first was a group of more than one hundred thousand owners of large, medium-sized, and small agricultural holdings. The second was a small group of rich peasants and small rural capitalists who had considerable influence in their own villages. Finally, the third category consisted of 1.5 million small-holding and landless peasants. The landowners had long had close ties with the merchants and real-estate owners in the urban areas.

In the 1960s and 1970s, economic development created and expanded modern occupational positions, forming the basis of the new middle class. Estimated at 1.8 million in 1977, the members of this class, after the bazaaris, were the most important political force in the country and provided a significant basis for radical Islamic opposition. This class consisted of civil servants, teachers and school administrators, engineers, managers, and white-collar workers. The expansion of universities also created a large number of politically conscious students. Many of the people who participated in various forms of revolutionary activities and radical politics were university students and/or had a middle-class background.[2]

The Politicization of the Bazaar

While the bazaaris enjoyed considerable influence under Mosaddeq, after the coup this influence not only waned but the regime's intervention in the economy in favor of the modern sector and foreign companies undermined their interests. Particularly disadvantaged by the economic restructuring of the postcoup period were those engaged in handicraft production, artisans, and shopkeepers. A 1957 law provided the guilds with legal status, stipulating the formation of the High Council of Guilds (Shura-ye ali-ye asnaf) consisting of their representatives.[3] The law, however, brought the guilds under government control by stipulating that the governor general would be the honorary chairperson of the High Council. The most important points of discussion between the guilds and the government centered around the guilds' annual taxes, foreign imports, and starting modern factories.[4] These discussions failed to produce policies in favor of the guilds, and the state's stabilization program, which led to recession in the early sixties, intensified pressures on their businesses. Further, the expansion of the banking system and other state credit institution, and the fairly rapid growth of a modern commercial sector in the sixties and the seventies, weakened the bazaar economy.[5]

The shah even went so far as to endorse the physical destruction of the bazaar, on the one hand, and the establishment of new shopping centers outside the bazaar, on the other. This was done in two ways: "Firstly by building new state schools, new housing and new shopping centers outside the Bazaar, while within the Bazaar streets were "widened"—a euphemism for imposing a modern grid-iron pattern of roads on the old narrow alleyways . . . Secondly it was done by the modernization of the banking system . . . To cut out the Bazaari middlemen, in 1976 the government sought to improve the nationwide distribution of foodstuffs, and conceived of building a new market in Tehran, based on London's New Covent Garden."[6] Later the shah admitted his contempt for the bazaaris: "The bazaaris are a fanatic lot, highly resistant to change because their locations afford a lucrative monopoly. Moving against the bazaars was typical of the political and social risks I had to take in may drive for modernization."[7]

Despite considerable expansion, the single-commodity export-oriented economy was highly vulnerable to fluctuations in the world oil market. Although relatively small, a sudden drop of about 12 percent in the international demand for Iran oil in the midseventies sent a fairly strong shock wave through the entire Iranian economy. This factor, plus externally induced inflation and the rise in the demand for various commodities that overwhelmed supplies, created considerable economic difficulties for the country. The state's strategy to manage these problems further worsened its relationship with the bazaar. To control inflation, the state launched a nationwide anti-price-gouging and antiprofiteering campaign, which was intensified in mid-1975. The bazaar was singled out as the scapegoat for the existence of high prices. In 1974–75, the anti-inflation campaign was launched, with the guilds as an enforcement agency. When the chambers of guilds proved to be uncooperative in implementing the government's measures, the minister of commerce dismissed some of the top guild leaders from chambers in Tehran and other parts of the country. Price levels were lowered by fiat from Tehran, and price lists were posted in shops and printed in newspapers. The government's imposition of price controls over goods and services in 1975 was another blow to the economic interests of small-scale tradespeople and artisans. In the subsequent two years, more than twenty thousand small businesses were fined or brought to court on charges of speculation and the violation of price regulations. The price control campaign had only a short-term effect: official indices went down for six months, but black-market prices for essential commodities rose sharply. On the whole, the campaign proved to be ineffective. But it considerably enhanced the merchants' and guilds' hostility toward the regime.[8]

The outbreak of violent street demonstrations against the regime in June 1963 and the Iranian revolutionary movement of 1977–79 should be understood against this background. The events of 1963 were particularly important in signifying the ulama-bazaar alliance against the shah. The land and social reforms of the early six-ties provided an opportune occasion for Ayatollah Khomeini and his followers to launch strong protests against the shah. The bazaaris, particularly those with a tra-ditional middle-class background, participated widely in these protests.[9] Although these protests were crushed and Ayatollah Khomeini was sent into exile, the ability of the religious opposition to attract a considerable number of people to its call gradually shifted the attention of the intellectual leaders away from secular opposi-tional ideologies and toward religion.

The Postcoup State: Repression, Bureaucratic Expansion, and Ideology

Economic reasons may explain the bazaaris' dissatisfaction with the shah and sup-port for the religious opposition.[10] However, it is necessary to go beyond narrow economic determinism and focus on the interactions between political and cultural forces in order to understand how class interests were transcended and a strong reli-gious revolutionary movement formed. This is particularly important because the bazaaris were among the supporters of the National Front before the coup. Why, then, did they abandon liberal nationalism and join the Islamic opposition? A part of the answer lies in the decline of secular discourse, including liberal-nationalist ide-ology, as a result of state repression. Right after the coup, the militant members of the National Front were executed or imprisoned or had to flee the country. The remainder made repeated efforts to revitalize the front within the same general pol-icy frame that it had occupied in the precoup period but found themselves weak-ened by a lack of foreign support. The United States proved to be a callous ally for liberal nationalism under Mosaddeq. And because of its close association with what were perceived as imperialist countries, the idea of democracy and pluralism became discredited among intellectual leaders. One may argue that the persistent efforts of the leaders of the National Front to get U.S. attention was a tactic that became increasingly ineffective, if not counterproductive, in regaining their former popular-ity among the political activists. The U.S. ties to the shah in the postcoup period constituted an insurmountable difficulty for liberal-nationalist thought. As a result, despite repeated efforts by the front's leaders after the coup, they were unable to play a leading role in the opposition movement.

For its part, the state relied heavily on its bureaucracy, repressive apparatus, and foreign support. It displayed little interests in forming alliance with indigenous social classes or groups. Although its developmental program resulted in a period of rapid economic growth and capital accumulation, it had quite opposite cultural outcomes, with debilitating effects on the regime's ability to survive. The land reform programs of the sixties, while eliminating the class of the "feudal" landowners, did not appreciably increase landownership among the peasants and provided the state with no solid basis of support in rural areas. The regime did not seriously attempt to form a strong alliance with the newly "liberated" peasant farmers. The liberal agricultural minister, Hasan Arsanjani, failed to tie small-scale farmers to the government through the newly established rural cooperatives. He went so far as to mobilize these farmers' cooperatives in a Congress of Rural Cooperatives in 1963, at which some 4,700 delegates gathered in Tehran. After days of speech making and meetings, the congress unanimously passed several resolutions that included the farmers' commitment to give their last breath to the protection of the constitutional monarchy, the demand that the government observe the UN charter on human rights, the call for the unity of the farmers and the rural cooperatives, the unanimous approval of the six laws offered in a referendum by His Imperial Majesty, and the appreciation of Arsanjani for his selfless efforts and sacrifice.[11] Arsanjani, however, was dismissed, and the regime's agricultural policies were revised to promote the unpopular rural corporations and agribusinesses. The opportunity of forging a link between the state and rural areas was thus missed.

Instead, the state bureaucracy served as an important mechanism for the control of civil society. Bureaucratic expansion was not only a result of the state's intervention in the economy, but also a means of co-opting the members of the opposition groups. Civil service positions were created and often handed out as political favors and rewards to opposition leaders for their conciliation and compromise with the regime. Furthermore, the shah frequently resorted to the tactic of "divide and rule" to insure his control of the state. One example of this tactic was creating new ministries and civil service posts with overlapping responsibilities. "This overlapping of function," says Marvin Zonis, "is not restricted to the gathering of information vital to the survival of the regime. Similar practices exist elsewhere in the bureaucracy. There is a Ministry of Economy and another for Development and Housing. Labor unions are the concern of the Ministry of Interior and the Ministry of Labor. Responsibility for the Literacy Corps is assigned to the armed forces and the Ministry of Education."[12]

Between the 1950s and 1975, the number of cabinet-level ministerial portfolios increased from eleven to twenty-seven. The bureaucratic organization of the state, however, was unable to perform the intermediary function of connecting the ruling monarch to the rest of the society. The shah did not allow serious interests to be represented by diverse groups and associations through the political process. Since the shah himself made all major decisions, no serious mechanism was left for the public to affect the scope and content of the activities of the government. Politics was thus depoliticized. Nor did the shah encourage the emergence of corporatist structures such as rural cooperatives or trade unions to represent their members' interests. As a result, the regime became somewhat detached from the civil society. This separation was even more amplified and exaggerated by the state's cultural policies and ideological orientation—a factor that contributed to the rise of Islamic revolutionary discourse from the sixties on.

State Ideology: Monarchy-Centered Nationalist Discourse

The regime's authoritarianism, intolerance of democratic freedom, and economic development strategies were all subjects of criticism in the opposition literature. Nevertheless, the most important factor shaping the oppositional discourse was the ideology of the state itself. It set the agenda for its challengers and defined their identity. Three books ostensibly written by the shah provided the cardinal parameters of the state's discourse: *Mission for My Country* (1960), *The White Revolution of Iran* (1967), and *Toward the Great Civilization* (1974). These works were to represent the shah's views on the past, present, and future of Iran, respectively.[13] The monarchy-centered nationalist discourse informed these works and underpinned the state's rites, symbols, and myths. In *Mission for My Country*, the shah hammered away at the idea that the monarchy had been essential for the country. Over the great time span of 2,500 years of continuous monarchy, said the shah, "the monarchy has brought unity out of diversity. We have always had differences of race, colour, creed, and economic and political situation and conviction; but under the monarchy the divergencies have been sublimated into one larger whole symbolized in the person of the Shah."[14]

Nationalism was another key parameter in the state ideology. In defending his own view of Iranian nationalism, the shah attacked both the communism of the Tudeh Party and the nationalism of the National Front. The former, in his view, were illegitimate not simply because they had sacrificed Iran's national interests for the sake of international communism, but because of their view of revolutionary change that stressed violence. Likewise, the shah considered Mosaddeq's conception of nationalism wanting not because he did not remain loyal to the monarchy. Mosaddeq's nationalism, he charged, was backward, negative, and counterproductive to Iran's interests. His "negative policies led straight to the sort of political and economic chaos which foreign agents found ideal for their purposes."[15] The shah, in contrast, portrayed his nationalism as positive: "a policy of maximum political and economic independence consistent with the interest of one's country."[16] But contrary to Mosaddeq, this policy "does not mean nonalignment or sitting on the fence."[17] While the shah criticized the British and Russians for their imperialistic schemes in Iran, he made positive reference to the United States: "We welcome American Point Four and military assistance, but only because it helps us to develop and strengthen Iran and to help ourselves and the wider cause of freedom. We welcome American business and commercial interests, but only where their presence in our judgment contributes to the same end. America has never tried to dominate us as the old imperialists did, nor would we tolerate that; and the same applies to our relations with all other countries."[18]

The land reform of 1963 put the communists and the liberals on the defensive. By labeling it the "White Revolution" or "The Revolution of the Shah and the People," the shah presented himself as a progressive monarch and champion of justice and equality. The shah's revolution was peaceful, propeople, and nonviolent, which was contrary to the communist revolution. "In recent years," wrote the shah in his second book, *The White Revolution*, "because of Iran's internal situation and her international position I felt an imperative need for a revolution based on the most advanced principles of justice and human rights that would change the framework of our society and make it comparable to that of the most developed countries of the world."[19] It was claimed that the revolution upheld two sacred principles: an emphasis on spirit and religion, and the preservation of individual and social freedom. "To realize these goals," said the shah,

> it was essential that land reform should take place and the feudal landlord
> and peasant system be abolished; that the relationship between workers and
> employers should be regularized so that labour should not feel exploited; that
> women—who after all make up half the population—should no longer be
> included with lunatics and criminals and deprived of their social rights; that
> the scourge of illiteracy should be removed so that illiterates who do not know
> how to defend themselves should know their rights; that nobody should die of
> disease nor spend their lives in misery and wretchedness through lack of treat-
> ment or care; that backwardness in the villages should be ended, and the
> undeveloped country districts should be connected with the rest of the coun-
> try; and in general that conditions in harmony with today's civilized world
> should prevail.[20]

In response to the protests of the ulama, which caused the riots of June 1963, the shah claimed that these riots "were inspired by reactionary forces led by an individual who claimed to be religious, even though his origin was obscure."[21] The shah was evidently referring to Ayatollah Khomeini who had preached against the reforms and called his followers to rise up against the shah's rule. From this date on the shah designated the events of June 1963 "the best example of the unholy alliance of the two forces of black reaction and red destruction."[22]

The state's discourse fell further away from Islam when the Iranian kingship was glorified and 2,500 years of continuous monarchy were extravagantly celebrated in 1971. This celebration was to establish a historical continuity between the past and the present. In an interview with Oriana Fallaci, the shah stated: "When there's no monarchy, there's anarchy, or an oligarchy or a dictatorship. Besides, a monarchy is the only possible means to govern Iran. If I have been able to do something, a lot, in fact, for Iran it is owing to the detail, slight as it may seem, that I'm its king. To get things done, one needs power, and to hold on to power one mustn't ask anyone's permission or advice. One mustn't discuss decisions with anyone."[23]

The Islamic calendar was changed to a monarchical calendar, whose beginning was officially set at the time when the first monarchy was established in Iran. The importance of religious holidays was downplayed, while new holidays were added to the calendar, including the shah's and his son's birthdays and the date of the implementation of the land reform.[24] Furthermore, in 1975 the shah abruptly dissolved all the "official" political parties and established a one-party system. His rule thus become explicitly totalitarian, as he required the public to show commitment to "Monarchy, Constitution, and the White Revolution" by joining the newly formed Rastakhiz Party.

In his third book, *Toward the Great Civilization,* the shah was jubilant. He boasted of Iran's progress from an impoverished, backward, and weak state to a developed and wealthy state with significant influence on world politics. He attributed these achievements to the pillars of the new Iranian society: the monarchical order, the constitution, and the revolution of the shah and the people. The monarchy guaranteed national unity, firmness in the power of leadership, military strength, political independence, and the significance of the country's international role. The constitution protected the democratic order and guaranteed the civil, political, and legal rights of all Iranians. The revolution of the shah and the people was the foundation of the all-encompassing socioeconomic transformation of society and determined the path and directed the process of the establishment and expansion of social justice, economic democracy, and democratic economy.[25] He stated that in Iran's democratic order "a complete individual freedom" was combined with "complete order and social discipline." There was no room for those who engaged in the acts of sabotage and destruction. These individuals were "instinctively ignorant and illogical." They were either "brainwashed" or "mentally ill." They were not allowed to engage in destructive and murderous activities against their own country under the guise of "the foolish and contradictory" ideology of "Islamic Marxism."[26]

To summarize, the ideology of the Pahlavi regime rested on a set of principles that specified its scope and boundaries with other ideologies and the normative expectations of the Iranian public. It was insisted that the monarchy was indispensable for Iran's national interests. Pre-Islamic kingship and ancient history were glorified, while the Islamic period was overlooked. In close alliance with the West, the state was portrayed as the agent of modernization and progress. These principles, however, were not a set of abstract ideas characterizing the general features of Iran's political order and having a diffuse and abstract function for national unity. The monarchy-centered nationalist discourse had an objective presence in a series of symbols, rites, and myths. The dates celebrating the anniversaries of the land reform and other reforms, including the anniversary of the forced unveiling of women by Reza Shah in 1936, the monarchical calendar, and the one-party system were all frequent reminders of the shah's totalitarian ideology. The prerequisite for being included in the country's polity was to accept these principles, to participate in the state's organized rites, and to categorically reject other competing ideologies. One thus could not retain the idea of monarchy yet debate or criticize the adequacy of the claims advanced by the state ideology or its policies. The shah was not "reasonable." There was no room for a qualified support for the monarchy or legitimate opposition. One was either with the shah or against him.

The Rise of Shi'i Revolutionary Discourse

Like other ideological producers, the precursors of the Islamic revolutionary movement made reference to the problem of political repression, the state's policies, the uneven distribution of resources, and the general socioeconomic condition of the country. What they said, however, could not be deduced simply from the exigencies of the existing social problems. This is true particularly in light of the fact that in the sixties and the seventies—the period during which the Islamic revolutionary ideology was formulated—Iran experienced unprecedented economic development. And the notion that Iran was suffering from economic backwardness and unjust or deteriorating social conditions cannot be reconciled with the reality of the country's extraordinary development. In fact, the expressions of the ideological producers were shaped as often by their own perceptions as by the reality of the social problems. If a significant section of the intellectual leaders found an Islamic solution meaningful, it was principally due to the very fact that they all faced the same ideological target—the secularist ideology of the monarchy, the periodic rituals of its propaganda machine, and the omnipresent symbols of the regime (the portraits and statues of the shah and the slogans written in public places for mass indoctrination). The discourse of the opposition became meaningful in its negation of the monarchy-centered nationalist discourse. The more the shah stressed secularism and the more he attempted to undermine the influence of the religious establishment, the more religious discourse became the defining identity of the opposition movement. The monarchy-centered nationalist and secularist discourse found its counterpart in the clergy-centered religious oppositional discourse. The absolutist power of the shah found its mirror image in the absolutism of the governance of the jurisprudent in Ayatollah Khomeini's revolutionary Islamic ideology.

The West and Westernization

The issues that were stressed forcefully in the state ideology—the West and Westernization, secularism and the glorification of Iran's pre-Islamic history and culture, the indispensability of the monarchy for Iran, and the social role and status of women—became in different ways the subjects of vindictive criticism by the precursors of revolutionary Islamic discourse. There is an astonishing historical parallel between the changes in the discourse of the regime in a secularist and often antireligious direction and the crystallization of revolutionary Islamic ideology in the sixties through the seventies. The dawn of this Islamic ideology was in the eclectic and contradictory messages of the sociopolitical and cultural writings of Jalal Ale-Ahmad (1923–69).[27] Ale-Ahmad was among the first intellectual leaders to present a systematic denunciation of the West that was later to epitomize the attitudes of the Islamic opposition on Westernization. Ale-Ahmad's anti-Western and proreligious orientation characterized his later work. Although he was from a clerical family—his father, Shaikh Ahmad, was a clergyman, and Ayatollah Taleqani was his paternal uncle—in the precoup period he grew up to become a secular writer and leftist activist, joining the Tudeh (Communist) Party. His works, particularly *Did-du Bazdid* and *Seh Tar,* had an explicitly antireligious tone. But in the sixties, he turned to religion. Among his many books and articles, three major works were directly related to political and cultural issues and reflected the core of his sociopolitical thoughts: *Seh Maqaleh-ye Digar (Three More Essays), Gharbzadegi (Westoxication),* and *Dar Khedmat va Khianat-i Roushanfikran (Concerning the Service and Betrayal of the Intellectuals).* Ale-Ahmad viewed these works as parts of a single self study of Iranian history and culture. *Gharbzadegi* represented a turning point in Ale-Ahmad's intellectual life, for it marked the beginning of his departure from Marxism, on the one hand, and his appreciation of the significance of Islam in society, on the other. In these works, Ale-Ahmad attempted to show the contradiction between the West and Islam, portrayed Westernization as a disease, and vociferously accused Westernizing intellectuals of betraying the nation and Islam. At the outset, he noted that Iran was not industrialized, and described what that meant for Iran: "forced by economics, politics, and that global confrontation between poverty and wealth, we must be polite and servile consumers of the products of western industry, or at best we must be satisfied, subservient, and low-paid repairmen for whatever comes from the west. It is this last which necessitates that we re-shape ourselves, our government, our culture, and our everyday lives into some semblance of a machine."[28] For him, the root of the problem was the contradiction between Islam and Western culture. In his attack on the West, Ale-Ahmad claimed that in its dealing with Iran, the West

> not only struggled against this Islamic totality (in the case of the bloody instigation of Shi'ism of Safavid times, in the creation of friction between us and the Ottomans, in promoting the Baha'i activities in the middle of the Qajar period, in the crushing of the Ottomans after the First World War, and finally in the opposition to the Shi'ite clergy during the Constitutional Revolution and afterwards . . .), but it also tried to as quickly as possible tear apart that unity which was fragmented from within and which only appeared whole on the surface. . . . It was our lot then to be the only ones, both in the guise and the reality of an Islamic totality, to stand in the way of the advance of European civilization (read: colonialism; Christianity), i.e., in the way of the drive to market [the products of] western industry. The stopping of Ottoman artillery outside of the gates of Vienna in the nineteenth [*sic*] century was the end of a prolonged event which had begun in 732 in Spain (Andalus). How can we view these twelve centuries of struggle and competition between East and West as anything but a struggle between Islam and Christianity?[29]

The emancipation of Iranian history and culture from Western cultural domination was Ale-Ahmad's solution. This emancipation involved a relentless attack on the secular intellectuals who had been the bearers of Western culture in Iran. Since the West was in conflict with Islam, it was clear that defending Islam was the only way to liberation and development. In his defense of Islam and critique of the West, Ale-Ahmad even argued that the execution of Sheikh Fazlullah Nuri during the Constitutional Revolution marked the triumph of Western domination of the country:

> Shaikh Nuri was not hanged as an opponent of the Constitutional movement (for in the beginning he was in fact a defender of it), but as a proponent of "the rule of the *Shariat*" and . . . as a defender of the integrity of Shi'ism. It was for this reason that in the wake of his death everyone was waiting for a writ to be issued from Najaf. And this was going on at a time when the leader of our west-stricken intelligentsia, Malkom Khan, was a Christian and Talebof was a social democrat from the Caucasus. In any case, from that day on we were marked with the brand of westitis. I consider the corpse of that great man [Nuri] hanging from the gallows, to be a banner bearing the emblem of the final victory of westitis over this country after 200 years of struggle.[30]

Ale-Ahmad then concluded that those who had translated the French constitution for Iran and those who had sacrificed Iran's national interests for the

Communist International were of the same type, responsible for the decline of Iran's historical and cultural identity.[31]

In *Dar Khedmat va Khianat-i Roushanfikran,* Ale-Ahmad developed a more detailed critique of the intellectuals. As he indicated, the treatise was inspired by the bloody demonstration of 1963 and in reaction to the indifference of the intelligentsia to the incident.[32] Ale-Ahmad attributed five characteristics to Iranian intellectuals: (1) having a Western lifestyle, (2) being irreligious or antireligious, (3) being educated, (4) being alienated from their local and traditional environment, and (5) having a scientific worldview.[33] He argued that the antireligious orientation of the intellectuals was a simple imitation of their European counterparts and was not rooted in Iranian culture or history. Critiques of religion in Europe, said Ale-Ahmad, were rooted in the Enlightenment (which had culminated in the French Revolution), caused by the Industrial Revolution and the development of science and technology, formed as reactions to the close association between the church and the state, and stemmed from the fact that a comprehensive system of laws on commerce and politics was absent in Christianity. In Iran, on the other hand, there was no enlightenment movement, no industrial revolution, and no significant connection between the state and religion. Moreover, Islam offered guidelines on virtually all aspects of social life. Finally, while the European intelligentsia had vast intellectual resources, a tradition of discovery, and inventions in laws, science, and philosophy, the Iranians had none of these. Therefore, they (Iranian intellectuals) were not authentic but uprooted imitators.[34] Ale-Ahmad then concluded his critique by suggesting that

> The intellectuals must decide between two alternatives:
> — Either putting an end to the westoxication, and in its stead attempting
>   to understand the native environment and problems, and making serious
>   efforts, worthy of an intellectual, to solve these problems by means of the
>   latest scientific methods; or,
> — Continuing the westoxication to the extreme, that is, a total reorganization
>   of the Iranian society according to the moral, political and social standards
>   of the West. This will result in a complete spiritual, national and cultural
>   annihilation of Iran from the face of the world.
>   In other words, the choice is between resisting colonialism or completely
> submitting to it. Submission to the western cultural domination is of course easy
> and beneficial. But resistance is hard and demands many sacrifices.[35]

That Ale-Ahmad's understanding of Iranian history, or Islamic history in general, was inadequate, if not flatly wrong, and that it reflected, in Adamiyat's assessment, a "confusion in historical thinking" is beside the point.[36] After all, when history becomes relevant for political action, it is not always the kind of history that is based on what actually happened but is often based on what political actors think happened. It is partly an actual history and partly self-recreated and self-remembered history. Ale-Ahmad's views became an accepted wisdom precisely because they offered a critique of the very culture that was promoted by an increasingly unpopular regime.

Ale-Ahmad's criticism of Western culture and defense of Islam were clothed in a general framework. On occasion, his criticisms appeared anachronistic and contrary to his own intellectual interests. In addition to his affinity with Marxism for certain part of his political activities, he was responsible for transmitting some of the major works of leading European authors. In Hamid Dabashi's apt assertions: "The fact that while Ale Ahmad severely criticized 'Westoxication' as a form of disease he himself, in his own highly alert discourse, was markedly 'West-stricken' is an acute, however ironic, testimony to his own insight. He, for example, criticized—and occasionally even ridiculed—the secular-minded intellectual's most exclusive attention to 'The Western' cultural heritage, at the expense of their own; and yet he himself was chiefly responsible for translating into Persian books by Sartre, Gide, Dostoyevsky, Camus, and others."[37]

To further underscore the eclectic and often contradictory messages that can be drawn from his career, Ale-Ahmad did what later became a taboo among revolutionary intellectuals and activists: he traveled to Israel and spoke approvingly of the Israeli experience: "For me as an Easterner, Israel is a model, [better] than any other model, of how to deal with the West. How to extract from its industries by the spiritual power of a [mass] martyrdom, how to take remunition [*sic*] from it and spend the capital thus obtained to advance the country, and how with the price of a short time of political dependency give permanence to our newly established enterprise."[38] He even displayed little identification with or sympathy for the Arabs. A love-hate attitude toward the Arabs and Arab culture has of course been one of the distinctive characteristics of Iranian intellectuals in the modern period, particularly from the second part of the nineteenth century until the middle of the twentieth. Ale Ahmad was no exception, and his approval of Israel was thus partly a reflection of his grievances against the Arab culture: "Having so much suffered at the hands of these rootless Arabs, I am happy to see the presence of Israel in the East. The presence of Israel that can cut off the oil pipe of the Arab sheikhs, and that can implant the seed of seeking justice and equanimity in the heart of every Beduin Arab and that can cause much headache for the illegitimate and archaic regimes. These rotten scales on the stem of the old but strong tree of Islam . . . ought to be blown away by the whirlwind awe of the Israeli presence so that I as an Easterner can rid myself of the tyranny of the puppet regimes installed by the oil [companies]."[39]

At any rate, Ale-Ahmad's disapproval of the West was not specific to any of its sociopolitical and cultural aspects save, perhaps, for its domineering character. He did not advance serious criticisms of the principles of social organization underpinning Western civilization. In the absence of such criticisms and in light of Ale-Ahmad's intellectual indebtedness to Western authors, we may thus postulate that his quarrel with the West was prompted by a certain Western lifestyle that he saw the Pahlavis were actively promoting and his fellow Iranians were eagerly imitating. His shift to Islamic subjects might have been due to a strong intuition that led him to discern "the sign of the times"—that the intellectual trend was shifting away from secularism and toward religion. The Pahlavis might have instilled that intuition in him.

Islam versus Secular Ideologies—Liberalism and Communism

In contrast with Ale-Ahmad, Ali Shari'ati (1933–77) offered not only a more direct and pointed criticism of Western ideologies—liberalism and communism—but a comprehensive reformulation of the sociopolitical view of Islam in a revolutionary direction. He was, in fact, an Islamic ideologue par excellence. The process of intellectual development in Shari'ati's thought also reflected its discursive context. True, Shari'ati was born into a clerical family. In his youth, he became a member of the Movement of God-Worshipping Socialists and of the center of the propagation of Islamic truth. After receiving a B.A. in Arabic and French from the University of Mashhad, he won a state scholarship to study in France. In 1959, he started graduate work in sociology at the Sorbonne in Paris, where he also joined the Freedom Movement (which was based on Islamic liberalism) and the Confederation of Iranian Students. Thus, when he criticized the intellectuals' attitudes toward religion, he was in fact defending his faith. He reiterated the view of the Egyptian Islamic modernist Abduh that "Europe abandoned religion and made progress, [while] we abandoned religion and went backward."[40] The attack on religion in Iran, said Shari'ati, "is different from the opposition of the educated people of Europe to religion. Opposition of the intellectuals to religion in Europe was rooted in their own experiences and knowledge of religion, the Middle Ages, and the church. The opposition of Iranian intellectuals to religion is rather based on a blind mimicking of the Europeans. . . . Our contemporary educated people understand neither Islam nor its history. They know only a European language and have translated the Europeans' judgment about their own religion [into Persian], and then imitation."[41]

For Shari'ati, religion was the most effective weapon to fight imperialism and Western cultural domination. He challenged Frantz Fanon on the question of religion and revolution. According to him, "Franz Fanon, whom I know personally and whose books I translated into Persian, was pessimistic about the positive contribution of religion to social movement. He had, in fact an anti-religious attitude until I convinced him that in some societies where religion plays an important role in culture, religion can, through its resources and psychological effects, help the enlightened person to lead his society toward the same destination toward which Fanon was taking his own through non-religious means."[42]

Nevertheless, the further development in his religious thought in the direction of an all-encompassing sociopolitical and cultural discourse cannot be attributed solely to his religious upbringing. There was more than one way that Shari'ati could have developed his understanding of the messages of Islam. Why did he move in the Islamic fundamentalist direction? Why did he fail to organize his reading of Islam in a manner similar to that of the nineteenth-century modernists in India and Egypt, or even to the Shi'i political modernism of Ayatollah Na'ini in the early twentieth century? We argue that the key factor in the development of his thought was the nature of the ideological target in opposition to which he developed his ideas. By 1967, when Shari'ati moved to Tehran to commence a lecture series at Huseiniyya Ershad, the Pahlavi regime had made considerable changes in the economic and social conditions of the country, its ideology was developing in a totalitarian direction, and its bureaucratic structure was expanding. Further developments in the state's ideology, including the glorification of Iranian pre-Islamic kingship and the celebration of 2,500 years of continuous monarchy in 1971, the change of the calendar from Islamic to monarchical, and the dissolution of all political parties and the establishment of a single-party system in 1975—all provided a clear-cut ideological target to focus on.

If in the early sixties Ale-Ahmad had sensed the changes in the demand side of the ideological market in favor of religious subjects, when Shari'ati entered the profession of religious education in the late sixties the popularity of religion was a matter of fact. He not only contributed to this popularity but by giving religion a modern conceptual scaffolding also managed successfully to draw a large secular audience to his intellectual movement. His approach was to launch a counter-offensive against both liberalism and Marxism, while somewhat haphazardly drawing from concepts and categories of liberalism, Marxism, and existentialism. He claimed that Islam transcended all these ideologies:

> Humanity arrived at liberalism, and took democracy in place of theocracy as its key to liberation. It was snared by a crude capitalism, in which democracy proved as much a delusion as theocracy. . . .
>
> The desire for equality, for liberation from this dazing whirl of personal avarice, so horrifyingly accelerated by the machine, led humanity into a revolt that resulted in communism. This communism, however, simply represents the same fanatical and frightening power as the Medieval church, only without God. It has its people, but they rule not in the name of the Lord but in the name of the proletariat.[43]

Likewise, he attacked the conservatives and the tendencies in the official religion that favored the status quo in historical Shi'ism. Shari'ati distinguished two versions of the religion: one was the Safavid Shi'ism, which was static and dormant, tied to the political power of the monarchy, and reactionary. The other was Alid Shi'ism—a progressive religion that would support a monotheistic classless society. The outcome of Shari'ati's intellectual exertions was a sociopolitical and religious exposition that was nothing short of a totalizing discourse whose development paralleled the process of the expansion of the state's monolithic ideology. For him, Alid Shi'ism represented a true Islam; it was a complete party. And his description of that totality rested on the notion that "'party,' in the general vocabulary of world intellectuals, is basically a unified social organization with a 'world view,' an 'ideology,' a 'philosophy of history,' an 'ideal social order,' a 'class foundation,' a 'class orientation,' a 'social leadership,' a 'political philosophy,' a 'political orientation,' a 'tradition,' a 'slogan,' a 'strategy,' a 'tactic of struggle,' and . . . a 'hope' that wants to change 'the status quo' in man, society, people, or a particular class, and establish 'the desired status' in its stead; and thus each party has two aspects of affirmation and negation: 'Thou shalt,' and 'Thou shalt not.'"[44]

This description is not too different from that of Hasan al-Banna's characterization of the Muslim Brothers. The difference, however, was that, contrary to the Egyptian ulama, the Iranian ulama were in opposition to the ruling regime. Thus, the notion that politically nonactive or proregime ulama were reactionaries was in line with the view of Ayatollah Khomeini and his followers, who were also opposing the secular regime. This fact alone had placed Ayatollah Khomeini in the category of Alid Shi'ism. In other words, the presence of the shah gave a semblance of unity and consistency to this otherwise heterogeneous and often contradictory Islamic movement. In fact, there were as many dissimilarities between Shari'ati's views and those of the ulama as there were between the Muslim Brothers and Sunni orthodoxy in Egypt.

The governing principles of Ale-Ahmad's and Shari'ati's intellectual projects revolved around merciless criticism of secular ideologies and a passionate defense of Islam. The description of Islam was couched in very general terms, and, perhaps owing to this generality, their works significantly contributed to the formation and dissemination of revolutionary religious ideology. They, however, did not have a specific political project. They did not offer a detailed presentation of what concrete form Islamic government should take in Iran, what procedures of rule making should be adopted, or who should have the ultimate authority under the Islamic system. Both were lay intellectuals, trained outside the religious institutions of the Shi'i establishment. Their defense of religion and attacks on Western culture were shaped by the pro-Western and secularist (and even antireligious) discourse of the intrusive state. In the same way that the domination of society by the monarch-ulama alliance in the nineteenth century had shaped the political and cultural outlooks of such intellectual leaders as Mirza Fath Ali Akhundzadah, Mirza Aqa Khan Kirmani, and Malkum Khan and directed them toward constitutionalism and liberal thought, the shah's break with the ulama and imposition of a Western cultural lifestyle on society resulted in the popularization of religion among opposition groups. While during the heyday of secularism early in the twentieth century the general tendency among intellectuals was to shy away from religion, in the era when secularism was appropriated by an exclusionary regime, religion increasingly became an attractive medium for political expression. It was thus not accidental for an intellectual leader like Ale-Ahmad to renounce Marxism and join the ranks of religious activists in the sixties.

Islam and Politics: The Governance of the Jurisprudent

Shari'ati received his secular education in Iran and at Sorbonne in Paris. He was involved in debates with the proponents of various secular ideologies. He was also addressing a predominantly secular audience, which was familiar with modern ideologies. He thus felt compelled to draw heavily from the categories of liberalism and communism in order to demonstrate the superiority of his faith. The regime's anticommunism and close ties to the capitalist West had given rise to the popularity of leftist politics among the educated youth. For Shari'ati, some sort of Islamic Marxism which demonstrated that Islam was striving toward the formation of a monotheistic classless society was an effective ideological resolution in order to bring youth under the banner of Islam. Whether Shari'ati succeeded in his efforts or his intellectual project was reduced to, in Dabashi's description, "rhetorical gibberish, were it to be dissected into its matters of fact"[45] are beside the point. Being a free lance intellectual, unconstrained by the discursive framework of organized Shi'ism, Shari'ati was free to expand the traditional discursive boundaries that were placed on the range of acceptable Quranic exegeses. It was the same type of freedom that enabled such diverse Muslim scholars as the Indian Sayyid Ahmad Khan to claim Islam's affinity with laissez-faire capitalism and the Syrians Mustafa as-Siba'i and Muhammad Mubarak with socialism.

Ayatollah Khomeini (1902–89), on the other hand, did not enjoy that kind of institutional freedom. He was trained in the very heart of Shi'i orthodoxy. He studied under the eminent jurist Ayatollah Sheikh Abdulkarim Ha'eri Yazdi, with whom he moved from Arak to Qom, where he established and maintained close ties with the leading ulama. Although he published on a wide range of subjects in Shi'i jurisprudence, Islamic philosophy and mysticism, Persian poetry, and political polemics, none of his works that appeared before the 1960s broke new ground in Shi'i sociopolitical thought. Perhaps the only work that displayed signs of political and intellectual activism was his *Kashf al-Asrar* (*Revealing the Secrets*, 1944), in which Khomeini took issue with Kasravi's secularism, rebutting his anticlerical statements.[46] Generally, his writings in this period reflected the conservative intellectual milieu of mainstream Shi'ism.

The change in Khomeini's political views from traditionalism to revolutionary activism was associated with the change in the country's sociopolitical conditions. In particular, the change in the triadic relationships involving the regime, the bazaar, and the ulama in the sixties and the seventies formed a favorable context for the rise of revolutionary Shi'ism. The shah not only definitively broke with the ulama but also antagonized the members of the classes that had historically close ties with them. As a result, the ulama found themselves united in resisting the secularizing and Westernizing policies of the state and in fighting for the protection of their economic interests and cultural prerogatives. They did not, however, display a political consensus. Their demands took a variety of forms. A group of the ulama led by Ayatollah Shari'atmadari took a somewhat liberal line by demanding that the shah must respect the constitution, reviving the old slogan that he must reign, not rule. Another group, led by Ayatollah Taliqani, took a more radical turn by toying with socialist ideas. Ayatollah Khomeini broke with the traditional view in Shi'i political theory by arguing for overthrowing the monarchy and establishing an Islamic government under the exclusive control of the supreme religious leader (i.e., the *faqih*). In all these efforts, the overriding concern was to uncover the most effective means of resisting the shah, and this political exigency appeared to have relaxed the traditional discursive boundaries placed on the ulama's sociopolitical expressions. The politics of resistance tended to take precedence over religious considerations.

Among these groups, Khomeini's political ideas signified a new development in Shi'ism. Like other ideological producers, Khomeini started with references to social problems, for example, political oppression, inequality, and the imposition of an unjust economic order. He blamed the "imperialists" and their "agents" for the condition of the Muslim people:

> Through the political agents they have placed in power over the people, the imperialists have also imposed on us an unjust economic order, and thereby divided our people into two groups: oppressors and oppressed. Hundreds of millions of Muslims are hungry and deprived of all forms of health care and education, while minorities comprised of all the wealthy and powerful live a life of indulgence, licentiousness, and corruption. The hungry and deprived have constantly struggled to free themselves from the oppression of their plundering overlords, and their struggle continues to this day. But their way is blocked by ruling minorities and the oppressive governmental structures they lead.[47]

Given the imposition of the undesirable political and economic conditions, Khomeini called upon Muslims not to remain silent and politically indifferent. He encouraged his followers to end the oppressive government. "How can we stay silent and idle today," he asked rhetorically, "when we see that a band of traitors and usurpers, the agents of foreign powers, have appropriated the wealth and the fruits of labor of hundreds of millions of Muslims—thanks to the support of their masters and through the power of the bayonet—granting the Muslims not the least right to prosperity? It is the duty of Islamic scholars and all Muslims to put an end to this system of oppression and, for the sake of the well-being of hundreds of millions of human beings, to overthrow these oppressive governments and form an Islamic government."[48]

These statements were consistent not only with the grievances of both the ulama and the bazaaris, but also with the fact that the shah was actively supported and maintained by Western powers. These facts, however, do not account for the formulation of Khomeini's distinctive political theory. How do we explain his political project, which gave absolute authority to the jurisprudent? Why did Khomeini, unlike Shari'atmadari, eschew demanding the implementation of the constitution? Why did he not follow the idea of Ayatollah Na'ini, who attempted to bridge the gap between Shi'ism and liberal ideas during the Constitutional Revolution? It is clear that Khomeini's political discourse was not an inevitable outcome of the development of Shi'i political theory. In fact, he was among the first learned religious scholars in Shi'ism to formulate the idea of a clergy-centered Islamic state. This was so because in Shi'ism only the imam is entitled to rule the Islamic community. After the disappearance of the twelfth imam there was no religious injunction in Shi'ism that gave the clergy the right to rule. "Khomeini's achievement," said Shahrough Akhavi, "was to mount a theoretical argument that empowered precisely the clergy to take over executive power and rule on the Imam's behalf until his return."[49] Khomeini's reference to evidence in the classic sources of Islamic law, however, proved difficult, because such sources did not authorize the clergy to exercise sovereign rule, but only to give rulings in technical disputes.[50] Thus, as Akhavi indicated, "Khomeini invoked reason as a source of law and maintained that, since the sources contained many references to the clergy as the 'fortresses of Islam' and the like, they were the logical referents when the sacred texts made mention of leaders of the community after the Prophet's death."[51]

This is not to argue that in the absence of a clear doctrine in classical Shi'ism on the sovereign authority of the clergy Khomeini's political project was illegitimate. For one thing, historical Islam, Shi'ism included, is replete with inventions of new ideas that became acceptable to the theologians, contributing to Islam's institutional development. For another, under the cultural onslaught of a secularist authoritarian regime, the ulama could be justified from their religious standpoint in coming up with a distinctly Islamic oppositional project. Khomeini was trying to save and protect a religious institution that was perceived not only by him and his colleagues but also by lay Muslim intellectuals like Ale-Ahmad and Shari'ati as being engulfed and overpowered by the shah's Westernization program. Given these historical exigencies, did it really matter for the beleaguered clergy whether there were injunctions in classical Shi'ism for or against the rule of the clergy? After all, Khomeini's objective was to establish the rule of the shari'a in society. This fact alone may lend credibility to the argument that his intellectual effort was consistent with the general Islamic tradition.

Nevertheless, to state that Khomeini's action was justified in terms of his desire to defend his faith is one thing. Explaining why he chose to develop a distinctively new absolutist Islamic theory of government is quite another. It may not be possible to pinpoint the nature of the thought process in Khomeini's mind. What seems clear, however, is that the outcome of that thought process—Khomeini's theory of government—did not escape the structuring power of the state ideology. In fact, there is a remarkable resemblance between the conceptual hierarchy underpinning his theory of government and that of the ideology of the monarchy—one became the mirror image of the other. Under the stifling monolithic culture imposed by the regime, the monarchy-centered nationalist discourse gave credibility to the clergy-centered Islamic discourse of Ayatollah Khomeini.

If the shah was the center of the regime's ideology, the nation was identified with the monarchy, and a true Iranian was defined in terms of allegiance to the institution of the monarchy, the constitution, and the principles of the revolution of the shah and the people, for Khomeini, on the other hand, a true Muslim was emphatically defined as anyone who believed in the authority of the ulama. Khomeini argued that the Quran and tradition gave "all the laws and principles needed by man for his happiness and perfection."[52] But "their execution and implementation depend upon the formation of a government."[53] The ulama's governance would be "an institution for ensuring the rigorous application of Shari'a to Muslim society."[54] Therefore, the jurisprudent "has the same authority that the Most Noble Messenger and the Imam had," except that his authority does not extend to other jurisprudents.[55] Khomeini's attempt to champion the cause of the ulama by equating the ulama's power with both Islam and the integrity of Iran are evident in many of his writings.

The rise and consolidation of the absolutist power of the jurisprudent (Ayatollah Khomeini) in the postrevolutionary period paralleled the progressive development of the shah's absolutism in the sixties and the seventies. This fact was clearly expressed by senior members of the Islamic regime after the revolution: "The legitimacy and legality of whatever is done and whatever institutions exist is due to the fact that they are buttressed by the *velayat-e* [vilayat-i] *faqih* [the governance of the jurisprudent]. As the *velayat-e faqih* is at the head of all affairs and main guarantor of the current laws of the country, it is the *divinely ordained duty of all the people* to follow every law which is passed and given to the Islamic government for execution. . . . Disobeying such a law is as forbidden (*haram*) as drinking wine is forbidden by Islam."[56]

As early as the spring of 1979, after the monarchy was overthrown, Ayatollah Shari'atmadari warned the public about the dangers of a monopoly of power, a single-party system, and the possibility of dictatorship. As for the necessity of the vilayat-i faqih, he claimed the such a system of rule was suitable only under exceptional circumstances:

> *Vilayat-i faqih* is for when there is no legitimate ruler in society like our situation right after the fall of the Shah. Under such a condition, therefore, the *faqih* determines the government. But if there is already a president and a parliament, and the president forms his cabinet and receives the vote of confidence from the parliament, then the constituted government is legitimate and may begin its work. In other words, the people's sovereignty is exerted through the parliament. In our revolution such a channel of exerting sovereignty was not available to the people. Therefore, the *faqih* determined the [provisional] government. Thereafter, with the election of the president and members of the parliament, the future government would begin its work with the vote of confidence from the parliament, and fall should the parliament vote otherwise.[57]

During the Constitutional Revolution, of which liberal secular ideas were the governing principles, the modernist ulama who attempted to bridge the gap between Islamic political theory and the idea of rational rule making gained considerable support. The traditionalists, led by Sheikh Fazlullah Nuri, who favored the old formula of the division of authority between the ulama and the monarch, were discredited. During the Iranian Revolution, in which liberal ideas gave way to anti-Western phrase mongering, it was people like Ayatollah Shari'atmadari who were discredited, while the antidemocratic Khomeini became the spokesperson of the revolution.

Islamic Fundamentalism, Women, and the Veil

The issue of women's social status and role in society was a major point of contention between the shah and the Islamic opposition. The encouragement of women to change their style of dress and participate in social activities was an important aspect of the Pahlavis' modernization policies. In 1936 Reza Shah ordered the unveiling of women. "My father," said Mohammad Reza Shah,

> strictly forbade any woman or girl to be seen veiled; if she were, the nearest policeman would request her to remove her veil, and if she refused he would

forcibly take it from her. Throughout Persia the wearing of the veil was abolished and remained so as long as my father reigned.

Persia thus became the second Moslem country (preceded only by Turkey)
officially to outlaw the veil. Every year the seventeenth of Dey—the Persian
month roughly corresponding to January—is celebrated by our women in
grateful remembrance of my father's work on their behalf.[58]

Following the forced abdication of Reza Shah by the Allies in 1941, this policy
was moderated, as some women preferred wearing the veil. "Strictly it was still illegal to do so," said the new shah, "but my Government and I decided to overlook
it. We preferred to see a natural evolution, rather than to force the pace."[59]

The issue of veiling gained publicity when Islamic fundamentalist groups,
encouraged by the political pluralism of 1941–53, began staging protest demonstrations against unveiled women and religious minorities, the Baha'is in particular. They also occasionally harassed unveiled women seen in public. One of these
groups engaged in terrorizing secular intellectuals and politicians and even assassinated Kasravi, Iran's leading critic of the religious establishment under Reza
Shah. Nevertheless, the religious movement in this period was far from the influence it attained after the fifties. With the rise of Islam as the dominant discourse
of the opposition, the issue of Islamic veiling gained an added significance. The
chief spokesperson of the new shift in the public attitude toward women was
Ayatollah Morteza Motahhari (1920–79). His influential book *The Problem of
Veiling* (1969) became the standard Islamic exposition on veiling during the
Iranian Revolution of 1977–79 and under the Islamic Republic in the postrevolutionary period.

At the outset, Motahhari argued that "besides the many practical deviations
that have been created in regard to veiling, this and other issues related to women
have become a vehicle for a group of impure individuals and mercenaries in order
to generate controversies about the holy religion of Islam, and our youth, not
properly guided from the religious standpoint, are influenced by these controversies."[60] He equated unveiling with nudity, and then reduced it to the level of
an epidemic by claiming that "without doubt the phenomenon of 'nudity' is the
disease of our era. Sooner or later this phenomenon will be recognized as a 'disease.'"[61] In outlining the position of Islam on veiling, Motahhari argued:

> In the problem of covering, or so-called veiling, the debate is not over whether
> it is good for a woman to appear covered or nude in public. The heart of the
> debate is whether a man's desires for a woman should be free. Should or
> should not a man have the right to enjoy any woman in any gathering to
> the highest degree save actual intercourse?

Islam, which views the spirit of the problem, says no. It is only in a family environment and within the legal framework of marriage accompanied with a series of heavy commitments that men may enjoy women as their legal spouses. In the public environment, the use of a stranger woman is forbidden. Outside the family, women are also forbidden to satisfy men's [sexual] desires in any form and by any means.[62]

Motahhari did not directly challenge the state's policies regarding the role of women in society. Nevertheless, his Islamic exposition on the necessity of veiling and its functions for both the "health" of society and gender relations was developed in clear opposition to the shah's promotion of unveiling and his modernization policies on this issue in general. In the course of the Iranian Revolution, many educated women began to wear the veil as a symbolic gesture to show their opposition to the shah's modernization.

TWELVE

Algeria: The Socialist Turn and Radical Islamism

Algeria's historical experience was in certain crucial respects similar to that of the other Islamic countries covered in this book. As in these countries, the rise of Islamic fundamentalism was a new development in the history of Algeria. It started with the breakdown of the religious-secular alliance between the ulama and the Western educated elite, who led the liberation movement against the French. It then developed into a strong protest against Ben Bella in 1964. It was further radicalized in reaction to the leftward shift in the economic and cultural policies of Houari Boumédienne in the early seventies. By the 1980s, militant Islamic fundamentalism had become the dominant religio-cultural movement in the country. One of the most important manifestations of these developments was the formation of the Islamic Salvation Front (FIS) in 1989 for the purpose of establishing an Islamic state in Algeria.

We seek the origin of radical Islamism in Algeria's social transformation in the postindependence period. We argue that the cultural and political dynamics that produced Islamic fundamentalism in Egypt, Iran, and Syria were also at work in Algeria: Economic development, the formation of a massive bureaucratic and administrative structure of the state, the spread of modern education, and changes in occupational profiles transformed Algeria's class structure and generated social groups that demanded economic benefits, political participation, and cultural enrichment. The nationalization of economic enterprises, agricultural reforms, and the unfavorable treatment of the private sector undermined, among other things, the interests of the Islamic institutions and the landowning class. The state's monopolization of the means of cultural expression and promotion of an official discourse on religion, culture, and society formed a clear target in opposition to which the disgruntled groups, aspiring members of the middle class, and newly educated individuals formulated their discourse. Because the control of the religious institutions and the promotion of an official Islam constituted a central element in the state's cultural policies, religion became politicized, and opposition to the state gradually shifted in the direction of radical Islamism. The economic difficulties of the eighties accelerated this process.

Religion and the Independence Movement

As had Egypt and Syria, Algeria came under Turkish regency in the early part of the sixteenth century, and with time the center of power shifted away from a circle of the indigenous elite and became concentrated in the *ojaq* (body) of the Janissaries, whose "small, ethnically distinct and jealously exclusive military caste, or the elites it supported, were able to rule, control, or neutralize for the better part of three centuries a native population of millions."[1] The decline of the Ottomans, coupled with Algeria's incorporation into the world capitalist economy and interstate competition, produced externally induced economic instabilities and structural transformation and contributed to political conflict among various indigenous forces. To give one prominent example, since France was Algeria's principle European trading partner, Napoleon's invasion of Egypt in 1798 disrupted Algeria's commercial relations with France and plunged its economy into a prolonged period of crisis.[2] The period between 1830 and 1871 began with the French invasion of the country, which led to Algerian resistance, and ended with the imposition of a colonial system on Algeria.

One of the most important components of the political and cultural response to imperialism in Algeria, as in other parts of the Islamic Middle East, was rooted in the Islamic identity of the nation.[3] The French assimilationist policy of 1865 failed because it required Algerians to renounce their Muslim civil status and agreed to live under French law. During the eighty years that the law remained in force only two thousand Muslims ever requested naturalization.[4] Nevertheless, despite the country's being under a colonial rule, the dominant Islamic movement of the early to the middle part of the twentieth century remained strongly committed to the project of political restraint and modernism. Inspired by the Egyptian Muhammad Abduh's visit to the country in 1903, a number of prominent Algerian Muslim scholars, such as Abdel Halim ben Smaia and Kamal Muhammad ben Mustafa, launched a new modernist approach to Islam. An indication of commitment to liberal ideas, scientific enlightenment, and tolerance was such impressive works by Kamal Muhammed as *La tolerance religieuse dans l'Islamisme* and *Les droits de la femme*. These reformers launched attacks in Algiers, Constantine, and Tlemcen on the "superstition" and "decadence" of the marabouts.[5]

In the 1920s, the Islamic reformist movement played a significant role in the Algerians' struggle for independence. In the view of its undisputed leader, Sheikh

Abdülhamid Ben Badis (1889–1940),[6] and two other prominent intellectual leaders of the movement, Bashir Ibrahimi of Bougie (1880–1965) and Shaykh Tayyib al-Uqbi of Biskra (1888–1960), Algeria's cultural predicament was similar to that of Egypt as described by Abduh. Like his, their project was to link the two different cultural orders: the modern culture of Europe and the genuine Algerian Islamic culture. On the one hand, they rejected the *evolues*'[7] notion that Algeria had to merge with France in order to develop culturally and economically in the same way that Abduh rejected the Egyptian Westernizers' desire to emulate Europe. On the other hand, they vigorously attacked the marabouts and brotherhoods for, in their view, promoting destructive heterodoxy and superstitions, and the official religious establishment for its narrow traditionalist juridical method and subservient attitudes toward the colonial authorities. As an alternative, they promoted the program of allegiance to Arab ancestors, the Arabic language, and the Islamic tradition. In rejecting the French notion that Algeria had never constituted a nation, Mubarak al-Mili produced the first national history of Algeria in Arabic, *Tarikh al Jaza'ir fil Qadim wal Hadith* (*History of Algeria in Antiquity and in Modern Times*) in two volumes between 1928 and 1932. Even more remarkable was the history of Ahmad Tawfiq al-Madani, published in 1932. His work, *Kitab al-Jaza'ir* (*The Book of Algeria*) began with a preface in which al-Madani pointed to the absurdity of proposing that two people with totally different customs, language, and history can be one. The preface concluded with the slogan "Islam is my religion, Arabic is my language, Algeria is my fatherland." This slogan, recited for years by pupils in the Quranic schools founded by the reformist movement, eventually became the official slogan of the Algerian independence movement.[8]

One of the most important organizational expressions of Islamic modernism was the Association of the Muslim Ulama of Algeria (Jam'iyyat al-ulama al-muslimin al-jaza'iriyyin), founded in 1931 and led by Ben Badis. The association's objectives were to spread modernist Islamic education in the country for both men and women, to push forward the idea of Algerian Islamic nationalism, and to liberate Algeria's Islamic institutions from the yoke of French colonial control. The French had confiscated the religious endowments (*habous*) in the 1830s and 1840s and assumed the obligation to finance the mosques and pay the salaries of the mosque personnel. While the reformist ulama used the French law of 1905 to demand the separation of religion and the state in Algeria, for the colonial authorities the application of the law to Algeria would not only deprive them of an important patronage item, but also give the control of the mosques and the habous to a hostile religious hierarchy. As a result, the French set up the Association Culturelle Musulmane (ACM) through which to manage religious affairs at the local level. "This arrangement," said Allan Christelow, "combined the worst of all worlds. It meant that the Muslim clergy . . . lost the prestige and economic security of being civil servants, and yet retained the stigma of being government lackeys."[9] The reformist ulama first led a campaign to boycott the official mosques and vilify the official clergy, then demanded the separation of religion and the state, and finally began to seize the mosques. Until mid-1957, when all the reformist schools were shut down by the French and all their assets were confiscated, the reformist ulama were the leaders of the Arabic and Islamic movement against French domination.[10]

During all these years, the leading ulama consistently showed their adherence to a modernist and moderate Islamic project, which remained unchanged even during the period of radicalization of the Algerian nationalism. Some of the articles published in *Le Jeune Musulman* displayed such an orientation. For example, in response to a *Le Monde* piece of August 30, 1942, which characterized Islam as an intolerant and obstructionist religion that had been expanded by force, requiring Arabs to "believe or die," one of *Le Jeune Musulman*'s articles indicated that the Quran instructed believers to respect other religions, that Moses and Christ were honored by Islam, and that Islam was based on equality, fraternity, and liberty.[11] In another article, a certain Omar Khalid took issue with Ernest Renan, who had argued in 1883 that Islam and science were incompatible. Khalid cited verses from the Quran in support of the notion that Islam commended science and teaching and that the Prophet instructed his followers to seek knowledge from the cradle to the grave.[12] In short, before independence, the dominant trend within the Algerian Islamic movement was moderate, closely connected to the nationalist movement, and involved in the spread of modern education and had a positive orientation toward Western learning.

Independence, won in 1962, ushered in a new era in the history of modern Algeria and a new episode for culture production, however. The rise and consolidation of the socialist-oriented authoritarian state paralleled the transformation of the Algerian religious movement from reformism to militant Islamic fundamentalism. It was first reflected in al-Qiyam, a movement formed in 1964 in opposition to the state's cultural policies and official Islam under both Ben Bella and Boumédienne. One of its leaders, Muhammad Khider, a founding member of the Front de Libération Nationale (FLN), was assassinated in 1967, and the movement as a whole was eventually suppressed by Boumédienne. Linked to al-Qiyam, another militant Islamic movement, Ahl al-Da'wa (People for the Call), was formed in the late seventies to express Algerians' dissatisfaction with many of the state's policies.[13] By the 1980s, militant Islamic fundamentalism became the dominant religio-cultural movement in the country. In 1989, the FIS was formed with the explicit purpose of establishing an Islamic state. The program of the FIS pointed to the ruling power's inability to manage the multidimensional crises shaking the country and the failure of different Western and Eastern ideologies, and suggested that Islam was the most reliable ideology that could address these crises and that the right politics must be based on the shari'a.[14]

Some prominent Islamicists have argued that there was continuity between the Islamic reformism of the preindependence period and the Islamic fundamentalism of the postindependence period. For example, Hugh Roberts claimed that the Algerian case exemplified Bruno Etienne's argument that radical Islamism in general derives its inspiration from the intellectual and spiritual renaissance of the Arab world stimulated by the teachings of the *salafiyya* movement (the Islamic movement modeled on the religious behavior of the early companions of the Prophet).[15] This continuity, in Roberts's view, is reflected in the attempts in both movements to purify Islam by attacking other trends in society that were viewed as being outside the Islamic path and "has been personified in two of its principal leaders, Sheikh Sahnoun and Sheikh Soltani, both of whom were active in Ben Badis's Association."[16] In addition, Abbasi Madani, one of the leaders of the FIS, was involved in the liberation struggle of the fifties. So was Mustafa Bouyali, an FLN veteran of the liberation struggle, who in 1979 founded the Group for the Defense against the Illicit to form an Islamic state in Algeria through the use of force. These examples, however, do not establish continuity between the two different episodes in the Islamic movement. We argue that in terms of discourse and sociopolitical orientation the radical Islamism of the eighties and the nineties was quite distinct and represented a new development in the Algerian Islamic movement.[17] The reformist ulama of the 1920s through the 1940s were positively predisposed toward Western learning and attempted to bridge the gap between Islam and modernity. They had little interest in establishing an Islamic state and even defended the separation of religion and politics. They displayed favorable attitudes toward the Islamic feminism of Qasim Amin. Even the first Algerian Muslim Congress of June 1936 came close to accepting the assimilationist thesis, with the reformist ulama supporting it on tactical grounds. The Islamic movement of the period after the seventies, on the other hand, rejected the Western model altogether and aimed at establishing an Islamic state.

This dramatic shift in the discourse and sociopolitical orientations of the Algerian Islamic movement was, as it were, formulated in an oppositional relation to the ideology of the state.[18] As was the case in twentieth-century Egypt, Iran, and Syria, the state's authoritarianism and exclusionary policies channeled oppositional activities through the medium of religion. A more crucial factor in the formation of the discourse of the Islamic opposition was the ideology of the state. The Algerian state's intervention in culture and control of religion to promote its own version of Islamic socialism contributed to the politicization of religion and the rise of militant Islamic fundamentalism.

The Rise of the Modern State and Social Transformation

As in other cases we have analyzed in this book, the key actor shaping culture and, at one remove, oppositional discourse in postindependence Algeria was the state. Although 1954–62 was the period of revolutionary struggle against French colonial rule, it was the postindependence state that brought about a real revolution in social relationships in Algeria. As the national state centralized and consolidated power, it embarked on a massive transformation of economic, social, and cultural relationships in the direction of a self-proclaimed Algerian socialism. In the course of over a decade after independence, Algeria was transformed into a country where political and military power merged and became concentrated in a small circle of the civil and military elite, extensive nationalization brought virtually all sectors of the economy under the control of this circle, economic policies were determined on the basis of technocratic, managerial socialist planning, culture and language were considerably Arabized, and socialism constituted the main ideological framework that shaped the state's economic policies and cultural orientation. Within this framework the state attempted to reorganize religious discourse and institutions to promote the idea of Islamic socialism.

The political conflicts among the constituting groups and factions of the FLN that existed during the revolutionary war surfaced as soon as independence was achieved. These conflicts, far from producing a pluralistic political structure in which diverse interests could be represented, resulted in a systematic exclusion of the defeated contenders and the increasing homogenization of the ruling elite.[19] From 1962 until 1990, when the secular intrusive state faced the effective challenge of the Islamic opposition, Algeria was ruled successively by three men and their clans: Ben Bella (1962–65), Boumédienne (1965–78), and Chadli Benjedid (1978–91). Following independence, the liberals favoring a multiparty system and market economy were pushed aside by leftist groups, who were partisans of various forms of state socialism. Among these groups, there was also a power struggle, as Ben Bella successfully defeated his rivals and transformed the elite heterogeneity of 1962 to a homogeneous power structure under his own control. His removal by Colonel Boumédienne in 1965 repeated the process.

The concentration of power and the homogenization of the ruling elite was a resolution of the problem of power produced by what Roberts described as "the disintegration of the wartime FLN into a plethora of factions representing clienteles rather than tendencies."[20] To achieve coherence in policy, Ben Bella attempted to reduce the number of factions within the regime in dealing with the challenges from the leadership of trade union (the Union Générale de Travailleurs Algériens— UGTA) over the autonomy of the union, from the head of the FLN, Muhammad Khider, over the power of the party vis-à-vis the government, from the group led by Ferhat Abbas and Ahmed Francis over the framing of the constitution, from the Kabyle opposition (i.e., the Front des Forces Socialistes—FFS), and from the Oujda clan.[21] This tactic failed, and Ben Bella was overthrown in a coup engineered and led by Boumédienne in 1965. While Boumédienne faced the same problem of power, his approach was quite different from that of Ben Bella. By effectively using his control of the army, he acted as the arbiter of the interplay of various factions. By the end of 1967, the internal profile of the regime was rationalized and the factions reduced to a manageable number. With political stability subsequently established, the regime was able to undertake a coherent policy making.[22]

Algeria's social and historical context might have been the cause of its failure to produce a liberal pluralistic system similar to that of postindependence Egypt and Syria after the end of the war of liberation and independence. Historians and commentators have used such concepts as Ibn Khaldun's *asabiyya*,[23] Weberian "sultanism,"[24] or the Arabic-Islamic notion of claimant, or *za'ama*,[25] to explain the rise of personal yet all-embracing—in fact, totalitarian—leadership in postindependence Algeria. Classical liberalism, on the other hand, was doomed because it rested on such alien notions as institutionalized power and representative process of government.[26] Finally, John P. Entelis argued that with colonialism and the revolution severely disrupting and undermining the traditional and religious bases of power, the principal sources of power in Algeria's technocratic system as a consequence became organizational in nature.[27] While the applications of these concepts may be debated, the undisputed fact of the politics of postindependence Algeria is the resolution of the problem of power in an authoritarian and exclusionary manner—a factor that significantly contributed to the radicalization of the Islamic movement.

Despite the populist rhetoric of the ruling elite, important policies affecting various aspects of Algerian society were decided by a relatively small yet stable civil and military elite with conspicuously little participation of the public. Although Boumédienne justified the coup against Ben Bella on the grounds that the latter had imposed a personal dictatorship on the country, his system of rule was no less authoritarian. The military, party, and administrative technocrats, who all shared a socializing background in the Armée de Libération Nationale, monopolized the state's critical military, mobilization, and managerial affairs. Using the crucial technical skills of this triad, Boumédienne maintained power, eliminated all organized opposition, and build a socialist state by creating the state's own institutions or by bringing under its control the existing associations, including the UGTA, women's organizations, and journalists' unions. The government did not tolerate any independent political organization outside the state. In 1969, the trade union movement was forced to become a branch of the FLN.[28] In 1966, the al-Qiyam movement was dissolved, and in 1970 an order was issued that prohibited al-Qiyam activities across the country. In 1971, the National Union of Algerian Students was also dissolved. And in 1976, private confessional education was suppressed, a measure which affected both Islamic and Christian schools.[29]

The three elements—the military, party, and administrative technocracy—forming the basis of Algeria's power elite were unevenly aligned, with the FLN being reduced to a minor, functionary role, while the military and the administrative elite were elevated to dominating positions.[30] The circulation of the elite under Boumédienne followed a somewhat rigid pattern according to which there was, in William Zartman's words, "elite circulation up and circulation out, but not circulation back in."[31] The weakening of the FLN as an intermediate organization connecting the state to the society and the rise of intrusive authoritarian rule dominated by a single individual naturally made the state a vulnerable target of ideological attack from below.[32]

Although the Arab socialism of the Algerian regime displayed close affinities with that of the Nassirites and Ba'athists, in certain crucial respects the Algerian state appeared astonishingly similar to the Pahlavi state. To be sure, from a foreign policy perspective, Algeria had a "nonaligned" pro-Soviet regime with a socialist orientation, while the Pahlavis were tied to the West, were anticommunist, and promoted capitalism. Further, the Algerian regime was a product of a national revolutionary war against a foreign colonial domination, while the shah's regime was installed by the U.S.- and British-engineered coup to suppress a nationalist movement and protect the interests of an international petroleum cartel. Finally, international capital had a favorable position in the Iranian economy in the prerevolutionary period, while the large-scale nationalization of foreign enterprises in Algeria was the key feature of the state's reorganization of the economy. Depending on one's ideological predilection, one may draw different political and ethical conclusions regarding the legitimacy of either the Algerian or the Pahlavi regime and the effectiveness of its socioeconomic and cultural policies. Nevertheless, from the perspective of Muslim intellectuals who were pursuing the distinctive Islamic objective of defending their faith against the onslaught of various forms of secular ideologies connected to an intrusive bureaucratic authoritarian state, these differences appear to have mattered little. Both regimes had a strong secular ideological orientation and were omnipresent in the social, cultural, and economic spheres of their societies. Both regimes implemented an agrarian reform that antagonized Islamic groups and the landowning classes, on the one hand, and failed to produce the expected results, on the other. The intermediate associations—including mass political parties—connecting both regimes to civil society became weak in the case of the Algerian FLN and nonexistent in the case of the Pahlavi regime. The comprehensiveness of the secular authoritarian state appears to have produced an all-inclusive movement of the Islamic opposition in both countries.

Economic Development, Class Formation, and the Educated Middle Class

Having achieved homogeneity and solidity, the postcoup ruling elite in Algeria embarked on a policy of extensive intervention in the economy and massive nationalization of foreign and domestic firms between 1966 and 1971. Nine foreign mining companies in 1966 and forty-five more foreign firms in 1968 were nationalized, and by the end of 1969 only about twenty French industrial enterprises, out of the seven hundred to eight hundred that existed in Algeria in 1962, remained under the control of their owners. This process continued with the nationalization of five foreign oil companies in 1970, 51 percent of all French oil companies operating in the country in 1971, and three more French industrial firms during 1971–72. The remaining foreign industrial enterprises in the country were nationalized in the period of the Second Four-Year Plan. This included twenty French and two Belgian enterprises, which were nationalized in 1974.[33] The nationalization of these companies expanded state control of the key financial, industrial, and agricultural sectors of the economy. The state gradually created a network of forty-five national industrial corporations, eight banking and financial organizations, and nineteen national offices to run the economy. Each company almost monopolized each branch of the economy, the most important of which was SONATRACH, the state-owned oil company founded in 1964.[34]

The reorganization of the economy, accompanied by an unprecedented economic growth, resulted in the transformation of the occupational structure, the generation of new employment opportunities, and demographic expansion from the 1960s through the 1980s. The population increased from 12.4 million in 1966 to 17.7 million in 1977 and to 25.4 million in 1990. The urban population increased from almost two million in 1950, or 22 percent of the total population, to 12.4 million in 1989, or 50 percent of the total population.[35] The number of students increased from 832,143 in 1963 to 1,941,020 in 1970 and then to 3,687,652 in 1978. In 1978, 145,066 were enrolled at the upper secondary level and 51,850 in the national universities.[36] In 1967, 40 percent of all students were on government scholarships, and the portion rose to 65 percent by 1978. The budget for scholarships increased eight-fold during the 1970–77 period alone.[37] During the Boumédienne period (1957–78), the country's occupational profile considerably expanded, as 1.11 million jobs were created, representing an increase of 64.5 percent during the period.[38]

The industrial public sector, including hydrocarbons and mining, substantially expanded: its share of total annual value added rose from 28.3 percent in 1967 to 44.5 percent in 1969. In terms of employment, of the total of 462,640 workers employed in the industrial sector in the late 1970s, 362,146 (79 percent) worked in the national industrial sector, 22,592 (4.5 percent) in the local public sector, and 77,900 (16.5 percent) in the private industrial sector.[39] The private sector, on the other hand, was treated with hostility in the first years of the postrevolutionary period (1962–66). Potential indigenous private investors were not only thwarted but also denounced as "'fat bourgeois' who should be 'unfattened in hot baths.'" Although the promulgation of the 1966 investment decree contributed to the rise of the private industrial sector,[40] the size of this sector remained minuscule compared to that of the state sector.

The process of economic reorganization drastically transformed Algeria's class structure. The economically dominant classes of French colons, large landowners, and international capitalists were dissolved, and a new, technocratic dominant class was gradually formed.[41] According to one analyst, "the members of the state bureaucracy shared interests with members of other strata, namely the army leaders, the professionals and the native Algerian landowners, which led to the maintenance of a stable alliance among them throughout the 1960s."[42] The proportion of the industrial workers in the total labor force increased from 13.4 percent in 1967 to 18.8 percent in 1978. The number of working women also rose and was diversified in this period. The number of fully employed and partially employed women in Algeria in 1977 (180,000) was approximately twice that of a decade before (93,000).[43] The rapid increase in the number of college students and college graduates facilitated by the government provision of scholarship naturally expanded the numbers of middle-class professionals.

Culturally, the rise of a distinctly Algerian middle class was aided by the Algerianization of the teaching staff of the educational institutions and the Arabization of their curriculum and language of instruction. The number of foreign teachers decreased from 7,212 out of 19,908 in 1963, to 4,859 out of 36,255 in 1968–69, and to 984 out of 76,025 by 1978, or 1.3 percent of the total. The Arabization of primary education began as early as 1963, when the teaching of the Arabic language was made compulsory in all programs and at every level. Before 1971, the Arabization of education proceeded by subject matter and by grade. Gradually a dual system emerged and took shape, particularly at the middle and high school levels. One was a bilingual section, and the other, an Arabic section. In the former the pupils were taught scientific subjects in French and other subjects in Arabic, while in the latter they were taught all subjects in Arabic, and French was taught as a foreign language.[44]

State Ideology and Cultural Change

Before the period of the revolutionary war, the Algerian nationalist movement was expressed in terms of a spectrum of views, ranging from moderate Islamic Arab nationalism to an assimilationist framework. With the shift in the politics of nationalism in the direction of armed struggle against the French—during which lower-middle-class, working-class, and even poor rural Algerians fought alongside the elite[45]—came a shift in the discourse of the movement toward radical ideologies. In fact, the war of liberation gave an impetus to socialist ideas. Socialism had already been discussed at the Soummam Congress as early as August 20, 1956. At this stage, however, reference to socialism was not extensive in the declarations of the leaders of the revolutionary movement, and the Tripoli program, made public in July 1962, contained a liberal version of socialism and mild social revolution, tempered with respect for Islam and tradition; the word "socialism" was not expressly used.[46] But in early August, about a month after independence (July 5, 1962), Ben Bella declared that "We want an Algerian socialism, born of our national experience and benefiting from the experiences of the socialist countries."[47] Although the invocation of the word "socialism" indicated a turning point in the ideological orientation of the new rulers of Algeria, for the public at large it meant bringing under socialist rule the land abandoned by the French settlers, which was perceived as an extension of the traditional *towiza*, or village mutual aid, practiced throughout the Maghrib; thus, no one saw any problem with the use of the term.[48] Moreover, the prevalence of extensive poverty and the fact that one out of two Muslim Algerians lived in a slum in the early sixties had made the idea of socialism highly attractive.[49] It reassured the thousands of squatters who had occupied the houses, villas, and industries of the fleeing Europeans.[50]

When the socialism of the new regime went beyond taking over the properties abandoned by the colons and Ben Bella began purging religious figures from the government during the first year of his presidency, criticisms were voiced from both within and outside the regime. Ben Bella justified his position by contrasting the ideas of neocolonialism and revolution. He lashed out at the opposition by arguing that "we maintain that either there is a revolution going on in this country—and we will be able to carry out our congress—and consequently we will be able to proceed with our forces on this path, or else that Algeria will become a revised and corrected version of all the other African governments that accept neocolonialism."[51]

Sensing public alarm at these radical pronouncements and wishing to appease the conservatives, Ben Bella took a religious puritan posture by introducing a series of measures, such as making the Ramadan fast and charity offering at the end of the month of Ramadan national duties on January 24, 1963, forbidding Muslims to drink alcohol during this month, raising taxes on alcohol, and referring to the principles of Tripoli which recognized Islam as the state religion.[52] Furthermore, to establish an Islamic precedent for its nationalization program, the Ben Bella regime instructed the minister of habous (religious endowment) to reinterpret the historical Islamic experience and the Islamic tenets in a fashion compatible with the idea of socialism. To this end, the minister of habous proclaimed that seventh-century Islam was an egalitarian revolutionary movement which retrogressed through the centuries. Ottoman Islam and its brother, the Islam of the marabouts and *zawaya* (analogous to monasteries) in North Africa, had a bourgeois or even reactionary nature. The antibourgeois Islam was the Islam of Medina when Muhammad and his successors were fighting the Meccan oligarchy.[53] The state official press pushed the theme further: "Islam no longer simply 'tolerated' socialism, it identified with it. In its first issue, *al-Ma'rifa* presented Abu Dharr, companion of the Prophet, as the father of socialism and promoter of class struggle. The daily *Sha'b* (*The People*), in an editorial described the Prophet himself as the advocate of a "revolution of the poor against the rich," sending the Mecca feudalists "through a Turkish bath."[54]

Taking up the idea of the Syrian leader of the Muslim Brothers Mustafa as-Siba'i,[55] the press of the National Union of Algerian Students offered in June 1963 religious commentary justifying the widespread nationalization: "The newspaper first cited the hadith—'Men are associated in three elements: water, fodder, and fire'—as evidence that Islam provided for the nationalization of certain natural goods. In particular, 'everything that is necessary to man is amenable to nationalization.' Turning to private property, the article recalled that Islamic law forbids greed (seizure or forced sale), that the habous is a kind of nationalization for religious purposes . . . It then concluded that Islam 'institutes socialization.'"[56] Using the Islamic concept of *ijma* and the notion of the infallibility of the community, Minister of Habous Tawfiq al-Madani (a leader of the former Association of Muslim Ulama of Algeria), in a speech delivered to inaugurate a new mosque in Bou Saada in 1964, pushed forward the idea that the socialist revolution was compatible with Islam since it was based on the will of the people. The principle of *ijma* contained the potential for reform, allowing Islam to adapt itself to changing conditions and eventually to get rid of tyrants or unjust and ineffective imams.[57]

Attempts to reinterpret Islam to fit the political requirement of the regime remained arbitrary and suspect because further changes in the regime's socioeconomic orientations made the previous interpretations redundant, and hence the relationship between religion and the postrevolutionary regime appeared one way—religious ideas were to change to justify the state's policy. Religion was not able to constrain the regime's behavior. When a wave of Marxist propaganda was released in Algeria in 1963 and the national press printed daily encomiums on the communist countries, and on Marx, Lenin, and Mao, people got the impression that the government was acting according to Marxism, and the notion of "Islamic socialism" came to be regarded as only a disguise for communism.[58]

By the end of 1964, secularism and state socialism had prevailed over Islam and other mainstream ideologies. French-speaking Muslims listening to Radio Algiers heard an evening variety program about evolution, explaining the world from the amoeba to man by way of the monkey. This was followed by a long and bitterly ironic denunciation of conservative religious leaders, referring to them as "these 'poor people' with rusty brains who think that the 'world has been created for man,' with the sun and moon to light him, animals to serve, and vegetables to feed him. Such a parody of the Quranic revelation was in direct conflict with the president's assurances and even more with the teaching of Islam in the schools."[59] The UGTA Arabic press was suspended without warning or comment for its proreligion editorials. Various representatives of independent movements lost their influence: Madani left the Habous Ministry, Sheikh Bayound was rumored to be in jail with other reformists, Hadj Naser was in voluntary exile, and Sheikh Ibrahimi had retired from public life. The purge of the old spiritual leaders neutralized the ulama, long considered to be the leading authorities of Algerian nationalism, pioneers of militant Arabism, and examples of the Muslim social ideal. "Their departure," as Raymond Vallin commented, "marked the end of an era that, in retrospect, might well appear as the golden age of Algerian Islam. For, through one of those ironies of which politics sometimes had the secret, the ulama, professional protestors who fought so long for freedom of religious practice, handed down to their successors, the Habous, a centralized state apparatus without equal in Islam, to our knowledge."[60]

The Boumédienne coup, while doing away with some of Ben Bella's excesses, did not change to any significant extent the structure, policies, and ideological orientation of the state. At the outset Boumédienne justified the coup as a revolutionary move against personalized power. He claimed that "the confusion and concentration of power and the liquidation of the revolutionary cadres have turned a policy of docility into a system of government. In trying to muzzle and tame the vital forces of the nation, in hardening and freezing the government bodies of the country, in hoping to create the myth of the 'providential man,' the dictator deliberately violated the revolutionary legitimacy."[61] Boumédienne further attacked Ben Bella's rule for creating "a sad legacy: the breakdown of authority into political and administrative fiefs, a demagogic conception of socialism, delinquency of the state, and paralysis of the party."[62] Hence, he stated:

> People of Algeria: In bringing an end to personal power, the Revolutionary Council has re-established revolutionary legitimacy. The continuity of the Algerian Revolution is henceforth ensured. . . .
>
> In this sense, socialism is part of our historical heritage. It did not have to await some demagogic make-believe to become a reality in our national policy. It is the expression of the will and aspirations of our people, the fruit of their revolutionary combat. . . . People of Algeria: On June 19, the Revolutionary Council took on historic commitments. Since June 19, the performance of the country's activities, the proper functioning of public affairs, have been handled normally, in security and order. . . . The swift downfall of the tyrant has ripped away the deceptive veil that concealed a sad reality.[63]

Revolution Culturelle et Revolution Socialiste

Insofar as Boumédienne justified his coup as a move against Ben Bella's exclusionary policies, usurpation of the people's rights, and personal dictatorship, diverse social groups and political organizations which were undermined by Ben Balla's high-handedness were satisfied to see him go. For the religious opposition, too, the coup, by overthrowing Ben Bella, removed an important source of concern. While Boumédienne suppressed al-Qiyam, he opportunistically managed to steal the religious issues of this movement by initiating a major campaign against the degradation of morals and the reassertion of the Islamic values in the fall of 1970.[64] "This campaign," said Hugh Roberts, "in its stigmatization of Western cultural values, its defense of the family, its conservatism concerning the position of women, and its attacks on alcoholism, 'cosmopolitanism' and 'semi-nudism,' echoed almost word for word many of the principal themes of *al-Qiyam's* agitation."[65] In this manner, Boumédienne appeared to be sympathetic to the concerns of conservative Muslims, succeeded in diffusing their opposition, and thus escaped the charge of infidelity to Islam. He failed, however, to acknowledge the autonomy of the Islamic movement outside the official religious framework set up and promoted by his regime.

The tactical nature of Boumédienne's Islamism was evident, for in the 1970s, he initiated a series of radical reforms under the rubrics *revolution culturelle* and *revolution socialiste*. The *revolution culturelle* was portrayed as a movement toward cultural authenticity. It signaled a shift in the state's cultural policies away from French to Arabic as the medium of communication in the public sector and the institutions of higher education. To be sure, Algeria's program of Arabization began with Ben Bella's Arabization of primary education in 1964, but in the *revolution culturelle*, Arabization became a real priority for the government.[66] One of the consequences of this renewed emphasis on Arabization about a decade later was a considerable increase in the number of Arabic university students and graduates who came either from the conservative background of new immigrants from rural areas or from the wealthier and better-educated conservative section of the urban area. For the latter group, a return to the Arabic-Islamic culture advocated by the Islamic opposition was certainly consistent with their interests, because it would make it possible for them to gain access to jobs that were monopolized by French-speaking Algerians.[67] The Arabization of the public administration and the state's economic sector did not keep pace with that of secondary and higher education, with the result that from the mid-1970s on there were large numbers of young Algerians educated in Arabic for whom employment opportunities were scarce. In particular, the large state corporations were generally disinclined to employ these graduates, preferring students who were fluent in European languages.[68] Naturally, this culturally discriminatory policy frustrated the Arabic-speaking graduates and gave credibility to the call of the religious opposition to return to authentic Arabic and Islamic values, and, in François Burgat and William Dowell's assessment, "the students who had followed Arabophone studies little by little identified themselves with the demands for a re-valuing of the Arabo-Muslim base, if only because these matched their most immediate professional occupations."[69]

Nevertheless, we must not overemphasize the significance of the *revolution culturelle* in fostering the rise of the Islamic opposition. This is because Islamic radicalism cut through Algeria's cultural divide. As Islamic activist Rashid Ben Aissa indicated, "The four students who in 1967 opened a mosque at university were Francophone. For several years the people listening to us were recruited from the French speakers, and I made my sermons in French. It is also very revealing of this quest for identity. The Arab-speakers only came later. For four or five years, the majority of the faithful were students from the faculties of science, which is to say the Francophones. On the other hand, the other faculties were completely de-Islamized. It is necessary to understand that at that time, the Arab press in Algeria was more violently anti-Islamic than the Francophone Moujahid."[70] Thus, the leftward shift in the state's policies appears to have been the crucial factor contributing to the shift in the oppositional discourse toward radical Islamic fundamentalism. Roberts's analysis of radical Islamism in Algeria is consistent with our analytical framework. Roberts has presented considerable materials in support of the argument that the left turn in Algerian politics beginning in late 1971, including the implementation of a wide-ranging program of radical social reforms, which Boumédienne described as *la revolution socialiste*, stimulated the rise of the Islamic opposition. These reforms involved, first, an assault by Boumédienne's regime on Muslim property. Whereas between 1965 and 1971 public property had expanded at the expense of foreign capital alone, the "agrarian revolution" promulgated on November 8, 1971, involved the nationalization of large estates, including the holdings of Muslim landowners, and the establishment of a collective farm sector. Such a large-scale nationalization of agricultural property alienated an important section of the Algerian public from the regime, a result not too different from what happened under the Pahlavi regime in the early 1960s. Aligned with the landowners, the conservative ulama launched a campaign against attacks on private property and became the spokespeople of the victims of the agricultural revolution. The landowners in turn contributed to religious institutions by funding the construction of mosques and other religious causes.[71] As a result, the attack on the regime's socialist ideology in Islamic terms gained credibility with the disgruntled property owners.

This left turn also resulted in the regime's closer relationship with the Algerian Communist Party and the socialist countries, which in consequence increased its vulnerability to opposition propaganda that the regime was governed by alien ideologies. Finally, the new course entailed the mobilization of the younger generation for the sake not of defending the regime against the external enemies but of rising against the internal enemies of the *revolution socialiste*. The regime thus developed and legitimized a radically critical attitude among the younger generation toward the existing bases of authority.[72] The students mobilized by Boumédienne were directed against the somnolent party and the corruption of parts of the administration. By late 1971, this new mobilization effort had resulted in the emergence of serious divisions within the regime and the breakup of the group of politicians who had formed its nucleus since 1965, the celebrated "Oujda clan." Kaid Ahmed was the first to go. He was then followed in late 1974 by the more substantial figure of the interior minister, Ahmed Medeghri, and in the summer of 1975 by Cherif Belkacem. These changes resulted in an increasing concentration of power in Boumédienne's hands, and by the mid-1970s he had succeeded in creating almost exactly the same circumstances as those surrounding Ben Bella in 1964, and a revival of Islamist agitation duly occurred.[73]

To be sure, in response to the demand of the Islamic opposition, Boumédienne conceded the demand for shura. And in 1976 a number of other concessions to Islamic sentiments were made, such as the outlawing of gambling in March 1976, the introduction of the Muslim weekend (Friday) in August of the same year, and reference to Islam as the state religion, even though no mention was made in the first draft of the national charter.[74] However, Boumédienne made no concession of substance and was determined to press on with his socialist program. He was committed to the project of social revolution, which for him meant the subordination of Islam to the will of the government and the abolition of it beyond its status as a constituent element of Algerian nationality.[75] The state not only considered itself the promoter of social justice and guarantor of social order, but the ultimate judge in deciding the proper form of ideological and religious expressions. According to Vatin, "the decision to impose socialism and to promote economic development (implying among other things a marked centralization of power and a dominant state bureaucracy) had to be passed on to the people through the same, well accepted language. There would be no real independence, it was proclaimed, without socialism and no socialism without Islam."[76]

The state-promoted national Islam in Algeria meant that the state monopolized religious affairs. In its attempt to promote the Arabic and Islamic values, it brought the Islamic institutions under its control and advanced it own version of the proper Islam. It nationalized Quranic schools as well as other institutions and appointed the imams, muftis, and Islamic judges.[77] According to Christelow, "After the war, the FLN substituted its apparatus for that of the colonial state. Having lost their property, and had their leadership killed or dispersed during the war, the Reformists were in no position to contest the official thesis that the separation of religion and state had simply been a problem of colonialism, no longer relevant now that independence has been regained. One might also suggest that the greatly increased role of the state in the economy undermined the private sector, which had been the main base of support for the Reformist Ulama."[78]

In short, Boumédienne's discourse, like that of Ben Bella, was militant, aimed at mobilizing the people in support of his state-centered socialist economic planning, anti-imperialist, revolutionary rhetoric, and secular Arab nationalist cultural policies. For him, the state was central for Algeria's economic development and national emancipation. This centrality rested on the notion that the national state was eternal, outside history, and any attempt to discredit the state was antinationalist. The state represented the general interests of society. The antistate activities of some groups, for him, were a colonial legacy. Boumédienne believed that resistance to a colonial state engendered the spirit of anarchy, a justifiable resistance to foreign domination whose first action was to try to destroy the Algerian state. What came from this was a spirit of revolution against all form of authority and power. This spirit of revolt, however, must disappear in the face of the national state. Boumédienne had no interest in "bourgeois" democracy, debates, and pluralism. Misery and underdevelopment would require quick action. His regime systematically referred to the people and emphasized the idea of solidarity and unity in order to promote socialism as a basis for absolute justice. It rejected, however, Marx's notion of class conflict: All the people had to work for the general interests of the country. The state's definition of socialism in the Algerian context transcended class division. While the capitalist worker spent his time trying to get his salary from his boss and did not care about the firm's profits, the socialist Algerian worker must care about the firm and the state because it was his own. Striking in the state sector was outlawed as an antinationalist act. People were all workers. The civil servant completing his tasks in his office was a worker, just like the officer or the permanent party worker. Each person lived of his labor and of his daily efforts. In sum, during his rule, Boumédienne monopolized public expression and power, without ever creating bridges between the state and the public. His failure to construct a dynamic party isolated the state from the people. As a result, his discourse was the only means of contact between him and society.[79] And it was this discourse that shaped the ideology of the Islamic opposition.

The State, Women, and Feminism from Above

As it was in other Islamic countries covered in this book, the status of women in Algeria was among the highly contested issues in the ideological debates among various groups. The issue of women in Algeria was also shaped by the specific context of the national struggle for independence and cultural authenticity. In the preindependence period, particularly between the two world wars, this debate was multisided and was informed by a plurality of positions. One was that of the French, whose "civilizational" mission was aided by a change in the attitudes of Algerian Muslims toward French schools. This change resulted in a significant increase in the number of Muslim students attending primary and secondary schools. In the 1930s, there were also schools for Muslim girls.

In the 1930s, the French mounted a campaign against the use of the veil and in defense of women's rights. The question of women, however, went beyond the conflict of the sexes, and the "battle of the veil" became another front in the cultural warfare between the colonial authorities and the Algerians who wanted to maintain their cultural distinction vis-à-vis the French.[80] People of the new middle-class background also held a position on women's questions similar to that of the French. These people were among the graduates of the French schools. In 1919, numbering scarcely one thousand, they were civil servants (among the most highly paid Algerians in the civil service), doctors, lawyers, teachers, pharmacists, and journalists. Included among them were also a few prominent businessmen in the port cities and the larger cities of the interior and a few industrialists who owned firms in the modern sector.[81] Yet the French and their supporters were not the only group defending women's rights.[82] Algerian nationalists, led by Emir Khaled, and later by other reformist leaders like Ferhat Abbas, were also involved in the Algerian women's movement. They were inspired by the nationalist and secularist position of Kemal Ataturk of Turkey. The dramatic changes in the law regarding the status of women adopted by the Turks were favorably received by Algerian reformers, who edited such journals as *La Voix de Humbles* and *La Voix Indigene* in the 1920s and 1930s. These journals also published the feminist views of the Egyptian Qasim Amin and the Tunisian Tahar al-Haddad. Finally, the reformist ulama, led by Ben Badis, defended the right of Muslim girls to an education.[83] The reformist spirit was captured by a young woman, Fatima Zuhra al-Najjar, who addressed a gathering at a Mawlid celebration in 1948, "calling on the men to cease resistance to girls' education because this was 'not the time for slowness and sluggishness. Rather this is an era of great speed, and people should arouse themselves, and prepare all their sons and daughters for a life of competition and struggle.'"[84]

After independence, however, the state incorporated some of the feminist ideas into its discourse, and official feminism from above became the only framework within which women's rights were expressed, debated, and defended. As early as November 15, 1964, a vigorous editorial in the new Arabic weekly *al-Shabab* (*The Youth*) stated: "Our revolution has not accepted and will not accept the subordination of women whatever the justification, whether in the name of a deviant notion of Islam, in the name of tradition, or in order to preserve special privileges."[85] Improving the condition of women became one of the professed objectives of the state's modernization program. In fact, women made some progress. They won a few seats in the communal and provincial elections of 1967 and 1969 and secured nine seats in the new National Assembly of 1977. In spite of the fact that nagging problems of unemployment and underemployment created very difficult conditions for job-seeking women, more than 180,000 women were in the work force by 1977, double the number employed in 1966. By the end of the

Boumédienne era, more than 1.5 million girls and young women were attending school.[86]

Chadli Benjedid, Economic Bust, and Conflict

The death of President Boumédienne in December 1978 marked not only the rise of a new leadership but also a definite change in the state's policy orientations. By disturbing the rigidly structured hierarchy of political power, this change in leadership created a breathing space which permitted the rise of an Islamic oppositional discourse. High-profile political opponents of the regime were released, several figures sympathetic to the Islamic agenda were appointed to the government, and politicians who were committed to Arabization took over the ministries of Information and Culture and of Primary and Secondary Education.[87] More important, the change in the state's economic policy from central planning toward economic decentralization and liberalization necessitated changes in the state's personnel and the decline of the leftist elements within the government. These in turn provoked the opposition of those who supported Boumédienne's socialist policies. The Berbers also considered Arabization a threat to their language, culture, and job prospects and rose in opposition to Chadli's cultural policies. These oppositions prompted Chadli to pursue a fairly tolerant approach toward the growing Islamic oppositional movement in 1979–82.[88]

Chadli's economic reform was, however, undermined by the country's vulnerability to economic fluctuations in the world oil market. Algeria was highly dependent on the export of oil, as about 98 percent of its foreign exchange earnings were generated by hydrocarbon sales.[89] The unprecedented increase in oil and gas prices in the seventies poured considerable financial capital into the Algerian economy. Oil and gas revenues jumped from $271.9 million in 1970 to $10,780 million in 1980.[90] But in the eighties the prices of crude oil plunged by more than two-thirds on the world market, causing a major drop in Algeria's revenues and foreign earnings. Such a dramatic decline threw the economy, hard put to satisfy the needs of a rapidly growing population, into a profound crisis. Given that Algeria had become dependent on the import of food as a result of the decline in agricultural self-sufficiency between the early sixties and the eighties, the sudden dramatic decline in the state's revenues paralyzed its ability to finance agricultural subsidies.

The economic difficulties of the 1980s considerably reduced the state's financial capacity to manage the economy. What is more, the liberalization measures implemented by the Benjedid government required cutting some government services and implementing certain austerity measures, which led to a substantial increase in the price of basic necessities. All contributed to the heightening of social discontent, the outbreak of riots, and the rise of the Islamic fundamentalist movement. Social tensions already evident in the late 1970s worsened through the 1980s, leading to the outbreak of serious riots in 1985, 1986, and 1988.[91] Further, a large segment of the working class also began showing their dissatisfaction with current conditions. For instance, the number of reported strikes rose from 72 in 1969 to 168 in 1973 and to 521 in 1977, before falling to 323 in 1978. It rose again to 870 by 1980. In 1969 only 2.7 percent of these strikes occurred within the public sector; this proportion rose to 15.7 percent in 1972, and to 36 percent in 1977 and 45.7 percent in 1980.[92]

The State and Islamic Oppositional Discourse

These economic problems might have caused the decline of the state's legitimacy, the expansion of social discontent, and the intensification of social unrest. Youth in particular were among the main followers of radical Islamism. This tendency was a result of limited educational and occupational opportunities for the youth. According to a study conducted in the mid-1970s, the son of an agricultural manager was thirty times more likely to enter a university than the son of a farm laborer, and the son of a technocrat or businessman was 285 times more likely. Noting that students at Algerian universities constituted a select group drawn from the most favored sectors of society, one observer described them as "the 1 to 3 percent of Algerians who are destined, because of their family and personal connections, acquired wealth and influence, type and level of education, multilingual fluency, and technical-scientific accreditation, to assume the top- and secondary-level positions in each of the principal institutional components of the technocratic system: government, party, military, bureaucracy."[93] As a result, poorly educated young men and women were no longer impressed by tales of their leaders' accomplishment in securing independence. "Young people no longer ask their elders what they did during the war," writes one analyst. "To them the war is a two hour weekly history lesson. They want to know, as one student bitterly stated . . . why more than half of them are jobless 'while we earn billions per year from natural gas, and [the former head of the ruling party] lives like a king.'" According to another report, the majority of the participants in the riots in Constantine in 1986 were born after independence, which was indicative of the fact that although they were exposed to a generation of socialist ideology, they were also exposed to "state corruption, social problems and political abuse." The overall cause of political alienation among students and others is defined by this scholar as the problem of the "three p's": "The core of the problem is the system of power, patronage and privilege that entrenched interests in the party, government and the economy are unwilling to sacrifice in the name of some larger good."[94] Owners of small businesses were also dissatisfied with the state's policies and were demanding a free market economy.[95]

The Islamic opposition movement naturally attempted to exploit these problems fully and mobilize supports for its agenda. In their turn, the youth activists and the disgruntled landowners and small business owners tended to provide the requisite social resources in support of the movement. These factors, however, do not explain the rise of radical Islamism as the dominant oppositional discourse. They do not because, on the one hand, the Islamic opposition movement emerged during the heyday of Algerian socialism and the state's triumphalistic economic nationalization and centralization—long before the difficulties of the eighties—and, on the other hand, disillusions with state socialism and demand for a free market economy do not necessarily entail support for a radical Islamic alternative. What factors did, then, contribute to the popularity of the discourse of Islamic fundamentalism? Why did liberal nationalism or Islamic reformism fail to become the dominant discourses of the opposition movement? To answer these questions, we trace the historical formulation of Islamic fundamentalist discourse on such diverse issues as socialism and secularism, culture and language, politics and government, and women in reaction to the development of various attributes of the state since the independence. The Algerian regime's intolerance of any independent political party and group channeled oppositional politics into the religious medium. To be sure, contrary to the Pahlavi state, the Algerian regime did not try to undermine the influence of religion in society and politics altogether. It rather aimed to promote an official religious discourse that was in keeping with its socialist policies. It actively competed with the Islamic groups in building mosques. Nevertheless, when the state failed to recognize the autonomy of the religious institutions, official Islam was perceived as a part of the regime's propaganda.[96] The more the regime attempted to impose its own version of Islam (i.e., Islamic socialism) on society, the more it contributed to the politicization of religion and the rise of Islamic oppositional discourse. As the regime attempted to declare the compatibility of Islam with socialism, the religious leaders began to express their concerns that it was imprudent, if not sacrilegious, to erase thirteen centuries of consensus on private property and fall into an arbitrary collectivism whose origins were foreign to Algeria and to Islam.[97] The more the ruling elite was identified with Western culture and the French language, the more Arabic and Islamic culture became the defining identity of the opposition.

Islam versus Western Ideologies—Socialism and Secularism

The al-Qiyam movement represented the first organized Islamic response to the state's socialism in the sixties. The movement initially benefited from the great division within the ruling elite. By 1964 Ben Bella had alienated a substantial portion of the former FLN leadership and was facing rebellions in several parts of the country. The socialist trend of his policies as well as his radical populist rhetoric had provoked unrest among the urban middle classes. His failure to secure the support of any prominent religious figure had further strengthened the Islamic opposition,[98] which was demonstrated when the leaders of al-Qiyam obliquely questioned the regime's religious and political orientation in a gathering of three or four thousand people in January 1964. As an alternative, they suggested a return to tradition and observance of Islamic moral codes.[99] The most prominent figures of the movement were Malek Bennabi and Muhammad Khider. The latter was one of the "nine historic chiefs," who were the foundering members of the FLN.[100] Sheikh Bashir Ibrahimi warned the government, "Our country is sliding nearer and nearer to hopeless civil war, an unprecedented moral crisis and insurmountable economic difficulties. Those governing us do not seem to realize that what our people aspire to above all is unity, peace and prosperity and that the theories on which their actions should be founded are to be found not in foreign doctrines but in our Arab-Islamic roots."[101] He also protested against the wearing of tennis skirts by young girls during a march in Algiers. The habous press also added in August 1964 that "the agents of atheism and Communism are paid propagandists who would like to soil the reputation of religion and its members. Beware! Impose your existence on the enemies, be witnesses in the Algerian society! Through your firmness and decisiveness, religion will win out."[102] The government responded in the Arabic newspaper of the UGTA by denouncing the sheikh and his followers vehemently as the "Ulama of Evil," enemies of socialism, and a "corrupt clique."[103]

A clear indication of the radicalization of the Islamic movement is reflected in an article published in its journal, *Humanisme Musulman*, in 1965, a declaration that was similar to the totalitarianism of Islamic fundamentalism in Egypt, Syria, and Iran. According to the article, "All political parties, all regimes and all leaders which do not base themselves on Islam are decreed illegal and dangerous. A communist party, a secular party, a Marxist party, a nationalist party (the latter putting in question the unity of the Muslim world) cannot exist in the land of Islam."[104]

The regime's further drift to the left in the early 1970s reinforced this process. The Islamic groups initiated what they considered the campaign for a double jihad: against the forces of international atheism, and in Algeria against the Francophone Marxist voluntary brigades that were leading the agricultural revolution and against the decadent morals of the West.[105]

Sheikh Abdul Latif Sultani (1902–84) was among the first who developed a somewhat systematic critique of the state's socialist policies. He published a virulent attack on the state's socialism in a pamphlet entitled *Mazdakism Is the Source of Socialism* in Morocco in 1974. He compared the regime's doctrine to that of Mazdak, leader of a sect of Persian heretics during the fifth century AD who were reputed to be libertine. Sultani also criticized the regime for the degradation of morals as the supreme evil, of which the consumption of alcohol, the mixing of sexes, the lack of consideration for religion, and even the cult of pre-Islamic Roman ruins were the expression.[106] According to Sultani,

These same harmful effects which were produced by the Mazdak sect in
Persian society (licentiousness, usurpation, injustice, etc . . .) are reproduced
[in the modern age] by socialism and Communism in the countries which are
afflicted by them. Injustice and debauchery in all forms are common there.
Liberties which call on the good and fight against evil are smothered there,
while those who want to do evil or aid it are given complete freedom.
Abandoned children are legion, the result of this promiscuity between the
sexes instituted under the cover of progressivism, of liberation and emancipation, etc. . . . King Choroes I the Great (Sassanid Emperor of the fourteenth
century before Jesus Christ) summed up the results: "The most vile species
mixed with the most honorable elements. The low people, who did not have
the audacity to reveal themselves before, had access to the most precious
women." [It is the same today], women go out in the streets with the finery
that has been given them, to meet whoever seems good to them, to speak with
who they want, to work in offices or elsewhere. But it is there that the evil and
corruption of society hides.[107]

Around the midseventies, another Muslim activist, Mahfouth Nahnah, who was
trained by Egyptian Muslim Brothers, also attacked the regime's socialist and secularist policies.

However, the regime's attempt to distance itself from communism in 1976, the
death of Boumédienne in December 1978, and the subsequent change in the state's
policies away from socialism and toward economic liberalization removed socialism
as an important target of ideological attacks from the agenda of Muslim activists,
although their literature contained criticisms of communism and materialist philosophy.

The issue of Western-inspired secularism and secular education remained the
central feature of the fundamentalists' critiques of the dominant order in Algeria.
Spearheaded by the Western-educated FIS leader Sheikh Abbasi Madani (1931–),
antisecularist arguments were more well reasoned and focused than issues related to
the economy and gender. Like his Iranian counterparts, Abbasi argued that the
decline of the Islamic world had been caused by its submergence in Western culture. Dubious Western theories and moribund promises of material well-being had
subjugated the minds of the people to accept secular ideas and overlook their
Islamic heritage. He vehemently attacked the secular intellectual leaders in Arab
countries who blamed the religion of Islam for the backwardness of Muslim societies. In his view, people like Michel Aflaq, Taha Hussein, Salama Musa, Tawfiq al-
Hakim, and Mustafa Kemal were imitators of Western thought, incapable of seeing
past their Western masters. These members of the elite manipulated the Muslim
people in order to facilitate the expansion of Western culture into the lands of

Islam. By training students and managers, the West tried to impose its ideas, principles, values, and way of life on Islamic countries. Furthermore, by spreading Western doctrines and ideas poisonous to Islam, these intellectuals had managed to divert attention away from the salutary ideas of authentic Muslim thinkers such as Mustapha Sadiq al-Rifa'i, Hassan al-Banna, Mustafa as-Siba'i, Muhammad Iqbal, Ben Badis, and Malek Bennabi.[108]

Abbasi cited examples from the history of Europe to show that religion did not have anything to do with backwardness. In France, he said, religion had never been absent from social and political life. Catholicism, Protestantism, and Judaism prospered in private schools. The separation of the spiritual and the temporal had never been complete. Nor did this separation eradicate religion as a system of values and beliefs. The aim in Europe was to break the power of the church and leave the way clear for the bourgeois revolution. Secularism was even essential for the blossoming of Christian education. Education flourished under the double sponsorship of religion and the arts. Many secular Arab Muslim thinkers attributed the success of the Western technological revolution and economic development to the decline of the church into the private sphere. Abbasi, in contrast, argued that the church had played a key role in Western development. The refusal of Muslims to refer to the Quran as the model for moral and social behavior and the avoidance of the Prophet's path were the causes of the decline of the Muslim world. No Islamic community could work properly without its basic values. This weakening of faith and the acceptance of foreign values and thoughts were the factors perpetuating Muslim backwardness.[109]

In the eighties, attacks by Islamic groups on secularism continued unabated. It was stigmatized as an imported ideology. It was denounced for representing a threat to Algeria's Islamic identity. The communists were rejected as being the disciples of Karl Marx, the man who claimed that religion was the opium of the people. The Islamic groups claimed that politicians tried to place Islam and secularism into the same equation, but these terms were irreconcilable and diametrically opposed. In secularism, God is put aside, while in Islam he is supreme. Secularism denied the Last Judgment, whereas Islam made it the end to all enterprises in this world.[110]

Women, the Veil, and the Mixing of the Sexes

A clear and well-articulated target tends to generate sophisticated and well-reasoned responses. The debates over secularism had a fairly long history in the Arab world. The pros and cons of the secularization thesis were known among educated individuals. The debates on this issue carried some substance—clear points of difference between the protagonists and antagonists of secularism, clear practical and policy implications, and identifiable lines of institutional separation between the realm of religion and the realm of the secular. It was thus not too surprising that the Islamic criticisms of secularism displayed, relatively speaking, some degree of theoretical rigor. The question of women could also elicit carefully reasoned responses. In India and Egypt in the last quarter of the nineteenth century, where the exclusion of women, female infanticide, maltreatment of women at home, and polygamy came under attack by such diverse people as the followers of the Enlightenment, the Westernizers, and the missionaries, the Muslim intellectuals' defense of their faith took the form of sophisticated treatises on Islamic feminism in the works of people like Mumtaz Ali and Qasim Amin.

In Algeria, in contrast, the Islamic fundamentalists' attacks on what they perceived to be a Western conception of womanhood was hopelessly unreflective and superficial. This is also understandable. In the totalitarian and despotic context of the Algerian state in the second half of the twentieth century, the dictator's talk of women's rights and freedoms could not be taken too seriously.[111] In practice, too, prowoman policies were often confined to her right to education, employment, movement, and dress and did not apply to the fundamental freedom to express herself, for such a freedom often entailed political freedom, something that was not tolerated by the ruling regime. A woman's rights in these areas, certainly not insignificant, were implemented from above by the ruling elite. Her presence in public without the veil thus became part of the state's propaganda to demonstrate its progressive nature. Nevertheless, this presence, perceived as indicative of the state's cultural dictatorship, became a target of ideological attack by Islamic opposition groups, which claimed that the state's real intention was the promotion of sexual laxity, nudity, and immorality. There are, however, differences among Algerian fundamentalists on the role and status of women in society. For Abbasi, a woman must obey the laws of silence. She must obey her husband. Abbasi was not against women working outside the home. He indicated that the Prophet's wife was engaged in commerce. He believed that women should not be marginalized, for they were the mothers of the nation, but he was against the mixing of the sexes.[112] Ali Belhaj (1956–), another FIS leader, had a more restrictive view of women's role in society. In a widely quoted interview in 1989, he stated that "The natural place of expression for women is the home. If she must go out, there are conditions: not to be near men and that her work is located in an exclusively feminine milieu. In our institutions and universities is it admissible to authorize mixing? It is contrary to Islamic morality. It is necessary to separate girls and boys and consecrate establishments for each sex. . . . In a real Islamic society, the woman is not destined to work and the head of state must provide her with remuneration. In this way she will not leave her home and consecrate herself to the education of men. The woman is a producer of men. She produces no material goods."[113]

In series of articles published in the literature of the Islamic groups on women's issues, the Western conception of gender equality was attacked because men and women had different characteristics and capabilities, making women rivals of men resulted in the decline of chastity and femininity, feminist ideology would marginalize her, and the mixing of the sexes in the universities and workplaces was contrary to Islam and would cause the decline of morals witnessed in the West. It was also argued that while Romans debated whether a woman was a person or demon, Muhammad claimed that she was the sister of man. Islam was the first religion to give her the right of expression, the right to vote, and the right to own property. She was absolutely free in choosing her husband. According to the Quran only what was "apparent" must be shown, that is, the face and hands. The Islamic woman must therefore cover herself. Any woman wearing "modern" clothes commits a very serious crime and should be punished. Women's freedom in the West did not bring them happiness. Western women who would use their bodies to promote themselves were free, but in this freedom they did not find happiness. Islamic women would be respected and treated as sacred, they would be recognized in society for their role in the family.[114]

The Islamic Alternative: The FLN versus the FIS

In the previous chapter, we attempted to show how monarchy-centered nationalist discourse generated its mirror image in the Islamic opposition movement—clergy centered Islamic revolutionary discourse. In the case of Algeria, it appears that the ideology of the national liberation front (FLN) also created something of its own mirror image in the Islamic Salvation Front. In the same way that FLN was composed of disparate groups united in the struggle for liberation of the nation, the FIS also united diverse Islamic groups for salvation through the Islamization of society and politics. As Abbasi Madani explained,

> It is a "front," since it affronts; and since it deals with a wide range of action and domain; it is the front of the entire Algerian people with all its layers and its vast territories. It is open to a variety of trends and ideas that despite the richness of this diversity constitute a coherent unity . . . ; the unity of interests, positions, and agreement. . . . It is the unity of a shared destiny.
>
> It is "Islamic," because it has a content, a method, a historical Islamic function. Islam is the goal from which we draw a model of change and reform, from which we draw our raison d'être and the reason for the continuity of our being, our being the best of the nation. . . .
>
> When it comes to "salvation," it is represented by the apostolic function, it is the salvation of the faith that takes us to the right path and prevents error; and by historical, economical, social, cultural, and civilizational function. It is the salvation of all to be all.[115]

The Islamic alternative portrayed in articles in *al-Munqidh*, the organ of the FIS, and the literature of other Islamic groups displayed a totalitarian discourse similar to the ideology of the postrevolutionary regime. In these articles, the Islamic state was presented as superior to the nationalist state. It was more moral and ethical. In one such article, written in French by a female activist with a doctorate in philosophy, modernism was equated with all the evils of Western society. She argued that modern ideologies such as "communism, socialism, capitalism, pragmatism, positivism, fascism, Nazism, Zionism, Arab Nationalism, Berberism, etc." all rejected transcendental values and saw truth and moral values as relative. Nationalism, which she attacked vehemently, would breed hatred of the other and the persecution of minorities. It was only an Islamic state that could create a counterbalance to modernism and absolute standards and values. The nationalist state could not have such standards because by definition it was modern.[116] The Islamic republic, however, was not the FIS's ultimate objective. In Ali Belhaj's words, "Our ultimate and strategic goal is the establishment of the Islamic Caliphate on earth . . . This will be done in stages . . . We will start with this country by founding an Islamic state in Algeria. After that we will work with our brothers in All Muslim countries, God willing, until the establishment of the Caliphate."[117] Likewise, "Abbassi Madani discussed the Caliphate that governs the whole Islamic *umma*. The state is only the guardian of the *shari'a*. It has three missions: a human mission which is to ensure the just implementation of prescribed rights and duties; a historical mission to maintain the unity and permanence of the Islamic *umma;* and a prophetic mission to promulgate and safeguard the heritage of the *shari'a*."[118]

The political universe of radical Islamism was based on a new set of concepts such as Islamic values, the spirituality and virtuousness of Islam, the superiority of the laws of the shari'a, the transcendental nature of the Islamic state, and decision making based on shura and ijtihad, which were juxtaposed in opposition to secularism, nationalism, Western culture, democracy, and pluralism. The relations among these concepts, however, would reproduce the image of a political regime not too different from the political system the Islamic activists were attempting to replace. In the same way that the socialist secular state did not tolerate political parties, pluralism, or any alternative to its philosophy, the Islamic state was totalitarian, authoritarian, and interventionist. There were variations in the views of the leaders of the Islamic movement, ranging from the rejection of democracy by Belhaj to the view espoused by the leadership of Hamas (a moderate Islamic movement with a strong following in southern Algeria in the early 1990s), which supported "shuracracy, a neologism coined by Sheikh Mahfouth Nahnah, as an Islamized version of democracy and some general stress on gradualism and pluralism.[119] As a whole, the ideology of the Islamic opposition appeared to have generated an authoritarian and monolithic discourse not too different from that of the regime.

THIRTEEN

Jordanian Exceptionalism:
The Alliance between the State
and the Muslim Brothers

In our analysis, we attempted to explain the contrast between Islamic modernism and Islamic fundamentalism in terms of variations in the nature of the discursive context and the state's intervention in culture. We argued that Islamic modernism in India, Egypt, and Iran emerged out of the pluralistic context of ideological debates and religious disputations among diverse groups where the state's intervention in culture remained minimal. And Islamic fundamentalism in Algeria, Egypt, Iran, and Syria originated from the monolithic discursive context imposed from above by an intrusive secular ideological state. The state's extensive interventions in culture politicized culture production and resulted in the formulation of political Islam. There is, however, an alternative explanation of this contrast, namely, the presence of a Western power in fostering modern discourses in Islamic countries. It may be argued that where this power was strongest, as it was in India and Egypt, Islamic modernism grew into a full-blown cultural movement. The same argument can also be made about the rise of Islamic reformism in French Algeria in the first half of the twentieth century. Where this power was relatively weak or absent, as in nineteenth-century Iran, Islamic modernism did not develop to any considerable extent. With the removal of direct foreign rule, the decline of Western hegemony, and the rise of the national state, favorable conditions thus emerged for Muslim self-assertions, one of the manifestations of which was the rise of Islamic fundamentalism.

The experiences of both Islamic reformist fundamentalism of the eighteenth century and the modernism of the nineteenth provide historical materials that cast doubt on this argument. They do so for several reasons. First, the reformist movement in Islam started in the eighteenth century, long before the establishment of Western hegemony in Islamic countries. The rise of the reformist fundamentalism of Shah Waliallah in India and Muhammad Ibn Abd al-Wahhab in Arabia exemplifies the desire for reform on the part of Muslim thinkers during the period when the ulama's power was on the decline. Moreover, Islamic modernist thought started in Egypt before the British occupation of the country. Finally, it is true that Islamic modernism in Iran was relatively weak, but Iran was among the first to make serious efforts to create a bridge between Islamic political theory and constitutionalism. All these facts indicated that attempts at rational analysis to adapt Islam to changing conditions of life were an integral part of the Islamic cultural tradition.

Jordan, however, may be a better case for testing our model. The history of the Islamic movement in this country displays a glaring contrast with the experience of Islamic fundamentalism in Algeria, Egypt, Iran, and Syria. The Jordanian movement has not only been peaceful and moderate but also defended the state against the challenges of radical ideologies in the fifties. Following the democratization process that was launched by the late King Hussein, the Jordanian Muslim Brothers (MB) participated in the 1989 elections. What is more, to reconcile their belief in the sovereignty of the shari'a and the secular framework established by the state, the Brothers made a keen political move in 1992 by forming the Islamic Action Front Party (IAFP).

The sole objective of the IAFP was to participate in the elections within the framework of the Political Parties Law and in a manner consistent with the general religious beliefs of the MB. The IAFP functioned as a "transmission belt" linking the general religious missions of the MB to the mundane issues facing Jordanian society and its political regime. The formation of the IAFP was also to resolve the tension between the sovereignty of the shari'a and the sovereignty of the electorate in a quasi-democratic state. At the same time, the very presence of the IAFP, solely preoccupied with political matters, and the MB, as a religious institution, was an implicit admission of the separation of political and religious leadership. What is astonishing about these developments in 1989–97 is that they reflected a secularization of the religious movement characterized by (1) organizational differentiation between the MB and IAFP and (2) the rationalization of religious discourse in a move from appealing to the shari'a to appealing to the electorate. All this happened while the Kingdom of Jordan remained a rentier[1] and an authoritarian and patrimonial state and had close and dependent ties to the West. Given that these characteristics are cited in the literature as contributing to the conflicts between religion and the state in other nations, a number of questions come to mind. How do we explain Jordan's exceptional religious experience? How did the Jordanian state manage to maintain a lasting coalition with the MB despite its undeniably close, and often dependent, ties to the West? What prevented the formation of a radical nationalist-religious alliance in Jordan similar to the one that overthrew the Iranian monarchy in 1979? What was the nature of the cultural space that made the coexistence of the Hashemites and the Brothers possible? What were the basic themes and symbolism of state ideology and their relationship with the religious outlooks of the MB? In what manner did the post-1989 democratization process affected the Brothers' politics and discourse?

In this chapter, we attempt to answer these questions in terms of the specific arrangement of the political, social, and cultural factors that came into play after the formation of the Kingdom of Jordan. These include the multiple, often contradictory, attributes of the Hashemite regime, the historical experience of the MB, the weakness of pan-Arab nationalism, and the late development of indigenous social classes. First, the Brothers were aware of the Hashemite dependence on the West and its "soft" and conciliatory approach toward Israel, but they had little ideological justification for engaging in a radical political movement against the monarch. Second, the merchants and landowners (who played influential roles in politics in other Islamic countries) were a late development in Jordan. Third, the rise of these classes in the course of the twentieth century was aided by the state's economic policies. Fourth, the alliance between the state and religion was reinforced by the active presence of such secular radical ideologies as Nasserism, Ba'athism, and communism, which challenged not only the institution of the monarchy but the MB as well.

The core of our argument in this chapter, however, is that the causal dynamic that explains the difference between Islamic modernism and fundamentalism is also applicable to the case of Jordan. That is, the Jordanian state has displayed heterogeneous features, having very limited interest in directly intervening in cultural and religious affairs. The democratization process launched by King Hussein generated a pluralistic environment and cultural dynamics that paralleled those experienced by the Islamic modernists in the late nineteenth century. As a result, during the 1989–97 period, the Jordanian MB began to display features which were a marked departure from the religious discourse and political orientations of their counterparts in other Islamic countries—tendencies toward moderation, secularism, and rationalization.

The Hashemite Kingdom of Jordan: Authoritarian Pluralism

The character of the Jordanian state provides a significant clue for uncovering the distinctive nature of the religious movement in the country and for understanding the dynamic of the alliance between religion and the state. The pertinent feature of the state that significantly affected the politics of religion was its institutional and ideological pluralism, which displayed diverse and often contradictory discourses connected to different apparatuses of the state. The point of unity of these discourses was in the institution of the monarchy. The state ideology reflected elements of Arab nationalism, Islamic conservatism, tribalism, pre-Islamic glorification, and Western modernism. Because of this very diversity, the state appeared differently to different segments of the Jordanian population. Although effective power resided with the king and selected members of Transjordanian elite, criss-crossing pressures emanating from these tendencies resulted in the state's pursuit of contradictory policies on significant regional issues. We may cite such varying evidence as (1) the regime's support for the Arab nationalists of the Istiqlal Party in Syria in the twenties, (2) the ensuing purge of the nationalists as a result of British pressure, (3) the free elections of 1956, (4) the abrogation of the Anglo-Jordanian treaty in 1957 and the consequent dismissal of the British commander of the Arab Legion, (5) Jordan's participation in the 1967 war, (6) the confrontation with Palestinian guerrillas in 1970, (7) the reorientation toward the West in the seventies, (8) the launching of democratization in 1989, (9) Jordan's "siding" with Iraq in the Persian Gulf War in 1991, and (10) the peace with Israel in 1994. While the post-coup Algerian, Egyptian, Iranian, and Syrian states pursued consistent policies, the sequence of the contradictory policies pursued by the Hashemites may be indicative of its responsiveness to crisscrossing pressures coming from different social and political forces. Such a plurality naturally prevented the kingdom from committing itself to a particular ideological blueprint.

Dependence on the British

The Jordanian state was formed in the historical context of British-French political rivalries, Turkish attempts to hold together the already fragile and segmented Ottoman Empire, the rise of Arab nationalism and the outbreak of the Arab revolt, and the Zionist movement, which, a generation later, culminated in the formation of the state of Israel in 1948. For the British, the creation of the Emirate of Transjordan under their general supervision was to provide a useful buffer state to prevent the French from expanding eastward after their occupation of Damascus in 1920.[2] For the founder of the country, Abdullah Ibn Hussein, the formation of the new state in 1923 was a partial realization of his revolutionary ambition. King Abdullah, however, remained heavily dependent on British support "that had allowed him to survive the tribal revolts and attacks of the 1920s and that kept his administration afloat despite the lack of taxable assets in Transjordan itself. Without Britain, it is fair to judge that neither Abdullah nor Transjordan in its formative years would have survived."[3]

Abdullah's dependence on the British grew out of sheer financial need and the necessity of protecting his kingdom from domestic and foreign foes. As a traditional Muslim committed to the pan-Arab nationalist cause, British constitutional democracy and social life had little appeal to him. For Abdullah, Transjordan was a stepping-stone for the formation of a greater Arab kingdom with Damascus as its capital.[4] There was already considerable resistance by the Syrians to the forced imposition of the French mandate on the country, and Abdullah's support for the Syrian Arab nationalists was in line with his plan to make this larger kingdom a reality. This greater aspiration was reflected in his first cabinet, which consisted entirely of nationalists who had previously served Faisal's two-year regime in Syria. The goal of these nationalists was the unification of Syria into one Arab state, independence for the states of Greater Syria and Iraq, and the rejection of foreign tutelage and Britain's Zionist policy in Palestine.[5]

Jordan's limited resources, tribal rebellions, and contention for regional leadership with neighboring Arab rulers, together with British and French colonial designs, had placed effective limits on Abdullah's aspirations. The king's weakness in the face of the threat of Saudi expansionism, his financial difficulties, and the Adwan tribal revolt further solidified his dependence on the British and the realization that his pan-Arabist project was merely a far-fetched fantasy. The British were apprehensive about Arab nationalism in general, and especially about Palestinian opposition to the mandate and the possibility that Wahhabism might galvanize anti-British sentiments in Palestine. They prevailed upon Abdullah to purge the Arab Legion and the Transjordan government of the nationalists of the Istiqlal Party and expel some of its prominent leaders from the country. With these expulsions, Transjordan was cleansed of most of the Arab nationalists whom Britain considered to be troublemakers. Contrary to Abdullah's original wish, the kingdom ceased to be the country of all Arabs, and the king's pan-Arab reputation was seriously tarnished.[6] When a revolt against the French broke out in Syria in 1925, Abdullah remained aloof from the struggle. His main problem was that Jordan did not have the demographic composition or social structure to sustain a nationalist movement of its own. It lacked cities, lacked a sizable middle class, and had not fostered the growth of a class of merchants and clerics, which were the source of nationalist movements elsewhere.[7]

The Bedouins and Transjordanians

In retrospect, however, purging the Arab Legion of the nationalists was crucial for the Hashemites' longevity. After all, nationalism in the Arab world hardly had the interests of monarchies at heart, and, for the politicized nationalist army, the monarch has always been a prime target. Weakening nationalism notwithstanding, this purge also helped the government counter the opposition of Jordanians to the extension of central government authority and their resentment of the predominance of non-Jordanians in the state administration. In the twenties, John Glubb, the British head of the Arab Legion, successfully and at times ruthlessly put down tribal insurrections, but in the thirties he brought the Bedouins into the army.[8] The Bedouins, in turn, were attracted to army careers because the British use of armored cars and aircraft had undermined this raid-loving people's supremacy in mobility.[9]

By the mid-1950s, the old economy of the Bedouins had given way to government employment, of which the chief form was service in the army.[10] By 1955, the army had absorbed practically all the young men of Bedouin or near-Bedouin tribes.[11]

King Hussein also patronized the Bedouins. They became the backbone of the military and a stabilizing force in the country, displaying their loyalty to the Hashemites on more than one critical occasion.[12] The retention of tribalism in the country's armed forces and political institutions is a significant element of historical continuity between the periods before and after the formation of the kingdom. Even the king was referred to as "sheikh of sheiks."[13] The political significance of the Bedouins made them an element in national identity. In the debates over the pros and cons of tribalism in Jordan, King Hussein himself expressed displeasure with journalists' arguments against tribal life. He asserted that whatever threatened the Jordanian tribes was forever a threat to Hashemite sovereignty.[14] The state's appropriation of tribal culture, both as the keystone of Jordan's national heritage and as its self-representation to the outside world, was institutionalized by the development of tourism and regionalized politics.[15]

The Muslim Brothers, Islam, and the Hashemites

The significance of the Bedouins in the national imagery, the regime's pro-Western orientation, references to pre-Islamic Jordan to emphasize the country's distinctive cultural heritage, which was supported by several remarkable archeological discoveries, and an increasing reliance on tourism as a crucial part of the state's strategy for development were all in varying degrees the subjects of the MB's criticism. Yet the MB had little Islamic justification to question the legitimacy of the regime because, notable as they were, these properties did not encompass the state's diverse ideological orientations. The Hashemites' unbroken descent from the house of the Prophet Muhammad and Abdullah's father's exalted position as the sharif of Mecca bestowed upon the kingdom substantial Islamic reverence. Furthermore, the ruling elite was not committed to secularism and did not exclude religious activists from employment in the state's bureaucracy. Abdullah's approval of the West was limited to the adoption of its military and administrative techniques.[16] He disliked foreign schools, banned women from appearing in public without proper Islamic dress,[17] and was an ardent anticommunist.[18] In 1945, he brought the MB under government protection and offered its secretary, Abdul Hakim Abdeen, a ministerial position.[19]

Interest Representation in the State Apparatuses

The Bedouin tribes and Transjordanians, the Palestinians, religious and ethnic minorities, the Hashemites' Western allies, and the MB had access to different apparatuses of the state. West Bank residents served as ministers in the ministries of Foreign Affairs, Agriculture, Economics, Education, and Development, even though the most powerful positions were reserved for Transjordanians.[20] The Jordanian policy toward the West Bank elite aimed to ensure that West Bank leaders had a share in government and would not be driven over into the opposition. However, the East Bank elements, who were loyal to the regime, remained in control of the most important foci of power.[21] Most of the key positions in the state bureaucracy and the military were reserved for Transjordanians. There are also disproportional representations of tribal areas in the parliamentary elections.

The Hashemites have also been consistent in dealing with the MB by combining a policy of conciliatory gestures toward the movement with a strict monitoring of its activities. Unlike other Arab nations, Jordan recognized the brotherhood officially, and its members were frequently co-opted into prestigious positions. In the 1950s, the former minister of the awqaf, Kamil Ismail al-Sharif, was one of the MB leaders in Egypt. The Brothers had substantial influence in the Ministry of Education.[22] Ishaq Farhan, the former leader of the IAFP, was the minister of education (1970–73), president of the University of Jordan (1976–78), and a member of the upper house of parliament.[23] In contrast with Algeria, Egypt, Iran, and Syria, the secularization process in Jordan proceeded quite slowly, and the 1952 constitution of Jordan gave religious courts jurisdiction in matters involving personal law such as marriage, divorce, inheritance, and child custody. Shari'a courts also had jurisdiction over matters pertaining to the awqaf.[24]

Class Formation: The Rise of the Landowners and Merchants

Political centralization and the establishment of state security forces facilitated the rise of landowners and merchants in Jordan.[25] Class formation in Jordan followed a pattern similar to the pattern in other Arab countries. Ottoman initiatives in the 1850s to establish administrative centers in Transjordan stimulated commerce and new village settlements. They also extended the land under cultivation, improved lines of communication, and provided a new level of security.[26] This trend, reinforced by development in the means of transportation, continued under the British mandate.[27] By the second quarter of the twentieth century, Transjordanian merchants emerged into the limelight as an active group conscious of their interests and powerful enough to voice their objections to the governmental policies they deemed unfavorable to their interests. In the quota system during the Second World War, a few wealthy merchants stood out as a "quota coterie," a cohesive group who controlled the Chamber of Commerce. These merchants had already established trading links and were well placed to take advantage of the quota allocation.[28] War profits and inflation introduced a class of merchant-moneylenders into the village, where settlement of titles had concurrently made it possible to mortgage land. Land also became more valuable as cultivation was extended, owing to high wartime prices for cereals.[29]

Another notable change in the Jordanian socioeconomic structure concerned land ownership, which was also introduced under Ottoman rule. By the 1920s, land ownership had become a source of power and wealth. It did not weaken tribalism, since effective control over land rested on a combination of tribal leadership and individual ownership of vast landed property.[30] Land ownership and the settlement of the Bedouin tribes went hand in hand with the state's attempts to establish its central authority. The state's land program emphasized individual land ownership to encourage members of the Bedouin tribes to become full-time farmers.[31] This development in property rights, however, provided a new form of class inequality and social tension.[32] To encourage the maintenance of smallholdings and to preserve small-cultivator ownership of much of the country's land, the government formulated the Mortgages Law in 1947.[33] This new land program had more positive political implications and was far more effective in buttressing the Hashemite regime's political standing than the more often cited personal dynamism of Jordan's monarchs. Indeed, land reform seems to have guaranteed the continuation of the monarchy during turbulent times.[34]

Economic Development, Social Differentiation, and the Rise of the New Middle Class

From the 1970s through the 1990s, rapid economic growth and the expansion of governmental programs stimulated the rise of a new middle class. Economic development in Jordan was associated with a far greater increase in the size of the state than any sector of the economy. For example, employment categorization for 1961 included agriculture, 35.3 percent; manufacturing and mining, 10.8 percent; trade and services, 21.7 percent; administration, professions, army, and public security, 18.8 percent; construction, 10.3 percent; and transport, 3.1 percent.[35] In the mid-1980s, the figures were as follows: industry, 12 percent; construction, 11 percent; transport, 9 percent; public administration, defense, and other services, 47 percent.[36] Although these categories are not quite comparable, considerable state expansion is indicated by an increase from 18.8 to 47 percent in employment in the public sector. A large segment of the Jordanian labor force was employed in the oil-producing Arab countries. In 1961, about 64,000 Jordanians were working outside the kingdom, but after the oil boom this number increased to 259,500 in 1975 and then to 539,232 in 1992.[37] This large expatriate labor force not only diminished the problems of unemployment, but also constituted a major source of revenue for the Jordanian economy: the remittances of the expatriate workers soared from $44.7 million in 1973 to $1,237,000 in 1984.[38]

This situation was not entirely without its own problems, since the Jordanian economy became vulnerable to fluctuations in oil prices due to varying world market demand and to sudden political crises affecting oil-producing countries. The decline in the world oil market that began in the late 1970s and Iraq's invasion of Kuwait caused the return of 350,000 Jordanians and Palestinians to Jordan in 1990–91. Within a few months, the kingdom's population increased by 10 percent, and the unemployment rate rose to unprecedented levels.[39] The sharp decrease in foreign grants and workers' remittances resulted in a growing deficit in the balance of trade.[40] This economic downturn contributed to social dissatisfaction among some groups, a source of increased popular support for the Islamic opposition movement.

The Society of the Muslim Brothers

In Egypt, Syria, Iran, and Algeria, the Islamic fundamentalist groups had a clear awareness of their cultural differences with the ruling regimes. In contrast, the Jordanian MB, from its foundation in 1945 up to the early seventies, did not exhibit any particular oppositional orientation or any major cultural grievances against the regime. Although it was founded by the Egyptian MB and derived its general Islamic understanding from the teachings of Hasan al-Banna, the Jordanian MB developed its own positions in response to the obstacles and opportunities it faced in the immediate social environment. Most important, Jordanian Islamic leaders did not share their Egyptian counterparts' pejorative depiction of the Hashemites;[41] nor did they become antimonarchical, as did the Egyptian MB.[42] Further, the ideological "neutrality" of the Jordanian regime under the democratization process created a condition that promoted the secularization of the MB. The appearance of twenty political parties, the publication of diverse newspapers and periodicals, electoral competition, and parliamentary debates generated a rather pluralistic intellectual market in which the Brothers no longer enjoyed the luxury of being the sole carrier of legitimate political discourse in society. To be sure, the regime was quite remote from the type of constitutional monarchy that existed in Western Europe, since it placed stringent limits on political liberties. The king enjoyed considerable power, and he ruled as often as he reigned.

Nevertheless, on a lower level of the hierarchy of power, there was still a considerable political space in which pluralism and debates among political groups on concrete issues were serious and consequential in shaping the policies of the government. In this political environment, the power of discourse was not solely determined by the organizational effectiveness of its carriers, but also by its ability to address concrete issues facing the public. And generalities such as that "Islam is the solution," that Jordan would be a better society if everybody observed the shari'a, and that all social ills emanate from Zionism and its Western allies or from emulating the decadent Western lifestyle became increasingly ineffective in rallying the Jordanian public to action. The Brothers made serious attempts to develop new ideas in response to stiff competition from other political parties. Moreover, the pluralistic context moved the MB in a secular direction, which entailed a rationalization of religious discourse and an organizational differentiation within the movement itself. The division of labor between the MB and the IAFP can be viewed as a practical admission of the necessity of separating political and religious leadership.

Traditionalism and Organizational Decentralization

The key factors determining the sociopolitical views of the MB in Jordan were the authoritarian pluralism of the Hashemites and the social context that promoted cooperation between the movement and the regime. Both King Abdullah and King Hussein patronized the Brothers. Moreover, merchants and property owners, having a favorable experience in Jordan and constituting the predominant group among the Brothers' activists in this period,[43] naturally directed the Brothers toward political moderation. In the 1940s and 1950s, preachers and emissaries of the Egyptian Brothers entered Jordan to promote the new branch of their movement, and merchants and other social notables were among their audience. In 1947, they provided funds for the foundation of the Islamic College in Amman, which was initiated by Haj Abdullatif Abu Qurah, the Jordanian MB's leader.[44] Several members of the country's elite (including the future King Hussein) were among its prominent students. By performing this educational function, the Brothers were able to claim an important patriotic accomplishment.[45]

In this period, the Brothers' teachings echoed the general ideas and principles developed by their Egyptian mentors. They claimed that their aims were to purify Islam, unify Muslim countries, develop the Islamic world in a direction that would assure an equitable distribution of wealth among Islamic nations, encourage charity to the poor, instill a spirit of Muslim patriotism in the population, and establish Islam as a global and competitive world culture. On politics, the Brothers held that religion and state were inseparable and that Islam was not only the personal religion of the individual but also the basis of law and order. Their positions on the social status of women and moral issues were austere and uncompromisingly traditional. Women should not use makeup or overadorn themselves. They should wear the veil and be forbidden to appear in public "half naked" (i.e., out of traditional garb). The secretary of the Brothers' Hebron branch went even further and urged the government to bar women from holding any position in its service. The MB also questioned the morality of the Jordanian broadcasting services for airing "immoral" songs and music.[46] In practical politics, the Brothers took no distinctive position. They were in complete agreement with the regime. Most of the members of their administrative bureau were of middle-class background and had no defined political affiliation. The most important members were Abu Qurah, a merchant, and al-Hajj Qasim al-Am'ari, a shop-owner. Said Ramadan, Abdul Hakim Abdeen, and Abdul Mu'iz Abdul al-Satar were emissaries from the Egyptian branch. The Society under Abu Qurah's leadership (1945–53) was also organizationally decentralized, each *jama'at* (society) having its own charitable purpose.[47] Generally, the political moderation of the Jordanian MB reflected the pragmatism of the Hashemites. The Islamic traditionalism of the MB embodied the state's conservatism. The MB's rejection of violence as a political method mirrored the Hashemites' abstention from bloodshed as a means of control.

When Jordan annexed the West Bank, the MB's membership was considerably transformed. Under the tutelage of the Egyptian leadership, the orientation of the Jordanian Brothers also changed from calling (inviting people to observe Islam or join the Islamic movement), personal improvement (*ad-da'wa wal islah*), and charity work to political activism and a distinctive program for social reform.[48] There were, however, only a few isolated instances in which moderation was not advocated. For example, one Egyptian emissary, Najah Juwaifel, was implicated in an Egyptian assassination attempt and fled to Jordan, where he tried to steer the Jordanian MB away from pragmatism and toward revolutionary activities. Juwaifel wanted to centralize the structure of the MB to give it a more political and military shape to mobilize against the British.[49]

Until 1954, the movement was under the control of the Egyptian leadership. Following Nassir's suppression of the Brothers in Egypt, the Jordanian branch elected its own leadership.[50] Its first by-laws were published in 1958, and the election of its first shura council followed in the same year.[51] From this period on, its organization gained a centralized structure, displaying astonishing similarities with the Marxist-Leninist parties. Figure 13.1 presents the organizational structure of the MB in Jordan.

Changes in the Ideological Context:
The Muslim Brothers and Arab Nationalism

Beginning in the late 1930s, Arab nationalism was gaining ground in different Arab countries, and by the early fifties, it had made a powerful entry into Jordan's political landscape. In the parliamentary elections of 1956, the National Socialists, led by Suleiman Nabulsi, formed the largest party in the House of Representatives, while the MB and Hizb al-Tahrir (an extremist party) together won only five seats. As the prime minister, Nabulsi promised to liberalize legislation and honor the government's agreement with "liberated Arab states." He followed a pro-Egyptian policy, abrogated the Anglo-Jordanian treaty, and signed the Arab Solidarity Agreement with Egypt, Syria, and Saudi Arabia. He organized rallies, in which resolutions that condemned the Eisenhower Doctrine and American policy in the Middle East were overwhelmingly approved, the severance of diplomatic relations with France (for its policies in Algeria) was endorsed, and Jordan's failure to support China's admission to the United Nations was protested. The Communist Party emerged from the underground, and the Soviet news agency, Tass, made its first appearance. The

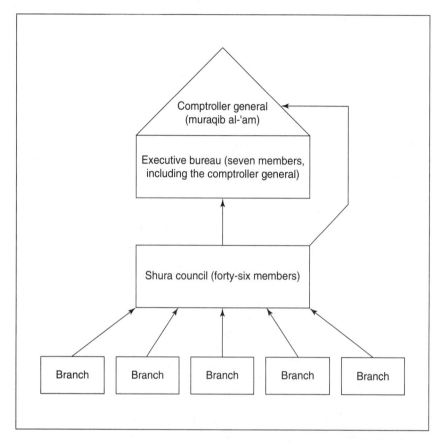

Figure 13.1. The organizational structure of the Muslim Brothers in Jordan. The MB consists of more than forty branches throughout the country. The branches elect the members of the shura council every four years. The shura council elects the comptroller general and the members of the executive bureau. According to the MB by-laws, candidates for the shura council must be over twenty-five years of age, active in the movement for at least five years, and educationally and ethically qualified to understand the principles of Islamic mission and should not have been arrested or convicted in the three-year period before their nomination. Women are banned from membership. Source: author's interview with the comptroller general, winter 2000; and Francesca Ciriaci, *Jordan Times,* July 11, 1998.

government also reorganized the army and the bureaucracy by replacing well-known royalists and supporters of conservative groups.[52]

Insofar as the objective of the nationalists was Arab unity, there was considerable overlap between them and the Hashemites. However, they differed on other issues. King Hussein's nationalism was pro-Western and anticommunist. He believed strongly that it was not in the Arab self-interest to incur the animosity of the "Free World."[53] Although he held that his nation was Arab first and Jordanian second, his pan-Arab nationalism rejected any unity dominated by the Egyptians.[54] Arab nationalism in this period, however, was as antimonarchical as it was anti-West. The nationalists had little love for the Hashemites, whom they considered reactionary agents of the West, and they would have been just as happy to see the Hashemites stripped of political power. Little wonder that they opted to abolish the monarchy, but this machination was thwarted by the military's unwavering loyalty to the king, the MB's support, and Jordan's steadfast upper classes.[55] The Arab nationalists' onslaught against the Hashemites and the menace of the Nassirite, Ba'athist, and communist forces in the country brought the regime closer to the Brothers. The latter, for their part, witnessing the stifling consequences of the rule of radical nationalism experienced by the Egyptian Brothers, were all too eager to ally themselves with the king in combating their common adversaries.[56]

The Decline of Arab Nationalism and the Rise of Political Islam

The decline of Nasserism and the idea of pan-Arab unity began before the defeat in the 1967 war. Nassir's domineering approach to inter-Arab relations (e.g., his interference in the Saudis' internal affairs, the involvement in Yemen's domestic conflict, and the short-live unification with Syria) had already disillusioned many of his Arab allies. The swift and disastrous defeat in the war, which brought back the painful memory of the ineptitude of the Egyptian army and the scandal of defective ammunition in the 1948 war, seriously damaged the legitimacy of pan-Arab nationalism.[57] The decline of Arab nationalism placed the Brotherhood in a favorable ideological climate. Further, the economic upswing and the expansion of educational opportunities, which by the early 1990s were indicated by 2,657 public schools, 1,384 private schools, 52 community colleges, and 18 universities,[58] changed the membership profile of the MB, as a large number high school, college, and university students joined its ranks.[59]

In 1970, the MB membership elected a new executive council that was sympathetic to the extremist ideas of the Egyptian Sayyid Qutb.[60] This was a turning point in the history of the Jordanian MB. At that time, many of its members were young or were in their early thirties and had participated in the *fedayeen* training camps. Two of the new council members who had been in the camps, Hammam Said and Muhammad Abu Farris, became well-known representatives of the "hawk" wing of the MB. With this new leadership came a fresh group of students, who were revolutionaries eager to fight Israel. A former fedayee, the University of Jordan professor Abdullah Azzam initiated an educational program, which involved setting up physical training and sport clubs, an activist approach in ad-da'wa efforts, and a more concentrated effort to recruit members in the mosques.

In addition to Azzam, Ahmad Nofal, Shaikh Theeb Anis, and the engineer Ahmad Azaideh had participated in the jihad camps. The MB appeared to be moving away from the politics of moderation and toward radicalism.

But the political and cultural context of Jordan was different from that of Egypt. The MB had had a favorable experience under the Jordanian regime, and the insinuation that the society was un-Islamic and dominated by a latter-day pharaoh were not taken seriously by most of its members, even though the extremists made much of the regime's pro-Western orientation. The new shura council and executive bureau (formed after the 1979 elections) reviewed Qutb's ideas, moderated Azzam's approach, formulated a new educational curriculum similar to the programs of the shari'a colleges and in the mainstream of Islamic seminaries, and excluded Sayyid Qutb's books.[61] Debates within the MB, however, resulted in the formation of two trends. One emphasized a closer interaction with political forces in society and dialogue with the government. The other took a more puritanical and politically isolationist approach, resisted involvement in governmental affairs, and suggested that the youth should be trained in Islamic education. To do otherwise might distract attention from the government's ineptitude and un-Islamic practices and would implicate the Islamic movement in the mistakes of the ruling authorities.[62] The pioneers of the first trend were Yousif al-Athem, Ahmad Azaideh, and Ishaq Farhan. The leaders of the second were Muhammad Abu Farris and Hammam Said. Other members such as Ali Hawmdeh, Ibrahim Kharaisat, and Muhammad Abul Rahman Khalifah (a former comptroller general) sided with the second trend.

Democratization: A New Discursive Framework

The two trends partly reflected the diversity in the social basis of the MB and were partly symptomatic of larger theological difficulties the movement was facing in Jordan. The Brothers were religious activists committed to reorienting the society from un-Islamic practices toward a political regime that conformed to the shari'a. For the merchants and shopkeepers that constituted the core leadership of the Brothers in the 1940s, their view of an Islamic order did not diverge from that of the regime. The Hashemites had impeccable credentials as Muslim leaders, and the Brothers felt little need to convince people in their immediate surroundings of the implicit superiority of their Islamic beliefs in creating a better society. But the social context in the 1990s was quite different from the context in the 1940s. A growing number of educated professionals with a modernist outlook occupied leading positions in the organizational hierarchy of both the MB and the IAFP.

In the political context of Egypt in the 1930s through the 1940s, Syria in the 1960s through the 1980s, Iran in the 1970s, and Algeria in the 1970s and 1980s many politically conscious members of the educated middle class turned to radical ideologies. The democratization process in Jordan, in contrast, removed the radical

option from politics. The government implemented several reforms to institution-
alize a new democratic change, including a revival of the parliament, the drafting
of the national charter to establish the framework for political activity, the repeal-
ing of martial law (which had been enforced in the aftermath of the 1967 war), and
the expansion of freedom and the commitment to pluralism and human rights.[63]
Democratization was especially facilitated when the king ended all legal and administrative ties to the West Bank in July 1988, reallocating responsibility for its
governance to the PLO. This dramatic act ended the kingdom's main source of
political and social tension.[64]

In order to establish a framework for transition to democracy, King Hussein
appointed a sixty-member royal commission in April 1990 to draft guidelines for
political party activity in Jordan. The commission included members representing
all political groups in the country and within months produced a written consensus in the form of the national charter. The charter was adopted in June 1991 at a
national conference of two thousand leading Jordanians.[65] The charter was a discursive framework for the foundation of democracy and pluralism in Jordan. It
defined the Jordanian identity, specified the character of the state, and spelled out
the will and the aims of the nation. It was carefully drafted to build a broad consensus among diverse political groups by defining Jordan's national identity in
terms of Arab and Islamic heritage, stressing the external factors that had undermined its nationhood, and overlooking the sources of internal division. It emphasized that the aims, principles, and objectives of the constitution would be best
realized by democracy. It reiterated that Jordan's system of government was parliamentary, monarchic, and hereditary. The Jordanian people were part of the Arab
nation. Islam was the religion of the state, and Islamic law was the principal source
of legislation. The Arabic language was the official language of the state. Jordanian
men and women were equal under the law. Tolerance and the recognition of the
right of others to disagree, respect for human rights, emphasis on economic development and social justice, and the elimination of external pressure or hegemony
were all endorsed.[66]

Colonels without Soldiers: A Strong Monarch and Weak Political Parties

There is an interesting correlation between monarchical power and prerogatives
and the strength of party politics. The power of one seems inversely correlated
with the strength of the other. The two institutions could not remain equally
powerful without producing political instability. During the heyday of liberal
nationalism in Egypt, the Wafd was in an uncompromising power struggle with
the king. Likewise, in the Iranian liberal-nationalist period (1941–53), the nationalist leaders demanded that the shah reign but not rule. In Jordan in the 1950s,
King Hussein dissolved the political parties when Arab nationalist politicians

tried to undermine his power. The Jordanian political pluralism of the 1990s saw a continuation of this rivalry, an imbalance of power between the monarch and the political parties.

Only a small percentage of Jordanians showed an interest in political parties. Surveys in 1995, 1997, and 1998 showed that about 2 percent of the respondents had ever been a member of any political party. At the time of the surveys, fewer than 1.1 percent held membership in a political party, and fewer than 2.7 percent intended to join a political party. Fewer than 0.5 percent indicated that they were members of the IAFP, and fewer than 0.6 percent indicated that they had intended to join the IAFP. This low level of political party affiliation among Jordanians seems to reflect a belief among respondents that none of the political parties represented their political, social, and economic interests. A large majority of Jordanians (between 81.5 and 91.3 percent) agreed on that point. Party affiliation declined between 1995 and 1998. Although this period is too short to support a firm conclusion, self-reports on party membership indicate a decline from 1.1 percent in 1995 to 0.4 percent in 1998 (table 13.1).

The Social Basis of the Islamic Action Front Party

The founding committee of the IAFP had 353 members. Of this number, 53 percent worked in the public sector. Middle-class professionals such as doctors, lawyers, engineers, pharmacists, managers, and journalists made up 30 percent of the total. Merchants, businessmen, and contractors were over 10 percent, and the remaining 6 percent included farmers, trade unionists, housewives, tribal figures, and mayors. It is notable that a fairly large percentage of the committee's members (37.5 percent) were from high-status groups such as medical doctors, lawyers, university professors, engineers, managers, pharmacists, and journalists.[67]

Similar data on the occupational and educational backgrounds of those who identified with the IAFP were derived from a randomly selected national representative sample of 1,169 Jordanians in 1999. Supporters of the IAFP tended to be more educated and of higher professional status than those who had no party preference. Table 13.2 shows the distribution of IAFP supporters by occupation. Professionals, technicians, associate professionals, legislators, senior officials, and service, shop, and sales workers were among those most likely to support the IAFP. This finding is consistent with the data on the occupational backgrounds of the leaders of the IAFP. One slight anomaly is that craft and related trade workers are represented somewhat less frequently among the IAFP supporters than among people with no party preference (10.64 percent versus 12.24 percent), which could mean the craft and trade workers were less politically active than workers in high occupational categories. This pattern may be due to the fact that many craft and trade workers tend to locate in traditional and conservative urban areas where people are more

Table 13.1. Political party affiliation and identification in Jordan in 1995, 1997, and 1998

	1995 (N = 2,000)	1997 (N = 973)	1998 (N = 1,306)
Affiliation with political parties:			
Respondents who were members of any party at any time	2.2	1.0	1.3
Respondents who were current members of any party	1.1	0.3	0.4
Respondents who were current members of the IAFP	0.5	0.4	0.2
Intention to join a political party:			
Respondents intending to join any political party	1.9	1.4	2.7
Respondents intending to join the IAFP	0.6	0.4	0.8
Party representation of political, social, and economic aspirations:			
Respondents whose views are most closely represented by the IAFP	11.4	5.8	9.4
Respondents whose views are most closely represented by other political parties	7.1	2.9	6.4
Respondents whose views are not closely represented by any party	81.5	91.3	84.2
Awareness of the IAFP:			
Respondents who mentioned the IAFP when asked, "Have you heard of any political party?"	42.6	28.1	26.2
Respondents who recognized the IAFP from a list of parties	34.6	33.9	41.0
TOTAL	77.2	62.0	67.2

Source: Public Opinion Surveys, Center for Strategic Studies, University of Jordan. Compiled by Tony Sabbagh.
Note: Figures are percentages of the total sample.

religious than the rest of the population. In table 13.2, the craft and trade workers who identified with a party unanimously supported the IAFP.

Table 13.3 summarizes the educational distribution of those who identified with the IAFP, other political parties, and no party. According to this table, people with intermediate or higher diplomas were among the most likely supporters of any political party, including the IAFP.

Table 13.2. Party representation of political, social, and economic aspirations in Jordan, by occupation

Occupation	Political Party Best Representing Respondent's Aspirations				Difference between IAFP and "No Party" (percentage)
	IAFP		No Party		
	Number	Percentage	Number	Percentage	
Members of the military	0	0.00	21	6.27	−6.27
Legislators, senior officials	4	8.51	14	4.18	4.33
Professionals	10	21.28	42	12.54	8.74
Technicians, associate professionals	8	17.02	42	12.54	4.48
Clerks	3	6.38	23	6.87	−0.49
Service, shop, and sales workers	9	19.15	57	17.01	2.14
Skilled agricultural and fishery workers	1	2.13	22	6.57	−4.44
Craft and related trade workers[a]	5	10.64	41	12.24	−1.60
Plant and machine operators	3	6.38	42	12.54	−6.16
Elementary occupations	3	6.38	24	7.16	−0.78
Unspecified	1	2.13	7	2.09	0.04
TOTAL	47	100.00	335	100.00	0

Source: Public Opinion Poll Unit, Center for Strategic Studies, University of Jordan, 1999.
Note: Sample size = 1,169.
[a]Craft and trade workers cited either the IAFP or no party as representing their aspirations; none cited other parties.

The Secularization of the Muslim Brothers

The new political pluralism and a weak social basis of support combined to move the MB in a secular direction. On the one hand, participation in electoral politics was contingent upon the acceptance of the national charter. That document was meant to guarantee individual liberty and check the government's arbitrary power, but it also prohibited revolutionary politics that sought an alternative to the constitution. On the other hand, success in electoral politics is based on the ability of a party to garner the most votes. Insofar as the Brothers were unable to win the majority, they had to decide whether to remain puritanical and politically less

Table 13.3. Party representation of political, social, and economic aspirations in Jordan, by education

| Educational Level | Political Party Best Representing Respondent's Aspirations | | | | | | Difference between IAFP and Rest of Sample (percentage) | Difference between Other Parties and Rest of Sample (percentage) | Total |
| | IAFP | | Other Parties | | Rest of Sample | | | | |
	Number	Percentage	Number	Percentage	Number	Percentage			
Illiterate	3	2.9	4	6.1	153	15.3	-12.4	-9.2	160
Able to read and write	7	6.9	2	3.0	89	8.9	-2.0	-5.9	98
Elementary	10	9.8	6	9.1	146	14.6	-4.8	-5.5	162
Preparatory	24	23.5	11	16.7	218	21.8	1.7	-5.1	253
Vocational apprenticeship	2	2.0	1	1.5	8	0.8	1.2	0.7	11
Secondary	19	18.6	19	28.8	180	18.0	0.6	10.8	218
Intermediate diploma	18	17.6	9	13.6	114	11.4	6.3	2.2	141
Bachelor's degree	14	13.7	10	15.2	76	7.6	6.1	7.6	100
Higher educational diploma	4	3.9	3	4.5	15	1.5	2.4	3.0	22
Unspecified	1	1.0	1	1.5	2	0.2	0.8	1.3	4
TOTAL	102	100.0	66	100.0	1,001	100.0	0.0	0.0	1,169

Source: Public Opinion Poll Unit, Center for Strategic Studies, University of Jordan, 1999.
Note: Sample size = 1,169.

influential or form political alliances with other groups and thus appear ideologically compromised. In Jordan, ideological inflexibility may diminish a party's popular support because considerations independent of ideology affect voting.

According to table 13.4, three of the most important factors in electing a candidate were the services the candidate rendered to his district (31.7 percent), his ability to air his view courageously (24.3 percent), and his academic qualifications (24.3 percent)—together 80.3 percent of the total. Only 12.9 percent of the voters considered the candidate's program and compatibility with their ideas the most important factors affecting their votes.

Jordan's shift to democracy was an opportunity for political participation that the MB fully exploited, but at the same time it unleashed a process that directed the religious movement toward secularization. This process was reflected in the double process of organizational differentiation and the rationalization of religious discourse. The first process involved the division of labor between the MB and the IAFP; the second refers to a change in the basis of legitimacy from appeal to the *shari'a* to appeal to the electorate.

Organizational Differentiation

The foundation of the IAFP resolved the legal problem the MB faced under the Political Parties Law of 1992. The pragmatic division of labor between the IAFP and the MB was unique in the history of the Islamic movement in Jordan, having far-reaching implications for the Brothers' view of the connections between the political and spiritual realms. The MB leadership preferred to remain an Islamic charity

Table 13.4. Most important factors affecting voters' decisions in the 1993 parliamentary elections in Jordan

Candidate's Characteristic	Number of Respondents Influenced by Characteristic	Percentage
Kinship	41	4.6
Political affiliation	22	2.5
Programs	57	6.4
Academic qualifications	150	16.7
Services rendered to his district	284	31.7
Ability to air his views courageously	218	24.3
Compatibility with respondent's ideas	58	6.5
Other considerations	23	2.6
Unspecified	44	4.9
TOTAL	897	100.0

Source: Public Opinion Poll Unit, Center for Strategic Studies, University of Jordan, 1993.

organization and not to become a political party subject to this law. As a solution, they decided to form the IAFP in a coalition with other Islamic political parties. The IAFP was exclusively concerned with politics, and the MB avoided being transformed into a political party. The MB continued carrying out its functions in professional associations, communities, and mosques, where it was predominantly concerned with social issues and reforming society through its calling (da'wa) and promoting a puritan ethic among individuals. In electoral competitions, the MB devoted all its social and organizational resources to the support of IAFP candidates. The Brothers thus appeared to have it both ways. On the one hand, as a religious organization, they were not subject to the Political Parties Law, which would have required it to disclose its sources of finance.[68] Their aim was to preach among the public in order to purify and Islamize society, and many members considered this to be a form of political work "from below." On the other hand, the IAFP used its mandate and parliamentary gains as a means to attain its Islamic objectives "from above."

The IAFP was a practical admission of the necessity of separating religious from political affairs. In his interview with the *Star*, Ishaq Farhan said, "the Islamic Action Front Party is an independent political party. It is independent administratively, financially and organizationally. The Muslim Brotherhood deals with Islam in general, and we are dealing with politics according to the Constitution, according to the law of the political parties, like other political parties in the country."[69] He also held that Islam and democracy were compatible, democratic values had roots in Islam, and "Western democracy could be shaped to the needs of the Islamic community and I think many of the values in democracy as applied in Jordan and [the values] in Islam as applied in the *Shura* concept have very much in common."[70]

The MB leadership, however, insisted on the unity of religion and politics. Abdul Majid Thunibat, the MB's comptroller general, stated that "the Muslim Brotherhood derives its legitimacy from Islam, which does not separate religion from politics and it has not stopped practicing political activities since 1946. . . . Islam is a religion and a state, a Koran and a sword."[71] From this viewpoint, the establishment of the IAFP was justified on practical grounds, that is, the Political Parties Law and the uncertainty of democracy in Jordan. For Hamazah Mansour, a member of the IAFP's executive bureau, the division of labor between the IAFP and the MB was

> rooted in the sociopolitical reality of Jordan. First, we cannot assume that democracy has a strategic value. I mean in the sense that it exists forever. Today we have democracy, tomorrow we may have martial law, and all political parties are shut down. Therefore, we need to have the MB, which is not a political party, to continue our religious work. Second, as a political party, the IAFP has a framework for Islamic activities within the existing party laws. By

law, we cannot discriminate against any Jordanian who wants to become a member of our party. Even a non-Muslim Jordanian can join the party. Third, there is, however, a division of labor between the MB and the IAFP. The MB activities are educational and directed toward individual self-improvement and jihad. The IAFP, on the other hand, is oriented toward political activities.[72]

Mansour's rationale is understandable. Nevertheless, if the IAFP is to remain an independent political party, as Farhan stated, and the MB an independent religious organization, the MB leadership must come to terms with the theological implications of this division of labor, either by modifying its Islamic conception of politics or by openly questioning the sovereignty of the parliament. Assuming that pluralism in Jordan will continue to develop and expand, the MB cannot have it both ways.

Rationalization of Religious Discourse: The Appeal to the Shari'a versus the Appeal to the Electorate

In addition to the organizational differentiation, there were changes in the manner in which the Brothers justified their political positions. These changes entailed a move away from a Shari'a-based deductive logic to inductive reasoning based on the dynamics of political debates over the concrete issues facing Jordanians. This process may be observed in the debates surrounding the actions of the MB's representatives in the Eleventh Parliament, the 1993 elections, and the boycott of the 1997 elections.

The Aftermath of the 1989 Elections

Following their success in the 1989 elections, the activists of the IAFP and the MB faced the difficult task of deciding how to address the economic problems of Jordan, on the one hand, and the question of whether the democratic framework set by the regime was, in the final analysis, acceptable to them. Their puritanism rather than the significance of concrete issues decided their politics. As a result, their representatives in parliament became the subject of ridicule by their rivals when they suggested that fathers should not be allowed to attend their daughters' functions in school because the mixing of the sexes was prohibited in Islam, or that the government should implement measures to stop the distribution, sale, and consumption of alcoholic beverages. The fourteen-point list the MB submitted to Prime Minister Mudar Badran (1982–91) as conditions for joining the government reflected what Ibrahim Gharaibih termed "a romantic vision of politics." "They included," said the *Jordan Times* reporter Francesca Ciriaci, "demands for enforcing Sharia . . . , including amending all legislation contradicting it, restoring personal funds deposited abroad in order to finance development projects and banning

alcohol sales to Muslims. . . . These actions alarmed many Jordanians, long accustomed to liberal policies and social tolerance."[73]

The Aftermath of the 1993 Elections

Political power often tends to muddle and distort rational processes of discursive
change. It is not simply that power distorts discourse to serve its interests. Power
also intervenes in the interaction between the processes of discursive formation and
practical experience. The Jordanian regime's manipulation of electoral laws and
enactment of new laws is a case in point. The most controversial piece of legislation the government implemented, allegedly to curb the MB's electoral success in
1989, was the one-person, one-vote law.[74] According to the interior minister, the
justification for this law was that "every one is equal. This law addressed the problem of inequality in the number of candidates the electorates could vote for in different districts. Before this law, in one district, people could vote for as many as
nine candidates, while in another district, for only one. This was not fair. The one-
person, one-vote law rectified this problem."[75] The critics, on the other hand,
argued that this law could not work under the prevailing condition that the number of parliamentary seats assigned for each electoral district was disproportionate
to its demographic weight.[76] The amendments to the 1993 Press and Publications
Law, which required weeklies to have a minimum paid-up capital of JD300,000
(around $440,000) was considered another legal hurdle that the government had
thrown in the way of political parties.[77]

These restrictive measures, imposed by a politically calculating government to
undermine the influence of opposition parties, introduced a new element into the
process of discursive change. The IAFP leaders, instead of blaming their fundamentalism in the Eleventh Parliament as the cause of their failure in the 1993 elections, blamed the government's laws and regulations. As a result, the organization's
resources were mobilized to change the government (i.e., the external conditions of
the movement) rather than the movement's discourse (which was probably equally
responsible for its shortcomings).[78]

The Government's Arbitrariness, Tourism, and the 1997 Boycott

The government's undemocratic practices prompted the MB and other opposition
parties to boycott the 1997 elections.[79] Participation of the Brothers in the boycott was
based on the realization that, given the governmental restrictions, the chances of their
electoral success were considerably diminished. It was also a move to repair the
Brothers' status in society, which was degraded by the charge that they had always been
the uncritical admirers of the regime. Nevertheless, the MB's avowed reasons for boy-
cotting the elections, far from being idealistic and religiously extremist, were based on
concrete concerns that were also shared by virtually all other opposition parties.

In the MB's statement of July 13, 1997, the appeal was no longer to the shari'a or the Quranic injunctions on immoral social behavior. It was rather to the degeneration of democracy and the rule of law between 1993 and 1997. The statement criticized the "one-person, one-vote" law; pointed to "a marked increase in arbitrary and unjustified arrests" by government security forces; alleged the prevalence of "administrative and financial corruption" at the highest levels; attacked "the Wadi Arab treaty" with the "Zionist State" that endangered Jordan's "existence, identity, sovereignty, independence and power"; testified to a sharp deterioration in economic conditions and to the danger of Zionist domination because "the laws that prohibit selling real estate to the Israeli enemies were abolished and new laws and decisions were issued to facilitate their ownership of the economic establishments"; questioned the domination of the executive authority over the judiciary; and criticized the government's cultural policies oriented toward normalization with the "Zionist Enemy" and a "weakening of the Islamic religious guidance."[80]

The Brothers' thinking on the inefficacy of electoral politics under governmental authoritarianism was indicative of their political refinement and departure from the more rigid fundamentalism of the earlier period. It also represented a noticeable shift in their discourse from symbolism and figurative behavior that were constructed in accordance with Islam (e.g., prohibition against both mixing of the sexes and alcohol consumption) to a realistic assessment of the concrete issues facing Jordanian society. More crucial and beyond the immediate political exigencies, the involvement of the MB in sociopolitical debates during the political pluralism of the 1990s had caused a more subtle change in the general sociopolitical and theological views of the prominent members of the MB. These changes were reflected in new attitudes toward such significant issues as (1) Islamic jurisprudence and an Islamic conception of knowledge versus Western science, (2) the duality of dar ul-Islam versus dar ul-harb and the issue of jihad, (3) the Western civilized order and the relationship between Islam and civilization, (4) the relationship between religion and politics, and (5) women and polygamy.

The views of the Brothers on Islamic jurisprudence, the duality of dar ul-Islam versus dar ul-harb, and Western civilization departed from Islamic orthodoxy and traditionalism. They also contained elements of modernity by displaying an orientation toward the rationalization of religious dogma. For Farhan, the shari'a provided only the general principles to guide mankind. "The more specific details of how to go about building the proper social order should be worked out within the specific historical context of the Islamic movement itself." Through the interaction between theory and practice, in his view, the movement would be able to "develop Islamic guidelines on the emerging problems of social life." Naturally, in his view, the gate of ijtihad was not closed and should not have been considered closed. No one can close the gate of independent reasoning within the general Islamic framework. Like all Islamic thinkers, Farhan believed that the Quran "encourages and directs the human mind to discover natural and social laws."[81]

The MB did not adhere to this orthodox methodology. With regard to *how* a consensus is to be formed (an issue about which Islamic orthodoxy was astonishingly silent), the MB adopted the method of modern political parties. Consensus was replaced by the ruling of the majority of the members of the shura council. While the presence of different trends within the MB was acknowledged and accepted, "all members and trends are obliged to kneel to the resolutions of the shura council and its executive bureau. In its deliberation, the shura council of course considers all the trends within our movement and adapts Islam to current situations."[82] The legitimacy of the Brothers' ruling was thus derived from the religious orientation of the members and not directly from the shari'a. This is because there was nothing Islamic in the *procedures,* and if a ruling turned to be Islamic, it was only because the individual members were devout Muslims. Insofar as one was concerned with the procedure for arriving at a collective ruling, the MB had little religiously based leverage to question the legitimacy of parliamentary rule.

On regional and international issues, the leaders of the Islamic movement had abandoned the traditional Islamic division of the world based on the opposition of dar ul-Islam and dar ul-harb. For them, this dichotomy had little relevance to the reality of the contemporary world. It was now obsolete. Again, according to Farhan, "this distinction is historical because in the past Muslims inhabited one place and non-Muslims another. Back then, it made sense to think of a place as being exclusively the abode of Islam. But now it does not make much sense to divide the world in terms of this duality. There are many Muslims who live in America. They are American citizens."[83] The Brothers held diverse attitudes on the West, ranging from a qualified appreciation of its material advancement to a straightforward condemnation of its social system. For Farhan, lack of spirituality was the major problem of the West. The West would be a better place if it adopted Islam:

> The issue is not replacing Western civilization with Islam. Once, this religion, uniquely, had a civilization of its own that contributed a lot to Western civilization including the advancement of science and scientific experimentation. There is no doubt that Western civilization has advanced. We appreciate its material aspects. We have a duty to cooperate with the West and learn from it, but we should not borrow or approve all its values. I do not think that the West believes that it has advanced because of Christianity or secularity. Nor do I believe that Muslims are backward because of Islam. Certainly, there are objective reasons for our backwardness such as, for example, Western

colonialization and the plundering of our resources by the West. . . . However, I think that Islam has a lot to offer to the Western world, and if it adopts Islamic values, it will fill the gaps created by its materialism and it will be perfect.[84]

Thunibat, on the other hand, had a rather apocalyptic forecast for the future of Western society, the United States in particular. The breakdown of the former Soviet Union, in his view, was not the triumph of democracy and market capital-ism. It was an instance of the downfall of the spiritless materialistic system to be followed by the destruction of American civilization. In his view, "the white man's civilization cannot continue because of its materialistic values and spiritual vacuity. It will destroy itself or will find someone to destroy it. We have already seen how materialistic competitions and spiritual hollowness brought down the communist system in Russia. The same is going to happen to American civilization. Like the Russian system, it will be destroyed from inside. This destruction is not farfetched. It is imminent."[85]

If the duality of dar ul-Islam versus dar ul-harb was obsolete, if Western scien-tific and technological progress was instructive for the construction of an Islamic society, and if Islam and democracy were congruent, then it was not altogether clear what it was in Western culture that contradicted Islam. It would be hard to justify the MB's anti-Western attitudes except on the grounds that the West supported Israel (the "Zionist enemy")[86] and was responsible for the colonial partitioning of the Arab territories. These may be good reasons for being critical of the West, but a distinctly Islamic critique that would address the inadequacy of the fundamental principles of Western society was conspicuously absent in the MB's discourse.

A clear expression of the MB's quarrel with the West revolved around the issue of women and gender relations. Western culture provided a target against which the Brothers developed and defended their conception of womanhood. The more conservative members of the MB displayed nothing new in their traditionalist and patriarchal conception of gender relations. They continued to assert that the woman's principal sphere of activity was in the home under the supervision of her male guardian, that Islam required gender segregation in the public arena, and that polygamy was a legitimate Islamic institution.[87] Nevertheless, the reasoning behind this conception was derived not from the shari'a but from the undesirability of "decadent" Western culture as a model for Jordan. Especially before the 1989 democratization, admonishing the public on the Western cultural "assault" on women was the central feature of the Brothers' discourse on women. In her study, Lisa Taraki provides ample evidence of the MB's position on this issue, citing the view of a female member of the Brothers: "The young Muslim woman could not resist [the Western cultural assault]. She began to imitate the Western woman, and went out of her home dressed but naked . . . under the pretext of liberation. She insisted on competing with men in all fields of life, claiming equality with them. But what was the result of all this? The woman was the one to lose. She lost the protective shadow of her home; she gained materially but lost her dignity. . . . But then came this sweeping tide, a call for a return to the pure spring, to Islam. A call for the return of the Muslim woman to her kingdom at home!"[88] In another statement, women were portrayed as objects of desire and their sexual attractiveness as their principal asset. The mixing of the sexes (*ikhtilat*) and going bareheaded and exposed (*sufur*) were condemned because they would give away women's principal asset: "Despite the intelligence of the gentle sex, its members have not woken to the fact that beautiful women are in the minority. So how did the majority prefer *al-sufur*, since inasmuch as it makes the beautiful few more attractive it detracts from the desirability of the ordinary many. . . . How do the less beautiful accept *al-sufur*, since it does nothing but rob them of the capital in the hearts of men, a capital generated by the *hijab* [veiling]? How do they accept that the more beautiful add this capital to their already large wealth?"[89]

In the post-1989 period, the Brothers exhibited a less restrictive view of women's social functions, although they did not question polygamy. The IAFP's platform called for "respecting women, their legitimate rights and their role in the development of society within the framework of Islamic virtues; and giving women access to participate in public life, and broadening the role of women's leadership in political life."[90] Farhan, the IAFP leader, stated that "the Front believes in the ability of women to assume all posts excepts for that of "head of state" (*Hakim 'Aam*). Thus, the Front does not oppose women becoming ministers, deputies or judges."[91] Even the MB's recent rationale for barring women from the organization was based on security concerns, not religion.[92]

Where the Brothers showed a marked departure from traditionalism and approach toward modernity was over the issue of democracy and the relationship between religion and politics. Some MB members contemplated the problem of how to reconcile the parliamentary principle of rational law with the principle of deriving the law from the shari'a. They asserted that a distinction should be made between democracy as a philosophy and democracy as a method. Islam is inimical to democracy because, said Muhammad Uwaideh, a leading member of the IAFP, "In democracy, the people are the reference or arbitrator, but in Islam, it is the Sharia (religious law) which is the reference or the arbitrator. In Islam, the people cannot either directly or through their representatives, endorse what the Sharia has prohibited or prohibit what the Sharia has endorsed. I believe that the criticism of democracy by Islamists focuses on democracy as a philosophy. . . . As for the methods and forms of democracy, they differ from one country to another. Generally speaking, these methods and forms do not contradict with Islam, as each country has its own way of expression and practice."[93]

This distinction, however, created political problems for the MB. Critics questioned its commitment to democracy because, in the final analysis, the Brothers were not really interested in establishing the rule of law. They were rather advocating legality within some form of theocracy. For example, Muhammad Ibn Mahfouz, the professor of Islamic studies at the University of Tunis, criticized Uwaideh because, in his view

> he [Uwaideh] decided, without reviewing the most important values and principles upon which democracy is based, that it is contradictory to Islamic jurisprudence, because the reference or arbitrator in the case of democracy is the people, while the reference or arbitrator in Islam is God. He only discussed democracy as a mechanism of government which Islamic movements could utilize through participation and party pluralism. He also suggested that democracy is preferable to dictatorial and repressive regimes, although Islam is the best. Therefore, the author indicated that the ultimate goal is to establish an Islamic regime and that democracy is one of the mechanisms or vehicles which could be utilized to achieve this ultimate goal. In other words, the function of democracy, according to him, is transitional.[94]

Mahfouz further stated, "we do not believe that such an outlook on Islam will be helpful even to Islam itself, because all philosophical, ideological, political and social theories which could not absorb theoretical and social evolution are eventually discarded by the people."[95]

In their more recent statements, however, the Brothers have become more emphatic regarding democracy. Thunibat went so far as to say, "our shura is equal to parliamentary democracy. We do not prevent an individual from expressing that the use of alcohol is OK because it promotes tourism. But this individual being able to pass a law in this regard is quite another matter.[96] Farhan, however, boldly admitted, "our political fiqh is not mature enough because of lack of experience in the last few centuries. We should work on it and develop it."[97] This is indeed a marked departure from the revolutionary assertions of the Brothers' commitment to the finality of Islam.

Episode and Discourse: Ideology, Target, and Practice in the Islamic World

One of the major aims of this study was to demonstrate the fundamental problem of the correspondence theory of ideology in light of historical cases of ideological production in the Islamic world. The notion that the production of ideas somehow corresponds to the reality of economic conditions, social differentiations, class relations, and group interests cannot be sustained against the manner in which the discourses of Islamic modernism, liberal nationalism, Arab nationalism, and Islamic fundamentalism were produced. We could not establish a direct connection between the production of these diverse discourses and the actions of the members of the groups and social classes to expand their economic interests, political power, and cultural privileges.

There was a degree of association between social classes and ideologies, however. The rise of Islamic modernism and liberal nationalism was associated with the rise in political and social influence of the merchants and landowners, and the rise of Islamic fundamentalism and Arab nationalism with the middle class. Liberal nationalism, in particular, had a closer class connection than other ideologies discussed in this book. Across Egypt, Iran, and Syria, liberal nationalism and parliamentary politics were tied to landowners and commercial classes. Nevertheless, this class support, far from providing liberal nationalism with the dynamism and vitality to develop further and be more effectively institutionalized (as class theory dictates), ended up discrediting it by particularizing the universalistic appeal it had had during the upsurge of nationalism and nationalist revolution.

As far as the backgrounds of the ideological producers are concerned, their major sources of employment were in the state bureaucracy as high-ranking officials, judges, and schoolteachers or professors in modern institutions of higher education. Religious institutions were also an important basis for both modernist and fundamentalist intellectual leaders, particularly in Iran. Across all these countries, social classes, religious institutions, and the state each in different ways contributed to the rise of these ideological movements. Among the three, however, the state appears to have played the most important role in the genesis of these ideologies. By establishing modern educational institutions, constructing and developing modern means of transportation and communication, and expanding its bureaucratic administrative organization, the modern state contributed to the creation of employment opportunity for ideological producers, the formation of networks among them, and the development of the institutional framework that helped them formulate and disseminate ideas. This fact further corroborates Wuthnow's finding on the centrality of the state in the formation of communities of discourses.

None of these social factors, however, explains how these diverse discourses were produced and their sociopolitical orientation took shape. For one thing, people with the same class backgrounds supported different ideologies in different historical episodes. To give one prominent example, the Iranian merchants of the bazaar were among the main supporters of constitutionalism and then liberal nationalism, but in the second half of the twentieth century they were among the major supporters of the religious opposition movement that overthrew the monarchy in 1979. Certainly, the bazaaris of the Constitutional Revolution were individuals different from the bazaaris of the sixties and the seventies, who supported the religious opposition. But what made them different was factors other than the nature of their vocation and even its physical site, which remained by and large invariant. People with the same class background even supported alternative (or even opposing) ideologies at a given historical juncture. Such was the case in Syria before the First World War, when a faction of the urban notables was in favor of Ottomanism while another faction supported Arab nationalism. Both Islamic fundamentalism and radical Arab nationalism were supported by middle-class individuals. Likewise, state expansion benefited people with diverse or even opposing ideological orientations. For example, the expansion of the state's bureaucracy in different ways benefited the harbingers of Islamic modernism, liberal nationalism, Arab nationalism, and Islamic fundamentalism. Therefore, it may not be possible to establish a correspondence between these ideological movements and the attributes of a class or the state.

For another thing, even in historically narrower and limited cases in which the support of a class for a given ideological movement can be clearly established, it is still hard to connect class dynamics to specific ideas directly. Even though liberal nationalism in both Egypt and Iran was supported by landowners and merchants, it is altogether unclear how the interests and desires of these people may have prompted the intellectual leaders, say, in Egypt to emulate Western ideas on secularism and nationalism and glorify ancient Egypt of the Pharaonic period or their counterparts in Iran to seek the key to Iran's progress in anticlerical secularism, anti-Arab Persianism, and the glorification of the country's ancient history. It is even more difficult to tie Islamic modernist or fundamentalist ideas to class interests. What further complicates making a causal inference from the connections between class and ideology is that class action did not always precede the rise of ideology. The rise of Egyptian dominant classes did not precede the rise of modern ideas in that country. In fact, the transformation of social relations and the rise of new social classes often went hand in hand with cultural change. It appears that the members of the politically weighty classes and the ruling elite contributed as much to the constitution of ideas as ideas contributed to their constitution as a notable or a political elite with certain "rights" and "responsibilities."

Episode and Discourse

The foregoing narrative revealed a historical pattern that was different from the pattern predicted by correspondence theory. Insofar as the generation of ideas is conceived as something that is produced, not inevitable, and that would require social resources to be produced and a social space to grow, our study supports Wuthnow's thesis on the significance of economic development and the mediating role of the state. To the extent that ideological production is conceived of as an outcome of debates, contrasting positions, conflict, and disagreements over a relatively small set of issues, our analysis of the origins of Islamic modernism, liberal nationalism, Arab nationalism, and fundamentalism supports Collins's model of intellectual creativity. We contend, however, that the episodic discourse model advanced in this book explains more fully how ideas are produced and how their social or political orientations take shape.

This study supports the notion that ideological production is a discontinuous process that proceeds in an episodic fashion. We contend that Islamic modernism, liberal nationalism, Arab nationalism, and Islamic fundamentalism were all in a broad sense the product of social transformations. However, the cultural change brought about by these transformations was not consistently and continuously connected to such objective changes as economic development, demographic expansion, social differentiation, and class and group formation. The setting for cultural change was structured by dramatic events or a conjuncture of historical events that interrupted the continuity of social life. These events had substantial impacts on the worldviews of culture producers. The swift reorganization of social life and rearrangement of the order of things that these events effected contributed to the generation of a new awareness and provoked an alternative way of thinking about sociopolitical issues among the intellectual leaders.

The rise of Islamic modernism in India followed the Sepoy Mutiny of 1857–59. The modern era in Egypt began after the Napoleonic invasion of the country in 1798–1801. Serious attempts at bridging Shi'ism and constitutionalism were made in Iran during the Constitutional Revolution of 1905–11. The Urabi rebellion (1879–82) and the subsequent British occupation of Egypt set the stage for the rise of Egyptian nationalism. The crisis of 1860 in Syria and the rise of the pan-Islamic despotism of Sultan Abdülhamid II (1876–1909) were events that stimulated the development of liberal Arabism among Syrian intellectual leaders. Pan-Arab nationalism emerged during and after World War I and in response to colonial partitioning of Arab territories. The development of constitutional thought in Iran followed a series of humiliating defeats in two wars with Russia, in 1813 and 1828, and debacles in Herat in 1837 and 1856, and the rise of economic nationalism followed the forced abdication of Reza Shah in 1941. Likewise, militant Islamic fundamentalism in Algeria, Egypt, Iran, and Syria became a dominant oppositional discourse during periods that started with military coups and subsequent changes in the regimes' overall policies.

Some of these episodes displayed clearly marked beginnings and endings, while others consisted of series of closely related events. For example, the events of 1857–59 were a clear indication of a new phase in the history of the Islamic movement in India, and the period between the coup of 1953 and the revolution of 1979 marked a distinctive episode in the social history of Iran. The beginning of Islamic modernism in Egypt, on the other hand, was not so clearly marked beyond the events surrounding Napoleon's invasion of the country and the rise of Muhammad Ali to power. The rise of liberal nationalism can also be traced to a series of events beginning with the formation of the Consultative Assembly of Delegates by Khedive Ismail in 1866, the khedive's problems with European creditors, and British intervention and then occupation of the country in 1882. Likewise, the decline of liberal nationalism and the rise of supranationalist ideologies, including Islamic fundamentalism, started in the late 1930s, but the military coup of 1952 abruptly ended the constitutional monarchy and created favorable conditions for the rise of Islamic extremism in Egypt.

Despite these differences in the clarity of the historical demarcations of the beginnings of episodes, the political, cultural, and social forces within each episode were distinctively arranged, giving rise to a distinctive regime of signification. In relation to this regime of signification, alternative discourses were produced. The rise and the domination of a new system of meanings in each episode significantly affected the worldviews of the ideological producers. During the heyday of liberal nationalism and secularism, for example, there were notable Muslim intellectual leaders who changed their cultural orientation so drastically that they even abandon clerical garb, while during the period of the rise of Islamic fundamentalism many lay intellectuals discarded secular ideologies to join the ranks of the religious activists. These dramatic changes in their outlooks occurred sometimes in parallel with the changes in the material conditions of their lives and sometimes without such material changes to any significant extent.

Cross-National Variation and Historical Discontinuity in the Production of Meaning

The parameters of our explanatory models—the variation in the discursive context from pluralistic to monolithic and the variation in the state's direct intervention in culture from minimal (i.e., in an ideologically neutral state) to extensive (i.e., in an ideological state)—accounts for both cross-national and historical variation in the production of ideas. Islamic modernism in India and Egypt emerged under conditions of a pluralistic intellectual market and a minimal state intervention in culture. This was true despite the existence of major differences in social structure between India and Egypt. India was religiously nonunified, culturally heterogeneous, and densely populated and had a complex system of social stratification and a differentiated system of colonial administration. Egypt, in contrast, was religiously unified, culturally homogeneous, and much less populous and had a simpler system of social stratification and a uniform system of political administration. Yet Muslim intellectual leaders, being involved in similar intellectual markets, arrived at Islamic modernist projects that were considerably alike. The weakness of Islamic modernism in Iran was associated with the absence of a major social transformation and discursive pluralism. The contrast between Iran and Egypt is particularly illustrative given the similarities between the two countries in social structure and religious experience in the early nineteenth century. In short, dissimilar social structures and historical experiences sharing similar proximate conditions produced similar ideologies (e.g., in India and Egypt), and countries sharing comparable social structure but dissimilar proximate conditions failed to create similar ideologies (e.g., Egypt and Iran).

The differences in the liberal-nationalist ideas of Egyptian, Syrian, and Iranian intellectual leaders were also related to the differences in the discursive context and the relations of this context to the ruling regime. In Egypt, British domination was the overriding concern, while Ottoman suzerainty had lost its significance. In Syria, on the other hand, the overriding concern was precisely that suzerainty. It was thus understandable for nationalism in Egypt to be Egyptian and territorial, while in Syria it revolved around the issue of Arab ethnicity. In one case, the intellectual leaders were facing a British physical presence in and domination of Egyptian territory, and this led to Egyptian territorial nationalism. In the other case, they were facing the changing nature of Ottoman domination, and that led to the rise of the Arabist identity. Repression under the Ottoman Empire also contributed to the development of pro-British attitudes among the Syrian émigrés in Egypt. In Iran, in contrast, the issue of foreign power was less significant than attempts to curb the ulama's power and monarchical absolutism. Iranian revolutionaries even used the British legation as a site for the sit-in that eventually forced the shah to ratify the Fundamental Law of the Constitution. Iran, like Egypt, experienced anti-British nationalism in the twentieth century; here again, the nature of this nationalism was related to the nature of British domination. In contrast with Egyptian territorial nationalism, the British control of Iran's oil industry gave rise to economic nationalism.

The similarities in Islamic fundamentalism across Algeria, Egypt, Iran, and Syria were also associated with similarities in the political and discursive context within which it emerged. Although these countries had considerable differences in history, culture, political structures, and the type of international alignment in which their regimes were involved, they astonishingly shared a comparable set of proximate conditions that promoted the rise of Islamic fundamentalism. All these regimes were intrusive, implemented a series of secular reforms, heavily intervened in the economy, and had extensive bureaucratic organizations. At the same time, all were authoritarian, and political power was personalized and often identified with the ruler. These regimes were also ideologically secular. A secular outlook was crafted to fit various forms of radical Arab nationalism and socialism in Algeria, Egypt, and Syria, and to fit the monarchy-centered nationalist discourse in Iran. The intervention of these states in religious affairs politicized religion, creating favorable conditions for the formulation of Islamic fundamentalist discourse.

Our model also explains the historical variation in ideological production in Egypt, Syria, and Iran, where we traced the process of ideological change since the nineteenth century. In Egypt, a historical sequence of Islamic modernism, territorial nationalism, moderate Islamic fundamentalism, and Islamic extremism was followed as Muslim scholars faced the diversity of discourses of the Azhar orthodoxy, the missionaries, the followers of the Enlightenment, and Westernizers in the second half of the nineteenth century; the domineering discourse of the British authorities about Egyptians' incapacity for self-rule in the decades before and after the beginning of the twentieth century; the secularist outlooks of intellectual leaders in the 1920s and 1930s; and the totalitarianism of Nassir's Arab socialism. In Syria, too, liberal Arabism, then radical Arab nationalism, and finally Islamic fundamentalism were the result of the efforts of the country's culture producers as they faced the sequence of obstacles represented by the authoritarianism of Sultan Abdülhamid, the Turkish nationalism of the Committee of Union and Progress, the French mandate and the colonial partitioning of the Arab lands, and the secular Arab socialism of the Ba'ath regime. Finally, in Iran, the change in the discourse of the intellectual leaders from anticlerical secularism and constitutionalism, to economic nationalism, and then to clergy-centered Islamic fundamentalism paralleled the change in the dominant regime of signification from monarchical absolutism and the ulama's obstructionism, to British economic domination, and then to monarchy-centered secular-nationalist discourse. These drastic cultural turns in the three countries also support our claim regarding discontinuity in the production of meaning. In all these cases, the shift from Islamic modernism to Islamic fundamentalism paralleled the change in the discursive context from intellectual pluralism to a monolithic discourse imposed from above by an intrusive secular ideological state.

Confounding Factors: Cultural Diffusion, Western Hegemony, and Modernism versus Fundamentalism

Islamic modernism and Islamic fundamentalism emerged in two different periods in world culture. In the first period, such seminal ideas as civilization, progress, evolution, and the test of civilization provided by the status of women characterized the key features of world culture. Europe was perceived as a civilized order, playing the leading role in worldwide trends toward a more humane, democratic, and prosperous society. Muslim thinkers used these ideas in formulating a modernist discourse to address the ideological obstacles facing their faith. In the second period, Western liberalism was challenged by such radical ideologies as communism, Fascism, and Nazism in Europe. While Fascism and Nazism produced their counterparts in various Islamic countries, it was communism that had the greatest influence on the thinking of culture producers. The rise of the international communist movement backed by the mighty propaganda machine of the socialist countries contributed to the change in the image of the West from a democratic and civilized order to an imperialistic system. The image of the West viewed according to the imperialism paradigm was that of an exploitative economic institution, decadent social order, and aggressive political system—all diametrically opposed to the features for which the Islamic modernists applauded the West. The Western support for dictatorial regimes in less developed countries naturally reinforced this image.

In the first period, the West enjoyed undisputed hegemony; in the second period, this hegemony was in a serious jeopardy. Is it possible that Islamic modernism was entirely shaped by the conditions of Western cultural dominance? Where it was strongest, notably in Egypt and India, was that not because these countries were under direct British colonial rule? Can it be that the overthrow of foreign rule and the decline of Western power in Muslim lands provided a favorable condition for the rise of Islamic fundamentalism? Insofar as Western hegemony means the popularity of the Enlightenment among Muslim intellectuals, this study in fact supports the notion that it shaped cultural movements in the Islamic world. If, on the other hand, the invocation of the role of Western hegemony in the production of discourse in Islamic countries is meant to tie Islamic modernism (and liberal nationalism) to various forms of power emanating from the West, without which this movement would not have emerged, this study questions the connection.

The intellectual leaders of Islamic modernism were not naive theoreticians incapable of understanding the reality of Western domination. They were aware of the aggressive nature of European powers and often criticized European intervention in the domestic affairs of their countries. Their worldviews, however, were shaped by the reality that they immediately faced. This reality included a degree of economic development and political stability, institutional support for intellectual activities, and a pluralistic intellectual context with minimal state intervention in cultural debates. These conditions directed Muslim thinkers, who also had interests of their own in reproducing conditions favorable to their intellectual activities, to engage in ideological reflection and abstraction in dealing with the multitude of issues raised by other contenders for the intellectual control of their society. Naturally, these thinkers preferred a moderate, reformist, and gradualist approach in addressing social problems. Their criticisms of the West notwithstanding, insofar as they believed in the civilized and progressive nature of the West—the dynamic nature of its science and technology, its democratic politics, the equality of its citizens, and its favorable treatment of women—in the final analysis their worldviews were still part of the same ideological universe that constituted Western societies. It was no accident that such modernist Muslim thinkers as Muhammad Abduh criticized al-Afghani for his preoccupation with politics, or that the reformist ulama in French Algeria found it in the interest of their movement to accept the principle of the separation of religion and politics.

The reality that Muslim intellectual leaders faced in intrusive secular ideological states was quite different. This reality was the control of cultural and sociopolitical affairs by state officials and secular ideologues. Educational institutions having been transformed into the state's instrument of indoctrination, Muslim intellectual leaders had no choice but to go underground. Under continued surveillance and the threat of arbitrary arrest and imprisonment, on the one hand, and the necessity of resisting the state's indoctrination, on the other, these leaders had little space for a systematic reflection in order to formulate a transcendental religious doctrine. The urgency of political struggle inadvertently resulted in the creation of an ideological system that became the mirror image of the state ideology.

It could be argued, however, that these interpretations are simply a logical reconstruction of the historical process of cultural change and cannot discount the significance of the Western presence in fostering the development of modern discourses in the Islamic world. To overcome this criticism, we consider Jordanian exceptionalism and the development of reformist movement in postrevolutionary Iran. These two cases demonstrate the emergence of different types of modernist discourse under the conditions specified by our model but in a historical context different from the conditions of nineteenth-century Western hegemony. Both cases show the development of new discourses which entailed the employment of rational analysis, the use of secular reasoning by Muslim thinkers cum political activists, and some sort of implicit recognition of the reality of secular politics.

Jordanian Exceptionalism and the Secularization
of the Islamic Movement

By demonstrating that the sociopolitical and cultural dynamics that explain the difference between Islamic modernism and fundamentalism also explain the contrast between Jordan, on the one hand, and Algeria, Egypt, Iran, and Syria, on the other, this study has attempted to discount the significance of Western powers in *directly* fostering the development of Islamic modernism in India and Egypt. Our contention was that it was the intellectual pluralism of the late nineteenth century that directly contributed to this development, not the reality of the Western presence in these countries.

We observed the secularization of the Jordanian Islamic movement in the 1989–97 period. This was reflected in the twin process of (1) organizational differentiation between the Society of the Muslim Brothers and the Islamic Action Front Party and (2) the move from the appeal to the shari'a to the appeal to the electorate in formulating policies. To be sure, in this period the Society of the Muslim Brothers in Jordan still had considerable similarities to its counterparts in Egypt and Syria, and broadly with the Islamic fundamentalist movements in other Islamic countries. It believed in the unity of religion and politics, which entailed the rejection of the secular order, questioned the modern conception of gender relations, and presented a critical, if not hostile, attitude toward the West. Although it has always maintained a politically moderate orientation, having a fairly peaceful relationship with the Hashemites, the movement as a whole has certainly been different from the Islamic modernism of the late nineteenth century. Moreover, the leaders of the Jordanian Muslim Brothers have not only failed to elaborate the implications of this development for the nature of the teachings of Islam on sociopolitical issues, but denied this change or its significance for their religious movement as well.

Nevertheless, given the turn toward extremism, political violence, and revolution in the Islamic movements of other countries, the change in the opposite direction in the Jordanian movement has both historical and theoretical significance for understanding how the nature of the intellectual market and the relation of this market to power shape the worldview and political orientation of a religious movement. We have attempted to connect this change to the nature of the Hashemite regime and its role in cultural and religious affairs. In contrast with the regimes of Algeria, Egypt, Iran, and Syria, the Jordanian regime remained nonideological and heterogeneous in the sense that different apparatuses of the states were connected to different, often contradictory, discourses. The state ideology reflected Arab nationalism, Islamic conservatism, tribal patrimonialism, pre-Islamic glorification, and Western modernism. Because of this very diversity, the state appeared to be different things to different segments of the Jordanian population. The cultural

orientation of the Hashemite regime was far from the rigid ideological predisposi-
tions of the regimes of Algeria, Egypt, Iran, and Syria.

Whether the change in the Jordanian Islamic movement will stimulate reflective thought and theoretical abstraction, resulting in a serious reexamination of
its worldview and the development of a full-blown Islamic modernist discourse,
depends on the persistence of political stability, economic development, institutional support, and a further development of culture. Certainly, the formulation of
a more abstract and transcendental discourse may require years of reflection and
research by the intellectual leaders of the movement—all these are contingent upon
both political stability and the availability of resources. One thing is clear: 1989–97
was a period of political stability marked by the prospect of peaceful settlement of
the Israeli-Palestinian conflict. The breakdown of the peace process, the intensification of the Israeli-Palestinian conflict, and the need for the Jordanian government
to maintain a cordial relationship with the West might have affected the nature of
the political context in Jordan and, at one remove, the worldview of the Islamic
movement. What form the future Islamic movement in the country will take and
what its specific sociopolitical message will be are hard to predict. If the democratization process is continued and if the country manages to maintain a degree of
political stability and economic development, it is logical to expect the move
toward modernity in the Islamic movement to gain increasing momentum.

The Religious State and Counterideology:
Secular Islam in Postrevolutionary Iran

The emergence of a strong reformist movement in postrevolutionary Iran is yet
another prominent example of the connection between a pluralistic political structure and the development of an Islamic modernist discourse in a sociopolitical
context quite different from nineteenth-century India and Egypt. It also lends
credibility to our argument regarding the dialogic nature of the interaction between
state ideology and the development of oppositional discourse. In chapters 9–12, we
contended that the secularism of the intrusive ideological state in Algeria, Egypt,
prerevolutionary Iran, and Syria was the key factor in the development of Islamic
fundamentalist discourse. Postrevolutionary Iran demonstrated the other side of
this equation in that the fundamentalism of the Islamic Republic had a secularizing effect on the discourse of the opposition movement.

Far from transcending the narrow ideological boundaries of the Pahlavis, the
Islamic Republic imposed a system of religious rules on society that rested on a particular, not universal, understanding of the shari'a. During the revolutionary period
of 1977–79, Islam transcended social differences among the participants in com-
munitarian relations. The universalism of the Islamic revolutionary discourse, however, did not mean that there was a shared understanding of the nature of the

postrevolutionary government, the social status of women, the sociopolitical function of religion, or the country's relationship with the outside world. It was universal precisely because it meant different things to different people. The political unity that was attained during the revolutionary movement was produced by a factor external to Islam: as long as the Shah, i.e., the common enemy, was present, diverse Islamic groups were united and the Islamic alternative to the ideology of the monarchy seemed uniform and consistent.[1] This unity, however, proved ephemeral and fleeting, and when concrete plans about the nature of the postrevolutionary regime emerged, disputes replaced harmony.

This is not to argue that Islam was incapable of furnishing a set of universal concepts to build a national consensus about Iran's postrevolutionary society. It would certainly have been possible for Ayatollah Khomeini and his associates to follow the project of the Islamic modernists of the earlier period, showing a more positive orientation toward democracy and rational rule making, a more egalitarian attitude toward gender relations, a less belligerent attitude toward the West, and a more inclusive understanding of Islam. Instead, they took a fundamentalist orientation. Through effective and large-scale repression of the opposition, they established a theocracy based on the governance of the jurisprudent. The ruling clerics attempted to transform the institution of Shi'ism into a monolithic religion controlled and guided by the state through the absolute power of the spiritual leader. They brought all the educational institutions under the government's control to promote the ethic and morality of their revolutionary Shi'ism. The mixing of the sexes was prohibited, and the universities and governmental offices were reorganized to ensure gender segregation. An Islamic dress code was imposed. Men were discouraged from wearing certain clothes, and women were not allowed to be seen public without the veil or their heads covered. Nor were they permitted to wear bright-colored dresses in public (appropriate colors being brown, black, blue, and gray). The moral police rigorously enforced the observance of the government's codes of conduct. Portraits of the spiritual leader replaced those of the shah, and Islamic revolutionary slogans came to replace the propagandistic statements of the prerevolutionary regime in public places. The mass media turned into the organ of the state's propaganda machine. As a result, the postrevolutionary state, far from achieving a transcendental Islamic regime, developed into an immanent ideological state.

Nevertheless, the structure and ideology of the Islamic Republic were quite different from those of Algeria, Egypt, prerevolutionary Iran, and Syria. The immanence and ideological nature of the state were moderated by a host of historical and ideological factors. Contrary to the Nassirite, Pahlavi, Ba'athist, and Boumedienne regimes, which all came to power through military coups, the Islamic Republic was an outcome of a popular revolution. The public demand for inclusion and political representation and the religious leaders' desire to establish a theocracy combined to produce a contradictory compromise in the structure of the Islamic Republic. Although considerably skewed in favor of the spiritual leader, the structural forces within the Islamic Republic were arranged in a fashion that would make the monopolization of power by the leader difficult. The personal power of Nassir, Assad, Boumédienne, and the shah appeared to have been much more extensive than that of the spiritual leader Ayatollah Ali Khamenei. There are, for example, the offices of the spiritual leader and the Constitutional Guardians versus the office of the president and the parliament, the revolutionary guards versus the army, and the religious overseers in various governmental offices versus the secular members of the civil service. The Islamic Republic, despite being an ideological regime, was an amalgam of religion and secularism. While the office of the spiritual leader derived its sovereignty from the shari'a, the presidency and the parliament derived theirs from the electorate. Further, from the religious and ideological viewpoint, we may consider the monolithic religious structure imposed from above after the revolution and defended by the office of the spiritual leader against the pluralistic historical tradition of the Shi'i ulama. The spiritual leader in Iran is not necessarily the most learned ayatollah in the country, and the most learned ayatollah in Shi'ism may not be interested in political involvement. The leaders of the Islamic Republic have thus far failed to force all the ulama to bow to the authority of the spiritual leader. Finally, the duality between the state and civil society, that is, the general conflict between the Islamic Republic and the demands of the public, particularly women and university students, for political power and inclusion generated yet another favorable context that undermined the concentration of power.

We may thus postulate that this structural and ideological pluralism may explain the rise of the current Islamic reformist movement, which has tended toward Islamic transcendentalism rather than toward fundamentalism and extremism. The reformist leaders in fact tried to occupy political positions within the pluralistic structure of the Islamic Republic in the presidential election of May 1997, the municipal elections of March 1998, the parliamentary elections of February 2000, and the runoff parliamentary elections of May 2000. We may further attribute to the dynamics of this structural and ideological pluralism the ideological reorientation of a significant group of Muslim scholars in a reformist direction. We have seen that some of the key figures leading the reformist movement were among the architects of the Islamic Republic: Abdul Karim Sorush, who is now defending Islamic democracy, was the principal theoretician of the Cultural Revolution that dismantled the institutions of secular education in the country in the early 1980s. Some of the reformist newspapers are run by activists who were involved in the anti-West demonstrations and the seizure of the U.S. embassy in Tehran. And some of the grand ayatollahs who were among the signatories of the institution of the governance of the jurisprudent are now part of the opposition, demanding political reforms. What is even more astonishing is that all these reformist groups are defending their democratic position in terms of their reading of Islam; traditional liberal democratic discourse plays only a minor role in legitimizing the demands for personal freedom and the rule of law.[2]

Power and the Production of Discourse

Political power is certainly an important factor in ideological production. The breakdown of the state-ulama alliance, the decline of the absolutist state, and the formation of the modern state were among the conditions of Islamic modernism. Among the conditions of liberalism was the weakness of monarchical absolutism, and of fundamentalism, the exclusionary policies of the intrusive secular ideological state. However, what is crucial for understanding the relation of power and discourse is not simply the reality of power or who wields the effective power. It is rather the nature of the interconnections between the power structure and the structure of the ideological market. When the realm of power and the market of ideas are differentiated from each other, that is, when power has remained within or retreated to the sphere of polity, defined by a set of procedures in terms of which the regime governs, the emergence and crystallization of historically significant issues follows the dynamic of ideological debates within the intellectual market, and the ideas being produced tend to have a social rather than a political orientation. The social function of power is thus a matter of social engineering, and the formulation of policy entails political conflict rather than ideological disputes. In this context, who actually wields effective power, while an important issue in politics, becomes secondary in the production of discourse. When, on the other hand, the use and the definition of the sphere of power of a regime intermesh with a certain discourse—that is, ideology permeates the administrative structure of the government—then the spheres of polity and culture tend to overlap. The social function of power becomes the reorganization of society according to the state's ideological blueprints. As a result, the king, the president, or the leader and every institution of the state are conjured up as the material embodiment of the regime's ideology and mission as, for example, the agent of progressive social change or the defender of peasants and workers, national emancipation, or the religious faith.

In the first case, the regime is nonimmanent, and in the second case, it is immanent.[3] An immanent regime presents itself as an organic whole; an injury to any of its constituting components is treated as an injury to the entire administrative body. To support the regime means supporting its entire body, and criticizing any aspect of the regime implies questioning its very essence and identity. The official political party is the vanguard of revolutionary change; the official media, the source of the truth; the state's strategy of economic and social development, the only way to realize national interests; and the leader himself, the essence of the

nation and protector of national independence. Questioning the party, the truth-
fulness of the state-controlled media, the state's economic policy, or the leader
would often mean questioning the entire regime. In an immanent regime, power is
everywhere.

The difference in the nature and function of power in India, Egypt, and Iran in
the late nineteenth century and in Algeria, Egypt, Iran, and Syria in the second half
of the twentieth century is one of the key factors that explains the difference between
Islamic modernism and Islamic fundamentalism. If Islamic fundamentalism had
been a reaction to Western domination and interference in the affairs of Muslim
countries, then this discourse should have emerged in the nineteenth century where
the West was dominating a large section of the Islamic world—Dutch-dominated
Indonesia, British India and Egypt, French Algeria and later Syria, and French and
Spanish Morocco. The rise of Islamic modernism under colonial domination in
many of these countries would have appeared counterintuitive and anachronistic.
Our analysis of the relation of power and the structure of the ideological market
under colonialism indicated that for Muslim intellectual leaders the question of who
had power mattered little, insofar as they could see that the problems facing their
faith and the anomalies related to their religious discipline were the result of intellectual dynamics that were outside of and unconstrained by the reality of political
power. Such appears to have been the case under British colonial rule in the late
nineteenth century. On the other hand, in the context of the secular ideological
intrusive state, where the ruling elite used power to promote a particular form of cultural and religious expression to realize its civilizational mission, intellectual leaders
opted for militant fundamentalism, as state cultural policies appeared to them mere
fabrications, a means to indoctrinate and control the public.

The immanence of the Algerian, Egyptian, Iranian, and Syrian regimes was the
key factor underpinning the generation of oppositional religious ideologies, which
were in certain crucial respect analogous to state ideology. Because under these
regimes qualified or partial opposition to the policies of the state meant total opposition, there could be only no opposition or total opposition. Because the criticism
of any aspect of an immanent state is equal to the negation of the entire regime,
oppositional ideologies unintentionally ended up developing into revolutionary
ideologies questioning the very essence of the state. (This is particularly true
because the religious oppositional movements were not initially revolutionary
movements in any of these countries.) If every aspect of the state was an embodiment of the core presupposition of the regime, the oppositional ideology branched
out to reflect the mirror image of state ideology: the state's symbolism tended
to generate opposition symbols, rituals to generate counterrituals, and totalistic
monolithic discourse to generate an equally totalistic monolithic oppositional ideology. Hence, secular nationalism, state feminism, and leader-centered discourses

led to the creation of religious fundamentalism, antifeminism, and leader-centered Islamic opposition.

Target: Something to Focus On

In their life course, ideological producers encounter a wide variety of issues, problems, events, and processes. Some of these may occur only in their particular life situations or immediate surroundings, while others are a part of the broader national or international environment. If these intellectuals were to think inductively, that is, constructing their views in terms of a careful assessment of the exigencies of social life as they experienced them individually, they would create such a wide and heterogeneous set of ideas that the intellectual field would appear chaotic and without order. This is particularly true in the history of the Islamic world in the modern period, where the intellectuals attempted to understand such major sociopolitical crises as the Napoleonic invasion of Egypt, the Indian Sepoy Mutiny of 1857–59, the crisis of 1860 in Syria, the war of independence in Algeria, the military coups in Egypt, Iran, and Syria, and the Iranian Revolution of 1979. Concepts such as a state of confusion or individual disorientation were used by intellectual leaders to describe these situations. The use of these concepts may be indicative of a lack of understanding of what was going on. They may also indicate that there were too many interpretations of the dynamics underpinning the unfolding events. How in the course of a few years did "confusion" and "disorientation" give rise to a relatively well-defined set of oppositional viewpoints? And how did the vast number of ad hoc interpretations gradually coalesced into a few manageable positions on the state of affairs?

For Collins, the development of thought involves a continued increase in the level of reflectivity and abstraction governed by the law of small number; that is, the multiplicity of ideological positions—the state of chaos and confusion—gives rise to the crystallization of a small number of carefully worked out and elaborated ideological resolutions. This may be true, but reflectivity and abstraction many not be the only mechanisms underpinning the law of small number. It is hard to attribute the rise of Islamic fundamentalism and Arab nationalism and the decline of territorial nationalism in Egypt in the forties to enhanced reflectivity and abstraction in ideological production, or the unanimity of a considerable segment of the Iranian educated elite on the formation of an Islamic system to some sort of transcendental abstraction that the ideologues of the Iranian Revolution of 1979 were able to manufacture. Further, inductive constraints (the limits that are imposed on one's expression by social forces) and deductive constraints (the organization and limitation of the thought process imposed by one's belief system) may not be enough to transform chaos into order. This is particularly true during times of crisis, when the social forces have become ineffective in constraining discourse or the belief systems have lost their validity. Besides the fact that both Islamic modernists and fundamentalists, for example, attempted, deductively, to draw from Islam, and liberal nationalists from various traditional or foreign perspectives on nation and nationalism, and that all these groups attempted, inductively, to allude to the Muslim community, the nation, and the land, it is still hard to explain the process of the formation of order in the production of discourse.

In our view, the key factor in the production of discourse is the nature of the *target* that the ideological producers encounter in their immediate sociopolitical environment. A target is an active ideological group that conveys through various means of expression—symbolic behavior, ritualistic act, written and verbal communication—certain ideas to the subject population for the intellectual control of society. The target structures chaos in the production of discourse. Contrasting targets structure social issues, and social issues mediate the relationship between ideas and the exigencies of social life and reduce the arbitrary nature of this relationship. Despite the vicissitudes of the social history of Muslim countries in the modern period, such significant issues as the status of the modern sciences vis-à-vis the Islamic sciences, the nature of political sovereignty, national identity, the status of women, and the relationship of the nation with the outside world constituted the invariant features of the cultural debates in these countries. Culture producers could have taken a wide variety of positions toward these issues. Their orientations, however, were structured by the existing ideological targets and the relations of these targets with political power. The variations in these targets were associated with the variations in their ideas. These targets reduced confusion, generated order, and framed the thought process in the production of discourse. Targets help ideological producers to stay focused.

In this book, we attempted to show the production of diverse discourses as a function of the kind of ideological targets intellectual leaders encountered in their sociopolitical environment. We began our analysis by considering the religious movements initiated by the ideas of Shah Waliallah and Muhammad Ibn Abd al-Wahhab in the eighteenth century. For them, Islamic orthodoxy and the religious rituals in vogue in their society were the immediate targets in opposition to which they formulated a reformist fundamentalist discourse. In nineteenth-century India and Egypt, the ulama had lost much of their exclusive cultural power. Such other ideological groups as missionaries, British Westernizers, and followers of the Enlightenment were also actively involved in expanding their cultural influence in society. In this diversified intellectual market, the following phenomena were apparent:

1.   The contenders formed ideological targets for one another, as the utterances of each side structured the utterances of the other.

2. The back-and-forth debates among these contenders were nonanony-
    mous, were systematic, and generated several historically significant issues,
    such as the role of the modern sciences, rational law, the social functions
    of religion, the best form of government, the status of women, and the
    nation's relationship with the outside world.

3. These issues posed serious difficulties for the Islamic belief system.

4. Muslim scholars advanced modernist resolutions of these issues. Far from
    reflecting the objective facts of social life, Islamic modernism was a dis-
    course consisting of a method of Quranic exegesis and a set of inter-
    connected positions on issues that gradually took shape as Muslim
    intellectuals debated these issues, tested the limits to their expression set
    by existing political and religious arrangements, negotiated various posi-
    tions, and reached an understanding of the acceptable Islamic resolutions
    that firmly connected their faith to modern culture.

Likewise, the variations in the ideological targets faced by liberal intellectual
leaders in Egypt, Syria, and Iran may explain the differences in their discourses. In
Iran, anticlerical secularism and constitutionalism were developed in response to
the dual targets of the ulama's obstructionism and the shah's absolutism. The economic nationalism of 1941–53 was developed in response to the British control of
Iran's oil industry. In this period, anticlerical secularism had become less significant
in nationalist discourse because it had already been appropriated by Reza Shah's
regime as a crucial element of its ideology. In Egypt, on the other hand, secularism
and constitutionalism went hand in hand with the issues of language and national
territory. Foreign domination, Turkish cultural influence, Ottomanism, the conception of political authority upheld by Islamic orthodoxy—all affected the views
of Egyptian ideological producers. However, the decline in the ulama's political
power under Muhammad Ali and thereafter, the gradual decline in Turkish cultural
influence, and the rise of Arabic as the national language removed the issues of
Turkish domination and the ulama's obstructionism from the agenda of the nationalist intellectual leaders. The decline of khedivial power following the British occupation and then Khedive Abbas's anti-British nationalism around the turn of the
century gave meaning to territorial nationalism and the glorification of the land of
Egypt in the rhetoric of nationalist leaders. For more reflective and sophisticated
thinkers not only British domination but also Ottomanism and pan-Islamism were
contrary to the ideas of nationhood and freedom.

The 1919 revolution in Egypt and the formation of a constitutional government
for a time removed British as the target of ideological attack by liberal-nationalist
ideologues, thereby unleashing the secular forces to launch a merciless attack on
Islam and Islamic history. The inability of the liberal-nationalist movement to

achieve total independence and its failure to pave the way for public participation in politics undermined its legitimacy, giving credibility to Islamic fundamentalism and Arab nationalism. In Syria, on the other hand, the pan-Islamic despotism of Sultan Abdülhamid and then a shift in the ideology of the Committee of Union and Progress toward Turkish nationalism stimulated the rise of liberal Arabism among political thinkers. The collapse of the Ottoman Empire removed many issues that were related, first, to Sultan Abdülhamid's arbitrary rule, then to the Ottomans' attempts to centralize power, and finally to Turkish nationalism from the intellectual agenda of the country's political thinkers. Instead, what these intellectual leaders faced was the colonial partitioning of the Arab lands and the artificial creation of Arab states by foreign powers—hence the glorification of Arab lands in the discourse of radical Arab nationalism.

Finally, the discourse of Islamic fundamentalism was also developed in oppositional relation to certain ideological targets—in this case, to the kind of obstacles Muslim activists faced in pursuing their religious objectives. In Egypt, the Muslim Brothers developed their ideas in opposition to the secularist outlook of intellectual leaders, and the rise of the religious extremism of Sayyid Qutb in the fifties and the sixties was in reaction to the repressive policies of Nassir's regime. In Syria, the Muslim Brothers expressed their opposition to the ruling regime in terms of the idea of Islamic socialism. With the coming to power of the Ba'athist Arab socialist party, the MB assumed an antisocialist and antistatist orientation. In Algeria also, the rise of radical Islamism was associated with the left-turn policies of the Algerian regime in the seventies. In Iran, Islamic fundamentalism was developed as a rejection of the shah's national secularism and glorification of pre-Islamic culture and kingship. Monarchy-centered nationalist secular discourse generated its opposing image in clergy-centered religious discourse.

In sum, the key factors in the actual production of discourse are the nature, the number, and the level of diversity of the targets ideological producers face. If we obtain an adequate picture of the role of the state in culture, the nature of the discursive field, and the kinds of ideological targets that are present in this field, we may be able to overcome indeterminacy and predict the process of ideological production.

Sociological versus Historical Explanations: Ideology and Practice

Our explanation of Islamic modernism, liberal nationalism, Arab nationalism, and Islamic fundamentalism was formulated in terms of the interplay of a series of sociopolitical and cultural forces in specific historical episodes. Although the episodes were conceptualized as discontinuous segments in the history of the Islamic world in the modern period, they were tied together in a broader dynamic that governed the interaction between the ideologies of the intellectual leaders and the practices of the ruling regimes. It is thus necessary to incorporate our sociological explanation into this broader historical process of ideological change in order to fully grasp the essence of what was at stake in the story that started with Islamic modernism and ended with fundamentalism. In our view, the theme of the story was quite simple and straightforward—secularism within the context of the encounter between the Western and Islamic cultural traditions.

Despite the Western domination of the Islamic world in the nineteenth century, the Islamic response to imperialism was not oppositional. This domination paralleled the establishment of Western cultural hegemony, which meant among other things the acceptance by Muslim intellectual leaders of the Europe-centered conception of secularism as a universal process of evolutionary change and historical progress. This secularist perspective was forcefully promoted in the Islamic world by people like James Mill, Macaulay, Muir, Hunter, Cromer, Morier, Renan, and other Westernizers connected to British and French colonial administrations. In addition, an important factor that promoted the rise of modern ideas among Muslim intellectual leaders was the existence of a discursive space produced by the admission of the reality of secular politics in historical Islam and the desirability of replacing the existing monarchical absolutism with a constitutional system. Not only in India and Egypt under the British and Algeria under the French, but also in independent Iran a leading section among the ulama accepted constitutionalism and rational rule making as a proper model of politics. A dominant trend within the religious establishment not only rebelled against the traditional conception of Islamic jurisprudence, but also allied with liberal-nationalist leaders, as the cases of Algeria, Egypt, Iran, and Syria demonstrated, in demanding constitutional change and democratic politics. Closely associated with Islamic modernism, the movements for the construction of the modern state in these countries were all directed, as it were, against the monarch's absolutism and colonial domination, not against the religious establishment. In Egypt, the Urabi rebellion (1879–82) and the nationalist revolution of 1919 reflected the grievances of indigenous forces against both the khedive and the British. The Iranian Constitutional Revolution (1905–11) was primarily directed against Qajar absolutism, even though anticlerical secularism was one of its essential components, and the modern revolutionary movement in Syria was in opposition to the Turks' attempt at administrative centralization and Turkification and then against the French mandate between the two world wars. In fact, the active involvement of an influential segment of the ulama in the movement for independence and for the construction of the modern state calls seriously into question the conflict between Islam and modernity.

However, the modernist ulama had serious reservations about the uncritical emulation of Western laws and customs, reservations that were not too different from those of Sir William Jones in India. Abduh, in particular, doubted the possibility of successfully transplanting European laws and institutions to Egypt. For him and other modernists, Islam contained the universal creed that could link the two cultures and form the moral basis of modern Egypt. What happened in Algeria, Egypt, Iran, and Syria in the twentieth century was contrary to Abduh's vision, however. Instead of using Islam as a source of legislation in a manner that was congruent with the people's customs and sensibility, the ideology of the ruling elite constituted the primary source of both legislation and state policies. Liberal nationalism and then Nassir's pan-Arab socialism in Egypt, the monarchy-centered nationalist discourse of the Pahlavis, Arab socialism in Algeria, and Arab Ba'athist socialism in Syria became the organizing principles of the modern state. These states were informed by a narrow, and often distorted, conception of secularism. While the ruling elite insisted on the separation of the state and religion, that separation did not entail the ideological neutrality of the state. As these elites attempted to undermine the influence of the religious institutions in their societies, they at the same time promoted their own discourses as substitutes for religion. Religion thus became politicized, as the conservative Islamic establishment resisted the loss of its traditional social functions and modern intellectuals sought in the institutional field of religion a cultural resource for formulating their discourse in oppositional relation to the ideology of the state.

Religion, Secularization, and the Modern State

The secularization project implemented by the state was based on a serious misconception regarding the relationship between religion and the state. According to the secularization thesis, drawn from the European experience of state formation and modernization, the separation of religion and the state is presumed not only as an inevitable outcome of modernization, but also a precondition for the development of rational rule making and democracy. Rooted in the Europe-centered rationalist school to which belonged Thomas Hobbes, James Mill, Jeremy Bentham, and J. S. Mill, among others, a view of human society and universal history of social evolution emerged in which religion was to wither away as society moved along the continuum of evolutionary process fueled by scientific progress, technological advancement, and industrial development. Scholars as diverse as the philosopher Ludwig Feuerbach and the psychologist Sigmund Freud pointed to the epiphenomenon of religion which was to disappear as scientific knowledge increasingly replaces ignorance. In his positivist project, the founder of sociology, Auguste Comte, also gave sociologists the role of supreme priests to guide society. The secularization thesis was further systematized in different ways in the works of the trinity of social theory—Durkheim, Marx, and Weber—in which the decline of religious belief was "scientifically" forecasted. Social progress was presumed to bring about the decline of the political, social, and cognitive functions of religion. In modern society, cultural change was thus perceived as an outcome of social differentiation produced by the dynamic of technological inventions and scientific breakthrough.

The secularization thesis gained a wide currency among twentieth-century intellectuals and policy makers in Algeria, Egypt, Iran, and Syria. Conscious of their intellectual superiority, confident of the correctness of their secular views, and having a deep conviction regarding the constraining role of the Islamic establishment and traditional culture, they launched cultural assaults on the ulama and Islamic institutions. These intellectual leaders attacked various aspects of the Islamic belief system by pointing to the inadequacy of its political and social theories, the alleged irrationality of the religious rituals, the outmoded methods of teaching and instructional materials used in the Islamic schools, and its unjustifiable support of the existing social hierarchy and of the institution of male domination. Likewise, policy makers often worked zealously to limit the sphere of activity of the Islamic groups, taking away their educational and social functions and bringing under the firm control of the government the economically resourceful institution of awqaf, and self-righteously imposed a state feminism on their societies from above. All these things were done in the name of progress and the civilizational needs of their societies. Secularism—be it in the form of liberal nationalism, Arab nationalism and state socialism, or monarchy-centered nationalism—then became the religion of the state. But the exclusionary policies of the state further undermined its legitimacy, giving credibility to the claims of the fundamentalist groups that the state was promoting alien ideologies.

State secularism of the twentieth century failed to produce a secular society, however. While organized religion in Algeria, Egypt, and Syria declined, new religious movements, often led by individuals who had received Western education, with mass followings and high levels of political activism emerged in these countries. In Iran, the traditional religious establishment coalesced with a new religious movement in bringing down the monarchy in the revolutionary movement of 1977–79.

We may argue that the development of the secular state in these countries was thus a sort of "aberration." This is so for two principle reasons. First, given that historical Islam accommodated secularism, the ruling elite's attempt to import a European model of secularism to their countries as a condition for development could not be justified. Second, the secularization project implemented in these Islamic countries was based on a misconception of what was really at issue regarding the development of the modern state.

The Ideological Neutrality of the Modern State

In the conflict between the state and religion that gave rise to Islamic fundamentalism interests certainly played a crucial role. Interests, however, did not determine the form and style of this conflict. Intellectually, the form of this conflict was rooted in a misguided secularization thesis. The uncritical application of this thesis by intellectual leaders and policy makers was a major contributing factor in the politicization of religion and the rise of religious extremism in Egypt from the 1930s on, and in Algeria, Iran, and Syria after the 1950s. True, modernization necessitated the institutional separation of the state and religion. But to explain why this separation was necessary, we need to address a more fundamental question: What was the nature of the function of the modern state that in fact necessitated this separation? Why is the state unable to function properly without being separated from religion? Although rational rule making was often posed in contradistinction to religious rules (which are not enacted but "discovered" or "recognized"), it is hardly defensible to argue that religious rules of behavior were irrational and less functional than interest-based legislation. Therefore, the juxtaposition of religious laws and positive laws in terms of the rationality and mutability of the latter may be misleading and biased against religious laws. Third, if the institutional separation of the state and religion was necessary because the state's laws were matters of social engineering and meant to be ideologically neutral—that is, they were provisional rather than being permanent, bound to time and place rather than being universal, and changed with changes in social circumstances rather than being unchangeable—then the notion of the separation of the state and religion was totally misconceived and misconstrued. This is because that from which the state had to be separated was not merely religion. The state in order to function effectively in representing the universal interests of society needed to be free from the constraints of weighty social forces, including the special interests of powerful social classes and status groups, the clergy, and the military not simply religion.

This notion had been well grounded in theories of liberal democracy since its first formulation in Bentham's conception of the liberal state as a utility maximizer for the entire society through its guarantee of a free market and provision of political utility (in the form of security of rights, security of property, and freedom of individual movement), in J. S. Mill's people's right to vote as a condition of maximizing human capacities, in T. H. Green's right to accumulate unlimited property as a requirement for the free development of individual personality,[4] and in James Madison's system of checks and balances. This notion was also echoed in Marx's approval of the French Revolution for freeing the state from "all manner of medieval rubbish, seignioral rights, local privileges, municipal and guild monopolies of provincial constitutions."[5] Marx's quarrel with theorists of liberal democracy was not over their project of constructing a state that represented the universal interests of society. It was rather over the fact that these theorists did not pay sufficient attention to political economy and that a democratic state in a capitalist society was not totally free. It was not free because of the insertion of the state into the economically organized social hierarchy of capitalism that constrained state action.

For Marx, the elimination of private property would provide the condition for the transformation of the state from a repressive institution for administering people to a system for administering things. Thus, what was at issue in political modernization was the state's freedom from all special interests, which in practice meant political inclusion and the equality of political voices in society.

The most fundamental problem of the secularization thesis was thus the state-versus-religion binary. If the thesis had any validity, secularization basically meant that the state, ideally, must bear no ideology. In this sense, the Algerian, Egyptian, Iranian, and Syrian cases were all aberrations, because the policy makers and the intellectual leaders associated with them, in their literal interpretation of secularization, simply substituted one discourse for religion as the ideology of the modern state. And by zealously undermining the social functions and influence of religion, they politicized religion, which led to the rise of militant fundamentalism.

Was it possible for the modern state to develop in the Islamic Middle East without politicizing religion? Was the experience of Algeria, Egypt, Iran, and Syria inevitable? This is where the case of Jordan comes in. The Jordanian state was certainly as modern as its Algerian, Egyptian, Iranian, and Syrian counterparts. Nevertheless, the process of its development produced a relationship between the state and religion that was quite different from the relationship in these other countries. The key factor, in our view, was that the Jordanian regime, in a comparative perspective, appeared to have been ideologically neutral, and its move toward democratization, beginning in 1989, created a political and cultural context in which the country's dominant Islamic movement exhibited signs of secularization.

The Secular Ideological State and Culture Production

A key factor in the politicization of culture in Algeria, Egypt, Iran, and Syria was the rise of the ideological state in these countries. This state not only claimed the monopoly of the legitimate use of the physical means of violence, to use Weber's terminology, but also a monopoly of the means and content of legitimate discourse. It adhered to an official ideology, appeal to which was the source of the state's regulatory and normative functions. Because of its very ideological nature, controlling culture and thought processes was among the state's top priorities. The state's ideology promoted a particular conception of history, defined the essence of the nation and national identity, identified the enemies and friends of the nation, promoted a particular form of language and style of expression, and subjected religious beliefs to its own particular cosmological doctrines. The state not only reorganized the educational institutions to serve its ideological objectives but also transformed the mass media and other means of communication into a propaganda machine. The calendar was reorganized, among other things, to specify celebrated dates and periodic rituals. The state's propaganda machine bombarded the public with its messages in murals, slogans on walls, and ideological statements on display objects for public consumption. The ideology of the state treated the nation and the state as one, transhistorical, eternal, and unchangeable. It narrowed the range of legitimate expression. The domain of politics and the realm of culture become identical. Cultural expression was at the same time political expression. Cultural opposition was also political opposition. Culture production was a political endeavor. An ideological state attempted to promote a conformist culture.

To be sure, all the states rested on certain ideological presuppositions—for example, democracy and individual sovereignty, constitutional monarchy, socialism and the exploitative nature of private control of productive wealth, the desirability of an Islamic republic and the sovereignty of the shari'a—which governed their rules of conduct. Insofar as these presuppositions were confined to such political matters as the process of selection of the political leaders and the members of legislature, circulation of the ruling elite, and the maintenance of order, they may be labeled ideologically neutral. On the other hand, when they were intended to govern virtually all aspects of social relationships, then the state could be considered ideological. An ideological state was discursively uniform and solidified. And the functioning of its apparatuses was often governed by a single principle. An ideologically neutral state was multiform and fragmented, and diverse principles often governed its different apparatuses.

Contrary to the secularization thesis, what was really at issue was not simply the separation of the state and religion. It was rather the freeing of the state from all forms of ideological entrapment. Insofar as the development of the modern state necessitated the freeing of its apparatuses from special interests—the monarch, the landed aristocracy, the clergy, and other status groups—in order to represent the universal interests of society, an ideologically neutral state was an expression of that universality. It was thus true that the development of the modern state necessitated its separation from religion. But it does not follow that in order for the state to develop, religious institutions must be reformed and their social functions narrowed. Implementing policies such as these was tantamount to substituting one ideological state for another and making secularism into an integral part of state ideology.

In sum, the sequence of historical events that gave rise to Islamic fundamentalism began with an Islamic-Western cultural encounter and continued through the establishment of Western hegemony, the formation of discursive pluralism, the rise of Islamic modernism, the development of liberal nationalism, the rise of the modern ideological state, the formation of a monolithic intellectual environment, and the rise of Islamic fundamentalism. In this sequence, if our analysis is correct, the main culprits in the genesis of religious extremism were the totalitarian despots who resided at the pinnacle of state power.

NOTES

Introduction

1. For an overview of the Islamicist perspective, see Mansoor Moaddel, "The Study of Islamic Culture and Politics: An Overview and Assessment," *Annual Review of Sociology* 28 (2002): 359–86.

2. For a discussion of the debates on colonial history, see a series of article published in *AHR Forum,* by Gyan Prakash, "Subaltern Studies as Postcolonial Criticism," *American Historical Review* 99 (December 1994): 1475–90; Florencia E. Mallon, "The Promise and Dilemma of Subaltern Studies: Perspectives from Latin American History," *American Historical Review* 99 (December 1994): 1491–1515; and Fredrick Cooper, "Conflict and Connection: Rethinking Colonial African History," *American Historical Review* 99 (December 1994): 1516–45.

3. Fred Halliday, *Islam and the Myth of Confrontation: Religion and Politics in the Middle East* (London: I. B. Tauris, 1996), p. 211. See also Moaddel, "Study of Islamic Culture."

4. Ernest Wallwork, "Religion and Social Structure in 'The Division of Labor,'" *American Anthropologist* 86, no. 2 (1984): 44; Guy E. Swanson, *Religion and Regime: A Sociological Account of the Reformation* (Ann Arbor: University of Michigan Press).

5. Karl Marx and Frederick Engels, "The German Ideology," in *Collected Works,* vol. 5 (New York: International Publishers, 1976), p. 36.

6. Ahmad Sadri, *Max Weber's Sociology of Intellectuals* (Oxford: Oxford University Press, 1992), p. 41. In Berger's explication, "Weber's understanding of the relation of ideas to history can be seen most clearly in his concept of 'elective affinity' (*Wahlverwandtschaft*), that is, of the way in which certain ideas and certain social processes 'seek each other out' in history." See Peter L. Berger, "Charisma and Religious Innovation: The Social Location of Israelite Prophecy," *American Sociological Review* 28 (1963): 950.

7. See Swanson, *Religion and Regime.*

8. Immanuel Wallerstein, *The Politics of the World-Economy: The States, the Movements, and the Civilizations* (Cambridge: Cambridge University Press, 1984), p. 5.

9. Partha Chatterjee, *Nationalist Thought and the Colonial World: A Derivative Discourse* (Minneapolis: University of Minnesota Press, 1993), p. 11.

10. See note 2.

11. David Harvey, *The Condition of Postmodernity* (Oxford: Blackwell, 1990), p. 302.

12. Ibid., p. 305.

13. Robert Wuthnow, "State Structures and Ideological Outcomes," *American Sociological Review* 50 (December 1985): 800.

14. Michel Foucault, *Discipline and Punish* (New York: Vintage Books, 1979), p. 23.

15. Timothy Mitchell, *Colonising Egypt* (Cambridge: Cambridge University Press, 1988).

16. Edward W. Said, *Orientalism* (London: Penguin Books, 1991), p. 12. This is not a judgment on Foucault's work in general. On the contrary, Foucault in *The Order of Things, Madness and Civilization,* and *The Archaeology of Knowledge* does stress the autonomy of culture and how fundamental cultural codes impose order upon experience. See also J. G. Merquior, *Foucault* (Los Angeles: University of California Press, 1985).

17. Terry, F. Godlove, Jr. "Interpretation, Reductionism, and Belief in God," *Journal of Religion* 69, no. 2 (1989): 185; D. Z. Phillips, *Religion without Explanation* (Oxford: Basil Blackwell, 1976); Gaston Richard, "Dogmatic Atheism in the Sociology of Religion," trans. Jacqueline Redding and W. S. F. Pickering, in *Durkheim on Religion: A Selection of Readings with Bibliographies and Introductory Remarks,* ed. W. S. F. Pickering (London: Rutledge & Kegan Paul, 1975).

18. Wallwork, "Religion and Social Structure."

19. Cited in ibid., p. 49.

20. Robert Wuthnow, "Rethinking Weber's View of Ideology," *Theory and Society,* 16 (1987): 123. See also Max Weber, *The Protestant Ethic and the Spirit of Capitalism,* trans. Talcott Parsons (New York: Scribner, 1958).

21. Louis Althusser, *Lenin and Philosophy* (London: New Left Books, 1971). Neo-Marxist theorists like Therborn, Przeworski, and Burawoy departed from subjectivism and stressed the material-based character of ideologies, the role of organizational structures, and how material condition structures rational choices among alternative ideas and strategies for workers. Yet the problem of the connection between ideology and material production has remained unresolved. See Michael Burawoy, "The Politics of Production and Production of Politics: A Comparative Analysis of Piecework Machine Shops in the United States and Hungary," in *Political Power and Social Theory,* ed. M. Zeitlin (Greenwich, Conn.: JAI Press, 1980), pp. 261–99; Adam Przeworski, "Material Bases of Consent: Economic and Politics in a Hegemonic System," in Zeitlin, *Political Power and Social Theory,* pp. 21–66; and Goran Therborn, *The Ideology of Power and the Power of Ideology* (London: Verso, 1980).

22. Victor W. Turner, *The Forest of Symbols: Aspects of Ndembu Ritual* (Ithaca, N.Y.: Cornell University Press, 1967), p. 30.

23. Weber, *Protestant Ethic.*

24. Talcott Parsons, *The Structure of Social Action: A Study in Social Theory with Special Reference to a Group of Recent European Writers* (Glencoe, Ill.: Free Press, 1949), pp. 563–78, *The Social System* (Toronto: Collier-Macmillan, 1951), pp. 496–535, *Societies: Evolutionary and Comparative Perspective* (Englewood Cliffs, N.J.: Prentice-Hall, 1966), pp. 20–27, *Politics and Social Structure* (New York: Free Press, 1969), pp. 55–57, and *The System of Modern Societies* (Englewood Cliffs, N.J.: Prentice-Hall, 1971), pp. 26–28. See also Marshall D. Sahlins and

Elman R. Service, *Evolution and Culture* (Ann Arbor: University of Michigan Press, 1960), p. 28; Elman R. Service, *Cultural Evolutionism: Theory in Practice* (New York: Holt, Rinehart & Winston, 1971), p. 25; and Parsons, *Politics and Social Structure*, pp. 55–57.

25. Hadely Cantril, *The Psychology of Social Movements* (New York: John Wiley & Sons, 1941); David Apter, ed., *Ideology and Discontent* (New York: Free Press, 1964); Chalmers Johnson, *Revolutionary Change* (Boston: Little Brown, 1966); William Kornhauser, *The Politics of Mass Society* (Glencoe, Ill.: Free Press, 1959); David C. Schwartz, "A Theory of Revolutionary Behavior," in *When Men Revolt and Why*, ed. James C. Davies (New York: Free Press, 1971), pp. 109–32; and Hans Toch, *The Social Psychology of Social Movements* (New York: Bobbs-Merrill Co., 1965).

26. Everett E. Hagen, *On the Theory of Social Change: How Economic Growth Begins* (Homewood, Ill.: Dorsey Press, 1962).

27. David C. McClelland, *The Achieving Society* (Princeton, N.J.: D. Van Nostrand, 1961).

28. Robert Wuthnow, *Communities of Discourse: Ideology and Social Structure in the Reformation, the Enlightenment, and European Socialism* (Cambridge, Mass.: Harvard University Press, 1989), p. 3.

29. Ibid., p. 535.

30. Ibid., pp. 1–22, 481, 530–31.

31. Ibid., p. 581.

32. Randall Collins, *The Sociology of Philosophies: A Global Theory of Intellectual Change* (Cambridge, Mass.: Harvard University Press, 1998), 38, 42, 791.

33. Ibid., p. 380.

34. Ibid., pp. 388, 379, 380.

35. Ibid., p. 791.

36. Ibid., pp. 791–92.

37. Collins abandoned the ethnocentrism of Western scholarship which considered Asia as exotic and "non-Western cultures as unique sensibilities running on distinctive inner logics" (ibid., p. 379). He showed that the long-run intellectual tendency in all philosophical traditions was toward raising the level of abstraction and reflexivity, even though each tradition was emanating from a different starting point: "issues of ritual propriety in ancient China, cosmological myth in India and Greece, theological disputes in early Islam" (p. 788). Collins rejected the unilinear evolutionism of the modernization perspective in favor of a multilinear evolution of different cultural traditions. By stressing the equal potential of all philosophical traditions to move in the direction of increasing abstraction and reflexivity, Collins's approach parallels Noam Chomsky's theory of universal grammar. Nevertheless, overcoming Europocentrism is one thing; glossing over serious differences among the world's cultural traditions is quite another. To explain differences in the world's cultural traditions requires positing intellectual creativity within the specific cultural and sociopolitical context of debates over historically significant issues. The variations in such contexts may explain the subtle differences in intellectual creativity across diverse traditions.

38. Jeffrey C. Alexander and Philip Smith, "The Discourse of American Civil Society: A New Proposal for Cultural Studies," *Theory and Society* 22 (1993): 156–57; Terence Hawkes, *Structuralism and Semiotics* (Berkeley: University of California Press, 1977), pp. 19–27; Ferdinand de Saussure, *Course on General Linguistics* (London: Duckworth, 1983).

39. This view is consistent with Herbert Blumer's symbolic interactionist perspective—that humans act toward things on the basis of the meanings they attach to them, and that these meanings arise out of social interactions. See Herbert Blumer, *Symbolic Interactionism: Perspective and Method* (Englewood Cliffs, N.J.: Prentice-Hall, 1969).

40. Michael Holquist, *Dialogism: Bakhtin and His World* (New York: Rutledge, 1990), p. 49.

41. Holquist, *Dialogism,* p. 21.

42. The creation of meaning through the medium of signs involves two levels that parallel the Saussurian binary, the opposition of language and speech. The first is the general rules and discursive codes that exist for all the adherents of a particular ideology. The second is the actual expression of opinions. For Saussure, the latter is unique to the individual speaker and resists generalization and therefore cannot be studied. The latter, on the other hand, lend itself to systematic studies and generalization. Here, we disagree with the Saussurian premise by arguing that the actual expression of meaning is systematic and follows a dialogical process, and it is amenable to systematic study and generalization.

43. Peter L. Berger and Thomas Luckmann, "Sociology of Religion and Sociology of Knowledge," in *Sociology of Religion,* ed. Roland Robertson (New York: Penguin Books, 1969), p. 70.

44. William Sim Bainbridge, "Social Influence and Religious Pluralism," in *Advances in Group Processes,* vol. 12 (JAI Press, 1995), pp. 1–18; Roger Finke and Rodney Stark, "Evaluating the Evidence: Religious Economies and Sacred Canopies," *American Sociological Review* 54 (1989): 1054–56.

45. Karl Mannheim, *Ideology and Utopia* (New York: Harvest, 1936), p. 80.

46. Hank Johnston, Enrique Larana, and Joseph R. Gusfield. eds., *New Social Movements: From Ideology to Identity* (Philadelphia:Temple University Press, 1994), p. 28; and William A. Gamson, *Talking Politics* (Cambridge: Cambridge University Press,1992).

47. William H. Sewell, Jr., "Historical Events as Transformations of Structures: Inventing Revolution at the Bastille," *Theory and Society* 25 (1996): 843.

48. The conception of social structure used in the present work conforms to that of Sewell's as consisting of both resources and rules. See William H. Sewell, Jr.,"A Theory of Structure: Duality, Agency, and Transformation," *American Journal of Sociology* 1 (July 1992): 1–29.

49. Morris R. Cohen and Ernest Nagel, *An Introduction to Logic and Scientific Method* (New York: Harcourt, Brace & Co., 1934), pp. 245–72.

50. A useful measure of discursive pluralism would be similar to the measure of religious pluralism employed in the literature of the sociology of religion. The pluralism index used in this literature equals 1 minus the Herfindahl concentration index (pluralism = $1 - \Sigma \rho_i^2$; where ρ_i is the proportion of all religious adherents in a country belonging to a particular religious group, i). On the basis of this definition, we may define discursive pluralism as 1 minus the sum of the squared proportion of all culture producers in a country belonging to a particular ideological movement. Unfortunately, the necessary data for constructing this measure are not available. See Finke and Stark, "Evaluating the Evidence"; Daniel V. A. Olson, "Religious Pluralism in Contemporary U.S. Counties: Comment on Finke and Sark," *American Sociological Review* 63, no. 5 (October 1998): 759–61; and Roger Finke and Rodney Stark, "Religious Choice and Competition: A Reply to Olson," *American Sociological Review* 63, no. 5 (October 1998): 761–66.

51. Cohen and Nagel, *Introduction to Logic*, pp. 261–65.

52. Charles Tilly, *Big Structures, Large Processes, Huge Comparisons* (New York: Russell Sage Foundation, 1984), p. 82.

53. An interesting case study that clearly demonstrated this process is Larson's examination of how the people of highland Madagascar came to understand and practice the Christianity introduced to them by British missionaries during the early nineteenth century. Larson argued that the native Malagasy grafted this new religion onto their language and existing religious practices. See Pier M. Larson, "'Capacities and Modes of Thinking': Intellectual Engagements and Subaltern Hegemony in the Early History of Malagasy Christianity," *American Historical Review* 102, nos. 4–5 (October 1997): 969–1002.

Chapter One

1. Aziz Ahmad, *Studies in Islamic Culture in the Indian Environment* (Oxford: Clarendon Press, 1964), p. 22.

2. For nineteenth-century critics of Islam see chapters 2–4. For an overview of the Islamicist perspective, see Moaddel, "Study of Islamic Culture," pp. 362–66. Among the Western Marxists who considered Islamic institutions a part of the ideological apparatus of the state is Perry Anderson, *Lineage of the Absolutist State* (London: Verso, 1979).

3. See Maxime Rodinson, *Islam and Capitalism* (London: Penguin Books, 1974); and Barbara Daly Metcalf, "Presidential Address: Too Little and Too Much: Reflections on Muslims in the History of India," *Journal of Asian Studies* 54, no 4 (November 1995): 951–67.

4. Reuben Levy, *An Introduction to the Sociology of Islam* (London: Williams & Norgate, 1933), p. 213; and Albert Hourani *A History of the Arab Peoples* (New York: Warner Books, 1991), pp. 158–59.

5. Reuben Levy, *Introduction to the Sociology of Islam*, pp. 236–37.

6. Ibid., pp. 237, 239, 245.

7. Ibid., pp. 255–60. Hallaq holds that the gate of ijtihad has never been closed in Islamic jurisprudence, and through Muslim history jurists often brought their own reasoning to pass a legal judgment. Although Hallaq's argument may modify our position regarding the limits to rational analysis, it does not question that modernists faced the resistance and criticisms of the orthodox ulama, each of whose members adhered to one of the four traditional schools. See Wael B. Hallaq, "Was the Gate of Ijtihad Closed?" *International Journal of Middle East Studies* 16 (1984): 3–41.

8. Moojan Momen, *An Introduction to Shi'i Islam* (New Haven, Conn.: Yale University Press, 1985), p. 185; Reuben Levy, *Introduction to the Sociology of Islam*, pp. 257–59.

9. *Encyclopaedia of Islam*, ed. H. A. R. Gibb (Leiden: Brill, 1960), 4:948.

10. Hamilton A. R. Gibb, "Al-Mawardi's Theory of the Khilafah," *Islamic Culture* 11 (1937): 291–302; and Erwin I. J. Rosenthal, *Political Thought in Medieval Islam: An Introductory Outline* (Cambridge: Cambridge University Press, 1958), p. 28.

11. Albert Hourani, *Arabic Thought in the Liberal Age (1798–1939)* (Cambridge: Cambridge University Press, 1983), p. 14.

12. Rosenthal, *Political Thought in Medieval Islam*, pp. 42, 239 note 34; S. A. Rizvi, "Islam in Medieval India," in *A Cultural History of India*, ed. Arthur Llewellyn Basham (Oxford: Clarendon Press, 1975), p. 283; Gholamhosein Ibrahimi Dina'nie, *Mantiq va Marifat dar*

Nazar-i Ghazali [Ghazali's View on Logic and Knowledge] (Tehran: Amir Kabir, 1991/1370), pp. 47–48.

13. Hourani, *Arabic Thought,* p. 15.

14. Ibid., p. 18. For a more detailed view of Farabi, see Richard Walzer, *Al-Farabi on the Perfect State* (Oxford: Clarendon Press, 1985).

15. *Encyclopaedia of Islam,* 4:945.

16. Ibn Khaldun, *The Muqaddhimah: An Introduction to History,* trans. Ranz Rosenthal (Princeton, N.J.: Princeton University Press, 1967), p. 385.

17. Hourani, *Arabic Thought,* p. 20.

18. Ibid., p. 21.

19. W. Montgomery Watt, "Shi'ism under the Umayyads," *Journal of the Royal Asiatic Society,* nos. 1–2 (1960): 158–72; Hamid Algar, *Religion and State in Modern Iran* (Berkeley: University of California Press, 1969).

20. Fereydoun Adamiyat, *Idi'olozhi-ye Nahzat-i Mashrutiyat-i Iran* [The Ideology of the Constitutional Movement in Iran] (Tehran: Payam Publications, 1976/1355), p. 197; Said Amir Arjomand, *The Shadow of God and the Hidden Imam* (Chicago: University of Chicago Press, 1984), pp. 109, 255.

21. It may not be a gross generalization to argue that the statement of Badre al-Din Ibn Jama'a (1241–1333), the Mamluks' official apologist, that "We are with whoever conquers" (cited in Hourani, *Arabic Thought,* p. 15), was also true in case of the official ulama of India and Iran.

22. *Shorter Encyclopaedia of Islam,* ed. H. A. R. Gibb and J. H. Kramers (Ithaca, N.Y.: Cornell University Press, 1953), p. 519.

23. Peter Hardy, "The Ulama in British India," in "Golden Jubilee Volume," *Journal of Indian History* (1973), p. 830.

24. *Shorter Encyclopaedia of Islam,* p. 520.

25. Sri Ram Sharma, *The Religious Policy of the Mughal Emperors* (New York: Asia Publishing House, 1962), p. 182.

26. Abdul Qadir Baudauni, *Muntakhab-ut-Tawarikh,* trans. G. S. A. Ranking, W. H. Lowe, and Sir Wolseley Haig (Calcutta, 1884–1925), 3:127; S. M. Ikram, *Muslim Civilization in India* (New York: Columbia University Press, 1964), p. 157.

27. Mortiza Raavandy, *Sair-i Farhang va Tarikh-i Ta'lim va Tarbiyat dar Iran va Orupa* [Cultural Change and the History of Education in Iran and Europe] (Rasht: Hidayat Publications, 1990/1369), p. 7.

28. Ibid., p. 8, *Encyclopaedia of Islam,* 5:1134; Ira M. Lapidus, *A History of Islamic Societies* (Cambridge: Cambridge University Press, 1988), p. 166.

29. Ikram, *Muslim Civilization in India,* p. 158.

30. Afaf Lutfi Marsot, "The Ulama of Cairo in the Eighteenth and Nineteenth Centuries," in *Scholars, Saints, and Sufis,* ed. Nikki R. Keddie (Berkeley: University of California Press, 1972), pp. 153–54; and Gabriel Baer, "Urbanization in Egypt, 1820–1907," in *Beginnings of Modernization in the Middle East: The Nineteenth Century,* ed. William R. Polk and Richard L. Chambers (Chicago: University of Chicago Press, 1968), p. 147.

31. Baer, "Urbanization in Egypt," p. 147.

32. Ann K. S. Lambton, *Landlord and Peasant in Persia* (London: Oxford University Press, 1953), pp. 126–27, and "The Persian Ulama and Constitutional Reform," in *Le shi'isme imamite,* ed. T. Fahd (Paris: Presses Universitaires de France, 1970), p. 249.

33. Lambton, *Landlord and Peasant*, p. 127.

34. Hardy, "The Ulama in British India," p. 834.

35. Ikram, *Muslim Civilization in India*, p. 157.

36. A. H. M. Nooruzzaman, "Rise of the Muslim Middle Class as a Political Factor in India and Pakistan, 1858–1947" (Ph.D. dissertation, University of London, 1964), p. 14.

37. Irfan Habib, *The Agrarian System of Mughal India (1556–1707)* (New York: Asia Publishing House, 1963), pp. 307–8.

38. Ibid., p. 299; Ibn Hasan, *The Central Structure of the Mughal Empire and Its Practical Working up to the Year 1657* (Lahore: Oxford University Press, 1935), chapter 8.

39. Habib, *Agrarian System of Mughal India*, p. 306.

40. Concerning the cultural policy and religious tolerance of prominent Muslim rulers, see H. G. Rawlinson, *India: A Short Cultural History* (New York: F. A. Praeger, 1952), p. 299; Sharma, *Religious Policy of the Mughal Emperors*, p. 49; Saiyid Athar Abbas Rizvi, "The Muslim Ruling Dynasties," in Basham, *Cultural History*, pp. 259–60; and William H. McNeill and Marilyn Robinson Waldman, *The Islamic World* (Chicago: University of Chicago Press, 1973), p. 373.

41. Ikram, *Muslim Civilization in India*, pp. 160–61.

42. C. A. Bayly, *Indian Society and the Making of the British Empire* (Cambridge: Cambridge University Press, 1988); Habib, *Agrarian System of Mughal India;* John F. Richards, "The Seventeenth-Century Crisis in South Asia," *Modern Asian Studies* 24, no. 4 (1990): 625–38.

43. See Satish Chandra, *Medieval India: Society, the Jagirdari Crisis, and the Village* (Delhi: Macmillan, 1982), pp. 46–75. See also Habib, *Agrarian System of Mughal India*, p. 320.

44. Richards, "Seventeenth-Century Crisis," p. 635.

45. Ibid, p. 637.

46. Bayly, *Indian Society*, pp. 3–4.

47. Ibid., p. 8; Surendra Gopal, "Nobility and the Mercantile Community in India, XVI–XVIIth Centuries." *Journal of Indian History* 50 (1972): 802.

48. Bayly, *Indian Society*, p. 5.

49. Ibid, pp. 9–10.

50. Ibid, p. 4; Farhat Hasan, "Indigenous Cooperation and the Birth of a Colonial City: Calcutta, c. 1698–1750," *Modern Asian Studies* 26, no. 1 (1992): 72, and "The Mughal Fiscal System in Surat and the English East India Company," *Modern Asian Studies.* 27, no. 4 (1993): 711–18.

51. Farhat Hasan, "Indigenous Cooperation," pp. 65–66.

52. Panayiotis J. Vatikiotis, *The History of Egypt*, 2nd ed. (Baltimore: Johns Hopkins University Press, 1980), p. 30.

53. Ibid., p. 50.

54. Afaf Lutfi Marsot, "The Role of the Ulama in Egypt during the Early 19th Century," in *Political and Social Change in Modern Egypt*, ed. P. M. Holt (London: Oxford University Press, 1968), p. 274.

55. Afaf Lutfi Marsot, *Egypt in the Reign of Muhammad Ali* (Cambridge: Cambridge University Press, 1984), p. 49.

56. Marsot, *Egypt in the Reign of Muhammad Ali*, p. 61; Vatikiotis, *History of Egypt*, p. 51; Daniel Crecelius, "Nonideological Responses of the Egyptian Ulama to Modernization," in Keddie, *Scholars, Saints, and Sufis*, p. 176.

57. Fred H. Lawson, "Social Origins of Aggressive Foreign Policy: The Case of Muhammad Ali's Egypt, 1800–1930" (Ph.D. dissertation, University of California, Los Angeles, 1982), p. 122.

58. Robert F. Hunter, *Egypt under the Khedives, 1805–1879: From Household Government to Modern Bureaucracy* (Pittsburgh: University of Pittsburgh Press, 1984), p. 17. See also Marsot, *Egypt in the Reign of Muhammad Ali*, pp. 185, 190; Lawson, "Social Origins," p. 211; Terence Walz, *Trade between Egypt and Bilad al-Sudan: 1700–1820* (Cairo: Institut Français d'Archeologie Orientale du Caire, 1978), p. 238–39, and "Asyut in the 1260's (1844–53)," *Journal of the American Research Center in Egypt* 15 (1978): 118; Peter Gran, *Islamic Roots of Capitalism* (Austin: University of Texas Press, 1979), p. 116; Albert Hourani, "The Syrian in Egypt in the Eighteenth and Nineteenth Centuries," in *Colloque International sur L'Histoire du Caire* (Cairo: General Egyptian Book, 1969).

59. Marsot, *Egypt in the Reign of Muhammad Ali*, pp. 66–73; Gabriel Baer, *A History of Landownership in Modern Egypt, 1800–1950* (London: Oxford University Press, 1962), pp. 1–7.

60. Marsot, *Egypt in the Reign of Muhammad Ali*, p. 67; Crecelius, "Nonideological Responses," p. 181.

61. Marsot, *Egypt in the Reign of Muhammad Ali*, p. 142; Baer, *History of Landownership*, p. 4.

62. Baer, *History of Landownership*, pp. 3–4.

63. Marsot, *Egypt in the Reign of Muhammad Ali*, p. 142; Gabriel Baer, *Studies in the Social History of Modern Egypt* (Chicago: University of Chicago Press, 1969), p. 38.

64. Ervand Abrahamian, "Oriental Despotism: The Case of Qajar Iran," *International Journal of Middle East Studies* 5 (1974): 11, 12.

65. John Foran, *Fragile Resistance: Social Transformation in Iran from 1500 to the Revolution* (Boulder, Colo.: Westview Press, 1993).

66. William M. Floor, "The Merchants (*tujjar*) in Qajar Iran," *Zeitschrift der Deutschen Morgenlandischen Gesellschaft* 126 (1976): 124–25.

67. "Correspondence Respecting the Persian Tobacco Concession," *Sessional Papers* 79 (1892): 211–12.

68. Fereydoun Adamiyat, *Shourish bar Imtiyaz'nameye Rizhi* [Rebellion against the Regie Concession] (Tehran: Payam Publications, 1981/1360), p. 13. See also Mansoor Moaddel, "Shi'i Political Discourse and Class Mobilization in the Tobacco Movement of 1890–92," *Sociological Forum* 7 (September 1992): 447–68.

Chapter Two

1. Here, we are referring to Kenneth Cragg, "The Tests of 'Islamicity,'" *Middle East Forum* 32 (November 1957), pp. 15–17, 33; and Kerr's discussions of procedural deficiency in the doctrine of the caliphate and Islamic jurisprudence. See Malcolm Kerr, *Islamic Reform: The Political and Legal Theories of Muhammad 'Abduh and Rashid Rida* (Berkeley: University of California Press, 1966), p. 10.

2. See Ann K. S. Lambton, "Justice in the Medieval Persian Theory of Kingship," *Studia Islamica* 17 (1963): 95–96; and Gustave von Grunebaum, *Medieval Islam: A Study in Cultural Orientation* (Chicago: University of Chicago Press, 1954), pp. 343–44.

3. Cited in Lambton, "Justice in the Medieval Persian Theory of Kingship," p. 104.

4. Aziz Ahmad, *Studies*, p. 201.

5. Hourani, *Arabic Thought*, p. 37.

6. Ibid., p. 38.

7. Gordon Nickel, "'The Grand Opening': Shah Wali Allah's [Waliallah's] Principles of Exegesis" (M.A. thesis, School of Oriental and African Studies, University of London, 1987), p. 3; G. N. Jalbani, *Teachings of Shah Waliyullah* [Waliallah] (Lahore: Sh. Muhammad Ashraf, 1967), p. 9; Qeyamuddin Ahmad *The Wahabi Movement in India* (Calcutta: Firma K. L. Mukhopadhyay, 1966), pp. 13–14.

8. Aziz Ahmad, *Studies*, p. 205.

9. Hafeez Malik, *Sir Sayyid Ahmad Khan and Muslim Modernization in India and Pakistan* (New York: Columbia University Press, 1980), p. 256; Aziz Ahmad, *Studies*, p. 209.

10. Aziz Ahmad, *Studies*, p. 205.

11. Ibid., p. 204.

12. Ibid., p. 205; Johannes Marinus Simon Baljon, Jr., *The Reforms and Religious Ideas of Sir Sayyid Ahmad Khan* (Lahore: Sh. Muhammad Ashraf, 1970), p. 2; Nickel, "The Grand Opening," pp. 1, 38; and Muhammad Iqbal, *The Reconstruction of Religious Thought in Islam* (London: Oxford University Press, 1934), p. 136.

13. Aziz Ahmad, *Studies*, p. 205.

14. Nickel, "The Grand Opening," p. 38.

15. Hourani, *Arabic Thought*, pp. 38, 53.

16. Aziz Ahmad, *Studies*, p. 210. See also Lapidus, *History of Islamic Societies*, p. 566. Lapidus has 1785 for Barelvi's birthday.

17. Sayyid Ahmad Barelvi, *Correspondence of Sayyid Ahmad of Barelvi* (London: India Office Library and Records, British Museum Oriental 6635, n.d.); Qeyamuddin Ahmad, *Wahabi Movement*, pp. 26–62, 326; P. Hardy, *The Muslims of British India* (Cambridge: Cambridge University Press, 1972), p. 54. For some, this movement was not primarily against the British, and Sayyid Ahmad Barelvi did not openly resist the East India Company in its territories. The movement turned against the British from 1840 on and participated in the 1875 mutiny (see Aziz Ahmad, *Studies*, p. 216). For others, however, Sayyid Ahmad Barelvi was clear in his mind that "his real adversaries were the English, 'the traders and venders of goods'" (see Qeyamuddin Ahmad, *Wahabi Movement*, p. 326).

18. Aziz Ahmad, *Studies*, p. 216; Qeyamuddin Ahmad, *Wahabi Movement*, pp. 177–272; Hardy, *Muslims of British India*, pp. 51–55.

19. Aziz Ahmad, *Studies*, p. 217.

20. Fazlur Rahman established a stronger connection between what he considered the "pre-Modernist" movement and Islamic modernism. The former, in his view, was a spiritual force based on an alignment of the ulama and Sufism that advocated the purification of the faith and insisted on independent and even original judgment in matters of religion. The modernists accepted these positions, with the difference that a further shift of emphasis toward positivism took place in their hands. See Fazlur Rahman, *Islam* (New York:

Doubleday, 1968), pp. 237–43; and Christian W. Troll, *Sayyid Ahmad Khan: A Reinterpretation of Muslim Theology* (New Delhi: Vikas Publishing House, 1978), pp. 24–25.

21. According to Troll, Sayyid Ahmad Khan shared "the religious aspiration of the *Mujahedin*—at least as far as returning 'to the sources,' the fight against innovation and the endeavour towards religio-social reform is concerned. But significantly, in the directly political injunctions of the Shari'a—for example, *jihad* and *khilafah* . . . evidence suggests that Sir Sayyid did not commit himself publicly, or that he was opposed to Indian 'Wahhabi' views and efforts in this field" (*Sayyid Ahmad Khan*, p. 57).

22. François Bernier, *Travels in the Mogul Empire* (New Delhi: S. Chand & Co., 1968), p. 439.

23. Cited in Francis Robinson, "Islam and the Impact of Print," *Modern Asia Studies* 27 (February 1993): p. 231.

24. Francis Robinson, "Islam and the Impact of Print," pp. 231–32; see also Marshall McLuhan, *The Gutenberg Galaxy: The Making of Typographic Man* (London: Rutledge & Kegan Paul, 1962); George Steiner, *Language and Silence* (London: Faber & Faber, 1967); G. Baumann, ed., *The Written Word: Literacy in Transition* (Oxford: Clarendon Press, 1986).

25. *Aligarh Institute Gazette* 10, no. 5 (January 29, 1875): 71. See also Muhammad Esmail Rizvani and Fatimeh Qaziha, *Khatirat-i Nasir ud-Din Shah Dar Safar-i Sivvum-i Farangistan* [The Memoirs of Nasir ud-Din Shah in His Third Trip to Europe] (Tehran: Saziman-i Asnad-i Melli-ye Iran Publications, 1992/1371), p. 22. A most astonishing phenomenon for Muslims was the West's remarkable technological achievements. A certain Haji Mulla Hadi Sabzivari (1797–1875), a prominent Iranian scholastic philosopher, when placed in front of the camera, was so fascinated and puzzled by how a photograph was made that for some time he tried hard to formulate an explanation of the process in terms of the traditional philosophical framework. See Ehsan Tabari, *Foroupashi-ye Nizam-i Sunnati va Zayeshi Sarmayedari Dar Iran* [The Decline of Traditional Order and the Emergence of Capitalism in Iran] (Stockholm: Tudeh Publishing Centre, 1975/1354), pp. 81, 86.

26. Abu Talib Khan Ibn Muhammad Isfahani, *Travels of Mirza Abu Taleb Khan in Asia, Africa, and Europe during the Years 1799 to 1803,* trans. from Persian by Charles Stewart (New Delhi: Sona Publications, 1972), preface, p. vii.

27. Ibid., p. 133.

28. Ibid., p. 110.

29. Ibid., p. 129.

30. Ibid., p. 134.

31. Ibid., p. 138.

32. Ibid., pp. 168–77.

33. Ibid., pp. 180–83.

34. Hourani, *History of the Arab Peoples,* pp. 304–5.

35. James Morier, *The Adventures of Hajji Baba, of Ispahan* (1824; reprint, London: J. M. Dent & Sons, 1914). The above quotation is from the preface to the 1937 edition (New York: Random House), no page.

36. Sir Walter Scott, "An Appreciation," in Morier, *Adventures of Hajji Baba,* p. ix.

37. Morier, *Adventures of Hajji Baba.*

38. Ibid., p. 67.

39. Ibid., pp. 8–87.

40. Ibid., pp. 88–89.

41. Ibid., p. 128.

42. Ibid., p. 248.

43. Scott, "Appreciation," pp. x–xi.

44. Morier, *Adventures of Hajji Baba*, p. 12.

Chapter Three

1. Barbara Daly Metcalf, "Too Little and Too Much"; and Hardy, *Muslims of British India.*

2. Aziz Ahmad, *Islamic Modernism in India and Pakistan: 1857–1964* (London: Oxford University Press, 1967), p. 103; Barbara D. Metcalf, *Islamic Revival in British India: Deoband, 1860–1900* (Princeton, N.J.: Princeton University Press, 1982).

3. Not only Sayyid Ahmad Khan, but also virtually all contemporary commentators on him stressed the magnitude of the opposition he was facing. The main opponents of the establishment of Aligarh College were Imad Ali, Muhammad Ali, and Ali Bakhsh, who procured *fatwas* from the ulama of various Indian cities, Mecca, and Medina, declaring him, "officially," among other things, "the *khalifa* . . . of the Devil himself who is intent upon leading Muslims astray," whose "perfidy is worse than that of the Jews and Christians." See Troll, *Sayyid Ahmad Khan,* pp. 20–21; and Altaf Husain Hali, *Hayat-i-Javed,* trans. K. H. Qadiri and David J. Matthews (Delhi: Idarah-i Adabiyat-i Delli, 1979; originally published in 1901), p. 541. Another of Sayyid Ahmad Khan's principal critics, Rashid Ahmad Gangohi, while conceding that Sayyid Ahmad Khan might be a well-wisher of Muslims, regarded his religious ideas as a "deadly poison" for Islam. See, Aziz Ahmad, *Islamic Modernism,* p. 106.

4. M. P. Jain, *Outlines of Indian Legal History* (Delhi: Dhanwantra Medical & Law, 1952), pp. 1–7.

5. Bayly, *Indian Society,* pp. 11, 18, 44, 46–47, 51, 61.

6. Aziz Ahmad, *Islamic Modernism,* pp. 13–14.

7. Duncan Forbes, "James Mill and India," *Cambridge Journal* 5, no. 1 (October 1951), pp. 19–33.

8. *Cambridge History of India* (1969), 6:96.

9. Sir William Jones, *The Letters of Sir William Jones,* ed. Garland Cannon, (Oxford: Clarendon Press, 1970), 2:794. See also J. Majeed, "James Mill's 'The History of British India' and Utilitarianism as a Rhetoric of Reform," *Modern Asian Studies* 24, no. 2 (1990): 209.

10. Geoffrey Theodore Garratt, "Indo-British Civilization," in *The Legacy of India,* ed. Geoffrey Theodore Garratt (Oxford: Clarendon Press, 1937), p. 398.

11. Forbes, "James Mill and India," p. 23.

12. Julius Richter, *A History of Missions in India,* trans. Sydney H. Moore (London: Oliphant Anderson & Ferrier, 1908), p. 186.

13. Garratt, "Indo-British Civilization," p. 398.

14. Ernest Binfield Havell, *Indian Sculpture and Painting* (London: J. Murray, 1928), p. 246.

15. Garratt, "Indo-British Civilization," p. 402.

16. Sir William Wilson Hunter, *The Indian Musalmans* (London: Trubner & Co., 1872), p. 136.

17. Jyotish Chandra Ghosh, "Vernacular Literatures," in Garratt, *Legacy of India,* p. 388.

18. Garratt, "Indo-British Civilization," pp. 400–401. Garratt cited several factors in the defeat of the Orientalists. "Bengal was an unlucky field of battle. There were few of those visible signs of Indian skill and energy which abound in many parts of the country. The local Muslims were uneducated, their Maulvis were the decadent hangers-on left over from the collapse of Mughal rule. Hinduism was seen at its worst in Bengal, and a new generation of British officials was at last awakening to some of its less defensible aspects. The younger Englishmen believed firmly that they were dealing with 'a decomposed society,' hopelessly corrupt, and they were supported in that idea by a group of reformist Bengalis, of whom Ram Mohan Roy was the best known. The 'suttee' controversy had important reactions . . . Besides the *sabamarana* rite, other unfortunate aberrations of Hinduism were coming to light, as the British administration spread and became more settled. Female infanticide was discovered to be prevalent; child marriages, untouchability, and such savage survivals as the *meriab* sacrifices added to the general prejudice" (pp. 399–400).

19. James Mill, *The History of British India,* vol. 1 (London: James Madden, 1848), p. 309; and John Millar, *The Origin of the Distinction of Ranks; or, An Inquiry into the Circumstances Which Give Rise to Influence and Authority in the Different Members of Society,* 3rd ed. (London: J. Murray, 1781).

20. Forbes, "James Mill and India," p. 29.

21. Ibid., p. 31.

22. "Mill, James," in *Encyclopaedia Britannica* (1993), 8:131. It may be noted that, as Forbes ("James Mill and India," pp. 22–23) indicated, the Evangelicals might have won the day for Anglicists and Westernizers without the support of the deist and rationalist James Mill. Before Mill, pioneers of Westernizing were in the field, including Westernizing Hindus like Ram Mohan Roy, whose pamphlet on the "idolatrous religion of the Hindus" was published in 1790.

23. Views similar to those of Macaulay and Mill were held by Christian missionaries "who saw in anglicizing the Indian the preliminary step to Christianizing him; and by progressive Indians such as Raja Ram Mohan Ray who sought the help of liberal ideas from Europe in order to combat the religious orthodoxies and social corruption of their country." See Ghosh, "Vernacular Literatures," p. 388.

24. M. P. Jain, *Outlines of Indian Legal History,* pp. 394–400; and *Parliamentary Papers* 12 (1831–32): 696.

25. M. P. Jain, *Outlines of Indian Legal History,* pp. 152–53.

26. Ibid., pp. 403–12.

27. The introduction of English laws to the Indian penal system was strongly resisted and in most cases proved abortive. See Rev. James Long, *Selections from Unpublished Records of Government for the Years 1748–1767 Inclusive* (1869; reprint, Calcutta: Firma K. L. Mukhopadhyay, 1973), pp. 567–68; and Abu Talib Khan, p. 158.

28. Richter, *History of Missions in India,* pp. 188–89.

29. "Female Infanticide," *Calcutta Review,* May–August 1844, pp. 372–73, 379.

30. Ibid., p. 441.

31. Ibid., p. 405.

32. Emperor Jahangir of Hindustan, *Memoirs of the Emperor Jahangueir,* trans. Major David Price (Delhi: Rare Books, 1970), p. 48.

33. "Biographies of Mohammed for India," *Calcutta Review* 17, no. 34 (1852): 387.

34. The Charter Act of 1833 also favored the missionaries because it permitted settlement in the company's territories without the formality of a residence license. See A. A. Powell, "Maulana Rahmat Allah Kairanawi and Muslim-Christian Controversy in India in the Mid-19th Century," *Journal of the Royal Asiatic Society* 1 (1976): 47; and *Parliamentary Papers,* House of Commons, Public Bills (1833), vol. 2.

35. Troll, *Sayyid Ahmad Khan,* p. 65.

36. Powell, "Maulana Rahmat Allah Kairanawi," pp. 42–43.

37. "The Mahommedan Controversy," *Calcutta Review* 4 (July–December 1845): 418.

38. "The Relation of Christianity to Islam, and the Coran in Its Last Meccan Stage," *Calcutta Review* 25, no. 50 (1855): 202, 214.

39. Cited in "Sprenger's Life of Muhammad," *Calcutta Review* 16, no. 32 (1851): 375; Aloys Sprenger, *The Life of Muhammad* (Allahabad, 1851).

40. *Calcutta Review,* 1852, p. 398.

41. *Calcutta Review,* 1845, p. 431.

42. Troll, *Sayyid Ahmad Khan,* pp. 60–61.

43. Cited in *Calcutta Review,* 1845, p. 426.

44. Ibid., p. 427.

45. *Calcutta Review,* 1852, p. 393.

46. Ibid., p. 405.

47. Ibid., p. 409. Some new converts also joined the ranks of the missionaries in criticizing Islam. A certain Reverend Imad-ud-din, baptized in 1866, was a convert from Islam to Christianity whose polemical *Tanqid al-khayalat* (1882–86) criticized the theological ideas of Sayyid Ahmad Khan. See Troll, *Sayyid Ahmad Khan,* p. 19.

48. Richter, *History of Missions in India,* p. 329.

49. Ibid., p. 330.

50. *Woman's Work for Woman,* April 1871, pp. 5–6; *Foreign Missionary Chronicle,* November 1834, p. 363.

51. Richter, *History of Missions in India,* p. 333.

52. Ibid., p. 337.

53. "Second Annual Report," *Woman's Work for Woman,* January 1873, pp. 3–4.

54. "Tenth Annual Report," *Woman's Work for Woman,* December 1880, p. 11.

55. Cited in "Mahommedan Controversy," *Calcutta Review* 4 (July–December 1845): 450.

56. Ibid., p. 447; Aziz Ahmad, *Islamic Modernism,* p. 26.

57. "Mahommedan Controversy," *Calcutta Review* 4 (July–December 1845): 468.

58. "The Mohammedan Controversy," *Calcutta Review* 17, no. 34 (1852): 412. These charges against Christianity were reiterated in Sayyid Ali Hasan's eight-hundred-page *Kitab-i Istifsar* [Book of Questions] (Lucknow, 1845).

59. Powell, "Maulana Rahmat Allah Kairanawi," pp. 46–47.

60. Ibid., p. 54.

61. Ibid., pp. 54–58; Aziz Ahmad, *Islamic Modernism,* pp. 26–27; "Mahommedan Controversy," *Calcutta Review* 4 (1845): 435–67.

62. Bayly, *Indian Society,* pp. 106, 120–21, 136,170–71, 178–79, 180; and Erik Stokes, *The Peasant Armed: The Indian Rebellion of 1857,* ed. C. A. Bayly (Oxford: Clarendon Press, 1986).

63. Rev. Robert Clark, *The Punjab and Sindh Missions of the Church Missionary Society,* 2nd ed. (London: Church Missionary Society, 1885), pp. 4–9; Richter, *History of Missions in India,* pp. 137–38; Aziz Ahmad, *Islamic Modernism,* p. 25.

64. Clark, *Punjab and Sindh Missions,* p. 12.

65. Sayyid Ahmad Khan, *The Causes of the Indian Revolt,* trans. G. Graham and A. Colvin (Lahore: Book House, 1873; first published in Urdu in 1859), pp. 21–23, 28–29, and appendix 1.

66. Ibid., appendix 2.

67. Richter, *History of Missions in India,* p. 203.

68. William Howard Russell, *My Indian Diary* (1860, reprint, London: Cassell & Co., 1957).

69. Hali, *Hayat-i-Javed,* p. 46.

70. Malik, *Sir Sayyid Ahmad Khan,* p. 76.

71. Troll, *Sayyid Ahmad Khan,* pp. xvii–xviii. Troll is less dramatic, however, than either Hali or Malik, arguing that "Sir Sayyid's concern for a 'purification' of Muslim religious practice in India goes back to the first half of his life, long before the events of 1857. . . . At that time neither 'the rationalistic outlook of nineteenth century scholarship in Europe' nor the religious estrangement of a class of young, western-educated Muslims had appeared—and it is these phenomenon that are held to have 'compelled' him into theology" (ibid., p. xviii).

72. Hali, *Hayat-i-Javed,* p. 64.

73. Sayyid Ahmad Khan, *Speeches and Addresses Relating to Muhammedan Anglo-Oriental College* (Aligarh, 1888), pp. 24–31.

74. "The Indian Philanthropist," *Aligarh Institute Gazette,* no. 39 (August 4, 1876): 475.

75. Aziz Ahmad, *Islamic Modernism,* pp. 40–41.

76. Hali, *Hayat-i-Javed,* p. 171.

77. Bashir Ahmad Dar, *Religious Thought of Sayyid Ahmad Khan* (Lahore: Institute of Islamic Culture, 1957), p. 140.

78. Aziz Ahmad, *Islamic Modernism,* pp. 42–43; Malik, *Sir Sayyid Ahmad Khan,* p. 29; Muhammad Hadi Hussain, *Syed Ahmed Khan: Pioneer of Muslim Resurgence* (Lahore: Institute of Islamic Culture, 1970), pp. 171–84; Troll, *Sayyid Ahmad Khan,* pp. 171–93.

79. Dar, *Religious Thought of Sayyid Ahmad Khan,* pp. 149–50; Hali, *Hayat-i-Javed,* p. 172.

80. Dar, *Religious Thought of Sayyid Ahmad Khan,* p. 156.

81. Cited in Muhammad Hadi Hussain, *Syed Ahmed Khan,* pp. 187–88.

82. Ibid., pp. 185–96; Aziz Ahmad, *Islamic Modernism,* pp. 45–49; Troll, *Sayyid Ahmad Khan,* pp. 188–93.

83. Malik, *Sir Sayyid Ahmad Khan,* p. 176.

84. Ibid., pp. 175–86.

85. Sayyid Ahmad Khan, "Selected Essays by Sir Sayyid Ahmad Khan from the Journal *Tahzib al-Akhlaq,*" trans. John Wilder (M.A. thesis, Hartford Seminary Foundation, 1972; from essays originally published in Urdu in 1870–76), pp. 12, 113 note 1; Aziz Ahmad, *Islamic Modernism,* p. 38; Baljon, *Reforms and Religious Ideas,* p. 33.

86. John Wilder, "Introduction," in Khan, "Selected Essays," p. 14.

87. Sayyid Ahmad Khan, "Selected Essays," p. 38.

88. Ibid., pp. 54–55.

89. Aziz Ahmad, *Islamic Modernism*, p. 38.

90. Sayyid Ahmad Khan, "Selected Essays," p. 85.

91. Hali, *Hayat-i-Javed*, p. 75. For a thorough analysis of Sayyid Ahmad Khan's commentary on the Bible, see Troll, *Sayyid Ahmad Khan*, pp. 58–99. See also Sir Thomas Walker Arnold, *The Preaching of Islam: A History of the Propagation of the Muslim Faith* (London, Constable & Co., 1913), pp. 408–27, 438–39.

92. Aziz Ahmad, *Islamic Modernism*, pp. 65–70.

93. Ibid., pp. 57–58.

94. Malcolm MacColl, "Are Reforms Possible under Mussulman Rule?" *Contemporary Review* 40 (August 1881): 257–81.

95. Moulvi Cheragh Ali, Moulvi, *The Proposed Political, Legal, and Social Reforms in the Ottoman Empire and Other Mohammadan States* (Bombay: Education Society Press, 1883), p. xxvii.

96. Ibid., pp. 3–8.

97. Ibid., p. 10.

98. Ibid., p. 11.

99. Khan, "Selected Essays," pp. 88–89.

100. Aziz Ahmad, *Islamic Modernism*, pp. 52–53.

101. Ibid., p. 128; Cheragh [Chiragh] Ali, *A Critical Exposition of the Popular "Jihad"* (Karachi, Pakistan: Karimsons, 1977), pp. lxxxiii–iv note 2.

102. Ibid., p. 72 note 40; Gail Minault, "Sayyid Mumtaz Ali and 'Huquq un-Niswan': An Advocate of Women's Rights in Islam in the Late Nineteenth Century," *Modern Asian Studies* 24, no. 1 (1990): 148; Barbara D. Metcalf, *Islamic Revival*, pp. 198–234.

103. Minault, "Sayyid Mumtaz Ali and 'Huquq un-Niswan,'" p. 152; Aziz Ahmad, *Islamic Modernism*, p. 72.

104. Minault, "Sayyid Mumtaz Ali and 'Huquq un-Niswan,'" p. 153.

105. Ibid., pp. 153–54.

106. Ibid., pp. 162–66; Aziz Ahmad, *Islamic Modernism*, p. 75.

107. Cheragh Ali, *Critical Exposition*, pp. i–xvi, 34, 40–41, 60, 76,192.

108. Ibid., pp. 194, 196, 203.

109. Numani Shibli, *Sirat al-Nabi*, trans. Fazulur Rahman (Karachi: Pakistan Historical Society, 1970/1330), pp. 5, 59–60.

110. Ibid., p. 295.

111. Ibid., p. 60.

112. Ibid., pp. 61-67.

113. Ibid., p. 68.

114. Muhammad Shibli Numani, *Omar the Great*, trans. Muhammad Saleem (Lahore: Sh. Muhammad Ashraf, 1962; originally published in Urdu in 1898), p. 5.

115. Ibid., pp. 13–23.

116. Ibid., pp. 167–73.

117. Ibid., pp. 187–95.

118. Muhammad Shibli Numani, *Alamgir,* trans. Syed Sabahuddin Abdur Rahman (Delhi: Idarah-i Adabiyat-i Delli, 1981; originally published in Urdu in 1911), pp. 71–78.

119. Aziz Ahmad, *Islamic Modernism,* p. 86.

120. Syed Ameer [Amir] Ali, *The Spirit of Islam* (London: Christophers, 1922), pp. 122–28; see also Ameer Ali, *A Short History of the Saracens* (New York: Macmillan & Co., 1955).

121. Ameer Ali, *Spirit of Islam,* p. 132.

122. Ibid., pp. xxxiii, lii.

123. Ibid., p. 247.

124. Ibid., p. 230.

125. Ibid., pp. 259–60.

126. Ibid., p. 264.

127. Aziz Ahmad, *Islamic Modernism,* p. 94.

128. Ameer Ali, *Spirit of Islam,* p. 274.

129. Ibid., pp. 210–11.

130. Ibid., pp. 211–15.

Chapter Four

1. J. Heyworth-Dunne, *An Introduction to the History of Education in Modern Egypt* (London: Frank Cass & Co., 1968), pp. 104–223, 253.

2. Vatikiotis, *History of Egypt,* p. 98.

3. Heyworth-Dunne, *Introduction to the History of Education,* pp. 144–45.

4. Khaled Fahmy, *All the Pasha's Men: Mehmet Ali, His Army and the Making of Modern Egypt* (Cambridge: Cambridge University Press, 1997).

5. Hourani, *Arabic Thought,* p. 53; Heyworth-Dunne, *Introduction to the History of Education,* pp. 144–45.

6. Heyworth-Dunne, *Introduction to the History of Education,* p. 168.

7. Fahmy, *All the Pasha's Men,* p. 315.

8. Edward William Lane, *An Account of the Manners and Customs of Modern Egyptians* (London: John Murray, 1871), 1:137.

9. Vatikiotis, *History of Egypt,* pp. 101–7, 183.

10. Ibid., pp. 179, 183, 186–87.

11. Evelyn Baring Cromer, *Modern Egypt* (New York: Macmillan Co., 1908), 2:141–42.

12. Charles Watson, *In the Valley of the Nile: A Survey of the Missionary Movement in Egypt* (New York: Fleming H. Revell Co., 1908), p. 208.

13. Andrew Watson, *The American Mission in Egypt: 1854–1896* (Pittsburgh: United Presbyterian Board of Publication, 1898), p. 361.

14. Charles Watson, *In the Valley,* p. 210.

15. Edith L. Butcher, *The Story of the Church of Egypt* (London: Smith, Elder, & Co., 1897), vol 2, p. 428.

16. "Saint Simon," in *The New Encyclopaedia Britannica* (1991), p. 334.

17. Hourani, *Arabic Thought,* p. 54; Heyworth-Dunne, *Introduction to the History of Education,* p. 145.

18. Jamal Mohammad Ahmed, *The Intellectual Origins of Egyptian Nationalism* (Oxford: Oxford University Press, 1960), p. 12.

19. Hourani, *Arabic Thought,* p. 69.

20. For an overview of the intellectual orientations of *Rawdat al-Madaris,* see Muhammad Abd al-Ghany Hasan and Abd al-Aziz al-Dosouqi, *Rawdat al-Madaris* (Cairo: al-Hayat al-Misriyya al-Aama al-Kitab, 1975).

21. Two Syrian Christians, Ya'qub Sarruf and Faris Nimr, founded *al-Muqtataf* in Beirut in 1876, but, weary of the everlasting vexation of the Ottoman officials, the editors emigrated to Egypt and continued the publication of the journal there. See Martin Hartmann, *The Arabic Press of Egypt* (London: Luzac & Co., 1899), pp. 11, 69–70. Farag, on the other hand, argues that the immediate reason for the departure of Sarruf, Nimr, and Makarius from Syria was the Lewis affair. These three were graduates of the Syrian Protestant College and early members of the anti-Turkish Secret Society of Beirut. See Nadia Farag, "The Lewis Affair and the Fortunes of al-Muqtataf," *Middle Eastern Studies* 8, no. 1 (January 1972): 73–83.

22. *Al-Muqtataf* 1 (1876): 133.

23. *Al-Muqtataf* 5 (1880): 10.

24. *Al-Muqtataf* 6 (1881): 313.

25. *Al-Muqtataf* 7 (1882): 2–6.

26. *Al-Muqtataf* 17 (1893), p. 101.

27. *Al-Muqtataf* 20 (1896): 161–65.

28. *Al-Muqtataf* 23 (1898): 801–5.

29. *Al-Muqtataf* 29 (1904): 1–8.

30. For example, see *al-Muqtataf* 2 (1877): 107, 208; and 7 (1882): 134.

31. *Al-Muqtataf* 1 (1876): 141, 174, 231, 276, 279, 268.

32. *Al-Muqtataf* 7 (1882): 2–6, 23, 57, 163.

33. *Al-Muqtataf* 1 (1876): 217.

34. *Al-Muqtataf* 10 (1885): 145–46. Rashi Rida also advocated the idea that Darwinism did not contradict the Quran. See *al-Manar* 8 (1906): 920.

35. See Abdel A. Ziadat, *Western Science in the Arab World: The Impact of Darwinism, 1860–1930* (London: Macmillan, 1986), pp. 26–27.

36. Ibid., p. 89. See also *al-Muqtataf* 30 (1905): 565.

37. *Al-Muqtataf* 1 (1876): 160; 4 (1879): 256; 8 (1883): 573; and 11 (1886): 486.

38. *Al-Muqtataf* 7 (1882): 279; 8 (1883): 7, 52, 53, 358, 469, 641, 548, 585.

39. *Al-Muqtataf* 10 (1885): 634, 676, 739.

40. *Al-Muqtataf* 11 (1886): 170, 232.

41. *Al-Muqtataf* 11 (1886): 355–60, 401. See also two commentaries on pages 745 and 748, and Shumayyil's rejoinder in 12 (1887): 50. Ya'qub Sarruf defended women's rights in his eulogy of Miriam Nimir Macarios (1860–87), a female activist (12 [1887]: 435). Other articles on women cover topics like "high esteem of women under the Pharaohs" (12 [1887]: 677), "women and elections" (13 [1888]: 624), a book on women's rights in Islam by the first inspector of Arabic science from the Ministry of Education (15 [1890]: 68), the claim that women's mental capability was weaker than men's (15 [1890]: 376–383), and the claim that women had smaller brains than men (16 [1891]: 643).

42. Cromer, *Modern Egypt,* 2:135.

43. Ibid., 2:139.

44. Ibid., 2:155.

45. Ibid., 2:157.

46. Ibid., 2:229. Milner expresses similar views about the Azhar: "So far as real knowledge and education goes, El-Azhar is, if not a dead, at least a dormant institution. . . . The only thing which really flourishes at the El-Azhar nowadays is the study of the Arabic language. Besides this there is nothing but a decrepit Theology and a still more decrepit Jurisprudence, both based entirely on the Koran and the commentaries of the old Arab doctors, both products of the scholastic method in its last stage of degeneracy." See Alfred Milner, *England in Egypt* (London: Macmillan, 1892), p. 364.

47. Cromer, *Modern Egypt,* 2:2, 228.

48. Ibid., 2:2, 230. Milner also stated that "imagine a people most docile and good-tempered in the world in the grip of a religion the most intolerant and fanatical" (Milner, *England in Egypt,* p. 5).

49. Wilfred S. Blunt, *Secret History of the English Occupation of Egypt* (1895; reprint, New York: Howard Fertig, 1967), p. 9. *Al-Muqtataf* (5 [1880]: 154) viewed British occupation as beneficial for Egypt. Most of the Syrian émigrés were dedicated to Westernization and had a strong influence on the climate of opinion in Egypt. See Jack A. Crabbs, Jr., *The Writing of History in Nineteenth-Century Egypt* (Cairo: American University Press, 1984), pp. 185–86; and Jamal Mohammad Ahmed, *Intellectual Origins,* pp. 30–31.

50. Charles Wendell, *The Evolution of the Egyptian National Image: From Its Origins to Ahmad Lutfi al-Sayyid* (Berkeley: University of California Press, 1972), p. 202.

51. Cited in Jamal Mohammad Ahmed, *Intellectual Origins,* p. 52.

52. In the first quarter of the nineteenth century, Lane witnessed the execution of a woman for apostasy. See Lane, *Account of the Manners and Customs,* 1:136–37. Cromer reported that the last person executed for apostasy by virtue of a decision of an Ottoman law court was an Armenian, who adopted Islam in 1843, subsequently repented, and returned to the Christian church. Lord Stratford, then ambassador at Constantinople, rose in all his wrath, and after some sharp diplomatic passages, extracted a declaration from the Porte that for the future no apostate should be put to death. Articles X–XII of the *Khatt-i Humayoun* in 1856 further ensured religious freedom. Cromer also reported that in Egypt he had to interfere once or twice to protect from maltreatment the Muslims who had been converted to Christianity by American missionaries. See Cromer, *Modern Egypt,* 2:137–38 note 2; and Stanley Lane-Poole, *The Life of the Right Honourable Stratford Canning* (London: Longmans, Green & Co., 1888).

53. Hourani, *Arabic Thought,* pp. 39–40, 53.

54. Charles Watson, *In the Valley,* p. 118. See also Susan Sachs, "American Headstones Tugging at Egypt's Memory," *New York Times,* November 8, 2000.

55. Andrew Watson, *American Mission,* pp. 31–32; Charles Watson, *In the Valley,* p. 118.

56. Charles Watson, *In the Valley,* p. 150.

57. Andrew Watson, *American Mission,* p. 360; Julius Richter, *A History of Protestant Missions in the Near East* (New York: Fleming H. Revell CompanyCo., 1910), p. 344.

58. Charles Watson, *In the Valley,* p. 78.

59. Ibid., p. 87.

60. Ibid., p. 92.

61. Ibid., p. 93.

62. Andrew Watson, *American Mission*, pp. 52–53.

63. Ibid., p. 436.

64. Ibid.

65. Charles Watson, *In the Valley*, p. 122.

66. Ibid., p. 123.

67. Charles Watson, *In the Valley*, pp. 172–73.

68. Charles R. Watson, *Egypt and the Christian Crusade* (New York: United Presbyterian Church of North America, 1907), appendix 4, pp. 274–75.

69. Cited in Sachs, "American Headstones."

70. Hourani, *Arabic Thought*, p. 144.

71. Ibid., p. 70; Hamid Enayat, *Sayri Dar Andisheh-ye Arab* [An Overview of Arabic Thought] (Tehran: Sipihr Printing Office, 1977), p. 28; Jamal Mohammad Ahmed, *Intellectual Origins*, p. 13. Tahtawi and students in the School of Languages translated over one thousand books into Turkish and Arabic. Personally, he listed twenty-eight works of various kinds which he wrote, translated, or edited. See Crabbs, *Writing of History*, pp. 72–74.

72. Enayat, *Sayri*, pp. 29–30; see also Rifa'a Rafi' Tahtawi, *Takhlis al-Ibriz ila Talkhis Bariz* (Cairo: al-Amir-ih, 1905), p. 133.

73. Hourani, *Arabic Thought*, p. 82.

74. Ibid., p. 75.

75. Ibid., p. 75.

76. Ibid., p. 109. Islamic modernism in the Middle East is associated with the life and work of al-Afghani. Born into a Shi'i family in a village close to Hamadan (Iran), he completed his education in Qazvin and Najaf. In his late teens, around 1857, he traveled to India, where he most likely first became acquainted with modern Western knowledge. From there, he went to Mecca and to Afghanistan, where he tried to persuade the Afghan king to ally himself with Russia against the British. He then moved to Istanbul and found a powerful protector, the reforming statesman Ali Pasha. He stirred controversy and the anger of the ulama when he elevated reason and philosophy to the level of revelation and prophecy. Expelled from Istanbul, he left for Egypt in 1871. Expelled from Egypt in 1879, he went to India for three years, after which he went to Paris, Iran, Russia, and back to Iran and ended up in Istanbul in 1892, where he remained until his death in 1897.

77. F. Guizot, *The History of Civilization*, vols. 1–3, trans. William Hazlitt (New York: D. Appleton & Co., 1890), first lecture, p. 24.

78. Ibid., pp. 72–73.

79. *Al-Urwa al-wuthqa* was an Arabic periodical published in Paris between March and October 1884, under the political directorship of al-Afghani and the editorial directorship of Muhammad Abduh. The journal was predominantly anti-British, containing about forty articles on British hegemony, government, and deception and the manner in which Great Britain dealt with other nations. There were also over twenty articles on Islam and Islamic civilization.

80. "Madi al-Umma wa Hadirouha wa Ilaaju ilaliha" [The past and present of the umma and the treatment of its malady), *al-Urwa al-wuthqa*, 1884, 45–60.

81. "Al-Wahdat al-Islami-yah" [Islamic unity], *al-Urwa al-wuthqa*, 1884, pp. 130–40.

82. "Al-Amal wa Talab al-Majd" [Hope and the pursuit of glory], *al-Urwa al-wuthqa*, 1884, pp. 151–62.

83. "Al-Qada wa al-Qadar" [Predestination], *al-Urwa al-wuthqa,* 1884, pp. 102–17.

84. "Answer of Jamal ad-Din to Renan," in *An Islamic Response to Imperialism: Political and Religious Writings of Sayyid Jamal ad-Din "al-Afghani,"* by Nikki R. Keddie (Berkeley: University of California Press, 1968), p. 183.

85. Ibid.

86. Ibid., p. 187.

87. Cited in Keddie, *Islamic Response,* p. 105.

88. Ibid., p. 73.

89. Ibid., pp. 37–38.

90. According to Hourani, "'The Sayyid,' he [Abduh] told one of his own disciples, 'never did any real work except in Egypt.' Instead of meddling in the intrigues of the palace at Constantinople, he should have tried to persuade the sultan to reform the system of education. He wrote something of this to al-Afghani himself who was angry, and their relations seem to have ended on this note. When al-Afghani died, he wrote no word of eulogy or affectionate commemoration." See Hourani, *Arabic Thought,* p. 158; and also *al-Manar* 8 (1906): 453–75.

91. Charles C. Adams, *Islam and Modernism in Egypt: A Study of the Modern Reform Movement Inaugurated by Muhammad 'Abduh* (New York: Russell & Russell, 1933), pp. 55, 64; Cromer, *Modern Egypt,* 2:179–81; *al-Manar* 8 (1906): 413, 462; Hourani, *Arabic Thought,* pp. 133–34; Enayat, *Sayri,* pp. 120–23. In a self-description of the objects of his career, Abduh indicated that "I later abandoned this question of political authority for fate to determine and for the hand of God to settle, for I realized that in such matters nations reap the fruits of what has been planted and cultivated over a long period of years, and that it is this planting with which we must now concern ourselves, with God's help." Cited in Kerr, *Islamic Reform,* p. 109.

92. Hourani, *Arabic Thought,* pp. 136–38.

93. Abduh admired Herbert Spencer, whom he visited in Britain, and translated his *Education* from a French version into Arabic. He had read Rousseau's *Emile,* Lev Tolstoy's novels and his didactic writings, David Friedrich Strauss's *Life of Jesus,* and the works of Renan. He had had some contact with European thinkers, written to Tolstoy on the occasion of his excommunication from the Russian Orthodox Church, and traveled to Europe, whenever he could, to renew his soul, as he said, and because it revived his hopes about the future of the Muslim world. See Adams, *Islam and Modernism in Egypt,* p. 67; *al-Manar* 8 (1906): 66; Hourani, *Arabic Thought,* pp. 135.

94. Hourani, *Arabic Thought,* pp. 139–40; Adams, *Islam and Modernism in Egypt,* pp. 97–99; Cromer, *Modern Egypt,* 2:180–81.

95. Adams, *Islam and Modernism in Egypt,* p. 110.

96. Hourani, *Arabic Thought,* pp. 148–49; Bryan S. Turner, *Weber and Islam* (Boston: Routledge & Kegan Paul, 1974), pp. 147–49; Adams, *Islam and Modernism in Egypt.*

97. Quran 2:252.

98. *al-Manar* 8 (February 10, 1906): 921–30; see also Adams, *Islam and Modernism in Egypt,* pp. 141–42.

99. Kerr, *Islamic Reform,* pp. 59, 111.

100. Ibid., p. 107.

101. See Adams, *Islam and Modernism in Egypt,* pp. 86–88; and Hourani, *Arabic Thought,* p. 144.

102. Cited in Adams, *Islam and Modernism in Egypt,* pp. 89–90. See also Donald M. Reid, *The Odyssey of Farah Antun: A Syrian Christian's Quest for Secularism* (Chicago: Bibliotheca Islamica, 1975), pp. 80–90.

103. In Hourani's assertion, "it is significant that both his controversies were concerned, not with the truth or falsity of Islam, but with its being compatible with the supposed requirements of the modern mind; and in the process, it may be that 'Abduh's view of Islam was itself affected by his view of what the modern mind needs." See Hourani, *Arabic Thought,* p. 144; and Reid, *Odyssey of Farah Antun,* pp. 85–86.

104. *Al-Muqtataf* mentioned the controversy about the relationship between Christianity and religion. See *al-Muqtataf* 15 (1891): 353–65, 425–32, 497–503; and Hourani, *Arabic Thought,* p. 162.

105. Cited in Adams, *Islam and Modernism in Egypt,* p. 244.

106. Hourani, *Arabic Thought,* p. 162.

107. Leila Ahmed, *Women and Gender in Islam: Historical Roots of a Modern Debate* (New Haven, Conn.: Yale University Press, 1992), pp. 134–37.

108. See Beth Baron, *The Women's Awakening in Egypt: Culture, Society, and the Press* (New Haven, Conn.: Yale University Press, 1992), pp. 14–16.

109. Cited in Leila Ahmed, *Women and Gender in Islam,* p. 140.

110. Adams, *Islam and Modernism in Egypt,* p. 22.

111. Qasim Amin, *The Liberation of Women,* trans. Samiha Sidhom Peterson (Cairo: American University in Cairo Press, 1992; originally published in Arabic in 1899), pp. 8–9.

112. Ibid., pp. 69–70.

113. Ibid., p. 7.

114. Ibid., pp. 42, 45, 76–79.

115. Ibid., p. 101.

116. Cited in Hourani, *Arabic Thought,* p. 168.

117. Cited in Jamal Mohammad Ahmed, *Intellectual Origins,* p. 50.

118. Ibid., pp. 50–51.

119. Leila Ahmed, *Women and Gender in Islam,* p. 156.

120. Ibid., p. 157.

121. Ibid., p. 155.

122. Ibid., p. 235.

123. See Minault, "Sayyid Mumtaz Ali and 'Huquq un-Niswan,'" pp., 147–72.

124. See Zeine N. Zeine, *The Emergence of Arab Nationalism* (Delmar, N.Y.: Carvan Books, 1973).

125. George Antonius, *The Arab Awakening: The Story of the Arab National Movement* (London: Hamish Hamilton, 1961), p. 95.

126. Cited in Hamid Enayat, *Modern Islamic Political Thought* (London: Macmillan, 1982), p. 54.

127. Sylvia G. Haim, ed., *Arab Nationalism: An Anthology* (Berkeley: University of California Press, 1962), p. 42.

128. Richard P. Mitchell, *The Society of the Muslim Brothers* (London: Oxford University Press, 1969), p. 39.

129. Cited in Jamal Mohammad Ahmed, *Intellectual Origins,* pp. 118.

130. Adams, *Islam and Modernism in Egypt,* pp. 259–68; Jamal Mohammad Ahmed, *Intellectual Origins,* pp. 117–19; Hourani, *Arabic Thought,* pp. 185–88, Enayat, *Modern Islamic Political Thought,* pp. 62–68.

131. Cited in Adams, *Islam and Modernism in Egypt,* p. 98.

132. Cromer, *Modern Egypt,* 2:180 note 1, also reported that Abduh encountered strong antagonism from the conservatives.

133. Crecelius, "Nonideological Responses of the Egyptian Ulama to Modernization," p. 187.

134. Hourani, *Arabic Thought,* p. 147.

135. Adams, *Islam and Modernism in Egypt,* pp. 261–62.

Chapter Five

1. Algar, *Religion and State;* Nikki R. Keddie, "The Roots of Islamic Power in Modern Iran," in *Scholars, Saints and Sufis,* ed. Nikki R. Keddie (Los Angeles: University of California Press, 1972).

2. Algar, *Religion and State,* pp. 33–40, note 43.

3. Mansoor Moaddel, "The Shi'i Ulama and the State in Iran," *Theory and Society* 15 (1986): 519–56; Charles Issawi, ed., *The Economic History of Iran, 1800–1914* (Chicago: University of Chicago Press, 1971), p. 17; and Lambton, *Landlord and Peasant,* p. 134.

4. Arjomand, *Shadow of God,* p. 65.

5. Mehdi Bamdad, *Tarikh-i Rijal-i Iran* [A Dictionary of National Biography of Iran] (Tehran: Zovvar Bookstore, 1968/1347), 2:375.

6. Nikki R. Keddie, "Peasants, 1900s," in Issawi, *Economic History of Iran,* p. 55.

7. Muhammad Reza Fishahi, *Vapassin Jonebesh-i Qoroun-i Vosta-ei dar Douran-i Feudal* [The Late Middle Ages' Movement in the Feudal Period] (Tehran: Elmi Printing Office, 1977/1356), pp. 63–81; Hadi Hairi, *Shi'ism and Constitutionalism in Iran* (Leiden: E. J. Brill, 1977), pp. 69–71.

8. Homa Natiq, "Sar Aghaz-i Eqtedar-i Eqtesadi va Siaci-ye Mollayan" [The rise of the political and economic dominance of the clergy], *Alefba* 2 (Spring 1983/1362): 43; Fishahi, *Vapassin Jonebesh-i Qoroun-i Vosta-ei,* p. 120.

9. Natiq, "Sar Aghaz-i Eqtedar-i Eqtesadi," p. 44.

10. Fishahi, *Vapassin Jonebesh-i Qoroun-i Vosta-ei,* p. 44.

11. Natiq, "Sar Aghaz-i Eqtedar-i Eqtesadi," p. 44.

12. Valentine Chirol, *The Middle Eastern Question; or, Some Political Problems of Indian Defence* (New York: E. P. Dutton & Co., 1903), p. 123.

13. Natiq, "Sar Aghaz-i Eqtedar-i Eqtesadi," p. 44; Lambton, "Persian Ulama," pp. 252–53.

14. Natiq, "Sar Aghaz-i Eqtedar-i Eqtesadi," p. 45.

15. Firouz Kazemzadeh, *Russia and Britain in Persia, 1864–1914* (New Haven, Conn.: Yale University Press, 1968), p. 188.

16. See Moaddel, "Shi'i Political Discourse," pp. 447–67.

17. "Correspondence Respecting the Persian Tobacco Concession," *Sessional Papers*, July 27, 1891.

18. Cited in Adamiyat, *Shourish*, p. 62.

19. According to some, the fatwas was forged by a group of merchants with the cooperation of Ayatollah Mirza Hasan Ashtiyani. See Adamiyat, *Shourish*, p. 75.

20. Cited in Sheikh Hasan Karbala'i, *Qarardad-i Rizhi-ye 1890* [The Regie Contract of 1890] (Tehran: Mobarizan, 1982/1361), pp. 68–69.

21. Algar, *Religion and State*, pp. 94–99; Ervand Abrahamian, *Iran between between Two Revolutions* (Princeton, N.J.: Princeton University Press, 1982), pp. 71–72; D. P. Costello, "The Murder of Griboedov," *Oxford Slavonic Papers* 8 (1957): 55–89, "A Note on 'The Diplomatic Activity of A. S. Griboyedov' by S. V. Shostakovich," *Slavic and East European Review* 40 (1962): 235–44, and "Griboedov in Persia in 1820: Two Diplomatic Notes," *Oxford Slavonic Papers* 5 (1954): 81–92; Natiq, "Sar Aghaz-i Eqtedar-i Eqtesadi," p. 55.

22. William W. Campbell, *A Memoir of Mrs. Judith S. Grant, Late Missionary to Persia* (New York: J. Winchester, 1844) p. 59.

23. Ibid.

24. Richter, *History of Protestant Missions in the Near East*, pp. 294–303.

25. "Second Annual Report of the Woman's Foreign Missionary Society of the Presbyterian Church," *Woman's Work for Woman*, January 1873, p. 9.

26. "Tenth Annual Report of the Woman's Foreign Missionary Society of the Presbyterian Church," *Woman's Work for Woman* 10, no. 12 (December 1880): 22.

27. Richter, *History of Protestant Missions in the Near East*, p. 304.

28. Ibid., p. 317.

29. Ibid., p. 318.

30. Cited in Abrahamian, *Iran*, p. 72; Samuel Greene Wheeler Benjamin, *Persia and the Persians*, Boston: Ticknor & Co., 1887), pp. 113, 342, 379.

31. Richter, *History of Protestant Missions in the Near East*, p. 304.

32. Samuel McChord Crothers, *Among Friends* (New York: Houghton Mifflin, 1910), pp. 180–81.

33. "Persia: Extracts from Mrs. Coan's Letter," *Woman's Work for Woman* 2 (September 1872): 175.

34. "Persia," *Woman's Work for Woman* 4, no. 1 (March 1874): 93.

35. Fereydoun Adamiyat, *Amir Kabir va Iran* (Tehran: Amir Kabir Publications, 1955/1334), pp. 192–93.

36. A missionary reported, "judging from all that we see and learn, such is the thirst for knowledge among the Armenians, and such also their dissatisfaction with their own schools as now carried on, that we should find no difficulty in establishing at once two schools, one for boys and another for girls." "Persia," p. 3.

37. Helen Easton Hoffman, "Are Persians Worth While," *Woman's Work: A Foreign Missions Magazine* 38, no. 12 (December 1923): 271.

38. Kasravi Tabrizi, *Tarikhi Mashruti-ye Iran* [The History of the Iranian Constitutional Revolution] (Tehran, 1977), p. 8.

39. Edward G. Browne, *A Year amongst the Persians* (London: Adam and Charles Black, 1893), p. 99.

40. Mongol Bayat, *Iran's First Revolution: Shi'ism and the Constitutional Revolution of 1905–1909* (New York: Oxford University Press, 1991), p. 35

41. Hairi, *Shi'ism*, p. 12.

42. Adamiyat, *Amir Kabir va Iran*, pp. 186–91.

43. Adamiyat, *Amir Kabir va Iran*, pp. 146–58; Bayat, *Iran's First Revolution*, p. 36.

44. Fereydoun Adamiyat, *Andisheh-ye Taraqi va Hukoumat-i Qanun: Asr-i Sipahasalar* [Progressive Thought and the Rule of Law: The Spahsalar Era] (Tehran: Kharazmi Publications, 1972/1351), p. 15.

45. Adamiyat, *Andisheh*, pp. 18–20; Bayat, *Iran's First Revolution*, pp. 36–37.

46. Adamiyat *Andisheh*, p. 16.

47. Ibid., pp. 21–22.

48. Ibid., pp. 17, 53–75.

49. Ibid., pp. 80–82.

50. Cited in ibid., p. 77.

51. Ibid., pp. 82–90.

52. Ibid., pp. 92–118.

53. Cited in Hairi, *Shi'ism*, p. 26.

54. Bayat, *Iran's First Revolution*, p. 37; Mirza Muhammad Khan Majd ul-Mulk, *Risala-ye Majdi-yya* (1870; reprint, Tehran: National Bank of Iran, 1942/1321).

55. Adamiyat, *Andisheh*, p. 153.

56. Abrahamian, *Iran*, pp. 65–66.

57. Adamiyat, *Andisheh*, pp. 172–89.

58. Algar, *Religion and State*, pp. 172–73.

59. Cited in ibid., p. 173.

60. Adamiyat, *Andisheh*, p. 267.

61. Algar, *Religion and State*, pp. 174–77.

62. Bayat, *Iran's First Revolution*, p. 38; Hairi, *Shi'ism*, pp. 30–43, 182–89.

63. Abrahamian, *Iran*, pp. 68–69.

64. Bayat, *Iran's First Revolution*, p. 44.

65. For more information on the causes and processes of the Iranian revolution, see Janet Afary, *The Iranian Constitutional Revolution, 1906–1911: Grassroots Democracy, Social Democracy, and the Origin of Feminism* (New York: Columbia University Press, 1996); Bayat, *Iran's First Revolution;* Edward G. Browne, *The Persian Revolution of 1905–1909* (New York: Barnes & Noble, 1910); and Abrahamian, *Iran.*

66. Browne, *Persian Revolution*, "The Fundamental Laws of December 30, 1906," pp. 362–71.

67. Browne, *Persian Revolution*, p. 148.

68. The Supplementary Fundamental Laws also consisted of the bill of rights and dealt with the separation of powers. Browne, *Persian Revolution*, "The Supplementary Fundamental Laws of October 7, 1907," pp. 372–84; see also comments by the British minister at Tehran, cited in Hairi, *Shi'ism*, pp. 215–16.

69. Browne, *Persian Revolution*, p. 127; Hairi, *Shi'ism*, pp. 152–54.

70. Cited in Abrahamian, *Iran*, p. 93. See also *Sur-i Israfil*, February 13, 1907; and "The Senate of the Ulama," *Habl ul-Matin*, June 18, 1907; "Defense," *Habl ul-Matin*, August 1, 1907.

71. Vanessa A. Martin, "The Anti-constitutionalist Arguments of Shaikh Fazlallah Nuri," *Middle Eastern Studies* 22 (April 1986): 182.

72. Sheikh Abd al-Nabi Nuri, *Tazkirah al-Ghafil wa Irshad al-Jahil* [A Reminder for the Negligent and a Guidance for the Ignorant] (1908), p. 2.

73. Ibid., p. 4.

74. Martin, "Anti-constitutionalist Arguments," pp. 191–92.

75. Nuri, *Tazkirah*, p. 7.

76. Ibid., pp. 7–9.

77. Mihdi Malikzadeh, *Tarikh-i Inqilab-i Mashrutiyat-i Iran* [The History of the Constitutional Revolution in Iran] (Tehran: Ilmi Publications, 1979/1358), 4:872–73; Hairi, *Shi'ism,* p. 199.

78. See Nazim ul-Islam Kirmani, *Tarikh-i Bidari-ye Iranian* (Tehran: Ibn Sina Publications, 1945).

79. Abrahamian, *Iran,* p. 95.

80. Malikzadeh, *Tarikh,* 6:1257–72.

81. Natiq, "Sar Aghaz-i Eqtedar-i Eqtesadi," p. 52.

82. Hairi, *Shi'ism,* pp. 73–76.

83. Browne, *Persian Revolution,* p. 406.

84. Adamiyat, *Idi'olozhi-ye,* p. 193.

85. Hairi, *Shi'ism,* p. 85; See also Nazim ul-Islam Kirmani, *Tarikhi Bidari-ye Iranian* [The History of the Awakening of Iranians] (Tehran: Ibn Sina Publications, 1945/1324).

86. Cited in Browne, *Persian Revolution,* p. 149.

87. Mirza Muhammad Hussein Na'ini, *Tanbih al-Umma wa Tanzih al-Millah* [The Admonition of the Umma and the Enlightenment of the Nation] (Baghdad, 1909). pp. 1–6.

88. Na'ini, *Tanbih,* p. 47; for a more detailed analysis of Na'ini's views, see Hairi, *Shi'ism,* chapters 3–6.

Chapter Six

1. For a concise summary of the nationalist views see Khaled Fahmy, *All the Pasha's Men,* pp. 12–24.

2. Ehud R. Toledano, *State and Society in Mid-Nineteenth Century Egypt* (Cambridge: Cambridge University Press, 1990), pp. 16, 21.

3. Fahmy, *All the Pasha's Men,* pp. 18–37, 43–47, 67–69, 73–75, 306–18.

4. Ibid., p. 19.

5. Ibid., p. 314.

6. This process was reinforced by Cromer's failure to draw outstanding Egyptians into the service of the government. See Zaheer Masood Quraishi, *Liberal Nationalism in Egypt: Rise and Fall of the Wafd Party* (Allahabad: Kitab Mahal, 1967), pp. 16, 25, 77–78; Jamal Mohammad Ahmed, *Intellectual Origins,* p. 52.

7. This is not to argue that landowners in general supported Urabi. Tawfiq had the backing of most of the Turco-Circassian landed elite, while Urabi had the backing of the indigenous army officers, many *umdas* and midlevel officials, members of the ulama, merchants, and some wealthy landowners. See Donald Malcolm Reid, "The 'Urabi Revolution and the British Conquest, 1879–1882," in *The Cambridge History of Egypt,* ed.

M. W. Daly (Cambridge: Cambridge University Press, 1998), p. 237. Schölch also presented the diversity of the people who signed the national manifestos (seventy-three government officials, ninety-three senior military officers, sixty members of the ulama, sixty members of the Majlis al-Nuwwab, forty-one merchants, and two Coptic and Jewish leaders). See Alexander Schölch, *Egypt for the Egyptians: The Socio-political Crisis in Egypt, 1878–1882* (London: Ithaca Press, 1981), p. 89. For a detailed and comprehensive analysis of Urabi movement, see Juan R. I. Cole, *Colonialism and Revolution in the Middle East: Social and Cultural Origins of Egypt's Urabi Movement* (Princeton, N.J.: Princeton University Press, 1993).

8. Vatikiotis, *History of Egypt,* pp. 107, 130–37, 148; Jacob M. Landau, *Parliaments and Parties in Egypt* (New York: Praeger, 1954), pp. 12, 20–22.

9. On how Europe inadvertently contributed to the rise of the Urabi revolution, Marsot argued that "had the two Powers not shown how easy it was to depose a ruler, even an absolute one like Ismail, and to replace him by another, perhaps Urabi would not have tried to emulate them." See Afaf Lutfi Marsot, *Egypt and Cromer: A Study in Anglo-Egyptian Relations* (New York: Praeger, 1968), p. 27.

10. Vatikiotis, *History of Egypt,* pp. 131–33.

11. Schölch *Egypt for the Egyptians,* denied that the Urabi movement was a revolutionary event. "Early in 1881, there was no storm brewing; revolution was not in the air. On 1 February 1881, the 'fallah' officers demanded nothing other than the abolition of the privileges of the Turco-Circassian *also* in the army" (p. 309). He further stated that " 'Urabi was not a revolutionary leader" (p. 310). While he believed that Egyptian nationalism provided the impulse, "the underlying idea was not that of an independent Egyptian national state. 'Urabi in particular was neither an Egyptian nor an Arab 'nationalist' " (p. 311).

12. Marsot, *Egypt and Cromer,* pp. 12–13.

13. France was espousing the cause of its bondholders in Egypt and the protection of the Suez Canal. England was more anxious to protect its interests in Egypt because 89 percent of all shipping sailing through the canal was British, and the canal was of strategic importance as the artery to India and the other colonies of the Far East. See Marsot, *Egypt and Cromer,* pp. 1–2. It is noteworthy that "before the occupation was decided upon Gladstone mentioned the rights 'of the foreign bondholders' as on a par with those of the Sultan, the Khedive, and the people of Egypt." See H. C. G. Matthew, *The Gladstone Diaries* (Oxford: Clarendon Press, 1990), 10:lxxii.

14. Nadav Safran, *Egypt in Search of Political Community* (Cambridge, Mass.: Harvard University Press, 1961), pp. 54–59.

15. Ibid., p. 57.

16. Marsot, *Egypt and Cromer,* pp. 96–97.

17. Arthur Goldschmidt, Jr., "The Egyptian Nationalist Party: 1892–1919," in Holt, *Political and Social Change in Modern Egypt,* p. 311.

18. Safran, *Egypt in Search of Political Community,* p. 60.

19. Jacques Berque, *Egypt: Imperialism and Revolution,* trans. Jean Stewart (London: Faber & Faber, 1967), pp. 147–48.

20. Berque, *Egypt: Imperialism and Revolution,* pp. 148–49.

21. Safran, *Egypt in Search of Political Community,* pp. 53–54.

22. According to Marsot, "Between the years 1882 and 1907 England made nearly one hundred and twenty declarations and pledges of its intention to evacuate Egypt, and at the same time initiated actions, each of which established its power in Egypt more securely." *Egypt and Cromer*, p. xi.

23. Milner, *England in Egypt*, p. 17.

24. Ibid.

25. Cited in Cromer, *Modern Egypt*, 1:342–43.

26. Cited in Marsot, *Egypt and Cromer*, p. 59.

27. Cromer, *Modern Egypt*, 1:343.

28. Ibid., p. 146.

29. Ibid., p. 147.

30. Ibid., p. 151.

31. Ibid.

32. Ibid., p. 153.

33. See Evelyn Baring Cromer, *Ancient and Modern Imperialism* (London: John Murray, 1910), p. 125.

34. Ibid., p. 127.

35. Ibid.

36. Donald M. Reid, "Cromer and the Classics: Imperialism, Nationalism and the Greco-Roman Past in Modern Egypt," *Middle Eastern Studies* 32, no. 1 (January 1996): 2.

37. Ibid., p. 5.

38. Cited in ibid., p. 7.

39. Milner, *England in Egypt*, p. 2.

40. Quraishi, *Liberal Nationalism in Egypt*, p. 25. Quraishi argued that having been deprived of high official posts by the Syrian Christians and the British, the Egyptian intelligentsia had developed anti-Syrian and anti-British attitudes. See ibid., pp. 16, 21.

41. Crabbs, *Writing of History*, pp. 185–86.

42. Jamal Mohammad Ahmed, *Intellectual Origins*, pp. 30–31.

43. As early as 1881, when Khedive Tawfiq claimed, "I am the Khedive of the country and shall do as I please," Urabi replied, "We are not slaves and shall never from this day forth be inherited." Cited in Jamal Mohammad Ahmed, *Intellectual Origins*, p. 25.

44. This was true despite the fact that by implementing certain administrative reforms proposed by the British, he restored a sound fiscal policy in the country, reorganized the judiciary, created the National Court, encouraged adult education, opened a law school and a new school of agriculture, and expanded irrigation works. See Vatikiotis, *History of Egypt*, pp. 199–200.

45. Marsot, *Egypt and Cromer*, p. 126; Goldschmidt, "Egyptian Nationalist Party," p. 310.

46. Marsot, *Egypt and Cromer*, p. 137.

47. Berque, *Egypt: Imperialism and Revolution*, pp. 248–49.

48. Goldschmidt, "Egyptian Nationalist Party," p. 319.

49. The situation of the British in Egypt became increasingly precarious in the twentieth century. First, they made themselves a visible target of ideological attack by eliminating all their Egyptian and European rivals. While the number of non-British foreign personnel working in Egypt was reduced, the number of British personnel actually increased, and they

got disproportionately high salaries. The total number of people employed in the civil service in 1882 was 52,974 Egyptians, drawing salaries aggregating £E1,648,503, and 1,067 Europeans, receiving £E305,096. Europeans thus constituted 2 percent of the service and drew 16 percent of the total pay. Excluding the armed forces, another British estimate placed the total number of civil servants at about 20,000, of whom 5 percent were Europeans. Finally, omitting customs, railways, and similar services, the total was said to be 10,000, of whom 8 percent were Europeans. In accordance with the policy of reducing the influence of other nations in Egypt, the number of non-English Europeans in the civil service continued to decline. By 1898 the number of Englishmen was 455, compared to only 299 in 1886. In addition, of course, they occupied the highest positions. Of 10,600 Egyptians in 1898 only 45 received a monthly salary of £E70 or more, whereas 47 of 455 Englishmen did. See Morroe Berger, *Bureaucracy and Society in Modern Egypt: A Study of the Higher Civil Service* (Princeton, N.J.: Princeton University Press, 1957), p. 31.

50. Four villagers were condemned to death, one to fifteen years' imprisonment, and others to shorter terms of imprisonment or to fifty lashes. See Jamal Mohammad Ahmed, *Intellectual Origins,* p. 62.

51. Cited in Jamal Mohammad Ahmed, *Intellectual Origins,* p. 63.

52. Berque, *Egypt: Imperialism and Revolution,* pp. 237–38.

53. Cited in Jamal Mohammad Ahmed, *Intellectual Origins,* p. 17.

54. Ibid., p. 18.

55. Cited in Wendell, *Evolution of the Egyptian National Image,* p. 135; al-Marsafi's main concern was also to pinpoint the weaknesses in the Egyptian society. He attacked the writers and the preachers in the mosques for want of sincerity and knowledge (Jamal Mohammad Ahmed, *Intellectual Origins,* p. 21).

56. Cited in Jamal Mohammad Ahmed, *Intellectual Origins,* p. 19.

57. Hourani, *Arabic Thought,* p. 194.

58. Ibid., pp. 200–207.

59. Cited in Safran, *Egypt in Search of Political Community,* p. 87.

60. Cited in Israel Gershoni and James P. Jankowski, *Egypt, Islam, and the Arabs: The Search for Egyptian Nationhood, 1900–1930* (Oxford: Oxford University Press, 1986), pp. 6–7.

61. Cited in ibid., p. 7.

62. Ibid., pp. 5–6; and Schölch, *Egypt for the Egyptians,* p. 312.

63. Schölch, *Egypt for the Egyptians,* p. 41.

64. Jamal Mohammad Ahmed, *Intellectual Origins,* p. 19; Landau, *Parliaments and Parties,* pp. 97–98.

65. For an interesting example of Nadim's satires, see Jamal Mohammad Ahmed, *Intellectual Origins,* p. 68.

66. Wendell, *Evolution of the Egyptian National Image,* p. 150.

67. Cited in ibid., pp. 152–53.

68. Ibid., p. 148.

69. Hourani, *Arabic Thought,* p. 197.

70. Cited in Wendell, *Evolution of the Egyptian National Image,* p. 153.

71. Ibid., p. 155.

72. Cited in ibid., p. 158.

73. Hourani, *Arabic Thought*, p. 173.

74. Cited in Wendell, *Evolution of the Egyptian National Image*, p. 234.

75. Hourani, *Arabic Thought*, p. 176.

76. Cited in Wendell, *Evolution of the Egyptian National Image*, p. 224.

77. Ibid., pp. 228, 230, 232; Hourani, *Arabic Thought*, p. 178.

78. Wendell, *Evolution of the Egyptian National Image*, pp. 225–26.

79. Cited in ibid., p. 233.

80. Ibid., p. 235.

81. Ibid., p. 230.

82. Ibid., p. 236.

Chapter Seven

1. C. Ernest Dawn, "The Formation of Pan-Arab Ideology in the Interwar Years," *International Journal of Middle East Studies* 20 (1988): 67–91.

2. For an overview of this debate see Adeed Dawisha, *Arab Nationalism in the Twentieth Century: From Triumph to Despair* (Princeton, N.J.: Princeton University Press, 2003); Rashid Khalidi, Lisa Anderson, Muhammad Muslih, and Reeva S. Simon, eds., *The Origins of Arab Nationalism* (New York: Columbia University Press, 1991); Eliezer Tauber, *The Emergence of the Arab Movements* (London: Frank Cass, 1993); Zeine, *Emergence of Arab Nationalism;* Philip S. Khoury, *Urban Notables and Arab Nationalism: The Politics of Damascus, 1860–1920* (Cambridge: Cambridge University Press, 1983); Antonius, *Arab Awakening;* C. Ernest Dawn, *From Ottomanism to Arabism: Essay on the Origins of Arab Nationalism* (Urbana: University of Illinois Press, 1973); Haim, *Arab Nationalism;* and Hourani, *Arabic Thought.*

3. Rashid Khalidi, "Ottomanism and Arabism in Syria before 1914: A Reassessment," in Khalidi, Anderson, Muslih, and Simon, *Origins of Arab Nationalism,* p. 51.

4. Christian P. Grant, *The Syrian Desert* (New York: Macmillan Co., 1968), pp. 45–78.

5. Tabitha Petran, *Syria* (New York: Praeger, 1972), p. 41.

6. See Hamilton A. R. Gibb, and Harold Bowen, *Islamic Society and the West: A Study of the Impact of Western Civilization on Moslem Culture* (London, 1950–57), vol. 1, pt. 1, p. 218; and Zeine, *Emergence of Arab Nationalism,* p. 9.

7. Khoury, *Urban Notables.*

8. Moshe Ma'oz, *Ottoman Reform in Syria and Palestine, 1840–1861: The Impact of the Tanzimat on Politics and Society* (Oxford: Oxford University Press, 1968), pp. 1, 4.

9. Petran, *Syria,* pp. 42–43.

10. There were also domestic and regional sources of Syria's economic strife, including the weakness of the Ottoman central government and the decline in order and security, the decline of the Persian economy, which dealt a blow to the transit trade in silk and other goods, and Napoleon's expedition in Palestine and the confusion and local wars that followed his retreat. See Charles Issawi, ed., *The Economic History of the Middle East, 1800–1914* (Chicago: University of Chicago Press, 1966), pp. 205–212.

11. Dominique Chevallier, "Western Development and Eastern Crisis in the Mid-Nineteenth Century: Syria Confronted with the European Economy," in *Beginnings of Modernization in the Middle East,* ed. William R. Polk and Richard L. Chambers (Chicago: University of Chicago Press, 1968), pp. 205–22.

374   NOTES TO PAGES 152–154

12. Ma'oz, *Ottoman Reform,* p. vi.

13. Lapidus, *History of Islamic Societies,* pp. 598–600; see also Ma'oz, *Ottoman Reform,* pp. 21–22, 27.

14. According to Antonius, the Egyptian occupation of Syria contributed to the rise of Arab nationalism. "The rule of tolerance established by Ibrahim had one unpremeditated result: it opened the door to Western missionary enterprise; and, by so doing, it gave free play to two forces, one French and the other American, which were destined between them to become the foster-parents of the Arab resurrection" (Antonius, *Arab Awakening,* p. 35).

15. Khoury, *Urban Notables,* p. 23. According to Salibi, "Damascene Muslims, like their coreligionists in other parts of the empire, had deeply resented the equal status which the *Tanzimat* extended to non-Muslims; and it was essentially this resentment which underlay the massacre of the Damascene Christians." See Kamal S. Salibi, "The 1860 Upheaval in Damascus as Seen by al-Sayyid Muhammad Abu'l-Su'ud al-Hasibi, Notable and Later *Naqib al-Ashraf* of the City," in Polk and Chambers, *Beginnings of Modernization,* p. 201.

16. Chevallier, "Western Development and Eastern Crisis," p. 220.

17. Khoury, *Urban Notables,* pp. 10–13.

18. Ibid., p. 6.

19. Antonius, *Arab Awakening,* pp. 59–60.

20. The missionaries also played an important role in the rise of Arab nationalism in Syria. According to Antonius, "the changes brought about by Ibrahim's policy gave the foreign missions their chance. They flocked to Bairut [*sic*] and thence radiated to the rest of Syria. The year 1834 appears to date a turning-point. The Jesuits had returned, the small American contingent was swelled by fresh arrivals, and a competition began between Catholic and Presbyterian, which attaining at times to the asperity of a duel, caused them to vie with each other for influence and supremacy, to set in train a revival of the Arabic language and with it, a movement of ideas which, in a short lifetime, was to leap from literature to politics" (Antonius, *Arab Awakening,* p. 37). Salibi reported that "the American University of Beirut, or AUB, originally established in 1866 as the Syrian Protestant College, had become the stronghold of the new, American-inspired brand of Arab nationalism. The American administration of AUB actually made a point of encouraging pan-Arab activism among its students." See Kamal S. Salibi, *The Modern History of Jordan* (New York: I. B. Tauris & Co., 1993), p. 172.

21. Khalidi, "Ottomansim and Arabism," pp. 55–61.

22. Chevallier, for example, argued that "merchants and bankers of Beirut and Aleppo expanded their businesses over the country while at the same time appealing to the criteria of Western liberalism" ("Western Development and Eastern Crisis," p. 221).

23. Dawn, *From Ottomanism,* p. 170.

24. Ibid., p. 173.

25. According to Khoury, the landowning bureaucratic class "began to assume its shape in the last half of the nineteenth century—that of a fairly well-integrated network of propertied and office-holding urban families which was to produce the political leadership in Damascus and other Syrian towns for several generations. And it was out of a struggle for power and position between two factions of this leadership that the idea of Arabism emerged as a political movement, one ultimately with widespread appeal in the Arab countries." See Khoury, *Urban Notables,* p. 1.

26. Bernard Lewis, *The Emergence of Modern Turkey* (Oxford: Oxford University Press, 1968), p. 335.

27. Zeine, *Emergence of Arab Nationalism,* p. 9.

28. Ibid., p. 61.

29. Ulrich W. Haarmann, "Ideology and History, Identity and Alterity: The Arab Image of the Turk from the 'Abbasids to Modern Egypt," *International Journal of Middle East Studies* 20 (1988): 177.

30. Zeine, *Emergence of Arab Nationalism,* p. 33.

31. See William L. Cleveland, *The Making of an Arab Nationalist: Ottomanism and Arabism in the Life and Thought of Sati' al-Husri* (Princeton, N.J.: Princeton University Press, 1971), p. 11. See also Antonius, *Arab Awakening,* pp. 45–51.

32. Lapidus, *A History of Islamic Societies,* p. 603.

33. Cleveland, *Making of an Arab Nationalist,* pp. 32–33. See also Ziya Gökalp, *Turkish Nationalism and Western Civilization: Selected Essays of Ziya Gökalp,* trans. and ed. Niyazi Berkes (London: George Allen & Unwin, 1959).

34. Uriel Heyd, *Foundations of Turkish Nationalism: The Life and Teachings of Ziya Gökalp* (London: Luzac & Harvill Press, 1950), p. 130.

35. This was the assessment of British Foreign Office. Cited in Zeine, *Emergence of Arab Nationalism,* p. 75. See also Great Britain, Foreign Office, *Handbooks Prepared under the Direction of the Historical Section of the Foreign Office,* no. 96 c & d, pp. 21–22.

36. Zeine, *Emergence of Arab Nationalism,* p. 79. Citing the work of Hanioglu, Khalidi indicates that the CUP was more intensely Turkish nationalist than most historians had assumed. It had a secret, purely Turkish, inner leadership group and inner membership unknown to those citizens who joined after 1908. See Khalidi, "Ottomanism and Arabism," p. 54.

37. Hourani, *Arabic Thought,* pp. 99–102.

38. See Antonius, *Arab Awakening,* pp. 45–47, 54–55; and Dawn, *From Ottomanism,* pp. 132–33.

39. "This idea was particularly widespread among the graduates of the American mission schools. . . . They were mainly Orthodox and Protestant Christians, and later Muslims and Druzes; for them, the independence of Lebanon meant the domination of the Maronites and of French culture, the pervading influence of the French government. The idea of 'Syria' seemed to offer them a chance of escaping from their position as a minority, without falling under a new domination." See Hourani, *Arabic Thought,* p. 276.

40. See Zeine, *Emergence of Arab Nationalism,* p. 55; and Antonius, *Arab Awakening,* pp. 79–80.

41. Hourani stresses this point in his discussion of Arab nationalism. See his *Arabic Thought,* pp. 260–323.

42. Dawn, *From Ottomanism,* p. 132.

43. Ibid., pp. 133–38; see also Haim, *Arab Nationalism.*

44. One observer indicated the prevalence of anti-Turkish attitudes in Jerusalem in the 1850s and 1860: "They are on this very account unable to comprehend how a Sultan of Turks, an alien race coming from Tartary, can rightly be regarded as Caliph (successor) of

Mohammed the Koreish Arab, or exercise the power of appointing or displacing the Shereef of Mecca." Cited in Hourani, *Arabic Thought*, p. 266.

45. Ibid., pp. 268–69.

46. See Sylvia G. Haim, "Alfieri and al-Kawakibi," Oriente Moderno 34 (1954): 331–34, and "Blunt and al-Kawakibi," *Oriente Moderno* 35 (1955): 132–43.

47. See Haim, *Arab Nationalism*, p. 42. For a more detailed analysis of political influence in the writings of al-Kawakibi and others see Elie Kedourie, "The Politics of Political Literature: Kawakabi, Azouri and Jung," *Middle Eastern Studies* 8, no. 2 (May 1972): 227–40.

48. Al-Kawakibi, however, did say that "if I had an army at my command I would overthrow Abdülhamid's government in 24 hours." Cited in Tauber, *Emergence of the Arab Movements*, p. 26.

49. Haim, "Alfieri and al-Kawakibi," p. 323, Hourani, *Arabic Thought*, p. 272.

50. Haim, "Alfieri and al-Kawakibi," pp. 324–31.

51. Hourani, *Arabic Thought*, p. 272. See also Dawn, *From Ottomanism*, pp. 138–40.

52. Haim, *Arab Nationalism*, p. 27.

53. Najib Azoury, a Christian Arab and formerly an Ottoman official in Jerusalem, became active in the closing years of Abdülhamid's reign. In Paris in 1904, he founded a society known as Ligue de la Patrie Arabe, whose declared object was to free Syria and Iraq from Turkish domination. He issued several fiery appeals calling upon the Arabs to rise in revolt. In the following year, he published (in French) a book under the title of *Le reveil de la nation arabe*. Two years later, having secured the collaboration of certain French writers of note, he started the publication (in French) of a monthly review entitled *L'Independence Arabe*, of which the first number appeared in April 1907 (Antonius, *Arab Awakening*, p. 98). Haim, however, suggests that Azoury was a shady character who may have been a French agent and taking money from French sources. See Haim, *Arab Nationalism*, p. 30; and Tauber, *Emergence of the Arab Movements*, p. 33.

54. Hourani, *Arabic Thought*, p. 279.

55. See Dawn, *From Ottomanism*, chapters 1–2.

56. Cited in ibid., p. 70. Translated by Dawn from the original source, Abdullah Ibn-al-Husayn, *Mudharkkarati* [My Memoirs], 1st ed. (Jerusalem: Matba'ah Bayt al-Muqaddas, 1945), appendix, p. 73.

57. Cited in Dawn, *From Ottomanism*, pp. 70–71.

58. Ibid., pp. 71–72.

59. Ibid., p. 72.

60. Ibid., p. 2.

61. Haim, *Arab Nationalism*, p. 35.

62. Gordon H. Torrey, *Syrian Politics and the Military: 1945–1958* (Columbus: Ohio State University Press, 1964), pp. 22–24; and Richard F. Nyrop, ed., *Syria: A Country Study* (Washington, D.C.: American University, 1972), p. 61.

63. Petran, *Syria*, pp. 70–71.

64. Eva Garzouzi, "Land Reform in Syria," *Middle East Journal* 17, nos. 1–2 (Winter–Spring 1963): 83.

65. Richard Bayly Winder, "Syrian Deputies and Cabinet Ministers, 1919–1959," *Middle East Journal* 17 (Winter–Spring 1963): 38.

66. Philip S. Khoury, *Syria and the French Mandate: The Politics of Arab Nationalism, 1920–1945* (Princeton, N.J.: Princeton University Press, 1987), pp. 20–21.

67. This was clear to President Woodrow Wilson. His principle of self-determination, of course, received wide recognition in the Arab world. The King-Crane Commission reported that, on the basis of 1,863 petitions it had received from representative town and village groups, it had determined that 73.5 percent demanded absolute independence for Syria, while 55.3 percent protested against article 22 of the covenant of the League of Nations (which entrusted the tutelage of the underdeveloped areas to advanced nations). Only 14.68 percent favored a French mandate. These were predominantly Lebanese Maronites, who had a special relation with France. Cited in Elizabeth P. MacCallum, *The Nationalist Crusade in Syria* (New York: Foreign Policy Association, 1928), p. 33.

68. See Salma Mardam Bey, *Syria's Quest for Independence: 1939–1945* (Reading, U.K.: Ithaca Press, 1994).

69. According to MacCallum, "French and Syrian standards of morality had so few points in common that it was sometimes difficult for individual French officials, not excluding some in highest places, to realize how deeply their official or private conduct sometimes offended Syrian susceptibilities. A certain disregard of public opinion in the matter of the moral traditions of the country, coupled with the personal arrogance of many of the French officials, created a bitterness of feeling that the exercise of a little more tact might easily have prevented. A crowning insult to Syrian self-esteem was the introduction of semibarbarous Senegalese troops in a mandated territory whose level of education and civilization was incomparably higher than that of Senegal." See MacCallum, *Nationalist Crusade,* p. 220.

70. Stephen Hemsley Longrigg, *Syria and Lebanon under the French Mandate* (New York: Octagon Books, 1972), p. 184.

71. See Khoury, *Syria and the French Mandate,* pp. 3–23.

72. See Jamil Mardam Bey, "Prologue: The Legacy of Equivocation," in Salma Mardam Bey, *Syria's Quest for Independence,* p. xi.

73. Khoury, *Syria and the French Mandate,* pp. 359–60.

74. Dawn, "Formation of Pan-Arab Ideology," p. 68.

75. Ibid., pp. 69–71.

76. Ibid., p. 75.

77. Ibid., p. 72.

78. Ibid., p. 74.

79. Ibid., pp. 72–75.

80. Haim, *Arab Nationalism,* p. 38.

81. Ibid., pp. 41–42.

82. Sati' al-Husri was born into a bureaucratic and commercial family. His father, Muhammad Hilal Ibn al-Sayyid Mustafa al-Husri, worked in the civil service of the Ottoman Empire. Sati' was educated in one of the leading schools of the Ottoman Empire. His early education took place in the home, where the language spoken was the Turkish of the educated Ottoman classes, as well as Arabic—not until 1919 did Sati' make Arabic his preferred language. In addition, he learned French from his two older brothers, Bashir Majdi

and Baidi' Nuri. He became an imperial civil servant and identified with the doctrine of Ottomanism. During his career as a schoolteacher and government official in the Balkans and later as a prominent educator in Istanbul, he had little contact with the various Arab societies which were active prior to the First World War. See Cleveland, *Making of an Arab Nationalist,* pp. x, 12–14.

83. Ibid., pp. 33–39.

84. Ibid., p. x.

85. Ibid., p. 92.

86. Cited in ibid., p. 99.

87. Ibid., p. 107.

88. Cited in ibid., p. 130. Al-Husri also criticized Egyptian intellectuals like Taha Hussein who tried to articulate a distinct modern Egyptian cultural identity based on the Pharaonic heritage (see ibid., pp. 136–37).

89. Ibid., p. 166.

90. Cited in ibid., p. 167.

91. Ibid., pp. 169–70. It was also cited in Sylvia G. Haim, "Islam and the Theory of Arab Nationalism," in *The Middle East in Transition,* ed. Walter Z. Laqueur (New York: Praeger, 1958), p. 283.

92. Haim, *Arab Nationalism,* pp. 44–45.

93. Author's phone interview with Ernest Dawn, May 14, 1999.

Chapter Eight

1. Fereydoun Adamiyat, *Andishaha-yi Mirza Aqa Khan Kirmani* [The Ideas of Mirza Aqa Khan Kirmani] (Tehran: Zar, 1978/1357), p. 264.

2. Abbas Amanat, *Pivot of the Universe: Nasir al-Din Shah Qajar and the Iranian Monarchy, 1831–1896* (Berkeley: University of California Press, 1997), p. xiv.

3. Ibid., p. 9.

4. Ibid., p. 10.

5. Ibid., p. xiv.

6. Ibid., p. 409.

7. Ibid., pp. 409–11, 415.

8. Bayat, *Iran's First Revolution,* pp. 76–80.

9. Ibid., p. 98.

10. Firoozeh Kashani-Sabet, *Frontier Fictions: Shaping the Iranian Nation, 1804–1946* (Princeton, N.J.: Princeton University Press, 1999), p. 226.

11. Ibid., p. 216.

12. Ibid., pp. 15–16.

13. Cited ibid., p. 37.

14. Cited in ibid., p. 38.

15. Cited in Adamiyat, *Andishaha-yi Mirza Aqa Khan Kirmani,* p. 271.

16. Fereydoun Adamiyat, *Andishaha-yi Mirza Fath Ali Akhundzadah* (Tehran: Kharazmi Publications, 1970), pp. 120–24.

17. Cited in ibid., p. 125.

18. Adamiyat, *Andishaha-yi Mirza Aqa Khan Kirmani,* pp. 272–74.

19. Ibid., pp. 278–80.

20. Adamiyat, *Andishaha-yi Mirza Fath Ali Akhundzadah*, pp. 69–73.

21. Ibid., pp. 74–89.

22. Cited in ibid., p. 118.

23. Adamiyat, *Andishaha-yi Mirza Aqa Khan Kirmani*, p. 276.

24. Ibid., pp. 42–45.

25. Ibid., pp. 45–49.

26. Cited in Adamiyat, *Andishaha-yi Mirza Aqa Khan Kirmani*, p. 245.

27. Adamiyat, *Andishaha-yi Mirza Aqa Khan Kirmani*, p. 256.

28. Ibid., p. 256.

29. Ibid., p. 359.

30. Ibid., p. 259.

31. Ibid., pp. 261–62.

32. Muhammad Mohit Taba-Taba'ie, *Majmu'ah-i Asar-i Mirza Malkum Khan* [The Collected Works of Mirza Malkum Khan] (Tehran: Ilmi Publications, 1980), 1:xxxi; and Abrahamian, *Iran*, pp. 65–66.

33. Abrahamian, *Iran*, p. 66; and Taba-Taba'ie, *Majmu'ah-i Asar-i Mirza Malkum Khan*, pp. 1–52.

34. Abrahamian, *Iran*, p. 66.

35. According to Adamiyat, "many of the mullas who had thought that constitutionalism meant handing over the affairs of the country to them were gradually realizing that it was to be otherwise." Cited in Afary, *Iranian Constitutional Revolution*, p, 96.

36. Bayat, *Iran's First Revolution*, p. 10.

37. Adamiyat, *Andishaha-yi Mirza Fath Ali Akhundzadah*, p. 116. Kirmani also expressed his opposition to the interventionist and colonial approaches of the Europeans and their prejudicial thinking about non-Westerners (see Adamiyat, *Andishaha-yi Mirza Aqa Khan Kirmani*, p. 241).

38. Cited in Afary, *Iranian Constitutional Revolution*, p. 55.

39. Ibid., p. 55.

40. Ibid., p. 54.

41. Abrahamian, *Iran*, p. 85; Afary, *Iranian Constitutional Revolution*, p. 57.

42. On July 15, 1910, Bihbahani was gunned down in his home by four members of the mujahidin who were associated with Haidar Khan Am Ughlu and the democrats. See Afary, *Iranian Constitutional Revolution*, p. 293.

43. Ibid., pp. 87, 91.

44. Abrahamian, *Iran*, pp. 102–3.

45. For an analysis of Reza Shah's educational, judicial, and religious policies, see Shahrough Akhavi, *Religion and Politics in Contemporary Iran* (Albany: State University of New York Press, 1980).

46. Kashani-Sabet, *Frontier Fictions*, p. 220.

47. Abrahamian, *Iran*, pp. 121–26.

48. Ahmad Kasravi, *Chihil Maqalah-i Kasravi* [Forty Essays by Kasravi], ed. Yahya Zoka-ie (Tehran: Kitab-Khaneh-i Tohuri, 1956/1335), pp. 3–6.

49. Ahmad Kasravi, *Dar Piramun-i Islam* [On Islam] (Tehran: Paydar Bookstore, 1969/1348), pp. 4–5.

50. Ibid., pp. 5–33.

51. Ibid., pp. 34–64.

52. Mansoor Moaddel, *Class, Politics, and Ideology in the Iranian Revolution* (New York: Columbia University Press, 1993), p. 35.

53. Cited in Rasoul Mehraban, *Gousheha-ie az Tarikh-i Moaser-i Iran* [Aspects of the Contemporary History of Iran] (Tehran: Otared, 1982/1361), p. 146.

54. The front's campaign for democracy was triggered by voting frauds in the fifteenth parliamentary election. In October 1949, Mosaddeq led a crowd of politicians, university students, and bazaar traders into the shah's palace to protest the lack of free elections. Once inside, the demonstrators elected a committee of twenty, headed by Mosaddeq, which soon became the nucleus of the National Front.

55. Moaddel, *Class, Politics, and Ideology*, pp. 41–42.

56. Ahmad Ashraf, "Bazaar-Mosque Alliance: The Social Basis of Revolts and Revolutions," *Politics, Culture, and Society* 1, no. 4 (Summer 1988): 548–59; Moaddel, *Class, Politics, and Ideology*, p. 116.

57. Cited in Moaddel, *Class, Politics, and Ideology*, pp. 43–44.

Chapter Nine

1. See Israel Gershoni and James P. Jankowski, *Redefining the Egyptian Nation, 1930–1945* (Cambridge: Cambridge University Press, 1995).

2. Richard P. Mitchell, *Society of the Muslim Brothers*, p. 232–33.

3. Ibid., pp. 209–31. See also Hasan al-Banna, *Five Tracts of Hasan al-Banna (1906–1949)*, trans. Charles Wendell (Berkeley: University of California Press, 1978), pp. 126–31.

4. Wendell argued that the MB represented "a continuation of the activist Pan-Islamic doctrine of Jamal al-Din al-Afghani and the early Muhammad Abduh" (al-Banna, *Five Tracts*, p. 3). While activism and the idea of Islamic unity are the common elements in the religious and political outlooks of al-Afghani and al-Banna, there is a world of difference between the two leaders in their attitudes toward modern discourses. Al-Banna did not have much interest in Western scholarship, and, contrary to Abduh and al-Afghani, he was not predisposed to consider such perspectives as those of Guizot, Spencer, Renan, and Comte in addressing the problems of his community.

5. A feddan is 1.04 acres.

6. Issawi, *Economic History of the Middle East*, pp. 366, 373.

7. Charles Issawi, *Egypt at Mid-century: An Economic Survey* (London: Oxford University Press, 1954), p. 61.

8. Ibid., pp. 59–60.

9. Hamied Ansari, *Egypt, the Stalled Society* (Albany: State University of New York Press, 1986.), p. 63.

10. Afaf Lutfi Marsot, *Egypt's Liberal Experiment: 1922–1936* (Los Angeles: University of California Press, 1977), p. 14.

11. Ibid., p. 205.

12. See Selma Botman, *Egypt from Independence to Revolution, 1919–1952* (Syracuse, N.Y.: Syracuse University Press, 1991), p. 83, table 3.

13. Issawi, *Egypt at Mid-century*, p. 208, table 22.

14. Ibid., p. 142.

NOTES TO PAGES 200–206   381

15. Marsot, *Egypt's Liberal Experiment*, p. 205.

16. Charles Issawi, *Egypt: An Economic and Social Analysis* (London: Oxford University Press, 1947), p. 173, and Safran, *Egypt in Search of Political Community*, p. 195.

17. Gershoni and Jankowski, *Redefining the Egyptian Nation*, p. 13.

18. Issawi, *Egypt at Mid-century*, p. 142.

19. Ibid., p. 140.

20. Gershoni and Jankowski, *Redefining the Egyptian Nation*, p. 13.

21. Safran attributed the decline of liberal politics to Egypt's uneven distribution of economic resources and the political supremacy of the big landed interests. In his view, the large landowners' "one-sidedness and selfishness had very few rivals in modern times. To list all the sins of omission and commission of the Egyptian ruling class during this period would be a depressing enterprise that would take us too far afield." See Safran, *Egypt in Search of Political Community*, p. 195.

22. There are alternative interpretations of the change in landownership. For Quraishi, "the Government's policy of encouraging the small land-holders, abolishing the last vestige of ownership, extending the cultivated area by breaking up of *Daira Sania* (Khedivial) estate of 280,000 feddans and forming several land companies with the object of reclaiming land and selling it to the peasants, and extending credit facilities and subdividing of land among heirs all helped to raise the number of landowners from 730 in 1825 to 1,556,000 in 1915" (see Quraishi, *Liberal Nationalism in Egypt*, p. 14). Ansari, on the other hand, cites several factors in the persistence of large holdings despite the natural fragmentation that might have occurred as a result of the Islamic law of inheritance: state land (Daira Sania and Domain land) was sold to the largest landowners because of their access to credit, the arable land that became available through land reclamation was divided into large parcels and sold to the largest landowners, and the small owners had to sell because they incurred huge debts (Ansari, *Egypt, the Stalled Society*, p. 74).

23. Gershoni and Jankowski argue that as producers and consumers of new discourses, these strata, through an ongoing negotiation with the intellectual elite, effected a change in the dominant nationalist discourse. See Gershoni and Jankowski, *Redefining the Egyptian Nation*, p. xiii.

24. Ibid., p. 1.

25. See M. M. Mosharrafa, *Cultural Survey of Modern Egypt* (New York: Longmans, Green & Co., 1948), part 2, p. 54.

26. All citations from Gershoni and Jankowski, *Redefining the Egyptian Nation*, pp. 3–7.

27. On February 28, 1922, the British government issued the Unilateral Declaration, which stipulated that Egypt was an independent and sovereign state but with four reservations, namely, imperial communications, the defense of Egypt, the protection of foreign interests and minorities, and the Sudan, to be settled through negotiation. See Marius Deeb, *Party Politics in Egypt: The Wafd and Its Rivals, 1919–1939* (London: Ithaca Press, 1979), pp. 56–57. Although his powers were curtailed, during the drafting of the constitution King Fuad managed to introduce changes that gave considerable power to the king. See Marius Deeb, *Party Politics in Egypt*, p. 60. The Wafd leadership was not free of autocratic tendencies either. On the contrary, considering itself the sole representative of the Egyptian nation, the Wafd considered the members of other parties and groups "dissenters" who worked against the nation's interests and aspirations (p. 135).

28. Deeb argued that in the early years following the 1919 popular uprising there were only two main forces: the British and the Wafd. The sultan had not yet emerged as a significant political force. The British alone backed Fuad because they thought he was probably the only member of the Muhammad Ali dynasty who was not anti-British. See Marius Deeb, *Party Politics in Egypt,* pp. 123–24. During the drafting of the constitution, King Fuad insisted that Egypt was not ready for a constitution or parliament and that one or two years of firm autocracy were still required. See Marius Deeb, *Party Politics in Egypt,* p. 59.

29. The Wafd's attitude, on the popular level, was antagonistic toward King Fuad. In both Cairo and Alexandria in March 1922 (following the declaration of independence on March 15, 1922), demonstrators shouted, "Down with the sultan" and "Long live Zaghlul." See Marius Deeb, *Party Politics in Egypt,* p. 57.

30. According to Deeb, the nominal independence of Egypt in 1922 limited the scope of direct action by the British and led them to pursue their policies indirectly. The British, however, resorted to direct action in 1924–25, 1926, 1927, and 1928, four times directed against the Wafd, and the fifth time, in 1925, against the king. See Marius Deeb, *Party Politics in Egypt,* pp. 127–28.

31. Issawi reported that the number of people employed in nonindustrial public services increased from 152,000 in 1927 to 171,000 in 1937. See Issawi, *Egypt at Mid-century,* p. 62, table 6.

32. According to one report, the number of Europeans in the Egyptian civil service dwindled to a handful in the first five years of the country's independence. See Morroe Berger, *Bureaucracy and Society in Modern Egypt,* p. 33.

33. The Egyptian University began as a private university in 1908 with Prince Ahmad Fuad as its first rector. See Donald Malcom Reid, *Cairo University and the Making of Modern Egypt* (Cambridge: Cambridge University Press, 1990), p. 1.

34. Reid, *Cairo University,* pp. 82–83.

35. Foreigners in the Ministry of Education actually rose from 163 in 1922 to 786 in 1936; most were foreign language teachers for the rapidly expanding state schools. Outside the Ministry of Education, however, the government's foreign employees dropped from 2,229 in 1922 to 440 in 1936. See Reid, *Cairo University,* p. 126. During Fuad's nineteen-year reign, the government sent 1,794 students abroad on study missions, and another 444 went between 1935 and the outbreak of World War II. Those who returned with doctorates slowly replaced their foreign mentors (ibid., p. 99).

36. Vatikiotis, *History of Egypt,* p. 310.

37. Reid, *Cairo University,* pp. 103–5.

38. Vatikiotis, *History of Egypt,* pp. 305–9.

39. Cited in Adams, *Islam and Modernism in Egypt,* p. 255.

40. Ibid., pp. 255–56.

41. Vatikiotis, *History of Egypt,* pp. 305–9.

42. Safran, *Egypt in Search of Political Community,* pp. 143–44.

43. Ibid., pp. 144–45.

44. Reid, "Cromer and the Classics," pp. 14–15.

45. Vatikiotis, *History of Egypt,* p. 311.

46. Ibid., pp. 306–7.

47. Al-Banna, *Five Tracts*, p. 5. For relevant textual evidence, see pp. 97, 109, 113. This is not to argue that al-Banna was influenced by the racism of Fascism or Nazism, as he stated, "if what is meant by 'nationalism' is racial self-aggrandizement to a degree which leads to the disparagement of other races, aggression against them, and their victimization for the sake of the nation's glory and its continued existence, as preached for example by Germany and Italy; nay more, as claimed by every nation which preaches its superiority over all others— then this too is a reprehensible idea" (see al-Banna, *Five Tracts*, p. 54).

48. Brynjar Lia, *The Society of the Muslim Brothers in Egypt: The Rise of an Islamic Mass Movement, 1928–42* (Reading, U.K.: Ithaca Press, 1998), p. 27.

49. Cited in ibid., p. 78.

50. Al-Banna, *Five Tracts*, p. 32.

51. Ibid., p. 34.

52. Cited in Zainab al-Ghazali, *Return of the Pharaoh: Memoir in Nasir's Prison*, trans. Mokrane Guezzou (Leicester: Islamic Foundation, 1994), p. xiv.

53. al-Banna, *Five Tracts*, pp. 48–49.

54. Ibid., pp. 49–50.

55. Ibid., p. 50.

56. Ibid., p. 50.

57. Ibid., pp. 53–54.

58. Ibid., p. 61.

59. Zainab al-Ghazali, *Return of the Pharaoh*, p. 226.

60. Ibid., p. 231.

61. Marius Deeb, *Party Politics in Egypt*, pp. 181–82.

62. Richard P. Mitchell, *Society of the Muslim Brothers*, p. 261. Al-Banna demanded total loyalty: "we would like our people to know that only he is fit to respond to this mission who comprehends it in all its aspects, and who devotes to it all that may be demanded of him in terms of his person, his wealth, his time, and his health. . . . it is a mission which does not tolerate divided loyalty, since its very nature is that of total unity, and whosoever is prepared to accept it will live through it as it lives through him." See al-Banna, *Five Tracts*, pp. 43–44.

63. Richard P. Mitchell, *Society of the Muslim Brothers*, p. 4.

64. Cited in Reid, *Cairo University*, p. 149.

65. Reid, *Cairo University*, p. 129.

66. Richard P. Mitchell, *Society of the Muslim Brothers*, pp. 37–38.

67. Marsot, *Egypt's Liberal Experiment*, p. 234.

68. Richard P. Mitchell, *Society of the Muslim Brothers*, p. 15.

69. Ibid., p. 16.

70. Ibid., pp. 16–26.

71. According to al-Banna, our understanding of Islam "is confined to God's Book, the Sunna of his Apostle, and the biographies of the early Muslim pietists" (see, al-Banna, *Five Tracts*, p, 47).

72. Richard P. Mitchell, *Society of the Muslim Brothers*, pp. 237–38.

73. Ibid., p. 246–47.

74. Ibid., pp. 114–15.

75. Lia, *Society of the Muslim Brothers*, pp. 279–80.

76. Richard P. Mitchell, *Society of the Muslim Brothers*, pp. 26–27. In early 1943, the situation was reversed, and the MB was allowed to function openly. The relationship with the Wafd's government, however, "alternated between the friendly and the hostile: surveillance and censorship, followed by periods of relative freedom" (ibid., p. 27).

77. Ibid., p. 33.

78. Ibid., p. 219.

79. Some claim that the MB's participation in the coup was to overthrow the monarchy as a step in reviving a great Muslim caliphate. The formation of the Free Army Officers was a result of the MB's activities in the army, and "Nasir and many of his fellow-officers who participated, later on, in the overthrow of King Faruq did, in fact, belong to the *Ikhwan* and swore allegiance to Hasan al-Banna and the head of the secret organization, Mahmud Labib, whom Hasan al-Banna appointed" (see Zainab al-Ghazali, *Return of the Pharaoh*, p. xviii).

80. Vatikiotis, *History of Egypt*, p. 417.

81. The first agrarian reform law of 1952 put the maximum limit for land ownership at 20 feddans per person. In 1958, the second land reform law put this limit at 300 feddans per family. In 1961, the third law lowered the limit to 100 feddans per person without mentioning the family. Then, in 1969, it was decided that the maximum was to be 50 feddans per person and 100 per family. One of the consequences of these reforms was an increase in the number of owners of medium-sized holdings (i.e., owners of over 20 feddans). The number of those who owned between 20 and 50 feddans rose from 22,000 in 1952 to 29,000 in 1964, and their property from 654,000 to 812,000 feddans (i.e., from 10.9 percent to 13.3 percent). See Nazih Nassif M. Ayubi, *Bureaucracy and Politics in Contemporary Egypt* (London: Ithaca Press, 1980), pp. 287–88.

82. Ibid., pp. 163–75; and Vatikiotis, *History of Egypt*, pp. 390–99.

83. Ayubi, *Bureaucracy and Politics*, p. 241, table 3, and p. 243, table 4.

84. Vatikiotis, *History of Egypt*, p. 401.

85. Adnan Ayyub Musallam, "The Formative Stages of Sayyid Qutb's Intellectual Career and His Emergence as an Islamic Da'iyah, 1906–1952" (Ph.D. dissertation, University of Michigan, 1983), pp. 78–79.

86. Ibid., pp. 251–52.

87. Zainab al-Ghazali, *Return of the Pharaoh*, pp. xx–xxi.

88. Musallam, "Formative Stages," pp. 101–8.

89. Sayyid Qutb, *Ma'alim fi al-Tariq* (Cairo: Maktabat Wahbah, 1964), pp. 214–15. Cited in Emmanuel Sivan, *Radical Islam: Medieval Theology and Modern Politics* (New Haven, Conn.: Yale University Press, 1985).

90. Cited in Sivan, *Radical Islam*, pp. 23–24.

91. See Sayyid Qutb, *Milestones* (Indianapolis: American Trust Publications, 1993); and William E. Shepard, *Sayyid Qutb and Islamic Activism: A Translation and Critical Analysis of Social Justice in Islam* (New York: E. J. Brill, 1996), p. xvii.

92. Cited in Sivan, *Radical Islam*, p. 30.

93. Ibid., p. 31.

94. Hasan Hanafi, "The Relevance of the Islamic Alternative in Egypt," *Arab Studies Quarterly* 4, nos. 1–2 (1982): 60–61.

95. Gilles Kepel, *Muslim Extremism in Egypt: The Prophet and Pharaoh*, trans. Jon Rothschild (Berkeley: University of California Press, 1985), p. 28.

96. See Zainab al-Ghazali, *Return of the Pharaoh.*

97. See Y. Haddad, "Sayyid Qutb: Ideologue of Islamic Revival," in *Voices of Resurgent Islam* ed. John Esposito (Oxford: Oxford University Press, 1983), pp. 67–98.

98. See Sivan, *Radical Islam.*

99. Dawn, "Formation of Pan-Arab Ideology," pp. 69–71.

Chapter Ten

1. Joseph H. Escovitz, " 'He Was the Muhammad Abduh of Syria': A Study of Tahir al-Jaza'iri and His Influence," *International Journal of Middle East Studies* 18 (1986): 294. See also David Commins, "Religious Reformers and Arabists in Damascus, 1885–1914," *International Journal of Middle East Studies* 18 (1986): 405–25; and Hisham Sharabi, *Arab Intellectuals and the West: The Formative Years, 1875–1914* (Baltimore: John Hopkins University Press, 1970).

2. See Andrew Rathmell, *Secret War in the Middle East: The Covert Struggle for Syria, 1949–1961* (London: I. B. Tauris, 1995), p. 9.

3. Petran, *Syria,* p. 85.

4. Patrick Seale, *The Struggle for Syria: A Study of Post-war Arab Politics* (London: Oxford University Press, 1965), p. 58.

5. Petran, *Syria,* p. 85; and A. R. Kelidar, "Religion and State in Syria," *Asian Affairs* 5, no. 1 (February 1974): 20.

6. For a comprehensive analysis of the historical situation of the peasantry in the socio-economic and political structure of Syria, see Hanna Batatu, *Syria's Peasantry, the Descendants of Its Lesser Rural Notables, and Their Politics* (Princeton, N.J.: Princeton University Press, 1999).

7. Kelidar, "Religion and State in Syria," p. 20.

8. Batatu, *Syria's Peasantry,* p. 102.

9. Ibid., p. 111.

10. Ibid., p. 323–24.

11. See Sami M. Moubayed, *Damascus between Democracy and Dictatorship* (New York: University Press of America, 2000), p. xi.

12. Gordon H. Torrey, *Syrian Politics and the Military,* p. 263.

13. Nyrop, *Syria: A Country Study,* pp. 30–31.

14. Batatu, *Syria's Peasantry,* p. 325.

15. Ibid., p. 325.

16. Seale, *Struggle for Syria,* p. 37.

17. John Galvani, "Syria and the Baath Party," *MERIP Reports* 25 (February 1974): 3–16.

18. Gordon H. Torrey, *Syrian Politics and the Military,* p. 82.

19. Mark Alexander (pseudonym for Walter Z. Lacqueur), "Communist Strategy in the Middle East," *Twentieth Century,* November 1951, p. 61.

20. Gordon H. Torrey, *Syrian Politics and the Military,* p. 150. See also Mustafa as-Siba'i, *Shtirakiat al-Islam* [Socialism of Islam], 2nd ed. (Damascus, 1960).

21. Cited in Seale, *Struggle for Syria,* p. 148.

22. Ibid., p. 149.

23. Robert W. Olson, *The Ba'th and Syria, 1947–1982: The Evolution of Ideology, Party, and State* (Princeton, N.J.: Princeton University Press, 1982), p. 3; and Kamel S. Abu Jaber, *Arab*

Ba'th Socialist Party: History, Ideology, and Organization (Syracuse, N.Y.: Syracuse University Press, 1966), p. 23.

24. Cited in David Roberts, *The Ba'th and the Creation of Modern Syria* (London: Croom Helm, 1987), p. 18.

25. Abu Jaber, *Arab Ba'th Socialist Party*, p. 27.

26. Petran, *Syria*, p. 90.

27. Itamar Rabinovich, *Syria under the Ba'th, 1963–66* (Jerusalem: Israel University Press, 1972), p. 10.

28. Ibid., p. 6.

29. Ibid., p. 15.

30. Robert W. Olson, *The Ba'th and Syria*, p. 17.

31. Rabinovich, *Syria under the Ba'th*, pp. 86–87.

32. Cited in ibid., p. 87.

33. Rabinovich, *Syria under the Ba'th*, pp. 89–90.

34. Cited in ibid., p. 109.

35. It should be noted that the main force behind the coup of March 8, 1963, was the Military Committee, which consisted of a group of army officers who were close to the Ba'ath Party but not formal members. Five officers, all of minority stock, constituted the leadership of the Military Committee: three were Alawis (Salah Jadid, Muhammad Umran, and Hafiz al-Asad), and two Ismailis (Abd al-Karim al-Jundi and Ahmad al-Mirr). After the coup, the Military Committee appealed to the veteran leaders of the Ba'ath Party, Michel Aflaq and Salah al-Din al-Bitar, requesting their sponsorship. Thus, between 1963 and 1966, they, alongside senior Sunni officers such as Armin al-Hafiz, served as window dressing for the military regime. See Eyal Zisser, "The 'Alawis, Lords of Syria: From Ethnic Minority to Ruling Sect," in *Minorities and the State in the Arab World*, ed. Ofra Bengio and Gabriel Ben-Dor (Boulder, Colo.: Lynne Rienner, 1999), pp. 129–45.

36. Ziad Keilany, "Socialism and Economic Change in Syria," *Middle Eastern Studies:* 9 (January 1973): 63; and Alasdair Drysdale, "The Asad Regime and Its Troubles." *MERIP Reports* 12, no. 110 (November–December 1982): 3.

37. Raymond A. Hinnebusch, "The Islamic Movement in Syria: Sectarian Conflict and Urban Rebellion in an Authoritarian Populist Regime," in *Islamic Resurgence in the Arab World*, ed. Ali E. Hillal Dessouki (New York: Praeger, 1982), pp. 140–41.

38. David Holmström, "Syria: Unity, Liberty, and Socialism," *Middle East International* 22 (April 1973): 11.

39. Kelidar, "Religion and State in Syria," p. 21.

40. Hinnebusch, "Islamic Movement in Syria," p. 159.

41. Kelidar, "Religion and State in Syria," p. 18.

42. Syrian Arab Republic, *Permanent Constitution of the Syrian Arab Republic* (Damascus: Office Arabe de Presse et de Documentation, 1973), p. 3.

43. Kelidar, "Religion and State in Syria," pp. 17–18.

44. Syrian Arab Republic, *Permanent Constitution*, appendix, pp. 1–3.

45. Syrian Arab Republic, *Permanent Constitution*, p. 2.

46. Kelidar, "Religion and State in Syria," pp. 18–19.

47. Umar F. Abd-Allah, *The Islamic Struggle in Syria* (Berkeley: Mizan Press, 1983), p. 93.

48. Ibid., p. 100.

49. Hanna Batatu, "Syria's Muslim Brethren," *MERIP Reports* (November/December 1982), p. 18.

50. Rabinovich, *Syria under the Ba'th*, p. 114.

51. Ibid., p. 116.

52. Hinnebusch, "Islamic Movement in Syria," pp. 157–59; and Abdul Latif Tibawi, *A Modern History of Syria* (New York: Saint Martin's Press, 1969), p. 415.

53. Batatu, *Syria's Peasantry*, pp. 269–70.

54. Ibid., p. 268.

55. Batatu, "Syria's Muslim Brethren," pp. 13–15.

56. Abd-Allah, *Islamic Struggle in Syria*, p. 203.

57. Ibid., p. 206.

58. Ibid., p. 139; Nikolaos van Dam, *The Struggle for Power in Syria: Sectarianism, Regionalism and Tribalism in Politics, 1961–1978* (New York: Saint Martin's Press, 1979), pp. 15. 101.

59. Abd-Allah, *Islamic Struggle in Syria*, p. 138.

60. Ibid., p. 214–18.

61. Ibid., p. 220.

62. Raymond A. Hinnebusch, *Authoritarian Power and State Formation in Ba'thist Syria: Army, Party, and Peasant* (Boulder, Colo.: Westview Press, 1990) p. 284.

63. Abd-Allah, *Islamic Struggle in Syria*, p. 221.

64. Ibid., p. 230.

65. Ibid., p. 235.

66. Ibid., p. 148.

67. Ibid., p. 141.

68. Hinnebusch, "Islamic Movement in Syria," p. 164.

69. Batatu, *Syria's Peasantry*, pp. 269, 274.

70. Ibid., p. 324.

71. Ibid., p. 260.

72. Galvani, "Syria and the Baath Party," p. 10.

73. Seale, *Struggle for Syria*, pp. 38–41.

74. Galvani, "Syria and the Baath Party," p. 11.

75. Keilany, "Socialism," pp. 64–65; and Fred H. Lawson, "Social Bases for the Hanna Revolt." *MERIP Reports* 12 (November/December 1982): 26.

76. Hinnebusch, "Islamic Movement in Syria,"pp. 157–58.

77. Batatu, "Syria's Muslim Brethren," p. 18.

78. Hinnebusch, "Islamic Movement in Syria," p. 166.

79. Van Dam, *Struggle for Power in Syria*, p. 15.

80. Hinnebusch, "Islamic Movement in Syria," p. 139.

81. Van Dam, *Struggle for Power in Syria*, p. 22.

82. Ibid., pp. 33–35.

83. Drysdale, "Asad Regime," p. 10.

84. Hinnebusch, "Islamic Movement in Syria," p. 161.

85. Batatu, "Syria's Muslim Brethren," p. 16; and John F. Devlin, *Syria: Modern State in an Ancient Land* (Boulder, Colo.: Westview Press, 1983), pp. 75–96.

Chapter Eleven

1. See Akhavi, *Religion and Politics in Contemporary Iran*, pp. 23–59; and Moaddel, *Class, Politics, and Ideology*, pp. 138–39.

2. This section is based on analyses presented in Moaddel, *Class, Politics, and Ideology*, chapter 3. See also Abrahamian, *Iran*, pp. 432–34; and International Labor Office, *Employment and Income Policies for Iran* (Geneva: ILO, 1973), p. 55, table 8.

3. See Iranian Government, *A'in-Nameh-ye Tashkil-i Itihadiyeh-ye Sinfi va Tanzim-i Umur-i Asnaf va Pishevaran* (Tehran: Mehr 1957/1336).

4. Leonard Binder, *Iran: Political Development in a Changing Society* (Berkeley: University of California Press, 1962), pp. 186–87.

5. Moaddel, "Shi'i Ulama and the State."

6. Robert Graham, *Iran: The Illusion of Power* (New York: St. Martin's Press, 1979), p. 221.

7. Mohammad Reza Pahlavi, *Answer to History*, trans. Michael Joseph (New York: Stein & Day, 1980), p. 156.

8. Moaddel, *Class, Politics, and Ideology*, p. 121; Michael M. J. Fischer, *Iran: From Religious Dispute to Revolution* (Cambridge, Mass.: Harvard University Press, 1980), pp. 121, 191; Ahmad Ashraf, "Bazaar-Mosque Alliance: The Social Basis of Revolts and Revolutions," *Politics, Culture, and Society* 1, no. 4 (Summer 1988): 557.

9. Moaddel, "Shi'i Ulama and the State," p. 545.

10. See Moaddel, *Class, Politics, and Ideology;* Misagh Parsa, *Social Origins of the Iranian Revolution* (New Brunswick, N.J.: Rutgers University Press, 1989); Abrahamian, *Iran;* Nikkie Keddie, *Roots of Revolution: An Interpretive History of Modern Iran* (New Haven, Conn.: Yale University Press, 1981).

11. Cited in Marvin Zonis, *The Political Elite of Iran* (Princeton, N.J.: Princeton University Press, 1971), pp. 58–59.

12. Ibid., p. 86.

13. Mohammad Reza Shah Pahlavi, *Bi Souy-yeh Tamaddon-i Bozorg* [Toward the Great Civilization] (Tehran, 1974), p. 6.

14. Mohammad Reza Shah Pahlavi, *Mission for My Country* (New York: McGraw-Hill, 1961), p. 327.

15. Ibid., p. 126.

16. Ibid., p. 125.

17. Ibid.

18. Ibid., p. 130.

19. Mohammad Reza Shah Pahlavi, *The White Revolution*, 2nd ed. (Tehran: Imperial Pahlavi Library, 1967), p. 2.

20. Ibid., pp. 17–18.

21. Ibid., p. 37.

22. Ibid.

23. Cited in Fred Halliday, *Iran: Dictatorship and Development* (Harmondsworth: Penguin Books, 1979), p. 58.

24. Mansoor Moaddel, "Ideology as Episodic Discourse: The Case of the Iranian Revolution," *American Sociological Review* 57 (June 1992): 363.

25. Pahlavi, *Bi Souy-yeh*, pp. 78–79.

26. Ibid., pp. 82–83.

27. Hamid Dabashi, *Theology of Discontent: The Ideological Foundation of the Islamic Revolution in Iran* (New York: New York University Press, 1993), p. 39.

28. Jalal Ale-Ahmad, *Plagued by the West (Ghrabzadegi or Westoxication)*, trans. Paul Sprachman (New York: Columbia University Press, 1982), p. 6.

29. Ibid., p. 9.

30. Ibid., pp. 32–33.

31. Jalal Ale-Ahmad, *Dar Khedmat va Khianat-i Roushanfikran* [Concerning the Service and Betrayal of the Intellectuals] (Tehran: Ravaq Publications, n.d.), p. 355.

32. Ibid., p. 15.

33. Ibid., pp. 49–50.

34. Ibid., pp. 261–72.

35. Ibid., p. 432.

36. Fereydoun Adamiyat, "Ashoftegy dar Fekr-i Tarikhi" [Confusion in historical thinking], in *Yadnamey-ye Jalal-i Ale-Ahmad* [For Jalal Ale-Ahmad] (Tehran: Pasargad, 1985/1363), pp. 538–50.

37. Dabashi, *Theology of Discontent*, p. 74.

38. Ibid., p. 68.

39. Ibid., p. 69. According to Dabashi, after the 1967 Arab-Israeli war, Ale-Ahmad's attitudes toward Israel became critical. Israel was no longer the hope of the East for emancipation from tyrant sheikhs, but an imperialist puppet, and the Arabs were not the historical enemies of the Persians, but their Muslim brothers (ibid., p. 70)

40. Ali Shari'ati, *Islamshenasi* [Islamology] (Mashhad: Tous, 1969/1347), p. 23.

41. Ibid., p. 23.

42. Ali Shari'ati, *What Is to Be Done?* trans. A. Alidust and F. Rajaee (Houston: Institute for Research on Islamic Studies, 1986), p. 19.

43. Ali Shari'ati, *Marxism and Other Western Fallacies: An Islamic Critique*, trans. R. Campbell (Berkeley: Mizan Press, 1980), p. 92.

44. Cited in Dabashi, *Theology of Discontent*: p. 117.

45. Ibid., pp. 103–4.

46. Ibid., pp. 409–12.

47. Ruhollah Khomeini, *Islam and Revolution: Writings and Declarations of Imam Khomeini*, vol. 2, trans. H. Algar (Berkeley: Mizan Press, 1981), pp. 49–50.

48. Ibid., pp. 50–51.

49. Shahrough Akhavi, "The Clergy's Concepts of Rule in Egypt and Iran," *Annals of the American Academy of Political and Social Science* 524 (November 1992): 100.

50. Ibid. See also Joesph Eliash, "Misconceptions Regarding the Juridical Status of the Iranian 'Ulama,'" *International Journal of Middle East Studies* 10:9–25.

51. Akhavi, "The Clergy's Concepts of Rule," p. 100.

52. Yann Richard, "Contemporary Shi'i Thought," in Keddie, *Roots of Revolution*, p. 207.

53. Khomeini, *Islam and Revolution*, p. 44.

54. G. Rose, "Velayat-i Faqih and the Recovery of Islamic Identity in the Thought of Ayatollah Khomeini," in *Religion and Politics in Iran*, ed. Nikki R. Keddie (New Haven, Conn.: Yale University Press, 1983), p. 180.

55. Ibid., p. 177.

56. Cited in Said Arjomand, *The Turban for the Crown: The Islamic Revolution in Iran* (New York: Oxford University Press, 1988), p. 182.

57. Cited in Moaddel, *Class, Politics, and Ideology,* pp. 207–8.

58. Pahlavi, *Mission for My Country,* p. 231.

59. Ibid., p. 232.

60. Mortaza Motahhari, *Mas'aleh-ye Hijab* [The Problem of Veiling] (Tehran: Islamic Society of Physicians, 1969/1347), pp. xi–xii.

61. Ibid., p. xii.

62. Ibid., pp. 66–67.

Chapter Twelve

1. John Ruedy, *Modern Algeria: The Origins and Development of a Nation* (Bloomington: Indiana University Press, 1992), p. 19.

2. Ibid., p. 40.

3. One of the earliest forms of resistance to the French was a Sufi brotherhood movement that was led by Amir Abd al-Qadir. See Mary-Jane Deeb, "Islam and National Identity in Algeria," *Muslim World* 87, no. 2 (April 1997), 115–16. And by the mid-1920s, the cultural nationalism of Sheikh Abdülhamid Ben Badis and the Association of the Ulama was one of the three main tendencies within Algerian political movements, the other two being the movement of the French-educated *evolues,* who sought equal rights for Muslims within the framework of French rule, and the revolutionary populist nationalism of the Etoile Nord-Africaine (1926–36) and its successor, the Parti du Peuple Algerien (PPA, 1937–54), both of which were led by the charismatic Messali Hadj. See *Cambridge Encyclopedia of the Middle East and North Africa,* s.v. "Algeria," p. 303.

4. Ruedy, *Modern Algeria,* pp. 75–6.

5. Ibid., p. 102.

6. See a series of short pieces on Ben Badis in *Le Jeune Musulman,* April 24, 1953, pp. 1, 6–7; May 8, 1953, p. 4; May 24, 1953, p. 4. Official tolerance of Ben Badis was partly due to French respect for his influential father, Mustafa, on whom Napoleon III had bestowed the Legion of Honor. The influence and wealth of his family in Constantine also facilitated his extensive studies abroad and contributed to the successful establishment of the various educational institutions by him. See Michael Willis, *The Islamist Challenge in Algeria: A Political History* (Reading, U.K.: Ithaca Press, 1996), p. 14 note 16)

7. The *evolues* were the intellectual counterparts of Egyptian Westenizers. Educated in the French schools and assimilated into the French manner and lifestyle, these educated Algerians, who numbered more than a thousand, were proponents of the assimilationist approach of the early twentieth century.

8. Ruedy, *Modern Algeria,* pp. 134–35.

9. Allan Christelow, "Ritual, Culture and Politics of Islamic Reformism in Algeria," *Middle Eastern Studies* 23, no. 3 (July 1987): 260.

10. Ibid., pp. 262–68.

11. See "La tolérance dans le Coran," *Le Jeune Musulman,* September 12, 1952, p. 4; September 26, 1952, pp. 6, 8.

12. See *Le Jeune Musulman*, July 25, 1952, pp. 1, 5; and also October 17, 1952, p. 4.

13. Mary-Jane Deeb, "Islam and National Identity in Algeria," p. 123.

14. See "The Islamic Action Salvation Front of Algeria," trans. Nicky Peters, in *Contemporary Debates in Islam: An Anthology of Modernist and Fundamentalist Thought*, ed. Mansoor Moaddel and Kamran Talattof (New York: Saint Martin's Press, 2000), pp. 273–313.

15. Hugh Roberts, "Radical Islamism and the Dilemma of Algerian Nationalism: the Embattled Arians of Algiers,' *Third World Quarterly* 10, no. 2 (April 1988): 560. See also Bruno Etienne, *L'islamisme radical* (Paris: Hachette, 1987).

16. Hugh Roberts, "Radical Islamism," p. 580.

17. The intellectual leaders often deny such charges. For example, Abbasi Madani argued that his movement was the continuation of the struggle to realize the dream of the liberation movement that started on November 1, 1954. This dream was to establish an independent state founded on Islamic principles, but the state that came to power after independence betrayed the revolution because it was based on secular and socialist principles. He reported that Ben Bella rejected his request for authorization to create an association similar to the association of the ulama that existed during the colonial period. In his view, Ben Bella was a personal despot. He was not married. He was cut off from the people, and opportunism caused his failure. Madani claimed that his participation in al-Qiyam was to continue the Islamic movement. The despotism of Boumédienne was even worse than that of Ben Bella. Boumédienne practiced political and military despotism of a kind that was unheard of in Algeria. He was also a single, ignorant man, cut off from the people, and inebriated by power. See "Entretien avec Abbassi Madani: Pour une nouvelle légalité islamique," *Politique Internationale*, no. 49 (automne 1990), pp. 177–92. In Madani's mind, there may not have been a difference between the Islamic movement before independence and the movement after independence, but even a cursory look at the teachings and orientations of the movement that was led by Ben Badis and those of the Islamic movement in the seventies and thereafter would demonstrate the extent of the difference. The first were moderate and eclectic, while the latter tended toward extremism and the rejection of all secular ideologies.

18. Roberts, however, did clearly demonstrate the development of the ideology of radical Islamism in reaction to the state's religious policies in the postindependence period, an argument similar to the theme of this book on the rise of Islamic fundamentalism.

19. For a detailed analysis of political conflicts in postrevolutionary Algeria, see David Ottaway and Marina Ottaway, *Algeria: The Politics of a Socialist Revolution* (Berkeley: University of California Press, 1970).

20. Hugh Roberts, "The Politics of Algerian Socialism," in *North Africa: Contemporary Politics and Economic Development*, ed. Richard Lawless and Allan Findlay (London: Croom Helm, 1984), p. 8.

21. Hugh Roberts, "Politics of Algerian Socialism," pp. 9, 42, notes 8–12.

22. Ibid., pp. 10–11.

23. Ottaway and Ottaway, *Algeria*, p. 282.

24. This concept was used by Jean Leca and Jean-Claude Vatin and was cited in Ruedy, *Modern Algeria*, p. 210.

25. P. J. Vatikiotis, "Tradition and Political Leadership: The Example of Algeria," in *Man, State, and Society in the Contemporary Maghrib*, ed. I. William Zartman (New York: Praeger,

1973), p. 310. Sharabi generalize the notions of *za'im* and *za'ama* to apply to all cases of revolutionary leadership in the Arab world. For him a *za'im* was " a savior, a hero, a symbol of national honor and freedom, and in possession of all power in the state." See Hisham B. Sharabi, "Power and Leadership in the Arab World," *Orbis* 7, no. 3 (Fall 1963): 590.

26. Vatikiotis, "Tradition and Political Leadership," p. 311–13.

27. John P. Entelis, "Algeria: Technocratic Rule, Military Power," in *Political Elites in Arab North Africa: Morocco, Algeria, Tunisia, Libya, and Egypt*, ed. I. William Zartman (New York: Longman, 1982), p. 110.

28. Farsoun, "State Capitalism in Algeria," *MERIP Reports*, no. 35 (February): 6.

29. The chronology of events is taken from Mustafa al-Ahnaf, Bernard Botiveau, and Franck Fregosi, *L'Algérie par ses islamistes* (Paris: Karthala, 1991), appendix 2.

30. Entelis, "Algeria," pp. 93, 95–96,

31. Cited in Entelis, "Algeria," p. 125.

32. In the words of one analyst who wrote in 1966, the FLN's "prestige has evaporated, and its national status has become largely symbolic." See William H. Lewis, "The Decline of Algeria's FLN," in Zartman, *Man, State, and Society*, p. 330.

33. Mahfoud Bennoune, *The Making of Contemporary Algeria, 1830–1987* (Cambridge: Cambridge University Press, 1988), pp. 124, 126, 130–32.

34. Ruedy, *Modern Algeria*, p. 216. Oil was discovered in the Sahara in 1956, became a considerable prize to be fought over by Algeria and the French, and contributed to the length of the war. Algeria saw this as the way out of its economic problems, and it played a large part in Algerian industrialization. See Monique Gadant, "Pétrole et société," *Peuples Méditerranéen*, January–March, 1984, pp. 105–26.

35. Karen Pfeifer, *Agrarian Reform under State Capitalism in Algeria* (Boulder, Colo.: Westview Press, 1985), p. 30.

36. Ruedy, *Modern Algeria*, p. 227, table 7.4.

37. Bennoune, *Making of Contemporary Algeria*, p. 229.

38. Ibid., p. 307.

39. Ibid., pp. 127, 159.

40. Ibid., p. 162.

41. According to Farsoun, "In the period after 1880 large French capitalist enterprises were set up in Algeria. The colony became completely dependent on and dominated by the metropole: the development of Algeria was organized in terms of the needs of France as its bourgeois rulers saw them. The first sector to fall under modern, large-scale colonial capitalism was agriculture, in which the most profitable sectors were concentrated in the hands of a small number of colons. As late as 1955, for example, of the 15 million acres of cultivable land, 25,000 Europeans owned 6.9 million acres." See Farsoun, "State Capitalism in Algeria," p. 3. Right after the independence, the economically dominant class in the urban area that consisted of "wealthy merchants, the small industrialists and the real estate owners, amounted to about 50,000 and controlled between 7,000 and 8,000 enterprises employing wage-labor." See Aissa Bennamane, *The Algerian Development Strategy and Employment Policy* (Norwich: Center for Development Studies, University of East Anglia, 1980), p. 94.

42. Farsoun, "State Capitalism in Ageria," p. 27.

43. Peter R. Knauss, *The Persistence of Patriarchy: Class, Gender, and Ideology in Twentieth Century Algeria* (New York: Praeger, 1987), p. 116.

44. Bennoune, 221–22.

45. Ruedy, *Modern Algeria*, 139.

46. Raymond Vallin, "Muslim Socialism in Algeria," in Zartman, *Man, State, and Society*, p. 50.

47. Maria Antonietta Macciocchi, "An Interview with Ben Bella," in Zartman, *Man, State, and Society*, p. 124.

48. Vallin, "Muslim Socialism in Algeria," p. 51.

49. See R. Descloitres, C. Descloitres, and J. C. Reverdy, "Urban Organization and Social Structure in Algeria," in Zartman, *Man, State, and Society*, p. 426.

50. Vallin, "Muslim Socialism in Algeria," p. 53.

51. Macciocchi, "Interview with Ben Bella," p. 125.

52. Vallin, "Muslim Socialism in Algeria," p. 51; and Willis, *Islamist Challenge in Algeria*, p. 39.

53. Vallin, "Muslim Socialism in Algeria," p. 51.

54. Ibid., p. 52.

55. Mustafa Siba'i, *Le socialisme en Islam* (Damascus, 1959), cited in *Orient*, no. 20 (4th quarter 1959): 117.

56. Vallin, "Muslim Socialism in Algeria," p. 53.

57. Ibid., p. 58.

58. Ibid., pp. 55–56.

59. Ibid., p. 60.

60. Ibid.

61. Houari Boumédienne, "The Third Anniversary of Algerian Independence," in Zartman, *Man, State, and Society*, p. 127.

62. Ibid., p. 127.

63. Ibid., p. 128.

64. This official Islamic campaign was directed against the West. A certain Mouloud Kassim claimed that all ills came from the West. See Ahmed Rouadjia, *Les frères et la mosquée: Enquête sur le mouvement islamiste en Algérie* [The Brothers and the Mosques: A Study of the Islamist Movement in Algeria] (Paris: Karthala, 1990), pp. 20–23.

65. Hugh Roberts, "Radical Islamism," p. 565. I have changed spelling from British English to American English.

66. See Rachida Yacine, "The Impact of French Colonial Heritage on Language Policies in Independent North Africa," in *North Africa: Nation, State and Region*, ed. George Joffe (London, Routledge, 1993), pp. 228–29.

67. See Jean-Claude Vatin, "Popular Puritanism versus State Reformism: Islam in Algeria," in *Islam in the Political Process*, ed. James P. Piscatori (Cambridge: Cambridge University Press, 1983), p. 100; Hugh Roberts, "Radical Islamism," p. 566; and Willis, *Islamist Challenge in Algeria*, p. 51.

68. See Hugh Roberts, "Radical Islamism," p. 566.

69. François Burgat and William Dowell, *The Islamic Movement in North Africa* (Austin: Center for Middle Eastern Studies, University of Texas at Austin, 1997), p. 257.

70. Cited in ibid., p. 257.

71. Al-Ahnaf, Botiveau, and Fregosi, *L'Algérie par ses islamistes*, pp. 24–28.

72. Hugh Roberts, "Radical Islamism," pp. 567–70.

73. Ibid., pp. 570–71.

74. Ibid., p. 573.

75. Ibid., p. 574.

76. See Jean-Claude Vatin, "Revival in the Maghreb: Islam as an Alternative Political Language," in *Islamic Resurgence in the Arab World*, ed. Ali E. Hillal Dessouki (New York: Praeger, 1982), p. 233.

77. Ibid., p. 234.

78. Christelow, "Ritual, Culture and Politics," p. 268.

79. This paragraph is based on Gadant, "Pétrole et société."

80. See Knauss, *Persistence of Patriarchy*, pp. 25, 27. See also also Frantz Fanon, *A Dying Colonialism* (New York: Evergreen Press, 1967).

81. Knauss, *Persistence of Patriarchy*, p. 47.

82. Some even argued that the French's efforts had produced a conservative backlash, as Knauss did: "if the French had not made such efforts to woo Algerian women from the influence of Algerian men, the use of the veil would possibly have become less frequent with the passage of time." Knauss, *Persistence of Patriarchy*, p. 29.

83. Knauss, *Persistence of Patriarchy*, pp. 49–52.

84. Christelow, "Ritual, Culture and Politics," p. 264.

85. Cited in Vallin, "Muslim Socialism in Algeria," pp. 61–62.

86. Ruedy, *Modern Algeria*, pp. 229–30.

87. Willis, *Islamist Challenge in Algeria*, p. 70.

88. Ibid., pp. 72–73.

89. Ruedy, *Modern Algeria*, 236.

90. Richard I. Lawless, "Algeria: Contradictions of Rapid Industrialization," in Lawless and Findlay, *North Africa*, p. 162, table 5.2.

91. Ruedy, *Modern Algeria*, p. 231; and Mark Tessler, "Alienation of Urban Youth," in *Polity and Society in Contemporary North Africa*, ed. I. William Zartman and William Mark Habeeb (Boulder, Colo.: Westview Press, 1993), pp. 73–74.

92. Bennoune, *Making of Contemporary Algeria*, 141.

93. Cited in Tessler, "Alienation of Urban Youth," p. 88.

94. All cited in ibid., p. 97.

95. See Luis Martines, *La guerre civile en Algérie 1990–1998* (Paris: Karthala, 1998).

96. See Rouadjia, *Les frères et la mosquée*.

97. Vallin, "Muslim Socialism in Algeria," p. 56.

98. Hugh Roberts, "Radical Islamism," p. 564.

99. Vallin, "Muslim Socialism in Algeria," p. 56. Other sources such as Roberts indicated the gathering numbered of about five thousand people (Hugh Roberts, "Radical Islamism," p. 564).

100. Hugh Roberts, "Radical Islamism," p. 563 and note 11.

101. Cited in Arslan Humbaraci, *Algeria: A Revolution That Failed* (London: Pall Mall Press, 1966), p. 237.

102. Vallin, "Muslim Socialism in Algeria," p. 59.

103. Ibid., p. 57.

104. See Hugh Roberts, "Radical Islamism," pp. 563–64.

105. Rouadjia, *Les frères et la mosquée* pp. 30–33.

106. Burgat and Dowell, *Islamic Movement in North Africa*, p. 250.

107. Cited in ibid., p. 251.

108. See "Entretien avec Abbassi Madani"; *La tribune d'octobre*, March 15–31, 1989, p. 6; *Algérie-Actualité*, no. 1252, October 12–18, 1989; *Al-Masar al-Maghribi*, March 26, 1990; al-Ahnaf, Botiveau, and Fregosi, *L'Algérie par ses islamistes;* and Jon Merrison, "The Doctrine and Discourse of Sheikh Abbassi: A Summary," unpublished manuscript, pp. 1–10.

109. "Entretien avec Abbassi Madani"; *La tribune d'octobre*, March 15–31, 1989, p. 6; *Algérie-Actualité*, no. 1252, October 12–18, 1989; *Al-Masar al-Maghribi*, March 26, 1990; al-Ahnaf, Botiveau, and Fregosi, *L'Algérie par ses islamistes;* and Merrison, "The Doctrine and Discourse of Sheikh Abbassi."

110. Al-Ahnaf, Botiveau, and Fregosi, *L'Algérie par ses islamistes*, pp. 21–22.

111. The lack of seriousness of the Algerian leaders concerning women's equality is best reflected in Algeria's Family Code, promulgated by the FLN in 1984. According to Slyomovics, this code reduced women to the status of minors, subject to the rule of father or husband, and presaged the remarkable mixture of nationalism and Islamism (an intellectual FIS-FLN accord) that secularists described much later as *le fascisme vert* (green fascism). See Susan Slyomovics, " 'Hassiba Ben Bouali, If You Could See Our Algeria': Women and Public Space in Algeria," *Middle East Report* 192 (January–February 1995): 11.

112. See *Al-Jaza'iriyya*, April 1989, pp. 4–11. I am indebted to Mohamed Farid Azzi for the summary.

113. Slyomovics, "Hassiba Ben Bouali," pp. 10–11. See also "Interview Abassi Madani à *Algérie-Actualité*: 'Les prochaines élections seront déterminantes . . .' " *Algérie-Actualité*, January 4, 1990, pp. 8–9; and *Jordan Times*, March 11, 1989, p. 4.

114. See Ahnaf, Botiveau, and Frégosi, *L'Algérie par ses islamistes*, pp. 239–66. These statements are based on materials published in *al-Mounquid* and other publications of Islamic groups in Algeria.

115. "C'est un 'front,' parce qu'il affronte; et parce qu'il a un large éventail d'actions et de domaines; c'est le front du peuple algérien avec toutes ses couches, et sur son vaste territoire. Il est ouvert à la variété de tendances et d'idées qui réalisent à travers la richesse de la diversité une unité cohérente . . . ; l'unité des intérêts, des positions et de l'accord. . . . C'est l'unité du destin commun.

"Il est 'islamique' d'appellation, parce qu'il a un contenu, une méthode, une fonction historique islamique. L'islam est un but auquel nous empruntons un modéle de changement et de réforme, et oú nous puisons notre raison d'être et les raisons de la continuité de notre être, l'être de la meilleure de nations. . . .

"Quant au 'salut,' il est représenté par la fonction apostolique, en tant que salut de la foi, celui qui méne à la voie droite et empêche l'erreur; et par la fonction historique, économique, sociale, culturelle et civilisationnelle. C'est la salut de tous pour être tout." Cited in Ahnaf, Botiveau, and Frégosi, *L'Algérie par ses islamistes*, p. 31.

116. Mary-Jane Deeb, "Islam and National Identity in Algeria," p. 125.

117. Cited in ibid.

118. Ibid., p. 126.

119. Kate Zebiri, "Islamic Revival in Algeria: An Overview," *Muslim World* 83, nos. 3–4 (July–October 1993): 215–19.

Chapter Thirteen

1. See Rex Brynen, "Economic Crisis and Post-Rentier Democratization in the Arab World: The Case of Jordan," *Canadian Journal of Political Science* 25, no. 1 (March 1992): 69–97.

2. Valerie Yorke, *Domestic Politics and Regional Security: Jordan, Syria and Israel* (Aldershot: Gower, 1988), p. 7; and Salibi, *Modern History of Jordan*, p. 88.

3. Mary C. Wilson, *King Abdullah, Britain, and the Making of Jordan* (Cambridge: Cambridge University Press, 1987), p. 3.

4. Mary C. Wilson, *King Abdullah*, p. 59; Salibi, *Modern History of Jordan*, p. 89.

5. Mary C. Wilson, *King Abdullah*, p. 62.

6. Ibid., pp. 72–79; Salibi, *Modern History of Jordan*, pp. 114–17; and Yorke, *Domestic Politics*, p. 10.

7. Mary C. Wilson, *King Abdullah*, p. 90.

8. Robert B. Satloff, *From Abdullah to Hussein: Jordan in Transition* (Oxford: Oxford University Press, 1994), p. 6.

9. Nasser H. Aruri, *Jordan: A Study in Political Development (1921–1965)* (The Hague: Martinus Nijhoff, 1972), pp. 31–32.

10. Uriel Dann, *King Hussein and the Challenge of Arab Radicalism: Jordan 1955–1967* (Oxford: Oxford U Press, 1989), p. 9.

11. Ibid., p. 10.

12. Yorke, *Domestic Politics*, p. 18; Aruri, *Jordan*, p. 30; and Raphael Patai, *The Kingdom of Jordan* (Princeton, N.J.: Princeton University Press, 1958), pp. 57.

13. Asher Susser, *On Both Banks of the Jordan River: A Political Biography of Wasfi all Tall* (Portland, Oreg.: Frank Cass, 1994), p. 5. See also Linda L. Layne, "Tribesmen as Citizens: 'Primordial Ties' and Democracy in Rural Jordan," in *Elections in the Middle East: Implications of Recent Trends*, ed. Linda L. Layne (Boulder, Colo.: Westview Press, 1987), pp. 113–51.

14. Cited in Linda L. Layne, "The Dialogics of Tribal Self-Representation in Jordan," *American Ethnologist* 16 (February 1989): 28. See also *Jordan Times*, January 28, 1985.

15. Layne, "Dialogics," p. 27.

16. Dawn, *From Ottomanism*, p. 72.

17. Hani Hourani, Taleb Awad, Hamed Dabbas, and Sa'eda Kilani, *Islamic Action Front Party* (Amman: al-Urdun al-Jadid Research Center, 1993), p. 9; and Awni Obaidi, *The Muslim Brotherhood in Jordan and Palestine, 1945–1970* (Amman: al-Urdun al-Jadid Research Center, 1991), p. 41.

18. Hourani et al., *Islamic Action Front*, p. 10; and Obaidi, *Muslim Brotherhood*, p. 40.

19. Hourani et al., *Islamic Action Front*, p. 9; and Obaidi, *Muslim Brotherhood*, p. 37.

20. Shaul Mishal, "Conflictual Pressures and Cooperative Interests: Observations on West Bank–Amman Political Relations, 1940–1967," in *Palestinian Society and Politics*, ed. Joel S. Migdal (Princeton, N.J.: Princeton University Press, 1980), p. 175.

21. Ibid., p. 178.

22. Yorke, *Domestic Politics*, p. 50.

23. Hani Hourani, Hamed Dabbas, Taleb Awad, and Omar Shniekat, *Jordanian Political Parties* (Amman: al-Urdun al-Jadid Research Center, 1993), pp. 29–30.

24. *Jordan Diary 1997* (Amman: International Press Office, 1997), p. 40.

25. See John Lewis Burckhardt, *Travels in Syria and the Holy Land* (London: John Murray, 1822), pp. 350–54.

26. Eugene L. Rogan. "Bringing the State Back: The Limits of Ottoman Rule in Jordan, 1840–1910," in *Village, Steppe and State: The Social Origins of Modern Jordan*, ed. Eugene L. Rogan and Tariq Tell (London: British Academic Press, 1994), pp. 51–52.

27. Abla M. Amawi, "The Consolidation of the Merchant Class in Transjordan during the Second World War," in Rogan and Tell, *Village, Steppe and State*, pp. 163–66.

28. Amawi, "Consolidation of the Merchant Class," pp. 174–75.

29. Mary C. Wilson, *King Abdullah*, p. 165. See also Doreen Warriner, *Land and Poverty in the Middle East* (London: Royal Institute of International Affairs, 1948), p. 80; Marcus Mackenzie, "Transjordan," *Journal of the Royal Central Asian Society* 33 (July–October 1946): 263; James Baster, "The Economic Problems of Jordan," *International Affairs* 31 (January 1955): 27.

30. Mary C. Wilson, *King Abdullah*, p. 57.

31. Timothy J. Piro, *The Political Economy of Market Reform in Jordan* (New York: Rowman & Littlefield, 1998), p. 23. See also Benjamin Schwadran, *Jordan: A State of Tension* (New York: Council for Middle East Affairs, 1959).

32. John Bagot Glubb, *Britain and the Arabs: A Study of Fifty Years 1908–1950* (London: Hodder and Stoughton, 1959), p. 173. See also Michael R. Fischbach, "British Land Policy in Transjordan," in Rogan and Tell, *Village, Steppe and State*, pp. 80, 106.

33. See Fischbach, "British Land Policy in Transjordan," pp. 106–7; IBRD, *Economic Development of Jordan*, pp. 130–31; Edgar Barton Worthington, *Middle East Science: A Survey of Subjects Other than Agriculture* (London: H.M. Stationery off., 1946), p. 15; and Warriner, p. 79.

34. Fischbach, "British Land Policy in Transjordan," p. 106. Gerber has also noted the connection between Hashemite longevity and land tenure. See Haim Gerber, *The Social Origins of the Modern Middle East* (Boulder Colo.: L. Rienner, 1987), p. 159.

35. Aruri, *Jordan*, p. 50, table 5.

36. Piro, *Political Economy of Market Reform*, p. 40.

37. Onn Winckler, *Population Growth and Migration in Jordan, 1950–1994* (Sussex: Academic Press, 1997), pp. 43, 48, 72. See also M. G. Quibria, "Migrant Workers and Remittances: Issues for Asian Developing Countries," *Asian Development Review* 4, no. 1 (1986): 82, table 1.

38. Winckler, *Population Growth and Migration*, p. 79, table 2.5.

39. Ibid., pp. 70–71.

40. Ibid., p. 91.

41. See Richard P. Mitchell, *Society of the Muslim Brothers*, p. 268.

42. Through much of his life, Banna seems not to have lost his loyalty to the Egyptian monarchy. However, the forces turned loose in the movement inevitably worked against the palace. The works of Muhammad al-Ghazali, the first of which appeared in 1948, could be regarded as indirect assaults on monarchical authority and reflections of the spirit of the

membership, if not of the leaders. This fact seems to have been clear to the palace, as the 1948 decree of dissolution shows. See Richard P. Mitchell, *Society of the Muslim Brothers*, p. 220.

43. Ammon Cohen, *Political Parties in the West Bank under the Jordanian Regime, 1949–1967* (Ithaca, N.Y.: Cornell University Press, 1982), pp. 163–65.

44. See Ibrahim Gharaibih, *Jama'a al-Ikhwan al-Muslimeen fil Urdun: 1946–1996* [The Society of Muslim Brothers in Jordan: 1946–1996] (Amman: al-Urdun al-Jadid Research Center, 1997), pp. 48–49, 51.

45. Author's interview with Ibrahim Gharaibih, a member of the Jordanian MB and IAFP, April 1998.

46. Ammon Cohen, *Political Parties in the West Bank*, pp. 179, 182.

47. Author's interview with Ibrahim Gharaibih.

48. Gharaibih, *Jama'a al-Ikhwan*, p. 59. There is no record of any military activity by the Jordanian MB during the period because the MB did not want to clash with the regime, contrary to the Egyptian branch (p. 63).

49. Author's interview with Ibrahim Gharaibih. Juwaifel left Jordan for Egypt in 1954 to support Nassir.

50. Interview with Yaya Shaqra, secretary of Abdul Majid Thunibat, the comptroller general of the Society of the Muslim Brothers, September 6, 1999.

51. Ibid.

52. Aruri, *Jordan*, pp. 136–37.

53. Hussein, King of Jordan, *Uneasy Lies the Head* (London: Heinemann, 1962), p. 78.

54. Ibid., pp. 74–75.

55. Ali Abdul Kazem, "The Muslim Brotherhood: The Historic Background and the Ideological Origins," in *Islamic Movements in Jordan*, ed. Julian Schwedler (Amman: al-Urdun al-Jadid Research Center, 1997), pp. 13–14.

56. Ammon Cohen, *Political Parties in the West Bank*, p. 152. See also Hanna Y. Freij and Leonard C. Robinson, "Liberalization, the Islamists and the Stability of the Arab State: Jordan as a Case Study," *Muslim World* 86, no. 1 (January 1996): 1–2; and Sami al-Khazendar, *Jordan and the Palestine Question: The Role of Islamic and Left Forces in Foreign Policy-Making* (Berkshire, U.K.: Ithaca Press, 1997), pp. 146–47.

57. Munitions exploded on the Egyptian soldiers before reaching the enemy (interview with Musa Kilani, spring 1997).

58. *Jordan Diary 1997*, pp. 25, 76.

59. Gharaibih, *Jama'a al-Ikhwan*, p. 76. The increase in petrodollars in oil-rich Arab countries is believed to have contributed to financing the Muslim Brothers. Nadir Sharif, the interior minister, indicated that the MB's major sources of support came from the poor areas in refugee camps. Financially, however, membership dues were not enough to cover all their expenses. When one of their leaders, who was also a member of parliament, died of cancer, the MB paid off all his debts, which were more than one hundred thousand dollars. The major source of finance came from the Persian Gulf states, Kuwait, and Saudi Arabia—in particular, not from the governments of these countries, but from rich Muslims, people like Osama Ben Laden from Saudi Arabia (author's interview with Nadir Sharif).

60. Kazem, "The Muslim Brotherhood," p. 23.

61. Gharaibih, *Jama'a al-Ikhwan*, p. 80. Abdul Majid Thunibat indicated that "Sayyid Qutb was a thinker of the Muslim Brothers. But we are not obliged to follow his ideas. Some of our members may find his ideas acceptable while others think otherwise. There are different trends within our movement. Nevertheless, all members and trends are obliged to follow the resolutions of the shura council and its executive bureau. These resolutions are of course based on the considerations of all the trends within our movement and the articulation of Islam with the current situations. The circumstances in which Sayyid Qutb developed his ideas did not coincide with ours. His ideas were the results of years of imprisonment, torture, and the particular conditions of Egypt. Al-jahili-yeh wat takfir (i.e., the idea of Sayyid Qutb) did not take root in Jordan, because our movement had a different political experience. Moreover, even the Egyptian branch went against his ideas. For example, Hasan Hudaibi, the leader of the Egyptian branch, attacked al-jahilyeh wat takfir, arguing that we are preachers, not judges." Author's interview with Thunibat.

62. Gharaibih, *Jama'a al-Ikhwan*, pp. 80–81.

63. *Jordan Diary 1997*, p. 43.

64. The democratic reforms were also a response to the deteriorating economic conditions of the country and the social upheavals of 1988–89.

65. *Jordan Diary 1997*, p. 44.

66. The principle that that Islam was the source of legislation was vague. It is unclear how Islamic law could be reconciled with the policies of a secular state. The constitution did not call for a body of Islamic jurists to oversee the process of legislation in order to ensure its conformity with Islam.

67. See Hourani et al, *Islamic Action Front*, p. 36.

68. See "Law No 32 For The Year 1992: Political Parties Law," pp. 331–35, *Jordan's Diary*, Article 6f and Article 19. The MB claimed that they were not a political party but a worldwide Islamic movement based on the teaching of Egyptian scholar and the founder of the brotherhood in Egypt, Hasan al-Banna, and therefore the law was not applicable to them.

69. *Star*, June 24, 1993.

70. Ibid.

71. Ibid.

72. Hamzah Mansour, interview with author, spring 1997.

73. Francesca Ciriaci, "Muslim Brotherhood Continues to Expand Popular Appeal despite Setbacks," *Jordan Times*, April 16–17, 1998.

74. According to article 46B of "Law No. 22 For the Year 1986: Law of Election to the House of Deputies," "The voter shall write the names of the candidates he wishes to elect on the Ballot Paper given to him by the Chairman of the Balloting Paper and shall return to the Ballot Box to deposit the Ballot Paper therein." Article 2B of the "Law Amending the Law of Election to the House of Deputies for the Year 1993" stated, "The voter shall write the name of the Candidate he wishes to elect on the Ballot paper given to him by the Chairman of the Balloting Panel and shall return to the Ballot box to deposit the Ballot Paper therein." See *Jordan Diary 1997*, pp. 335–52. This law thus ended the previous voting system, whereby voters were entitled to as many votes as the number of parliamentary seats allocated for their district.

75. Interview with Nadir Rashid, interior minister, spring 1997.

76. See Hani Hourani and Hussein Abu-Rumman, *The Democratic Process in Jordan* (Amman: al-Urdun al-Jadid Research Center, 1996), pp. 105–6. Hamzah Mansour criticized the government for the undemocratic nature of the law. He said, in America, everybody has representation; everybody is equal in the election process. In Jordan, there is no proper criterion for dispensing that equality. What we have here is something like that every 20,000 people have the same representation as every 100,000. Districts with 100,000 and 20,000 are treated the same and are represented equally. If people in Jordan are all equal, then why do we have quotas for Caucasians, Christians, the Bedouins? If we are going to have quota, why should it not be proportional to their population? Presently, 11 percent of the parliamentary seats are reserved for Christian minorities, while they constitute only 3 percent of the total population" (interview with Hamzah Mansour, spring 1997).

77. For an interesting commentary on this law see Rami G. Khouri, "State and Press: Mutual Irresponsibility on the Dizzying Road to Arab Liberalism," *Jordan Times*, October 21, 1997.

78. According to Hamzah Mansour, "the idea of one-person, one-vote was formed and implemented under the influence of the United States. There was a commonality of purpose between Jordanian and American governments to combat the Islamic movement. The government has in the past disturbed and disorganized the IAFP's electoral campaigns." Mansour, interview with author, spring 1997. Many other leading members of the MB and IAFP shared Mansour's assessment.

79. Proboycott groups released a "national salvation plan" for political, social, and economic reforms. They opposed the Arab-Israeli peace process, insisted on the abolition of the one-person, one-vote law, and demanded the total independence of the judiciary from the executive branch of the government. *Jordan Times*, October 21, 1997, p. 3.

80. *Why Does the Muslim Brotherhood Boycott the 1997 Parliamentary Elections: A Statement to the People* (Amman: Muslim Brotherhood Headquarters, July 13, 1997). The pragmatic nature of this statement is even more evident when one considers that although the MB fiercely opposed the 1994 peace treaty with Israel, its leadership did not include its abrogation among the conditions for participating in the elections (see Ciriaci, "Muslim Brotherhood").

81. Ishaq Farhan, interview with author, spring 1997.

82. Ibid.

83. Ibid.

84. Ibid.

85. Abdul Majid Thunibat, interview with author, April 1997.

86. For the Muslim Brotherhood the Palestine problem was central. It has described the Jews as "dishonest," "the defilers of the prophets," "liars," "God's adversaries," "corrupt," and a "deadly enemy" (Khazendar, *Jordan and the Palestine Question*, p. 139)

87. This conception was prevalent among the "hawk" wings of the MB. Hammam Said advanced a traditionalist and literal interpretation of gender relations in Islam when he simply reiterated the Quranic verse "al-mar'u qavvamuna il-an-nissa'" (men have authority over women) (interview with author).

88. Cited in Lisa Taraki, "Jordanian Islamists and the Agenda for Women: Between Discourse and Practice," *Middle Eastern Studies* 32, no. 1 (January 1996): 144.

89. Cited in Taraki, "Jordanian Islamists," p. 145.

90. Cited in Hourani et al. *Islamic Action Front*, p. 32.

91. Ibid., p. 21.

92. Thunibat stressed that women were barred to protect them from being harassed by the state's security forces. Interview with author, spring 2000).

93. Hourani and Abu-Rumman, *Democratic Process in Jordan*, p. 318.

94. Ibid., p. 323.

95. Ibid.

96. Thunibat, interview with author, April 1998.

97. Ishaq Farhan, interview with author, April 1997.

Conclusion

1. See Moaddel, "Ideology as Episodic Discourse," p. 368.

2. See, for example, Abdul Karim Soroush and Mohsin Kadivar, *Monaziri darbar-ye Pluralism-i Dini* [A Debate on Religion Pluralism] (Tehran: Salam Newspaper, 1999/1378); and Mohsin Kadivar, *Nazariyyeh Doulat dar Fiqh-i Shi'eh* [Theory of the State in Shi'i Jurisprudence] (Tehran: Nay, 1977/1376).

3. For a discussion of the relationship of immanent to nonimmanent regimes and ideology, see Swanson, *Religion and Regime.*

4. See C. B. MacPherson, "Politics: Post-Liberal-Democracy," in *Ideology in Social Science*, ed. Robin Blackburn (New York: Vintage, 1972), pp. 17–31.

5. Karl Marx, "Civil War in France," in *Selected Works*, by Karl Marx and Frederick Engels (New York: International Publishers, 1977), p. 289.

BIBLIOGRAPHY

Abd-Allah, Umar F. 1983. *The Islamic Struggle in Syria.* Berkeley: Mizan Press.

Abrahamian, Ervand. 1974. "Oriental Despotism: The Case of Qajar Iran." *International Journal of Middle East Studies* 5:3–31.

———. 1979. "The Causes of the Constitutional Revolution in Iran." *International Journal of Middle East Studies* 10:381–414.

———. 1982. *Iran between Two Revolutions.* Princeton, N.J.: Princeton University Press.

Abu Jaber, Kamel S. 1966. *Arab Ba'th Socialist Party: History, Ideology, and Organization.* Syracuse, N.Y.: Syracuse University Press.

'Abul Fazl, Allami. 1873. *The Ain I Akbari.* Translated by H. Blochmann. Calcutta: Baptist Mission Press.

Abu Talib Khan Ibn Muhammad Isfahani. 1972. *Travels of Mirza Abu Taleb Khan in Asia, Africa, and Europe during the Years 1799 to 1803.* Translated from Persian by Charles Stewart. New Delhi: Sona. Originally published in 1814.

Adamiyat, Fereydoun. 1955/1334. *Amir Kabir va Iran.* Tehran: Amir Kabir Publications.

———. 1970. *Andishaha-yi Mirza Fath Ali Akhundzadah.* Tehran: Kharazmi Publications.

———. 1972/1351. *Andisheh-ye Taraqi va Hukoumat-i Qanun: Asr-i Sipahsalar* [Progressive Thought and the Rule of Law: Sipahsalar Era]. Tehran: Kharazmi Publications.

———. 1976/1355. *Idi'olozhi-ye Nahzat-i Mashrutiyat-i Iran* [The Ideology of the Constitutional Movement in Iran]. Tehran: Payam Publications.

———. 1976. *Idi'olozhi-ye Nahzat-i Mashrutiyat-i Iran* [The Ideology of the Constitutional Movement in Iran]. Tehran: Payam Publications.

———. 1978/1357. *Andishaha-yi Mirza Aqa Khan Kirmani* [The Ideas of Mirza Aqa Khan Kirmani]. Tehran: Payam Publications.

———. 1981/1360. *Shourish bar Imtiyaz'nameye Rizhi* [Rebellion against the Regie Concession]. Tehran: Payam Publications.

———. 1985/1363. "Ashoftegy dar Fekr-i Tarikhi" [Confusion in historical thinking]. In *Yadnamey-ye Jalal-i Ale-Ahmad* [For Jalal Ale-Ahmad]. Tehran: Pasargad.

Adams, Charles C. 1933. *Islam and Modernism in Egypt: A Study of the Modern Reform Movement Inaugurated by Muhammad 'Abduh*. New York: Russell & Russell.

Adhikari, G. 1943. *Pakistan and Indian National Unity*. Bombay.

Afary, Janet. 1996. *The Iranian Constitutional Revolution, 1906–1911: Grassroots Democracy, Social Democracy, and the Origin of Feminism*. New York: Columbia University Press.

Ahmad, Aziz. 1964. *Studies in Islamic Culture in the Indian Environment*. Oxford: Clarendon Press.

———. 1967. *Islamic Modernism in India and Pakistan: 1857–1964*. London: Oxford University Press.

Ahmad, Aziz, and G. E. Von Grunebaum. 1970. *Muslim Self-Statement in India and Pakistan, 1857–1968*. Wiesbaden: Otto Harrassowitz.

Ahmad, Qeyamuddin. 1966. *The Wahabi Movement in India*. Calcutta: Firma K. L. Mukhopadhyay.

Ahmed, Jamal Mohammad. 1960. *The Intellectual Origins of Egyptian Nationalism*. Oxford: Oxford University Press.

Akhavi, Shahrough. 1980. *Religion and Politics in Contemporary Iran*. Albany: State University of New York Press.

———. 1992. "The Clergy's Concepts of Rule in Egypt and Iran." *Annals of the American Academy of Political and Social Science* 524 (November): 92–102.

al-Ahnaf, Mustafa, Bernard Botiveau, and Franck Fregosi. 1991. *L'Algerie par ses islamistes*. Paris: Karthala.

Ale-Ahmad, Jalal. 1982. *Plagued by the West (Ghrabzadegi or Westoxication)*. Translated by Paul Sprachman. New York: Columbia University Press.

———. n.d. *Dar Khedmat va Khianat-i Roushanfikran* [Concerning the Service and Betrayal of the Intellectuals]. Tehran: Ravaq Publications.

Alexander, Bobby C. 1991 "Correcting Misinterpretations of Turner's Theory: An African-American Pentecostal Illustration." *Journal for the Scientific Study of Religion* 30, no. 1:26–44.

Alexander, Jeffrey C., and Steven Seidman. 1990. *Culture and Society: Contemporary Debates*. Cambridge: Cambridge University Press.

Alexander, Jeffrey C., and Philip Smith. 1993. "The Discourse of American Civil Society: A New Proposal for Cultural Studies." *Theory and Society* 22:151–207.

Alexander, Mark [Walter Z. Lacqueur]. 1951, "Communist Strategy in the Middle East." *Twentieth Century*, November.

Algar, Hamid. 1969. *Religion and State in Modern Iran*. Berkeley: University of California Press.

Ali, M. Athar. 1993. "The Mughal Polity: A Critique of Revisionist Approaches." *Modern Asian Studies* 27(4): 699–710.

Alloula, Malek. 1986. *The Colonial Harem*. Minneapolis: University of Minnesota Press.

Alnaf, M., Bernard Botiveau, and Frank Fregosi. 1991. *L'Algerie par ses Islamistes*. Paris: Karthala.

Althusser, Louis. 1971. *Lenin and Philosophy*. London: New Left Books.

Amawi, Abla M. 1994. "The Consolidation of the Merchant Class in Transjordan during the Second World War." Pp. 162–86 in *Village, Steppe and State: The Social Origins of*

Modern Jordan, edited by Eugene L. Rogan and Tariq Tell, London: British Academic Press.

Ameer [Amir] Ali, Syed. 1922. *The Spirit of Islam.* London: Christophers.

———. 1955. *A Short History of the Saracens.* New York: Macmillan & Co.

———. 1968. *Memoirs and Other Writings of Syed Ameer Ali.* Edited by Syed Razi Wasti. Lahore: Peoples Publishing House.

Amin, Qasim. 1992. *The Liberation of Women.* Translated by Samiha Sidhom Peterson. Cairo: American University in Cairo Press. Originally published in Arabic in 1899.

Anderson, Perry. 1979. *Lineages of the Absolutist State.* London: Verso.

Ansari, Hamied. 1986. *Egypt, the Stalled Society.* Albany: State University of New York Press.

Antonius, George. 1961. *The Arab Awakening: The Story of the Arab National Movement.* London: Hamish Hamilton.

Apter, David, ed. 1964. *Ideology and Discontent.* New York: Free Press.

Arendt, Hannah. 1958. *The Origin of Totalitarianism.* Cleveland: Meridian Books.

———. 1965. *On Revolution.* New York: Viking Press.

Arjomand, Said Amir. 1984. *The Shadow of God and the Hidden Imam.* Chicago: University of Chicago Press.

———. 1988. *The Turban for the Crown: The Islamic Revolution in Iran.* New York: Oxford University Press.

———, ed. 1984. *From Nationalism to Revolutionary Islam.* Albany: State University of New York Press.

Arkoun, Mohammad. 1988. "Algeria." Pp. 171–86 in *The Politics of Islamic Revivalism: Diversity and Unity,* edited by Shireen T. Hunter. Bloomington: Indiana University Press.

Arnold, Sir Thomas Walker. 1913. *The Preaching of Islam: A History of the Propagation of the Muslim Faith.* London: Constable & Co.

Aruri, Nasser H. 1972. *Jordan: A Study in Political Development (1921–1965).* The Hague: Martinus Nijhoff.

Asad, Muhammad. 1987. *This Law of Ours and Other Essays.* Gibraltar: Dar Al-Andalus.

Ashraf, Ahmad. 1970. "Historical Obstacles to the Development of a Bourgeoisie in Iran." In *Studies in the Economic History of the Middle East,* edited by M. A. Cook. London: Oxford University Press.

———. 1988. "Bazaar-Mosque Alliance: The Social Basis of Revolts and Revolutions." *Politics, Culture, and Society* 1, no. 4 (Summer): 548–59.

Ashraf, Mujeeb. 1982. *Muslim Attitudes towards British Rule and Western Culture in India.* Delhi: Idarah-i Adabiyat-i Delli.

Ayubi, Nazih Nassif M. 1980. *Bureaucracy and Politics in Contemporary Egypt.* London: Ithaca Press.

Azimi, Fakhreddin. 1989. *Iran: The Crisis of Democracy.* London: I. B. Tauris.

Badawi, Muhammad A. Zaki. 1978. *The Reformers of Egypt.* London: Croom Helm.

Baer, Gabriel. 1962. *A History of Landownership in Modern Egypt, 1800–1950.* London: Oxford University Press.

———. 1968. "Urbanization in Egypt, 1820–1907." In *Beginnings of Modernization in the Middle East: The Nineteenth Century,* edited by William R. Polk and Richard L. Chambers. Chicago: University of Chicago Press.

———. 1969. *Studies in the Social History of Modern Egypt*. Chicago: University of Chicago Press.

Bainbridge, William Sim. 1995. "Social Influence and Religious Pluralism." Pp. 1–18 in *Advances in Group Processes*, vol. 12. JAI Press.

Baljon, Johannes Marinus Simon, Jr. 1970. *The Reforms and Religious Ideas of Sir Sayyid Ahmad Khan*. Lahore: Sh. Muhammad Ashraf.

Bamdad, Mehdi. 1968/1347. *Tarikh-i Rijal-i Iran* [A Dictionary of National Biography of Iran]. Vol. 2. Tehran: Zovvar Bookstore.

Banna, Hasan al-. 1978. *Five Tracts of Hasan al-Banna (1906–1949)*. Translated by Charles Wendell. Berkeley: University of California Press.

Barelvi, Sayyid Ahmad. n.d. *Correspondence of Sayyid Ahmad of Barelvi*. London: India Office Library and Records (Oriental 6635).

Baron, Beth. 1994. *The Women's Awakening in Egypt*. New Haven, Conn.: Yale University Press.

Baster, James. 1955. "The Economic Problems of Jordan." *International Affairs* 31 (January): 26–35.

Batatu, Hanna. 1982. "Syria's Muslim Brethren." *MERIP Reports* (November/December), pp. 12–20, 34, 36.

———. 1999. *Syria's Peasantry, the Descendants of Its Lesser Rural Notables, and Their Politics*. Princeton, N.J.: Princeton University Press.

Baudauni, Abdul Qadir. *Abdul Qadir Baudauni, Muntakhab-ut-Tawarikh*. 1884–1925. Translated by G. S. A. Ranking, W. H. Lowe, and Sir Wolseley Haig. Vol. 3. Calcutta.

Baumann, G., ed. 1986. *The Written Word: Literacy in Transition*. Oxford: Clarendon Press.

Bayat, Mongol. 1991. *Iran's First Revolution: Shi'ism and the Constitutional Revolution of 1905–1909*. New York: Oxford University Press.

Bayly, C. A. 1983. *Rulers, Townsmen and Bazaars: North Indian Society in the Age of British Expansion, 1770–1870*. Cambridge: Cambridge University Press.

———. 1988. *Indian Society and the Making of the British Empire*. Cambridge: Cambridge University Press.

Beinin, Joel, and Zachary Lockman. 1987. *Workers on the Nile*. Princeton, N.J.: Princeton University Press.

Bengio, Ofra, and Gabriel Ben-Dor, eds. 1999. *Minorities and the State in the Arab World*. Boulder, Colo.: Lynne Rienner.

Benjamin, Samuel Greene Wheeler. 1887. *Persia and the Persians*. Boston: Ticknor & Co.

Bennamane, Aissa. 1980. *The Algerian Development Strategy and Employment Policy*. Norwich: Center for Development Studies, University of East Anglia.

Bennoune, Mahfoud. 1988. *The Making of Contemporary Algeria, 1830–1987*. Cambridge: Cambridge University Press.

Berger, Morroe. 1957. *Bureaucracy and Society in Modern Egypt: A Study of the Higher Civil Service*. Princeton, N.J.: Princeton University Press.

Berger, Peter L. 1963. "Charisma and Religious Innovation: The Social Location of Israelite Prophecy." *American Sociological Review* 28:940–50.

Berger, Peter L., and Thomas Luckmann. 1969. "Sociology of Religion and Sociology of Knowledge." Pp. 61–73 in *Sociology of Religion,* edited by Roland Robertson. New York: Penguin Books.

Bernier, François. 1968. *Travels in the Mogul Empire.* New Delhi: S. Chand & Co.

Berque, Jacques. 1972. *Egypt: Imperialism and Revolution.* New York: Praeger.

Bhadra, Gautam. 1988. "Four Rebels of Eighteen-Fifty-Seven." Pp. 129–75 in *Selected Subaltern Studies,* edited by Ranajit Guha and Gayatri Chakravorty Spivak. Oxford: Oxford University Press.

Binder, Leonard. 1962. *Iran: Political Development in a Changing Society.* Berkeley: University of California Press.

Bjorkland, J. Bernard. 1956. "The American Mission as a Causal Factor in the Growth of the Protestant Community of Egypt from 1854–1900." B.A. thesis, Department of History, American University, Cairo.

Blackburn, Robin, ed. 1972. *Ideology in Social Science.* New York: Vintage.

Blumer, Herbert. 1969. *Symbolic Interactionism: Perspective and Method.* Englewood Cliffs, N.J.: Prentice-Hall.

Blunt, Wilfrid S. 1895. *Secret History of the English Occupation of Egypt.* Reprint, New York: Howard Fertig, 1967.

Bonne, Alfred. 1955. *State and Economics in the Middle East.* London: Routledge & Kegan Paul.

Botman, Selma. 1991. *Egypt from Independence to Revolution, 1919-1952.* Syracuse, N.Y.: Syracuse University Press.

Boumédienne, Houari. 1973. "The Third Anniversary of Algerian Independence." Pp. 127–30 in *Man, State, and Society in the Contemporary Maghrib,* edited by I. William Zartman. New York: Praeger.

Brown, Arthur Judson. 1936. *One Hundred Years.* New York: Frelming H. Revell.

Browne, Edward G. 1910. *The Persian Revolution of 1905–1909.* New York: Barnes & Noble.

Brynen, Rex. 1992. "Economic Crisis and Post-Rentier Democratization in the Arab World: The Case of Jordan." *Canadian Journal of Political Science* 25, no. 1:69–97.

Burawoy, Michael. 1980. "The Politics of Production and Production of Politics: A Comparative Analysis of Piecework Machine Shops in the United States and Hungary." Pp. 261–99 in *Political Power and Social Theory,* edited by M. Zeitlin. Greenwich, Conn.: JAI Press.

Burckhardt, John Lewis. 1822. *Travels in Syria and the Holy Land.* London: John Murray.

Burgat, François, and William Dowell. 1997. *The Islamic Movement in North Africa.* Austin: Center for Middle Eastern Studies, University of Texas at Austin.

Butcher, Edith L. 1897. *The Story of the Church of Egypt.* London: Smith, Elder & Co.

Butterworth, Charles E. 1982. "Prudence versus Legitimacy: The Persistent Theme in Islamic Political Thought." Pp. 84–114 in *Islamic Resurgence in the Arab World,* edited by Ali E. Hillal Dessouki. New York: Praeger.

Camic, Charles. 1991. "Book Reviews: *Communities of Discourse.*" *American Journal of Sociology* 97, no. 1:210–14.

Campbell, William W. 1844. *A Memoir of Mrs. Judith S. Grant, Late Missionary to Persia.* New York: J. Winchester.

Canfield, Robert L., ed. 1991. *Turko-Persia in Historical Perspective.* Cambridge: Cambridge University Press.

Cantril, Hadely. 1941. *The Psychology of Social Movements.* New York: John Wiley & Sons.

Chandra, Satish. 1982. *Medieval India: Society, the Jagirdari Crisis, and the Village.* Delhi: Macmillan.

Chatterjee, Partha. 1993. *Nationalist Thought and the Colonial World: A Derivative Discourse.* Minneapolis: University of Minnesota Press.

Cheragh [Chiragh] Ali, Moulvi. 1883. *The Proposed Political, Legal, and Social Reforms in the Ottoman Empire and Other Mohammadan States.* Bombay: Education Society Press.

———. 1977. *A Critical Exposition of the Popular "Jihad."* Karachi: Karimsons.

Chevallier, Dominique. 1968. 'Western Development and Eastern Crisis in the Mid Nineteenth Century: Syria Confronted with the European Economy." Pp. 205–22 in *Beginnings of Modernization in the Middle East,* edited by William R. Polk and Richard L. Chambers. Chicago: University of Chicago Press.

Chirol, Valentine. 1903. *The Middle Eastern Question; or, Some Political Problems of Indian Defence.* New York: E. P. Dutton & Co.

Chopra, Pran Nath. 1963. *Some Aspects of Social Life during the Mughal Age (1526–1707).* Agra: Shiva Lal Agarwala & Co.

Christelow, Allan. 1985. *Muslim Law Courts and the French Colonial State in Algeria.* Princeton, N.J.: Princeton University Press.

———. 1987. "Ritual, Culture and Politics of Islamic Reformism in Algeria." *Middle Eastern Studies* 23, no. 3 (July): 255–73.

Ciriaci, Francesca. 1998. "Muslim Brotherhood Continues to Expand Popular Appeal despite Setbacks." *Jordan Times,* April 16–17.

Clancy-Smith, J. 1994. *Rebel and Saint.* Berkeley: University of California Press.

Clark, Rev. Robert. 1885. *The Punjab and Sindh Missions of the Church Missionary Society.* 2nd ed. London: Church Missionary Society.

Cleveland, William L. 1971. *The Making of an Arab Nationalist: Ottomanism and Arabism in the Life and Thought of Sati' al-Husri.* Princeton, N.J.: Princeton University Press.

Cohen, Ammon. 1982. *Political Parties in the West Bank under the Jordanian Regime, 1949–1967.* Ithaca, N.Y.: Cornell University Press.

Cohen, Morris R., and Ernest Nagel. 1934. *An Introduction to Logic and Scientific Method.* New York: Harcourt, Brace & Co.

Cohen, Norman J., ed. 1990. *The Fundamentalist Phenomenon.* Grand Rapids, Mich.: William B. Eerdmans.

Cole, Juan R. I. 1993. *Colonialism and Revolution in the Middle East: Social and Cultural Origins of Egypt's Urabi Movement.* Princeton, N.J.: Princeton University Press.

Collins, Randall. 1998. *The Sociology of Philosophies: A Global Theory of Intellectual Change.* Cambridge, Mass.: Harvard University Press.

Commins, David. 1986. "Religious Reformers and Arabists in Damascus, 1885–1914." *International Journal of Middle East Studies* 18:405–25.

Cooper, Fredrick. 1994. "Conflict and Connection: Rethinking Colonial African History." *American Historical Review* 99 (December): 1516–45.

"Correspondence Respecting the Persian Tobacco Concession." 1892. *Sessional Papers* 79:211–12.

Costello, D. P. 1954. "Griboedov in Persia in 1820: Two Diplomatic Notes." *Oxford Slavonic Papers* 5:81–92.

———. 1957. "The Murder of Griboedov." *Oxford Slavonic Papers* 8:55–89.

———. 1962. "A Note on 'The Diplomatic Activity of A. S. Griboyedov' by S. V. Shostakovich.'" *Slavic and East European Review* 40:235–44.

Coward, Rosalind, and John Ellis. 1977. *Language and Materialism.* London: Routledge & Kegan Paul.

Crabbs, Jack A., Jr. 1984. *The Writing of History in Nineteenth-Century Egypt.* Cairo: American University Press.

Cragg, Kenneth. 1957. "The Tests of 'Islamicity.'" *Middle East Forum* 32 (November): 15–17, 33.

Crecelius, Daniel. 1972. "Nonideological Responses of the Egyptian Ulama to Modernization." Pp. 167–210 in *Scholars, Saints, and Sufis,* edited by N. R. Keddie. Berkeley: University of California Press.

Cromer, Evelyn Baring. 1908. *Modern Egypt.* New York: Macmillan Co.

———. 1910. *Ancient and Modern Imperialism.* London: John Murray.

Crothers, Samuel McChord. 1910. *Among Friends.* New York: Houghton Mifflin.

Curzon, George N. 1892. *Persia and the Persian Question.* Vol. 1. London: Longmans Green.

Dabashi, Hamid. 1993. *Theology of Discontent: The Ideology Foundation of the Islamic Revolution in Iran.* New York: New York University Press.

Dann, Uriel. 1989. *King Hussein and the Challenge of Arab Radicalism: Jordan 1955–1967.* Oxford: Oxford University Press.

Dar, Bashir Ahmad. 1957. *Religious Thought of Sayyid Ahmad Khan.* Lahore: Institute of Islamic Culture.

Davies, James. C. 1962. "Toward a Theory of Revolution." *American Sociological Review* 27:5–18.

Davis, Kingsley. 1951. *The Population of India and Pakistan.* Princeton, N.J.: Princeton University Press.

Davison, Roderic H. 1990. *Essays in Ottoman and Turkish History.* Austin: University of Texas Press.

Dawisha, Adeed. 2003. *Arab Nationalism in the Twentieth Century: From Triumph to Despair.* Princeton, N.J.: Princeton University Press.

Dawn, C. Ernest. 1973. *From Ottomanism to Arabism: Essay on the Origins of Arab Nationalism.* Urbana: University of Illinois Press.

———. 1988. "The Formation of Pan-Arab Ideology in the Interwar Years." *International journal of Middle East Studies* 20:67–91.

Deeb, Marius. 1979. *Party Politics in Egypt: The Wafd and Its Rivals, 1919–1939.* London: Ithaca Press.

Deeb, Mary-Jane. 1997. "Islam and National Identity in Algeria." *Muslim World* 87, no. 2 (April): 111–28.

Dekmejian, Hrair R. 1985. *Islam in Revolution: Fundamentalism in the Arab World*. Syracuse, N.Y.: Syracuse University Press.

Descloitres, R., C. Descloitres, and J. C. Reverdy. 1973. "Urban Organization and Social Structure in Algeria." In *Man, State, and Society in the Contemporary Maghirb*, edited by I. William Zartman. New York: Praeger.

Dessouki, Ali E. Hillal, ed. 1982. *Islamic Resurgence in the Arab World*. New York: Praeger.

Deutsch, Karl W. 1961. "Social Mobilization and Political Development." *American Political Science Review* 55:493–514.

Devlin, John F. 1983. *Syria: Modern State in an Ancient Land*. Boulder, Colo.: Westview Press.

Dion, Leon. 1959. "Political Ideology as a Tool of Functional Analysis in Socio-political Danamics: An Hypothesis." *Canadian Journal of Economics and Political Science* 25 (February–November): 47–59.

Donati, Paolo R. 1992. "Political Discourse Analysis." Pp. 136–67 in *Studying Collective Action*, edited by Mario Diani and Ron Eyerman. London: Sage Publications.

Drysdale, Alasdair. 1982. "The Asad Regime and Its Troubles." *MERIP Reports* 12, no. 110 (November–December): 3–11.

Eagleton, Terry. 1991. *Ideology: An Introduction*. London: Verso.

Edwardes. S. M., and H. L. O. Garrett. 1962. *The Mughal Rule in India*. Delhi: S. Chand & Co.

Eliash, Joesph. "Misconceptions Regarding the Juridical Status of the Iranian 'Ulama.'" *International Journal of Middle East Studies* 10:9–25.

Enayat, Hamid. 1977. *Sayri Dar Andisheh-ye Arab* [An Overview of Arabic Thought]. Tehran: Sipihr Printing Office.

———. 1982. *Modern Islamic Political Thought*. London: Macmillan.

Entelis, John P. 1982. "Algeria: Technocratic Rule, Military Power." Pp. 92–143 in *Political Elites in Arab North Africa: Morocco, Algeria, Tunisia, Libya, and Egypt*, edited by I. William Zartman. New York: Longman.

Escovitz, Joseph H. 1986. "'He Was the Muhammad Abduh of Syria': A Study of Tahir al-Jaza'iri and His Influence." *International Journal of Middle East Studies* 18:293–310.

Esposito, John L. 1984. *Islam and Politics*. Syracuse, N.Y.: Syracuse University Press.

Esposito, John L., Yvonne Yazbeck Haddad, and John Obert Voll. 1991. *The Contemporary Islamic Revival*. New York: New York University Press.

Etienne, Bruno. 1987. *L'islamisme radical*. Paris: Hachette.

Evans, Peter, Dietrich Rueschemeyer, and Theda Skocpol, eds. 1985. *Bringing the State Back In*. New York: Cambridge University Press.

Fahmy, Khaled. 1997. *All the Pasha's Men: Mehmet Ali, His Army and the Making of Modern Egypt*. Cambridge: Cambridge University Press.

Fanon, Frantz. 1967. *A Dying Colonialism*. New York: Evergreen Press.

Farag, Nadia. 1972. "The Lewis Affair and the Fortunes of al-Muqtataf." *Middle Eastern Studies* 8, no. 1 (January): 73–83.

Farsoun, Karen. 1975. "State Capitalism in Algeria." *MERIP Reports*, no. 35 (February): 3–30.

Fazlur Rahman. 1968. *Islam*. New York: Doubleday.

Feshahi, Muhammad Reza. 1977/1356. *Vapassin Jonbesh-i Qoroun Vosta-ei dar Douran-i Fe-oudal* [The Last Middle Ages' Movement in the Feudal Period]. Tehran: Muhammad Hasan Elmi Printing Office.

Finke, Roger, and Rodney Stark. 1989. "Evaluating the Evidence: Religious Economies and Sacred Canopies." *American Sociological Review* 54:1054–56.

———. 1998. "Religious Choice and Competition: A Reply to Olson." *American Sociological Review* 63, no. 5 (October): 761–66.

Fischer, Michael M. J. 1980. *Iran: From Religious Dispute to Revolution.* Cambridge, Mass.: Harvard University Press.

Fishbach, Michael R. 1994. "British Land Policy in Transjordan." Pp. 80–107 in *Village, Steppe and State,* edited by Eugene L. Rogan and Tariq Tell. London: British Academic Press.

Floor, William M. 1975. "The Guilds in Iran: An Overview from the Earliest Beginning till 1972." *Zeitschrift der Deutschen Morgenlandischen Gesellschaft* 125:99–116.

———. 1976. "The Merchants (*tujjar*) in Qajar Iran." *Zeitschrift der Deutschen Morgenlandischen Gesellschaft* 126:101–35.

Foran, John. 1993. *Fragile Resistance: Social Transformation in Iran from 1500 to the Revolution.* Boulder, Colo.: Westview Press.

Forbes, Duncan. 1951. "James Mill and India." *Cambridge Journal* 5, no. 1 (October): 19–33.

Foucault, Michel. 1972. *The Archaeology of Knowledge.* New York: Pantheon.

———. 1979. *Discipline and Punish.* New York: Vintage Books.

Frechtling, L. E. 1938. "The Reuter Concession in Persia." *Asiatic Review* 34, no. 119 (July): 518–33.

Freij, Hanna Y., and Leonard C. Robinson. 1996. "Liberalization, the Islamists and the Stability of the Arab State: Jordan as a Case Study." *Muslim World* 86, no. 1 (January).

Fulbrook, Mary. 1983. *Piety and Politics: Religion and the Rise of Absolutism in England, Wurttemberg and Prussia.* Cambridge: Cambridge University Press.

Furet, Francois. 1981. *Interpreting the French Revolution.* New York: Cambridge University Press.

Gadant, Monique. 1984. "Pétrole et société." *Peuples Méditerranéens,* January–March, pp. 105–26.

Galtung, Johan. 1971. "A Structural Theory of Imperialism." *Journal of Peace Research* 8, no. 2:81–117.

Galvani, John. 1974. "Syria and the Baath Party." *MERIP Reports* 25 (February): 3–16.

Gamson, William A. 1992. *Talking Politics.* Cambridge: Cambridge University Press.

Garratt, Geoffrey Theodore. 1937. "Indo-British Civilization," Pp. 394–422 in *The Legacy of India,* edited by Geoffrey Theodore Garratt. Oxford: Clarendon Press.

Garzouzi, Eva. 1963. "Land Reform in Syria." *Middle East Journal* 17, nos. 1–2 (Winter–Spring): 83–90.

Geertz, Clifford. 1968. *Islam Observed: Religious Development in Morocco and Indonesia.* New Haven, Conn.: Yale University Press.

———. 1973. *The Interpretation of Culture.* New York: Basic Books.

Gerber, Haim. 1987. *The Social Origins of the Modern Middle East.* Boulder, Colo.: L. Rienner.

Gershoni, Israel, and James P. Jankowski. 1986. *Egypt, Islam, and the Arabs: The Search for Egyptian Nationhood, 1900–1930*. Oxford: Oxford University Press.

———. 1995. *Redefining the Egyptian Nation, 1930–1945*. Cambridge: Cambridge University Press.

Gharaibih, Ibrahim. 1997. *Jama'a al-Ikhwan al-Muslimeen fil Urdun: 1946–1996* [The Society of Muslim Brothers in Jordan: 1946–1996]. Amman: al-Urdun al-Jadid Research Center.

Ghazali, Shaikh Muhammad al-. 1991. *Sayhat Tahdir Min Du'at al-Tansir* [A Warning Scream against Missionaries' Call]. Cairo: Dar al-Sahwa.

Ghazali, Zainab al-. 1994. *Return of the Pharaoh: Memoir in Nasir's Prison*. Translated by Mokrane Guezzou. Leicester: Islamic Foundation.

Ghosh, Jyotish Chandra. 1937. "Vernacular Literatures." Pp. 369–93 in *The Legacy of India*, edited by Geoffrey Theodore Garratt. Oxford: Clarendon Press.

Gibb, Hamilton A. R. 1937. "Al-Mawardi's Theory of the Khilafah." *Islamic Culture* 11:291–302.

———. 1947. *Modern Trends in Islam*. Chicago: University of Chicago Press.

Gibb, Hamilton A. R., and H. Bowen. 1950. *Islamic Society and the West*. London: Oxford University Press.

Glubb, John Bagot. 1959. *Britain and the Arabs. A Study of Fifty Years, 1908–1958*. London: Hodder & Stoughton.

Godlove, Terry F., Jr. 1989. "Interpretation, Reductionism, and Belief in God." *Journal of Religion* 69, no. 2:184–98.

Gökalp, Ziya. 1959. *Turkish Nationalism and Western Civilization: Selected Essays of Ziya Gökalp*. Translated and edited by Niyazi Berkes. London: George Allen & Unwin.

Goldschmidt, Arthur, Jr. 1968. "The Egyptian Nationalist Party: 1892–1919." In *Political and Social Change in Modern Egypt*, edited by P. M. Holt. London: Oxford University Press.

Gopal, Ram. 1959. *Indian Muslims: A Political History*. London: Asia Publishing House.

Gopal, Surendra. 1972. "Nobility and the Mercantile Community in India, XVI–XVIIth Centuries." *Journal of Indian History* 50:793–802.

Graham, G. F. I. 1885. *The Life and Work of Syed Ahmed Khan*. Edinburgh: William Blackwood & Sons.

Graham, Robert. 1979. *Iran: The Illusion of Power*. New York: St. Martin's Press.

Gran, Peter. 1979. *Islamic Roots of Capitalism*. Austin: University of Texas Press.

Grant, Christian P. 1968. *The Syrian Desert*. New York: Macmillan Co.

Great Britain. Foreign Office. *Handbooks Prepared under the Direction of the Historical Section of the Foreign Office*.

Grunebaum, Gustave von. 1954. *Medieval Islam: A Study in Cultural Orientation*. Chicago: University of Chicago Press.

Guizot, F. 1890. *The History of Civilization*. Vols. 1–3. Translated by William Hazlitt. New York: D. Appleton & Co.

Gupta, Ashin Das. 1985. "Indian Merchants and the Western Indian Ocean: The Early Seventeenth Century." *Modern Asian Studies* 19:481–99.

Gurr, Tedd R. 1970. *Why Men Rebel*. Princeton, N.J.: Princeton University Press.

Haarmann, Ulrich W. 1988. "Ideology and History, Identity and Alterity: The Arab Image of the Turk from the 'Abbasids to Modern Egypt." *International Journal of Middle East Studies* 20:175–96.

Habib, Irfan. 1963. *The Agrarian System of Mughal India (1556–1707)*. New York: Asia Publishing House.

Haddad, Yvonne Y. 1982. "Islam: 'The Religion of God.'" *Christianity and Crisis* 42 (November 15): 354–58.

———. 1983. "Sayyid Qutb: Ideologue of Islamic Revival." Pp. 67–98 in *Voices of Resurgent Islam*, edited by John Esposito. Oxford: Oxford University Press.

Hagen, Everett E. 1962. *On the Theory of Social Change: How Economic Growth Begins*. Homewood, Ill.: Dorsey Press.

Haim, Sylvia G. 1954. "Alfieri and al-Kawakibi." *Oriente Moderno* 34:331–34.

———. 1955. "Blunt and al-Kawakibi." *Oriente Moderno* 35:132–43.

———, ed. 1962. *Arab Nationalism: An Anthology*. Berkeley: University of California Press.

Hairi, Hadi. 1977. *Shi'ism and Constitutionalism in Iran*. Leiden: E. J. Brill.

Hali, Altaf Husain. 1979. *Hayat-i-Javed*. Translated by K. H. Qadiri and David J. Matthews. Delhi: Idarah-i Adabiyat-i Delli. Originally published in 1901.

Hallaq, Wael B. 1984. "Was the Gate of Ijtihad Closed?" *International Journal of Middle East Studies* 16:3–41.

Halliday, Fred. 1979. *Iran: Dictatorship and Development*. Harmondsworth: Penguin Books.

———. 1996. *Islam and the Myth of Confrontation: Religion and Politics in the Middle East*. London: I. B. Tauris.

Hamdi, Kamel. 1991. *Ali Benhadj, Abassi Madani, Mahfoud Nahnah, Abdellah Djaballah: Differents ou differends?* Algiers: Chihab.

Hanafi, Hasan. 1982. "The Relevance of the Islamic Alternative in Egypt." *Arab Studies Quarterly* 4, nos. 1–2:54–74.

Hardy, Peter. 1972. *The Muslims of British India*. Cambridge: Cambridge University Press.

———. 1973. "The Ulama in British India." In "Golden Jubilee Volume," *Journal of Indian History*, pp. 821–45.

Hartmann, Martin. 1899. *The Arabic Press of Egypt*. London: Luzac & Co.

Harvey, David. 1990. *The Condition of Postmodernity*. Oxford: Blackwell.

Hasan, Farhat. 1992. "Indigenous Cooperation and the Birth of a Colonial City: Calcutta, c. 1698–1750." *Modern Asian Studies* 26, no. 1:65–82.

———. 1993. "The Mughal Fiscal System in Surat and the English East India Company." *Modern Asian Studies* 27, no. 4:711–18.

Hasan, Ibn. 1935. *The Central Structure of the Mughal Empire and Its Practical Working up to the Year 1657*. Lahore: Oxford University Press.

Hasan, Muhammad Abd al-Ghany, and Abd al-Aziz al-Dosouqi. 1975. *Roudat al-Madaris*. Cairo: al-Hayat al-Misriyya al-Aama al-Kitab.

Hasan, Saiyid Nurul. 1973. *Thoughts on Agrarian Relations in Mughal India*. New Delhi: People's Publishing House.

Hasan, Sayyid Ali. 1845. *Kitab-i Istifsar* [Book of Questions]. Lucknow.

Havell, Ernest Binfield. 1928. *Indian Sculpture and Painting*. London: J. Murray.

Hawkes, Terence. 1977. *Structuralism and Semiotics*. Berkeley: University of California Press.

Heyd, Uriel. 1950. *Foundations of Turkish Nationalism: The Life and Teachings of Ziya Gokalp*. London: Luzac & Harvill Press.

Heyworth-Dunne, J. 1968. *An Introduction to the History of Education in Modern Egypt*. London: Frank Cass & Co.

Hinnebusch, Raymond A. 1982. "The Islamic Movement in Syria: Sectarian Conflict and Urban Rebellion in an Authoritarian Populist Regime." Pp. 138–69 in *Islamic Resurgence in the Arab World,* edited by Ali E. Hillal Dessouki. New York: Praeger.

———. 1990. *Authoritarian Power and State Formation in Ba'thist Syria: Army, Party, and Peasant*. Boulder, Colo.: Westview Press.

Hoffman, Helen Easton. 1923. "Are Persians Worth While?" *Woman's Work: A Foreign Missions Magazine* 38, no. 12 (December): 270–72.

Holmström, David. 1973. "Syria: Unity, Liberty, and Socialism." *Middle East International* 22 (April): 11–13.

Holquist, Michael. 1990. *Dialogism: Bakhtin and His World*. New York: Routledge.

Holsti, Ole R. 1968. "Content Analysis." In *The Handbook of Social Psychology,* edited by Gardner Lindzey and Elliot Aronson. 2nd ed. Reading, Mass.: Addison-Wesley.

———. 1969. *Content Analysis for the Social Sciences and Humanities*. Reading, Mass.: Addison-Wesley.

Holt, Peter M., ed. 1968. *Political and Social Change in Modern Egypt*. London: Oxford University Press.

Hooglund, Eric. 1991. "Government and Politics." Pp. 182–220 in *Jordan: A Country Study,* edited by Helen Chapin Metz. Washington, D.C.: Library of Congress.

Hourani, Albert. 1969. "The Syrian in Egypt in the Eighteenth and Nineteenth Centuries." In *Colloque international sur l'histoire du Caire*. Cairo: General Egyptian Book.

———. 1983. *Arabic Thought in the Liberal Age (1798–1939)*. Cambrige: Cambridge University Press.

———. 1991. *A History of the Arab Peoples*. New York: Warner Books.

Hourani, Hani, Taleb Awad, Hamed Dabbas, and Sa'eda Kilani. 1993. *Islamic Action Front Party*. Amman: al-Urdun al-Jadid Research Center.

Hourani, Hani, Hamed Dabbas, Taleb Awad, and Omar Shniekat. 1993. *Jordanian Political Parties*. Amman: al-Urdun al-Jadid Research Center.

Hourani, Hani, and Hussein Abu-Rumman. 1996. *The Democratic Process in Jordan*. Amman: al-Urdun al-Jadid Research Center.

Humbaraci, Arslan. 1966. *Algeria: A Revolution That Failed*. London: Pall Mall Press.

Hunt, Scott A., Robert D. Benford, and David A. Snow. 1994. "Identity Fields: Framing Processes and the Socioal Construction of Movement Identities." Pp. 185–208 in *New Social Movements: From Ideology to Identity,* edited by Hank Johnston, Enrique Larana, and Joseph R. Gusfield. Philadelphia: Temple University Press.

Hunter, Robert F. 1984. *Egypt under the Khedives, 1805–1879: From Household Government to Modern Bureaucracy*. Pittsburgh: University of Pittsburgh Press.

Hunter, Shireen T. 1984. *The Politics of Islamic Revivalism*. Bloomington: Indiana University Press.

Hunter, Sir William Wilson. 1872. *The Indian Musalmans*. London: Trubner & Co.

Husayn, Abdullah Ibn-al-. 1945. *Mudharkkarati* [My Memoirs]. 1st ed. Jerusalem: Matba'ah Bayt al-Muqaddas.

Hussain, Asaf. 1983. *Islamic Movements in Egypt, Pakistan and Iran.* London: Mansell Publishing.

Hussain, Muhammad Hadi. 1970. *Syed Ahmed Khan: Pioneer of Muslim Resurgence.* Lahore: Institute of Islamic Culture.

Hussein, King of Jordan . 1962. *Uneasy Lies the Head.* London: Heinemann.

Hussein, Mahmoud. 1973. *Class Conflict in Egypt, 1945–1970.* New York: Monthly Review Press.

Hussein, Taha. 1954. *The Future of Culture in Egypt.* Translated by Sidney Glazer. New Washington: American Council of Learned Societies.

Ibn Khaldun, Abd al-Rahman. 1967. *The Muqaddhimah: An Introduction to History.* Translated by Ranz Rosenthal. Princeton, N.J.: Princeton University Press.

Ibrahimi Dina'nie, Gholamhosein. 1991/1370. *Mantiq va Marifat dar Nazar-i Ghazali* [Ghazali's View on Logic and Knowledge]. Tehran: Amir Kabir.

Ikram, S. M. 1964. *Muslim Civilization in India.* New York: Columbia University Press.

———. 1966. *Muslim Rule in Indian and Pakistan.* Lahore: Star Book Depot.

Inalcik, Halil. 1973. *The Ottoman Empire: The Classical Age, 1300–1600.* Translated by Norman Itzkowitz and Colin Imber. New York: Praeger Publishers.

International Labor Office. 1973. *Employment and Income Policies for Iran.* Geneva: ILO.

Iqbal, Muhammad. 1934. *The Reconstruction of Religious Thought in Islam.* London: Oxford University Press.

———. 1973. *Speeches and Statements of Iqbal.* Compiled by A. R. Tariq. Lahore: Sh. Ghulam Ali & Sons.

"The Islamic Action Salvation Front of Algeria." 2000. Translated by Nicky Peters. Pp. 273–313 in *Contemporary Debates in Islam: An Anthology of Modernist and Fundamentalist Thought,* edited by Mansoor Moaddel and Kamran Talattof. New York: Saint Martin's Press.

Issawi, Charles. 1947. *Egypt: An Economic and Social Analysis.* London: Oxford University Press.

———. 1954. *Egypt at Mid-century: An Economy Survey.* London: Oxford University Press.

———. 1963. *Egypt in Revolution: An Economic Analysis.* London: Oxford University Press.

———, ed. 1966. *The Economic History of the Middle East, 1800–1914.* Chicago: University of Chicago Press.

———, ed. 1971. *The Economic History of Iran, 1800–1914.* Chicago: University of Chicago Press.

Jahangir, Emperor of Hindustan. 1970. *Memoirs of the Emperor Jahangueir.* Translated by Major David Price. Delhi: Rare Books.

Jain, M. P. 1952. *Outlines of Indian Legal History.* Delhi: Dhanwantra Medical & Law.

Jain, M. S. 1965. *The Aligarh Movement: Its Origin and Development, 1858–1906.* Agra: Sri Ram Mehra & Co.

Jalbani, G. N. 1967. *Teachings of Shah Waliyullah.* Lahore: Sh. Muhammad Ashraf.

Jazani, Bijan. 1973. *The Socio-economic Analysis of a Dependent Capitalist State.* London: Iran Committee.

Johns, Anthony H. 1987. "Indonesian: Islam and Cultural Pluralism." Pp. 202–29 in *Islam in Asia: Religion, Politics and Society,* edited by John L. Esposito. New York: Oxford University Press.

Johnson, Chalmers. 1966. *Revolutionary Change.* Boston: Little Brown.

Johnston, Hank, and Bert Klandermans. 1995. *Social Movements and Culture.* Minneapolis: University of Minnesota Press.

Johnston, Hank, Enrique Larana, and Joseph R. Gusfield, eds. 1994. *New Social Movements: From Ideology to Identity.* Philadelphia: Temple University Press.

Jones, Sir William. 1970. *The Letters of Sir William Jones.* Edited by Garland Cannon. Oxford: Clarendon Press.

Jong, F. de. 1978. *Turuq and Turuq-Linked Institutions in Nineteenth Century Egypt.* Leiden: E. J. Brill.

Kader, Abdel. 1987. *Egyptian Women in a Changing Society, 1899–1987.* London: Lynne Rienner.

Kadivar, Mohsin. 1977/1376. *Nazariyyeh Doulat dar Fiqh-i Shi'eh* [Theory of the State in Shi'i Jurisprudence]. Tehran: Nay.

Kapil, Arun. 1995. "Algeria's Crisis Intensifies: The Search for a 'Civic Pact.'" *Middle East Report* 25 (January–February): 2–7, 28.

Kaplan, Lawrence. 1992. *Fundamentalism in Comparative Perspective.* Amherst: Unviersity of Massachusetts Press.

Karbala'i, Sheikh Hasan. 1982/1361. *Qarardad-i Rizhi-ye 1890* [The Regie Contract of 1890]. Tehran: Mobarizan.

Kasravi, Ahmad. 1956/1335. *Chihil Maqalah-i Kasravi* [Forty Essays by Kasravi]. Edited by Yahya Zoka-ie. Tehran: Kitab-Khaneh-i Tohuri.

———. 1969/1348. *Dar Piramun-i Islam* [On Islam]. Tehran: Paydar Bookstore.

———. 1977. *Tarikhi Mashruti-ye Iran* [The History of the Iranian Constitutional Revolution]. Tehran.

Katzenstein, Mary Fainsod. 1995. "Discursive Politics and Feminist Activism in the Catholic Church." Pp. 35–52 in *Feminist Organizations: Harvest of the New Women's Movement,* edited by Myra Marx Ferree and Patricia Yancey Martin. Philadelphia: Temple University Press.

Kazem, Ali Abdul. 1997. "The Muslim Brotherhood: The Historic Background and the Ideological Origins." In *Islamic Movements in Jordan,* edited by Julian Schwedler. Amman: al-Urdun al-Jadid Research Center.

Kazemzadeh, Firouz. 1968. *Russia and Britain in Persia, 1864–1914.* New Haven, Conn.: Yale University Press.

Keddie, Nikki R. 1968. *An Islamic Response to Imperialism: Political and Religious Writings of Sayyid Jamal ad-Din "al-Afghani"* Berkeley: University of California Press.

———. 1971. "Peasants, 1900s." Pp. 54–57 in *The Economic History of Iran, 1800–1914,* edited by Charles Issawi. Chicago: University of Chicago Press.

———. 1972. "The Roots of Ulama Power in Modern Iran." Pp. 211–29 in *Scholars, Saints, and Sufis,* edited by Nikki R. Keddie. Los Angeles: University of California Press.

———. 1981. *Roots of Revolution: An Interpretive History of Modern Iran.* New Haven, Conn.: Yale University Press.

Kedourie, Elic. 1966. *An Essay on Religious Unbelief and Political Activism in Modern Islam.* London: Fank Cass & Co.

―――. 1972. "The Politics of Political Literature: Kawakabi, Azouri and Jung." *Middle Eastern Studies* 8, no. 2 (May): 227–40.

―――. 1976. *In the Anglo-Arab Labyrinth.* Cambridge: Cambridge University Press.

―――. 1980. *Islam in the Modern World.* New York: Holt, Rinehart & Winston.

Keilany, Ziad. 1973. "Socialism and Economic Change in Syria." *Middle Eastern Studies* 9 (January): 61–72.

Kelidar, A. R. 1974. "Religion and State in Syria." *Asian Affairs* 5, no. 1:16–22.

Kepel, Gilles. 1985. *Muslim Extremism in Egypt: The Prophet and Pharaoh.* Translated by Jon Rothschild. Berkeley: University of California Press.

Kerr, Malcolm. 1966. *Islamic Reform: The Political and Legal Theories of Muhammad 'Abduh and Rashid Rida.* Berkeley: University of California Press.

Khader, Bichara, and Adnan Badran, eds. 1987. *The Economic Development of Jordan.* London: Croom Helm.

Khalidi, Rashid. 1991. "Ottomanism and Arabism in Syria before 1914: A Reassessment." In *The Origins of Arab Nationalism,* edited by Rashid Khalidi, Lisa Anderson, Muhammad Muslih, and Reeva S. Simon. New York: Columbia University Press.

Khalidi, Rashid, Lisa Anderson, Muhammad Muslih, and Reeva S. Simon, eds. 1991. *The Origins of Arab Nationalism.* New York: Columbia University Press.

Khazendar, Sami al-. 1997. *Jordan and the Palestine Question: The Role of Islamic and Left Forces in Foreign Policy Making.* Berkshire, U.K.: Ithaca Press.

Khelladi, A. 1992. *Les islamistes algeriens face au pouvoir.* Algiers: Editions ALFA.

Khomeini, Ruhollah. 1981/1360. *Hokumat-i Islami* [Islamic Government]. Tehran: Islamic Republic.

―――. 1981. *Islam and Revolution: Writings and Declarations of Imam Khomeini.* Vol. 1. Translated by H. Algar. Berkeley: Mizan Press.

Khouri, Rami G. 1997. "State and Press: Mutual Irresponsibility on the Dizzying Road to Arab Liberalism." *Jordan Times,* October 21.

Khoury, Philip S. 1983. *Urban Notables and Arab Nationalism: The Politics of Damascus, 1860–1920.* Cambridge: Cambridge University Press.

―――. 1987. *Syria and the French Mandate: The Politics of Arab Nationalism, 1920–1945.* Princeton, N.J.: Princeton University Press.

Kirmani, Nazim ul-Islam. 1945/1324. *Tarikhi Bidari-ye Iranian* [The History of the Awakening of Iranians]. Tehran: Ibn Sina Publications.

Knauss, Peter R. 1987. *The Persistence of Patriarchy: Class, Gender, and Ideology in Twentieth Century Algeria.* New York: Praeger.

Kornhauser, William. 1959. *The Politics of Mass Society.* Glencoe, Ill.: Free Press.

Kulke, Hermann, and Dietmar Rothermund. 1986. *A History of India.* London: Routledge.

Lambton, Ann K. S. 1953. *Landlord and Peasant in Persia.* London: Oxford University Press.

―――. 1963. "Justice in the Medieval Persian Theory of Kingship." *Studia Islamica* 17:91–119.

―――. 1970. "The Persian Ulama and Constitutional Reform." Pp. 245–68 in *Le shi'isme imamite,* edited by T. Fahd. Paris: Presses Universitaires de France.

Landau, Jacob M. 1954. *Parliaments and Parties in Egypt.* New York: Praeger.

Lane, Edward William. 1871. *An Account of the Manners and Customs of Modern Egyptians.* London: John Murray.

Lane-Poole, Stanley. 1888. *The Life of the Right Honourable Stratford Canning.* London: Longmans, Green & Co.

Langer, Suzanne. 1951. *Philosophy in a New Key.* Cambridge, Mass.: Harvard University Press.

Lapidus, Ira M. 1988. *A History of Islamic Societies.* Cambridge: Cambridge University Press.

Larrain, Jorge. 1983. *Marxism and Ideology.* London: Macmillan Press.

Larson, Pier M. 1997. "'Capacities and Modes of Thinking': Intellectual Engagements and Subaltern Hegemony in the Early History of Malagasy Christianity." *American Historical Review* 102, nos. 4–5 (October 1997): 969–1002.

Lawless, Richard I. 1984. "Algeria: Contradictions of Rapid Industrialization." In *North Africa: Contemporary Politics and Economic Development,* edited by Richard Lawless and Allan Findlay. London: Croom Helm.

Lawless, Richard, and Allan Findlay eds. 1984. *North Africa: Contemporary Politics and Economic Development.* London: Croom Helm.

Lawson, Fred H. 1982. "Social Bases for the Hanna Revolt." *MERIP Reports* 12 (November–December): 24–28.

———. 1982. "Social Origins of Aggressive Foreign Policy: The Case of Muhammad Ali's Egypt, 1800–1930." Ph.D. dissertation, University of California, Los Angeles.

Layne, Linda L. 1987. "Tribesmen as Citizens: 'Primordial Ties' and Democracy in Rural Jordan." In *Elections in the Middle East: Implications of Recent Trends,* edited by Linda L. Layne. Boulder, Colo.: Westview Press.

———. 1989. "The Dialogics of Tribal Self-Representation in Jordan." *American Ethnologist* 16 (February): 24–39.

———, ed. 1987. *Elections in the Middle East: Implications of Recent Trends.* Boulder, Colo.: Westview Press.

Lazreg, Marina. 1994. *The Eloquence of Silence: Algerian Women in Question.* New York: Routledge.

Lelyveld, David. 1978. *Aligarh's First Generation: Muslim Solidarity in British India.* Princeton, N.J.: Princeton University Press.

Lenin, V. I. 1977. "What Is to Be Done? Burning Questions of Our Movement." Pp. 347–529 in *Collected Works,* vol. 5. New York: International Publishers.

Levy, Marion J., Jr. 1966. *Modernization and the Structure of Society.* Princeton, N.J.: Princeton University Press.

Levy, Reuben. 1933. *An Introduction to the Sociology of Islam.* London: Williams & Norgate.

Lewis, Bernard. 1968. *The Emergence of Modern Turkey.* Oxford: Oxford University Press.

———. 1993. *Islam in History.* Chicago: Open Court.

———. 1993. *Islam and the West.* Oxford: Oxford University Press.

Lewis, William H. 1973. "The Decline of Algeria's FLN." Pp. 330–39 in *Man, State, and Society in the Contemporary Maghirb,* edited by I. William Zartman. New York: Praeger.

Lia, Brynjar. 1998. *The Society of the Muslim Brothers in Egypt: The Rise of an Islamic Mass Movement, 1928–42.* Reading, U.K.: Ithaca Press.

Long, Rev. James. 1869. *Selections from Unpublished Records of Government for the Years 1748–1767 Inclusive.* Reprint, Calcutta: Firma K. L. Mukhopadhyay, 1973.

Longrigg, Stephen Hemsley. 1972. *Syria and Lebanon under the French Mandate.* New York: Octagon Books.

Lunt, James. 1989. *Hussein of Jordan: Searching for a Just and Lasting Peace.* New York: William Morrow & Co.

Lybyer, Albert K. 1913. *The Government of the Ottoman Empire in the Time of Suleiman the Magnificent.* Cambridge, Mass.: Harvard University Press.

MacCallum, Elizabeth P. 1928. *The Nationalist Crusade in Syria.* New York: Foreign Policy Association.

Macciocchi, Maria Antonietta. 1973. "An Interview with Ben Bella." Pp. 124–26 in *Man, State, and Society in the Contemporay Maghirb,* edited by I. William Zartman. New York: Praeger.

MacColl, Malcolm. 1881. "Are Reforms Possible under Mussulman Rule?" *Contemporary Review* 40 (August): 257–81.

Mackenzie, Marcus. 1946. "Transjordan." *Journal of the Royal Central Asian Society,* vol. 33 (July–October).

MacPherson, C. B. 1972. "Politics: Post-Liberal-Democracy." In *Ideology in Social Science,* edited by Robin Blackburn. New York: Vintage.

Madfai, Madiha Rashi al-. 1993. *Jordan, the United States and the Middle East Peace Process, 1974–1991.* Cambridge: Cambridge University Press.

Majd ul-Mulk, Mirza Muhammad Khan. 1870. *Risala-ye Majdi-yya.* Reprint, Tehran: National Bank of Iran, 1942/1321.

Majeed, J. 1990. "James Mill's 'The History of British India' and Utilitarianism as a Rhetoric of Reform." *Modern Asian Studies* 24, no. 2:209–24.

Malik, Hafeez. 1980. *Sir Sayyid Ahmad Khan and Muslim Modernization in India and Pakistan.* New York: Columbia University Press.

Malikzadeh, Mihdi. 1979/1358. *Tarikh-i Inqilab-i Mashrutiyat-i Iran* [The History of the Constitutional Revolution in Iran]. Tehran: Ilmi Publications.

Mallon, Florencia E. 1994. "The Promise and Dilemma of Subaltern Studies: Perspectives from Latin American History." *American Historical Review* 99 (December): 1491–1515.

Mannheim, Karl. 1986. *Ideology and Utopia.* New York: Harvest.

Ma'oz, Moshe. 1968. *Ottoman Reform in Syria and Palestine, 1840–1861: The Impact of the Tanzimat on Politics and Society.* Oxford: Oxford University Press.

Marcus, Abraham. 1989. *The Middle East on the Even of Modernity: Aleppo in the Eighteenth Century.* New York: Columbia University Press.

Mardam Bey, Salma. 1994. *Syria's Quest for Independence: 1939–1945.* Reading, U.K.: Ithaca Press.

Marsot, Afaf Lutfi. 1968. "The Role of the Ulama in Egypt during the Early 19th Century." Pp. 264–80 in *Political and Social Change in Modern Egypt,* edited by P. M. Holt. London: Oxford University Press.

———. 1968. *Egypt and Cromer: A Study in Anglo-Egyptian Relations.* New York: Praeger.

———. 1972. "The Ulama of Cairo in the Eighteenth and Nineteenth Centuries." Pp. 149–66 in *Scholars, Saints, and Sufis,* edited by Nikki R. Keddie. Los Angeles: University of California Press.

———. 1977. *Egypt's Liberal Experiment: 1922–1936.* Los Angeles: University of California Press.

———. 1984. *Egypt in the Reign of Muhammad Ali.* Cambridge: Cambridge University Press.

Martin, Vanessa A. 1986. "The Anti-constitutionalist Arguments of Shaikh Fazlallah Nuri." *Middle Eastern Studies* 22 (April): 181–96.

Martines, Luis. 1998. *La guerre civile in Algerie, 1990–1998.* Paris: Karthala.

Marty, Martin E., and R. Scott Appleby. 1991. *Fundamentalisms Observed.* Chicago: University of Chicago Press.

Marwell, Gerald, and Pamela Oliver. 1984. "Collective Action Theory and Social Movement Research." Pp. 1–28 in *Research in Social Movements, Conflicts and Change,* edited by Louis Kriesberg. Greenwich, Conn.: JAI.

Marx, Karl. 1977. "Civil War in France." In *Selected Works,* by Karl Marx and Frederick Engels. New York: International Publishers.

Marx, Karl, and Frederick Engels. 1975. "The Holy Family." Pp. 1–211 in *Collected Works,* vol. 4. New York: International Publishers.

———. 1976. *Collected Works.* New York: International Publishers.

———. 1976. "The German Ideology." In *Collected Works,* vol. 5. New York: International Publishers.

———. 1977. *Selected Works.* New York: International Publishers.

Matthew, H. C. G. 1990. *The Gladstone Diaries.* Vol. 10. Oxford: Clarendon Press.

———. 1976. "The German Ideology." Pp. 19–116 in *Collected Works,* vol. 5. New York: International Publishers.

Maududi, Abul Ala. 1960. *The Islamic Law and Constitution.* Lahore: Islamic Publications.

McAdam, Doug. 1994. "Culture and Social Movements." Pp. 36–57 in *New Social Movements: from Ideology to Identity,* edited by Hank Johnston, Enrique Larana, and Joseph R. Gusfield. Philadelphia: Temple University Press.

McClelland, David C. 1961. *The Achieving Society.* Princeton, N.J.: D. Van Nostrand.

McLuhan, Marshall. 1962. *The Gutenberg Galaxy: The Making of Typographic Man.* London: Routledge & Kegan Paul.

McNeill, William H., and Marilyn Robinson Waldman. 1973. *The Islamic World.* Chicago: University of Chicago Press.

McVey, Ruth. 1983. "Faith as the Outsider: Islam in Indonesian Politics." Pp. 199–225 in *Islam in the Political Process,* edited by James Piscatori. Cambridge: Cambridge University Press.

Mehraban, Rasoul. 1982/1361. *Gousheha-ie az Tarikh-i Moaser-i Iran* [Aspects of the Contemporary History of Iran]. Tehran: Otared Publications.

Melasuo, Tuomo. 1992. "How to Understand Islamism in Algeria." *Nordic Research on the Middle East* 2:56–70.

Merquior, J. G. *Foucault.* 1985. Los Angeles: University of California Press.

Metcalf, Barbara Daly. 1982. *Islamic Revival in British India: Deoband, 1860–1900.* Princeton, N.J.: Princeton University Press.

———. 1995. "Presidential Address: Too Little and Too Much: Reflections on Muslims in the History of India." *Journal of Asian Studies* 54, no. 4 (November): 951–67.

Metcalf, Thomas R. 1994. *Ideologies of the Raj.* New Cambridge History of India, vol. 3, bk. 4. Cambridge: Cambridge University Press.

Metz, Heleh C. 1989. *Jordan: A Country Study.* Washington, D.C.: Library of Congress.

Migdal, Joel S., ed. 1980. *Palestinian Society and Politics.* Princeton, N.J.: Princeton University Press.

Mill, James. 1848. *The History of British India.* Vol. 1. London: James Madden.

Millar, John. 1781. *The Origin of the Distinction of Ranks; or, An Inquiry into the Circumstances Which Give Rise to Influence and Authority in the Different Members of Society.* 3d ed. London: J. Murray.

Milner, Alfred. 1892. *England in Egypt.* London: Macmillan.

Milton-Edwards, B. 1991. "A Temporary Alliance with the Crown: The Islamic Response in Jordan." In *Islamic Fundamentalism and the Gulf Crisis,* edited by James P. Piscatori. Chicago: Fundamentalism Project, American Academy of Arts and Sciences.

Minault, Gail. 1990. "Sayyid Mumtaz Ali and 'Huquq un-Niswan': An Advocate of Women's Rights in Islam in the Late Nineteenth Century." *Modern Asian Studies* 24, no. 1:147–72.

Mishal, Shaul. 1980. "Conflictual Pressures and Cooperative Interests: Observations on West Bank–Amman Political Relations, 1940–1967." In *Palestinian Society and Politics,* edited by Joel S. Migdal. Princeton, N.J.: Princeton University Press.

Mitchell, Richard P. 1969. *The Society of the Muslim Brothers.* London: Oxford University Press.

Mitchell, Timothy. 1988. *Colonising Egypt.* Cambridge: Cambridge University Press.

Moaddel, Mansoor. 1986. "The Shi'i Ulama and the State in Iran." *Theory and Society* 15:519–56.

———. 1989. "State Autonomy and Class Conflict in the Reformation (Comments on Wuthnow, *ASR,* December 1985)." *American Sociological Review* 54:472–74.

———. 1992. "Ideology as Episodic Discourse: The Case of the Iranian Revolution." *American Sociological Review* 57 (June): 353–79.

———. 1992. "Shi'i Political Discourse and Class Mobilization in the Tobacco Movement of 1890–92." *Sociological Forum* 7 (September): 447–68.

———. 1993. *Class, Politics, and Ideology in the Iranian Revolution.* New York: Columbia University Press.

———. 1993. "The Egyptian and Iranian Ulama at the Threshold of Modern Social Change: What Does and What Does Not Account for the Difference." *Arab Studies Quarterly* 15, no. 3:21–46.

———. 2002. *Jordanian Exceptionalism: An Analysis of State and Religion Relationships in Egypt, Iran, Jordan, and Syria.* New York: Palgrave.

———. 2002. "The Study of Islamic Culture and Politics: An Overview and Assessment." *Annual Review of Sociology* 28:359–86.

Moaddel, Mansoor, and Kamran Talattof, eds. 2000. *Contemporary Debates in Islam: An Anthology of Modernist and Fundamentalist Thought.* New York: Saint Martin's Press.

Moghadam, Valentine M. 1993. *Modernizing Women: Gender and Social Change in the Middle East*. London: Lynne Rienner.

Momen, Moojan. 1985. *An Introduction to Shi'i Islam*. New Haven, Conn.: Yale University Press.

Moosvi, Shireen. 1987. *The Economy of the Mughal Empire*. Delhi: Oxford University Press.

Morier, James. 1824. *The Adventures of Hajji Baba of Ispahan*. Reprint, London: J. M. Dent & Sons, 1914.

Morray, J. P. 1980. *Socialism in Islam*. Monmouth, N.J.: Insitute for Theoretical History.

Mosharrafa, M. M. 1948. *Cultural Survey of Modern Egypt*. New York: Longmans, Green & Co.

Mostowfi, Abdullah. 1942. *Tarikh-i Edjtemai va Edari-ye Doureh-ye Qajarieh* [The Social and Administrative History of the Qajar Period]. Vol. 1. Tehran: Zovvar Bookstore.

Motahhari, Mortaza. 1969/1347. *Mas'aleh-ye Hijab* [The Problem of Veiling)]. Tehran: Islamic Society of Physicians.

Moubayed, Sami M. 2000. *Damascus between Democracy and Dictatorship*. New York: University Press of America.

Moussalli, Ahmad S. 1992. *Radical Islamic Fundamentalism: The Ideological and Political Discourse of Sayyid Qutb*. Beirut: American University of Beirut.

Muir, Sir William. 1923. *The Life of Mohammad*. Revised by T. H. Weir. Edinburgh: Johan Grant.

Munson, Henry, Jr. 1988. *Islam and Revolution in the Middle East*. New Haven, Conn.: Yale University Press.

Musallam, Adnan Ayyub. 1983. "The Formative Stages of Sayyid Qutb's Intellectual Career and His Emergence as an Islamic Da'iyah, 1906–1952." Ph.D. dissertation, University of Michigan.

Mustafa, Abdel-Rahim. 1968. "The Breakdown of the Monopoly System in Egypt after the 1840s." Pp. 291–307 in *Political and Social Change in Modern Egypt,* edited by Peter M. Holt. London: Oxford University Press.

Nadwi, Abul Hasan Ali. 1969. *Western Civilization, Islam and Muslims*. Lucknow: Academy of Islamic Research and Publication.

Na'ini, Mirza Muhammad Hussein. 1909. *Tanbih al-Umma wa Tanzih al-Millah* [The Admonition of the Umma and the Enlightenment of the Nation]. Baghdad.

Nasr, Seyyed Hossein. 1964. *An Introduction to Islamic Cosmological Doctrines*. Cambridge: Harvard University Press, Belknap Press.

Natiq, Homa. 1983/1362. "Sar-Aghaz-i Eqtidar-i Eqtisadi va Siaci-ye Mollayan" [The rise of the political and economic dominance of the clergy]. *Alefba* 2 (Spring): 40–57.

Neuhouser, Kevin. 1989. "The Radicalization of the Brazilian Catholic Church in Comparative Perspective." *American Sociological Review* 54 (April): 233–44.

Nickel, Gordon. 1987. "'The Grand Opening': Shah Wali Allah's Principles of Exegesis." M.A. thesis, School of Oriental and African Studies, University of London.

Noer, D. 1973. *The Modernist Muslim Movement in Indonesia: 1900–1942*. Oxford: Oxford University Press.

Nooruzzaman, A. H. M. 1964. "Rise of the Muslim Middle Class as a Political Factor in India and Pakistan, 1858–1947." Ph.D. dissertation, University of London.

Nuri, Shaikh Abd al-Nabi. 1908. *Tazkirah al-Ghafil wa Irshad al-Jahil* [A Reminder for the Negligent and a Guidance for the Ignorant]. Tehran.

Nyrop, Richard F. 1972. *Syria: A Country Study.* Washington, D.C.: American University.

Obaidi, Awni. 1991. *The Muslim Brotherhood in Jordan and Palestine, 1945–1970.* Amman: al-Urdan al-Jadid Research Center.

Oberschall, Anthony. R. 1973. *Social Conflicts and Social Movements.* Englewood Cliffs, N.J.: Prentice-Hall.

Olson, Daniel V. A. 1998. "Religious Pluralism in Contempory U.S. Counties: Comment on Finke and Stark." *American Sociological Review* 63 (October): 759–61.

Olson, Robert W. 1982. *The Ba'th and Syria, 1947–1982: The Evolotion of Ideology, Party, and State.* Princeton, N.J.: Princeton University Press.

Ottaway, David, and Marina Ottaway. 1970. *Algeria: The Politics of A Socialist Revolution.* Berkeley: University of California Press.

Pahlavi, Mohammad Reza. 1961. *Mission for My Country,* New York: McGraw-Hill.

———. 1967. *The White Revolution.* 2nd ed. Tehran: Imperial Pahlavi Library.

———. 1974. *Bi Souy-yeh Tamaddon-i Bozorg* [Toward the Great Civilization]. Tehran: Iranian Government.

———. 1980. *Answer to History.* Translated by Michael Joseph. New York: Stein & Day.

Parsa, Misagh. 1989. *Social Origins of the Iranian Revolution.* New Brunswick, N.J.: Rutgers University Press.

Parsons, Talcott. 1949. *The Structure of Social Action: A Study in Social Theory with Special Reference to a Group of Recent European Writers.* Glencoe, Ill.: Free Press.

———. 1951. *The Social System.* Toronto: Collier-Macmillan.

———. 1964. "Evolutionary Universal." *American Sociological Review* 29:339–57.

———. 1966. *Societies: Evolutionary and Comparative Perspective.* Englewood Cliffs, N.J.: Prentice-Hall.

———. 1969. *Politics and Social Structure.* New York: Free Press.

———. 1971. *The System of Modern Societies.* Englewood Cliffs, N.J.: Prentice-Hall.

Patai, Raphael. 1958. *The Kingdom of Jordan.* Princeton, N.J.: Princeton University Press.

Peacock, James L. 1978. *Purifying the Faith: The Muhammadiyah Movement in Indonesian Islam.* Menlo Park, Calif.: Benjamin/Cummings.

Pelsaert, Francisco. 1925. *Jahangir's India: "Remonstrantie" of Francisco Pelsaert.* Translated by William Harrison Moreland and Pieter Geyl. Cambridge: W. Heffer & Sons.

Petran, Tabitha. 1972. *Syria.* New York: Praeger.

Petrushevsky, Ilya Pavlovich. 1985. *Islam in Iran.* Albany, N.Y.: SUNY Press.

Pfander, Rev. C. G.. 1862. *Mizan-ul-Haqq: Treatise on the Controversy between Christains and Muhammedans* [in Persian]. London: W. M. Watts.

Pfeifer, Karen. 1985. *Agrarian Reform under State Capitalism in Algeria.* Boulder, Colo.: Westview Press.

Phillips, D. Z. 1976. *Religion without Explanation.* Oxford: Basil Blackwell.

Piscatori, James P., ed. 1983. *Islam in the Political Process.* Cambridge: Cambridge University Press.

Piro, Timothy J. 1998. *The Political Economy of Market Reform in Jordan.* New York: Rowman & Littlefield.

Powell, A. A. 1976. "Maulana Rahmat Allah Kairanawi and Muslim-Christian Controversy in India in the Mid-19th Century." *Journal of the Royal Asiatic Society* 1:41–63.

Prakash, Gyan. 1994. "Sualtern Studies as Postcolonial Criticism." *American Historical Review* 99 (December): 1475–90.

Przeworski, Adam. 1977. "Proletariat into a Class: The Process of Class Formation from Karl Kautsky's 'The Class Struggle' to Recent Controversies." *Politics and Society* 7:373–401.

———. 1980. "Material Bases of Consent: Economic and Politics in a Hegemonic System." Pp. 21–66 in *Political Power and Social Theory,* edited by M. Zeitlin. Greenwich, Conn.: JAI Press.

Quandt, William B. 1969. *Revolution and Political Leadership: Algeria, 1954–1968.* Cambridge, Mass.: MIT Press.

Qudddus, Syed Abdul. 1991. *The Islamic Revolution.* Lahore: Wajidalis.

Quibria, M. G. 1986. "Migrant Workers and Remittances: Issues for Asian Developing Countries." *Asian Development Review* 4, no. 1: 78–99.

Quraishi, Zaheer Masood. 1967. *Liberal Nationalism in Egypt: Rise and Fall of the Wafd Party.* Allahabad: Kitab Mahal.

Qureshi, Saleem M. 1960. *Jinnah and the Making of a Nation.* Karachi.

Qutb, Sayyid. 1964. *Ma'alim fi al-Tariq.* Cairo: Maktabat Wahbah.

———. 1993. *Milestones.* Indianapolis: American Trust Publications.

Raavandy, Mortiza. 1990/1369. *Sair-i Farhang va Tarikh-i Ta'lim va Tarbiyat dar Iran va Orupa* [Cultural Change and the History of Education in Iran and Europe]. Rasht: Hidayat Publications.

Rabinovich, Itamar. 1972. *Syria under the Ba'th, 1963–66.* Jerusalem, Israel University Press.

Rahman, Fazlur. 1968. *Islam.* New York: Doubleday.

Rath, Kathrine. 1994. "The Process of Democratization in Jordan." *Middle Eastern Studies* 30 (Jluly): 530–57.

Rathmell, Andrew. 1995. *Secret War in the Middle East: The Covert Struggle for Syria, 1949–1961.* London: I. B. Tauris.

Rawlinson, H. G. 1952. *India: A Short Cultural History.* New York: F. A. Praeger.

Rawlinson, Sir Henry, ed. 1875 "Concession of the Persian Government to Baron Reuter (Abstract)." App. 5, pp. 391–94, in *England and Russsia in the East.* London: J. Murray.

Reed, Stanley. 1991. "Jordan and the Gulf Crisis." *Foreign Affairs* 70 (Winter): 21–35.

Reid, Donald Malcolm. 1975. *The Odyssey of Farah Antun: A Syrian Christian's Quest for Secularism.* Chicago: Bibliotheca Islamica.

———. 1990. *Cairo University and the Making of Modern Egypt.* Cambridge: Cambridge University Press.

———. 1996. "Cromer and the Classics: Imperialism, Nationalism and the Greco-Roman Past in Modern Egypt." *Middle Eastern Studies* 32, no. 1 (January): 1–29.

———. 1998. "The 'Urabi Revolution and the British Conquest, 1879–1882." Pp. 217–38 in *The Cambridge History of Egypt,* edited by M. W. Daly. Cambridge: Cambridge University Press.

Richard, Gaston. 1975. "Dogmatic Atheism in the Sociology of Religion." Translated by Jacqueline Redding and W. S. F. Pickering,. In *Durkheim on Religion: A Selection of*

Readings with Bibliographies and Introductory Remarks, edited by W. S. F. Pickering. London: Routledge & Kegan Paul.

Richard, Yann. 1981. "Contemporary Shi'i Thought." In *Roots of Revolution: An Interpretive History of Modern Iran,* by Nikki Keddie. New Haven, Conn.: Yale University Press.

Richards, John F. 1990. "The Seventeenth-Century Crisis in South Asia." *Modern Asian Studies* 24, no. 4:625–38.

Richter, Julius. 1908. *A History of Missions in India.* Translated by Sydney H. Moore. London: Oliphant Anderson & Ferrier.

———. 1910. *A History of Protestant Missions in the Near East.* New York: Fleming H. Revell Co.

Rizvani, Muhammad Esmail, and Fatimeh Qaziha. 1992/1371. *Khatirat-i Nasir ud-Din Shah Dar Safar-i Sivvum-i Farangistan* [The Memoirs of Nasir ud-Din Shah in His Third Trip to Enrope]. Tehran: Saziman-i Asnad-i Melli-ye Iran Publications.

Rizvi, Saiyid Athar Abbas. 1975. "The Muslim Ruling Dynasties." Pp. 245–93 in *A Cultural History of India,* edited by Arthur Llewellyn Basham. Oxford: Clarendon Press.

———. 1975. "Islam in Medieval India." Pp. 281–65 in *A Cultural History of India,* edited by Arthur Llewellyn Basham. Oxford: Clarendon Press.

———. 1982. *Shah 'Abd al-Aziz.* Camberra: Ma'rifat Publishing House.

Roberts, David. 1987. *The Ba'th and the Creation of Modern Syria.* London: Croom Helm.

Roberts, Hugh. 1984. "The Politics of Algerian Socialism." In *North Africa: Contemporary Politics and Economic Development,* edited by Richard Lawless and Allan Findlay. London: Croom Helm.

———. 1988. "Radical Islamism and the Dilemma of Algerian Nationalism: The Embattled Arians of Algiers.'" *Third World Quarterly* 10, no. 2 (April): 556–89.

Robertson, Roland, ed. 1969. *Sociology of Religion.* Baltimore: Penguin.

Robinson, Francis. 1993. "Islam and the Impact of Print." *Modern Asia Studies* 27 (February): 229–51.

Rodinson, Maxime. 1974. *Islam and Capitalism.* London: Penguin Books.

———. 1985. *Marxism and the Muslim World.* New York: Monthly Review Press.

Roff, Willaim R., ed. 1987. *Islam and the Political Economy of Meanings.* Berkeley: University of California Press.

Rogan, Eugene L. 1994. "Bring the State Back: The Limits of Ottoman Rule in Jordan, 1840–1910." In *Village, Steppe and State: The Social Origins of Modern Jordan,* edited by Eugene L. Rogan and Tariq Tell. London: British Academic Press.

Rogan, Eugene L., and Tariq Tell, eds. 1994. *Village, Steppe and State: The Social Origins of Modern Jordan.* London: British Academic Press.

Rose, G. 1983. "Velayat-i Faqih and the Recovery of Islamic Identity in the Thought of Ayatollah Khomeini." In *Religion and Politics in Iran,* edited by Nikki R. Keddie. New Haven, Conn.: Yale University Press.

Rosenthal, Erwin I. J. 1958. *Political Thought in Medieval Islam: An Introductory Outline.* Cambridge: Camridge University Press.

Rouadjia, Ahmed. 1990. *Les frères et la mosquée: Enquête sur le mouvement islamiste en Algérie* [The Brothers and the Mosques: A Study of the Islamic Movement in Algeria]. Paris: Karthala.

Rousseau, Richard W., ed. 1985. *Christianity and Islam: The Struggling Dialogue*. Scranton, Pa.:Ridge Row Press.

Roy, Olivier. 1994. *The Failure of Political Islam*. Cambridge, Mass.: Harvard University Press.

Ruedy, John. 1992. *Modern Algeria: The Origins and Development of a Nation*. Bloomington: Indiana University Press.

Russell, William Howard. 1860. *My Indian Mutiny Diary*. Reprint, London: Cassell & Co., 1957.

Sadri, Ahmad. 1992. *Max Weber's Sociology of Intellectuals*. Oxford: Oxford University Press.

Saeed, Javaid. 1994. *Islam and Modernization: A Comparative Analysis of Pakistan, Egypt, and Turkey*. London: Praeger.

Safran, Nadav. 1961. *Egypt in Search of Political Community*. Cambridge, Mass.: Harvard University Press.

Sahlins, Marshall D., and Elman R. Service. 1960. *Evolution and Culture*. Ann Arbor: University of Michigan Press.

Said, Edward W. 1991. *Orientalism*. London: Penguin Books.

Salibi, Kamal S. 1968. "The 1860 Upheaval in Damascus as Seen by al-Sayyid Muhammad Abu'l-Su'ud al-Hasibi, Notable and Later *Naqib al-Ashraf* of the City." In *Beginnings of Modernization in the Middle East: The Nineteenth Century*, edited by William R. Polk and Richard L. Chambers. Chicago: University of Chicago Press.

———. 1993. *The Modern History of Jordan*. New York: I. B. Tauris & Co.

Saran, Parmatma. 1941. *The Provincial Government of the Mughals*. Allahabad: Kitabistan.

Satloff, Robert. B. 1986. *Troubles on the East Bank: Challenges to the Domestic Stability of Jordan*. New York: Praeger.

———. 1994. *From Abdullah to Hussein: Jordan in Transition*. Oxford: Oxford University Press.

Saussure, Ferdinand de. 1983. *Course on General Linguistics*. London: Duckworth.

Savory, Roger M. 1979. "The Problem of Sovereignty in an *Ithna Ashari* ('Twelver') Shi'i State." *Middle East Review* 11 (Summer): 5–11.

Sayeed, Khalid Bin. 1963. "Religion and Nation Building in Pakistan." *Middle East Journal* 17, no. 3 (Summer): 279–91.

Sayyid Ahmad Khan. 1873. *The Causes of the Indian Revolt*. Translated by G. Graham and A. Colvin. Lahore: Book House.

———. 1888. *Speeches and Addresses Relating to Muhammedan Anglo-Oriental College*. Aligarh.

———. 1972. "Selected Essays by Sir Sayyid Ahmad Khan from the Journal Tahzib al-Akhlaq." Translated by John Wilder. M.A. thesis, Hartford Seminary Foundation.

Schmitter, Phillippe C. 1974. "Still Century of Corporatism?" *Review of Politics* 36:85–131.

Schölch, Alexander. 1981. *Egypt for the Egyptians: The Socio-political Crisis in Egypt, 1878–1882*. London: Ithaca Press.

Schudson, Michael. 1989. "How Culture Works: Perspectives from Media Studies on the Efficacy of Symbols." *Theory and Society* 18:153–80.

Schwartz, David C. 1971. "A Theory Revolutionary Behavior." Pp. 109–32 in *When Men Revolt and Why*, edited by James C. Davies. New York Free Press.

Scott, Sir Walter. 1914. "An Appreciation." In *The Adventures of Hajji Baba, of Ispahan,* by James Morier. London: J. M. Dent & Sons.

Seale, Patrick. 1965. *The Struggle for Syria: A Study of Post-war Arab Politics.* London: Oxford University Press.

Service, Elman R. 1971. *Cultural Evolutionism: Theory in Practice.* New York: Holt, Rinehart & Winston.

Seton, Rosemary. 1986. *The Indian "Mutiny," 1857–58: A Guide to Source Material in the India Office Library and Records.* London: British Library.

Sewell, William H., Jr. 1992. "A Theory of Structure: Duality, Agency, and Transformation." *American Journal of Sociology* 1 (July): 1–29.

———. 1996. "Historical Events as Transformations of Structures: Inventing Revolution at the Bastille." *Theory and Society* 25:841–81.

Sharabi, Hisham. 1963. "Power and Leadership in the Arab World." *Orbis* 7, no. 3 (Fall): 583–95.

———. 1970. *Arab Intellectuals and the West: The Formative Years, 1875–1914.* Baltimore: Johns Hopkins University Press.

Shari'ati, Ali. 1969/1347. *Islamshenasi* [Islamology]. Mashhad: Tous.

———. 1980. *Marxism and Other Western Fallacies: An Islamic Critique,* translated by R. Campbell. Berekeley: Mizan Press.

———. 1986. *What Is to Be Done: The Enlightened Thinkers and an Islamic Renaissance.* Translated by A. Alidust and F. Rajaee. Houston: Institute for Research on Islamic Studies.

Sharma, Sri Ram. 1962. *The Religious Policy of the Mughal Emperors.* New York: Asia Publishing House.

Sheikholislami, Reza. 1971. "The Sale of Offices in Qajar Iran, 1858–1896." *Iranian Studies* 4 (Spring–Summer): 104–18.

Shepard, William. 1982. *The Faith of a Modern Muslim Intellectual: The Religious Aspects and Implications of the Writings of Ahmad Amin.* New Delhi: Indian Institute of Islamic Studies.

———. 1996. *Sayyid Qutb and Islamic Activism: A Translation and Critical Analysis of Social Justice in Islam.* New York: E. J. Brill.

Shibli Numani, Muhammad. 1962. *Omar the Great.* Translated by Muhammad Saleem. Lahore: Sh. Muhammad Ashraf. Originally published in Urdu in 1898.

———. 1970/1330. *Sirat al-Nabi.* Translated by Fazulur Rahman. Karachi: Pakistan Historical Society.

———. 1981. *Alamgir.* Translated by Syed Sabahuddin Abdur Rahman. Delhi: Idarah-i Adabiyat-i Delli. Originally published in Urdu in 1911.

Shwardan, Benjamin. 1959. *Jordan: A State of Tension.* New York: Council for Middle East Affairs.

Siba'i, Mustafa. 1959. *Le socialisme en Islam.* Damascus.

———. 1960. *Ishtirakiat al-Islam* [Socialism of Islam]. 2d ed. Damascus.

Sivan, Emmanuel. 1985. *Radical Islam: Medieval Theology and Modern Politics.* New Haven, Conn.: Yale University Press.

Slyomovics, Susan. 1995. "'Hassiba Ben Bouali, If You Could See Our Algeria': Women and Public Space in Algeria." *Middle East Report* 25, no. 192 (January–February): 8–13.

Smelser, Neil J. 1963. "Mechanisms of Change and Adjustment to Change." Pp. 32–54 in *Industrialization and Society*, edited by B. F. Hoselitz and W. E. Moore. The Hague: Mouton.

———. 1963. *Theory of Collective Behavior*. New York: Free Press of Glencoe.

Smith, Donald E. 1974. *Religion and Political Modernization*. New Haven, Conn.: Yale University Press.

Smith, Wilfred Cantwell. 1963. *Modern Islam in India*. Lahore: M. Ashraf.

Snow, David A., and Robert D. Benford. 1988. "Ideology, Frame Resonance, and Participant Mobilization." In *From Structure to Action*, edited by Bert Klandermans, Hanspter Kriesi, and Sidney Tarrow, vol. 1 of *International Social Movement Research*. Greenwich, Conn.:JAI Press.

Soroush, Abdul Karim, and Mohsin Kadivar. 1999/1378. *Monaziri darbar-ye Pluralism-i Dini* [A Debate on Religion Pluralism]. Tehran: Salam Newspaper.

Sprenger, Aloys A. 1851. *The Life of Muhammad*. Allahabad.

Steiner Goerge. 1967. *Language and Silence*. London: Faber & Faber.

Stepan, Alfred. 1985. "State Power and the Strength of Civil Society in the Southern Cone of Latin America." Pp. 317–43 in *Bringing the State Back In*, edited by Peter Evans, Dietrich Rueschemeyer, and Theda Skocpol. New York: Cambridge University Press.

Stokes, Erik. 1986. *The Peasant Armed: The Indian Rebellion of 1857*. Edited by C. A. Bayly. Oxford: Clarendon Press.

Susser, Asher. 1994. *On Both Banks of the Jordan: A Political Biography of Wasfi all Tall*. Portland, Oreg.: Frank Cass.

Swanson, Guy E. 1967. *Religion and Regime: A Sociological Account of the Reformation*. Ann Arbor: University of Michigan Press.

Swidler, Ann. 1986. "Culture in Action: Symbols and Strategies." *Ameican Sociological Review* 51 (April): 273–286.

Syed, Anwar Hussain. 1982. *Pakistan, Islam, Politics and National Solidarity*. New York.

Syrian Arab Republic. 1973. *Permanent Constitution of the Syrian Arab Republic*. Damascus: Office Arabe de Presse et de Documentation.

Tabari, Ehsan. 1975/1354. *Foroupashi-ye Nizam-i Sunnati va Zayeshi Sarmayedari Dar Iran* [The Decline of Traditional Order and the Eemergence of Capitalism in Iran]. Stockholm: Tudeh Publishing Centre.

Taba-Taba'ie, Muhammad Mohit. 1980. *Majmu'ah-i Asar-i Mirza Malkum Khan* [The Collected Works of Mirza Malkum Khan]. Tehran: Ilmi Publications.

Tahtawi, Rifa'a Rafi.' 1905. *Takhlis al-Ibriz ila Talkhis Bariz*. Cairo: al-Amir-ih.

Tal, Lawrence. 1993. "The Israeli-PLO Accord: Is Jordan Doomed?" *Foreign Affairs* 72:45–58.

Talbot, Cynthia. 1995. "Inscribing the Other, Inscribing the Self: Hindu-Muslim Identities in Pre-colonial India." *Comparative Studies in Society and History* 37:692–722.

Taraki, Lisa. 1996. "Jordanian Islamists and the Agenda for Women: Between Discourse and Practice." *Middle Eastern Studies* 32, no. 1 (January): 140–58.

Tauber, Eliezer. 1993. *The Emergence of the Arab Movements*. London: Frank Cass.

Tessler, Mark. 1993. "Alienation of Urban Youth." In *Polity and Society in Contemporary North Africa*, edited by I. William Zartman and William Mark Habeeb. Boulder, Colo.: Westview Press.

Therborn, Goran. 1980. *The Ideology of Power and the Power of Ideology.* London: Verso.

Tibawi, Abdul Latif. 1969. *A Modern History of Syria.* New York: Saint Martin's Press.

Tilly, Charles. 1978. *From Mobilization to Revolution.* Reading, Mass.: Addison-Wesley.

————. 1984. *Big Structures, Large Processes, Huge Comparisons.* New York: Russell Sage Foundation.

Titus, Murray T. 1990. *Islam in India and Pakistan.* Karachi: Royal Book.

Toch, Hans. 1965. *The Social Psychology of Social Movements.* New Yorks: Bobbs-Merrill Co.

Torrey, Charles. 1892. "The Commercial-Theological Terms in the Koran." Ph.D. dissertation, University of Strassburg; Leiden: E. J. Brill.

Torrey, Gordon H. 1964. *Syrian Politics and the Military: 1945–1958.* Columbus: Ohio State University Press.

Troll, Christian W. 1978. *Sayyid Ahmad Khan: A Renterpretation of Muslim Theology.* New Delhi: Vikas Publishing House.

Turner, Bryan S. 1974. *Weber and Islam.* Boston: Routledge & Kegan Paul.

Turner, Victor W. 1967. *The Forest of Symbols: Aspects of Ndembu Ritual.* Ithaca, N.Y.: Cornell University Press.

Vallin, Raymond. 1973. "Muslim Socialism in Algeria." Pp. 50–64 in *Man, State, and Society in the Contemporary Maghirb,* edited by I. William Zartman. New York: Praeger.

van Dam, Nikolaos. 1979. *The Struggle for Power in Syria: Sectarianism, Regionalism and Tribalism in Politics, 1961–1978.* New York: Saint Martin's Press.

Vatikiotis, Panayiotis J. 1973. "Tradition and Political Leadership: The Example of Algeria." In *Man, State, and Society in the Contemporary Maghirb,* edited by I. William Zartman. New York: Praeger.

————. 1980. *The History of Egypt.* 2nd ed. Baltimore: Johns Hopkins University Press.

Vatin, Jean-Claude. 1982. "Revival in the Maghreb: Islam as an Alternative Political Language." Pp. 221–50 in *Islamic Resurgence in the Arab World,* edited by Ali E. Hillal Dessouki. New York: Praeger.

————. 1983. "Popular Puritanism versus State Reformism: Islam in Algeria." In *Islam in the Political Process,* edited by James P. Piscatori. Cambridge: Cambridge University Press.

Wallace, Mackenzie D. 1883. *Egypt and the Egyptian Question.* London: Macmillan & Co.

Wallerstein, Immanuel. 1984. *The Politics of the World-Economy: The States, the Movements, and the Civilizations.* Cambridge: Cambridge University Press.

————. 1990. "Cultural Change and Historical Capitalism." *Contemporary Sociology* 19:337–39.

Wallwork, Ernest. 1984. "Religion and Social Structure in 'The Division of Labor.'" *American Anthropologist* 86, no. 2:43–64.

Walz, Terence. 1978. "Asyut in the 1260's (1844–53)." *Journal of the American Research Center in Egypt,* vol. 15.

————. *Trade between Egypt and Bilad al-Sudan: 1700–1820.* Cairo: Institut Français d'Archeologie Orientale du Caire.

Walzer, Richard. 1985. *Al-Farabi on the Perfect State.* Oxford: Clarendon Press.

Warriner, Doreen. 1948. *Land and Poverty in the Middle East.* London: Royal Institute of International Affairs.

Waterbury, John. 1983. *The Egypt of Nasser and Sadat.* Princeton, N.J.: Princeton University Press.

Watson, Andrew. 1898. *The American Mission in Egypt: 1854–1896*. Pittsburgh: United Presbyterian Board of Publication.

Watson, Charles R. 1907. *Egypt and the Christian Crusade*. New York: United Presbyterian Church of North America.

———. 1908. *In the Valley of the Nile: A Survey of the Missionary Movement in Egypt*. New York: Fleming H. Revell Co.

Watt, W. Montgomery. 1960. "Shi'ism under the Umayyads." *Journal of the Royal Asiatic Society,* nos. 1–2:158–72.

———. 1988. *Islamic Fundamentalism and Modernity*. London.

Weber, Max. 1958. *The Protestant Ethic and the Spirit of Capitalism*. Translated by Talcott Parsons. New York: Scribner.

Wendell, Charles. 1972. *The Evolution of the Egyptian National Image: From Its Origins to Ahmad Lutfi al-Sayyid*. Berkeley: University of California Press.

Wherry, Rev. Elwood Morris. 1907. *Islam and Christianity in India and Far East*. New York: Fleming H. Revell Co.

Willis, Michael. 1996. *The Islamist Challenge in Algeria: A Political History*. Reading, U.K.: Ithaca Press.

Wilson, Mary. C. 1987. *King Abdullah, Britain, and the Making of Jordan*. Cambridge: Cambridge University Press.

———. 1994. "Jordan: Bread, Freedom, or Both?" *Current History* 93 (February): 87–90.

Wilson, Rodney, ed. 1991. *Politics and the Economy in Jordan*. London: Routledge.

Winckler, Onn. 1997. *Population Growth and Migration in Jordan, 1950–1994*. Sussex: Academic Press.

Winder, Richard Bayly. 1962–63. "Syrian Deputies and Cabinet Ministers, 1919–1959." *Middle East Journal* 17 (Autumn 1962): 407–29; 17 (Winter–Spring 1963): 35–54.

Worthington, Edgar Barton. 1946. *Middle East Science: A Survey of Subjects Other Than Agriculture*. London: H. M. Stationery Office.

Wuthnow, Robert. 1985. "State Structures and Ideological Outcomes." *American Sociological Review* 50 (December): 799–821.

———. 1987. "Rethinking Weber's View of Ideology." *Theory and Society* 16:123–37.

———. 1989. *Communities of Discourse: Ideology and Social Structure in the Reformation, the Enlightenment, and European Socialism*. Cambridge, Mass.: Harvard University Press.

Yacine, Rachida. 1993. "The Impact of French Colonial Heritage on Language Policies in Independent North Africa. " In *North Africa: Nation, State and Region,* edited by George Joffe. London: Routledge.

Yorke, Valerie. 1988. *Domestic Politics and Regional Security: Jordan, Syria and Israel*. Aldershot: Gower.

———. 1990. "A New Era for Jordan?" *The World Today,* February, pp. 27–31.

Zaret, David. 1985. *The Heavenly Contract: Ideology and Organization in Pre-revolutionary Puritanism*. Chicago: University of Chicago Press.

———. 1989. "Religion and the Rise of Liberal-Democratic Ideology in 17th-Century England." *American Sociological Review* 54 (April): 163–79.

Zartman, I. William, and William Mark Habeeb, eds. 1993. *Polity and Society in Contemporary North Africa*. Boulder, Colo.: Westview Press.

Zebiri, Kate. 1993. "Islamic Revival in Algeria: An Overview." *Muslim World* 83, nos. 3–4 (July–October): 203–26.

———. 1993. *Mahmud Shaltut and Islamic Modernism.* Oxford: Clarendon Press.

Zeine, Zeine N. 1973. *The Emergence of Arab Nationalism.* Delmar, N.Y.: Caravan Books.

Ziadat, Abdel A. 1986. *Western Science in the Arab World: The Impact of Darwinism, 1860–1930.* London: Macmillan.

Zisser, Eyal. 1999. "The 'Alawis, Lords of Syria: From Ethnic Minority to Ruling Sect." Pp. 129–45 in *Minorities and the State in the Arab World,* edited by Ofra Bengio and Gabriel Ben-Dor. Boulder, Colo.: Lynne Rienner.

Zonis, Marvin. 1971. *The Political Elite of Iran.* Princeton, N.J.: Princeton University Press.

INDEX

Abadan, 107
Abbas II, 137, 138
Abbas Mirza, 110
Abbas, Ferhat, 270, 282
Abbasids, 33, 34, 209
Abbasi Madani, 5, 269, 288–91;
    antisecularist, 287; discussed caliphate, 291;
    explained FIS, 290; leader of FIS, 269
Abd-Allah, Umar F., 386
Abd al-Majid, Sultan, 77
Abd al-Raziq, Ali, 3, 98, 99, 100, 208, 213;
    Islam and the Principles of Authority, 76
Abd al-Wahhab, Muhammad Ibn, 28,
    43–45, 293, 335
Abdeen, Abdul Hakim, 297, 301
Abduh, Muhammad, 2–3, 76, 89–91, 99,
    101, 131, 154, 176, 215, 327; British rule in
    principle unacceptable, 80; and con-
    cepts of *ibadat, mu'amalat,* and *kafir,*
    90; criticized al-Afghani, 79; discourse
    constrained by British presence, 89;
    doubted the possibility of successfully
    transplanting European laws, 90;
    expressed sympathy for Wahhabism, 45;
    and Islam as the true sociology, 91;
    modernist project, 90; Mufti of Egypt,
    76; took issue with European writers,
    80–81, 99; true society based on the
    teaching of Islam, 93
Abdul al-Satar, Abdul Mu'iz , 302
Abd ul-Azim Shrine, 185
Abdul Aziz, 44

Abdülhamid II, sultan, 137, 141, 147,
    153, 160–61, 195, 323, 337; Ottomanism,
    157–62; pan-Islamic despotism, 157–62
Abdul Hayy, 44
Abdul Kazem, Ali, 398
Abdullah, King, 295–99
Abdullah, Amir, 166
Abd ul-Latif Khan, 72
Abidin Palace, 214
Abrahamian, Ervand, 187, 189, 352, 379, 388
Abu Bakr, 73
Abu Dharr, 276
Abu Farris, Muhammad, 304
Abul Fazl, Allami, 36
Abu Hanifa, 32
Abu Jaber, Kamel S., 386
Abu Qurah, Haj Abdullatif, 301
Abu-Rumman, Hussein, 400
Abu Talib Khan, Mirza, 47–48; British
    progress, 48; praised monogamy and
    European women, 47; visit to House of
    Commons, 47
Adamiyat, Fereydoun, 171, 253, 350, 352,
    368, 378
Adams, Charles C., 364
ad-da'wa wal islah, 302
Addison, Joseph, 65
Afary, Janet, 187, 368
Aflaq, Michel, 227–28
agha, 152
Aghasi, Mirza, 182
aghawat, 152

433